The Rise of Hindu
Authoritarianism

Achin Vanaik is a writer and social activist, a former professor at the University of Delhi and Delhi-based Fellow of the Transnational Institute, Amsterdam. He is the author of numerous books, including *The Painful Transition: Bourgeois Democracy in India*, also from Verso.

The Rise of Hindu Authoritarianism

Secular Claims, Communal Realities

ACHIN VANAIK

VERSO
London • New York

For Anish and Samar

This updated and expanded edition is based on Achin Vanaik's
The Furies of Indian Communalism, first published by Verso 1997

First published by Verso 2017
© Achin Vanaik 2017

1 3 5 7 9 10 8 6 4 2

Verso
UK: 6 Meard Street, London W1F 0EG
US: 20 Jay Street, Suite 1010, Brooklyn, NY 11201
versobooks.com

Verso is the imprint of New Left Books

ISBN-13: 978-1-78663-072-8
ISBN-13: 978-1-78663-073-5 (UK EBK)
ISBN-13: 978-1-78663-074-2 (US EBK)

British Library Cataloguing in Publication Data
A catalogue record for this book is available from the British Library

Library of Congress Cataloging-in-Publication Data
A catalog record for this book is available from the Library of Congress

Typeset in Galliard by MJ&N Gavan, Truro, Cornwall
Printed and bound by CPI Group (UK) Ltd, Croydon, CR0 4YY

Contents

Acknowledgements

First let me express my gratitude on two counts to Perry Anderson. When he last visited India and on seeing the changing political climate then, he had urged me to rework and update my 1997 study to make it a more contemporary reader for an audience at home, and especially abroad, to achieve a better understanding of this rising spectre of Hindu communalism. But it was the reception in progressive Indian circles of his 2013 book *The Indian Ideology* that stirred me sufficiently to get on with what I had earlier considered doing, but for one seemingly valid reason or the other, kept putting off. What surprised and even dismayed me was not that strong disagreements with his book had been voiced by prominent intellectuals belonging to a left and left-liberal milieu. But why was there no acknowledgement by these critics of the great political value of a text that so systematically, comprehensively and lucidly punctured the smugly false self-image that far too many Indian liberals (let alone right-wingers) carried of their country?

It brought home to me that progressive thought in and about India had now come to inhabit a basically post-Marxist space much more concerned to reveal the distinctiveness of an Indian 'civilization' and 'culture' which 'Western'-inspired conceptual frames (like Marxism) are presumably incapable of adequately appreciating. Among those holding such a view, many an exaggeration of the quality of Indian modernity and secularity has followed. Hence the implied riposte carried by the subtitle of this book. My own analytical spectacles remain those of a Marxist – which is not to deny the necessity of thinking through, across, beside and beyond the Marxist tradition as well, for Marxism is not and does not claim to be a theory of everything.

This book would not have the shape it does if I had not learned so much from my interactions with many people. These include the Sarkars, Tanika and Sumit, as well as my comrades from the Centre of Marxist Studies that we collectively set up a few years ago to promote an anti-bureaucratic and anti-Stalinist commitment to the project of bringing about a truly democratic socialism. My thanks to Anil Chaudhury, Wilfred D'Costa, Vivek Chibber, Kunal Chattopadhyay, Soma Marik, Mihir Desai, Archana Agarwal, Sushovan Dhar and Bodhisatwa Ray. A special debt is owed to my political-intellectual interlocutor of well-nigh three decades, as well as my close friend and inspiration in shared activism, Praful Bidwai, who passed away in June 2015. He is sadly missed. Thanks are also due to Barbara Harriss-White and Leo Panitch of *Socialist Register*. The annual issues for the years 2009 and 2015 carried my two articles on India. A few passages taken from them, but now duly reworked, updated and expanded, have been incorporated in Chapters 1 and 5. Nor can I forget Sebastien Budgen and Duncan Ranslem of Verso; the first for his encouragement and for keeping me to necessary timetables, the second for his painstakingly thorough and scrupulous copy-editing that has made an often dense text both more precise in the laying out of its arguments and freer of errors.

Last, but far from least, I am grateful for the encouragement and support I have always had from my partner Pamela, to whom I dedicated my first book, and my sons Anish and Samar, to whom I dedicate this one.

Introduction

It was in 1997 that I first undertook a book-length study of what I then called the 'communal phoenix' that was rising to cast its 'shadow over India's body politic'.[1] This had been preceded in 1990 by a wider-ranging overview of India's economy, polity and society, in which I had devoted a full chapter, titled 'Communalism and Hindu Nationalism', to this growing and disturbing problem.[2] If, between 1947 and 1990, the advance of political Hindutva (roughly 'Hinduness') had been relatively slow, although accelerating from the mid 1980s, it was in the 1990s – following the Ram Janmabhoomi, or Ram Temple movement (the single greatest mass mobilization since the era of the independence struggle), culminating in the destruction of the Babri Masjid in the town of Ayodhya in December 1992 – that the transformative power of Hindu communal forces in India really became apparent. This event focused the minds of many Indian intellectuals and activists committed to the preservation and promotion of secularism, and I noted with approval in *The Furies of Indian Communalism* (henceforward; *Furies*) that, as a result, the work of many Indian intellectuals had helped raise the quality of the general debate on secularism above existing theoretical and political levels, even worldwide.

Some two-and-a-half decades later, what do we find? Between 1998 to 2004, the Bharatiya Janata Party (BJP) – the electoral–political wing of the collective cohort of Hindu nationalist forces called the Sangh 'Parivar' (Family) – became the hub of the coalition governments that ruled in Delhi. The BJP had become a normalized and respectable political force governing either on its own or in alliances within several Indian states. While the trajectory of the Congress has moved from single-party dominance at the centre to requiring alliances to form the national government, finally reaching its nadir so far in the 2014 general elections, the trajectory of the BJP has been the reverse – from alliance partnerships to single-party majority rule – and it has replaced the Congress as the biggest national-level political force.

---

1 A. Vanaik, *The Furies of Indian Communalism: Religion, Modernity and Secularization* (London, 1997).
2 A. Vanaik, *The Painful Transition: Bourgeois Democracy in India* (London, 1990).

This electoral rise both in the provinces and at the centre is part of a wider cultural–ideological advance, and of a deeper implantation in the country's structures and institutions.

This political journey of the Sangh Parivar must cause a retrospective reassessment of the secular claims that have often been made for India, in relation to the nature of both the state and society. In *Furies*, I wrote that

> even among those concerned to defend secularism, secularization and the secular, the focus of attention has been mostly on the character, practice and ideal of the secular state, on its laws and its affirming ideology. Much less has been written about the secularization of Indian civil society – its advances and retreats, its possibilities and obstacles, its desirability or undesirability. That there is a secularization process going on 'in the background' is generally conceded, but it is the secularity of the state and the ideology of secularism that have been foregrounded in most intellectual discussion. It is generally here that theoretical advances and new insights have been provided[3].

Since I believed (and continue to believe) that the longer-term battle to defeat communalisms and fundamentalisms must be waged on the terrain of civil society, where the democratic process must be stabilized and secularization deepened, I hoped that the balance of theoretical and analytical attention would shift towards civil society, and towards increased talk of the need for the further secularization of Indian life, even as concern to preserve such secularity as the Indian state had already achieved would remain salient because of the then more immediate threat presented by the forces of Hindutva to ascend to state power. Surely, subsequent developments – the BJP coming to office for six years, then receding from control of central state power for a decade, but finally bouncing back with even greater electoral popularity and no longer constrained by the need for coalition partners – should have led to increased concern about the weakness of the secularization process in civil society, and indeed to a reassessment of the secular credentials of the state itself?

To a limited extent, this has indeed happened, and this book is part of that trend. But there remains a need – which lies outside my competence to address – for the development of serious historical narratives about the secularization process in this part of the world.[4] Such narratives could serve

---

3 Vanaik, *Furies*, p. 4.

4 While historians and sociologists in Europe have provided illuminating narratives of Europe's secularization process, there is much less of this in the subcontinent. There are those who, perceiving secularization as the 'gift of Christianity', deny its applicability to geographical India. There are others who identify secularity with tolerance, and emphasize the unique tolerance of India past and present. Others still provide straightforwardly secular histories – or, more recently, histories tracing the rise of communalism. The sociological approach to the study of religion is well established in the West, but less so in

as a more accurate diagnosis of the 'Indian condition', to which the search for ways to deepen secularism and secularization could be better directed. To talk of the Indian condition in this way – as if it is in need of serious medicines, or even surgery – is of course offensive to a significant portion of intellectuals at home and abroad, and even to some, like the anti-secularists, who are also hostile to Hindutva. But the latter would hold secularism and the secular state partly or fully responsible for the rise of communalism and religious fundamentalism. Having some overlap with their arguments (though its extent varies from thinker to thinker) is an intellectual current which, under the influence of postmodernist/post-Marxism/postcolonial theory, would argue that there are 'multiple secularisms' corresponding to 'multiple modernities'. That is to say, an adequate understanding of the problems of specific societies requires much more specific understandings of those societies and their cultural and religious traditions, legacies and continuities. A very distinctly Indian form and understanding of secularism therefore exists, from which others can learn. Western-imposed notions of secularism are thus a problem, if not a danger.

There is therefore something of a division even between defenders of secularity. How should it be understood? How far should it go? What is its relation to democracy? How should it be pursued, or avoided? Hindutva's rise today might easily inspire more hostile criticism of India's colonial past, especially of the National Movement era, and also of the character of the cultural nationalism that preceded the emergence of political nationalism associated with it. This is certainly my view, though this study does not seriously investigate this colonial past. However, the other side, at its politest, would criticize this approach for being a disabling one-sidedness that refuses to understand the much more complex relationship between religion and secularity in the Indian context. The implications of these different approaches are discussed in the relevant chapters.

Like *Furies*, this book discusses Hinduism, Hindu nationalism and Hindu communalism, but makes only peripheral references to minority communalisms, or to Islamic India. Leaving aside an unnecessarily defensive attempt to establish appropriately liberal credentials by 'balancing' my preoccupation with majority communalism with a study (and condemnation) of minority communalisms, I believe that the text as it stands will prove to be of some value. My main obsessions are the secularity of the Indian state and the secularization of Indian civil society. India cannot become an Islamic state; it can certainly become a Hindu state. If secularization – understood as relative decline in religious influence and in the importance of religious identity – is to proceed apace, then it must above all address that religious

---

India with regard to its premier religion, Hinduism. There has been more emphasis on sociological and anthropological studies of Hindus, which has led to more interest in folk Hinduism and caste practices. But philosophical approaches still dominate the study of Hinduism and its place in Indian life.

system, Hinduism, which purports to describe the beliefs, rituals and practices of the overwhelming majority of the population.

The issue of minority communalism, its sources and directions, becomes
more obviously relevant in studies whose focus lies elsewhere, such as on
Kashmir and its impact on the rest of the Union; or in studies of the current
turmoil within significant sections of the Muslim population in India. Quite
clearly, however, no practical perspective for combating majority communalism can be complete without insisting simultaneously on combating minority
communalisms, particularly Muslim communalism. Any perspective on how
best to combat Muslim communalism would be greatly enhanced by an
in-depth historical and sociological analysis of Muslim communalism and its
complex relationship to lived and doctrinal Islam.

Such a major exercise is also important because of the new pressure
exerted by powerful circles in the West and in India, even beyond the
Hindutva crowd, to carry out a demonization of Islam. Islam-baiters both
in India and the West push a set of common themes – Islam is basically
intolerant; Islam shapes the Muslim mind more than anything else; an Islam
in crisis is creating an increasingly monolithic *ummah* or worldwide community of believers. But the biggest spur towards demonization of Muslims
and Islam is the shamefully dishonest and one-sided discourse on terrorism
that has emerged since the 11 September 2001 attack on the Twin Towers
in New York. The destabilizations caused by the initial backing of al-Qaeda
in Afghanistan against the former Soviet Union, followed by the invasions
of Iraq (1991, 2003) and of Afghanistan (2002) after the Soviet collapse,
had primed the US for a higher level of military unilateralism, the Western
air assaults in Libya and Syria, and support for Arab dictatorships and Israel,
unleashing what has been aptly called a 'clash of barbarisms'. The primary
catalyst for this now well-established feedback relationship between state
and non-state terrorisms has been the US-led West, though this does not
excuse the terrorism or brutalities of Islamic groups and states.

The most common form and meaning of terrorism is that it is an act, a
method, a technique, a tactic, and as such is adopted and deployed by the
individual, the group and larger collectivities, including the apparatuses of
the state. Terrorism by states, internally or externally, is far more devastating
in terms of civilian casualties. But the label of 'state terrorism' is applied
selectively and hypocritically to a few states outside the West. The 'Global
War on Terror' (an absurdity in that one cannot wage a war on a tactic or
technique) not only legitimizes the use of one kind of violence and terrorism
in the name of fighting another; it is also one of the more effective ideological banners today for the pursuit of US and Western imperial interests.
Moreover, given that Russia (in Chechnya), China (in Xinjiang) and India
(in Kashmir) all face secessionist pressures from Muslim-populated regions,
and are themselves aspiring if not already imperial powers, though of a lesser
order, they all see some value in using the discourse of 'Islamic terrorism'.

But in the case of Hindutva, unlike for the others, the identification of Islam and Muslims with terrorism serves to strongly reinforce its *foundational* ideology and purpose. This is why exposing the 'Global War on Terror' as a fraud and opposing the demonization of Islam and Muslims are even more important in the Indian context.[5]

This book is divided into three parts, besides the Introduction. Part I contains Chapter 1, which outlines the communalization of the Indian polity between independence and the 2014 general elections. The chapter stresses the fact that the Congress struggle for independence under the leadership of Gandhi had a Hindu nationalist dimension of considerable weight, even as it also had a secular dynamic. Both secularism – a normative ideal – and communalism – the name given to a form of religio-political conflict of great negativity and danger – are to be understood as modern phenomena. It is in this chapter that the importance of secularizing civil society in India is first broached, while it is pointed out that particular relationships of secularization–desecularization are connected to particular patterns in the state–society relationship. The process of secularization is therefore a complex one that, by operating in a wider political economy of capitalist development, frequently, and in various contexts, suffers from interruptions, halts and even reverses. It is not unilinear.

Chapter 1 also provides a capsule survey of the Sangh Parivar's parent body, the Rashtriya Swayamsevak Sangh (National Volunteer Corps), or RSS, and of some of its major affiliates. In keeping with my emphasis on the importance of the secularization of civil society, I draw attention to a valuable recent account of the process of production and dissemination in print of a homogeneous Brahminical version of Hinduism – a version that exists within 'offical' Indian nationalism. This process certainly prepared the ground, especially in north India, for mass receptivity to many of the basic themes underpinning the ideology of the Sangh. Following independence, the Sangh Parivar culturally implanted itself among sections of the Dalits ('downtrodden' – the self-appellation used in preference to 'untouchables') and Adivasis (tribals), despite its upper-caste doctrinal biases.

Insofar as the electoral rise of the BJP since the 1980s has been more a function of the decline of Congress than the reverse process holding, my survey of the sources and likely effects of this decline precedes my account of the BJP's own rise. No such narrative, however, can refrain from highlighting the Ram Janmabhoomi Campaign, lasting from roughly 1989 to 1992, in the context of Mandal politics. The Mandal Commission Report

---

5 For a detailed critique of the Global War on Terror, both in relation to its function as an ideological banner for US imperialism and for the internal inconsistencies in the discourse on terrorism, see my 'Political Terrorism and the US Imperial Project', in A. Vanaik, ed., *Selling US Wars* (Northampton, MA, 2007), published in India as *Masks of Empire* (New Delhi, 2007).

proposing reservations for intermediate or 'backward castes' was presented in 1979 to the then post-Emergency Janata government but was only applied by the V. P. Singh government in 1990. The expansion of the reserved quota for central government jobs beyond those already available for Dalits and Adivasis (15 percent plus 7.5 percent respectively) by an additional 27 percent quota for the benefit of the intermediate or 'backward castes' (in officialese referred to as 'Other Backward Classes' or OBCs) and who otherwise at 52 percent of the total population make up the single-largest caste bloc in the country antagonized the upper castes, thereby weakening any project of constructing a cross-caste Hindu unity. This made the Ram Janmabhoomi Campaign all the more necessary. This chapter also discusses the quantitative and qualitative changes in the character of the 'great Indian middle class' (in fact, in relative terms more an elite of massive proportions than anything else) as a key social base for Hindutva and other right-wing forces and projects. This is presented along with an account of national coalition governments, wherein the BJP becomes not only a normalized political force but one whose fluctuating electoral fortunes can be mapped on an ascending trend-line up to the breakthrough of 2014.

If there is one strategic lesson to be drawn from this and later chapters, it is futility of placing any hope in the prospect that the Congress – in large part responsible for Hindutva's rise – might effectively confront the BJP/Sangh.

Part II constitutes the theoretical heart of the book. It retains most of the theoretical material presented in *Furies*. Since much water has passed under the theoretical bridge since then, it includes not only an updating and revision of the previous text, but a great deal that is completely new. My intention is both to strengthen my previous argument and to question and criticize claims made since then from various directions of an Indian state and society whose remarkable secularity, supposedly, was formerly less understood and appreciated.

Chapter 2 is titled 'Religion, Modernity, Secularization' (note *secularization*, not secularism). Although communalism is made possible by the modernizing–secularizing process, there is an undeniable sense in which secularization and secularism are antidotes to the communal disease. But in understanding secularization, the key point of reference is not communalism but religion. However, amid contending notions of secularization, it is necessary to choose and account for one's alignments. I have sought to defend the classical notion of secularization – relative decline in religious influence – as a *fact* in modernity everywhere. Its further deepening in societies like India is a definite *possibility* – but one that will have to be fought for. Finally, I endorse the *desirability* of such relative decline in religious influence and in the importance of religious identity. I did not start out with the idea of launching such a defence: it emerged out of my inquiries, rather than guiding them.

It gradually became clear to me that a defence of the classical view of secularization required an understanding not only of the nature and functions of religion, but also of how modernity has transformed the ways in which culture and society have interacted both with religion and with each other. Chapter 2 is the most abstract and explicitly theoretical chapter, but it is indispensable to the architecture of the book. In it I argue against the claim that, even in modernity, religion is necessarily central to culture and to society, or that, beyond some soon-to-be-reached or already-reached limit, secularization understood as the continuing decline of religious power and influence no longer holds good and indeed would not even be desirable. Religion and modernity, some say, must be strongly conjoined for the good of human society.

By theoretical rather than historical argument, Chapter 2 builds a plausible case for the validity of the secularization-as-decline thesis. It does so by distilling and then contesting the strong arguments of those who are its opponents. Of course, the most convincing way to establish that the substantial secularization of Indian society is already an indisputable fact, and that further secularization is a real possibility, is to provide an *historical* narrative of the secularization process in India. We have secular histories of India, but not specifically histories of the secularizing process in India. What I have written, therefore, is something like an abstract prolegomenon to this still unfulfilled project, which at least calls attention to its importance.

While a subsection in the chapter deals with the Marxist understanding of religion-as-ideology, I have not felt particularly beholden to that tradition in my effort to 'understand religion'. Religion always has ideological functions, and it has thus become something of a Marxist convention to invoke Gramsci's remarkable insights into 'hegemony' and 'ideological domination'. His observations on religion emerged from his studies on Italian Catholicism and its place in the construction of an Italian national culture. But the strength of the Marxist approach is also its weakness. Religion has ideological functions, but it goes far beyond them. Of course, immortalizers or near-immortalizers of religion ignore, soft-pedal or deny the ideological dimension, and it is here that the Marxist approach remains a useful reminder of the ever-present link between religious discourses and practices and social and political power.

But there is much more to be said in areas where the contribution of the Marxist tradition is much more limited. So Gramsci features in my survey, but in a minor role. He had a core understanding of religion that was deep and broad, but his thoughts on the matter took a specific direction because of his preoccupation with the how and why of fascism and fascist ideology – and of course with what should be done about it. More important for me has been the influence of another Marxist intellectual and activist closer to our own times: Raymond Williams.

In the religion–culture–society relationship, the middle term is the pivot. Later in his career, Raymond Williams worked with a notion of culture – as a 'realized signifying system' – that contrasted with his earlier, more anthropologically inclined notion of a 'whole way of life'; the former remains the best starting point for investigating complex modern societies, at least for my purposes. Williams also later dropped his treatment of 'culture in common' and 'common culture' as synonymous. Common culture was now contrasted with the essentialist notions of culture as would be suggested by the term 'culture in common'. Cultural essentialism is a basic assumption of those who would contest the value of secularization and secularism for India, and must be opposed and refuted.[6]

In modernity, the production and diffusion of symbolic goods is much more institutionalized, and extends further over time and space, than ever before, because of the revolution in the technologies of mass communication. The result has been the creation, really for the first time, of something we now call a *mass* culture connected to the mass media. In short, it may be that the mediatization of culture has come to play a central role in the secularization of culture. To the extent that such mediatization strengthens public forms of religiosity, the overall direction taken by the secularization process across different societies therefore becomes more variable. So what basically happens to religion in modernity? What should we now be wanting and fighting? What is it feasible to want and fight for now?

One of the key questions in the historical discussion of modernity has always been whether it is industrialization which happens to be capitalist, or

---

6 R. Williams, *Culture* (London, 1981), and *Resources of Hope* (London, 1989).

There is another kind of essentialist claim, different from cultural essentialism. Will religion always be essential for most or many people, no matter how much success there is in the construction of the desired socialist future? This question is not broached in the chapter, but, given the now increasingly widespread view that religion will easily outlive Marxism, and even socialism, some observations may not be amiss. Even if the relationship of religion to culture and society in the course of modernity is accepted as historical and contingent, what about the spiritual dimension of human existence, and religion's relationship to it?

It is even more difficult to theorize the spiritual than to theorize the religious, or the religious experience. But clearly the spiritual experience is not congruent with the religious experience, though it may take that form. A spiritual feeling is probably not capable of full description or theorization. It is experienced as an exceptionally heightened sense of self in relation to something – so heightened that, in some key respect, it is ineffable or indefinable. (Charles Taylor in his magnum opus, *A Secular Age*, [Cambridge, MA, 2007], calls it a 'fullness'.) It is not for Marxists to deny the existence of the spiritual experience, but only to point out that its sources can be, and are, many, and that a positive and healthy modernity enhances the sources and the possibilities of the spiritual.

It can be experienced in a religious form, so a fully atheist Marxist utopia is neither necessary nor desirable. But it also has other sources and forms – the sense of awe a scientist may have in the course of his explorations; the impact of a piece of music; the intensity of an emotion experienced in a relationship of friendship or love; the sense of wonder at nature's beauty. If there is no warrant for the Marxist to deny all value to religion and the religious experience, there is also no warrant for the immortalizer of religion to insist on a privileged relationship of the religious to the spiritual.

capitalist industrialization per se that constitutes the fundamental process of modernity as it has unfolded. Marxists such as Perry Anderson and Robert Brenner correctly insist on the latter view.[7] Theorists of power, including Anthony Giddens and Michael Mann, hold to the former view – as indeed do theorists of rationality and of cognitive transformations as the driving force of modernity, such as Max Weber and Ernest Gellner.[8] But all of these six figures would subscribe to what Gellner called the 'Big Ditch' view of a profound and decisive *rupture* created by the advent of modernity in the trajectory of specific societies, and in the processes of world history itself. They would share many understandings of the relationship of modernity to tradition, which is really the principal terrain of investigation in Chapter 2.[9]

This question of 'rupture' is fundamental for anyone wishing to situate herself within the modernity–tradition debate in India. There are three possible lines of argument. India, it can be claimed, is still basically a traditional society. A second view is that India is a society in transition between tradition and modernity. A third view, to which I subscribe, is that India has long been pursuing its own trajectory of modernity, different from that in the West but incomprehensible without reference to it. It is not that 'traditional' institutions, beliefs, values and practices do not exist, but rather that they can no longer do so in the 'old' way, and that this itself constitutes a decisive change. Even in the long history of pre-modernity, there is always change as well as continuity, but ordinary people's 'lived experience' of both (of time and space) was very different then from what happened after the impact of

---

7 The Anderson-Brenner riposte to neo-Weberian arguments about the separation of 'power accumulation' from 'capital accumulation' is a powerful one. In feudalism it is precisely the form taken by production relations that necessitates power accumulation in order to enhance capital accumulation. P. Anderson, *Lineages of the Absolutist State* (London, 1974); R. Brenner, 'The Social Basis of Economic Development', in J. Roemer, ed., *Analytical Marxism* (Cambridge, 1986).

8 In the Indian context, Gandhians and neo-Gandhians like the anti-modernist Ashis Nandy, former director of the Centre for the Study of Developing Societies, New Delhi, hold a similar view of modernity as industrialism – rationalism, abstracting from its capitalist character. The 'enemy' is thus science, rationality and Western materialism. Mahatma Gandhi saw colonialism as flowing from Western materialism rather than from capitalism.

9 The answer to the question: 'What is the duration of tradition?' can be variable. Also, what is supposed to represent the continuity of a tradition from pre-modernity to modernity depends on what is defined as essential to tradition, and on who does the defining. Historically, what was defined as tradition was decided by its custodians, and thus inseparable from questions about the distribution of social and cultural power. In modernity the essentialism of tradition is also decided by the 'observer' of tradition. So modernity also has its traditions.

Tradition is a special way of organizing time (and space). In pre-modern society, the historical sense is less linear (though not absent), and depends more on the organization of collective social memory. As Anthony Giddens points out, the 'authenticity' of tradition comes not from its accuracy in capturing the past – the most traditional societies are oral cultures that can never accurately capture a true past. Instead it comes from the fact that it is 'the very medium of the "reality" of the past'. It is this status of tradition that is disrupted. A. Giddens, U. Beck and S. Lash, *Reflexive Modernization* (Oxford, 1994), pp. 93–4.

modernity. Ordinary life now takes place in a whole new world, and entails
being a very different kind of person.

Modernity destroys tradition, but it also reworks and 'preserves' it,
thereby providing the objective basis for many intellectuals who reflect on
modernity, to adopt a Nostalgia Paradigm. This paradigm is characterized
by its sense of history as decline, and by a feeling that wholeness and autonomy have been lost. These are, in fact, new feelings created by new times.
But the essential point is that traditions recently invented, and older ones
reworked, continue to be important in modernity itself. Even so, as time
passes the destructive and inventive processes in regard to these traditions
reach qualitatively higher levels than ever before. Traditions in the pre-
modern sense are always linked to localism and local communities, which is
why, over any wide territorial expanse, such as pre-modern India, the existence of a traditional society is always the existence of traditional societies,
in the plural. As the era of modernity proceeds, the crucial local contexts
within which tradition thrives are undermined as never before by modernity's principal characteristic: capitalist globalization.[10]

India has escaped none of the processes of modernity in its various phases.
It simply experiences them in its own uneven and combined way. The idea
that India fundamentally remains a traditional society is simply an absurdity; and that of its being in transition between tradition and modernity is
not much better. India's encounter with modernity came through colonialism. It is only in the earliest phase of this encounter that it is legitimate
to talk of a *truly indigenous* resistance. During this initial contact, there
is 'primary' resistance to protect recently affected ways of life. But once
indigenous society is irrevocably changed, there can be only 'secondary'
resistance – resistance within the terms of modernity, even when it seeks to
refute it.

Those who rework tradition after this encounter with colonialism are
themselves influenced by criteria brought to India by colonialism. The
'internal' criteria of Indian tradition never suffice for the necessary reworking. The reinterpretations and reworkings are carried out by members of
the elite, but popularized in ways never available or attempted before, and
therefore large masses of ordinary people begin to develop a new awareness
of, and allegiance to, what are supposed to be their enduring traditions.[11]
The first serious reworkings of tradition in response to modernity took place
in a context (colonialism) marked by a sense of defeat. This meant that there
was strong pressure on those carrying out this reworking both to rationalize

---

10 Giddens emphasizes the globalization, not the capitalism. But he is right when he
claims that this globalization runs directly counter to tradition, which 'controls space
through its control of time'. Instead, globalization controls time through its control of
space. Ibid., p. 96.

11 For a subtle analysis of this point, see J. Alam, 'Tradition in India under Interpretive Stress', *Thesis Eleven* 39 (1995), issue on 'India and Modernity: Decentring Western
Perspectives'.

the colonial victory and to find within its traditions distinctive and relatively untouched sources of 'Indian superiority'.

It is one thing to assert that India and other societies outside the advanced industrialized world have long since been 'condemned to modernity', and therefore to insist on finding modernist solutions to contemporary problems. It is another thing, however, to ignore the inadequacies and ugliness that accompany this modernity. Here it is the *capitalist* character of modernity that becomes a crucial source-bed for generating these evils – and understanding this helps us to explore ways to overcome them. Neither pre-modernist indigenisms nor postmodernist meanderings offer much in this respect. They only serve to obscure and disarm. Since both the anti-modernist and the postmodernist see industrialism, scientific rationality and the rise of the nation-state as the principal characteristics of modernity, both let capitalism itself off the hook. Socialism and Marxism are dismissed as having no relevance to their respective projects. For the postmodernist, the issue is no longer even the evils of modernity. The way to counter the advocacy of these false trails cannot be a simple argument in favour of an unproblematic modernity. It has to be the defence of a *critical* and *modest* modernity, in which a critical and modest Marxism assuredly has a place.

Charles Taylor, in his remarkable book, gives capitalism a very minor role in explaining the advent of what he calls *A Secular Age*.[12] This huge tome is a work of great erudition that has many virtues. According to Taylor, the defining characteristic of the new secular age is that masses of people can now subscribe to what he calls an 'exclusive humanism' – in other words, to an ultimate vision or goal of human flourishing alone. There has been a religious decline compared to the past, but new forms of religiosity have also emerged, producing a religious re-composition rather than any simple, linear process of religious decline. So far, so good.

But he locates the primary source for the emergence of the secular age (or 'secularity 3', as he calls it) principally in the emergence of a religious individualism developed in the course of Christian moral teachings before, but especially after, the impact of the Reformation. This laid the basis for the rise of a less religious 'secular subjectivity', and a resulting shift towards an 'immanent self' that can now prioritize an exclusive humanism above all else. For all his emphasis on the changes in the 'background conditions' of Christian beliefs, this remains a strongly ideational explanation, and it has been strongly criticized. Another line of criticism is that even this story of the centrality of Christian teachings ignores how these were themselves shaped by historical encounters with the non-Western and non-Christian world.

Taylor's text has been taken up here for two main reasons. It is perhaps the most important recent historically informed yet theoretical effort to

---

12 See the reference to Taylor's book in note 6 above.

insist on the conjoining of religion with modernity for the greater public good. It is not just that his method for understanding the emergence of a secular modernity can be criticized, but that what flows from his study – with regard to both the issue of secularization and the political project of the pursuit of greater human flourishing – must, in my view, be rejected. He sees further secularization as undesirable because of the 'three maladies of immanence'. Since immanence means a narrowing of our world-view to exclude the possibility of transcendence, this leads to a) the loss of meaning in this world; b) the absence of ways to solemnize and highlight (as religion does) the rites of passage in one's life-cycle; and c) a reduction in our capacity to cope with the emptiness of ordinary life.

Given that Taylor is known widely for his writings on multiculturalism, it is not surprising that he subscribes to the view that there are 'multiple modernities', and therefore 'multiple secularities'. His work has no doubt pushed many thinkers towards predominantly cultural understandings of modernity – or, rather, of various modernities – in which Difference with a capital D becomes the single most important signpost in studying the past, and in proposing future courses of action to pursue the now 'multiple emancipatory projects' that are especially relevant in the societies of the non-Western world, including India. And if Western secularism is rooted in its religious past, as Taylor purports to have shown, could this not also be the case for India, especially in relation to its dominant religion, Hinduism? Despite the recognition that, insofar as all these societies are modern and therefore there is something common and new about them, the temporal distinction between past and present becomes less important than the spatial difference between cultural/civilizational entities. As a phenomenon characterized above all by the rate, depth and scope of change with which it is associated – sharply distinguishing it from pre-modernity – modernity itself becomes less significant than the cultural continuities with the past possessed by each of these entities, which together make up a modern plurality of societies. What better way is there, then, of trying to understand the hybridities of each of these social orders and of our pluralistic world?!

For those holding such a perspective it is not just that the modernity of Indian secularism is subject to challenge, or that undue praise may be heaped on its distinctive character and quality, but that the nature of today's modernity on a global scale is itself misrecognized by them in harmful ways. All modernity is hybrid, and the process of hybridization not only does not stop within modernity, but becomes more dynamic. This raises the question of what is the main source of this dynamism, affecting even the cultural–ideational domain. It is, in fact, a capitalism that creates processes that unify *and* differentiate as never before.[13] Today, for the first time ever, three

---

13 If the view of Perry Anderson is that all modernity is hybrid, for Bruno Latour hybridity means that we have never been modern. See A. Dirlik 'Thinking Modernity

historically unique horrors co-exist: 1) Mass immiseration and physical human suffering are produced by malnutrition, ill health and early mortality, as well as by the presence of mass illiteracy, whose remediation would be an important contributor to the securing of much greater personal dignity. What makes all of this so different from the past is that there is now no *global* scarcity of necessary resources available to eliminate these deprivations; 2) The very existence of the human species, in very large part or as a whole, is threatened by multiple ecological disasters; 3) The same threat is offered by potential nuclear or biological warfare.

The first two of these threats can be directly connected to the nature of contemporary capitalism; the third more indirectly to global capitalism and the system of multiple nation-states that currently sustains it, and also partly expresses its uneven and combined character of development. What the paradigm of multiple modernities (and its cousin 'connected histories') does is to downgrade the power and reality of a universalizing capitalism (never a totalized state of affairs) in shaping the era we are living in, as well as the responsibility it has for generating these unique yet universal dangers.[14] Surely this means that we have to pursue a universal project of emancipation – a collective alternative modernity (not in the plural) based on the transcendence of capitalism? It is no surprise that Taylor, for one, has no such vision – indeed, that he pursues nothing more than a social-democratic welfarist humanization of capitalism as far as his concerns about political economy go. Instead, what must be pursued is a global multicultural order (a fitting goal for one who is among the most important theorists of multi-culturalism) that brings together a plurality of cultural (and religious) visions consonant with the reality of multiple modernities (or even 'alternative modernities') in a framework of mutual respect and equality. It is this that is all-important, and it can come from an overlapping consensus on common ends, even as the reasons for arriving at those ends may differ. This for Taylor and his many admirers would be the desired precondition for successfully installing greater collective human flourishing.

Chapter 3 explores concepts that are the bread-and-butter terms of discourse on Hindutva and communalism. These include terms like 'Indian civilization', 'Indian culture', 'Hinduism' and 'caste'. Even those who line up on opposite sides in their attitude to Hindutva and secularism often share

---

Historically: Is "Alternative Modernity" the Answer?', *Asian Review of World Histories* 1: 1 (2013), pp. 5–44.

14 The literature on 'multiple modernities' is now considerable. An important reference point was the special issue of *Daedalus* 129: 1 (2000), whose inaugural text was S.N. Eisenstadt, 'Multiple Modernities'. Recent post-colonial writings have echoed this theme. Indian-origin contributions include S. Kaviraj, 'An Outline of a Revisionist Theory of Modernity', *European Journal of Sociology* 46: 3 (2005); H. Mukhia, 'Subjective Modernities', Occasional Paper for *History and Society* (new series) at the Nehru Memorial Museum and Library, New Delhi, 2013. For the 'connected histories' approach, see G. Bhambra, 'The Possibilities of, and for, Global Sociology: A Postcolonial Perspective', *Postcolonial Sociology, Political Power and Social Theory* 24 (2013); pp. 295–314.

similar understandings of these key concepts and their interrelationships. Consequently, there are all too often unwarranted concessions to votaries of Hindutva and to anti-secularists (those who oppose both Hindutva and 'Westernized' secularists).

I dispute the idea of a centuries-long Indian civilization, and of some essentialist Indian culture beholden to Hinduism. I further dispute the view that Hinduism is a 'single, religious fabric' or 'comprehensible whole', even though it has undeniably been subject to a process of singularization in the last two hundred years that is currently gathering ever greater pace – making it much more amenable, however for the purposes of communal mobilization. Caste as a *pan*-Indian phenomenon is also relatively recent, so neither Hinduism nor caste can be said to constitute the essential elements of a putative Indian civilization and culture of long standing. Such essentialism is usually accompanied by an excessively benevolent rendering of Hinduism (its 'mystique of tolerance'), and even of the caste system.

There is in this chapter a brief deconstruction of the ideological structure of Hindutva discourse. The way the forces of Hindu communalism manipulate cultural, political, social and economic themes of various kinds to construct *practical* and *mobilizing* ideologies at various moments, for different purposes and audiences, is always a highly flexible, mobile and complicated affair – indeed, sometimes erratic. I have confined myself to the much simpler task of portraying the relatively inflexible 'chain of reasoning' that makes up the more abstract intellectual construct of Hindutva that then informs and guides the more practical forms taken by the ideological arguments and claims of the different variants of Hindu nationalism. These versions have been softer and harder, milder and more virulent in their political thrust and orientations.

Recognition that there have been such Hindu nationalist variants becomes particularly important because the remarkable rise of the Sangh and its understanding of Hindutva raise an unavoidable question. Can we understand this advance in state and society, on the political, social and cultural fronts, without re-examining and reassessing the validity of earlier claims about the secularity of the National Movement, of the Congress and its leaders, of the nature of the Constitution that emerged from the predominantly upper-caste Hindu membership of the Constituent Assembly – in short, of the much-praised character of Indian secularism? If this Indian secularism has merits from which Western secular states and societies can learn, what about its comparative shortcomings? Since writing *Furies*, I have felt the need to present a new and much more critical take on the Constitution and on the secular claims made for the Indian state, emphasizing even more strongly the need for Indian society to be secularized, and therefore to reach a more modest evaluation of its comparative virtues.

When it comes to the views of key thinkers who are opposed to Hindutva yet critical of a 'Westernized' understanding of secularism as something unsuited to and even dangerous for India, the work of four such theorists was taken up in *Furies*. They were Bikhu Parekh, T. N. Madan, Ashis Nandy and Partha Chatterjee. While Parekh and Madan have sought in the intervening years to further develop their views and judgements on this issue, the theoretical concerns of the latter two have moved elsewhere, and they have added little of note to their earlier positions. The influence of all of them in elite public discourse, among NGO activists, and within academia at home and abroad, has endured if not grown. This is not a function of their organizational and political power, as it is in the case of the forces of political Hindutva. It is much more directly a function of the persuasiveness of their ideas in a milieu marked by the decline of Marxist intellectual influence, the dilemmas of liberal modernism, the rising popularity of postmodernist thinking and of forms of postcolonial theorizing that demand nothing less than an epistemic revolution to overthrow Western conceptual impositions (including much if not all of Marxism) that prevent a proper understanding of non-Western societies and cultures.

One of the earliest Indian thinkers who argued along these lines is the psychologist Ashis Nandy, who on the issue of secularism and India has been a self-declared 'anti-secularist' and 'anti-modernist'. I have devoted considerable space to criticizing his views, in the most directly polemical passages in the book. Of course, the more recent reflections of Parekh and Madan are also addressed.

The anti-secularists are decidedly unhappy with even the liberal democracies, not because these systems are capitalist or insufficiently democratic but because their 'liberalism' enshrines a conscious separation of private meaning from public legitimacy. A primarily political language of legitimation has emerged in contrast to the pre-modern, supposedly more wholesome inseparability of the private and public orders of meaning. For the Indian anti-modernist taking his cue from Gandhi, the sources of evil in modern life rest not on social factors but on a particular view of the ultimate purpose and meaning of man. Modern civilization is said to be based on a false theory of man.[15] Ancient civilizations, in which a religious culture was allowed proper sway, were soul-centred. They had a spiritualism at their core, anchored by a notion of the transcendent, and thus did not suffer from the debilitating dichotomies of mind/body, or soul/body, characteristic of modern man.

Gandhi's judgement of modernity was not historical or sociological, but psychological, moral and philosophical – though he made no serious attempt to understand philosophy or psychology. This is where Nandy, a relatively uncritical defender of Gandhi's thought (whose uncritical approach in fact

---

15 See P. Chatterjee, *Nationalist Thought and the Colonial World: A Derivative Discourse?* (New Delhi, 1986), Chapter 4. Chatterjee, though not an anti-modernist, sees Gandhi as subjecting civil society to critique rather than Western modernization. In fact, at a deeper level evident in Chatterjee's own analysis, Gandhi's critique rests on a theory of man himself.

reduces the complexity and stature of a figure like Gandhi), can step into the breach. Furthermore, the growth of communalism (not so much in the first fifteen years after Indian independence, but certainly later) is seen by the anti-secularists as evidence of the increasing divorce of the Indian political and social elite from the masses. This Westernized and secular elite speaks a different language from that of the authentic Indian, found for the most part in the villages.

This is a truly surprising claim. Indian democracy in action has in fact produced a form of democratic culture more imbued with an indigenism that can be appropriated by communal forces. Sudipta Kaviraj has perceptively observed that, since the 1960s, Indian politics have undergone a massive alteration in style, language and modes of behaviour, far more effectively reflecting the cultural understandings of rural Indian society, rather than the Westernist cultivation of the elite that inherited power in the Nehru years.[16]

One can attribute the origins of communal politics not simply to tradition, nor simply to modernity, but to changing patterns within modernity. The arguments of the anti-secularists and anti-modernists are both false and dangerous, not least because they legitimize the proposition that a 'religious community', which is insufficiently differentiated internally, is a vital, operative, bottom-line 'political unit'.[17] Support for this view also came from another important source – some leading lights of the Subaltern Studies group, notably Partha Chatterjee, its most important theorist after the founding figure and original inspirer of the group, Ranajit Guha. Guha provided the original theoretical rationale for seeing Subaltern Studies as a distinct school within the wider field of Indian historiography, and for defining its purposes and ambitions. His *Elementary Aspects of Peasant Insurgency in Colonial India* was the first book-length study representing this new historiography.[18]

Partha Chatteree's *Nationalist Thought and the Colonial World: A Derivative Discourse?* and *The Nation and Its Fragments: Colonial and Postcolonial Histories* were the major book-length studies that emerged from the later Subaltern Studies group, and in particular expressed its theoretical trajectory. Chatterjee's 1994 article in the *Economic and Political Weekly*, 'Secularism and Tolerance', continued in the direction set by the second of these books, confirming how close he had come to the indigenism of Nandy and his programme for organizing religious tolerance, though without quite accepting Nandy's anti-modernism.[19] Since then, Chatterjee has been extremely

---

16 S. Kaviraj, 'Religion, Politics and Modernity', in U. Baxi and B. Parekh, eds, *Crisis and Change in Contemporary India* (New Delhi, 1995), p. 313.

17 Even a critic of anti-secularists and anti-modernists like Akeel Bilgrami conceded this point. A. Bilgrami, 'Two Concepts of Secularism: Reason, Modernity and Archimedean Ideal', *Economic and Political Weekly*, 9 July 1994.

18 R. Guha, *Elementary Aspects of Peasant Insurgency in Colonial India* (New Delhi, 1983).

19 Chatterjee, *Nationalist Thought*; P. Chatterjee, *The Nation and its Fragments:*

prolific, bringing out several books on varied topics, and has declared that it is time to move beyond the concerns of the Subaltern Studies group – without, of course, repudiating the theoretical insights derived within it. Indeed, from being a key representative of that school of historiography, he has become a key figure in postcolonial theory, whose continued assault on the Enlightenment values of universalism and reason remains very influential for students of India, even as his 1994 article remains his most direct engagement with the issue of Indian secularism.

In *Furies*, I included a section on Subaltern Studies, as a necessary prelude to evaluating Chatterjee's essay on 'Secularism as Tolerance'. This has now been removed. So much has since been written on it and, if the best initial critique of the theoretical turn taken by Subaltern Studies was by Sumit Sarkar, Vivek Chibber's *Postcolonial Theory and the Specter of Capital* (2013) constitutes the most powerful and scrupulously argued critique of those key theorists of the Subaltern Studies group whose writings have been perceived as being among the most coherent and illustrious contributions to postcolonial theorizing more generally. Chibber's book-length critique of these theorists and their writings has been so effective that it has rendered further criticism otiose.[20]

The last part of Chapter 3 takes up the task of clarifying the distinctions between religious fundamentalism, religious nationalism and communalism. Although the most dangerous forces within Hindu communalism (the right-wing reactionary formations of the RSS and its front organizations, and the BJP) explicitly espouse Hindu nationalism, there are a range of Hindu nationalisms. Theirs is the most pernicious kind, posited as it is on hostility to the Muslim 'other'. Moreover, the danger represented by this Hindu Right is not just cultural, or directed only against Muslims or other religious minorities, but is mobilized politically against the majority of ordinary Hindus themselves.

By identifying themselves as Hindu nationalists, these forces of the Hindu communal Right clearly wish to disguise the wider and deeper danger they represent. A major part of their overall project is (a variant of) Hindu nationalism, and there is no real problem in referring to it as such – provided this

---

Colonial and Postcolonial Histories (New Delhi, 1994); Chatterjee, 'Secularism and Tolerance', *Economic and Political Weekly*, 9 July 1994.

20 Chatterjee, (ibid.); S. Sarkar, 'The Decline of the Subaltern in Subaltern Studies', in his *Writing Social History*, (Delhi, 1997). See also S. Sarkar, 'An Anti-Secularist Critique of Hindutva', in *Germinal* (New Delhi) I (1994); S. Sarkar, 'Orientalism Revisited: Sadian Frameworks in the Writing of Modern Indian History', *Oxford Literary Review* 16: 1–2 (1994); 'Subaltern Studies: Historiography and Thompsonian Social History', in *Writing Social History* (New Delhi, 1998); V. Chibber, *Postcolonial Theory and the Specter of Capital* (London, 2013). For another excellent, more recent and broader critique of postcolonial studies (including its theoretical indebtedness to Subaltern Studies), see V. Kaiwar, *The Postcolonial Orient: The Politics of Difference and the Project of Provincialising Europe* (Chicago, 2015). Not surprisingly, both Chibber and Kaiwar are non-dogmatic Marxists, insisting on the continuing power of Marxism as an extraordinarily powerful research agenda for understanding and thereby helping to transform the contemporary world order.

larger danger of the Hindu communal Right is clearly recognized, and the multiple sources of its resurgence properly analysed.

In Part III, Chapter 4 addresses how not to perceive the forces of Hindu communalism, while Chapter 5 discusses how to situate it within the overall context of economic, political and social changes in India. Chapter 4 is probably the most iconoclastic from the perspective of the Indian Left. Easily the dominant view within the Indian Left and among Indian Marxists is that, in the Hindu communal Right, we have been witnessing the rise and growing danger of an Indian fascism. It can hardly be denied that the Hindu Right has certain fascist characteristics, but otherwise I have long dissented from this general view. Apart from two new and extended subsections, one taking up the more recent studies of fascism and another on the Left debate on fascism in India, the rest of this chapter contains only minor amendments since the publication of *Furies*. The fact that the BJP-led coalition government ruled from 1998 to 2004 at the centre without establishing anything remotely like a fascist dictatorship stands as a vindication of my prognosis and, I would argue, of my general analysis of why it was not correct to characterize the forces of Hindutva as fascist, despite its undeniable fascist aspects. However, the failure of a fascist dictatorship to emerge has not led those who insisted that an Indian fascism was indeed on the march to embark on any reappraisal of their earlier position. Rather, it has led only to further rationalizations and justifications of their original stance concerning the reality of Indian fascism. Readers will have to judge for themselves the merits of the respective positions of these thinkers and myself.

The way in which the enemy is characterized and understood can affect the conduct of the long-term struggle against it. Much depends, obviously, on what one understands by 'fascism', and this is by no means a straightforward question. Most sensible Marxist and bourgeois attempts to understand fascism involve serious investigation and reconstruction of the histories of 'actually existing fascism'. To be thorough, this enterprise would have to be comparative; and it would have to start with what is universally accepted as the primary raw material – the histories of fascist movements and regimes in inter-war Europe, the proper study of which would include delving into the pre-war and late-nineteenth-century histories of the countries and the continent in question. This approach is not the special insight of Marxists, but simple common sense.

Thereafter, however, differences emerge. There is no simple positivism that can be deployed in such historical investigation and reconstruction. There is already a framework of assumptions and biases that guides this research, decisively shaping any final assessment – and which, at least for those more self-consciously aware of this and wanting to be internally consistent, constitutes a coherent operating paradigm. It matters a great deal whether it is a Marxist or non-Marxist who is doing the historical reconstructing, and if a Marxist, what kind of Marxist she is. Such prior alignments shape the scope and method of historical research, the directions of investigation, the weights assigned to different causal factors, and the generalizations that emerge from such a study. Either one is keenly aware not only about the various methodologies concerning the historical study of fascism between Marxists and non-Marxists, but also about the differences between those calling themselves Marxist, or one is not.

Greater self-consciousness on this score encourages sensitivity to the value of another, secondary level of discussion about fascism, addressing a broader field of enquiry. It seeks to grasp the guiding frameworks behind different approaches, and to understand why there are different theories of fascism, why different thinkers theorize as they do (and why they think they are right), and, finally, whether or not it is possible amid these contending understandings to establish accepted standards of adjudication. Discussion of this sort leads to a greater awareness of the difficulties in developing a completely convincing theory of fascism, to a better understanding of one's own basic orientation on the issue, and to a greater capacity for self-criticism and intellectual humility in presenting one's own argument. These are some of the reasons why I have engaged in such a discussion in this chapter. But the most valuable purpose of such an exercise is that one becomes much more aware of the problem of *competing* 'fascist understandings' or 'fascist minimums' or 'fascist essences' or 'generalizations about the nature of fascism', and that one must have good reasons for choosing one's own alignments.[21]

Of course, most good studies of the actually-existing fascisms of the inter-war period, whether of bourgeois or Marxist provenance, provide generalizations about the *essential* nature of the fascist beast. This can he understood as establishing the basic dynamic of fascism, or the proper dialectic between the international and the national, or defining its key characteristics, or whatever. The point is that it is regularly done, and in turn becomes a crucial guiding frame for investigating other possible fascisms in different times and places. But how do we adjudicate between different Marxist understandings of contemporary 'fascist threats'? The crucial reference point remains *historical* fascism and the subtlety and power with which it was analysed by outstanding Marxist thinkers and activists of the time – the classical Marxist tradition.

If there is no methodological escape from the 'imperative of definition', there are nonetheless different ways of going about this. One advantage that Marxists should have over non-Marxists is a greater inclination towards recognizing that a phenomenon like fascism must be understood

---

21 This effort reinforced my respect for the classical Marxist understanding of fascism, which emerges from studies by major Marxist thinkers of the inter-war period, and the work by those Marxists coming later who chose fidelity to that tradition, such as the late Ernest Mandel. It is precisely this respect that makes me so sceptical of the value of a spatial extension of the fascist paradigm to backward and dependent countries.

as something *in motion*. Their definition of fascism must not be static, but dynamic. Weberians, neo-Weberians and Marxists correctly recognize the need for definition, and can therefore engage in shared talk of the 'fascist essence' or the 'fascist minimum'. But Marxists must not, in pursuit of this intellectual–political responsibility, make the Weberian-influenced mistake of postulating 'ideal types'. Precisely because fascism must be understood dynamically, I have insisted in this chapter that fascism must be seen as a *unity of three moments* – namely, when out of power, when in power, and in its transition from one to the other. This is why the historical key to grasping its 'essence' or 'minimum' is provided above all by Germany and Italy, while other historical examples of fascist-like movements provide important but partial insights. Both structure and agency must be incorporated – both the putative fascist actor and the context in which it operates, as well as the interrelationship between the two *where the context was and is*, both domestic and international.

The best classical Marxist understandings respected this methodological necessity, and tried to integrate all of these three dimensions. Fascism was not only linked closely to the contradictory workings of capitalism in the imperialist era, thus remaining a recurring tendency or possibility as long as capitalism and imperialism exist, but was a highly *distinctive*, indeed extreme, form of resolution of not just any or many kinds of capitalist crisis, but of the most exceptionally acute form. The fascist state was not just a very authoritarian form of right-wing, reactionary nationalism in power, but a very special kind of authoritarian state representing the most *extreme form of political central-ization* (the 'political expropriation of the ruling bourgeoisie') necessitated by the exceptional severity of the crisis faced by capitalism in the country concerned. Hence, though fascist victory i.e., the capture of a state was *rare*, it had a profound *qualitative* impact both domestically and internationally.

In assessing the possibilities of fascist emergence in more recent times, the question of bourgeois democracy inserts itself. During the inter-war years there was nothing like the *mass appeal* (as an ideal to be striven for) that bourgeois liberal democracy acquired after World War II. This was in great part because liberal-democratic forms of political rule endured in capitalist countries – and not only there. Where these forms of rule sustained themselves, it was because of a deep mass commitment to their preservation and strengthening. In most of South America, a continent in which independent nations emerged almost everywhere after the 1830s, authoritarian rule was common till the 1970s. Thereafter, bourgeois democracy has become the norm. While, after the collapse of the communist bloc, the mass appeal of a socialism that would seek to overturn class rule even in its more ruthless neoliberal guise has greatly diminished, even as the mass aspiration to establish liberal-democratic forms of political rule (albeit capitalist) against existing authoritarianisms has greatly spread and grown. The banner of socialism has been largely replaced by that of democracy. One has to come to terms with this new reality globally and nationally: the mass emotional and political appeal of achieving and sustaining a national-political system of liberal democracy is itself a crucial new barrier to the resuscitation of the kind of exceptionally intense emotional identification of masses with a supreme leader so characteristic of fascism (both as a movement and as a state form), which was so often able to pass as the expression (and institutionalization) of a 'truer and deeper kind of democracy'.

Furthermore, fascism is not just the strongest form of national reaction, but the strongest form of *international* reaction. That is what historical fascism was, and it is astonishing that Third World Marxists subscribing to the notion of fascism in the Global South can so flippantly and casually ignore this. Fascism's victory and years in power represented the consolidation of a most dramatic right-wing shift in the relationship of class forces not only nationally, but also internationally. This could only be the case because the terrain on which that victory took place – the national territories of Europe – included advanced *imperialist* countries. Hungary and Romania, where strong fascist movements existed in the inter-war period, might not qualify as imperialist countries, but their movements were part of the penumbra of European fascism, whose central zone (Italy and Germany) was imperialist, and thus gave the fascist threat its distinctive character. Victory for these movements in Hungary or Romania would have resulted in regimes better characterized as something like semi-fascist, registering their different and lower order in relation to Italian and German fascism.

In this text, I have sought to emphasize the qualitatively different *global* impact in this respect of, say, a fascism victorious in the United States and the supposed clerical fascism of Iran. The impact of 'fascism' in a backward country is so enormously different from, and weaker in depth, scale and consequences for human history than, fascism in an advanced country that it makes no sense to see them both as species of the same genus. But this has not stopped some leftists and Marxists in South Asia from perceiving fascist dangers even in the small island country of Sri Lanka, as represented by the now defunct Liberation Tigers of Tamil Eelam ('Tamil Tigers'). The classical Marxist tradition had a powerful sense of the great importance of this point – hence its recognition that fascism proper was a phenomenon of imperialist countries only.

The dominance of the Stalinist and Maoist traditions in India has been so strong that one should not be surprised that respect for the classical Marxist tradition generally is much weaker. If the theory of Socialism in One Country (even a backward country) has not been repudiated, then why not also a Fascism in a Backward Country? At least some Indian and Third World Marxists have had sufficient respect for the power of the classical Marxist analysis of historical fascism to talk not of Indian fascism, but of a danger that is semi-fascist, quasi-fascist, and so on. In Chapter 4, I have queried even these usages. They are certainly preferable to talking of the danger of an 'Indian fascism', but, if used, should be understood only as a rough descriptive label. India today, however, is clearly not in the same league as most backward developing countries, but is widely recognized as an 'emerging capitalist power'. This is sensible enough. But is it now to be understood as an imperialist power to which the application of the label of fascism, could be considered appropriate? Certainly, its foreign policy behaviour over decades in South Asia and its near environs has been expansionist and aggressive. But perhaps it would be more accurate to see it today as more of a 'regional imperialism-in-the-making' than as an established imperial power. But it would take more than such a change in India's global status from the past to justify the use of the label of fascism.

The key issue here has to do with the forms that fascism can take. Can we talk of fascism taking different forms? Clearly, we can. Can we talk of fascism taking a great many different forms? This is much more problematic – indeed, highly dubious. Can we talk of there being virtually no limit to the forms fascism can take? Cannot fascism, like capitalism itself, at least potentially be universalized to all and any capitalist country? To advance this claim is to so stretch the concept of fascism as to render it little more than a term of abuse. It is, in fact, to disregard the actual historical meaning and significance of fascism. A theory that universalizes the possibility of fascism and believes itself to be a Marxist peerspective constitutes a fundamental revision of the classical Marxist view. Such revisionism should not be automatically ruled in error. But too many in and around the major Left parties in India who partake in such revisionism either do not believe or do not know that they are so engaged. Or if they do know, they feel no obligation to justify it in relation to the classical view. The classical view does not rule out the temporal extension of the fascist danger beyond the inter-war period, tied as it is to the crisis-prone rhythm of world capitalist accumulation. But it does rule out its spatial extension to backward, dependent capitalist countries. I strongly endorse this circumspection.

I have also suggested in this chapter that the use of the fascist paradigm to understand contemporary right-wing threats even in the advanced capitalist and imperialist countries is questionable. But here I am more open to changing my assessment if sufficiently convincing counter-arguments are forthcoming. But I suspect that, whether one is arguing for its growing irrelevance or continuing relevance to an understanding of what is happening or possible in imperialist countries, there are *objective* reasons for this difficulty in exercising a decisive verdict either way. One major reason for this uncertainty is that there will be very different assessments about how durable the structures of bourgeois democracy are in these countries.

The period of original fascism was the period of the most serious global crisis that had ever been faced by modern capitalism – the crisis of its *internal* dynamic of capital accumulation, rather than in such matters as its impact on the global ecological balance. As the late Eric Hobsbawm forcefully reminded us, it is only if we recognize the unique depth of this crisis that we can understand why this period saw, on one hand the first successful proletarian revolution and the rise of powerful communist movements and parties across the industrialized world and, on the other, the emergence of fascism on such a scale.[22] Fascism represented not just the most polarizing counterforce to communism – which had emerged as the antidote to capitalism, thereby lending its own impetus to this very crisis – but also the most serious danger ever to liberal-democratic capitalism and the most advanced values born of the great bourgeois revolutions and the Enlightenment. According to Hobsbawm, actually-existing fascism presented so much greater a danger to liberal-democratic advanced capitalism than did the actually-existing backward communism in Russia that only a 'bizarre' alliance between liberal democracy and communism was able (barely) to save the day.[23]

Clearly, the inter-war period witnessed a very distinctive kind of structural crisis within capitalism, and suffered very distinctive forms of conjunctural crises, giving rise to distinctive forms of barbarism and reaction, and calling forth distinctive forms of resolution to those crises. It is now common currency on the Marxist Left (and elsewhere) to point to a three-phase pattern of capitalist evolution in the twentieth century.[24] Indeed, it is the structuring principle for making those kinds of political–ideological generalization that Marxists are wont to invoke. But this particular pattern of Great Depression – Long Boom – Long Downturn was never *anticipated* by Marxists. More precisely, no Marxist ever predicted the years of the Long Boom or the Golden Age. All analysis of this period was in some way *post facto*.

This failure has some bearing on current discussions about the 'fascist danger'. It suggests the existence of serious problem areas in the Marxist analysis of capitalism and imperialism, regardless of the fact that it is almost certainly superior to alternative analyses of the 'nature of the epoch' or of world capitalism. Many Marxists fared much better when it came to explaining why the Long Boom would not last, and predicting its end. Thus there has been little dispute that, after the early 1970s, world capitalism entered a Long Downturn, whatever its shorter-term cycles of accumulation and growth. This downturn would lay the foundation for the likely rise of a new

---

22 E. Hobsbawm, *The Age of Extremes* (London, 1994).

23 Quite the weakest part of Hobsbawm's book (ibid.) was his inadequate treatment of Stalinism. The other side of his determination to emphasize the importance of this 'bizarre' alliance and of the historic role of Stalinist Russia in defeating fascism is his inadequate emphasis on Stalinist culpability in enabling the rise of fascism to power in Germany, and in Europe generally, at least up to the 1935 Comintern turn towards Popular Frontism. Nazism could have been defeated by a united left in Germany, and in that process Germany might have become ripe for proletarian revolution. Even for Spain, Hobsbawm has not adequately addressed Stalin's reactionary and disarming role. That is why Trotsky was right to emphasize that the period of fascist possibilities was also necessarily and simultaneously the period of revolutionary possibilities.

24 For Hobsbawm, these phases were the Age of Catastrophe (1914–45), the Golden Age (1945–73) and the Landslide or Crisis Decades of 1973 and after.

period of widespread political and ideological reaction. Whether this downturn has continued right up to the present, or whether there was a new, longer-term upturn in the 1990s that only ended with the Great Recession of 2008–12, has also become a matter of some dispute on the Left. But it remains valid to note a connection between prolonged economic decline and the authoritarian momentum of various political dislocations.

Again, no Marxist anticipated or predicted the speed or manner of communist collapse, caused above all not by external pressures but by internal failings of the communist societies. The international capitalist context ensured that backward socialisms (if they did not extend to advanced countries) could only be 'holding operations' – but not when or how they would stop holding. We should not make too much of such 'grand' predictive failures – which were, after all, not a Marxist monopoly. But they do suggest, at the very least, that there are some significant weaknesses in the Marxist understanding of the current phase of imperialism.

Without adequately grasping the nature of this recent imperialist downturn, the simple assertion that there are new forms of fascism that correspond to the new phase of imperialist accumulation means little. Some will agree and some will not. Others, including myself, will suggest that the period of political reaction that we are now undergoing has given rise (and will continue to give rise) to new kinds of barbarism which, because they share some characteristics with old forms of barbarism (fascism), tempt some to consider them as fascisms. Even the concrete 'dialectic' of international – national elaboration, which is supposed to explain why there exists a fascist danger in a given country, presumes exactly that level of competence which Marxists should be highly cautious about claiming – that they have a sufficiently adequate grasp of the 'international context' and of the nature of current neo-imperialism. Our Marxist predecessors in the inter-war period, by contrast, had a much surer grasp of the nature of their period.

Of course, political struggle cannot 'wait' for sounder analysis of the nature of the enemy before commencing. It is not only in studying it but also in fighting it that one can develop a better understanding of the enemy. The last part of Chapter 4 addresses this issue in general, and specifically in relation to India. The questions this section seeks to answer are simple and directly programmatic: What difference does it make to strategic and tactical perspectives of struggle against the enemy whether we consider it fascist or not? And what should these perspectives be?

Chapter 5 offers a survey of the contemporary political scene. It covers the results of the 2014 general elections, highlighting the replacement of the Congress by the BJP as the country's central point of political reference. Nevertheless, the Indian polity remains in flux, as it has been since the late 1960s. Much has changed since the first two decades after independence, when Congress dominance went effectively unchallenged. The sources of this continuing flux derive largely from the complex interweaving of six processes (outlined in this chapter) that have both helped to promote Hindu communalism and created obstacles for it.

There has been an overall fulcrum shift to the right – economically, culturally, politically – and the key argument of this concluding chapter is that, unlike some battles, the war against the Hindu right cannot be won on the cultural and electoral fronts alone. To bury Hindu communalism for good, one has to oppose much more than Hindu communalism – all the more so because the persistent failure of India's neoliberal-driven economy, which Modi has sought to strengthen further, is in fact exacerbating the problem that makes him most vulnerable: the insufficient number of decent jobs, and therefore adequate livelihoods, for the multitude. It is this that will generate mass discontent, providing the groundswell for possible change of a more progressive kind that can encompass positive developments in the cultural and political domains. But here it will be the practices of living politics – of mobilization and organization – that will decide the direction taken by popular anger and frustrations. What are the forces that can channel these energies, and to what ends?

This certainly does not mean that one should downgrade, let alone dismiss, the Sangh's agenda for change on the fronts of education, public culture or its pursuit of its longstanding 'trident' of issues – namely, abrogation of Article 370, regarding the autonomous powers of Jammu and Kashmir province; imposing its particular version of a Uniform Civil Code; and building the Ram Temple in Ayodhya. Of course, these efforts must be strongly resisted. Our shorter-term goal is to halt and reverse the fortunes of the BJP/Sangh in the arena of electoral politics. But the growing acceptability of themes associated with Hindutva and the greater respectability of the Sangh in society at large have given these forces a confidence that its longer-term goal – that of carrying out its wider transformative project of installing a Hindu Rashtra, entailing the permanent inferiorisation of religious minorities – is achievable, despite the objective difficulties arising out of the country's unique social diversities. This has to be countered by the invocation of an opposing transformative project and vision.

What might that be? A de-communalisation and a much greater secularization of civil society is urgently required. But can this be separated from the broader effort to oppose Indian capitalism in the name of pursuing a socialist alternative? Since, in my view, this is what is necessary, the last part of Chapter 5 offers some thoughts on 'Secularism, Socialism and the Building of an Anti-Neoliberal Platform' as the way to move forward, for which the development of a new Left is vital. It is the *pursuit* of this project that is all-important, and it may be hoped that successes along the way will open up new possibilities and new energies that can bury the threat of Hindutva, and even provide an opportunity to secure what has for some time now been regarded as 'improbably possible' – the inauguration of a genuinely socialist project!

PART I

1

The Communalization
of the Indian Polity

*From Independence to
the 2014 Elections*

The spectre of growing communalism haunts India today. In the battle for the soul of Indian nationalism, various positions have been staked out. First, there are those who insist that Indian nationalism must rest on cultural and psychological foundations of an impeccably Hindu provenance. Second, there are those who insist that Indian nationalism must derive from secular principles. Notwithstanding the problems of precise definition, the term 'secular' does possess an agreed meaning: state neutrality with regard to religion. In multi-religious India, this can mean either a fundamental separation of the state from religious activity and affiliation, or impartial state involvement on issues relating to the religious interests of different communities. In practice, 'Indian secularism' has been a mixture of the two. For this writer, the result is an unsatisfactory attempt to reconcile essentially incompatible approaches. A third position holds that, because secularism is in origin a profoundly Western, or at least un-Indian concept, it is at odds with the reality of non-Western, non-Christian existence in general, and with the Indian genius in particular. What is needed is not secularism, nor Hindu nationalism, but an anti-secularism that opposes factitious attempts at separating religion from politics and the state, and instead encourages the use of the 'authentic' resources of faith to sustain a sociopolitical culture with a deeper tolerance of diversity and pluralism than 'Western secularism' can ever generate.

Religion itself is the key resource in the struggle against communalism. State-centred theories of how to engineer the social good (the modern secular state) are themselves the problem – the stimulus behind communalism. To these must be counterposed the resources of a religiously suffused and plural civil society. This Indian anti-secularism is confined mostly to academic rather than activist debate. But this train of thought has proved to be something of a forerunner and stimulant to the growing popularity in intellectual circles of postcolonial theorizing that would now seek to understand the conjoining of religion and Indian modernity in ways that 'Westernized' conceptions of secularism are not capable of apprehending. That this mixed character of state secularism, because weighted in favour of impartiality rather than separation, has proved to be a success as well as being a testimony to the distinctiveness of Indian secularism.

These competing claims provide the context for the following reflections on communalism and nationalism. To fight communalism, we must understand what it is and how it grows. To fight it in the name of a secular nationalism requires us to understand nationalism as well, to know what it does and does not share with communalism.

The Pattern of Modern Nationalism

There is a widespread consensus that nationalism is a modern phenomenon attendant upon the emergence of capitalism, though its longevity has undoubtedly surprised those who thought the globalizing tendencies of capitalism would render nationalism increasingly anachronistic. But what is 'nationalism', the 'nation', 'nationality'? Up to and including the period of post-1945 decolonization, nation formation and the emergence of nation-states has mostly taken place in four waves.[1] There was first what the late Benedict Anderson called the creole or settler nationalism of the New World, in which language was not the *differentia specifica* of nationhood and nation-state formation.[2]

Then came the linguistic-based territorial nationalisms of western and eastern Europe, in which national yearnings were also related to the later dissolution of the Hapsburg, Ottoman and Tsarist multinational empires. In the twentieth century came the tide of anti-colonial nationalisms, whose boundaries of resistance coincided in almost all cases with the seemingly artificial border demarcations of colonial administrative convenience. In these 'new' nations, nation-state formation was more clearly connected to the existence of self-conscious national movements intent on expressing a distinct national culture and history that could not always, or even often, be congruent with the spread of some single indigenous language or ethnic group.

More recently, we have seen not only the resurgence of the supposedly resolved 'older' nationalisms, but also the emergence of post-colonial nationalisms whose *raisons d'être* are new and cannot be ascribed to the distorting legacies of colonial rule. Such is particularly the case with South Asia – Bangladesh, the national movements in Pakistan, Tamil nationalism in Sri Lanka, and the secessionist struggles in India's north-east, in Punjab and Kashmir.

---

1 The fifth wave emerged after the break up of the USSR, Yugoslavia and the collapse of communism in eastern Europe.

2 B. Anderson, *Imagined Communities* (London, 1983).

There is an important lesson here: there is no single feature or identifiable factor common to all nationalisms, to all nations, to all nation-state
formations. Though many cultural characteristics occur in different nationalisms, they never combine in any immutable package of 'national markers'.
Furthermore, no single characteristic is ever indispensable. Nations (and
nationalisms) are *not* intrinsically secular categories. They can rest on exclusivist racial, tribal or religious claims. Indeed, in India religious groups
have been among the strongest candidates for nationhood – as testified to by secessionist struggles in Kashmir and Punjab, and in the fact of
Partition itself.

The early stirrings of Indian nationalism, whether as political movement,
national identity or national ideology, owed much to the 'Hindu Renaissance' of the nineteenth century. Hindu nationalism was important in
promoting a national identity, though it was not the only factor and was
contested by wider-ranging interpretations of Indian culture and history.
There is always a cultural struggle involved in the creation of a nation or
nationality, which is best understood either as Anderson has defined it – as
an imagined political community – or (better still) as Kohn understood it –
as a cultural entity, lodged above all in consciousness, striving to become a
political fact.[3]

This cultural struggle is sharper for the 'new' nations, where nation formation is more directly tied to a national movement intent on fostering a
national identity based on indigenous cultural roots. It is this latter capacity
that has given nationalism the edge over socialism, largely explaining why
successful socialist revolutions after Russia's in 1917 took root by way of
a merger with nationalism, either anti-colonial or anti-imperialist in thrust
(Japanese imperialism in the case of China, French imperialism in the case of
Indochina, American imperialism in the case of Cuba).

The purpose of this brief excursus into the nature of the newer nationalisms in general, and into Indian nationalism in particular, is to establish
on *prima facie* grounds the plausibility of the following proposition: the
period when an anti-colonial national identity was being forged was also
the period when the Indian polity was being communalized, and the
Congress-led National Movement cannot escape most of the responsibility
for this. This conclusion stands opposed to those currents of Indian historiography that insist on the essentially anti-communal character of the Indian
National Movement.

Here Gandhi's role comes into dispute. How central was his use of religious idiom and his personal 'saintliness' in generating a mass following for
the Congress? Was his religiosity peripheral or central to the formation of
a winning political strategy for independence – a Gramscian 'war of movement' hinging on an escalating series of compromises? Was it the source of a

---

3 H. Kohn, *The Idea of Nationalism* (New York, 1944).

mere communal tinge, or does he as the principal leader of the Congress-led National Movement bear a great deal of the responsibility for the tragedy of Partition? On the other hand, did he not speak the 'language of the masses' with a force that no one else could approximate?

Gandhi did not so much speak the language of the masses as speak in the language of the Hindu masses. The religious qualifier here is crucial. Gandhi was the one Congress leader to hold out to the very end against Partition, which was subsequently carried out amid a terrible bloodbath. But he cannot be absolved of much of the blame for that tragic denouement. Kathryn Tidrick, in what is the single most powerful exposition on the life and thought of Gandhi, has this to say about the aftermath of Partition:

> Gandhi and many others shared the blame for these horrors. Despite his unorthodoxy, despite his friendships and alliances with Muslims, he was a 'Hindu' politician, incessantly invoking Rama and publicly embracing the ascetic practices associated with Hindu holiness. The message he wanted India, as a nation, to broadcast to the world was a mixture of Hinduism and Christianity, philosophically alien to Islam. He never disassociated himself sufficiently from the Hindu communalist wing of Congress. He always seemed ready to blame the Muslims for communal disorders … Communal feeling, however high-mindedly invoked, was a tiger he could not ride.[4]

Even among the non-Muslim masses, the distinction between speaking 'for' and 'in' is fundamental. Gandhi helped to create an important 'Congress link' between local-level grievances (and leaders) and the pan-Indian struggle against a centralized colonial state. But it was a link over which he did not exercise much control. Historians of the subaltern have pointed out the frequent discrepancies between what Gandhi espoused and the way his exhortations or directives were interpreted to fit popular perceptions of the meaning of their struggles.[5] Since the socially oppressed of India are no more naturally prone to permanent non-violence towards, and class conciliationism with, their social oppressors than the socially oppressed elsewhere, Gandhian principles of *ahimsa* (non-violence) and 'trusteeship' (class paternalism) were in part forged precisely to serve as control mechanisms.

The link also provided for a two-way interpenetration of identities. Most historical work has stressed the seeping downwards of a 'national identity',

---

4 K. Tidrick, *Gandhi: A Political and Spiritual Life* (Noida, 2008), p. 309. Tidrick's work, which is the first such study to highlight the decisive impact of late Victorian esoteric Christianity on Gandhi's personality, has never received the attention it deserves from the broad community of Gandhi-scholars and admirers, either in India or abroad – no doubt because of its iconoclastic character.

5 R. Guha and G. Chakravorty Spivak, eds, *Selected Subaltern Studies* (New York, 1988). See especially G. Pandey, 'Peasant Revolt and Indian Nationalism'; and S. Amin, 'Gandhi as Mahatma'.

so that obscure villages and unknown villagers could come to identify themselves with the National Movement as Indians as well as retaining their more
spatially restricted identities. Sandra Freitag is one of the few who have
emphasized the opposite process: how local-level identities generalized and
spread upwards to influence even the character of the National Movement.[6]

In the north, unlike in the west and south (where linguistic and anti-
Brahmin caste identities were rather more important), the dominant community identity was often religious in character. Here the development
and expansion of a common religious identity was not the passive product
of colonial machinations, but was meshed into local cultural and political
practices, themselves undergoing change in a dynamic socioeconomic and
political context. Even before Gandhi, Congress efforts to widen its local
support base meant building on existing cultural cleavages and perceptions
consolidating religious identities. That the Congress-led National Movement did have an important secular dimension tied to aspirations of some
of its key leaders is not in dispute. But the growing weight of historical evidence would strongly suggest that any easy separation between nationalism
and communalism during the colonial period is frankly untenable.[7]

Communalism

While the characterization of nationalism as a modern phenomenon is
widely accepted, even if the *ethnies* on which certain ethnic nationalisms are
based have a much longer history, the same cannot be said of communalism. Nevertheless, it is best understood in this way, and thus as qualitatively
different from the politico-religious tensions and conflicts of pre-modern,
pre-capitalist, pre-colonial times. The idea that the separation of the political from the religious is a viable proposition had to await the emergence of
generalized market relations (generalized commodity production), which
enabled a decisive separation between the political and economic spheres of
existence, and thus an emerging civil society.

That political life and whole areas of social existence should become

---

6 S. Freitag, *Collective Action and Community* (Oxford, 1989).

7 Even as Jinnah's Muslim League characterized Muslims as a 'nation', this was quite
compatible with the establishment of a confederal India containing Muslim-majority and
Hindu-majority provinces with delegated authority and power. Ayesha Jalal has perceptively pointed out that 'Muslim difference' was not and could not be translated into
an encompassing 'Muslim politics'. Similarly, the Congress actually combined secular
and Hindu conceptions of nationalism while professing to stand for an unequivocal
secular nationalism, as against the Muslim League's communal nationalism. See A. Jalal,
'Exploding Communalism: The Politics of Muslim Identity in South Asia', in S. Bandyop-
adhyay, ed., *Nationalist Movement in India: A Reader* (New Delhi, 2009). A powerful
critique insisting that the cultural core of Indian nationalism was a Vedic Brahminism is
to be found in G. Aloysius, *Nationalism without a Nation in India* (New Delhi, 2007).
Aloysius also presents an unsparing view both of Gandhi as a person and of his leadership
of a movement that, he argues, consciously sought to sustain the pre-colonial hierarchies
associated with the caste system. See especially Chapters 4, 5 and 6.

relatively autonomous from each other marks a decisive transition, providing the foundation for the *relative* decline and compartmentalization of
metaphysical and religious thought. The private world of 'meaning' and the
public arena of 'legitimacy' were substantially separated. Secularism is itself
a modern ideology promoting the notion that the separation of the political
from the religious is a positive ideal.

It is because of this pre-established point of reference – the secular ideal –
that communalism has a distinctly negative connotation, itself testifying to
its more modern character. Communalism may not be straightforwardly
counterposed to nationalism, but it is more easily contrasted with secularism.
There is another, more important reason for emphasizing the modernity of
communalism. In the era of modern mass politics, religious politics has a
strength that is qualitatively greater and more dangerous than its equivalent
in the pre-modern era. The distinguishing characteristic of modern politics
is the decisive significance of mass mobilization, mass appeal and popular
legitimization of elite rule.

This is not something found only in the democracies. It is crucial for
authoritarian and quasi-democratic regimes as well. Here the capacities for
mass mobilization are weaker, and the relationship between popular sanction
and elite governance less direct. But even dictatorships must pay attention
as never before to moulding and influencing popular perceptions. Centralized control over key networks of communication is the sine qua non of
political monolithism. Ruling classes, whether by coercion or persuasion,
or both, justify their dominance in the name of maintaining or extending
the 'national popular interest'. This stands in contrast to the legitimations
sought by the absolutisms and monarchisms of the past. The politics of communal appeal today are in an altogether different register from the politics of
religious appeal in the past.

Having affirmed communalism's modernity, what then of its meaning?
The term 'communal' was first used by British colonialists simply to describe
'communities of interest', including religious groups. It is in the context of
the 1906–09 debates around constitutional reform in India and the issue
of separate electorates for Muslims that the term 'communal' was given a
negative connotation of bigotry, divisiveness and parochialism, because such
separate representation was deemed anti-national and anti-modern.[8] Communalism in a religiously plural society is a highly complex phenomenon
which it is risky to try to confine within a single definition. But it is among
other things a process involving competitive de-secularization (a competitive striving to extend the reach and power of religions), which – along with
non-religious factors – helps to harden divisions and create or increase tensions between different religious communities. Here greater importance is

---

8 See S. Tejani, *Indian Secularism: A Social and Intellectual History* (New Delhi,
2007), pp. 115–16.

granted to religious forces, religious identity, religious competition and religious ideologies, as well as to religious imbrication in popular, folk and elite cultures. The development of a strong collective religious identity among Hindus, Sikhs, Muslims and Christians is a necessary but insufficient condition for the growth of communalism. Non-religious factors are not excluded as important causal factors, but are often misperceived in religious terms. If we are to comprehend communalism properly, we must undertake a comprehensive examination of both the religious and secular in Indian society.

Communal Politics

Focusing on the specific problem of communal politics, we are immediately confronted with two broad questions. First, what lies behind the appeal of communalism? Though the identity crisis of an urban middle class undergoing modernization and partial Westernization has made it receptive to such appeals, their origin has usually been elitist, and disseminated for achieving and promoting secular purposes and goals. There is considerable authority in the instrumentalist argument that religion, whether in the form of faith or ideology, has little to do with the formation of such an appeal – beyond the obvious point that some of its symbols, myths and devotional themes are selectively misappropriated.

Here a 'materialist' analysis of the sources of communalism would reveal the role of the colonial state in deliberately exacerbating the communal divide. Competition for jobs created tensions between the Hindu and Muslim urban middle classes and elites. In post-independence India, attention would no doubt be focused on the socioeconomic changes that have taken place in many Indian towns possessing a sizeable Muslim population, as a result of Gulf remittances, the growing export demand for handicrafts and artisanal products, and other expressions of uneven development that have clearly disturbed traditional patterns of dependence between Hindu traders and Muslim artisans. Similarly, the effects of the Green Revolution in Punjab are not without communal resonance for the Sikh kulak and Hindu trader. Then again, there is also the upward economic and political mobility of the agrarian bourgeoisie, of these mostly upper echelons of the intermediate castes having their social and emotional reflection in a greater striving towards association with a broader Hindu identity. While such explanations are important, they are only part of the story.

There is also a second question: What accounts for the success of the communal appeal? Here it becomes impossible to maintain any artificial separation between 'true' or 'folk' religion, on the one hand, and communalism on the other. For what unites 'folk' and 'elite' religion, its 'authentic' and 'inauthentic' forms, is something intrinsic to the nature of all of the main world religions – Judaism, Islam, Christianity, Buddhism and Hinduism. We are here on the socio-psychological terrain of identity, of the relationship (never static) between religious belief and the socio-psychic need to anchor one's sense of self, or more correctly one's senses of selves.

Among the many functions of religion and religious belief, this is now arguably the crucial one, and is common to all believers from whatever social strata. While the claims of a religious philosophy or ethics can be universal, this function of identity fixation, or affirmation, must always be particularist. A believer is Hindu or sub-Hindu, Christian or sub-Christian, Islamic or sub-Islamic, and so on, even if this particularist identity can itself be an expansive one. The communal appeal thus derives much of its formidable character not just from the resources of power accumulated by the one making the appeal, but also from the importance of religious identity in the psychic health of the receiver. But this is not to invest it with incontestable powers.

The importance of religious identity is historically and socially variable. Where substantial secularization of state and civil society has taken place, religious identity in social – and psychic – life is less important, and the communal appeal correspondingly less attractive. Since the formation and expansion of religious identity 'from below' takes place largely in civil society, secular emphasis concerning state and civil society needs to be inverted.

Outside of the advanced West, in much of West, South and Southeast Asia there have been far more complex patterns of development in the relationship between modernization and secularization, on one hand, and de-secularization, on the other. Even in those social formations dominated by the capitalist mode of production, no single pattern of evolution explains the overall process of secularization of different social formations. Particular social formations possess specific combinations of the secular and non-secular emerging from their particular histories.

In the later modernizing societies of the post-colonial countries, where the state played a more important role in carrying out a forced industrialization, there is all the more reason to expect sharper disparities between the modernizing and secularizing pretensions of the state and the slower-changing realities of civil societies. In Iran under the Shah, efforts to secularize the state and its laws, while not without merit or effect, did not so much reduce overall religious influence as *displace* it onto civil society, in certain respects reinforcing its power there. It remained a latent force fully capable of resurfacing and encroaching on the state domain, as the post-Shah Iranian experience shows. Post-communist Poland is perhaps another, more qualified example.[9] In Turkey, the Kemalite revolution

---

9 The relationship between secularization and de-secularization need not be a 'dialectical' one, in which they are two moments of the same process. It can also be one of adjacency or juxtaposition with minor feedback loops. These two processes can respectively pertain to distinct spaces: the state and civil society; to distinct ethnic groups: Britons of Asian and of non-Asian origin; or to dominant and dominated classes. See B. S. Turner, *Religion and Social Theory*, (London, 1991).

resulted in significant displacement of religious influence, and not just overall decline.

In India, a non-denominational state with substantially secularized laws, resting on an insufficiently secular Constitution, coexists with a civil society in which religious influence is pervasive. It is a situation that gives rise to a profound tension. Despite the flawed secularity of the Indian state, it remains an obstacle to fulfilling the strongest ambitions of Hindu communalism. Its secularity must be strengthened. But the crucial challenge lies elsewhere, in civil society itself. In this respect one is struck by the contrast between the United States and the UK. The secular Constitution of the former (with its 'wall of separation' between religion and the state) compares favourably with the theocratic trappings of the British state. But British civil society (with the exception of Northern Ireland) bears no comparison to America, where church membership is high if not growing, and church influence on government, community and social life is far more pervasive and powerful.[10]

Even in Western secular societies, there is considerable variation in the extent to which different states and civil societies are secularized. If in protestant western Europe church membership is declining overall (though religion retains its importance for the life-cycle rituals marking birth, the transition to puberty, adolescence, adulthood, marriage and procreation, and death), in the US and eastern Europe it is probably increasing. Possibilities for further secularization would seem to be intimately tied to the fate and future of civil society.

The progressive decline of religious influence in this realm (as in much of western Europe) does not signify its progressive abandonment in personal and family life. In that respect, the expectations of many mainstream sociologists in the 1950s have not been borne out. But insofar as religious identity occupies a decreasingly significant role in everyday life, in those collective endeavours that form such a large part of people's economic, political and social routine, the politics of religious identity loses much of its purchase. Where this is not the case, secular gains might over a longer time-span prove more ephemeral. This relationship between secularization and desecularization, between state and civil society, holds an obvious lesson for any practical programme of struggle against communalism in India. Winning this struggle will entail a long-term battle on the terrain of civil society, and

---

10 Durkheimian sociologists who believe that the United States in some sense holds the mirror to the future of secularization elsewhere have developed the notion of 'Civil Religion', i.e. the American Way of Life, which binds the country. This is an ethos encompassing those of the three main faiths, Protestantism, Catholicism, Judaism, and is significantly shaped by them, particularly Protestantism. For criticisms of the civil religion argument in its strong version, see Turner, *Religion and Social Theory*; R. K Fenn, 'Religion, Identity and Authority', R. Robertson and B. Holzner, eds, *Identity and Authority*, (Oxford, 1980); and, from another angle, D. Martin, *The Religious and the Secular*, (London, 1969). See also the subsection titled 'Secularization Once Again', in Chapter 2, below.

it is because the forces of Hindu nationalism and communalism have been far better organized on this terrain that the country is in its current plight. Credit here, if one can call it that, must be given to the organizations that make up what is called the Sangh Parivar (see below). But first, what about the anti-secularism that would take its distance from both Hindu nationalism and secularism?

For a society that knows no linguistic, cultural or conceptual equivalent to the notion of secularism, how is such an idea to become meaningful beyond the circle of a narrow, Westernized elite, without an imposition which, understandably and legitimately, would evoke popular resistance? The problem of 'cultural translatability' is a very real one.[11] However, it is one thing to raise the question: 'How can one judge societies and cultures from outside their own terms of reference, norms and systems of meaning?' It is quite another to replace this serious if plaintive query with the closed-minded, aggressive reprobation: 'How dare one judge cultures from the "outside"?', as the Indian anti-secularist (and not just her) is wont to do. Such extremism allows no space for willed and purposeful societal change, brought about partly by universal capacities to judge, discard and select from a range of human practices, beliefs and values – change that becomes broader as more cultures meet, cross-fertilize, and even clash.[12]

Each history and culture gives meaning to a notion of change by way of a common horizon of reference involving a notion of progress, with a small 'p'. And surely histories now flow into and diverge from History. We no longer live in a time of parallel, isolated histories, if we ever did, and there is much to be gained, for example, from the universalization of ideas and practices associated with the goals of mass political democracy, and gender and racial equality. Where cultures, in the name of their distinctive traditions, oppose such processes, they are likely to lose out in the long run, not due to alien imposition but because each society possesses a critical self-awareness. People do learn from their own history and, when it becomes possible, from the cultural, historical 'other'.

Should secularization be considered a desirable universal? The anti-secularist says: No! He would eschew the extravagant quest for understanding and appreciation across religious divides and settle more modestly for the 'mutual tolerance' that emerges out of the 'lived relations' between different religious communities.[13] But does this answer anything? How is the

---

11 T. N. Madan, 'The Concept of Secularism', paper presented at the National Seminar on Secularism in India, organized by the Indian Academy of Sciences and the Tata Institute of Social Sciences, 25–27 September 1989.

12 See the excellent critique of relativism by S. P. Mohanty, 'Us and Them: On the Philosophical Bases of Political Criticism', *Yale Journal of Criticism* 2: 2 (1989).

13 The Indian experience shows that the relationship between religious pluralism, individualism and secularism is much more complicated than in the standard US-based model, where religious pluralism has strong connections to the privatization of religious concerns, the absence of church–state conflict, and the immigrant nature of US society.

communal challenge to be met? By counterposing to it a 'positive' anti-secularism? As a tactical perspective, the use of faith as the main resource against communalism might seem appropriate and necessary in the Indian context; but as a strategy it is disastrous.

The anti-secularist, like many a secularist, insists on retaining an instrumentalist view of the relationship between religion and communalism. She must separate religion into its tainted and untainted parts, using the latter against the former: the *ethical resources* of religion thus constitute the most important armoury in resisting communalism. It is the 'good' politics of religious appeal versus the 'bad' politics of religious appeal, and isn't the Mahatma not an exemplar of the effectiveness of this strategy?

As well as 'over-valuing' (to put it politely) Gandhi's effectiveness during the National Movement, and ignoring the issue of how to 'institutionalize' anti-communalism, this attitude betokens a fatal strategy, fighting as it does on the terrain of the Hindu communalist. For reasons that go to the heart of the function and purpose of religious faith, the communal appeal will prove stronger. Humans do not believe because above all else they wish to be good, but because above all else they wish to find a home in the world and the cosmos. Because religion is a world-view providing more than ontological solace (a moral ethic, an epistemology), its ontological function by association no doubt becomes even more powerful. Religious morality gives power to religious identification, but it is the latter which is primary. Communal politics tries to link itself explicitly to the deepest psychic needs of identity enhancement and stabilization, besides which questions of religiously sanctioned good or bad behaviour cannot have the same power and appeal. The anti-secularist, by refusing to outlaw the 'politics of religious identity' as a strategic goal, helps to extend and consolidate its legitimacy.

Both the communalist and the anti-secularist are moved to take their respective approaches partly because of a shared overestimation of the power and importance of religion. A world completely without religious faith may be inconceivable, contrary to certain versions of Utopia. But even at its strongest point – the issue of identity – religion has retreated. To venture a global generalization subject to spatial and social variation, the most important contemporary form of a 'social we' is not religion, caste, ethnicity, gender or any 'primordial' identity. Nor is it class. It is nation and

---

Interestingly, where some American sociologists see Christianity as the source of secularization and democracy, some Indian scholars see Hinduism as the source of secular and democratic impulses in India. If Christianity is the master-key to world history, Hinduism is the master-key to Indian evolution! Both modern Christianity and modern Hinduism call attention to their 'innate tolerance'. It has been said that Christian ecumenicalism represents the laying of ground rules to rationalize intra-Christian religious competition. In the past, Hinduism's renowned 'tolerance' was the result of its lack of self-consciousness and the very absence of a 'Hindu' coherence, or any notion of a 'Hindu community'. Caste (an expression of social intolerance) was the organizing principle. Today's self-consciously avowed claim of tolerance by Hindus is more often than not the intolerant expression of feelings of religious superiority to the Semitic faiths, especially Islam.

nationality. The most powerful is not the same as the most enduring. Like all historically constituted identities, it is subject to transcendence, decline and death.

From our perspective, though, the salient question is: Why is the power of nationalism so great? Numerous forms of transnational identification and mobilization – class, gender or sisterhood, racial or black solidarity, Third Worldism, the pan-religious loyalties of an earlier era – have all suffered ignominious defeat when they have sought to confront nationalism head-on. We have yet to develop an enduring and widespread internationalist sentiment or sense of belonging that goes beyond the emotions of charitable concern and vague fellow-feeling.

The Hindu 'revivalist', it should be noted, cannot dare to challenge nationalism in the name of a higher or stronger allegiance to a wider pan-Asian Hinduism. The references to an ancient geography of Hinduism stretching from the Middle East to the Southeast Asian archipelago can focus emotions on the 'Muslim Betrayal' via Partition (the 'rape of Mother India') and on the expansive 'grandeur' of Hinduism's past. But, fundamentally, it is ammunition to help culturally redefine the foundations of the Indian Union. The Hindu 'revivalist' does not confront nationalism in the name of a *greater* religious loyalty, but seeks to co-opt the former.

This exceptional character of nationalism surely lies in its unique combination of politics and culture, of civic power (for example, the importance of citizenship) and identity. For the first time, the nation-state (through the principle of equal citizenship rights) invests ordinary people with an authority and importance that is historically unique. To date, the zenith of popular individual empowerment is political citizenship, whose frame of operation is the nation-state or the multinational state.[14] Moreover, the state itself, within its territorial confines, is the most powerful of all authority structures, and can therefore, through its policies and practices, make a much greater positive difference in the lives of its 'national citizens' than can religious institutional loyalties, It is the historical failure, above all, of the supposedly secular Congress to promote and institutionalize a secular and democratic nationalism that has allowed the forces of Hindu nationalism to gain the ground they have. It is in this sense that the historic and historical decline of the Congress better explains the rise of the BJP than vice versa – a topic in need of further elucidation. But to gain a proper sense of how the communal ground was laid before, as well as after the emergence of the BJP, a brief

---

14 Supra-nationalism, to be stable and enduring (as in western Europe), must retain the institutional foundations of this popular empowerment. If it is to survive, it cannot go backwards. Indeed, it will have to offer more than what has so far been achieved if it is not to be merely another label for a loose confederation of national structures of political power only slightly diluted by the requirement to come together in this way. A truly supra-national, unified Europe will have to be more secular, not less. As it is, the likelihood of Turkey being invited to become a full member of the EU is remote, partly because of widespread unease about bringing in a Muslim nation.

survey of the Sangh Parivar is required. The BJP, after all, is the electoral-political vehicle set up by the Sangh, whose parent body is the RSS.

The Sangh Parivar

A distinction must therefore be maintained between the party expression of political Hindutva – the BJP – and the wider array of forces comprising organized Hindu nationalism and communalism. Though the BJP's fortunes have fluctuated, Hindu communalism's impact, and that of the ideology of Hindutva, have had a steadier upward trajectory. There have been periods of stasis, in which the graph of its movement showed prolonged plateaus. But it is difficult to perceive any serious slump in its fortunes once the country got over the trauma of the assassination of Mahatma Gandhi in 1948, for which Hindu communal organizations and attitudes were held directly or indirectly responsible.

But despite the steady if slow rise of organized Hindutva (meaning above all the RSS, founded in 1925), it is only in the last thirty or so years, from the mid 1980s, that the Sangh 'Parivar' or 'Family' has grown to menacing proportions. This includes the group of organizations controlled or influenced by the RSS, such as the BJP, the VHP (World Hindu Council), the lumpenised storm-troopers who are members of the Bajrang Dal (Lord Hanuman's Army), the ABVP (the all-India student's wing), the Rashtriya Sevika Sangh (national women's wing) and the Sangh-controlled major trade union federation, the Bharatiya Mazdoor Sangh (BMS). Indeed, though the cadre strength of the RSS since its birth has steadily risen, by the mid 1970s this growth was so far short of its historical expectations that the RSS had lost much of its élan, and was suffering from serious internal organizational problems. Its real impact, culturally, politically or organizationally, on the Hindu society within an India to whose total transformation it was committed remained limited.

To say that its efforts were limited is not to understate the nevertheless significant inroads made by the RSS and its constellation of affiliates (formed after independence), especially in the cities and towns of the populous Hindi heartland states of north India. The Sangh had secured a network of dedicated cadres, including full-timers (*pracharaks*), and had established branches in the few thousands. It had participated in struggles (including involvement in communal riots) to promote Hindi in the Devanagari script, ban cow slaughter and push other Hindutva-related themes. It had succeeded in propagating a singular Brahminised Hinduism in which the *Bhagavad Gita* is the key text for shaping a proper 'Hindu life'.[15] The

---

15 The RSS subscribes to Advaita Vedanta (non-dualist monism), first formulated by Shankaracharya around 800 AD, where the Vedanta itself is based on the Upanishads, supposedly divinely inspired. According to Advaita the material world is created by a spiritual energy emanating from a Universal Soul (Brahma), with which the individual soul

problem was that, despite decades of patient work since the formation of
the RSS, the *gap* between these achievements and its expectations was still
so huge – unsurprising in a country of India's size, population and social
complexity.

The subsequent dramatic rise of both the Sangh and the BJP from the
late 1970s has in fact forced a re-evaluation of the fruits of its activities, both
during its pre-independence past and in the early decades thereafter. This
has involved a much more critical assessment of the Congress-led National
Movement and of the communal bigots hosted by it, who were pro-
Hindutva but saw the Congress as the only vehicle for achieving influence
and power. There were others, less communalist but sympathetic nonetheless to many of its views and values. It is a fact that the wing of Hindu
conservatives within the Congress (among the most prominent of which
were Sardar Patel and Madan Mohan Malaviya) would have liked the RSS
and Hindu Mahasabha to dissolve themselves within the Congress, not only
because they shared a number of similar views but because they thought
this absorption would also help moderate Hindu extremism.[16] New work
has uncovered the developing relationship between many Hindu rulers of
princely states and the Hindu right, the former being seen as embodiments
of Hindu masculinity and martial values. Even today, historical links with
the princes of Madhya Pradesh and Rajasthan have been electorally and
organizationally helpful to the BJP.[17] Most interestingly, from the late 1990s
onwards a host of new studies have emerged shedding light on the creation
of a 'Hinduised public sphere' and the role played by the media – 'print
Hinduism'– from the early twentieth century until today, and by television
and the Indian language newspaper revolution since the 1970s. The emergence of social media and its use by the Hindutva brigade will no doubt
provide ample fodder for further studies of this kind.

One of the most important studies on print Hinduism has focused on the
'Gita Press', set up in 1926 to propagate Sanathan Hinduism, which argues
that what is most required for the country's rejuvenation from foreign
rule and degeneration generally is the revival of the virtues of an ancient
Hinduism, as embodied in classic texts, and the social order it established,

can potentially merge through a 'march to perfection'. One must follow one's dharma or
duty (established by one's jati or sub-caste) and the law of karma, which determines the
next birth and death cycle. But it is possible to escape the law of karma to become a world
renouncer – the enlightened sage detached from the world, mastering the Upanishads –
and realize the unity of self and Brahma through meditation.

16 It is no surprise that the current Modi regime has publicly incorporated Malaviya
and Patel in the Sangh's pantheon of nationalist heroes. This is for both doctrinal reasons
and because the RSS, although consciously staying out of the National Movement, can
thereby indirectly claim to have shaped the course of the independence struggle.

17 See I. Copland, 'Crucibles of Hindutva? V. D. Savarkar, the Hindu Mahasabha and
the Indian Princely States', in J. McGuire and I. Copland, eds, *Hindu Nationalism and
Governance* (New Delhi, 2007). A top BJP leader, currently chief minister of Rajasthan, is
Vasundhara Raje Scindia, who comes from the former ruling dynasty, the Scindias.

from which there has been a serious decline into a current darker age. This, rather than the more reformist-minded Hinduism of sects like the Arya Samaj and Brahmo Samaj, is the message that this press has consistently conveyed through its various publications.[18] Ideologically motivated, and not primarily profit-oriented, it has promoted a homogeneous Brahminised Hinduism through its many cheap but high-production publications, as well as views on various themes including the banning of cow slaughter, the promotion of Sanskritised Hindi, the depiction of Muslims as foreigners and sexual predators, and so on, that have always been identified with the Hindu right, and particularly with the more hard-core Hindu nationalists.[19]

The *Gita*, containing the dialogue between Lord Krishna and Arjun in the epic *Mahabharata*, is presented not as allegory but as gospel, while the *Ramayana* epic is presented in only one version – that of Tulsidas's *Ramcharitmanas*. As of February 2014, 71.9 million copies of the *Gita* have been sold; 70 million of the Ramcharitmanas; 19 million of religious texts from the Puranas, Upanishads and other ancient scriptures; 94.8 million of other tracts and monographs on the duties of ideal Hindu women and children; and over 65 million of stories of the mythic past of revered Hindu saints, deities and heroes, as well as biographies and devotional songs. Gita Press has published in all the major Indian languages, and also in English (for both the domestic readership and the Indian diaspora), while its influence has obviously been strongest in the Hindi-speaking north.

A religious monthly, *Kalyan*, has featured since its inception in 1926 both as the vehicle for ecumenical views on Hinduism and the purveyor of the particular line of Gita Press. Any number of stalwarts from the world of politics, academia and business have been frequent contributors to this monthly, including Mahatma Gandhi, former presidents Rajendra Prasad and S. Radhakrishnan, and notables of the far right such as Golwalkar of the RSS and S. P. Mookerjee of the Hindu Mahasabha.[20] This ecumenism was of

---

18 A. Mukul, *Gita Press and the Making of Hindu India* (Noida, 2015). Other major texts are V. Dalmia, *The Nationalization of Hindu Traditions* (Delhi, 1997); A. Rai, *Hindi Nationalism* (New Delhi, 2001); F. Orsini, *The Hindu Public Sphere 1920–1940: Language and Literature in the Age of Nationalism* (New Delhi, 2002); and F. Orsini, *Before the Divide: Hindi and Urdu Literary Culture* (New Delhi, 2010). The Gita Press is the only indigenous press of colonial times that remains operational.

19 Mukul says that the Gita Press played a crucial role 'in creating a unified face of Hinduism … without diluting its stance on core principles of sanathan Hindu dharma such as caste divisions and the responsibilities of women that included grounding the male child in Hindu morality [and the] depiction of Muslim men as the "other" – libidinous, sexually dissipated and voluptuously lustful – from whom Hindu women had to be protected at all costs.' Mukul, *Gita Press*, p. 29.

20 The editor and public face of *Kalyan* from 1926 to his death in 1971 was H. P. Poddar, who had a love–hate relationship with Gandhi. Hostility first arose in 1932, over Gandhi's campaign to end untouchability through the advocacy of unrestricted intermingling and coercive temple entry, both being anathema to Poddar. At times of communal strife, the line of the journal was always unequivocally against Muslims. Nevertheless, Gandhi, for all his periodic differences with Poddar, appreciated the journal's contribution to raising awareness about Hinduism. Even three years after their falling-out over

course within the framework of a 'neo-Hinduism' that called for the regeneration of a Hindu society being threatened in one way or the other, even as the sources of these threats were different for different contributors, and not always the Muslim 'other'. This neo-Hinduism has also been called the 'civic religion of India's ruling elites'.[21] The journal has a current circulation of around 200,000, though it must be said that today, with competition from a variety of other sources, the Gita Press is no longer as pre-eminent as it once was.

The subsequent growth of the print and electronic media have on balance helped to create a more Hinduised and communal public sphere. In India the print media have grown explosively, alongside the expansion of television. Non-English papers and journals far outpace English-language ones, in both numbers and circulation. The big Hindi dailies of north India are owned by upper-caste families, or have corporate heads who are broadly sympathetic to many Hindutva themes, and the journalists employed by them are fully aware of limitations imposed by ownership on the course and content of their professional work. There is an explosion of Hindu religious channels on television, featuring all kinds of god men and women. The screening of long-running TV serials of the *Ramayana* and *Mahabharata* epics between 1987 and 1990 greatly helped to 'authorize' and popularize one upper-caste Hindu version of the epics, amid what had historically been a dazzling array of different versions appropriate to specific contexts and times. Certainly, the Sangh leadership was very aware of the contribution of these TV performances in the generation of a somewhat favourable public mood and attitude to its Ram Janmabhoomi campaign of those times, which culminated in the 1992 demolition of the Babri Masjid in Ayodhya – the supposed birthplace of the God-king Rama. Even the film industry – especially the Hindi-Bollywood sector, though it is more ecumenical and in earlier times sought to present a more composite view of Indian culture – has on balance certainly not harmed, and may have gently supported, the Hindutva project.

The Sangh has always paid more attention than any other political force to the capacity and power of the media in all its forms to shape public attitudes, and has therefore sought to expand its own control and influence on this terrain.[22] Combined with the success of the VHP in establishing a

---

the Poona Pact of 1932, Gandhi wrote to Poddar saying: 'What you are doing through *Kalyan* and Gita Press is a great service to God. I feel I am part of what you are doing because you consider me your own and I consider you mine' (ibid., p. 51). Two political figures whose thinking was strongly opposed by Gita Press were Nehru and Ambedkar.

21 G. Larsen, *India's Agony Over Religion* (Delhi, 1997), p.257.

22 For serious studies of the connection between the media (print and pictorial) and the growth in influence of Hindutva ideology, see A. Rajagopal, *Politics After Television: Hindu Nationalism and the Reshaping of the Public in India* (Cambridge, 2001); R. Jeffrey, *India's Newspaper Revolution: Capitalism, Politics and the Indian-Language Press* (London, 2000); R. Jeffrey, 'Grand Canyon, Shaky Bridge: Media Revolution and the Rise of "Hindu Politics', in McGuire and Copland, *Hindu Nationalism and Governance*.

widening religious network of sadhus and sect leaders, the end result has been the entrenchment of displays of public religiosity, with the increased presence of Hindu religious leaders of various kinds making pronouncements on political issues. Most active religious leaders associated with the VHP are modern gurus – in other words, first- or second-generation gurus, but not modern in the sense of holding or propagating liberal values. Although the VHP was formed in 1964, like the other affiliates of the Sangh, really, it began to grow rapidly from the late 1970s. It was relaunched in 1979, since when it has often been the spearhead of various ethnic mobilizations. Christophe Jaffrelot has called the strategy of the VHP (and of the RSS) one of 'stigmatization and emulation' of its erstwhile religious opponents – Christians and Muslims who have an ecclesiastical structure of sorts. Thus the effort to portray and push a singular Hinduism is often referred to as its 'semitization' or 'syndicalization'. The VHP has sought with some success to set up its own ecclesiastical-like structure for Hindus, since various religious leaders and temple institutions have seen not only that the Sangh is promoting the cause of Hinduism but that association with it brings prestige, material support and more followers.[23]

Two other areas where the Sangh has achieved relative success, here too in more recent times, are among tribals and Dalits. In 1952, it formed the Vanvasi Kalyan Ashram (VKA), or Centre for Tribals' Welfare. But this remained a single unit for two-and-a-half decades, until the massive growth of its branches took place, between 1978 (after the end of Emergency) and 1992 (demolition of Babri Masjid). At 80 million, India has the world's largest indigenous population, and the term 'Adivasis' used to identify them means the 'indigenous' or 'original people'.[24] This is one reason why the Sangh insists on calling them 'Vanvasi' or 'forest-dwellers', since tribal existence cannot be said to have preceded the Aryans, as the originators of not just Hindu India but in some Hindu nationalist accounts of civilization itself. Today, the RSS claims the involvement of the VKA in over 17,800 projects, and contacts with over 51,000 tribal villages in twenty-eight states and two Union territories.[25] The aim is to make the tribals see themselves as part of the Hindu fold, in opposition to Muslims and particularly Christians – the latter having been partially successful in their missionary work, both through their cultural–religious activities providing a measure

23 Two important recent studies of the RSS and Sangh Parivar are C. Jaffrelot, ed., *The Sangh Parivar: A Reader* (New Delhi, 2005); and P. Kanungo, *RSS's Tryst with Politics: From Hedgewar to Sudarshan* (Delhi, 2003). An earlier and also important study – Christophe Jaffrelot, *The Hindu Nationalist Movement and Indian Politics: 1925 to 1990s* (New Delhi, 1999) – is a more general survey of Hindu nationalist forces from the colonial period to the 1990s.

24 Censuses in the colonial period categorized tribals as animists. It is after independence that the government, under the influence of 'nationalist anthropologists', categorised them as 'Hindu'.

25 Sohini Chattopadhya, 'Exclusive: Inside a Hindutva Hostel: How RSS Is Rewiring the Tribal Mind', 17 December 2015, available at catchnews.com.

of social dignity and through the provision of healthcare, education and general livelihood support.

The VKA's main focus is on education. The National Rural Employment Guarantee Scheme (NREGS), first set up by the United Progressive Alliance (UPA) government of 2004–08, has enhanced earnings in many tribal areas, as well as promoting lower-level employment opportunities. This created a stronger desire among tribals for education. The VKA has stepped into this breach, since the Sangh has always prioritized work more generally on the fronts of education, communications and culture. Saffronizing education by controlling the teaching of the young – saffron being the emblematic colour of political Hindutva – has always been a crucial objective going well beyond the tribal population.[26] These tribal schools teach from class V to X, and sometimes to the final year of secondary education, or class XII. Some of these schools have hostel facilities, mainly for tribal boys, and these hostels also act as nodal points for tribal school children over a wider expanse. Maths, English and science are taught alongside Sanskrit and a Hindutva-ised history, while due attention is paid to readings from the *Gita* and to the singing of 'patriotic' songs. Tribal heroes of the past are incorporated in such a way as to portray them as Hindus, while nature-gods are re-described as manifestations of Hindu gods. A significant proportion of full-timers of the VKAs are from tribal ranks. The Sangh sees its mission as not just Hinduizing, but 'civilizing' tribals, which means inculcating lifestyle standards which represent a break from tribal practices and traditions, and are more in tune with the upper-caste Hindu-inflected ethos of the Sangh. These conversion efforts have seen considerable success. They have secured for the BJP a degree of political-electoral support in states with a high proportion of tribal inhabitants. Another, more negative indication has been the occasional involvement since the beginning of the 1990s of tribals in communal assaults on Muslims and Christians.

The Sangh has also had a measure of success in creating a more 'Hinduised Dalit identity'. The aim has been to bring about a certain degree of Dalit acceptance of a Brahminical code of values and norms, thereby generating social harmony among all Hindus. While there have been studies of how the Sangh, through welfare activities – especially provision of low-cost and sometimes free schooling for lower castes – has sought to extend its popularity, far less attention has been paid to the overlap between the two kinds of identity politics that have become so much stronger in the last few decades – Dalit cultural politics and Hindutva ideology.[27] It is true that

---

26 The latest available data on the schools run by the Sangh state that, by 2003, there were 14,000 such schools catering to 1.7 million students, with around 73,000 teachers. See C. Jaffrelot, *Religion, Caste and Politics in India* (New Delhi, 2010), p. 193. These schools have been federated under an organization called Vidya Bharati (Indian Knowledge), which also covers 250 intermediate colleges and around twenty-five institutes of higher education and training colleges. See Wikipedia entry: 'Vidya Bharati'.

27 One of the few recent works in English that has looked at the cultural activities of

there has been a degree of overlap. The Bahujan Samaj Party (BSP) has been the principal political vehicle of certain sub-castes of the Dalits, and has sought to engage in cultural politics by generating collective Dalit pride in the past, placing selective emphasis on certain folk memories, stories and heroes, both historical and mythical. Here the purpose has been to highlight caste oppression, and the need to unite against it. While this has consolidated considerable Dalit support behind the BSP, the electoral need to make alliances with non-Dalit upper-caste groups has meant that there has had to be a certain moderation of caste and cultural antagonisms. That is to say, a consistent or out-and-out assault on Hinduism and Brahminism has had to be avoided. Mayawati, the female leader of the BSP, has found it useful to appropriate the past of Dalit myths in ways that highlight female figures in revolt. Moreover, although she is herself a Buddhist convert, it is telling that there has so far been no mass conversion of a kind that has increased the percentage of Buddhists in the country as a whole – though this may change, of course. Proportionally speaking, the data from the latest Census of 2011 shows a stagnant Buddhist population. Furthermore, the BSP represents only a proportion of Dalits, though a sizeable one (the Jatavs, who constitute 12 per cent of the near 21 per cent of Dalits in the biggest Indian state of Uttar Pradesh, are its key support base). Moreover, this representation is mostly confined to the north of the country, from which it has so far been unable to break out.

The fact is that there has always been some fertile ground even among the lower castes for Hindutva to make inroads. While resentment of upper castes, and therefore dissent, is one part of the Dalit and lower-caste reality, another has always been the desire to be accommodated, accepted and respected by the upper castes. Many non-Dalit lower and middle castes (separated from Dalits by the line of 'impurity') have throughout history sought cultural mobility upwards within the Hindu fold, through processes of Sanskritization and Kshatriya-ization. In the 1980s and 1990s, the Sangh treated Dalits as a homogeneous bloc. The effort was to appropriate Dalit histories (real and imagined) as reflected in their folk tales, memories, myths, legends, and so on, as part of a larger web of Hindu cultural legacies and traditions. Dalit heroes were presented as reincarnations of Hindu deities, and their stories often woven into a narrative that connected them to the unifying figure of Lord Rama. The Sangh also sought to inflect these Dalit legends in a more militaristic and anti-Muslim direction, circulating propaganda material which claimed that untouchability and lower-caste oppression did not precede but arrived with Muslim invasions and rule.

A subsequent shift away from treating Dalits as one bloc led to much more localized cultural interventions appropriate to specific and differentiated local histories, issues, myths, legends and heroes of particular

---

the Sangh aimed at winning over Dalits is B. Narayan, *Fascinating Hindutva: Saffron Politics and Dalit Mobilisation* (New Delhi, 2009).

sub-castes. This included Sangh celebrations of days important to local Dalit groups, as well as invitations to Dalit leaders to inaugurate other Hindu functions, thereby enhancing their status and prestige. The strategy now was to pursue the 'Hinduization of local spaces, local history and the local past'.[28] By doing this, the Sangh could help reduce the frequency of, or even prevent, occasional social gatherings that provided local 'common spaces' for celebration involving both Dalits and Muslims, whose socioeconomic circumstances were not very different from those of the Dalits. Again, these longer-term efforts in civil society have paid dividends in electoral politics – and again, as in the case of tribals, what was once inconceivable is no longer so: the occasional involvement of Dalits in anti-Muslim riots.

Nevertheless, areas of tension remain, and will not be easily surmounted despite the Sangh's highly publicized examples of inter-caste dining between Dalits and select pro-Hindutva upper-caste groups. For one thing, the Sangh wants to maintain middle- and upper-caste leadership in its broad Hindutva activities. For another, there remains a basic conflict between the influential views (especially at an all-India level) of anti-caste thinkers like Bhimrao Ambedkar, Jyotiba Phule and Erode Venkata Ramasamy (better known as Periyar), who were uncompromisingly critical of Hinduism even as the Sangh tries in particular to co-opt the iconic figure of Ambedkar as a great Hindu and later Buddhist leader. Rather than directly challenging their anti-caste views and asserting the superiority of its own Brahminised conception of Hinduism, the Sangh tries to side-step this tension, addressing Dalit resentments by incorporating them within its broader 'Hindu community', through the assertion of a wider discourse of not just development, but a more inclusive nationalism against both non-Hindu minorities and liberal and left 'anti-national' critics.[29]

As the parent body and principal coordinator of the Parivar as whole, the RSS has also grown in terms of the number of both its *shakas* (neighbourhood branches) and its membership.[30] It initially attracted mainly adolescent youths, coming overwhelmingly from urban Hindu upper castes and middle- and lower-middle-class backgrounds. They are provided with spaces for physical recreation and convivial cultural gatherings for recitals and storytelling. The more serious regulars are slowly absorbed, and given physical training and a politico-religious catechism.[31] But the effectiveness

28 Ibid., p. 19

29 B. Narayan, 'Dalits and the Remaking of Hindutva', *The Hindu*, 25 January 2016.

30 The RSS retains a measure of control by assigning its trusted members, and particularly its full-timers, to important official positions in the various affiliated bodies. These deputies link with each other and report back to the RSS hierarchy, to which they are obedient. So, although there are often tensions between the various organizations within the constellation, there is a mechanism for their moderation and mediation, so that matters rarely become out of control.

31 For detailed accounts of the internal structure and organization of the RSS, see Kanungo, *RSS's Tryst with Politics*; and W. K. Anderson and S. D. Damle, 'RSS: Ideology, Organization and Training', in Jaffrelot, *Sangh Parivar*, as well as their older book, *The*

of the RSS as an inspirational and highly disciplined cadre organization rests largely on the mystique of the *pracharak* system, in which the self-sacrificing, ascetic and committed pracharaks who vow to remain unmarried, thereby declaring their dedication to the cause above all other temptations. They have been termed the spinal cord of the whole organization.[32]

In 1977, the number of *shakas* stood at around 10,000. By 2003 it had risen to 33,758, with over 2 million cadres, according to the figures provided by the RSS. Though there is no other way of ascertaining the real numbers, these can be taken as broadly accurate.[33] The latest figures indicate that there are 56,859 *shakas*, representing substantial growth, as might be expected after the Modi election victory of mid 2014.[34] Perhaps more important is the proliferation of all kinds of associations much more loosely controlled by the RSS. These include groups representing different professional occupations, such as lawyers, accountants, and so on, as well as other niche groupings; but what is important is that they extend their loyalties to the Sangh, and to the fulfilment of the Hindutva project. This final goal remains elusive, but what is disturbing is that there is no other force comparable to that represented by the Sangh Parivar and its sympathizing groups, nor any that can boast ideologically motivated activism on a comparable scale. It is the objective

---

Brotherhood in Saffron: The Rashtriya Swayamsevak Sangh and Hindu Revivalism (New Delhi, 1987).

32 A few thousand *pracharaks*, or full-time organizers, dedicate their lives to make the RSS function. They must be bachelors whose family is the RSS, as well as being ideologically totally committed. This entails a spartan, ascetic existence, since they are not just the key organizers but the living exemplars of the ideals of the RSS itself – its 'new men'. They are supposed to be the best and the most dedicated of cadres, and become *pracharaks* through the most careful selection. However, social transformations inside and outside the RSS have reduced the quality of potential recruits to this status, as well as much reducing the attractions of self-sacrificing *pracharak*-dom, though one-time *pracharaks* at a certain point can leave to pursue more normal family life and vocations. Even the upsurge in RSS popularity over recent years has not been able to overcome this internal problem of the *pracharak* system. However, as if in compensation, recruitment into the growing number of affiliates of the Sangh as a whole has grown. It may be that the RSS in future will have to think about making changes in tune with the changing times. In 2015 there was already talk of changing the basic uniform of white shirts and khaki shorts for a more contemporary style, and in August 2016 wearing a white shirt with full brown trousers was made compulsory for members.

33 Jaffrelot, *Sangh Parivar*, 'Introduction'.

34 A. Mukherji, 'RSS is on a Roll: Number of Shakas Up 61% in 5 Years', 16 August 2015, at timesofindia.indiatimes.com. Shaka meetings are held daily, where attendance rose by 29 per cent; weekly, where attendance shot up by 61 per cent; and monthly, where attendance rose by 40 per cent. Some 5,524 shakas were claimed to have been added in 2015. See S. K. Ramchandran, 'Check Anti-National Activities in Varsities', *Hindustan Times*, 12 March 2016. According to this report, the proportion of students in these shakas is 65.6 per cent, with another 25.3 per cent comprising entrepreneurs and professionals under the age of forty. This is somewhat misleading, in that youth involvement is largely transitory and unstable. The number of youth who become more hard-core members or supporters is considerably smaller than the number who come and go, showing a much weaker form of commitment to Sangh ideology, even as Hindutva's influence in the general population has broadened. Correspondent for the *Asian Age*, 'RSS Shakas Unable to Attract Youth', 10 July 2016.

complexity of India, rather than the current power wielded by any organized counter-force, that constitutes the biggest obstacle to Hindutva.

Ideological instrumentalism

Hindutva in its most complete form – including its particular appropriation of Advaita or non-dualism from the broader and far-from-unified field of Hindu philosophical thinking – is the more intellectualized and abstract construct which motivates the practice of the Sangh Parivar. But the set of ideas that must guide its practice, while related to this larger body of thought, is not congruent with it. The former has to have a simpler, more concrete and *politically* directed structure and content. It has to be capable of mobilizing on a large scale, and therefore of arousing passions and emotions, and prompting identifications of self-interest, in ways that Hindutva proper would find much more difficult.

The fundamental premise of Sangh ideology is that Indian resurgence, and ultimately salvation, can only be brought about by the self-conscious unity of Hindus as a religious–cultural grouping. How, then, might Hindus be united, given the peculiar character of Hinduism? There are only two ways, and both have been pursued. One has to establish a principle of coherence and unification that is either *internal* to Hinduism or *external* to it. The only halfway-plausible candidate for the first approach is the construction of a loose and accommodating Brahminism. But this kind of construction of a more singular Hinduism can only take the Sangh so far. As a principle to bind all Hindus together, it is not strong enough; its tensions with the more popular forms of practice and worship prevent it from forming the powerful social glue that is needed.

The other approach – establishing an external principle of coherence – is more promising, because it does not intervene within Hinduism to make choices, but instead posits an opponent for all Hindus regardless of their various beliefs and practices. This approach is absolutely central to the Sangh Parivar's task of constructing the desired Hindu unity. Using such a principle, Hindus can aspire to be united not by what they are supposed to share but by what they oppose – even to the point of hostility. Indeed, the more strongly emotional the common opposition to the external 'other' or 'enemy', the stronger is the desired unity likely to be.

Given India's history, the only feasible candidate for this role of hostile 'other' to Hindus are Muslims and Islam. But the logic does not end here. How, after all, is this hostility to be constructed among Hindus in twentieth-century pre-independence India, and thereafter? For the last 150 years, and particularly after 1947, it is impossible to argue that Muslims have directly dominated and oppressed Hindus and Hinduism.

The ideological strategies for constructing such hostility are limited. First, there is the stratagem of pushing a particular historical interpretation of the past. After all, a somewhat plausible case can be made about Muslim persecution of Hindus and the denigration, and even desecration, of the symbols and institutions of Hinduism in the past – but only insofar as the distinction between Muslim rulers and ordinary Muslims can be soft-pedalled or elided. That is to say, the objective is somehow to make today's community of Muslims responsible for past 'crimes'. Hence the argument that today's Muslims must acknowledge the presumed iniquity of Babar at Ayodhya by agreeing to its replacement with a temple; by refusing to endorse this, they themselves become 'guilty' of disrespecting and antagonizing today's Hindus, who merely seek to correct this putative historical injustice.

What can be claimed to unite elite Muslim rulers with ordinary Muslims, either in the past or today? Islam itself, of course. Culpability, then, resides in the character of Islam and the way in which it constructs Muslimness and influences Muslim behaviour in India. Islam is not usually directly attacked; the Sangh Parivar can even genuflect on occasion to the positive aspects of Islamic doctrine and life. But the charge against it is always present, whether disguised or overt. Indeed, in today's climate of Islamophobia about terrorism, it has become easier to decry Islam as such.

The Sangh often resorts to double-speak, insisting that it is not against Muslims. How can it be? After all, Muslims are by birth and blood Hindus. Insofar as culture is also tied to matters of birth and blood, this is tantamount to saying that the 'true' culture of Muslims is Hindu. In the view of the Sangh, it is thus said to be 'unfortunate' that Muslims refuse to recognize this, and what it entails. The Sangh therefore claims that it 'respects' Muslims, though not because they are Muslims and believe in Islam, but rather because, in a more fundamental sense, they are *not* Muslims – in other words, *in spite of* Islam and Muslimness! So Muslims are *Babar ke Aulad*, or the 'children of Babar', and to be condemned as such; or they are not the children of Babar, but actually Hindus who have betrayed their heritage, and thus should be condemned on that account. Either way, they lose.

An interpretation of India's past stressing its essential Hinduness and the iniquities wrought by Muslims can readily arouse a level of emotional hostility and a desire to construct a Hindu 'unity', but it can only go so far. A politics of historical revenge is certainly a part of the Sangh's current political and ideological armoury. But among contemporary Hindus the cultivation of a strong sense of anger against Muslims must be based primarily on *present* grievances. Since it is difficult for even the most diehard RSS cadre to argue that Muslims directly dominate Hindus today, how is this to be done? The Sangh can try to arouse a sense of fear or deprivation among Hindus. To a limited extent, cross-border terrorist attacks into India by Muslim combat groups, as have happened from time to time, can be used to arouse fear about Indian Muslims, who are portrayed as sympathizers. In the current global climate of growing Islamophobia, this course will be no doubt be adopted more frequently. But it still has stubborn limits.

As for arousing a sense of deprivation, given the subordinate position of the overwhelming bulk of Muslims in Indian society, this is more difficult than trying to arouse a sense of grievance or righteousness among Hindus against Muslims. Given the absence of direct dominance by even a small section of Muslims, this can best be done by shifting the angle of attack. Muslims are not attacked for being directly oppressive of Hindus, just as racist whites do not attack the minority black community in Britain for being directly oppressive of whites. In both cases, the Hindu communalist and white racist attack is launched against the state for *favouring* Muslims and blacks, respectively.

The necessary sense of grievance or indignation is cultivated by invoking the principle of 'unfairness of treatment' by the state as between 'majority' and 'minority' communities, for which *partial* responsibility is transferred not only to leaders of the minority community, or others who would justify such 'unbalanced treatment' – for example, secularists or white anti-racists – but also to ordinary members of the minority community, or communities, themselves. What provokes anger here is not that Muslims benefit from such 'favouritism', but simply the fact of supposed favouritism. Thus BJP and Sangh leaders have no difficulty in arguing that the absence of a Uniform Civil Code or the general policy of 'minority-ism' (as they call it) pursued India's secular state does not help Muslims, but perpetuates their backwardness. They can also don the mask of a more sincere friend of Muslims than their supposed allies among secularists and progressives.

The structural logic of the Sangh's practical ideology demands that the notions of minorityism and 'appeasement of Muslims' become central to the strategy for uniting Hindus psychologically and emotionally – and therefore, it is to be hoped, culturally and politically. What remains, then, is to make the accusation persuasive through the selective appropriation and treatment of those issues wherein a minimally plausible case can be constructed to show the state or particular parties as guilty of perpetuating minorityism. Hence the constant, and often innovative search by the Sangh Parivar for issues through which this basic message can be pushed.

But it is necessary to remind ourselves that what must be explained is not the 'newness' of the Sangh Parivar's ideological message, but the *new receptivity* to one it has pursued for decades. It is here that the issue of Congress decline must be situated, even as the Sangh must be credited with the ability to take advantage of the new, more favourable political environment in which it has found itself. As we shall see, the political trajectory of the BJP, and of its earlier incarnation as the Jan Sangh, was not without fits and starts, detours and diversions, beginning in the mid 1970s.

The Historic Decline of the Congress

Virtually every major political development in recent times bears the stamp imposed by a basic structural malady expressed in a double dilemma. The historic decline of the Congress party has taken place at a time when no political formation has been able to replace it in its historical role. The overall result is an unprecedented political and ideological vacuum, and a politics of extreme flux as competitors strive to cannibalize the space formerly occupied by the Congress. Whatever the partial or temporary successes enjoyed by one competitor or another, they have proved neither stable nor significant enough to make any single force the new fulcrum of Indian political life in the way that the Congress was for so many years after independence. But the Bharatiya Janata Party (BJP) today is the strongest candidate to take up that role.

If the era of 'one-party dominance' at the centre is long gone, neither is there any visible prospect that a stable two- or three-party competitive system at the national level might institutionalize itself. Most importantly, it has become clear that some kind of bourgeois centrist formation is not fated, by the sheer complexity and segmented character of Indian society, always to rule at the centre. Therein lies the principal danger. An accelerated Hindu communalization of the Indian polity has taken place, and with it comes a stronger authoritarian thrust. If the political rise of the lower castes has led some to talk of India's 'Second Democratic Revolution', then the political rise of Hindutva forces threatens the credibility of this claim. The term 'authoritarian democracy' remains a good way of characterizing the Indian polity – only the authoritarian dimension has grown stronger.[35]

The basic mould of plebiscitary politics and centrist rule, which encompassed the range of possible regimes for so long, is now so seriously weakened that the future has become far more open-ended and unpredictable.[36] The single most important reason for this turn of affairs has been the scale and depth of the decline of Congress. The general trajectory has been visible for a long time, beginning in the late 1960s; but, until recently, the gradient of its decline was not steep. Moreover, the three alternatives to Congress rule at the centre – the Janata Party (1977–80), the Janata Dal (1989–90) and the United Democratic Front, or UDF (1996–98) – were also centrist formations, and in the first two cases gave way to Congress rule again, while the UDF, the last non-Congress, non-BJP government, was succeeded by a BJP-led coalition.[37]

---

35 I first used this term to describe the Indian polity in my text on India's political economy, A. Vanaik, *The Painful Transition: Bourgeois Democracy in India* (London, 1990), and it seems more appropriate now than ever.

36 Indian politics remains plebiscitary in one sense – most parties, excluding the BJP, base their appeal not on ideology but on issues that seem to be of current relevance. On the general plebiscitary character of Indian politics until 1989, see my ibid., Chapter 2.

37 The Charan Singh government (1979) and the Chandrasekhar government

It was plausible, therefore, to assume (a) that a generally non-polarized framework of plebiscitary centrist domination in some form would still hold sway; and (b) that the Congress, though weakened and no longer enjoying sole star billing, would nonetheless remain an important player. The prospect of a post-Congress India still seemed more a matter of distant speculation than an immediate prospect.

The depth and severity of the crisis facing the Congress party only became evident after 1989, upsetting all calculations and perspectives concerning the future direction of Indian politics. It was the 1991 elections, during which the leader of the Congress party and former prime minister, Rajiv Gandhi, was assassinated, that indicated the arrival of a new phase in Indian politics. Hitherto the endemic instability of the polity had been expressed in a series of wave elections, bringing to power either the Congress or a patched-up centrist rival – the Janata Party, and later the Janata Dal. The increasing volatility of voter behaviour expressed itself in sharp swings behind one or the other centrist formation, motivated negatively by disillusionment with one side, and positively by receptivity to a new issue-based (rather than programme-based) appeal by the other.[38]

Though the accession to power of the Janata Dal in 1989 as a minority government had indicated the shape of things to come, it was the 1991 elections that broke this pattern. For the first time in its history, the Congress formed only a minority government. Where wave elections and strong parliamentary majorities had once expressed underlying instabilities, deepening political instability was now to express itself through the emergence of parliamentary instabilities as well. The Congress party in power established a parliamentary majority by engineering defections, but the writing was on the wall. Coalition governments or unstable minority governments were becoming a marked feature of national-level politics.

More importantly, Indian politics was becoming more polarized, the space for traditional centrist politics was shrinking fast, and the Congress was declining rapidly, despite its rule since 1991. So serious has been the decline of the Congress that, after the 2014 election results, it is no longer out of place to wonder whether its crisis is terminal, or whether India is entering a post-Congress future. Confident requiems for the Congress should still be avoided, however. Matters remain too much in flux, and inherently unpredictable.

But the crisis of the Congress is sharper than most observers have so far perceived. It would be tempting but misconceived to draw reassuring parallels with the longevity of populist political formations – for example, in certain Latin American countries.[39] The Congress may still survive as a

(1990–91) were purely interim arrangements, of little consequence. They had no electoral mandate, emerging only as a result of parliamentary manoeuvrings.

38 Vanaik, *Painful Transition*

39 For the cyclical changes in the fortunes of Latin American populist parties, see

significant force in Indian politics; a more than hundred-year-old party does not cave in so easily. And the segmented character of Indian society continues to favour broadly centrist formations over other, more polarizing ones. But if the Congress is to survive, it must do so in a new form. The old Congress is dying, even if no definitive epitaph can yet be written. A new Congress has yet to emerge.

Socially, the Congress party's pre-eminence rested on its ability to combine solid upper-caste support with enduring loyalty from the ranks of the 'core minorities' in many parts of the country. This term refers to Dalits, Adivasis and Muslims where the first two are also referred to as Scheduled Castes (SCs) and Scheduled Tribes (STs) which is Constitutionalese for those social groups listed in official schedules as entitled to reservations in government jobs and educational institutes as well as having reserved electoral constituencies, The rise of the backward or intermediate castes and the consolidation of their votes weakened the electoral impact of the traditional pattern of Congress support. But what really undermined the Congress was its increasing abandonment by those sections that had long supported it.

The loyalty of upper castes – Brahmins and forward castes (above the OBCs in caste ranking but below Brahmins) – was most important in the north, and especially in the all-important state of Uttar Pradesh, which provides the single largest number of seats (eighty) to the national parliament, the Lok Sabha. In Uttar Pradesh, 12 per cent of the population are Brahmins, who also make up some 40 per cent of the country's Brahmins. Together with the forward castes, they constitute around 25 per cent of the state's electorate. Generally, dominance at the centre has required dominance in the northern states, whose order of importance is: Uttar Pradesh, Bihar, Madhya Pradesh, Rajasthan. There were periods in the 1980s when the Congress could compensate for loss of support in the north by gains in the south. But this only disguised the seriousness of Congress's declining support among upper castes, because such gains took place in the context of wave elections. With that era now receding, Congress's dilemma is revealed in its true, stark proportions.

In north India, the upper castes have shifted to the BJP, with some sections favouring regional parties. But it was the eroding hold on the core minorities that dealt a body blow to Congress's claim to be the country's true national party. Today the electoral behaviour of these groups is characterized by considerable volatility, with non-Congress alternatives preferred more often than not. Since, proportionally speaking, the defection of upper castes has been considerably greater than that from below, a reduced and weakened Congress became, in 2004 and 2009, a party whose electoral

---

M. Löwy, ed., *Populism in Latin America*, Notebooks for Study and Research 6 (Amsterdam, 1987). Certain one-time populist formations, like Argentinian Peronism, reorganized themselves on a totally different right-wing basis. They have made the transition to a new type of party, while the Congress has not.

support was relatively more concentrated among the core minorities and poor, even as it pursued a more right-wing, neoliberal policy orientation.[40]

After the demolition of the Babri Masjid, and with the Congress ever more willing to accommodate itself to Hindu communalism, Muslim alienation from the Congress is greater than ever. But even besides this, one of the most important developments in recent times has been the remarkable new ferment that is taking place within the Muslim community. The enormous pressure political Hindutva has exerted on Muslims has heightened internal frustrations. The failure of traditional (usually religious) authorities to provide necessary protection and succour has been cruelly exposed. The overall result is a greater willingness than ever to reject or outflank the traditional leadership elements among Muslims. This new willingness to question the traditional leadership and the norms it has laid down for how Muslims must organize their lives is a positive development in Indian political life. It does not yet amount to a major self-assertion by Muslims in the larger context of Indian politics, but it does indicate a newer independence in political thinking, reflected in a much greater willingness to change political alignments from what they have been in the past.

The social base for this new upsurge of reform has, of course, been the emergence and consolidation of a sizeable Muslim middle class, substantially making up for the vacuum in north India created by the earlier migration of this stratum to Pakistan after Partition. There is now a significant layer of young Muslims born three-and-a-half to four decades after independence for whom the issues of the pre-Partition era, and the traditional concerns advocated by the Muslim leadership in that period and in the first decades after independence, seem increasingly irrelevant. They constitute an important reservoir in which activists for social and political reform can be found.

This Muslim middle class began to flex its muscles in the early 1970s, pressing towards secular issues of reform that could help their social, educational and economic advancement. Thus issues such as preserving the status of Urdu (which, for various reasons related to the communalization of north Indian politics for over a century, had come to be seen symbolically as a 'Muslim' issue) were of much less concern to them than the promotion of measures that, symbolically or otherwise, led not to a politics of self-conscious isolation and separateness, but towards greater integration in the secular institutions of market, polity and higher education.

---

40 As for the BJP, it has overtaken the Congress as the most favoured repository of votes for the upper castes and upper classes. In the 2004 general elections, 43 per cent of the upper castes voted for the BJP, compared to 21 per cent for the Congress. Among peasant proprietors, 25 per cent voted for the BJP compared to 23 per cent for the Congress. Among OBCs, the vote share was approximately the same, while among Dalits, Adivasis, Muslims, Sikhs and Christians, the Congress did consistently and significantly better. Among the upper-middle class, the BJP secured 31 per cent of votes, compared to 26 per cent for the Congress; among the lower-middle class, the Congress secured 28 per cent to the BJP's 25 per cent; while among the poor and very poor, the Congress did considerably better.

This secularizing thrust was set back, to the benefit of the traditional leadership pursuing its usual politics of the 'Muslim community', precisely because of the upsurge of communal Hindu politics from the middle and late 1970s onwards. A Muslim politics otherwise has little *raison d'être* in a country as diverse as India, in which the shared cultural characteristics among members of a local community (Hindu and Muslim) or region have been greater than those supposedly shared between members of a single religious community between such localities and regions.

Two factors, however, stand as the primary obstacles to the steady dismantling of such a politics of Muslimness: first and foremost, the defensive self-consciousness and fear among Muslims created by the growth and impact of Hindu communalism (especially the polarizing effects of communal riots); and second, the 'unifying' issue of Muslim Personal Law. The launching by Hindutva of such a major onslaught on Muslim Personal Law, and the demand for its replacement by a Uniform Civil Code, has made an issue of gender equality and social reform into one of 'Muslim identity'.[41] Establishing how best to deal with the issue of community-based Personal Laws, in communities that might be religious, tribal, sect-based, and so on, has become an important part of the current struggle to de-communalize Indian society and politics.

For scheduled castes, the Congress no longer stands for anything with which it can identify. Other regional formations are just as capable of pushing a vote-catching populism, and of doing so with greater credibility. The very fact that scheduled castes gave their loyalty to the Congress for so long makes the Congress's failure to address their needs adequately all the more reprehensible, and is now a powerful barrier to Congress efforts to reclaim such support. Moreover, unprecedented Dalit assertiveness has transformed the parameters of Indian electoral politics as they were formerly understood. The Congress has suffered most from this upsurge of Dalit power and independence.

Even support from scheduled tribes, which make up around half of the country's Dalits, has proved impermanent. In states like Gujarat, which contains disproportionately high numbers of tribals, the Congress base has been greatly eroded, with the BJP gaining at its expense. In other states, too, other parties, whether regional or having nationalist pretensions, have gained ground.

The historically accumulated prestige of Congress among the core minorities was an asset that many observers felt could not be easily squandered even by a feckless leadership. But that is exactly what has happened. It is what makes the crisis of the Congress so acute, and its revival on newer terms so urgent if it is to restore its status as a major actor in the organization

---

41 Political Hindutva would like a Uniform Civil Code compatible with what it believes should be the fundamental principles governing Hindu family life and gender relations.

of Indian political life. The one glimmer of hope it clings to even today, when it has been reduced to its lowest parliamentary ebb in comparison to other non-BJP parties, is that it has a stronger national presence that it hopes will attract tactical voting support from the core minorities at the Lok Sabha level.

Ideological disarray

The ideological disarray of the Congress has been the inevitable corollary of its political and electoral decline – part cause and part consequence. The old Nehruvian Consensus that has collapsed was based on a loose acceptance of four principles – socialism, democracy, secularism and non-alignment. Domestically, socialism represented a form of social democracy – a state-driven capitalism combined with a limited paternalist welfarism. But it also embodied a certain value commitment to social justice and greater equality, which acted as a benchmark for judging policies. Secularism meant, at a minimum, a commitment (despite variant interpretations of secularism) to preserving a non-denominational, religiously non-affiliated state. Externally, non-alignment represented the effort to maximize national independence in foreign policy by avoiding formal or serious informal alignments with either bloc in the Cold War era.

The collapse of the Nehruvian Consensus was primarily due to a failure to implement those principles effectively; but from the 1980s, accelerated by the collapse of the Communist bloc, the principles of socialism, secularism and non-alignment have come to be widely and increasingly criticized, or even rejected altogether, while India's claim to being the world's largest democracy is more frequently and bombastically proclaimed than ever before. In a sense, India's experience is an expression of the widespread disillusionment created by the failed promise of developmentalism in most Third World countries in the post-colonial era.

The internal reasons for Congress decline include the following:

- the rise of rich farmers looking for political expression outside the Congress, and of a much larger category of aspiring capitalist farmers who followed their leadership;
- the rise of significant tensions between the industrial and agrarian elites;
- the growth and consolidation of an industrial elite lacking commitment to the development of an indigenous industrial base and strong technological self-reliance, and on the look-out for greater collaboration with foreign capital;
- the shift within the dominant coalition, with the big bourgeoisie becoming more powerful and successful in imposing its strategic vision on India's desired future;
- support for this elite by growing sections of the bureaucracy;

- the rise of a criminalized, lumpenized business class linked to the black economy, tax evasion and speculation;
- the steady transformation of the urban 'middle class' and professionals, who lost progressivist inclinations as they became more self-centred, hedonistic and consumerist in their aspirations;
- the rise of a lumpen political elite;
- generational change in the Congress leadership;
- rising (but unmet) expectations and the increasing electoral volatility of the core minorities;
- growing federalist pressures in the Indian polity, leading to the rise of all kinds of non-Congress regional political formations;
- the increasing lop-sidedness of the Indian economy, with its uneven growth pattern, sectorally and geographically; and
- the ever starker inability of the Indian economy to meet the basic needs of the poor, whose absolute numbers remain huge.

Ideologically, then, the Congress has simply drifted. It has accommodated itself to winds whose force and direction have been governed by factors beyond its control. In three fundamental areas – foreign policy, secularism and the economy – the Congress shifted significantly to the right, thereby pushing the centre of gravity of Indian politics as a whole in that direction. On the issue of secularism, the BJP/Sangh took up the running from the mid 1980s, and there is little doubt that the Congress reinforced this trend by pursuing a perspective that is accurately characterized as 'pale saffron', in keeping with much of its past behavior, saffron being the emblematic colour of political Hindutva.

This trend has extended beyond the more explicit Congress use of the 'Hindu card' – a practice that surfaced most obviously with Indira Gandhi in regard to Punjab, Kashmir and elsewhere. Under Narasimha Rao, the Congress for the first time in its history organized a de facto alignment with the BJP (before the destruction of the Babri Masjid), to stabilize its rule at the centre. This further legitimized Hindutva politics, and encouraged the forces of political Hindutva in its Ayodhya campaign. Indirectly, the Congress bears a great deal of the blame for the destruction of Babri Masjid. It could see what was coming, and should have done much more to prevent it, and legally and politically punishing those responsible for these communal crimes, which included the unleashing of widespread anti-Muslim pogroms in the wake of the demolition.[42] That it did none of these things reflected

---

42 The Congress government and BJP both produced 'White Papers' which, as expected, absolved the Congress and the BJP/Sangh combine respectively of responsibility for the demolition. For the only independent judgement of the event by three respected retired senior judges, see the report of the *Citizen Tribunal on Ayodhya* (Delhi, May 1994). The judgement found the Sangh Parivar guilty of premeditated conspiracy in destroying the mosque, and the Congress central government guilty of failing to prevent this demolition when it had been forewarned by its intelligence agencies.

its inordinate concern not to go against what it perceived as widespread pro-Hindutva sentiments among Hindus. The politics of expediency and cowardice were of greater consequence than any politics of principle.

Given that the Congress record in preventing communal riots through all the decades after independence, and in punishing those responsible for such outbreaks, has been so abysmal, this perhaps should not have come as a surprise. Indeed, this past history gives great force to the argument that the biased, upper-caste Hindu character of the Congress itself, from the days of the National Movement onwards, even in the changed circumstances of post-colonial political evolution would only pave the way for a more full-blown Hindutva to emerge. But the fact that, over time, there would be a further communal degeneration of the Congress does suggest that, in the early post-independence era of Nehru, it did possess more élan and confidence in reinforcing the secular credentials that it had consciously awarded to itself.[43]

The New Economic Policy (NEP) inaugurated by the Congress in 1991 was not the outcome of a wide internal debate within parliament, or among the press or the general public. It was a fait accompli brought about by a narrow circle of top politicians and high-level bureaucrats, in conjunction with key decision-makers within the IMF and World Bank. The NEP not only represented a right-wing shift in economic thinking, but was inspired by the most conservative form of neoclassical economic thinking – neoliberalism. A Congress leadership in any case bereft of all ideological moorings, and further disarmed by the collapse of the communist bloc – and therefore presumably of the socialist paradigm – responded to an immediate balance-of-payments crisis by endorsing a 'long-term solution' to what was essentially a short-term problem. This proposed 'solution' was itself highly ideological – a triumphalist neoliberalism which, in the Indian case, demanded rapid privatization of the public sector; removal of strategic control over the domestic operations of the market by the state; external liberalization, and removal of controls over all kinds of foreign capital flows; devaluation; the reduction of trade barriers, and a renewed emphasis on exports (especially of primary commodities); reduced taxes; and a decline in 'unproductive' government expenditure (social welfare). The ideological recoil from bad socialism was so strong that it led to the widespread endorsement of bad capitalism.

---

43 Even so, evidence of the presence of this serious communalist streak in the composition of the Congress was provided when, in 1948, to ensure the accession of Hyderabad province into the Union, the Indian army carried out what is, in terms of casualties (well over 20,000 dead), the worst ever anti-Muslim pogrom to date.

Searching for a new centrism

The only serious attempt to establish a new strategic foundation for Indian centrism, in this situation of political and ideological disarray in old centrism (dominated by the Congress), was made by V. P. Singh, the former prime minister of the short-lived (1989–90) Janata Dal minority government. He had the acumen to realize the nature of the problem, and to propose the most feasible solution. But he lacked the organizational ability to institutionalize a coherent force or party capable of enacting this politics of a new centrism. However, he was the one Indian political leader of any stature who in recent times had such a strategic vision, because he understood the implications of two important developments in Indian politics to have emerged in the preceding decades. These are the unprecedented assertiveness on the part of Dalits, and the 'forward march' of the backward or intermediate castes, or Other Backward Classes (OBCs), as they are also called. Admittedly, these OBCs are led for the most part by their upper layers.

V. P. Singh's platform of 'social justice', as symbolized by Mandalism, however much it was an anathema to the Indian elite and to the urban middle classes and professionals, was one expression of this new strategic vision. During the Janata Party regime (1977–80), a Commission was set up under the chairmanship of a parliamentarian, B. P. Mandal, to suggest improvements to the condition of what the Constitution called the 'Socially and Educationally Backward Classes' (SEBCs), which mainly referred to the intermediate castes or OBCs below the forward castes and above the scheduled castes and scheduled tribes. The Mandal Report, as it came to be known, was submitted at the end of 1980, and recommended quotas in central government jobs and higher educational institutions in the public sector in proportion to the size of this group, which, according to the last caste-based census of 1931, was around 52 per cent of the total population. The Supreme Court, taking note of the fact that there were already 22 per cent quotas for scheduled castes and scheduled tribes, ruled that no more than a 27 per cent quota could be reserved for OBCs, so that total quotas would not constitute a formal majority. This report was shelved until August 1990, when the V.P. Singh government decided to accept its recommendations, leading to mass protests, especially by upper-caste youth and triggering counter-demonstrations in its support. The BJP, which was supporting the government from the outside, was deeply alarmed. It withdrew support, on the grounds that enacting the report's recommendations would divide Hindus along caste lines, when its goal was to unify Hindus religiously, across boundaries of caste – precisely the purpose for which the Ram Janmabhoomi campaign had been launched in the first place.

Though V. P Singh and his party were brought down, the next Congress minority government of Narasimha Rao, seeing widespread support for the report from numerous regional parties relying on OBC votes, passed its recommendations, thereby providing for OBC quotas in central government jobs. Since then, OBC quotas of 27 per cent have been extended not only to all central government bureaucratic services, but also to central higher education institutions, and are also applied to student intakes and initial appointments to the lowest-rung teaching positions.

Given the sheer numerical weight of OBCs, all parties, including the BJP and the Left, have subsequently accepted the effective Mandalization of Indian politics. It is not as if these quotas (for the most part filled by the upper ranks of the OBCs) have transformed the lives of the poor and most backward of the OBCs, as distinct from modestly increasing the number of middle-class OBCs in much the same way as had happened for a section of scheduled castes and scheduled tribes. But no political party today, regardless of what this or that ideologue might say, can openly oppose Mandalism and what it represents, except to their grave disadvantage. The forward march of the 'Backwards' (a shorthand term commonly used for designating the OBCs) and the new assertiveness of Dalits are indisputably factors of great importance, which any political party wishing to expand its authority and power must now take into account and try to come to terms with.

What V. P. Singh and his Janata Dal sought to do, though without success, was to consolidate a new electoral and social foundation for centrism. No longer should it rest, as the old Congress had done, on an amalgam of upper castes and core minorities; instead it should rely on the Backwards and the core minorities, and in doing so provide a more stable foundation for a new centrism than even that enjoyed by the old centrism. The principal strategic problem is that the category of Backwards is socially differentiated and electorally heterogeneous. Ultimately, the most stable and powerful foundation for a new centrism – whose fulcrum would correspond to what, given mass deprivation, would appear to be the more 'natural', left-leaning centre of gravity of Indian politics – would have to rest on a non-antagonistic alliance between core minorities, and the very sizeable lower and middling sections of the Backwards. Instead, what has emerged has been an electoral alignment of sorts between the upper sections of the OBCs and sizeable sections of the core minorities.

This has proved to be an unstable situation, because the social and class relations between the two groups – particularly between the upper Backwards and the Dalits – are all too often highly antagonistic. The upper sections of the Backwards in rural India are, in class terms, usually rich farmers or aspiring capitalist family farmers, coexisting uneasily with tenants and agricultural labourers coming for the most part from the core minorities and the lower sections of the OBCs. As the agriculture sector shrinks more of these upper sections of the OBCs are becoming owners of small and medium sized businesses exploiting lower caste labour. To put it another way, while objectively speaking the more likely centre of gravity of Indian political life should be left-of-centre, in fact it has rarely been so. Social tendencies and pressures are not the same as political tendencies and pressures, and it is the latter that

determine where the centre of gravity will in fact come to rest. The direction a society takes is never decided by its average consciousness – in other
words, by the consciousness of the people as some amorphous mass – but
above all by the consciousness of its leading strata and elements: the articulate, the mobilizers of the mobilized, and secondarily the minority among
the masses who are the mobilized. This is precisely why capitalist and elitist
development has taken place in India, although the objective terrain is so
favourable to socialism and egalitarianism. Political mobilization and struggle decide the direction a society takes; thus, while the votes of rural India
decide which force comes to power, urban and semi-urban India decides, by
and large, what that force stands for and how it behaves in power.

The historical decline of the Congress had its most obvious and sharpest
expression at the level of the states. Rivals to the Congress emerged, came
to power, and in some cases displaced the Congress as the natural party of
government, or natural pole of reference. In any case, a host of other factors
have led (despite more laws justifying central intervention in the states, and
despite the inadequate decentralization of economic and financial powers)
to a more federalist and decentralized practice of politics. Regional leaders
and parties have begun to exercise greater national influence. It is in this
wider framework of Dalit assertion, Muslim ferment, OBC pressures and
regional pulls that we must situate the rise of the BJP, and of the forces of
political Hindutva, where 'Hindutva' denotes the strongest form of Hindu
nationalism.[44]

In India, failed developmentalism is obvious enough at the socio-
economic level. Its major political reflex has been systemic instability, while
ideologically it is symbolized by the collapse of the hegemony of the Nehruvian Consensus. The BJP and the forces of Hindu communalism have
benefited most from the ensuing ideological and political vacuum, partly
because of certain intrinsic strengths. They possess the most ideologically
coherent, organized and disciplined cadre force in the country, in the shape
of the RSS,[45] which has steadily burrowed its way into the pores of civil
society in many parts of the country. BJP and Sangh ideology can claim
a considerable degree of legitimacy from its continuity with the cluster of
ideological values that guided and informed the National Movement.

Most of all, the BJP has benefited from offering a coherent political
and ideological alternative to the Congress. The left has also been such an
alternative, but its more regional character and identification has been a
handicap. The BJP has been more nationally dispersed, and has always been

---

44 There are variants of Hindu nationalism that are not as stark or aggressively hostile
to Muslims as the Sangh variant. See the subsection on 'Hindutva' in Chapter 3, for more
on this.

45 Serious book-length studies of the RSS in English have been surprisingly rare.
There is the older text of W. K. Anderson and S. D. Damle, *The Brotherhood of Saffron*
(Delhi, 1987). More recent texts, mentioned above, include Jaffrelot, *Hindu Nationalist
Movement*; Jaffrelot, *Sangh Parivar*; and Kanungo, *RSS's Tryst with Politics*.

a more significant factor in the heartland of Hindi-speaking states, which have been disproportionately more important than other regions in determining the shape of national politics. In short, it has been so positioned as to be the most likely beneficiary of the decline not just of the Congress, but of the politics of old centrism.

The Political Rise of the BJP

For the first two decades after independence, the considerable success of India in institutionalizing democratic rule and carrying out a degree of welfarist industrialization enabled the Congress to survive as the dominant political institution. Indeed, the Congress and its leadership oversaw this period of successful transition to a relatively stable democracy. A variety of factors were responsible for the subsequent emergence of the peculiar paradox of India's polity – endemic political instability encased within a macro-framework of remarkable democratic durability. A democratic political system had been institutionalized with strong mass commitment to its preservation. But there was a partial decay and mutation of various democratic institutions, including the legislature, the civilian bureaucracy, the judiciary and the press – not to mention the routinization of undemocratic (frequently violent) practices at lower levels of governance.

Above all, the principal overseer of political stability, the Congress, had entered a period of slow but steady decline. For decades a Congress alliance with rural landed elites had assured it decisive control over the countryside, while it also carried a populist appeal among the poorest sections. Given the enormously segmented character of Indian society – no other country in the world is criss-crossed by such a range of community affiliations and identities – the Congress was the centrist formation par excellence, the one party appealing to the widest cross-section. To be stable, Indian political democracy could not rest on some unachievable two-party competitive system, but seemed to require the constant popularity of a dominant centrist formation.

Challenges from above and below undermined this Congress dominance. Historically, the electoral base of the Congress rested on the Brahmins and forward castes, along with the core minorities, that is, the Muslims, the Dalits (untouchables) and the Adivasis (tribals) of both the hills and the plains. The very success of Indian development in the first two decades transformed the situation. New rural elites from the middle or backward castes, as they were also called, emerged and pressed for their aims, both within and outside the Congress party. At the same time, growing expectations made the support of large sections of the core minorities for the Congress increasingly insecure. The Congress itself had also transmogrified. In the first two decades after 1947, the Congress had moved from being a mass movement and organization to being an increasingly corrupted party of governance by patronage. Organizationally, it had become an electoral machine to be cranked up around the time of various local, regional and national contests.

The crisis of Congress hegemony became obvious, and therefore the inauguration of the era of endemic political instability took place in the late 1960s, when for the first time in its post-independence history the Congress party split, with Indira Gandhi's wing proving triumphant. The Emergency of 1975–77 is best understood as Gandhi's failed attempt to resolve the endemic crisis of bourgeois instability through an authoritarian transformation of the polity. But this failure only meant that it became clearer how *not* to tackle the problem of instability. It was the Emergency, and the mass-scale anti-corruption movement that preceded and partly provoked it, that gave the forces of Hindutva an unexpected lease of life. Until the 1977 elections, the Bharatiya Jan Sangh (BJS), set up in 1951 with RSS support, had been peripheral to Indian politics. When it became part of an anti-Congress, non-Left coalition, temporarily welded into a single centrist party called the Janata Party, it made a decisive break from its undistinguished political past. In fact, the role of the RSS in resisting the Emergency (a role they were literally pushed into by Gandhi's attack on them, in order to give the Emergency a 'progressive' image), and before that its cadre participation in the anti-corruption 1974–75 JP Movement (named after its leader, a revered Gandhian, Jay Prakash Narayan), helped the Jan Sangh to secure the single largest share of parliamentary seat allotments within the Janata Party.[46] Between 1977 and 1979, the Jan Sangh was able for the first time to place its own people in many key sections of the central bureaucracy, and to use state resources to benefit itself and its parent organization, the RSS.

When the Janata Party broke up over the issue of affiliation of members of parliament to the RSS, it was clear that, if a centrist party was to be genuinely centrist, then it could not countenance the kind of political and organizational loyalties of its MPs to an extra-party entity such as the RSS, which was not subject to the control of the Janata Party itself. The Janata Party was to break up over the unwillingness of the Jan Sangh to sever its links with the RSS, an extra-parliamentary organization with no commitment to the Janata Party as such. This led to the formation of the breakaway party, the Janata (Secular), in mid 1979. Given this disarray, the Congress under Gandhi was able to win the 1980 election through the promise of bringing back stability of rule. This contrasted with the mishmash of the Janata party, whose former components had split into various formations and had become marginalized. The Janata (S) won forty-one seats. The Jan Sangh remained part of the rump Janata Party, which won thirty-one seats. Out of these, the Jan Sangh won sixteen – much less than the ninety-three it had won in 1977, but closer to the twenty-two it gained in 1971.

46 Of the Janata Party's total tally of 298 Lok Sabha parliamentary seats, 93 went to candidates loyal to the former BJS.

The dilemma now facing the Jan Sangh (which had reconstituted itself independently as the Bharatiya Janata Party) was the classic one. Given the highly segmented character of Indian society, how could any non-centrist party hope to win, or even fare well electorally? Should the BJP weaken or strengthen its links with the RSS, whose agenda could not be the same as that of a political party, even one with a formal commitment to Hindutva? The RSS would support even the Congress (as it has already done on occasion) if it felt that this would promote the advancement of Hindu cultural nationalism of the kind it desired in civil society. Should the BJP try to be the party of the 'Great Hindu *Rally*', or should it try to be the Hindu equivalent of a right-wing Christian Democratic party of western Europe – only more Hindu than Christian Democracy is Christian, and less democratic? Should the BJP move towards the centre of the Indian political spectrum, thereby diluting its Hindu nationalist and communalist message? Or should it, by tying itself more strongly to the parent cadre organization, the RSS, swing towards a more aggressive and communalist posture?

The answer came soon enough. Between 1980 and 1984, the BJP had sought to weaken its links with the RSS, to move to the centre, and to dilute its ideological message through advocacy of a largely incomprehensible 'Gandhian Socialism'. This eventually gave way to 'Integral Humanism', a term coined by Deen Dayal Upadhyaya, a Hindu nationalist leader of less self-confident times. The 1984 elections were the turning point. The BJP fared dismally, winning only two seats. L. K. Advani replaced the 'moderate' A. B. Vajpayee; there was a change of orientation to a more aggressive, extreme and open form of Hindu nationalism. From 1984 onwards, the BJP was a party looking for issues on which to peg its messages. It would now seek to extend its social and political base by moving right, actively pursuing the politics of polarization on the issues of secularism and the cultural self-definition of the Indian nation and state.[47]

Moreover, the pivot of 'mainstream' Indian politics was open to being shifted quite considerably. Indeed, deeper social transformations had fertilized the ground for certain kinds of cultural–religious activities and identifications that could benefit the Sangh Parivar. The BJP was aware of this, but the shift in its political strategy after 1984 was determined more by the failure of the alternative politics it had pursued between 1980 and 1984 than by any deep-seated or calculated analysis it had made of the potential dividends to be garnered by making such a strategic shift. Moreover, the 1980–84 failure greatly strengthened the control and influence of the RSS

---

47 That the BJP advanced by moving to the right refuted the principal thesis concerning its future growth prospects proposed in Bruce Graham, *Hindu Nationalism and Indian Politics* (Cambridge, 1990). However, Graham was not wrong in pointing out the existence and continuity of the basic tension between wanting to represent the Great Hindu Rally and wanting to dilute this thrust if it seems this can bring about or further consolidate central power.

over the party, naturally pushing it towards a more communalist politics. As the BJP became stronger, the relationship of forces between itself and the RSS would of course change. But at this point in time the precondition for the BJP to become stronger was greater subservience to the RSS.

Of the underlying social transformations that the BJP would now take into consideration, one of the most important was the rise of the intermediate castes, which now sought greater economic and political power, as well as upward cultural mobility. One avenue for achieving the latter was not just Sanskritization, but identification with and reworking of a wider Hindu identity. This was reflected in the great appeal of a series of religious-cultural events and activities, including the various *yagna yatras* or processions that took place through the late 1970s and early 1980s. Moving across many of the provinces or states of the Indian federation these long processions, religious cavalcades and pilgrimages linked up rural with semi-urban and urban India around common symbols of reverence and loyalty. The Vishwa Hindu Parishad (VHP) or World Hindu Council, originally set up as another front organization of the RSS, was instrumental in organizing such *yatras*. As it grew in strength, spectacularly so in the 1980s, the VHP also developed a considerable authority of its own, separate from that of the RSS. It is seen by many to be even more aggressively cultural-nationalist and explicitly anti-Muslim in its attitudes than the RSS.

By the mid 1980s, the BJP was beginning to make its mark as the 'party of the future'. In a context of deepening uncertainty and flux, the BJP and the Sangh Parivar were the one collective force that had the organizational means, ideological clarity and inclination to pursue the politics of sustained mass mobilization. The aim was not simply to search for events and issues to mobilize around. There have been many such mass mobilizations since 1947. It was a search to highlight or create those events and issues which could function as exemplary expressions of an already pre-conceived ideological perspective for which there was now a more receptive environment.

Major mass mobilizations and mass campaigns like the 1974 Railway Strike, the J. P. Movement (1974–75), the electoral campaign to reject Emergency rule (1977), and V. P. Singh's anti-corruption (Bofors) campaign (1989) were issue- or event-based activities that essentially defined the character of the participants. The combatant parties could derive some overall ideological colouring, but this was necessarily of a very loose kind. The politics of such mass mobilizations defined primarily what the instigators and organizers were against, rather than what they stood for – certainly not in any broad, programmatic or ideological way.[48]

---

48 Another party that has jumped onto the Hindutva bandwagon is the Shiv Sena in Maharashtra, an organization comprising a high proportion of goons and lumpen elements, which was initially promoted by Bombay industrialists and the Congress government of Maharashtra in the 1970s to launch physical attacks on communist control and influence among that city's working class. The failure of the CPI (the split with the

This was not the case with the mobilizational politics of the Sangh Parivar. As their acolytes and ideologues have repeatedly asserted, theirs was for the first time since the National Movement an *ideological politics of mass scope* – an attempt, partly successful, *to alter the mainstream agenda itself.* For once, they were right. Far-left insurgency movements have also pursued intensely ideological politics, but these have operated at the margins of general political life.

In the early 1980s, religious front organizations of the RSS, most notably the VHP, had carried out a series of mass-mobilizing pilgrimages of a half-religious, half-cultural nature, aimed at consolidating a common Hindu identity. The forces of Hindu communalism were the only formations confident of carrying out such mass mobilizations. And between 1984 and 1989 the BJP could claim considerable success in spreading its messages. But what was missing was an issue that could put Muslims in the dock and allow the Sangh to go to town on the issue of 'Muslim appeasement' by the Indian state, and thus simultaneously arouse a strong sense of Hindu deprivation and grievance. They were soon to be rewarded.

The absence of a Uniform Civil Code (UCC) of even an optional nature has been a concession to a Muslim fundamentalist leadership adamant about the sanctity of a conservatively interpreted Sharia. Meanwhile, a refusal of governments to carry out a purge of predominantly Hindu paramilitary forces, which have themselves attacked Muslim communities, has been the other side of this picture. In 1986 the issue of a UCC came up when the Supreme Court insisted that the provisions of the Indian penal code on maintenance took precedence over Sharia for an elderly Muslim divorcee, Shah Bano, who had petitioned it. The Congress government's decision to overturn the ruling legislatively in favour of preserving Muslim Personal Law sparked mobilization by Hindu communalist forces and counter-mobilization by fundamentalist Muslim leaders. This transformed what was essentially an issue of women's

---

CPM did not help) to confront the Shiv Sena effectively by direct physical counter-attacks paved the way for the latter's rise and the communists' decline, even before the transition of Bombay, from 1990 onwards, to becoming Mumbai – a de-industrialised centre of commerce, finance and entertainment with very little union presence and an irrelevant Left. See P. Bidwai, *The Phoenix Moment: Challenges Confronting the Indian Left* (Noida, 2015), pp. 85–88.

The Shiv Sena's principal calling card has always been its claim to being the promoter and protector of Marathas, advocating a 'sons of the soil' approach and defending 'Maharashtrian pride'; for its first decades of existence, it was therefore against even Hindu outsiders from the north, south or elsewhere taking jobs and benefits in Bombay, and in the state as a whole. From the 1990s, the Shiv Sena, seeing the BJP rise, sought to broaden its base by promoting Hindu nationalism, but has never had the organizational or ideological resources to outplay the Sangh in this regard. The end-result is that the BJP, once the junior partner of the Shiv Sena, over time has become the senior partner, and currently rules in Maharashtra. The Shiv Sena, to maintain its distinctiveness, is now pushing 'Maharashtrian-ness', and is currently in many respects more critical of the BJP than is the Congress. But, given its political DNA, it remains a regional force only, and one that is so far losing ground even at this level to the BJP.

oppression by personal laws of all kinds into a battleground of identity politics between 'appeased' Muslims and 'aggrieved' Hindus – although the victims of such a government decision were Muslim women and children.

To counter-balance this concession to Muslim communalism, the government now allowed an injustice that had lain dormant to become explosive. For decades before independence, there had been a localized belief, unsubstantiated by any serious empirical evidence, that a temple dedicated to Lord Rama at his presumed birthplace – a mythical site in the town of Ayodhya – had been destroyed by the first Mughal Emperor, Babar, in the sixteenth century, and a mosque built in its place. Muslims rightly regarded the shrine as a mosque that had long been desecrated by the surreptitious placement of Hindu idols in December 1949, after which they were denied access by New Delhi 'in the interests of maintaining law and order', though elementary justice demanded that there be full restoration of its status as a mosque. But locks were also placed on the shrine, denying access to Hindus for worship. But after the Shah Bano affair, to appease Hindu communalists, the Congress government in 1986 removed the locks, allowing Hindus such access.

The Ram Janmabhoomi campaign

This decision enabled the RSS, BJP and VHP to spearhead a remarkable campaign for the destruction of the mosque and its replacement by a new temple dedicated to Lord Rama, as a symbol of respect for 'Hindu wishes' desecrated by past 'Muslim perfidy'. All those, including the state, opposing this were 'appeasing' Muslims, and were contemptuous and hostile to 'Hindu sentiment'. This campaign was among the most significant in India's post-independence history. It polluted the political and democratic atmosphere of Indian society, delivering huge dividends to the forces of Hindu communalism, though in time it was to offer diminishing returns.

The VHP launched the Ayodhya campaign in the early 1980s, and controlled it until 1988. The BJP's adoption of the campaign meant that the VHP, a rag-tag coalition of assorted sadhus, leaders of obscure Hindu sects and plain fanatics, had become much more important within the RSS-led 'family'. The RSS consolidated a particularly close relationship with the BJP from the mid 1980s onwards. At the RSS's goading, the BJP astutely exploited the potential offered by the mosque/temple issue, first to mobilize people politically on a mass scale, and second to combine non-parliamentary activism with its parliamentary work, thus bringing the pressure of its mass campaign to bear on the weak V.P. Singh administration that had emerged as a minority Janata Dal government in the 1989 general elections. Singh, had come to power on an anti-corruption platform, in response to Rajiv Gandhi's involvement in the Bofors arms-selling scandal.

The peak of the BJP's Ayodhya campaign, and the unmasking of the Sangh Parivar's ruthlessly authoritarian, communalist and anti-secular face, were yet to come. Nonetheless, by 1989 the BJP, standing independently in the elections, won eighty-eight seats, propping up a minority Janata Dal government that it would soon enough bring down. The Singh government depended on both the Left (consisting primarily of the communist parties) and the BJP for its survival. The BJP had by then identified the mosque/ temple issue as a high-priority item on its agenda. The elevation of the issue also expressed a qualitative change in the relationship between the party and its 'sister' organizations in the Sangh Parivar – the VHP, the Bajrang Dal and the RSS.

By mid 1990, numerous forms of mobilization by the Sangh Parivar could be identified: the collection of 'consecrated' bricks from villages and towns in a symbolic gesture of support for the planned construction of a Rama temple on the alleged site of the birth of Lord Rama (Ram Janmabhoomi) at Ayodhya; public meetings where fiery anti-Muslim rhetoric would flow freely; and processions of *Ram jyotis* – literally oil lamps dedicated to Rama, which would be organized late at night, often in a provocative fashion to threaten violence and aggression against Muslims in the neighbourhood.

In parts of north India, an overtly militant and particularly menacing form of mobilization was organized: the wielding and brandishing of the *trishul*, or trident – Lord Shiva's weapon – and its use as a symbol of a new, militant Hindu consciousness. A whole industry mushroomed, manufacturing prop-aganda material – posters, stickers and mini-*trishuls*, as well as colourful and fanciful accounts of ancient and medieval Indian history.

In the autumn of 1990, the BJP multiplied the scale of mobilization many times over, and imparted to it a particularly aggressive edge in the form of L. K. Advani's *rath yatra* – literally, a chariot tour, which covered more than half of the country. The chariot – an imitation of ancient horse-drawn carts from the *Mahabharata* (in reality, a decked-out Toyota van) – took Advani to more than twenty communally sensitive cities, as well as hundreds of small towns and villages, where volunteers could drum up support and organize rallies and public meetings on an overtly anti-Muslim platform of hatred and vituperation. Advani boldly displayed the election symbol of the BJP – the lotus flower – on the *rath*, and made no effort to conceal the link between the *yatra*, religion and politics.

The *rath yatra* left a trail of violence and devastation in its wake. From the beginning, the *yatra* was calculated to provoke: there were accompanying rituals using human blood; the most horrifying and belligerent chants and slogans were raised; and Muslim-owned shops and names were openly tar-geted. V.P. Singh came under pressure from the Left and from secular sections of the media to ban the *yatra*, because it was deliberately provoking violence.

Singh dithered, vacillating between promising tough action and trying to placate the BJP leadership. Ultimately, and belatedly, Advani was arrested and his march halted – not by the central government, but by the gov-ernment of Bihar, then also under Janata rule. As soon as Advani was arrested, the BJP announced that it was withdrawing support for Singh in parliament. By September, the government was tottering, and counting its last days. In October, the VHP launched another offensive, this time in Ayodhya itself. It organized a *karseva*, or voluntary service, to make a symbolic beginning to building a temple. Unwilling to prevent it, although it was in blatant violation of court injunctions against a change in the site's status, the government allowed *karsevaks* to gather in large numbers right next to the Babri mosque. On 30 October, a frenzied mob climbed over the compound wall of the mosque, and some volunteers planted saffron flags on one of the domes. A weak and vacillating government had allowed the forces of extreme right-wing communalism to score a victory. No one was prosecuted for this criminal act.

The Singh government was followed by an unstable Congress-supported regime headed by Prime Minister Chandrasekhar, which soon made way for elections in May 1991. The Congress returned to power in a minority government without Rajiv Gandhi, who was assassinated during the election campaign. The new prime minister, Narasimha Rao, was a weak compromise candidate never known for his firmness, and was in favour of a 'soft Hindutva' rather than a principled secular approach. The BJP made handsome gains: it won 119 seats, as against 88 in 1989. Its share of the national vote rose to over 20 per cent, way beyond expectations, breaking all previous patterns of sudden surges in electoral support. Thanks to the fragmentation of the rest of the non-Congress vote between factions of the splintered Janata Dal, the BJP emerged as the single largest party of opposition in the lower house of parliament. It also took power in the state of Uttar Pradesh, where Ayodhya is located. Rao's greater proclivity towards appeasement, his dependence on non-Congress MPs in crucial parliamentary votes, and his weakness within the ruling party were cynically exploited by the BJP's leaders, who extracted concession after concession. A situation of collaboration or informal alliance between the BJP and the Rao faction of the Congress soon emerged, permitting the BJP to tilt the scales in its favour time and again.

An important factor sustained this informal alliance. In mid 1991, the government embarked on a new right-leaning economic policy, which was strongly opposed by the Left. The BJP broadly endorsed the policy, which meshed with its own orientation, although some of its hard-core RSS leaders had reservations about its emphasis on the liberalization of foreign investment and trade. Rao came to depend increasingly on the BJP for support for his policy in and out of parliament. By 1992, the BJP commanded a degree of political influence far exceeding its numerical weight in parliament, politics and society. It used this influence deftly, through the media and the bureaucracy, to advance its Ram Janmabhoomi campaign, calculating that the effete and vacillating Rao government would not be willing or able to stand its ground against the Sangh's strategy of physical encroachments into Ayodhya.

In July 1992, the Sangh undertook a *karseva* to construct a platform on a plot of land within the mosque complex, as part of its temple-construction campaign. The government's response to this patently illegal and provocative move was supine. It allowed the platform to be built, thus legitimizing the encroachment, and pleaded with obscure religious leaders and sadhus to urge reason upon the leaders of the agitation. The post-July run-up to the demolition of the Babri mosque, which took place on 6 December 1992, is a story of retreat after ignominious retreat by the government; further intrusion by the BJP; negotiations and special pleading with an unrelenting Hindu communalist leadership; disinformation and dissimulation by the government; and deception, manipulation and rogue tactics on the part of the BJP and its allies. Subsequent disclosures make it plain that the government had adequate warning from its own intelligence agencies, as well as from the Hindu communalist leaders with whom it was negotiating, of a planned assault on the Babri mosque on 6 December. But it failed to take precautionary measures – to deploy adequate central paramilitary troops, secure injunctions from the courts, or to arrest BJP-VHP leaders, who were engaged in a conspiracy to destroy the mosque. The carnage of 6 December, consisting of the demolition of the mosque and anti-Muslim riots, sent shock-waves throughout the country. The BJP parliamentary leadership's first response was apologetic: Advani resigned as leader of the opposition in the Lok Sabha, and the chief minister of Uttar Pradesh also quit. But the party soon moved to a more defiant, militant posture, justifying what had happened and blaming the lethargic legal system for its inability to resolve the Ayodhya dispute.

December 1992 marked the peak of the BJP's militant activism. After the demolition, it proved more difficult for the BJP to maintain a steady upward swing. It could not mobilize for the construction of a temple as effectively as it had over destroying a 'hated symbol'. Instead, its regional spread was subjected to reverses and partial recuperations. The most significant barrier to its spread was the emergence of multi-caste alliances related to lower-caste assertiveness in the north of India. This historic political trend, which started in the south in the 1930s, had now reached the north. It has been an integral part of the social reform movement in the country. Given the growing awareness of their rights among Dalits and OBCs, this trend seems irreversible.

The trend had received a strong boost in 1990, when the New Delhi government under V.P. Singh announced the acceptance of a 1978 report of the Mandal Commission on OBCs (see above), which recommended, as we have seen, that 27 per cent of all government jobs be reserved for OBCs in addition to the 15 and 7.5 per cent respectively provided for the Dalits and Adivasis by the Indian Constitution. Singh's announcement of the implementation of the Mandal Report touched off a furore in the north, with upper-caste Hindus taking to the streets. The agitation had the side effects of both protecting the existing pattern of quotas for the Dalits and Adivasis from being seriously attacked (a tendency that had been developing before the Mandal furore) and alarming them sufficiently to motivate them to explore connections with the political representatives of the OBCs. The practical effect of implementation was very limited – some 50,000 new central government jobs would have been affected annually. The real significance of the report lay in its symbolic impact.

Thus political formations of the lower and middle castes received a great fillip. Such a caste alliance pays powerful electoral dividends, provided it can be sustained. Muslims, OBCs and Dalits represent roughly 14, 52 and 15 per cent of the Indian population, respectively. If even half of them back a party or alliance formation, it can expect to win. The *rath yatra*, which so polarized Indian politics, was launched by the BJP partly as a fearful response to the impact of the Mandal Report, which would set lower against upper castes, thus enormously weakening the effort to establish a consolidated Hindu vote. The anti-caste struggle, then, is vital to the effort to de-communalize and transform Indian society in a more secular, humane and socialist direction.

In a narrowly partisan sense, the Babri Masjid–Ram Janmabhoomi Ayodhya campaign did for the Sangh and the BJP what the Dandi Salt March had done for the Congress-led National Movement. But, whereas the latter helped unite the country against colonial rule, the former polarized and divided the country as never before. Nevertheless, it has over time been accepted, and in the longer term, far from damaging the BJP, can now be seen as a massive political success that propelled the party and the Sangh to national prominence, and undoubtedly extended their mass support far beyond what they had previously achieved.

With the demolition of the Babri Masjid on 6 December 1992, the Sangh fulfilled its professed goal, and maximized the political benefits of that campaign. Had it timed its demolition closer to the 1996 general elections, might it not have made more gains? This is uncertain. Sustaining such a campaign for so long at the same level of intensity was problematic. In fact, the accelerating intensity of the campaign throughout 1992 had already made further procrastination difficult. What is clear is that the BJP and the rest of the Sangh Parivar had to fulfil its promise at some time, or else risk a serious erosion of its credibility.

The Era of Coalition Rule at the Centre (1996–2014)

The five general elections from 1971 to 1989 all resembled referenda.The winning slogans offered were, chronologically, 'Remove poverty' (1971), 'End Emergency' (1977), 'Bring back stability' (1980), 'Save the country' (1984, after Indira Gandhi's assassination), and 'End corruption' (1989). In the absence of any clear and convincing ideological perspective from any side, the electorate was presented with issue-based differentiation between the main claimants to power. This pattern began to change with the rise of the strongly ideological BJP, and the RSS behind it. The 1996 elections were not like a referendum, nor were those that followed. In the six elections between 1971 and 1996, power was delivered to either the Congress or a centrist alternative – usually a patchwork formation united by anti-Congressism, rather than by any positive principle. The Congress lost three times, but the alternative to it did not last a full term. Congress's massive parliamentary victories, a function of the first-past-the-post system in 1971 and 1984, were themselves, ironically, indicative of the growing volatility of voter support, which could swing massively from one referendum-like election to the next. In 1991, for the first time in its history, the Congress came to power as a minority government. A specifically parliamentary instability had been added to the general problem of endemic political instability, until the Rao government engineered the necessary defections.

This new pattern of parliamentary instability was reaffirmed in the 1996 elections, in which the Congress was ousted, but its replacement – a United Democratic Front government of non-Congress, non-BJP parties – could only rule with the outside support of the Congress, which had garnered 140 seats. For the first time, the BJP had become the single largest component of the Lok Sabha, with 161 seats. It was invited to form the government, but during its thirteen days in power could not secure the required support for a working majority, and had to step down. It was replaced by the UDF, which held 192 seats. This brief and undistinguished interlude was over by March 1998, when the Congress precipitated another election. During the eighteen months of UDF rule, the first prime minister, Deve Gowda, the former chief minister of the state of Karnataka, had to give way under Congress pressure to I.K. Gujral, a former bureaucrat who had been foreign minister under Gowda.

The 1998 poll results were a shock to the Congress, which for the first time since independence lost two consecutive Lok Sabha elections, winning 141 seats, compared to the BJP's 182. This time the BJP had overcome its former 'pariah' status, and had forged a coalition with regional parties, indicative of the fact that the BJP had for the first time become 'normalised', its fundamentally communalist character now a matter of minor political consequence for most regional parties, barring those of the Left. The National Democratic Alliance (NDA), led by the BJP, secured a slim majority of thirteen seats, and was therefore pulled down by the eighteen MPs of the All India Anna Dravida Munnetra Kazhagam (AIADMK), one of the two contending parties in the state of Tamil Nadu, because its demand for the sacking of the ruling and rival Dravida Munnetra Kazhagam (DMK) in Tamil Nadu was not met by the centre. Both are parties standing for regional Tamil pride and are splits from the original political formation.

The fact that the BJP, and the Sangh behind it, had to bear the greatest responsibility for the series of communal riots, in which several hundred – mostly Muslims – had died before and after the demolition of the Babri Masjid, was no longer of much consequence. This commitment to violence, both practical and symbolic (the one decisive policy change the BJP carried out during its 1998–99 tenure was expressed in the nuclear tests that took place in May 1998), has caused no serious damage to its political credibility, its ability to forge alliances with other regional parties, or to its cultural, ideological and institutional influence in civil society. And, as we will see, the terrible anti-Muslim pogrom overseen by Narendra Modi's Gujarat government in February 2002, would also do no lasting damage either to the future prospects of the BJP/Sangh or to those of Modi himself.

The 1999 election results gave the NDA a comfortable majority, the BJP securing 183 seats and the Congress down to 114. This government lasted the full five years, to 2004 – when, against all expectations, it lost to the Congress-led coalition. The Congress now realized that its days of hoping to come to power on its own were finally gone, and that it would now carefully have to construct winning pre-poll alliances with other parties. The next two administrations, spanning the periods 2004–09 and 2009–14, also witnessed coalition governments of the UPA, led this time by the Congress, which also lasted their full terms.

During this first period of continuous BJP rule (1998–2004), the Vajpayee-led government made one dramatic change on the foreign policy front, ending the posture of nuclear ambiguity that had been in place since the 1974 'peaceful nuclear tests', and going openly nuclear. New Delhi then had to rectify the temporary damage done to the Indo-US strategic relationship, the search for which the Rao government of 1991–96 had begun after ditching the older policy of declared if not actual nonalignment, but which had nonetheless precluded a longer-term strategic association with the United States. The other advance made by the BJP was to deepen significantly India's relationship with Israel. A rapprochement had begun under Rao, who for the first time since 1947 had established full diplomatic relations. But to this newer strategic orientation the BJP added its own anti-Muslim ideological dimension. First, the Kargil War led India to seek military supplies and help from Israel on a hitherto unprecedented level, and it was no accident that the first ever visit to India by an Israeli premier, Ariel Sharon (the 'butcher of Shabra and Shatila') took place in 2003, under this administration. On the economic front, the BJP-led government would simply continue in the neoliberal direction that had been initiated by earlier Congress rule. This created a certain tension with the RSS, since Hindu nationalism had formerly entailed a certain commitment to the pursuit of economic nationalism.

To understand why this accommodation by the BJP to neoliberalism took place – which the RSS in due course broadly accepted – one has to turn to the rising importance of what has been misnamed the 'Great Indian Middle

Class' (IMC). If many of the characteristics of the Indian polity today have been shaped by a churning from below, it is also the case that many of the policies pursued by governments since the mid 1980s have continued to be shaped by the urban elites in India, and those aspiring to such status. Liberalization, as it is commonly termed, has certainly 'liberated' the attitudes, values and aspirations of this middle class. It is this broad category that is the most important social anchor for the new economic policies that justify and promote Indian integration into the world economy on strongly neoliberal lines.

But how big is this middle class? And what is new about it? Unlike in the advanced, highly urbanised, industrial democracies, where the statistical classification of social groups is done with reference to verified employment incomes and tax liabilities, in India there is no equivalent way of obtaining adequate statistics about the employment patterns and incomes of the vast mass of people. This is true of rural India, but also of the urban but informal sectors of employment. Even in urban areas, taxation yields are very limited, because of the lack of knowledge about taxable incomes and because of the huge amounts of 'hidden' or 'black' money and wealth. Thus, even as there are large numbers of fairly well-off urbanites like shopkeepers, traders, and so on, who do not fall into the tax net, of those who do (including the very rich), many are under-taxed because the sources of their varied incomes (from the black economy) are not known in full.

Since tax statistics are so unreliable, recourse is usually made to the assessments of research institutes, of which the National Council for Applied Economic Research (NCAER) is the best regarded. Though judgements are unavoidably impressionistic and somewhat arbitrary, data collected on consumption patterns are used to assess the size of the IMC, which is not altogether inappropriate since the preoccupation with certain forms of 'high' consumption and the lifestyles associated with them is the common characteristic of this social category. But consumption data are nowhere near as useful as reliable income statistics (themselves absent) for the purposes of grading social groups into 'classes', as these are conventionally understood. What should be obvious, however, is that, unlike in more developed societies, the middle classes of India are not a median or near-median category. That is to say, they are not economically situated somewhere in the rough middle of the population. According to the latest (2010) NCAER estimates, by 2016 this IMC would be around 267 million, while other sources pitch this figure closer to 300 million.[49] Even if this elite was between 15 and 20 per cent, or even less, it would, in absolute numbers, still be very sizeable – exceeding, in years to come, the entire population of the third most populous country in the world, the United States. Unsurprisingly, this 'mass elite' continues to enjoy very considerable influence in shaping government

---

49 See Wikipedia entry: 'Standard of Living in India'.

policy, as well as the values and discourses of institutions ranging from the press to the judiciary – institutions whose governing bodies are themselves overwhelmingly dominated by members of this elite. But, relative to the whole population, it is small and lacks the role of middle classes in most developed societies, where a more genuinely median middle class acts as a substantial buffer between the dominant classes and the sizeable layer of dominated and lower classes. It acts as the large social constituency that the upper classes seek to woo, especially ideologically, in order to stabilise their own position. This stability is reinforced by the ability of significant numbers of this middle class to move upwards to join the ranks of the rich, and sometimes the very rich.

In India there is no such buffer. The oppressed and exploited lower classes are much larger, and therefore the political churning from below that is taking place – and that represents the main source of optimism about the future of India – is much more threatening to this IMC, which consequently feels insecure, frustrated, fractious and resentful. Indeed, its new proclivity towards belligerence and hedonism – aspects of an inward turn – is partly a response to this sense of challenge it senses from below. There thus exists a paradox, in which the IMC dominates the corporate world, the bureaucracy, the media and the domain of professionals, enjoying a disproportionate influence on the policy direction of government, but lacks any dominion over the democratic *process*. No matter how much it might be favoured by policy outcomes, there are always also policies it finds threatening. The existence of an electoral process over which it has no control always carries the threat that in some significant way its position may be undermined.

The comparison that the IMC makes between itself and the most prosperous one-third in the advanced industrial societies is of great importance. All elites see their self-interest not as something distinct from or counterposed to the 'national interest' as defined by the state, but as effectively synonymous with and expressive of it. The changing character of this elite over time plays a crucial role in establishing the character of elite nationalism in any given period. And elite nationalism always contests other notions, ideologies and projects of nationalism, in an effort to establish itself as the official nationalism purveyed by the government and as the dominant form and conception of nationalism in society at large.

Elite nationalism today

Elite Indian nationalism today is very different from what it was in the first two decades after independence, when the involvement of this elite and middle class in the National Movement, with its progressive commitments and values, was still a living memory that provided an influential legacy. Most notably, it is today more thoroughly communalized and anti-democratic, more deeply contemptuous of the values of social concern and sympathy for the disadvantaged and poor, than ever before. There is no better indicator of the character of the Indian elite than its response to what can be considered the pivotal events of India's post-independence history: the establishment of Emergency Rule between 1975–77; the V. P. Singh government's partial implementation of the Mandal Report's recommendations in 1990; the destruction of Babri Masjid in December 1992; the crossing of the nuclear Rubicon in May 1998; and the Gujarat Pogrom of 2002.

It is easy to forget, more than a quarter of a century later, that, by a comfortable majority, the urban middle class came around very quickly to supporting the Emergency, welcoming its claims to bringing about 'discipline', removing unsightly urban slums, and banning strikes and other forms of civil disturbance. Even the ruthless programme of compulsory sterilization, which never touched the elite or middle classes, was justified on the basis that population growth was a 'problem' that needed to be tackled on a 'warfooting'. The rapidity and ignominiousness with which the Emergency regime collapsed soon led this same middle class to condemn the Emergency once it was over, and to declare that it had been a political tragedy. But only those with short memories will take this middle-class attempt at retrospective self-absolution at face value.

On the Mandal issue, the depth and scale of the hostility to the Singh government's support for quotas in central government jobs for OBCs, in addition to the time-honoured quotas already existing for Dalits and tribals, had to be seen to be believed. Understood by all sides, the central issue was politically symbolic. As we have seen, when this measure fully implemented, less than 50,000 jobs were affected. But the issue enhanced the already rising power of the OBCs. The upper castes and classes, were virtually united in their opposition to Mandal, but the shock troops of the anti-Mandal agitation were upper-caste youth from the lower-middle classes. Despite the intensity of these protests, the Mandalization of Indian politics is now sullenly accepted by the upper castes and classes, even as they remain uneasily watchful about further OBC encroachments.

On the destruction of the Babri Masjid, the IMC has been more divided. One section of the elite, committed to liberal, secular values, was greatly disturbed. Then there is a layer of hard-core supporters who approved of this act, and has recruited from among a younger generation born later, which has little or no living memory of the Ram Janmabhoomi campaign, or even of the 2002 Gujarat pogrom, but for various reasons is strongly attracted to the 'hard' cultural nationalism of the Sangh Parivar and the BJP. Among a significant layer of 'pale Saffronites', there was considerable shock at the physical and symbolic violence displayed during this period, the openly contemptuous defiance of the constitution and the law, and the contradiction between the public commitment of the BJP to using only peaceful means to achieve its ends and the actual course of events. This layer will not abandon the BJP – they despise the Congress more – but continues to feel uneasy with some of the behaviour of both the Sangh and BJP. Its members are happy to accept and endorse a 'soft Hindutva', but are worried that the adoption of too strident an ideological orientation could cause major social turmoil and upheaval. They may feel that Muslims and other religious minorities have been 'pampered', and that the Sangh talks much sense; but they do not want continuous or large-scale riots, or other forms of social and political backlash.

Excluding the hard-core layer, these sections of the middle class, whether secular-minded or 'soft Hindutva', have two shared characteristics. They respect 'order', and therefore are naturally inclined to follow power in their own self-interest. They also have a strong propensity to discern moderation and rectitude in dominant powers, however weak the basis for such an assessment might be. There is a desire on the part of the more secular-minded and democratically committed section of the middle class to believe that such moderate trends exist, and are gaining ground within the BJP and Sangh. The 'soft Hindutva' brigade, for its part, wishfully imagines the dominant practices, behaviour and orientation of the BJP and Sangh as expressive of its own character and orientation.

But such flagrant wishfulness is integral to the nature of the middle classes, whose dominant function in society is usually to be the 'servitors of power', and thereby win some small share in the exercise of that power. The middle class, however, is never the key locus of power in society. Today, almost twenty-five years after the demolition of Babri Masjid, the middle class has for the most part come comfortably to terms with the ideology and prac- tice of Hindutva. A reservation sometimes registered is that there should be no 'excesses', as they are disruptive to business. But even here there is some leeway; on occasion it may be useful in the longer term (whatever the more immediate tensions) to teach 'them' – meaning Muslims – 'a lesson'. Certainly, the BJP and the Sangh have partially succeeded in reshaping the public 'common sense' on matters of democracy and secularism.

In ideological manoeuvres that have secured substantial and growing resonance in Indian society, democracy has been redefined as Hindu major- itarianism, and secularism as a false and anti-Hindu, minority-favouring construct.[50] The BJP/Sangh has carried out an assault on democracy as a governing principle by seeking to redefine it as a species of majoritarianism – the fulfilment of the wishes and potential of a supposedly natural majority,

---

50 Some empirical evidence for this is given in a post-2004 election survey that showed how Hindutva, through over two decades of sustained communalist propaganda and practice, had gained substantial adherence from the middle and upper sections of society to a 'new common sense' characterized by 'a) a majoritarian viewpoint, b) high expression of religiosity, c) insistence on maintaining group boundaries, d) lack of sharp awareness or knowledge about blatantly communal events, e) mild disapproval of minority interests, and f) a weak association between these and partisanship as far as support to the BJP is concerned'. According to this survey, more Hindus vote for the BJP than for the Con- gress (in 2004, 40 per cent compared to 35 per cent), and this support is stable, i.e. the BJP does not require communal campaigns to sustain it. See S. Palshikar, 'Majoritarian Middle Ground?', *Economic and Political Weekly*, 18–24 December 2004.

the Hindus. It thus seeks to destroy the fundamental underpinning of political democracy: the concept of an Indian citizenship that must necessarily be abstracted from the possession of any particular attribute (religion, race, language, and so on) that is not in principle universally available and achievable, regardless of communitarian loyalties. One of the crucial checks to prevent such 'natural' majorities from achieving undue influence is the institutionalization of minority rights. The BJP, however, attacks the very principle of minority rights as representing unwarranted privilege. It is not specific abuses of such rights that are attacked – which may be reasonable enough – but the very principle on which they are based.

Similarly, the BJP seeks to carry out its assault on secularism and the secular state through redefinition. Once secularism is redefined as tolerance, the truly secular state comes to mean the truly tolerant state. From here it is an easy step to advocating a Hindu *rashtra*, and implicitly a Hindu state, or one which is in some basic sense affiliated to the 'majority religion'. After all, Hinduism, it is claimed, is the most tolerant of all religious systems, and is therefore the most conducive to true secularism. Those who oppose the idea of a Hindu *rashtra* or Hindu state, but propose a reinterpretation of secularism as tolerance provide powerful legitimacy to the overall project of the BJP and the Sangh Parivar, even if they would themselves be shocked by the resulting political denouement.

On the nuclear bomb, the Indian media and most of the IMC not only accepted the new status but, to greater or lesser extent, gloried in it. It was seen as a desirable and necessary expression of the new, more assertive India – a symbol of newfound pride, as well as a means of exercising greater global power and achieving greater security. Unlike other landmark events – the Emergency, Mandalization, Hindutva, and the attack on secularism – the issue of the nuclear bomb does not yet touch in any significant way the lives of the vast majority of the population. There are no domestic 'penalties' to worry about if the middle class adopts an immoral and aggressively nationalist pro-bomb posture. Whatever else the acquisition of the bomb may or may not mean, like slavery, colonialism or apartheid, its endorsement cannot be defended on moral grounds. The decision to cross the nuclear Rubicon was status-driven, not threat-driven. It was changed self-perceptions – specifically the changed character of elite Indian nationalism – not changes to perceived external threats, that explain why India went openly nuclear. It is not accidental that the only party which has been demanding an Indian bomb since the 1950s (the BJP and its previous incarnations) should have taken this decision when it finally arrived in power.[51] Its motivation was simple: the bomb is needed in order to fulfil the Hindutva

---

51 As far as I am aware, I was the only person in the public domain to say in my book, written in 1994 and published a year later, that if the BJP came to power they would very likely go nuclear. See A. Vanaik, *India in a Changing World: Problems, Limits and Successes of its Foreign Policy* (New Delhi, 1995), p. 123.

mission of constructing a strong India as Savarkar argued, by 'uniting Hindus and militarizing Hindu-dom'.

Among sections of the elite, the response to the tests of 1998 was frenzied – a near-hysteria of self-congratulatory hype and hyperbole: India had finally 'stood up'; it had acquired 'mega-tonnes of prestige' – and so on. The nature of this response was extremely revealing. It bespoke not a mature, relaxed, confident nationalism, but its opposite – an immature, anxious, insecure, belligerent nationalism desperate to find some source of pride and self-aggrandizement – and finding it in the acquisition of the bomb.

This search for self-esteem, for signs of an India 'coming of age' in a world where not enough 'respect' is shown to it, has led to a curious side-effect: the NRI phenomenon. Non-resident Indians (NRIs), especially the professionals of the United States, have become the exemplars of the 'successful'. After migration to the United States, most educated Indians are seen as having achieved great success, measured in terms of high status and earnings. It is seen as evidence of what elite Indians can achieve if they are not hemmed in economically by archaic state controls and hostility to the inspirational ideal of wanting to become as rich as possible. The same thinking insists on how much better things would be if only Indians were not hemmed in socially by the pressure from below of a claque of other forces, and therefore allowed to progress politically by making no concessions to populism.

This admiration for the NRI is a strange form of 'nationalist' adulation and role-modelling. What is most striking about the first-generation NRI professionals who migrate to the United States is that they mostly come from the top 5 per cent of Indian society, and would have remained a part of this elite had they stayed behind, enjoying high status and income relative to other Indians. They have simply exchanged one elite position for another, non-Indian one, primarily in order to earn more money, secure more material comforts and a higher international status. And they have been perfectly happy to 'defect' from India on this account. That this very category of people should now have become envied role-models for the Indian elite left behind, but always keen to acquire Green Cards for themselves and aspiring family members, speaks volumes about the self-serving character of this elite Indian nationalism. It is equally interesting that the deeds of successful members of the Indian diaspora abroad are 'nationalised', become a source of pride for Indians at home. An obvious corollary is that any kind of international achievement by Indians, no matter how trivial or superficial, also becomes a pretext for nationalistic glorification.[52]

---

52 It is no surprise that it was under this first BJP-led NDA government that a special 'Pravasi Bharatiya Divas' (Overseas Indian Day) was inaugurated in 2001, to highlight and commemorate the achievements abroad of the Indian diaspora. The constituency New Delhi had in mind was that of rich, professionally successful, mostly upper-caste Hindus from North America, Western Europe and Oceania. Dual citizenship was then proposed to be given in 2003 to those of Indian origin in the US, the UK, Canada and Australia – but of course not to the descendants of Indian indentured labourers or

Such is the character of today's Indian middle class. It will no doubt strike many readers as unduly harsh and negative – but it is a clear-eyed assessment that carries a particular strategic-political message. The task of creating a better and more humane India in the coming period cannot be achieved through this IMC, but only against and in spite of it. Some reason for optimism about the country's future is afforded by the fact that India is still not like the advanced Western democracies, where what has been called the 'two-thirds' or 'one-third plus one-third' society prevails, in which one-third of the population prospers while another third merely copes, and the remaining third is in far worse state than it was during the West's own period of mass prosperity, the Golden Age of 1948–73. Even this characterization may be mistaken; the recent Occupy Movement's slogan,'We are the 99 per cent', may in fact be closer to the mark. Even if one understands the 'two-thirds society' analysis as a benchmark for comparison, India is closer to being an 'iceberg' society, with one-eighth prospering and the remaining seven-eighths either just coping (in the limited upper echelons), or failing to do so entirely. Perhaps 'three-quarters society' is the most fitting term to describe India. At any rate, the main point is that the persistence of mass suffering and privation means the necessary (if not always sufficient) condition for provoking the eruption of progressive forms of social struggle is ever present. This provides a clear basis for hope in radical social change for the better.

Communal violence and the Gujarat pogrom

The fifth landmark event listed above was the Gujarat pogrom of 2002.[53] It is not as if violence in India is abnormal – far from it. Independent India has always posed something of an enigma. Barring the two-year interlude of Emergency Rule (1975–77) – when the Indian state was still less authoritarian and ruthless than the average Latin American or African dictatorship up to that date – India stands out as a developing country displaying a remarkable durability and stability of democratic institutions and processes at the national level. Yet, at a closer scale of magnification, few developing countries can match the frequency, scale and intensity of either routinized or episodic violence that exists in India. This structural paradox raises disturbing questions about the relationship of such violence to the existing order – and its utility for that order. Any comprehensive study of violence in India must therefore range over an extraordinarily wide terrain of interacting relationships, recognizing its various forms and sites.

---

migrants to Southeast Asia, Africa or the West Indies. This promise, however, has yet to be fulfilled, since it aroused some controversy at home.

53 One of the best accounts of this pogrom is presented in A. Basu, *Violent Conjunctures in Democratic India* (Cambridge, 2015), Chapter 5. In its own right, this book is methodologically innovative in the way it charts the rise of the BJP politically, and in explaining its swings between relative moderation and belligerent militancy, temporally and spatially.

Amid the welter of different typologies of violence and approaches to understanding it, from the socio-psychological to the most abstractly structural–functional, it is Hindu communal violence against Muslims, and the rise of Hindutva with which it is connected, that has done most to reshape the trajectory of Indian politics and the behaviour of the Indian state. There are of course multiple forms and sources of violence. A brief if schematic list would be as follows: 1) criminal and gang violence; 2) sectarian intra-group violence, such as between Shias and Sunnis; 3) patriarchal violence; 4) inter-ethnic violence, such as between Kuki and Naga tribes; 5) socioeconomically motivated violence associated with class oppression, resistance and struggle; 6) ethno-national, or secessionist violence; 7) communal violence; 8) officially sponsored and directed violence, executed by the apparatuses of the state, at the central level and lower administrative levels, arising from declared or undeclared policy and simultaneously reinforcing caste, class, gender and ethno-national oppressions. These categories are ideal types; in practice the forms of violence are invariably mixed.

While caste and class relations are essentially vertical, gender relations are both horizontal and vertical. Violence against women has a scale, depth and frequency that is simply unmatched by any other kind of violence. While caste and class violence also have a normalized and quotidian character, gender violence is uniquely pervasive. It is not just episodic and collective, but has a distinctive familial, individualized and privatized character. It traverses all boundaries, and all other forms of political violence also express themselves in specifically gendered ways – the rape, beating and humiliation of women being part of the process of establishing the dominance of class, caste, ethnic group or government forces. What is more, violence against women is intimately connected to the more collective forms of periodic violence. The human emotions that lead to such 'sudden extremes' simmer in the cauldron of everyday social relations and practices.[54] Yet the very universality, pervasiveness and constancy of the oppression of women, in and across all social relations, tends to deprive it of the more specific charge and power whose accumulating force in particular historical circumstances can significantly alter the political trajectory of a state and society. This is precisely what the accumulating forces of Hindutva since the early 1980s have been able to accomplish.[55]

---

54 See the fine compilation, A. Basu and S. Roy, *Violence and Democracy in India* (Kolkata, 2007). For an important study that explores the relationship between women and Hindutva, either as victims or allies, see T. Sarkar and U. Butalia, eds, *Women and the Hindu Right* (New Delhi, 1995). The very low female-to-male sex ratio in India is testimony to the extraordinarily institutionalized character of women's oppression. B. Harriss-White provides a specific study of this. See 'Girls as disposable commodities in India', *Socialist Register 2009* (London. 2008).

55 For a fuller discussion of the normality of violence in India, in which the question of communal violence is also situated, see A. Vanaik, 'India's Paradigmatic Communal Violence', *Socialist Register 2009* (London, 2008).

In terms of sheer numbers, Hindutva is the biggest religious nationalist movement in the world. For nearly three decades after independence,
Hindutva's salience remained low. The horrific legacy of the Partition genocide; the assassination of Mahatma Gandhi by a Hindutva devotee; the
political and ideological dominance of the Congress party (purporting to
uphold the principles of socialism, secularism, democracy and nonalignment); the defeat and dismemberment of Pakistan in 1971 – all contributed
to this reality. From the 1970s onwards, the process of Congress decline
and growing disillusionment with the principles that the first prime minister, Jawaharlal Nehru, had helped to establish, became unmistakable. New
forces emerged, which nonetheless failed to re-establish a stable non-Congress form of centrist rule. All this began to pave the way for the rise of
Hindutva. It is not an accident that, parallel to this emergence (a) a fairly
dramatic escalation occurred in Hindu–Muslim riots; (b) the overwhelming
majority of victims (deaths and injuries) were Muslims; and (c) the police
and paramilitaries were among the principal perpetrators of the violence.

The officially recorded figures speak for themselves. Between 1954 and
1963, the average annual number of Hindu–Muslim riots stood at 60.6,
and the average annual number of deaths at 34.4 persons. Between 1964 and
1979, the respective figures were 319.2 riots and 260.2 persons. Between
1980 and 1988 the figures had risen to 534.1 riots and 416.6 persons. In
the six years after 1988 for which figures are available (1989–93, plus 2002),
there was an annual average of 528 deaths.[56] The emergence of lower-caste
and women's movements have at least made the high recorded figures of
atrocities against them something of an embarrassment for higher political
authorities, and forced some kind of acknowledgement of failure on their
part. But when it comes to the predominantly Muslim victims of communal
violence, there is no such acknowledgement from the culpable state authorities or parties – in other words, the Sangh.

Paul Brass's argument that 'riots are dramatic productions, creations of
specific persons, groups, and parties operating through institutionalised
riot networks within a discursive framework of Hindu–Muslim communal
opposition and antagonism that in turn produces specific forms of political
practice that make riots integral to the political process' is entirely correct.[57]
In other words, whatever their triggers, communal riots are organized and
not spontaneous phenomena. Moreover, the most developed and organized
perpetrators are the Sangh Parivar and other militant Hindu organizations. Brass outlines the three phases through which the organization of

56 Compiled from the Table 'Hindu–Muslim Riots and Resulting Victims', in
Jaffrelot, *Hindu Nationalist Movement*, p. 556. I have changed the 1993 figure of 558 to
874, to include victims in the March riots of that year in Mumbai, and added the rough
estimate of 2,000 for deaths in the Gujarat pogrom of February 2002, before taking the
annual average to 528.
57 See P. Brass, *Forms of Collective Violence* (New Delhi, 2006); P. Brass, *The Production of Hindu–Muslim Violence in Contemporary India* (New Delhi, 2003).

communal violence passes: preparation/rehearsal, marked by the presence of 'fire-tenders' who keep inter-group tensions stoked; activation/enactment, undertaken by 'conversion specialists' who are the on-the-ground mob mobilizers and leaders; and finally, the aftermath of communal violence events, in which the 'blame displacers' – comprising politicians, intellectuals and members of the media – help shift the discourse away from the suffering of victims on to 'problems of governance', and who implicitly or explicitly justify the violence. Little wonder, then, that the perpetrators invariably avoid prosecution even when they are identified. Deaths in such riots or pogroms are caused by mob frenzy and police killings, as well as by individuals carrying out cold-blooded brutalities independently of collective action.

The spur for much of this communal violence, as Steve Wilkinson has shown, is electoral competition.[58] His empirical work on state and town variations in the incidence and duration of ethnic and communal riots comes to the conclusion that minorities will be protected only when it suits ruling or aspiring political parties at the state level to woo the Muslim vote. In the south of India, where there have been strong backward caste movements and therefore greater intra-Hindu competition, the votes of Muslims become more important, and they are safer. But Wilkinson's belief that intra-Hindu competition will increase as a result of the Dalit and OBC upsurges in the north, and that this will lead to an eventual decline in Hindu–Muslim riots, is over-optimistic, to say the least. Current statistical trends on communal violence tell a different story, while the growing communalization of the general political–ideological environment in the north has created popular expectations that such violence will repeatedly occur, and should occasion no great alarm or surprise. This is apparently because, to some degree, there is a 'pampering' of minorities, especially Muslims, in the quest for their 'vote banks'. So, it is claimed, there is no fundamental flaw in Indian democracy, but an understandable 'Hindu resentment' that basically *reacts* against this alleged pampering, even if the reactions are sometimes 'excessive'. In other words, as both Brass and Wilkinson understand so well, it is the political dimension that is decisive – namely, the role played by the Sangh Parivar and the success it has had in transforming its ideological constructs into a proliferating public 'common sense'.

In her important study, Amrita Basu makes the powerful point that it is not just negative factors, such as institutional weaknesses of various kinds, that must be taken into account, but that it is often the very strength of organizations and institutions that promotes such violent eruptions. She causally links her 'independent variable' of anti-minority violence to five key dependent variables and their interactions: (i) internal party unity or factionalism; (ii) the nature of the relationship between the party (BJP) and its

---

58 See S. I. Wilkinson, *Votes and Violence: Electoral Competition and Communal Riots in India* (Cambridge, 2004).

cohort movement-structures; (iii) whether the BJP is in power (as part of a coalition or on its own) at the state level; (iv) whether the BJP is in power at the centre (in a coalition or on its own); (v) the range, character and caste composition of opposing parties and movements.[59]

The police and paramilitary forces are invested with all necessary legal powers to prevent riots from taking place through pre-emptive action, and, when riots start, to bring them swiftly to an end. If, despite this, there are frequent and sustained communal riots, it is because the police, at the behest of the political leadership in the states concerned, have either remained silent spectators or even participated in the riots. While many a prominent spokesperson from the Muslim community has called for a more religiously mixed police force, this is really of very limited value. At most, a more diverse police force can create a somewhat less prejudiced atmosphere in police ranks; but widespread and strong biases reflecting existing prejudices and stereotypes among the general population remain. No wonder, then, that, despite low Muslim representation in the army, Muslim leaders have much greater trust in it, and repeatedly call for its deployment during riot situations. The structure of the police is like that of Indian society – a very small national ruling elite, a comfortable regional middle class, and a mass of the poor – 90 per cent of all police are constables or head constables.

But achieving a more religiously mixed police force is not the answer. In Andhra Pradesh, the share of Muslims among the police is 16 per cent, or about double the percentage of Muslims in the state. Yet in every major riot since 1978, the police have exhibited partisan behaviour against Muslims. In Kerala and West Bengal, where the proportion of Muslims in the police is far below their proportions in their respective state populations, the frequency of riots is low, and police behaviour impartial. In West Bengal, this is because the Communist Party (Marxist) or CPM-led Left Front – which also includes the other big mainstream left party, the Communist Party of India (CPI) – was in power for thirty-four years, from 1977 to 2011 and able to set a certain pattern of police behaviour in that state. In Kerala, it is because these two left parties and the Muslim League factions feature in coalition governments. In Bihar and Uttar Pradesh, where the police have a notorious reputation of holding strong communal prejudices, they have behaved impartially when the highest civilian authorities, like chief ministers Lalu Prasad Yadav, Nitish Kumar (Bihar) and Mulayam Singh Yadav have demanded it.[60]

On February 27, 2002, the Sabarmati Express, jam-packed with Hindutva activists and supporters returning from Ayodhya, had one of its passenger cars burnt, allegedly by Muslim locals, just as it pulled out of Godhra station in Gujarat – although there are other claims that the fire started inside the

---

59 Basu, *Violent Conjunctures*.
60 O. Khalidi, *Khaki and Ethnic Violence in India* (New Delhi, 2003); and K. S. Subramanian, *Political Violence and the Police in India* (New Delhi. 2007).

bogey. Fifty-eight people died, including women and children. Days earlier, on their journey to Ayodhya – the site of periodic agitations calling for the construction of a Ram temple to begin – Hindutva activists had already raised the communal temperature by their anti-Muslim sloganeering and generally hooliganish and intimidatory behaviour. Similar behaviour on their return journey had raised tensions to a high pitch among local Muslims along the train route. According to eyewitnesses at Godhra station, the molestation of a Muslim girl on the platform and the terrorization of a Muslim tea-vendor lit the spark that led to the torching of the car. There are some doubts as to the source of the fire, some reports claiming that it started from a portable stove inside the bogey. But even if the cause was the assault from outside, it was still a spontaneous event by unidentified locals. What followed was the most politically consequential pogrom in post-independence India.

Over the next few days and weeks, the Gujarat state government, headed by Chief Minister Narendra Modi – a rabid Hindutva ideologue and former *pracharak* of RSS – carried out a massive pogrom and reign of terror. Mobs numbering in the thousands were unleashed, while the police according to eye-witness accounts were told to remain aloof. At least 2,000 Muslims were butchered. Muslim-populated localities in cities, towns and villages through-out much of the state, as well as Muslim-owned shops and businesses, were torched and destroyed. Over 150,000 people were displaced, and had to take refuge in makeshift camps set up by a few Muslim and non-Muslim civic associations. Pregnant women were skewered, others gang-raped and then burned to death. The scale of violence was enormous, but always selective and carried out with remarkable speed. This was only possible because of several months of prior preparation and planning. Muslim homes and busi-nesses had been geographically identified; transport had been made ready, and gas cylinders and other combustible materials stocked. Distribution of venomous and hate-spewing pamphlets had been underway for some time.[61]

This was easily the worst communal pogrom since the Partition holocaust.[62] Moreover, for all his shedding of crocodile tears over the event,

---

61 The most detailed account of what happened was given by the Concerned Citizens' Tribunal in its two-volume report, *Crime Against Humanity: An Inquiry into the Carnage in Gujarat – Findings and Recommendations* (Mumbai, 2002). The official National Human Rights Commission subsequently endorsed the principal findings of this report after making its own inquiry.

62 While the 1984 anti-Sikh pogrom in the wake of the assassination of Prime Minister Indira Gandhi by her Sikh bodyguards took some 3,000 lives, there remains a profound political difference between the two events. The latter took place in a context of secession-ist tensions relating to the movement for Khalistan, or separate Sikh homeland – tensions in which the killing of Gandhi was an act of vengeance for the prior assault by the Indian army on the holiest of Sikh shrines – the Golden Temple in Amritsar – where the leader of the Khalistan agitation, Sant Bhindranwala, had taken final refuge. The assassination triggered the pogrom. That this was a one-off event has been confirmed by the rela-tive ease with which harmonious Hindu–Sikh relations have been re-established. The Khalistan movement has completely faded away, and never enjoyed the support of more than a small minority of Sikhs. Hindu–Sikh relations are simply not comparable to those

when push came to shove, the then prime minister, A.B. Vajpayee, rational-ized the pogrom, declaring that it was but a reaction to the Godhra event. Vajpayee has always been the moderate face of the Sangh, who could appeal to a wider cross-section of the Indian public – but one who has rationalized and justified, in one way or another, the most brutally decisive acts of the Sangh: the Ram Janmabhoomi campaign, the Pokharan II explosions, and the Gujarat pogrom; and on whose watch (1998–2004) at the centre the first sustained efforts were made to saffronise education – with the introduc-tion, for example, of new Hindutva-ised school textbooks. The real measure of how normalized the BJP has become is the fact that Vajpayee, who was given the country's highest civilian award – the Bharat Ratna – is widely seen by the public media and much of the secular and liberal intelligentsia of the country as a statesmanlike figure, only a little short of the stature of Nehru and Gandhi![63]

Far from Modi and his senior political, bureaucratic, judicial and police cohorts being held criminally responsible, he actually profited politically. Modi first became chief minister in October 2001 not by facing a public election but through appointment in a party reshuffle organised by the BJP's central leadership. His return with an increased party majority in the December 2002 state elections testified to the normalization of communal-ism in Gujarat. Modi was then re-elected for an unprecedented second and third time in 2007 and 2012. This success in Gujarat not only made him a potential future prime ministerial candidate for the BJP, but also seemed to confirm the view that a hard-line posture towards Muslims – even to the extent of communal violence against them – could be electorally and politically beneficial for the party.

One must also recognize that communal violence can bring in a com-mercial layer of supporters, because riots all too often have a real economic function. Indeed, one of the more important background conditions that are conducive to many such riots breaking out where they do is the existence of economic competition between entrenched Hindu entrepreneurs, traders and contractors and a rising layer of Muslim entrepreneurs, small proprietors and investors. Many such Muslims are beneficiaries of steady remittances from abroad, or are returnees who have accumulated savings from work in the Gulf States and elsewhere. Time and again, the consequences of

---

between Hindus and Muslims, while the Hindu Right is more prone to seeing the Sikh community as the historical sword-arm against Muslims, and as a natural ally, than as any kind of hostile opponent.

63 In his New Year's message in 2002, Vajpayee defended the Ram Temple movement as an expression of 'national sentiment'. In his address of 17 December 2002 to the BJP Parliamentary Committee, Vajpayee blamed Muslim leaders for not 'sufficiently' con-demning the Godhra Massacre. He has always declared himself loyal to the RSS, taking no part in the National Movement. He has stated unequivocally not only that Hindutva is liberal and secular, but that '[t]his Indianness or Bharatiya (which is no different from Hindutva) is what we should all celebrate and further strengthen'. See V. Venkatesan, 'A Secular Veneer', *Frontline*, 18–31 January 2003.

communal riots have included the economic devastation of such Muslim competitors. There is a Hindu propertied class that benefits from such violence, and has every reason to give solid political, as well as financial and material support to Hindutva forces. The late Asghar Ali Engineer, perhaps the single most diligent chronicler of communal riots in India, repeatedly pointed out that such riots take place in towns where there is a substantial percentage of Muslims, well above the national average of 14 per cent but also well below a majority or near-majority of the local population. Such violence hardly ever takes place where Muslims constitute such a small proportion that they cannot pose any kind of economic or political challenge.[64] But what was not anticipated, even by Engineer, was that 2002 would initiate a new phenomenon – the spread of riots to villages – and that this pattern would be repeated thereafter. This was true, for example, in the 2013 and 2015 communal incidents in Uttar Pradesh, which were of lowintensity, but deliberately orchestrated.

Several years later, rehabilitation and compensation remain incomplete and inadequate. The Gujarat police, judiciary and government have shown more alacrity in arresting 'suspects' and charging them for the Godhra 'conspiracy' than in pursuing those involved in the pogrom that followed. The higher echelons of the police and bureaucracy remain unpunished, while the top leaders of the Sangh Parivar responsible for the carnage have never been touched. The Congress – the main opposition party in Gujarat – played a negligible role in providing succour to the victims when it was most needed. Neither at the state or national level has the Congress, since 2002, dared to carry out a genuine and serious campaign highlighting this horror, or vigorously declaring its opposition to Hindu communalism, or warning that Gujarat has become a laboratory for a type of violence that can be unleashed elsewhere.

Leaving to one side the debate about whether the Sangh Parivar constitutes a fascist force, and whether India has been facing or will face the danger of a fascist takeover and transformation, there is no dispute within the Left about the fact that the Sangh has fascist characteristics. This is most evident in the way it organizes mass violence as a spectacle, and how, for its devoted cadres and supporters, such ethnic cleansing is experienced as cathartic and celebratory. But the Sangh also speaks in different voices to different audiences, often making skilful use of the language of democracy.

The Sangh's periodic deployment of communal violence has played an

---

64 See A. A. Engineer, ed., *Communal Riots in Post-Independence India* (Hyderabad, 1984). For an acute analysis of the material background to the Gujarat pogrom of 2002, see B. Harriss-White, *India's Market Society* (New Delhi, 2005). She points out that, in eastern Gujarat villages, poor tribals attacked Muslim moneylenders on behalf of the Sangh. Economic exploitation alone does not explain this, since elsewhere it is Hindu middlemen who exploit tribals. But local implantation of Hindutva activists and sustained communal propaganda against Muslims may combine with economic resentments to create such brutalized tribal behaviour.

important part in the expansion of its popularity and influence; but it also has its downside. Its greatest gains socially have been among the Indian 'middle class' – especially among professionals and those with college credentials. This section of society is comfortable with the Sangh's anti-Muslim sentiments, but it is also worried by the 'disturbances' created by riots and the possibility of 'retaliatory' violence.[65] Future violence by the Sangh must be contextually sensitive – that is, carefully calibrated to achieve its desired gains, in social terrains that have been carefully surveyed and properly prepared for. Such violence must be occasional, controllable, and as far as possible presented as a reaction to some issue or event – and therefore more easily justifiable.

Though the Congress was in power for ten years, between 2004 and 2014, it made little progress on the matter of communalism. Neglect and indifference are what most marked the attitude of the two Congress-led UPA governments. Economic and foreign policy took centre-stage. There was no effort (apart from reversing the NDA changes to school textbooks) to address the dangers presented by Hindu communalism. It was as if the mere fact of the BJP being out of power for so long would prove decisive in derailing these forces. Certainly, the Sangh was shaken by this hiatus. But the idea that the organizations of Hindutva were thereby facing some kind of crisis was an illusion that too many observers of liberal and even left persuasion were prepared to entertain. The main reason for this false perception lay in the widespread failure or refusal to recognize that the Indian state was never as secular as it claimed; that many of the beliefs held by Hindu communalists had secured substantial public assent; that the Congress was not a party either capable of or interested in launching a serious struggle against Hindu communalism, given not only its historical character, but a function also of the view of far too many of its leaders (and members) that they could not afford to alienate 'Hindu sentiment'.

These two Congress-led governments were far more concerned to push the neoliberal economic agenda; to consolidate the Indo-US strategic relationship as embodied in the Indo-US Nuclear Deal; to marginalize the mainstream Left, which had been pressing it in uncomfortable directions during the first UPA term; to marginalize and destroy the extra-parliamentary Left, namely the Naxalites, which the Manmohan Singh government in 2006 declared to be the single biggest national security threat, well ahead of the forces of Hindu communalism – or, as he called it, a 'virus' needing to be 'eliminated'. This is not a directive that would be aimed at the BJP or Sangh, though many liberal voices do call for the link between the two to be greatly weakened, or even severed, so that the BJP can become a more moderate,

---

65 In the last couple of years, there is some evidence that, for the first time, Indian Muslims may have become involved in public bomb blasts, as well as becoming recruits to transnational terrorist groups.

albeit religiously inflected right-of-centre party. After all, the greatest class gain for the Sangh is undoubtedly the new acceptability and legitimacy it has gained in the eyes of big capital, and from the corporate-controlled public media. The BJP is seen as no different from the Congress in being committed to promoting the interests of big capital in the name of creating a strong India. True, the Sangh's willingness to carry out anti-Muslim violence is a matter of unease, but only that. The protection of profit-making is far more important than the protection of Muslims. Little wonder, then, that even after the Gujarat pogrom, only a year later in February 2003, one of the premier bodies representing the collective interests of the Indian capitalist class, the Confederation of Indian Industry, had no hesitation in inviting Narendra Modi to address the chieftains of Indian capital, while Gujarat remains a favoured destination for investment by Indian and foreign capital.

The most desirable political recipe for capital – domestic and foreign, large, medium and small – is the institutionalization of two capitalist parties that can be trusted to pursue similar pro-business policies, as well as a foreign policy commensurate with these needs, and which can secure sufficient domestic legitimacy from the wider populace. If the progressive Hinduization of the polity can help to secure this, then so be it. Politically speaking, then, the ideal formula would be the emergence of a stable situation in which, alongside the BJP, there is a reasonably healthy Congress party capable of being the alternative pole or hub of government authority, as and when the electoral pendulum swings its way. This would be the best guarantee (even with coalition arrangements of some kind) of the necessary order from which capital and its middle-class base might benefit most handsomely, and be more confident of being able to contain the various pressures and upsurges from below.

Alas, the 2014 election results have so decimated the Congress, and its internal structure is so factionalized, that even this desired political formula seems currently unrealizable, and therefore the spectre of continuous social upheaval remains a powerful and disturbing one. Meanwhile, the Hindutva train – in reality, several trains on multiple tracks – continues to chug along. It has already covered enormous ground, and continues to move forward, albeit at varying speeds, and with stops, occasional reverses, and restarts. Of course, the forward march of Hindutva is a socio-political process that interacts with other important socio-political processes, such as the rise of a massive 'Indian middle class', the continuing forward march of the OBCs, the unprecedented assertiveness of Dalits, an angry Muslim ferment, and the regionalization of the Indian polity. All this constitutes an unpredictable and highly complex amalgam that will continue to shape the Indian polity for the foreseeable future.

PART II

2

Religion, Modernity, Secularization

Four Notions of Secularization

The word 'secular' comes from the Latin *saeculum*, which first meant 'age', 'great span of time' or 'spirit of the age'. Once this becomes a term of contrast, there is then ordinary or profane time and there is the 'higher' time of God's eternity, each having their distinctive affairs, and institutions devoted to the concerns of that particular domain or sphere of existence. But this 'higher' time also intervened in ordinary time, so one could not have the same sense of time – of it being linear, homogenous and empty – as in modernity. There thus existed two worlds, the temporal and spiritual. This was the birth within Christian discourse of the notion of relative separation or disengagement, with the spiritual order ultimately remaining decisive. Ever since, the 'secular' and the 'religious' have been mutually constituted. As a modern category, discussions of the secular in relation to the religious can take the form of a philosophical, legal–political or cultural discourse.[1]

The term 'secularization' emerged after the Peace of Westphalia in 1648, and originally referred to the transfer of ecclesiastical lands to civic control. To secularize was thus to 'make worldly'. By the nineteenth century, and in the still powerful flush of Enlightenment values, Britain's G. L. Holyoake coined the term 'secularism' to define an ideology and movement wherein social (and individual) morality, formerly determined by the transcending principles of religion, was now to be determined by reason, and anchored to the good of men and women in this life. Agnostic or indifferent to religion, this version of secularism acquired a more atheistic slant through Holyoake's disciple, Charles Bradlaugh. But secularism as a rationalist movement, whether agnostic, indifferent or atheistic, soon stalled. It ignored rather than confronted religion or religious discourse.

Capitalist industrialization, the rise of science and of the Enlightenment, the emergence and consolidation of civil society – in short, modernity –

---

1 J. Casanova, 'The Secular, Secularizations, Secularism', in C. Calhoun, M. Juergensmeyer and J. Van Antwerpen, eds, *Rethinking Secularism* (New York, 2011).

posed the question of religion anew. How did religion, specifically Christianity, relate to modernity's emergence? What was its place in the new
dispensation? 'Religious change' in the West (the original location of capitalist modernity and the secular state) was an incontestable fact, and the
notion of secularization was the registration of this fact. Broadly speaking, to
this day, three notions of secularization have vied, singly or in combination,
for controlling emphasis.

There is the concept of secularization as the decline of religious institutions, beliefs, practices and consciousness, of their loss of social significance.
Then there is the concept of relative separation. Other terms to signify more
or less the equivalent process are disengagement, differentiation, compartmentalization. Here there is lateral shrinkage in the social space occupied
or influenced by religion, and an implied reallocation of religious functions
in the polity, society and culture. The third notion is intimately connected
to the growing importance of rational thought and activity. This dynamic
implies newer claimants to intellectual and moral authority other than the
traditional religious systems. It implies growing bureaucratization and
routinization in forms of organization. Secularization here means greater
rationalization of thought and behaviour. This kind of secularization can
take place within as well as against religious systems – for example, in the
view that Protestantism is a more secularized form of Christianity.[2]

The last two notions are to be distinguished from the first.[3] Those subscribing to the first notion of secularization as religious decline can accept
the second and third as complementary facets of the secularization process.
Those subscribing to the second and third notions need not (and many
sociologists of religion do not) accept the first notion, either definitionally
or as an accurate historical evaluation.[4] Intellectually, a great deal is at stake
in this conceptual divide – nothing less than one's understanding of the
general place of religion in modernity, society and culture, of the very nature

---

2 Where Catholicism is all-encompassing, Protestantism shrinks the scope of the
sacred. Christianity is divested of 'mystery, miracle, magic'. There is God on one side
and fallen humanity on the other, and the only miracle is grace. Protestantism, especially
Calvinism, reduces religion to its 'essentials'. See P. Berger, *The Social Reality of Religion*
(London, 1969).

Larry Shiner's typology of concepts of secularization (decline, this-worldliness, disengagement, transposition, desacralization) is effectively reducible to the three outlined
above. See L. Shiner, 'The Concept of Secularization in Empirical Research', *Journal for
the Scientific Study of Religion*, Fall 1967.

3 This is Weber's 'disenchantment of the world'. Durkheimians accept this, but need
not accept that it means an overall decline in religious influence. Reallocation of religious
functions can mean loss of breadth, but also an increase in depth.

4 Among the most forceful opponents of the secularization-as-decline thesis are
P. Glasner, *The Sociology of Secularization* (London, 1977); and D. Martin, *A General
Theory of Secularization* (Oxford, 1978); D. Martin, *The Dilemmas of Contemporary Religion* (Oxford, 1978); D. Martin, *The Religious and the Secular* (London, 1969). For a
later restatement of Martin's views, see 'The Secularization Issue: Prospect and Retrospect', *British Journal of Sociology*, September 1992.

of humans, culture and society, and therefore of the possibilities of future social and cultural change.

What is generally not in dispute is the fact of some overt shrinkage in the social space occupied by religion, at least when compared to the past; the concomitant fact of greater influence in everyday life of rational processes unknown or less used in the past; and the fact or desirability of a 'basic separation' between religion and the state.[5] But this consensus does not concede either the fact or desirability of separating religion from *all* politics, nor the fact or desirability of the decline of religion in civil society.

Moreover, the emergence of a secular state in Western democracies was more a practical consequence of a specific historical experience than an institutionalization of an abstract secular ideal. It partly represented the lessons learned by both church and state from a history of debilitating religious sectarian strife, the terrible 'wars of religion' of the sixteenth and seventeenth centuries. But the 1648 Peace of Westphalia, which brought those wars to an end, did not inaugurate the emergence of the secular state; rather, it institutionalized the principle of 'who rules, his religion', denoting a partnership between church and state. It was more the struggles against religious conformism after 1648 that paved the way for the emergence of the secular state in Europe.[6]

What *is* in dispute is the meaning of the secularization of civil society (outside the domains of formal political governance) and of culture. Contending notions of secularization are here inseparable from contending notions of religion. The difficulties in defining, discussing or agreeing about secularization are clearly related to the same difficulties with respect to religion.

But before skating on the treacherously slippery ice of 'understanding religion', a more recent, fourth notion of secularization must be taken up. This Indian contribution is the product of its specific history. In a context where there was no equivalent to the Enlightenment experience, where the values associated with liberal democracy and nationalism were imported, secularism was perceived as the unifying principle mediating between and collating different religious communities, in order to forge a common struggle for

---

5 Even in the United States, with its sharp separation of church and state, laws grant a few special favours, such as in regard to taxation, to religious personnel. This is true also in Europe, where there is often a formal state affiliation to a particular church. Even in increasingly multi-religious France, 80 per cent of the budget of private Catholic schools is provided by the state. According to Alfred Stepan, the twenty-seven members of the EU (Croatia became the twenty-eighth in 2013) all fund religious education; 89 per cent offer religious education in state schools, though not always compulsory; 44 per cent fund the clergy; and 19 per cent have established religions, including Anglicanism in England, Lutheranism in Denmark, Finland, and Norway, and Orthodoxy in Greece. See A. Stepan 'The Multiple Secularisms of Modern Democratic and Non-Democratic Regimes' in Calhoun et al., *Rethinking Secularism*, p. 117. The issue of what is meant by 'basic separation' will be taken up in Chapter 3.

6 Ibid., pp. 14–20.

national liberation. Secularism was the invocation of the principle of religious tolerance, itself romanticized as constituting the cultural or spiritual essence of an ancient and enduring Indian civilization. Here secularization was not a registration of religious change. Unlike in the West, where secularization and secularism are related but not congruent terms, secularization was all too often treated here as more or less a synonym for secularism. Both terms were used to characterize 'a state of affairs', an enduring feature over time rather than a coming to terms with any process of religious change. The Indian usages of the terms 'secular', 'secularism' and 'secularization' invoked images of an unchanging religious–spiritual–cultural essence.

Like its Western democratic counterpart, the Indian secular state would be religiously impartial. This impartiality, however, would be ensured not by abstinence from religious affairs, but by its 'fair' involvement on India's multi-religious terrain. In practice, and by constitutional provision, the difficulties of successfully institutionalizing such a notion meant that the Indian state did not represent that sharp a contrast from the broad Western model. The secularity of the Indian state is correctly characterized as something of an admixture in theory; less so in practice. It institutionalized separation in law while endorsing some degree of state intervention in religious affairs in the interests of 'public order, health and morality'.[7]

But its political practice all too often involved an active balancing of favours to various religious communities. Legal sanctions regarding the degree to which the state can intervene in religious affairs vary, reflecting divergent specific histories. There is now a large and growing literature about 'varieties of secularism'. Insofar as the term secularism is supposed to represent a principle of statecraft (what is sometimes referred to as 'political secularism', to distinguish it from secularism as an ideology of morals), the general principle of a basic (if never complete) separation of the state and of government from religion holds, even as there will be different degrees of separation.[8] There is, even in the most secular states, some small

---

7 Article 25 of the Constitution guarantees freedom of conscience, propagation and worship subject to 'public order, health and morality'. Lack of clarity and agreement over the meaning of secularism ensured that the word 'secular' was deliberately excluded from the (1949) Constitution, and was inserted only in 1976. Partly because of political compromises with Muslim religious leaders, the Common Civil Code was brought into the Constitution, but included under the Directive Principles. There was an ongoing dispute about education in the National Movement period, between those like Bal Gangadhar Tilak, who felt a Hinduized educational syllabus was essential to establish cultural nationalism and anti-colonial pride, and those like Mahadev Govind Ranade, Gopal Krishna Gokhale and Gopal Ganesh Agarkar, who wanted a modern, science-related education to overcome debilitating superstition and make progress. Gandhi effected a compromise embodied in Articles 28 and 38, whereby all minorities, including religious ones, could set up educational institutions of their choice and apply for state funding. Only those schools *wholly* maintained by such funding would, as a principle, avoid religious instruction.

8 The normative and political dimensions of secularism are obviously connected, in that the all-encompassing ethical question of how one is to live necessarily raises the narrower question of how one is to live politically with others.

overlap.[9] The permanent invariant is that, in cases of conflict between religion and the state, faith is not above the law. Final powers of arbitration are given to the state.

In the Indian context, the overdetermination of the notion of secularization by the idea of tolerance did mean that the question of the secularization of civil society was never posed in the same way as in the West. Whether Indian civil society was, could be or needed to be secularized were effectively non-questions since, for most, the tolerance (i.e. secularism) of Indian society was treated as axiomatic, despite the communal horrors of Partition. It is only in recent years, with the fragility of Indian secularism having been revealed, that the issues of secularism and secularization have been seriously inserted into the intellectual and theoretical agenda.

The political importance of this debate is obvious. How can one hope to fight successfully for something unless one is clear what one is supposed to be fighting for? Amid contending notions, one must choose and explain why. It is my contention that the classical concept of secularization – the declining influence of religion – needs to be strongly defended as something that has taken place, and whose furtherance is desirable (though not certain) in countries like India, where the pernicious caste system is sacralized. I talk of secularization rather than secularism because the key referent of the latter is the state, whereas my greater preoccupation is with civil society. The substantial and enduring secularization of civil society is itself the best way to preserve and deepen the state's existing secularity, and to secure wider acceptance of secularism as a political doctrine. Since, in the short run, maintaining and deepening the secularity of the Indian state is also vital, there can be no gainsaying the importance of those discourses concentrating on secularism, as distinct from secularization.

To understand communalism, it is necessary to understand secularization. But to understand the latter, it is crucial to understand religion and its role and place in society: specifically in the era of modernity. As the title of this chapter indicates, religion, modernity and secularization must therefore be the central themes under investigation. Having pointed out that there are contending views on secularization, I have also suggested that there are contending notions of religion to which they are connected, which produces a definitional issue of some importance.

However, it would be a serious error to select and then defend at all costs any particular definition of religion. What is more important is (a) to understand the pitfalls of certain definitions or ways of understanding

---

9 This being the case, there is an excessive enthusiasm among many Indian secularists for tightening up certain kinds of state behaviour, such as eliminating religious inauguration ceremonies at state functions, and ending media relays of religious music, functions, and so on. Some forms of such behaviour can be curtailed or eliminated. But to do so is *not* to make the Indian state significantly more secular. In fact, a misplaced zeal for using the secular broom in this way can also be counterproductive.

religion – what I have called, respectively, the assassination and immortalization of religion, that is, its imperishability in time and space for all human life, individual and social; and (b) to recognize that modernity introduces everywhere a shift in the relevance of religion from a social to a more personal domain of human existence. It is not that the personal and the social are easily separable, but persevering readers will get my drift when they come to the appropriate subsection in this chapter.

Any defence of the feasibility and desirability of further secularization has to try to expose the inadequacies and limitations of religion, even as it must also acknowledge its strengths. One is not talking of the elimination of religion.[10] In particular, one must successfully argue against the view that religion is *unavoidably central* to culture and/or society. Thus, religion, culture and society – and their inter-relationships – in our times must also be scrutinized. The subsection on 'Culture and Society' (preceded by an assessment of the not exclusively Marxist notion of religion as ideology) explores this terrain. Those who subscribe to the thesis that religion is central to culture and society (hence: What price secularization?) have very little choice but to subscribe to some kind of 'social coherence' or 'social cement' theory of society, in which religion is the key cementing agent. But those who subscribe to a social cement thesis have more flexibility. They do not have to subscribe to the view that religion is unavoidably central to culture and society. I have suggested that all coherence models of society are less plausible than other approaches grappling with the 'problem of order' in society. This conclusion simultaneously strikes a body blow against the centrality-of-religion thesis, and powerfully reinforces the view that further secularization, understood as religious decline, is indeed feasible.

Yet another temptation has been to understand the relationship between culture and society deterministically. On this understanding, there is thought to be either a 'cultural programming of society' (in which religion is often seen as the key cultural programmer) or a 'social programming of culture' (the 'dominant ideology' thesis is the Marxist variant of this approach). Since an appropriate understanding of culture is vital for engaging in this

---

10 A more democratic and therefore humane society is one where a religious way of life and belief is one option among others, provided it is compatible with freedom for others to worship or not, and with the complete absence of discrimination on any grounds, religious or non-religious. Casanova rails against what he calls 'secularist secularity', by which he means any claim to being 'liberated from religion' – Calhoun et al., *Rethinking Secularism*, p. 60. But this skirts the fact that greater rationality of thought does require some degree of 'liberation' from religious beliefs, and that the question of feeling liberated 'from' as well as being liberated 'by' will also be a personal one, depending very much on specific existential circumstances, experiences and beliefs. Moreover, religious systems themselves must undergo some degree of internal change in keeping with the reality of epistemological and moral progress and change. This is not to give a purely positive judgement to modernity – far from it, since both the positive and negative aspects of modernity are of an altogether different order from those of a less secular and more religious past. But the positive transformations and possibilities opened up by modernity must at least be recognized and adapted to.

discussion, I have had to clarify my own thinking. Clearly, the term 'culture' has various meanings, which is its strength. How best to understand it depends upon what one is trying to explain or distinguish between – for example, art and culture, market and culture, or, as in this case, culture and society. On this question I have been decisively influenced by the later Raymond Williams. Cultural essentialism of any kind – and most immortalizers of religion tend to be cultural essentialists – is the bane of any serious attempt to understand the increasingly complex and dynamic nature of the relationships between religion, culture and society in modernity.

The next subsection, 'Religion in Modernity', explores the basic role of religion today. Here it is the question of identity that becomes paramount. It becomes necessary to focus on religious identity and its relationship to other identifies, and to point to the peculiarities and limitations of religious identity. Further secularization means the further decline in the importance of religious identity. This is both possible and desirable. Religion should become more privatized, and religious affiliation more of a free choice. Respect for religious pluralism demands as much. But I do not claim that it must or should become progressively more marginal, or should or will disappear. The view that religion reasserts its centrality to human society in modernity, but differently than in its pre-modern past – namely, through some unique capacity to stabilize the human personality – is also rejected.

Charles Taylor's 2007 text on how the secular age emerged in the West has had a major impact on all subsequent discussions about secularism, and is therefore taken up for discussion, followed by a dissection of other arguments against the secularization-as-decline thesis. The final subsection returns to the inadequacies of the specifically Indian notion of secularism, or secularization, as 'tolerance'.

The Definitional Issue: Assassins and Immortalizers

Modernity has been the most formidable challenge yet to religion. Religious systems have responded by carrying out internal reforms in beliefs and practices, so as to reassert their contemporary relevance. They have also responded by adopting modern means to pursue traditional goals and values. But perhaps the most striking tribute to the power of modernity is the spawning of the study of religion itself. Religion has come to be seen as a distinct entity distinguishable from other spheres of existence, and a new mass awareness has developed of its existence in different forms, as various religions and religious systems.

Religion, not God (s), is the focus of such self-conscious scholarship. There is more than an echo here of Nietzsche's 'God is dead, long live religion'. In Weber's striking observation, the modern man or woman seems no longer able to live with religion or to live without it. She now needs to name and understand it, where once there was unreflective acceptance of its reality, indeed of it *as* reality.

The definitional issue, then, can hardly be dodged. Seeking definitions of such complex, multidimensional phenomena as religion is always a risky affair. Definitions chop reality up in different ways. They can be too broad or too narrow. They can bring too much into their field of vision or leave too much out. They draw boundaries in the dark with more than a hint of arbitrariness. It may well be more fruitful to 'talk about' religion, or to recognize that the most interesting insights lie in the overlaps between different definitions. This refusal to make too much of definitions is wise.

But what other way than by adopting, however cautiously, working definitions is there of securing some more or less useful entry point into the domain of inquiry? Weber explicitly stated that a definition of religion would be the end-result of his monumental comparative researches into the world religions. But he, too, had to begin with an implicit definition and a distinctive approach: *verstehen*, understanding from within, religion as the meaning in a meaningless world, sociology as the interpretive study of society. The real problem here with definitions is that, useful as they may be as points of entry, they may too strongly fix the points of exit. They may assign or invite conclusions and evaluations in an excessively deterministic manner.

Peter Berger, one of the most respected modern theorists of religion, warned against 'assassination by definition'.[11] He had in mind those negative definitions which easily lend themselves to abusive ideological usage: religion as 'the disease of language' (Max Müller), or as 'false consciousness' (many Marxists, though not Marx), or as 'imperfect philosophy' (Edward Burnett Tylor and other nineteenth-century positivist anthropologists), or as 'the childhood of man' (Freud). For Berger, such biased approaches consistently fail to preserve that necessary balance in the assessment of what religion is and does, and of its involvement in the relationships both between humans and nature and between humans themselves.

Yet the very same charge can be levelled against Berger. Like others, he was prone to immortalization through definition. This would apply to all those definitions which ultimately root religion in the anthropological condition – in other words, in the notion that in our essence we are inescapably religious animals. For Durkheim and many influenced by his sociology, this immortalization is routed through society. We are social animals, and the sacred–religious is the ineradicable form of the social relationship between the individual and the group, constituted, as it has to be, as a 'moral community'. Other immortalizing definitions see human social existence as inconceivable without 'overarching values', and see religion in anything

---

11 P. Berger, 'Some Second Thoughts on Substantive versus Functional Definitions of Religion', *Journal for the Scientific Study of Religion* 13: 2 (June 1974).

providing them, or in whatever confers a strongly solemn sense of identity, or in the capacity to transcend one's biology.[12]

Immortalizing religion effectively renders the idea of secularization-as-decline as, at best, of very limited value. Its bias towards endorsing a 'strong coherence' model of culture and society should be obvious.[13] To investigate religion is to investigate what it is and what it does. There can be two ways of defining what it is. Real definitions look for an essence. They are evaluative, and ask to be judged by their truth. While this may be appropriate for the study of some or many religions, it seems impossible to establish an essence common to *all* religions or worshippers. Nominal definitions are descriptive. But description can be from the outside or inside. Outsider descriptions are more likely to be non-evaluative and cautious in assessing religion's relationship to society and culture.[14]

Insider descriptions generally belong to the hermeneutic–phenomenological school: 'To believe is to understand, to understand is to believe.'[15] The religious experience or faith must be understood in its own terms. Historians of religion and cultural anthropologists often favour this approach, but it has also received considerable impetus from philosophy's 'revolution

---

12 R. N. Bellah, 'Religious Evolution', in A. Robertson, ed., *Sociology of Religion* (Harmondsworth, 1969); H. Mol, *Identity and the Sacred* (Oxford, 1976); T. Luckmann, *Life-World and Social Realities* (London, 1983). For a general survey, see B. Wilson, *Religion in Sociological Perspective* (Oxford, 1982).

13 This is a strongly contested claim, and if these critics are right then a significant scepticism is cast over the validity of that notion of religion, which the coherence model presumes.

14 Two examples of such outsider descriptions are those by Anthony Giddens and Martin Southwold. According to Giddens, the characteristics of all religions are symbols evoking reverence and awe among believers who practise rituals. However, Giddens seems to accept Durkheim's unconvincing attempt to separate magic sharply from religion. His definition would also exclude non-ritualistic religions like the early and more austere forms of Hinayana Buddhism. A. Giddens, *Sociology* (Oxford, 1991), Chapter 14.

Southwold, unlike Giddens, eschews any attempt to establish properties fitting all religions. Using the distinction between a monothetic class (where all members share a common bundle of attributes) and a polythetic class (where all members have some but not all of the attributes belonging to that class), he places religion in the latter class. He lists some twelve attributes, a few of which, like belief in supernatural beings and ritual practices, are near universal: (1) central concern with godlike beings and human relations with them; (2) a dichotomy of the world into the sacred and profane, and central concern with the sacred; (3) orientation towards salvation from 'mundane' existence; (4) ritual practices; (5) beliefs not logically or empirically demonstrable, but held as a matter of faith; (6) an ethical code, supported by such beliefs; (7) supernatural sanctions on infringements on that code; (8) a mythology; (9) a body of scriptures, or an exalted oral tradition; (10) a priesthood or specialist religious elite; (11) association in a 'moral community'; (12) association with an ethnic or similar group. See M. Southwold, 'Buddhism and the Definition of Religion', *Man* 13 (1978).

Apart from the purposes of formal classification, such descriptive definitions hardly aid further investigation into the really interesting questions regarding religion. What, for example, are its more important dimensions ?

15 See discussion of the hermeneutic approach to religion in B. Morris, *Anthropological Studies of Religion* (Cambridge, 1987). See also J. A. Saliba, *Homo Religiousus in Mircea Eliade* (Leiden, 1976).

of language'. Religion and culture have come to be seen, above all, as symbolic orders, meanings embodied in symbol systems. For example, religion is perceived as sacred symbols synthesizing the 'ethos' of a people's culture.[16] Humans are said to have a natural propensity to symbolize; symbolic systems are said substantially to constitute reality. The way is cleared for the over-valuation and near-immortalization of religion. Here religion is said to provide meaning and order. What is ignored is that religion is in part an 'ideology', and operates not simply on the terrain of meaning but on the *intersections* between meaning and power.

The idea of religion as above all 'the religious experience' or 'faith' raises at least two problems. It generally forecloses further investigation into that experience or faith itself. The individual subjectivity, the religious actor or believer, is at the epicentre of the religious enterprise. To grasp religion is to understand (as much as one can) through empathy the subjective purposes, feelings and responses of the believer, not to judge them. The religious experience is beyond truth and falsehood. Yet this claim cannot be secured beyond all doubt. The notion of experience *is* open to cognitive investigation. Experiences and identities have epistemic status. What goes into them – beliefs, values, desires – has epistemic status. These elements do not have complete freedom from error. An experience is a 'pattern of salience', one way of 'processing information' so there can be better or worse, truer or falser experiences, as judged by a 'weak' principle of objectivity and therefore more accurate, more explanatory, more humane readings of the world.[17]

Faith is not simply to be accepted as given and impenetrable to the outsider, but must be theorized as much as possible. There is bad faith and good faith, and it is an abnegation of intellectual, moral and political responsibility *not* to argue with faith, especially if it is bad faith.[18] It is one thing to

---

16 C. Geertz, 'Religion as a Cultural System', in R. Bocock and K. Thompson, eds, *Religion and Ideology* (Manchester, 1985). Geertz's definition of religion is '1) a system of symbols which acts to 2) establish powerful, pervasive, and long-lasting moods and motivations in men by 3) formulating conceptions of a general order of existence and 4) clothing these conceptions with such an aura of factuality that 5) the moods and motivations seem uniquely realistic'. His definition of culture is 'an historically transmitted pattern of meanings embodied in symbols, a system of inherited conceptions expressed in symbolic forms by means of which men communicate, perpetuate and develop their knowledge about and attitudes towards life' (ibid., pp. 3–4).

17 S. P. Mohanty, 'The Epistemic Status of Cultural Identity', *Cultural Critique* 24 (Spring 1993).

18 This point was particularly significant in the context of the reactionary, right-wing Hindu nationalist political campaign over the Ram Janmabhoomi–Babri Masjid issue. Historians, many from the Jawaharlal Nehru University (JNU), mostly liberal and left-wing, provided strong historical evidence and argument against the idea that Babar had destroyed any temple (let alone one that had been constructed to worship Ram) in order to build a mosque. These JNU historians were attacked not only from the Right but from sections of the Left as pursuing a typically leftist, insensitive and elitist initiative. These historians were daring to argue with faith, although the faith that a Ram temple existed and had been destroyed was itself *constructed*, and had become a mass belief only over the decade of the 1980s.

stress the difficulties of this task, or to recognize that even in bad faith there is a component central to faith that must be acknowledged and respected even when it makes bad faith so resistant to change. But it is something else to so elevate the importance of faith as to deny the necessity and usefulness of its interrogation, or to assume this can *only* be done from a position of sympathetic detachment from within.[19]

The second problem is a paradox. The outsider supposedly can only go so far in the effort to understand from within, especially when such understanding is attempted across cultural and religious divides. If the problem of cultural untranslatability precludes all but the hermeneutical approach, how is the claim to the correctness of this tradition of scholarship to be validated? How is one to confirm that it is a religious experience in the first place? Some level of translation always takes place, otherwise meaningful communication across linguistic divides would be impossible. Once this is acknowledged, the thin end of the investigative wedge has been inserted. There can be no logical objection to the idea that a better translation and a better understanding of not just the individual actor but her context are always available in principle. Given competing translations and understandings even *within* a cultural or religious system, what reason is there to assume that decisive arbitration here must rest with the religious actor alone?

Durkheim, father of the functionalist definition of religion, said that its

---

The point is not that such a 'rationalist exposure' could by itself (in the absence of mass political counter-mobilization against the forces of Hindutva) check the construction of bad faith, or even play a major role in doing so. But that this effort was a morally, intellectually and politically important one that was necessitated by the very deliberate and systematic construction of bad faith on such a wide scale.

See also J. V. Spickard, 'For a Sociology of Religious Experience', in W. H. Swatos Jr, ed., *A Future For Religion?* (Delhi, 1993). Spickard puts forward a typology of different notions of religious experience. He concludes that religious experiences and emotions cannot be separated from the ideas and context by which they are explained. For example, one does not first speak in tongues and then join an assembly, but the other way around. Quite his most interesting idea is that experiences are 'inner patterns of time' – patterns, or experiences, that can be learned and shared.

19 This was certainly the inclination of Mircea Eliade. For a sensitive and subtle exploration of the question of faith in the Indian context, see R. Bharucha, *The Question of Faith* (New Delhi, 1993). Bharucha is justifiably more sympathetic than I am in his treatment of the issue of faith, because his basic orientation is different. My own more limited programme is to attack the excessive valorization of faith and the refusal to recognize its inescapable imbrication with issues of ideology and power. Bharucha takes this imbrication as given, but nonetheless wishes to explore the variability in the relationship between religion-as-faith and religion-as-ideology, and is more concerned to understand the 'ambivalences of faith' and the 'enigmas of faith'.

Whereas my political project is to defend a particular notion of secularization-as-religious-decline, and therefore contest the idea of the social centrality of religion (including its 'faith' and 'other' components), Bharucha's political project is to establish the necessity of fighting for the secular on the terrain of religious discourse itself – a project requiring a more sensitive appreciation of religion–faith and its resources. I concur with his view about the need to fight for the secular on the religious terrain itself. But I am less sanguine about the *degree* of usefulness of such a project. I would certainly subordinate it strategically to the struggle for secularization outside the terrain of religious discourse.

importance lay in what it does, not in what it says or claims. A distinction must be made between its manifest and latent functions, and it is the latter that are decisive in the proper comprehension of religion. Religious practices (for example, rituals) were much more important than beliefs or doctrine. The latter could be false; but the heart of religion, its role, could not be. Durkheim's functionalist approach marked a paradigm shift, profoundly altering twentieth-century thinking on religion. The centre of gravity shifted from the philosophy to the sociology of religion.[20] Its great flaw was that it left out the subjective dimension. What about religion's relationship to the ultimate conditions of individual existence – the problems of pain, suffering, death?

Unlike Durkheim, Weber did address 'meaning of life' questions. So most modern sociologists of religion have sought to wed the approaches and insights of Weber and Durkheim. They have sought to elaborate on what religion is and what religion does, to deal with substantive as well as functional issues. The real line of division in the definitional issue seems to be between the substantivist and functional approaches, each having either a psychological or sociological bias.[21]

Where psychological substantivists talk of the 'religious experience', sociological substantivists make one such experience – belief in supernatural beings, for example – the cornerstone of their definition.[22] Psychological functionalists stress religion's role in cognition (explaining the unknown), or see religion as a compensatory mechanism, or as human projection come to life (alienation, reification), rooted either in the anthropological condition or in social need. Sociological functionalists view religion as that which has ultimate significance for a social group, or which integrates it. This integration can be system-cohering where the system is culture and/or society. Alternatively, religion as a form of ideological discourse can be seen as legitimating oppression. In the first case, religion is usually seen as helping to

---

20 Indian studies of Hinduism have largely escaped this paradigm shift. Most remain obsessed with the philosophy of Hinduism, especially as embodied in the Vedas. Between contemporary anthropological studies of Hinduism and caste, and Vedantic philosophizing, the historical sociology of Hinduism has been by contrast a casualty of sorts. Romila Thapar's writings, within her time frame of ancient India, constitute a magnificent exception.

21 Luckmann, *Life-World and Social Realities.* This is a fine insight of his.

22 One of the most sophisticated of such sociological substantivists is Alexander Saxton; see A. Saxton, *Religion and the Human Prospect* (New York, 2006; repr. New Delhi, 2007). Controversially, he makes religion universal, and defines it as 'belief in superhuman and supernatural but anthropomorphic spiritual power (s) functioning in (or over) nature' (p. 51), or, even more concisely, as 'belief in anthropomorphically benevolent spiritual beings in and over nature' (p. 180). His use of the term 'supernatural' means he draws a sharper line between nature and the 'beyond', in a way that is much more characteristic of Christianity than, say, lived and practised Hinduism. His approach has a strong functionalist dimension as well, since he believes that such beliefs helped people to cope with the consciousness of the inevitability of death peculiar to the human species, which, along with the 'problem of evil' and suffering, would otherwise be psychologically and socially highly destabilizing. Religion was thus a universal adaptive mechanism.

create a universe or canopy of meaning, in which meaning-creation and organization is also the creation of 'order'.[23]

Obviously, this division between substantivists and functionalists is not sharp. Who does not believe in some social function of religion? Many if not most substantivists (Berger supported the phenomenological approach) have strong functionalist accents. But the converse is less likely to hold. Not surprisingly, in our post-Enlightenment era of greater scepticism about the 'divine order of things' and notions of 'divine will', religion is more often asked to justify itself by reference to what it does. A *general* defence of religion must focus on the similarities between religions, and this is what functionalism does. Functionalist definitions promote large-scale theories of religion, and open up the prospect of comparative studies. Substantivists have shorter-range theories; they provide more focus on differences between religions, and are more empirically oriented. But functionalist definitions can encapsulate substantivist ones. They see as religion all that substantivists do (ideology, value system, and so on) and more – sometimes too much more.[24] Substantivists, then, are also likely to be 'moderate' functionalists, but rarely non-functionalists or 'extreme' functionalists.

Immortalizers or near-immortalizers of religion, however, cut across the substantivist–functionalist boundary. Marx, a substantivist (religion as ideology) and a psychological functionalist (religion as alienation) was not an immortalizer. Freud, a psychological functionalist, was not an immortalizer. Admittedly, sociological functionalists, in their overwhelming number, are. Religion presumably has crucial immortal or near-immortal properties, because its role is *irreplaceable* – not because it necessarily plays a great many roles. The question of religion's immortality and omnipotence is in the end dependent as much on one's broader understanding of culture and society as it is on one's specific understanding of religion. For Marxists, that relationship has been mediated by the concept of ideology.

Religion as Ideology: Marxists and Others

The common thread among Marxists is that religion is an ideology, though what various Marxists mean by ideology is not uniform. Nonetheless, in seeing it as ideology, Marxist discussion is conducted on the terrain of ideas, doctrine, discourse, and so on, and their impact on individual and society. This contrasts with the Durkheimian, functionalist emphasis on practice and ritual as the heart of religion. Thus, certain Marxist approaches come quite close to modern non-Marxist cognitive understandings of religion.

Marxist historical sociology, which has sought to explain the riddle of Western superiority, or why capitalism first emerged and flourished in

---

23 Berger, *Social Reality of Religion*.
24 Luckmann, *Life-World and Social Realities*.

Western Europe and then extended itself globally, has also taken in the study of world religions. What was the role of specific religious systems in encouraging or obstructing the emergence of capitalism out of the pre-capitalist incubator? This was also Weber's project, but because he gave an un-Marxist primacy to the world religions as the 'switchmen' who decided the tracks along which civilizations would move (though powered by the engine of 'social interests'), he sought to carry out major comparative studies of the world religions themselves.

Marxists, though they studied Islam and the Islamic world (Maxime Rodinson, for example) as a counterpoise to colonialist and orientalist historiography, were never tempted to emulate Weber in the same way. The empirical foundations for Marxist theorizations about religion have been anthropological studies of tribal religions and systems of magic, the Judaeo-Christian biblical tradition, or the rise and spread of Christianity. It is only more recently that one can talk of Marxists making sketches on a wider canvas. In the Marxist tradition as it stands, the specifically Christian experience constantly risks being transmogrified into the general characteristics of religion per se.

Much Marxist work on religion has been of two types.[25] It has consisted of commentaries on or developments of Marx and Engels's approaches; or of applications of these to specific cases – as in Kautsky's study of Christianity. But more recently, clearly motivated by liberation theology and radical Christian grassroots movements in Latin America (the only large area that was both overwhelmingly Christian *and* colonized), there has been a deeper effort to appreciate the utopian and redemptive dimensions of religious thought and doctrine. Thus there has been an attempt to recover within the Marxist tradition those currents which drew some inspiration from the Romantic rebellion against the excesses of Enlightenment rationalism and anti-clericalism, saw important positive convergences between Marxist and Christian millenarianism, or stressed the compatibility of the moral philosophy of religion with Marxism.[26]

It is also the case that a number of Marxist thinkers, past and present, have had such a serious engagement, both intellectual and emotional, with the Biblical tradition, theology and the church that it has left indelible imprints on their Marxism. Perhaps the best study currently available of this engagement is by Roland Boer, in the first three volumes of his five-volume *Criticism of Heaven and Earth* series.[27] The Marxists whose works

---

25 M. Löwy, *Marxism and Liberation Theology – Notebooks for Study and Research* 10 (Amsterdam, 1988).

26 M. Löwy, 'Revolution against "Progress": Walter Benjamin's Romantic Anarchism', *New Left Review* I/152 (July–August 1985). See also references in M. Löwy, *Marxism and Liberation Theology*. E. Bloch, *L'athéisme dans le Christianisme* (Paris, 1978); L. Goldmann, *The Hidden God* (London, 1955); L. Boff and C. Boff, *Theologies de la Liberation* (Paris, 1985); G. Gutiérrez, *Theologie de la Liberation-Perspectives* (Brussels, 1974).

27 Roland Boer, *Criticism of Heaven and Earth*, 5 vols (Leiden, 2013).

are put under the microscope, revealing their often intense involvements, range from Kautsky and Luxemburg in the early twentieth century, right through Bloch and the Frankfurt School theorists such as Horkheimer, Benjamin and Adorno, to those of our own times, such as Jameson, Eagleton, Žižek, Löwy and many others, some of whom, while not calling themselves Marxists, have certainly been influenced by the Marxist tradition.[28]

What about Marx's own understanding of religion? Boer's fourth volume is devoted specifically to the writings of Marx and Engels, tracing the hundreds if not thousands of allusions both made to Christian theology. Indeed, Boer says it was religion as theology (and therefore, one might add, as ideology) that preoccupied Marx. While Boer's study is among the widest-ranging studies anywhere of the evolution of the duo's thinking and of their divergent concerns – Engels was more impressed by the revolutionary origins of Christianity, and sought to explore this history, whereas Marx's development of the notion of fetishism can be traced to his earlier interest in religious work on idolatry – it is the issue of 'religion as ideology' that will be the specific focus here.[29] Marx's understanding of this was in important respects different from that of Engels. 'False consciousness' is used by the latter; never by the former. Marx was more of a Hegelian, understanding the origin of religion as alienation, while Engels was more of an anthropological positivist, seeing the believer as a failed rationalist, and discerning the origin of religion in the misunderstanding of nature and its forces.

Early Marx sees religion as alienation, later Marx as ideology – but he did not abandon his early notion.[30] Ideology concealed alienation. Insofar as Marxists continue to see religion as a strong, or 'basic', form of alienation, they and immortalizers, or near-immortalizers, often have strikingly convergent views about the power and importance of religion. Peter Berger's alienation model of religion, involving the dialectic of externalization, objectification and internalization of man's own thought-products, is explicitly Hegelian. For him, 'religion is the audacious attempt to conceive of the entire universe as meaningful'. It is the positing of a 'sacred cosmos' which transcends and includes man, and 'locates his life in an ultimately meaningful order'.[31]

But, no matter how positive this positing of a sacred cosmos might be (and for Berger it is highly positive), it remains a mystification and falsification

---

28 Vol. I looks at Ernst Bloch, Walter Benjamin, Louis Althusser, Henri Lefebvre, Antonio Gramsci, Terry Eagleton, Slavoj Žižek and Theodor Adorno. Vol. II is on Lucien Goldmann, Frederic Jameson, Rosa Luxemburg, Karl Kautsky, Julia Kristeva, Alain Badiou, Georgio Agamben, Georg Lukács and Raymond Williams. Vol. III focuses on Max Horkheimer, E. P. Thompson, G. E. M de Ste Croix, Michael Löwy, Roland Barthes, Gilles Deleuze, Félix Guattari and Antonio Negri.

29 In his fourth volume, *Criticism of Earth* (Leiden, 2012) Boer says Marx came across the idea of fetishism in the early ethno-anthropological work of one Charles de Brosses, and later made use of the concept in his economic writings. See 'Introduction', p.6.

30 J. Larrain, *Marxism and Ideology* (London, 1983).

31 Berger, *Social Reality of Religion*, p. 26.

of the world – a human thought product *given* reality by man through alienation–reification: 'All human productions are, at least potentially, comprehensible in human terms. The veil of mystification thrown over them by religion prevents such comprehension.'[32] Gramsci, in one of his formulations, described religion in a way that has a definite affinity with Berger's view of religion as an 'audacious' project: 'Religion is the most gigantic utopia, that is, the most gigantic "metaphysics" that history has ever known, since it is the most grandiose attempt to reconcile, in mythological form, the real contradictions of historical life.'[33]

But Gramsci's emphasis on religious reconciliation of the 'real contradictions of historical life' shows how Marxist approaches depart from Berger, Durkheim, and even Weber. For he is saying that it performs an ideological function, as well and at least implicitly serving specific social interests and relations of power. It is the notion of religion as ideology that links the Marxist understanding of religion to questions of social power and social order. But this social order is understood not merely or primarily in terms of how the *individual* is to relate to society, and the cognitive presuppositions for this – the 'ordering of meaning', society and culture being 'universes of meaning' – but in terms of how specific social groups, such as classes, *impose* their social order or control social conflict, and in terms of the intellectual and ideational preconditions for the dominance of these groups. This, in fact, is the most important insight provided by the Marxist approach to religion.

Religion is many things, and plays many roles. But it also has ideological functions which are *negative* – functions that serve oppressive group interests. The ordering of meaning in society, or *nomization*, is never neutral or wholly positive, but mediated through social relations. We are not simply individuals alone in the cosmos; each one of us is also an 'ensemble of social relations'. All attempts to understand religion and the religious quest which insist on the *individual* mind being the decisive point of departure are likely to be dangerously misleading, because they obscure this ideological dimension.[34]

Whatever the origin of the religious impulse, and whatever the unprecedented existential dilemmas of the modern individual (faced with alternative

---

32 Ibid., p. 90.

33 A. Gramsci, *Selections from the Prison Notebooks*, ed. Q. Hoare and G. Nowell Smith (London, 1971), p. 405.

34 I have adopted Berger's terms 'nomization' (ordering of meaning) and 'cosmization' (ordering of the cosmos) as useful shorthands (Berger, *Social Reality of Religion*). Berger's own individual–social dialectic is unsatisfactory. His triad of externalization–objectification–internalization sees society as externalization–objectivation, and internalization as the 'reappropriation in consciousness' of society. This is what Roy Bhaskar calls a dialectical model of 'society forms individuals forms society', which, he argues convincingly, fails because individual and society are *not* related as in a dialectic. Society comes first for any given individual, and confronts him as a given. This is precisely the point about religion. See R. Bhaskar, *Reclaiming Reality* (London, 1981), Chapter 5.

forms of cosmization, nomization and social legitimation to those of a religious system), religious systems, for most of their lifetimes, have confronted humans as a *given*. Their power over humans is not the result of an individual *choice* to 'order meaning' or 'make sense of her society or the world' in a religious way, but more the expression of that individual's existence as an 'ensemble of social relations'. Over these religiously legitimated social relations – their power distribution, their durability and strength – that individual has no say. Over their reproduction or transformation, she has some say.

For Marx, religion was a *form* of ideology, and ideology was a 'specific mode of being of ideas'. Ideology is always ideas, but ideas are not always ideologies. Marx had a negative and restricted conception of ideology.[35] It is negative because ideology is a distortion of real contradictions in the world. It is restricted because there are many more distortions and errors than ideology can cover or speak of. So the relationship between ideology and non-ideology is not a simple positing of falsity against truth. Moreover, ideology distorts real contradictions in different ways. It denies contradictions, misunderstands them, displaces or dilutes them, and by doing so serves the social interests of those who benefit from this general misrepresentation.

Marx does not have an interest theory of ideology, or of religion. He does not have a functionalist *explanation* of ideology or religion. He does not claim that the origin or purpose of ideology or religion is to serve special interests. He simply points out that it *also* has this function. He *attributes* this role; he does not *explain* ideology or religion by this function.

Marx's understanding of ideology develops further complexities. Ideology is the inversion in consciousness of an inverted reality. It is the 'inverted reflection of an inverted reality which results in negation of the latter inversion.'[36] Inverted reality comes about through alienation. Alienation is the inversion of an objectified social practice. Ideology is the further distortion – inversion in consciousness – of this already inverted reality. It is in this sense that religion is the basic form of alienation and the first form of ideology. And it is in this sense that the critique of religion must, above all, be the critique of the conditions (inverted reality) that give rise to it in the form of alienation and ideology.

Marx and Engels believed that the era in which religion could play a progressive role was over. There was, therefore, little reason for them to devote too much further effort to investigating either religion in general or any specific religion. They took this view for two reasons. First, they held a negative conception of ideology, which itself was to be rejected or exposed as distortion. Therefore religion as a form of ideology could not provide

---

35 Larrain, *Marxism and Ideology.*
36 Ibid.

resources in the struggle against ideology. Religion was an *obstacle* to progress; it could not be a *weapon* of progress.

Second, this view fitted their understanding of the transition from pre-capitalist societies to capitalist ones. This was a movement from societies where relations of dependence and exploitation were transparent, and therefore more in need of sacralizing systems of legitimation (religions), to a mode of production where such relations were obscured and no longer transparent. This facilitated the emergence of other kinds of non-religious, non-sacralizing ideologies. Secular bourgeois ideologies would become more important, and their most important counterpoint would be secular socialist ideas (not socialist 'ideology'). Religious discourse would have little role or place on this new battlefield of ideas and social forces. Where religious ideology sought to *justify* the existence of hierarchy and dominance, bourgeois political ideology sought to obscure and deny the existence of this dominance.

One of the strongest criticisms of the treatment by Marx and Engels of religion as ideology is made by Alexander Saxton. Marx and Engels equate religion to ideology and see ideological constructions as a set of obfuscations and mystifications that serve to camouflage the interests of ruling groups. In which case they are implying that religion emerges at a later stage in the evolution of societies when they become more stratified, indeed class-divided societies. That, at any rate, is the charge made by Saxton against the masters and it is a reasonable one given that religion in some form *precedes* the emergence of stratified class societies. Religion, cannot then just be an ideology in the sense understood by Marx and Engels, although it does substantially become that in a class-divided society, when religious elites emerge and align themselves with political elites or seek to maintain their own social position through religiously rooted arguments, justifications and claims. But a more damaging criticism of the notion of religion as ideology is that Marx and Engels could never perceive of religion as a possibly liberating force for the working class in a capitalist society (they did concede this for occasions in the pre-capitalist past) but only as a barrier to the development of a progressive and revolutionary class consciousness – a completely one-sided and therefore mistaken view.

Such an approach shows itself incapable of recognizing that religious belief can continue to play a liberating role under capitalism – for example, in Latin America; and it is a view that can also act as a barrier to alliances (within the working classes) with sections that remain religiously committed, since class and revolutionary consciousness does not require complete rejection of religion and the role it plays, which goes beyond ideological mystification, and for which Marxism has no answers – personal solace in the face of death, the loss of a loved one, and some other forms of emotional suffering.[37] Saxton

---

37 A. Saxton, *Religion and the Human Prospect*, Chapter 11.

correctly points out that religious belief does not preclude escape from class exploitation, nor always generate clerical hierarchies that make such escape impossible.[38]

It is likely that the rise of mass working-class parties in Europe promoted a positive or neutral conception of ideology. Corresponding to its growing class strength, the notion of a 'class point of view' became more important. Clashes of ideas sharpened, and the notion of confronting a ruling-class ideology with a working-class counter-ideology became increasingly legitimate among socialists. Whatever the explanation for this shift from a negative to a positive or neutral concept of ideology, it was complete by the time of Luxemburg, Lenin and Trotsky, and finds its most fruitful developments in the thought of Gramsci, for whom 'hegemony' and 'ideological subordination' became closely related concepts.

Here, the work of Boer is particularly illuminating. Gramsci drew from his interrogation of the workings of the Catholic Church in Italy, and from Christianity more generally, various crucial insights. Christian ecumenism – the coming together of Protestant denominations and orthodox churches (but not the Catholic Church) – could provide lessons for forging a left unity of parties and communist currents. Similarly, the processes and practices of Christian conversion would highlight the role played by the clergy as 'organic intellectuals', and how proselytization was effective in different ways in winning over targeted intellectual layers, or in creating intellectuals of a new type, or in creating over a prolonged period structures that eventually condition belief and lead to successful and rapid mass conversion. Of course, Gramsci recognized the profound limits of the hegemony exercised by Christianity, and the Catholic Church in particular, in that it would religiously sanctify private property and class division as God's will. But he was also greatly impressed by how the Protestant Reformation uplifted and transformed the whole of society: the intellectual and moral reform it was able to carry out could provide insights for Communists as well. The construction of hegemony overseen by the state always required intellectuals to mediate between ruling and subaltern groups and classes, thereby universalizing ruling-class values. Leadership is when a particular social class, for example the working class, can successfully universalize its ideas and understandings to create the national–popular.[39]

As far as the issue of religion is concerned, the shift towards the positive or neutral conception of ideology has had a generally beneficent impact. Marx's restricted concept of ideology promoted a restricted conception of religion. It tended to ignore the importance of religious practice and its significance in symbolic–cultural life. It certainly promoted too one-sided an emphasis on religion as illusion, as distorted consciousness. But Marx's concept

38 Ibid., p. 226, n. 27.
39 Boer, *Criticism of Heaven and Earth*, Vol. I, Chapter 5, on Gramsci.

cannot be reduced simply to false consciousness (though Engels and many other Marxists were not as subtle). For Marx, religion was the expression of real needs, but it misconstrued those needs and then 'answered' them in a way that helped to perpetuate both the needs and their misconstrual. Moreover, for Marx capitalism was both de-sacralizing and dehumanizing. If the former meant a significant degree of secularization, the latter meant that capitalism would also create the conditions conducive to newer forms of religiosity.

Religion thus reproduced its conditions of existence and its role, but in historically shaped ways. Religion did not posit a false world as an *alternative* to the real world, but rather a way of relating to a real world through belief in a false world. To risk an oxymoron, religion was not a false consciousness, but a false real consciousness – a false way of experiencing real lived relationships as these themselves changed over time. Experiences are always real, in that they exist; but they can still have a false epistemic status.

The sophistication Marx could extend to the notion of ruling-class ideas (not ideology) was effectively denied to religion. Whereas the ideas of the ruling class could be undistorted (if self-serving) expressions of practice, ideology, and religion as a form of ideology, could only be distorted expressions of practice. But even a notion of religion as more than ideology, as belonging to the set of ruling-class ideas, is clearly insufficient. This would sociologically limit the concept to the ruling class, just as Marx's notion of religion as ideology epistemologically limits it to distorted ideas.

The strong criticism of Marx's concept is (a) that it sees religion as primarily a form of knowledge; and (b) that it distinguishes too sharply between different forms of knowledge: ideology and non-ideology, science and ideology, ruling-class and subordinate-class ideas. Religion, even understood as a form of knowledge, cannot be so easily compartmentalized.

Though Marx and Engels paved the way for a study of religion in relation to social power, their negative definition links it more strongly to oppressive social groups. The idea of religion as a social opium might suggest that religion legitimates oppressive-class rule by enveloping it in hazy mystification, and that it simultaneously acts as a palliative for the oppressed classes. What is lost from view is religion's capacity to provide a Utopian motivation to rebel – something that Engels was quite willing to admit when talking of religion in the past. Liberation theology is a sharp reminder that religious belief, doctrine and sensibility can still inspire progressive social movements. Religion, even as a form of knowledge, belongs to a wider domain of ideas, or 'signification'.

According to the more positive or neutral conception of ideology, this field of signification can be the domain of ideational conflict. This looser, more general conception of ideology frees the study of religion from the corsets imposed by a restricted and negative conception, allowing something more closely approximating religion's truer place in the realm of human affairs. But the critical edge of the Marxist approach to religion can also be lost in this loosening of epistemological and sociological stays. Retaining a fundamental emphasis on the relationship between meaning and power, and on ongoing conflicts in the field of signification, is essential.

There is much to be said for linking ideology to asymmetrical relations of power, for understanding ideology as 'meaning in the service of power'. Meaning is understood not as beliefs, but as signification. So ideology is much more than a belief system, and not necessarily as coherent. It belongs to the realm of language and discourse rather than to the realm of beliefs, and is embodied in everyday practices and routines.[40]

Those Marxists seeking to defend Marx's notion of religion have had to greatly broaden the notion of ideology itself. In doing so, they risk so expanding its conceptual boundaries as to make it increasingly less different in scope and nature from culture. Furthermore, what is distinctive about religion tends to get lost.[41] These are real dangers, not always avoided.[42]

At most, ideology should connect meaning and power, but not necessarily in a relationship of 'service'. Ideology lies between 'explicit doctrine' and 'lived experience'. There is an *ideological formation* which can be looked at from many angles. This formation is multi-layered and criss-crossed, having more and less articulated levels. Religion is one such (part of an?) ideological formation, a 'way of bringing to bear the most fundamental questions of human existence on a uniquely individual life'.[43]

---

40 J. B. Thompson, *Studies in the Theory of Ideology* (Cambridge, 1984); J. B. Thompson, *Ideology and Modern Culture* (Oxford, 1990). Thompson's notion of 'meaning in the service of power' is thus brought closer to Althusser's understanding of ideology as more a matter of habit than conscious thought. But where the latter saw ideology as affixing identities (interpellations), the former links it more strongly to specific social groups. Thompson's conception is broader than Marx's, but, like Marx's, is also determinedly critical. It is epistemologically lenient but sociologically strict. However, if Thompson's view is accepted, then religion clearly cannot be a *kind* or *form* or *subset* of ideology. It is more than that, though it obviously has ideological functions.
41 S. Feuchtwang, 'Investigating Religion', in M. Bloch, ed., *Marxist Analysis and Social Anthropology* (New York, 1975). For Feuchtwang, ideology is Althusser's 'lived relations', and religion is a kind of ideology. 'The study of religion is part of the study of ideology, indeed it is part of that study which represents it par excellence' (p. 66); '[R]eligion "is a shared reality", it is both a system of ideas about reality and a means of communicating those ideas' (p. 62). Feuchtwang criticizes the 'subjective idealist' sociology of religion – for example, the hermeneutical school – and he himself seeks to provide a wider 'theory' (ideology) from which the 'concept' of religion can be derived. In the end, however, he admits that he has not been able to show what is peculiar to religion as a kind of ideology.
42 Eagleton prefers to remain agnostic about epistemological and sociological approaches to understanding ideology, only railing against too narrow or too broad definitions of ideology. Different definitions have their differing values and purposes, and that, he says, is often good enough. There is no essentialist notion of ideology. By accepting a variety of conceptual usages, we recognize that we are dealing with a category whose variant meanings comprise a family of resemblances. T. Eagleton, *Ideology* (London, 1991), p. 50.
43 On the same page, Eagleton tries to clarify further: 'Religion consists of a hierarchy of discourses, some of them elaborately theoretical (scholasticism), some ethical

There is a tendency among modern Marxists to exaggerate the importance of ideology and culture – a mental reflex among socialists towards
capitalist stabilization and the general absence of revolutionary working-class
behaviour in the advanced capitalist countries. But the linguistic turn in philosophy makes a more generous re-evaluation of the role of ideology and
cognition in social life unavoidable. The question, however, is how far this
should be taken. Over-generosity here can make a mockery of the Marxist
insistence (howsoever subtly qualified) on the primacy of economic survival.

And what of the ideological terrain itself? Is it not occupied by various
ideologies?[44] These are not unitary class ideologies, but different discourses
(ideologies are 'clusters' or 'discursive chains' coexisting, partially merging,
and competing with each other). An ideology constructs individuals as
subjects, and also as ideological communities with or without the help of
a systematized, explicit body of doctrines. Here, religion is once again a
kind of ideology, and ideology is a subset of culture. Culture is a system
of symbols, so religion/ideology is an *aspect* of this symbolic system. The
key aspects here are those which interpellate subjects (affix identity) and
construct imagined ideological communities. Ideologies may or may not
have political significance, depending on whether they help to sustain existing relations of power. The more disinterested or natural the ideological
community appears, the more it overrides the contradictions of social life.
Nationalism is perhaps the most powerful example of such an ideological
community – the inheritor of this mantle from kinship loyalty and the religious community of the past.

The notion of religion as a form of ideology, then, is a reasonably productive and defensible one, provided a positive or neutral conception of
ideology is employed. Later Marxist understandings are to be preferred to
earlier ones. The Marxist approach offers a launching pad for a serious investigation of the connection between social position and religious beliefs and
experiences, and of the relationship between religious discourses and the
preservation of social and political power. But since religion is also more
than this, there are important aspects of its role and impact that tend not to
be treated with sufficient sensitivity. In developing a better understanding
of religion in modernity, of religion in culture and society, one has to think
through and beyond the Marxist tradition.

But whether ideology should be understood in a critical sense or in a positive or neutral sense, or whether one can abstain from so choosing and leave

---

and prescriptive, others exhortatory and consolatory (preaching, popular piety); and the
institution of the church ensures that each of these discourses meshes constantly with the
others, to create an unbroken continuum between the theoretical and the behavioural'
(ibid., p. 50). Christianity seems to figure inordinately as Eagleton's model of an organized religion, and it is far from clear how useful his approach is compared to others.
See also R. Boer, *Criticism of Heaven and Earth*, Vol. I, Chapter 6 on 'The Apostasy of
Terry Eagleton'.

44 K. Thompson, *Beliefs and Ideology* (London, 1986).

it to be determined by context, are not matters that hinge on the question of how best to understand religion. They hinge much more on the relative analytical usefulness of critical and positive conceptions of ideology for more general purposes. They depend more on how ideology, understood in these contrasting ways, can be separated from and used to understand culture and society. To make ideology nearly coterminous with culture damages such endeavours, and risks immortalizing religion. Here it may well be that the critical conception of ideology as 'meaning in the service of power' proves more useful. If this view were adopted, then it would be necessary to make adjustments to the conceptualization of religion and of its relationship to ideology. But there would be no 'loss' to speak of. Religion would now simply straddle ideology and culture, rather than being immersed in culture (and society) via ideology. The really important questions concern the relationship between religion, on the one hand, and culture and society, on the other.

Culture and Society: The Problem of Order

The immortalization of religion would not be so questionable a procedure if its advocates were only suggesting that religion is likely to endure for ever because, for some or many, it will remain the most desired way of coping with the individual's ontological dilemma, so that the more individualized functions of religion will endure even as modernity renders its social functions more tenuous and problematic. Immortalizers, however, generally claim much more.[45] They assert religion's *inescapable centrality* to culture and society. Religion is either coterminous with or at the heart of any and all human cultures. Furthermore, religion is crucial to society because it is indispensable to the securing and maintenance of social order.

This is the most common form of the social cement thesis. Three types of relationship are involved here: between religion and culture, between religion and society, and between culture and society. Culture and society are analytically (though not empirically or in reality) separable. But, more often than not, proponents of the social cement thesis do not rigorously explicate the analytical difference between the two.

For some (usually sociologists and social anthropologists), society is the decisive term, and is intrinsically human: culture is subsumed by it. For others (most often culturalists and cultural anthropologists), culture is the ultimate human reality, and society its vehicle. Some understand religion as the human capacity for symbolic self-transcendence beyond biology – an understanding that eternalizes religion, making it effectively coterminous

---

45 To allow that a few may escape the hold of religion altogether is to let in the thin end of the wedge. The few can become some, some can become many, and the argument of eternality is weakened. Better to insist dogmatically that the atheist or the self-consciously non-religious or anti-religious individual is nonetheless a religious animal.

with any symbolic conception of culture itself.[46] Others are more qualified. Culture is the capacity for such symbolic self-transcendence.[47] The fact of mortality is the important source of 'culture, that huge and never stopping factory of permanence'.[48] Culture is seen as basically beyond reason. So far religion has been the pre-eminent cultural practice. In modernity, it is conceded, this undergoes some change, and philosophy can replace religion. Changing cultural responses to the problem of finitude mean the value and importance of the specifically religious antidote can diminish. Religion is but one *form* of that capacity.

Theoretically, this allows for the possibility of non-religious kinds of culture. But rarely is any better substitute envisaged. Culture subsumes society. Society comes out of but is then the condition for culture's production and reproduction. There can be no question of disorder in society because society *is* order. Society's key purpose is nomization (the ordering of meaning), and its stability is best attained when cosmization (ordering of the cosmos) reinforces nomization. Religion as a mode of cosmization is exceptionally powerful and stable because it is reverential and sacred, evoking awe. It is a 'sacred legitimation' that unites nomos and cosmos. Dharma, then, far from being unique (as claimed by innumerable savants of Brahminical Hinduism), is but the 'high' Indian version of religious–sacred cosmization–nomization. What is distinctive about dharma is its incredibly detailed and elaborated character. Dharma, along with the karma–samskara complex, provides a unique way of handling the theodicies of suffering and happiness, enclosing them with complete symmetry, providing a *simultaneous* legitimation of the conditions of all social strata. This is the most conservative form of high religious legitimation of social hierarchy yet devised.

Whether or not religion is inescapably central to society, then, depends on whether alternative modes of cosmization–nomization, alternative legitimations, are possible and as effective. Berger, the foremost proponent of this view, recognized that religious theodicies have become more implausible in modernity, and thus religious forms of cosmization–nomization are weakened. There are alternative modes (for example, science), but they are not better. If modernity makes it *possible* for religion no longer to be central, society is likely to imperil itself, if it thinks it can find an adequate non-religious replacement. Hence Berger's ambivalent attitude to modernity, and his fear and scepticism about secularization if this is taken to suggest a continuing process of religious decline. Not only is society order, but order

---

46 Luckmann, *Life-World and Social Realities.*
47 Berger, *Social Reality of Religion;* Z. Bauman, *Mortality, Immortality and Other Life Strategies* (Oxford, 1992).'*Transcendence* is what, everything having been said and done, culture is about. Culture is about expanding temporal and spatial boundaries of being, with a view to dismantling them altogether' (Bauman, *Mortality, Immortality,* p. 5).
48 Bauman, *Mortality, Immortality,* p. 4.

is also human nature.[49] In true Durkheimian fashion, the only serious conflict allowed for is that between individual and society. Intermediate social
groups and their conflicts do not come into the picture.

From a substantivist perspective, Berger was as deeply committed, indeed
more so, to a social coherence model as any Parsonian functionalist who sees
religion as providing the normative order cohering society. Only the routes
are different. Functionalism sees society's normal state as a healthy equilibrium, like that of a biological organism. Disturbance sets off a dynamic that
has its wellspring in shared moral values and norms that aim to establish a
new equilibrium. Most functionalists see religion as the main source of this,
but some accept that another mechanism besides religion can do the job.[50]

Others would say another kind of religion needs to emerge – for example,
an American Civil Religion – in which the relationship is inverted. Culture is
no longer based on religion, but religion on culture. This is a convoluted way
of recognizing the declining influence of religion in the US yet preserving
its claim to social centrality. What is noticeable in the functionalist approach
(where religion is linked to society) and the phenomenological–hermeneutic
approach (where religion is linked to culture) is that an unshaken commitment to the social cement thesis is accompanied by a distinctly shakeable
consensus on religion as an essential or major component of that cement.
Modernity has created uncertainty about religion's social role even among
those seeking to conjoin religion and modernity.

One could go further, as Saxton does. Now, for the first time in human
history, we are faced with the possible devastation of the human species itself
through nuclear or biological warfare and/or ecological disaster. In this situation, religion, he says, can no longer be the 'saving resource' or adaptive
mechanism it was in the past, when it could make the issue of finitude at
least bearable through some promise of individual salvation, and through the
postulation of a more powerful and important world of benign (as well as
not so benign) spirit beings. There is, of course, no empirical foundation for
religion's truth. That truth lay in the 'will to believe', or faith, which Saxton
says helped humans survive in different collective units despite rivalries of
religious and other kinds. But now, given these two new great evils that
threaten the very existence of the human species (and much else), knowledge must trump faith if there is going to be the building of a wide enough
global community of action between believers and non-believers to tackle

---

49 Berger, *Social Reality of Religion*; N. Abercrombie, 'Knowledge, Order and Human
Autonomy', in J. D. Hunter and S. C. Ainlay, eds, *Making Sense of Modern Times: Peter L.
Berger and the Vision of Interpretive Sociology* (London, 1986). See P. Berger, *The Sacred
Canopy: Elements of a Social Theory of Religion* (New York, 1967). 'The anthropological
presupposition for this is a human craving for meaning that appears to have the force
of instinct. Men are congenitally compelled to impose a meaningful order upon reality'
(Berger, *Sacred Canopy*, p. 22).
50 See discussion of Merton in R. A. Wallace and A. Wolf, *Contemporary Sociological
Theory* (Englewood Cliffs, NJ, 1986).

these two evils effectively. Here the foundational principle of all religions – namely, the supremacy of faith and the promise of some kind of salvation regardless of terrestrial events – is becoming a profound barrier to the development of the necessary resources to guarantee the survival of humanity in the future.[51] In short, religious influence on humans must diminish. Even to believe that it is central to society (whatever its role in the past) would constitute a grave danger.

The religion-is-central-to-society formula is generally the result of a double fusion: religion is fused with culture, and culture with society. This second fusion or the cultural programming of society is the source of the 'social integration' or social cement thesis. The first fusion establishes religion as the key cultural programmer.[52]

The second fusion, an intellectual one, is inscribed in the conceptual tools developed and deployed, even though these may be empirically legitimized through anthropological field research or sociological enquiry. Raymond Williams points out that a general conception of culture only emerges after the Industrial Revolution as a reaction to the general character of change and to the increasingly felt need for general designs.[53] Seventeenth- and eighteenth-century Romanticism, with its rejection of strong notions of progress and reason, fostered a notion of culture 'beyond reason', as in part symbolically expressive of a people's basic and enduring values, perhaps best captured through recognition of the 'informing spirit' of its religion and culture. Nineteenth-century anthropology, with its notion of culture as a 'whole way of life', made culture coterminous with or broader than society. This reinforced the idealist tenor of Romantic conceptions of culture, which by the late eighteenth century treated it no longer as a noun of 'process', of 'tending' ('to cultivate'), but as a noun of configuration or generalization of the 'informing spirit'.[54] This was now extended to a whole way of life. But it also stimulated a *descriptive* conception of the whole way of life, its artefacts, habits, customs, and so on, that promoted comparative cultural studies and systems of classification.

The most important twist was supplied in the 1960s, after the decline of behaviourism. Recognizing that human action was not so much a response to external stimuli or constraints as the result of internal representation of the external environment was an advance. From being 'out there', culture came to be seen more as 'in the mind'. Ever since, a cognitive conception of culture – in particular a semiotic or symbolic conception – has dominated the field of culture theories.

---

51 A. Saxton, *Religion and the Human Prospect*, Chapters 13 and 14.

52 There is also the 'social programming of culture'. Where this is the central emphasis, as in the dominant ideology thesis among certain Marxists, we have a weaker and much less religiously inclined version of the social integration argument.

53 R. Williams, *Culture and Society* (Harmondsworth, 1971), Conclusion.

54 R. Williams, *Keywords* (London, 1988), pp. 87–93.

Allying itself to the anthropological notion of a whole way of life, a strongly idealist conception of culture has resurfaced at a considerably higher level of sophistication than before. Symbols are seen as not just partly but sub-stantially or overwhelmingly constitutive of reality itself. The problem lies not with a symbolic conception of culture but with the exorbitation of the symbolic order. Society is seen no longer as a nexus of economic, political and cultural–ideological relationships, or as their structured totality, but as an *organized* system of meaning to be decoded through an understanding of the '*shared* system of symbols/meaning', itself organized by a unifying principle that is discoverable. Culture has a unity, a definite patterning, even an essence, or at least a distinctive ethos, rooted for the most part in col-lective tradition. This is a more developed cousin to the more traditional Durkheimian view of society as a 'structure of social ties informed by a moral consensus'.

Such a sweeping notion of culture–society–symbolic order is strongly inclined towards endorsing the indispensability of religion as its particularly powerful, if not decisive axis. Religious or sacred symbols 'condense' the values of a culture. What is important is not faith in God (s), but faith in faith, and the role of faith and worship in society. The self-consciousness and self-questioning of modernity may lead us to question God, but if society is to cohere we must encourage the 'worshipping of our worshipping'.[55] What is lost sight of here is that religious symbols do not just 'condense', they also 'refer' – in other words, they make truth-claims and serve legitimating func-tions. The social cement thesis repeatedly de-emphasizes (where it does not altogether ignore) the epistemological status of religious claims, as well as religion's functions in legitimating prevailing social relationships of power.

In all such notions, there is little place for cultural contradictions and inconsistencies. Insofar as they exist, they are supposed to do so at a sec-ondary level in a framework of overall cultural coherence. Otherwise, by definition, neither culture nor society could survive or reproduce itself. The more segmented, fractured, layered, complex and *messy* our notion of a culture, or of a cultural space or zone, the more difficult it is to sustain the view that religion's relationship to culture is essential and permanent, rather than contingent.

To assert the contingency of this relationship does imply that religion has not been and cannot be crucial and enduring. It is only to contest the claims of religion to complete ubiquity and incorrigible omnipotence. It is to refuse to close off possibilities, and to be open to the prospects and conse-quences of cultural change and transformation. It is to have a more *dynamic* notion of culture, and it is hardly surprising that more static notions of culture prima facie should seem more appropriate to pre-modern cultures

---

55 This is precisely what Saxton attacks as being disastrous for the future. Knowledge must trump faith on a wide enough scale to ensure the preservation of the human species. The relevant chapter passages are also referred to in note 51, above.

and societies. A give-away about the close relationship between the notions of religion and culture conceptualised in more static terms, is provided by the striking fact that no pre-modern religion (certainly not the world religions) has had a strong concept of terrestrial progress before it made contact with Enlightenment thinking.

Raymond Williams was more aware of these problems than most. Williams, like others, also held to a cognitive/symbolic concept of culture. But where he was inclined to see culture as 'process', others had a broader and more static vision of culture as a 'class of things shared', a 'state of affairs'. Williams moved away from an earlier, more anthropologically inclined view of culture as a whole way of life to a more restricted one, which he felt was more appropriate for modern societies, at least.

The sources for this shift lay in his greater sensitivity to the very distinctive problems posed by modernity of complexity and change. Culture was better seen not as a whole way of life, but as a 'realized signifying system' that is not as all-encompassing as simply a 'signifying system'. A 'realized signifying system' included 'manifest signifying systems', or the more obviously cultural practices. But it also incorporated the interrelationship between 'manifest' and 'non-manifest' systems. Either more manifest cultural practices were dissolved in less manifest ones whose main purposes were not cultural but nonetheless had an inescapable cultural dimension, or 'other' practices were dissolved into manifest cultural practices, lending them certain non-cultural dimensions.[56]

Whatever the difficulties and ambiguities here, it was his way of distinguishing between the more and the less cultural, of grasping how the more cultural can shade into the less cultural, and then into the almost non-cultural. It was Williams's way of insisting on the inescapability of a cultural materialism and of a materialist culture – of, for example, the culture of the economy and the economy of a culture. In contrast, the whole-way-of-life notion, or any too exaggerated notion of the cultural–symbolic order, created at least two major problems.

How is one to speak of the more or less cultural, if, in a move paralleling Foucault's dissolution of the notion of power, everything everywhere is cultural? Similarly, what then lies outside culture? The only answer could be nature. The result is a radically polarized conception of the relationship between culture and nature, when in fact modernity renders their relationship even more complex and multifaceted in comparison to the already multilayered relationship between the two in all but the most primitive (pre-tribal) of societies. Implicitly, Williams was warning of the dangers of an analytical conflation or near-conflation of culture with society, and of an essentialist or too homogeneous view of culture itself – a view encouraged by the thesis that there is a fusion between religion and culture.

---

56 R. Williams, *Culture* (London, 1981).

To talk of a cultural zone or space is to employ an heuristic whose worth is guided by the specific purposes of the project for which it is chosen. Any cultural area always comprises many cultures coexisting, connecting, repelling one another and clashing, thus creating a shifting balance of cultural forces. One can talk of the tone or ethos of a culture provided it is kept in mind that this is always the temporary resultant emerging out of a cultural field of force always subject to transformation and change; that within that space there are ethoses as well as ethos. Any cultural space comprises dominant, residual and emergent cultures, and generational, temporal and spatial tensions of a cultural kind. To talk of a culture as if it were largely sealed, uniform and a long-enduring entity is to risk mistaking the heuristic for the real thing, which is always characterized by far more complexity, openness and flux, especially in modernity.[57] For our times, there can be few more plausible understandings of culture, cultures and cultural spaces than those proposed by Williams. His approach also focuses attention directly on issues concerning asymmetries in cultural power and the desirability of cultural democratization.

What of the difference between culture and society? Or between a cultural and a socio-cultural system? Especially after the ascendance of a cognitive concept of culture, the crucial difference is that society consists of persons and their interrelationships, while culture does not. Nor does culture comprise thoughts, for only persons have thoughts. Thoughts and feelings are culturally determined, but do not belong to culture as such. Culture comprises propositions or meanings abstracted from particular individuals, encoded in symbols. The cultural system does not have a knowing subject; the socio-cultural system does.[58] Persons, however, are involved in asymmetrical relationships of power that have institutional embodiments which help create a territorial space over which such power hierarchies operate in a structured and not merely haphazard way.

The geographical shapes or boundaries of such societies have never been easy to establish. Indeed, some historical sociologists would do away altogether with the notion of society before the advent of modernity, and prefer to talk of 'overlapping socio-spatial networks of power'. Accordingly, this network has distinct dimensions of ideological, economic, military and political power.[59] After the emergence of an international system of

---

57 Thompson, *Beliefs and Ideology*, Chapter 4. Thompson uses the metaphor of 'the archaeology of culture': 'The notion of an archaeology of culture is useful in so far as it suggests that it is necessary to excavate different layers of culture which are in a sense discontinuous. Culture studies have frequently lapsed into a "wholistic" and deductivist approach which views the parts of culture as explicable and decodable as parts of a whole, totality, or system. Find the principle that binds the whole, the code that unlocks the system, and the elements can be explained by deduction' (p. 106).

58 M. Archer, *Culture and Agency: The Place of Culture in Social Theory* (Cambridge, 1988).

59 M. Mann, *The Sources of Social Power*, Vol. I (Cambridge, 1988).

nation-states, societies have become more visibly bounded, and are largely congruent with the territorial boundaries of a given nation-state. Certainly, it is this national-territorial totality that most of us have in mind when using the term 'society' today.[60]

Whatever clarity of definition or degree of resolution a society has, it seems to owe it more to political and administrative factors than to cultural ones. To understand how society exists, survives and reproduces itself, one must look at a whole complex of variables and levels of human existence and human relationships, especially at the political level. One cannot simply assume that the key to the whole construct lies in the domain of the cultural or, even more narrowly, in the domain of religion.

The search for the sources of order or stability in a society is to be conducted at the level of the *social* itself, or in the socio-cultural system as a whole, and not purely or primarily at the level of the cultural system. Social order is not a simple or straightforward function of meaning. It has as much, if not more, to do with issues of power, and therefore with matters of social tension, dominance and conflict, as it has to do with issues of cultural and moral norms, values and beliefs. One should expect cultural tensions and contradictions (including religious differences) to have some discernible relationships to social stratification and conflict, which indeed they do and have always done.

Existential dilemmas are not uniform, or the same for everyone. They bear a definite relationship to social position: religious needs differ, and the poor probably have always been more concerned with problems of health, wealth, prosperity, security, solace and self-respect in the face of deprivation, and therefore with what religion has had to offer in these respects.[61] The more ethereal visions of 'religious essence', and abstract enunciations of its 'morally binding' character over society, have generally been connected to elitist conceptions of society, and to justifications for elite dominance.[62]

---

60 For the term 'national–territorial totality', see F. Halliday, 'State and Society in International Relations: A Second Agenda', *Millennium* 16: 2 (1987).

61 B. S. Turner, *Religion and Social Theory* (London, 1991); B. S. Turner, *Body and Society* (London, 1984).

62 In an important article that seeks to carefully dissect variations in the secular state, and rightly to critique those versions of secularism that seek to 'eliminate religion from public life and from politics more generally', Rajeev Bhargava makes the claim that 'the most significant feature of most religions [is] that they encourage their members to choose to live a disciplined, restricted, rule-bound, desire-abnegating life', and that these are 'the constitutive features of most religions'. One can accept that there can and should be space for religion-based activism in public political life, even as one demands a basic separation of religion from the state, without endorsing this unbalanced assessment of the virtues of religious life. Most people are believers for both good and bad reasons related to how this helps them to cope practically with the problems and dilemmas of everyday life. This also requires coping at emotional and attitudinal levels which often involves accepting unwarranted prejudices about others. See R. Bhargava, 'Rehabilitating Secularism', in Calhoun et al., *Rethinking Secularism*, pp. 100–1.

When there is downward conflation of the cultural system with the socio-cultural system, then social integration is identified with cultural integration. This promotion of the Myth of Cultural Integration of a society is an untenable move, because the cultural system (which excludes persons) can have only a logical, not a causal, coherence. There are only logical relations in a cultural system (including logically inconsistent relations), but no causal relations. It is illegitimate to read off from logical coherence in a cultural system causal coherence or consensus in a socio-cultural system.[63] The 'grip of tradition' over a society, insofar as it can be said to exist, comes from social factors, not from cultural integration.

Structural functionalists believed that value-patterning through role-expectation led to this cultural integration, though they might differ on whether or not religion functionally integrates the other parts (morality, art, philosophy, and so on) of a cultural system (and therefore of society). For functionalists, coherence is established through practices and activities. Structuralists in the twentieth century believed in invariant properties of the mind. Such invariant properties cohere culture, which coheres society. Here, the organizing mechanisms are located in the mind, in the unconscious – for example, in myth. Religion, then, is a 'necessary myth', since social mythology is vital to cohering society. Religion, it is argued, will be a better, more humane kind of social cement than non-religious forms of social mythology, because of its transcendent dimension.[64]

Whatever the case for pre-modern societies with low social differentiation and slower rates of change, in respect of modern societies there are grave problems with the standard social coherence models. Empirical evidence alone suggests a much more complex picture of reality. Most people have beliefs that are inconsistent and often incoherent, and behave in inconsistent ways. If culture is related to how we think and behave, then cultural inconsistency, contradiction and incoherence are widespread and irrefutable facts of life. It is also true that there is popular allegiance to certain symbols, values and beliefs that favour the status quo, and therefore the stability (on elite terms) of society.

But the overall picture is much more contradictory, far less uniform, evincing far less 'committed' consent than suggested by the social cement or consensus models, which ignore power relations. Such models do not

---

63 Archer, *Culture and Agency*. In fact, all kinds of combinations are possible – for example, high logical consistency in elite culture can exist within a society of low causal consensus.

64 This is the view of David Martin, one of the foremost opponents of the secularization-as-decline thesis. See, in particular, *Religious and the Secular*. The 'socially necessary myth' argument tends to confuse the social power of *belief* in illusions with the social power of illusions themselves. Some Durkheimians avoid this by focusing on practice, not the beliefs. Others, who take a substantivist view, are more prone to this confusion. Symbols stand apart and exercise power. But precisely because they are human-made and because belief in them is retractable, they are not so stable a source of power in modernity.

explore the *origins* of normative agreement. They disregard or de-emphasize questions concerning *who benefits* from the social order. They clearly favour the status quo.

In truth, the social cement 'mixture' can have varying compositions. The adhesive strength of the mixture, or the degree of consensual attachment it creates, can vary from the strongly active to the highly passive. Legitimation requires a strongly active form of consent. The role of religion in legitimating the public order has indisputably, though unevenly, declined. Even Third World theocracies or confessional states are, in a longer historical view, more on the defensive now that republican and democratic alternatives exist, and are clearly feasible.

In general, the strength of social cement is a function of (a) the degree of development of the infrastructure of communication, and (b) the existence of options regarding morals, values and beliefs. If, in the pre-modern era, the weakness of the first was compensated for by the relative absence of the second, in the modern period, the rapid development of the first and the 'mediaization of modern culture' is compensated for (and its homogenizing tendencies countered by) the substantial flowering of the second.[65] There were more chances of getting away with the idea of a cultural essence harmonizing society on some higher Olympian plane of spirituality when those tensions and conflicts were class struggle, wars and revolutions – in other words, largely political and economic in character. But from the second half of the twentieth century, the notion of a harmonizing culture is all the more out of place when the terrain of culture – language, value, identity, experiences, life-styles, and so on – is criss-crossed by tensions and conflicts as never before; when the 'politics of life choices' has joined the 'politics of life chances' on the stage of human struggle.[66]

There are four possible sources of social order: consensus; rational choice; coercion, or fear of punishment; and lack of *unified* dissensus. Undoubtedly all elements are present in some measure. But models of social stability differ sharply in the weight they assign to each component. The object of criticism here – consensus models (which are the only ones prepared to give religion such a central role) – are convincing neither on theoretical nor on empirical grounds, even in the more stable, advanced capitalist democracies, where there has been most empirical testing of such claims.

The average person, it seems, is more likely to have a stretched value-system, with a low degree of commitment to all values. Moreover, there is a clear difference between the abstract and the situational. The more abstract and far removed from familiar routines the values and beliefs in question, the more likely that the average person will go along with dominant views. The more situational and directly relevant the values or beliefs in question,

---

65 Thompson, *Ideology and Modern Culture.*
66 A. Giddens, *Modernity and Self-Identity* (Oxford, 1991).

the stronger will be the correlation between that person's views and his social position, and the more likely that these will be in dissonance with, or only weakly supportive of, dominant views.

The rational-choice argument sees social order as the result of interactional bargaining between self-maximizing agents. Compliance here is based neither on fear nor on consensus, but on pragmatic assessments of self-interest. But this 'exchange theory' model of social order does not explain why interests are what they are, because it does not consider context – they just are, and are taken as such. Its methodological individualism assumes what must be explained. The result is a form of tautological reasoning. Why do people tailor their interests and ambitions so as not to challenge a social order in which the majority is disadvantaged? They do not challenge because it pays them not to. How do we know it pays not to? Because they do not challenge!

The third source – coercion, or fear of punishment – is an important explanation of social stability or order.[67] But it is when this is combined with the fourth source that we reach the most plausible perspective. Most people do not see themselves as victims most of the time. To do so would be to block avenues of self-respect that make life liveable, and in some sense worthwhile. People are not self-pitying sufferers, or straining at the leash, as it were – constrained only or primarily by fear. It is not so much active consensus but acquiescence – the passivities born of routines and habits, or the 'dull compulsions of economic relations' – that helps to secure social order and social reproduction.

It is not that society has core values (which may or may not be anchored by religious practice and belief) upon which there is consensus, but that whatever consensus about values or beliefs exists pertains to specific roles.[68] This is a vision of society as more like an orchestra whose members are 'trained' (through socialization processes) and 'persuaded' (through sanctions and rewards) to play their respective parts, than of society as a choir happily singing the same song. But the training is never complete, and the persuasion is never irresistible. What keeps society in some sense together is not consensus, but a lack of a unified dissensus, a counter-consensus, challenging the social order. For normal functioning, active agreement is not necessary. Passive acceptance of the existing order of things is enough. The

---

67 Since our concern here is assessing how central religion and culture are to the preservation of social order, the very important issue of the relationship between political order and social order is not taken up, though the principle of coercion is basic to matters concerning the creation of political order, which is itself vital to the establishment of social order. Here, a distinction must be made between 'force' and other forms of coercion, since there are different ways of punishing and threatening short of the physical. For a study on how the 'ordering of force' (the authorizing of its use in relation to other forms of coercion) is basic to the constitution of political order, and thus of social order, see S. Bromley, 'Politics and the International', in A. Anievas, ed., *Marxism and World Politics: Contesting Global Capitalism* (New York, 2010).

68 Thompson, *Ideology and Modern Culture*.

weakness of negative factors is more relevant to the explanation of social normality and order than the strength of positive ones.

The Marxist variant of the social cement argument is the 'dominant ideology' thesis – a form of upward conflation of the socio-cultural system with the cultural system. Instead of normative consensus, there is a 'manipulated' cultural consensus. Instead of the cultural programming of society, there is the social programming of culture. Ruling-class solidarity leads to a wider social solidity. Another Marxist variant, with less affinity to Durkheim and more to Weber, is Critical Theory's argument about the diffusion and dominance of technocratic consciousness in advanced capitalist societies.

The dominant ideology thesis, however, is available for application over a far wider range of societies, geographically and historically. Among the earlier and still severest critiques of the dominant ideology thesis was that of Abercrombie, Hill and Turner.[69] It has acted as an important brake on the slide of Marxist thought in the last few decades down a distinctly culturalist slope. Abercrombie, Hill and Turner did not deny that there is a dominant ideology, or ideologies, only that it does not have the power that its proponents who, following the Marx of *The German Ideology*, claim. Abercrombie, Hill and Turner employed theoretical and empirical criticisms. Certainly, the empirical evidence in post-war advanced capitalisms supports the notion of a highly 'contradictory consciousness' among the working class.

Theoretically, the dominant ideology thesis has too many loose ends. It is much easier to talk of its existence than to specify accurately what it is – its full content and range. Though the dominant ideology is said to incorporate and pacify dominated classes there is, unsurprisingly, considerable disagreement over the degree of such incorporation and pacification. Finally, the mechanisms for transmitting the dominant ideology and carrying out a more or less unidirectional indoctrination are not as impervious to the social tensions and cultural contradictions of capitalism as the dominant ideology thesis must assume.

The dominant ideology is strong enough to be a significant obstacle to the construction of a collective counter-ideology of the oppressed, but no stronger. This is akin to the claim that the putative social cement is not much more than slightly toughened social plaster, which nonetheless is generally sufficient to make difficult or prevent collective mobilization and unification amid the numerous scatter-points of dissent in society.

Marxist critics plausibly suggest that the dominant ideology has always been much more important in solidifying the dominant class or social bloc whose lines of communication are shorter, and whose class self-consciousness is generally greater, than is the case with the subordinate classes. In feudalism, the weakness of communications infrastructure would have made

---

69 N. Abercrombie, S. Hill and B. S. Turner, *The Dominant Ideology Thesis* (London, 1980).

lordly hegemonic control over peasants and serfs trickier but for the alliance with religious elites. In today's capitalist state, there is greater diffusion of the dominant ideology, and perhaps greater assent to some of its themes among subordinate classes – in other words, greater partial incorporation. But the role of the dominant ideology in solidifying the dominant class or ruling bloc itself is considerably weakened. This is because differentiation within the ruling bloc is greater and, when added to the pressure of over a century and a half of class and ideological contestation, this renders the dominant ideology less solidifying. Much, however, depends on the social relationship of forces between dominant and subordinate classes. The greater the pressure and challenge from below, the more likely it is that sections and fractions within the ruling blocs will disagree among themselves. The weaker such resistance, the more sturdy the dominant consensus – nationally and globally – is likely to be among elites.[70]

In rejecting the extravagant claims of ideology, religion and culture in society, Abercrombie, Hill and Turner argued that they were actually following in the footsteps of Marx (*The German Ideology* being an aberration), and even of Durkheim and Weber. Others will not agree. Durkheim, after all, is the progenitor of the original social cement thesis. But he did also believe that, with the advent of modernity, one was moving from the realm of 'mechanical solidarity' to that of an 'organic solidarity', in which the functional division of labour counted for much more than the notion of core values or '*conscience collective*'.[71] Certainly, in his tracing of the evolution of legal codes and systems, he was also tracing the growing disjunction between morality and religion, even as he held to the view that, in some basic though perhaps minimal sense, the two were inseparable.[72]

---

70 The period since the 1980s has seen the global ascendance of neoliberalism, which has not been decisively shaken even by the global 'Great Recession' of 2008–12. For one of the earliest articles highlighting this ascendance, see P. Anderson, 'Renewals' in *New Left Review* II/1 (January–February 2000).

71 Abercrombie et al. *The Dominant Ideology Thesis* give more importance, in the general structure of Durkheim's thought, to his *The Division of Labour* than to his *The Elementary Forms of Religious Life*.

72 Insofar as morality refers to codes of social relationships that in some measure involve reciprocity between people, then, as Saxton points out, 'Religion is not conceptually necessary to explain the origin of social morality.' Saxton, *Religion and the Human Prospect*, p.72. Such reciprocal codes of behaviour were necessary and conducive to group survival and continuity, and in this respect one could even say that animals and insects have a social morality of sorts that is instinctual and, unlike that of humans, not really capable of systematic change and development of a kind that indicates moral progress. But the point is that egalitarian hunter-gatherer societies would have had their own codes of reciprocity, even though it was not yet tainted by the existence of a religious elite, or by association with those at the top of a more stratified society. Though not its original source, Saxton argues that primitive religion can nevertheless be said to have helped sustain such moral codes of behaviour, and, when more unequal and stratified societies emerged, would have played a role in maintaining social discipline.

Saxton believes religious monism – for example, the *advaita* doctrine of Vedic Hinduism – and monotheism evolved from early animism and polytheism. Although this Vedic/Brahminical Hinduism allows for a multiplicity of gods and goddesses, he controversially

Probably the safest approach is simply to accept Durkheim's work as being located at a point of transition, a coming-to-grips with the challenge of modernity for society and religion, with the ultimate direction of his own thought processes still open and unclear. Even as he emphasized the centrality of *some* notion of religion to society, he acknowledged the diminished role in modern life of religion as recognized until then. We cannot know if he would have been in sympathy with the direction taken by subsequent Durkheimians. But Abercrombie, Hill and Turner are on strong ground in claiming that Parsons's more determined commitment to the centrality of the normative consensus became the symptomatic and most influential interpretation of the Durkheimian legacy.

The case of Weber is more straightforward. He may have felt Calvinism explained the origins of capitalism. He would not have claimed, however, that it or any other religious creed would explain the maintenance and reproduction of capitalism. The world was being progressively disenchanted through the rise of technocratic–bureaucratic rationality. Human society and culture were being progressively compartmentalized. The decline of religion meant the effective loss of culture's gyroscope – the source of stable definitions of society and the self. The dilemma of the modern woman or man was loss of meaning and a deepening sense of inauthenticity.

If Weber and Durkheim seem to have had a strong sense of the historical firebreak created by modernity, this sense has not always been so manifest in their followers. However central or stabilizing religion may have been to culture and society in the pre-modern era, modernity is characterized by a rate, scope and depth of change that must upturn all arguments that emphasize modernity's basic *continuity* with tradition and traditional societies. The upshot must be a profound re-evaluation of the relationships between religion, culture and society; a recognition that these are much more likely than not to be qualitatively different from the relationships claimed to operate between them in the past.

We have seen that the social coherence or consensus model is singularly unimpressive in understanding modern societies. That alone is enough to strongly dispute the claim of immortalizers or near-immortalizers of religion about the *unavoidable* centrality of its role in culture and society. Of the past, with its slower rhythms of change, we might concede the fact of such centrality. But, even there, we do not know enough empirically (and may never know enough) to arrive at confident conclusions. Much of what we do know is from textual sources that are strongly biased towards elitist versions of the power, importance and meaning of specific religions and religious systems. If it is plausible that, in much of pre-modernity, each religion was

---

and unconvincingly insists that this does not make it fundamentally different from mono-theism because the essence of both is belief in an 'undifferentiated creative force'. Thus his basic definition of 'religion' is universal, allowing for no exceptions spatially or temporally, even as it accommodates further religious evolution and change (Chapter 5).

more thickly integrated into a culture or cultural space, it is also plausible that the space over which such thickness operated was much smaller. So there was a greater expansion of Christianity over pagan Europe in the era of industrialization than before. The greater thinness of religion's connection to culture is the obverse side of the greater spread of a particular religious system. As modernity progresses, there are greater obstacles presented even to this lateral spread.

Raymond Williams suggested that one should not look for a universal schema to explain the relationship between culture and society.[73] The force of this proposition, if one accepts it, is a real and powerful one. Openness and change are thereby marked on the scroll of the future. There is no fixed relationship between religion and culture, religion and society, or culture and society. Even if such fixities were true of the past, they need not be so of the future. I hope enough has been said already to establish that it is not true even of the present.

Religion in Modernity: The Question of Identity

If modernity forces a change in the role of religion, as it assuredly does, then what is the direction of this change? It is the more individual functions of religion rather than its social functions that become increasingly important, even as we acknowledge that there is no easy separation between the individual and society. Has the manifest function of religion (salvation) become more important than its latent function (social binding)?[74] Even if this is perceived as a universal trend, it is the case that the process is uneven and that religious resurgences are often related to a felt need in insecure circumstances to stress one's community loyalties. But it is also true that religious influence on the individual, especially in late modernity, is no longer so necessary for binding her to society – nationalism has proved a more powerful form of collective bonding than religion. Nor, indeed, is religion any longer so important to control sexuality (women's bodies) through religious sanction so as to assure transmission of property rights, since family-owner capitalism has been overtaken to a greater or lesser extent by corporate capitalism.[75]

In the most industrialized, urbanized societies today, religion is not so much the 'texture' of life as a 'filling up of the interstices'. In countries like India, the picture is much more combined and fuzzy. But it nonetheless constitutes a significant break from its own past.[76] Neither India nor

73 Williams, *Culture*.
74 Wilson, *Religion in Sociological Perspective*.
75 Turner, *Body and Society*.
76 Kaviraj talks of the transition from a 'thick' religious identity to a 'thin' one, by which he means a shift away from a situation in which 'religious identity was anchored in beliefs spread across a wide variety of levels' These ranged from contemplations about the nature of existence, to the rationales for carrying out detailed ritual practices. S. Kaviraj,

other Third World societies have escaped modernity's powerful impact. The more important individual functions of religion in modernity have to do with questions of identity (individual and group) and meaning. It is the relationship between religion and individual subjectivity that becomes paramount – but subjectivity itself changes along with modernity.[77]

The modern personality is in crucial ways different from the pre-modern personality. The impact of modernity on identity-availability and identity-formation is new. The nature and place of religious identity in society is different. But what is identity? Given the connection between identity and culture, a cognitive approach to culture makes it virtually compulsory to adopt a cognitive theory of subjectivity and identity. This approach links identity to an interactional concept of consciousness in which consciousness is a world of meanings, but 'is less something "within" us than something around and between us'.[78]

A good starting point is Erik Erickson's definition: 'The term identity connotes both a persistent sameness within oneself (self-sameness) and a persistent sharing of some kind of essential character with others.'[79] This

---

'Religion, Politics and Modernity', in U. Baxi and B. Parekh, eds., *Crisis and Change in Contemporary India* (New Delhi, 1995), p. 167.

77 Bellah, 'Religious Evolution'. Bellah presents an evolutionary schema of religion as a symbol system that evolves historically and linearly in relation to the growing 'concrete-ness of the self'. The causal mechanism behind this is the impact of growing structural complexity on the self, and on the sense of its relationship to nature and society. The measure of this (the criteria of religious change) are symbols, forms of action, types of organization. Each of these changes character in the evolutionary progression from prim-itive religion, through its archaic, early modern and modern forms.

In primitive religion, there are mythical symbols, no separation of real from mythical worlds, fluid organization, 'acting out'. In archaic religion there is more specification of the mythical symbol system, more activity in the real world; hierarchical organizations and cults emerge and there are new 'ways of seeing'. In historic religion there is the simplifi-cation of myth, more religious action for providing salvation while differentiated religious communities arise with growing tensions between them. In early modern religion there is symbolic concentration on the direct relation between believer and transcendence; the internal qualities of the believer become more important than acts; religious organiza-tion gets simplified and can now take the form of the collectivity of the 'elect' and of those outside. In modern religion at a time when the Kantian revolution has taken place means the possibilities of religious symbolization are made infinite and with the atrophy of religious organization, individuals formulate their own religious solution.

Bellah is committed to the eternality of religion because of its unbreakable link, through symbols, to the 'ultimate' values of humans. But others sympathetic to his schema (for example, Luckmann, *Life-World and Social Realities*) do admit that, in modernity, these 'ultimate' values are important with respect to the *private* individual. Bellah's schema is inflexible, and glorifies Christianity as the religion most compatible with modernity because it is world-affirming rather than world-renouncing. He seeks to establish a *contin-uum* with respect to changes in subjectivity, which certainly underestimates, and possibly aims to deny, the *ruptural* character in the transformation of personality caused by the emergence of modernity. But he is not wrong to historicize the question of subjectivity and its relationship to religion, nor to claim that the 'sense of the self' is not the same but can change decisively with decisive changes in social structure.

78 Eagleton, *Ideology*, p. 194.

79 E. Erikson, *Identity and Anxiety* (New York, 1960), p. 30. See also E. Erikson, *Identity and the Life Cycle* (Indiana, 1959). 'Ego-identity, then, in its subjective aspect, is

'essential character' which is *held* or *shared* (sameness within oneself cannot be sameness in all respects, but has to be some *relevant* notion of sameness) refers to what consciousness is about – namely beliefs, values, desires.[80] It refers to some set of these held and shared. A variation on this cognitive definition is the point made by the Canadian philosopher Charles Taylor, that to be a person or self is to exist in a space defined by distinctions of worth – that is, against a background of strong evaluation. Human beings are strong evaluators, and identity is intimately connected to issues of self-worth – hence the particular sensitivity with which one must handle it even in casual discussion and argument. Identity involves *commitment* in a framework of values. Identity is not the same as belonging, because belonging *comes* from what is held and shared.

This is clearly a socio-psychological conception of identity. But there can be a difference in bias towards either a more sociological or a more personality-centred understanding.[81] The above definitions as they stand are too mentalist, leaning too much towards a Cartesian separation between mind and body, mind and brain. They benefit from qualification in two respects. A more physicalist concept of identity is required. This would not refute or replace the cognitive concept of identity, but be a necessary addendum.

Each person's psychological make-up comprises a core psychological domain having minimum mental capacities for reasoning, emotion, and so on, which are universally shared. And there is also a distinctive psychological domain comprising the distinctive elements of consciousness, including beliefs, values and desires. Both what is shared and what is distinctive together help to make up personal identity.[82] But what makes these capacities and their exercise in forms of consciousness one's own cannot be the capacities or forms which are available to and shareable with others, but their physical emplacement in one's *own* brain. An exact biological clone having my exact capacities and beliefs, values, desires, is still not me. The cognitive theory of identity makes it totally interactional, and states that there is no 'I' that is not at the same time, actually or potentially, part of a 'we'. The physicalist conception of identity is a reminder that there is a part of 'I-ness'

---

the awareness of the fact that there is a self-sameness and continuity to the ego's synthesising methods and these methods are effective in safeguarding the sameness and continuity of one's meaning for others' (*Identity and the Life Cycle*, p. 23). In Erickson's psychoanalytic approach, identity is ego-identity.

80 See R. Bhargava's talented exposition in 'Religious and Secular Identities', in Baxi and Parekh, eds, *Crisis and Change in Contemporary India*.

81 'Personality' remains an unresolved and disputed term in psychology.

82 See in particular P. Unger's discussion of 'dispositional psychology' in *Identity, Consciousness and Value* (Oxford, 1990). Perry Anderson, in talking of Derek Parfit's studies, suggests that it is the material background of genetic engineering, not the ideational background of the 'instability of language', that influences Parfit's concept of identity. This is certainly true of Unger, who acknowledges Parfit's strong influence in his development of a physicalist–naturalist concept of identity. P. Anderson, 'A Culture in Contraflow', *New Left Review* I/182 (July–August 1990).

which is *not* shareable. There is no complete merger of the individual and society. There is an irreducible element of I-ness which is materially (physically), not ideationally or 'spiritually', located. Even so, the construction of personal identity is always simultaneously the construction of a social identity. And once the physicalist (materialist) case is accepted, the really interesting things to investigate are best dealt with in and by the cognitive approach.

The second qualification has to do with recognizing the three separate aspects of the self–society relationship. There is an individuation dimension as well as an individuality dimension in the construction of subjectivity. There are conferred identities, as well as more freely chosen and constructed ones. Individuation is strongly related to social control and authority (authority figures, authority symbols). Insofar as a sense of self first emerges from a sense of separateness on the part of the infant from the mother, which is coupled with a sense of dependency, individuation is the name of this process. An infant has desires, but it does not have beliefs or values. The transition from infancy to childhood, adolescence, and then adulthood is also a movement on the individuation–individuality continuum towards the latter pole.

Identifying one's environment, being identified by one's environment, and identifying *with* one's environmentare three distinct processes. The second (having identity or identities conferred) can come before the first – for example, at the point of birth.[83] The first is the infant individuation process; and the third is where the individuality dimension of identity-construction is most prominent. All social identities are, of course, place- and thing-related.

A strong individuality theory of subjectivity is more appropriate for the post-infant than for the infant phase in the human life-cycle. It is also more appropriate for the modern personality than for the pre-modern individual, because the transition from traditional life to modernity also sees a qualitative leap in the individualization of personality related to the qualitatively greater range of beliefs, values and desires available, and the greater possibilities of choice between them that now exist. This is not the least nor the only impact of modernity on identity.

Identities are rational and theoretical constructs having epistemic status. There can be false and bad identities, because what makes up identities has epistemic status. Identities act as psychic filters. They are ways of reading the world. They make sense of our experiences and shape them, but are also inputs into the construction of experiences.[84] Identity is located at the

---

83 C. F. Grauman, 'On Multiple Identities', *International Social Science Journal* 35 (1983). To be identified is to receive ascription from others. The two most powerful forms of such conferred or ascribed identity are those that 'make one belong' and those that 'make one responsible'.

84 Mohanty, 'Epistemic Status of Cultural Identity'.

juncture between individual and environment. Sociology emphasizes the socialization process: the internalization of social mores in the individual to stabilize society. Identification theory in psychology is the view from the other side, with the emphasis on internalization of mores and identity-construction to meet individual needs.[85]

Humans *must* have identity for psychological well-being and stability. There is a need for identity or identification that is as powerful as any other human need or instinct.[86] And it is a need that is always answered in some form through situational–cognitive processes. Between identity and behaviour is motivation. Identities motivate; the need for an identity does not.[87]

This need for identity exists for personal–social, not for cosmic–meaning reasons. Religious identity per se is neither inescapable nor essential, but identity is. Psychological security comes from having an identity. It does not presume anything more than that. It does not presume a stable social or cosmic order. It does not presume *particular* identities or world-views. Incoherent world-views might be sufficient. Infant individuation *is* closely connected to external reliability, predictability and order.

But the transition from individuation to individuality is also the realization of the ability to live and cope with uncertainty and unpredictability. In earlier pre-modern times cosmization could more easily reinforce nomization. There is now no automatic or necessarily desirable relationship between cosmization and nomization or in their function in securing individual psychic order. The modern Age of Doubt does not imply a stronger tendency towards psychic disorder. Rather, newer forms of psychic disorder emerge, such as compulsive behaviour. But nor is there a weakening of the resources for securing psychic order. The modern age does imply a more continuous and frequent process of psychic reordering – a more frequent and multiple negotiation and renegotiation of identities that make up the self. There is a 'structured totality' of identities that make up the self, not, as postmodernists would have it, a fragmented self. But this structured totality is not fixed. It is endlessly revisable.

---

85 For a fine exposition of Identification Theory, see W. Bloom, *Personal Identity, National Identity and International Relations* (Cambridge, 1990).

86 Giddens, *Modernity and Self-Identity*. Giddens talks of 'ontological security' for psychic normality – the first process of infant individuation whereby it develops a 'protective cocoon'. This comes about only through an initial and fundamental act of *trust*.

Given that there is a biological drive towards identification, is it primary or secondary? George Herbert Mead's view was that it was primary – biologically programmed and awaiting a trigger. For Freud it was secondary – emerging out of the infant's experience of dependency and the discovery that identification is the way to ensure primary gratification and resolve primary anxieties. Either way, identification is unavoidable.

87 Gerry Cohen is quite right on this score. The motivating power of identity (identities), he points out, bears some proportionate relationship to the strength of the need(s) answered by that identity or identities. G. Cohen, *History, Labour, and Freedom* (Oxford, 1988), Chapter 8.

The new *revisability* of identities on a scale, and with a depth and frequency unknown before, is yet another tribute to the impact of modernity.[88]
Just as society is uniquely dynamic, the self too is uniquely dynamized. But
this does not necessarily mean more psychic disorder or greater fragility
of identities. Humans are both objects and subjects. The very notion of
subjectivity carries this dual meaning. We are subject–actors; we are subject–
objects of more powerful actors. Identity's object dimension relates to the
boundary question. To have a particular identity is necessarily to establish
difference from other identities, to be defined by this difference over which
one has no control. The subject dimension is related to matters of trust and
commitment, an active investment of oneself in an identity involving the
anchoring of emotions. It is this active investment that gives such power to
strongly held identities. Yet modernity forces more frequent negotiations
and affirmations, with respect to both the boundary question and the trust
dimension.

There are distinctive identity problems of modernity, but these have to
do not with the brittleness or fragility of modern identities, but with their
flexibility and revisability.[89] Modern identities can be as deeply held as those
of the past. They are not more fragile, but more changeable because of the
greater self-reflexivity of the individual today.[90] Identities in modernity are
not more unstable, but are stable identities worn more lightly (if need be,
more insistently, aggressively and regularly), in innumerable hues, 'cut' in a
great variety of ways, composed of a greater range of 'fabrics'.

---

88 This revisability brings in the question of history and its vital relationship to identity. A sense of where one is connects to a sense of where one is coming from. A Hindu
communalism seeking to establish a new sense of 'Hinduness' must necessarily seek to
revise history.

89 Mol, *Identity and the Sacred*. Religion strengthens the 'fragile frame of identity'.
Mol makes the false claim of greater brittleness of identity in modernity because he wants
to make a case for the necessity and importance of religion in modernity through its
relationship to subjectivity. For Mol, religion is the sacralization of identity, or its fixa-
tion/affirmation, which is carried out through the anointment of that identity with the
awesome power of reverence, i.e. sacrality. It is thus the best guarantee of psychological
well-being, the best – or among the best – answers to the distinctive identity problems
and crises of modernity. The stabilization of society (nomization) is decisively connected
to the stabilization of the cosmos (cosmization).

There are distinctive identity problems in modernity, but Mol's approach is not the best
way to grasp or address them. His is a nostalgia for a world that can never return, and this
is revealed most starkly in his warrant for 'closed-mindedness'. Identity defence, he says,
requires strong boundary defence, and this in turn involves prejudice, or pre-judging.
Such closed-mindedness is good because it preserves order.

90 Giddens, *Modernity and Self-Identity*. Self-reflexivity is a new kind of self-
consciousness expressing itself in (a) heightened self-monitoring, and (b) self-revisability
in the light of new knowledge, which in modernity is a continuous and highly speeded-up
process. Identities are much more likely to be 'adopted' rather than 'handed down'. While
journals, travelogues and diaries are certainly a feature of the past, it is 'generally accepted
among historians that the writing of autobiographies (as well as biographies) only developed during the modern period' (p. 76). For the autobiography is 'not merely a chronicle
of elapsed events' but a document of self-monitoring and self-reflexivity: a 'corrective
intervention into the past' (p. 72).

Charles Taylor notes the emergence of the modern identity in the seventeenth century.[91] Pre-modern cosmologies saw the world as bestowed with meaning and morality. The world is as it is because it is as it should be: strong certitude arising from a closed order. The world's existence was the fulfilment of some scheme, divine or transcendent. It had a teleologically established rhythm or order which wars, plagues, and so on, did nothing to disrupt. Modernity destroys the certitudes of custom and tradition. But, contrary to Enlightenment hopes, it does not replace these with certitudes of its own that are as strong. Knowledge and reason have led to growing uncertainty, indeed to the institutionalization of radical doubt, to a multiplicity of claimants to authority. The claims of these authority systems are partial, and religion, the system which has come closest to making a claim to *absolute* authority, must itself lose some ground and reduce the scope of its own claims to a less absolute or complete level. God may not after all have made the world in seven days. Brahminism's cosmic clock (our time of degeneration or *kaliyug*) may best be taken as a philosophical metaphor rather than as an empirical claim about the actual historical process. The role of religion in modernity is subject to relativization, but the existence of uncertainty also creates a space for religion's resurgence as a form of psychological reassurance. But this refutes neither the fact of religion's relativization nor its inability to play the same role as in the past, or to do so as intensely.

In modernity, the connection between nomos and cosmos is greatly weakened. Social order and cosmic order, personal or social meaning and cosmic meaning, are no longer so strongly connected. Personal and social meanings are elevated in importance, while the domain of cosmic meaning suffers relative demotion. This is not just because science and rationality have emerged to offer an alternative explanation of the cosmos. It is even more the consequence of the emergence of new notions of control and progress. Society perceives new vistas of possible and actual progress, while the self glimpses a new horizon of fulfilment. The challenge to religion in respect of cosmization is paralleled by challenges in respect of nomization.

There are more and newer ways of making sense of both society and the cosmos. And new notions of progress and fulfilment create a new and stronger preoccupation with the social rather than the cosmic order, encouraging new hopes of moulding society and the self in desired directions. This is a partial compensation for Weberian despair over the 'loss of meaning'. Not only does the meaning-of-life-in-society question become more tenuously connected to the meaning-of-life-in-the-cosmos question; it also becomes the more important question, the major testing ground upon which religion must prove its modern efficacy. And there is more than just the religious means of meeting the former need. Traditional, usually religious ideas

---

91 C. Taylor, *Philosophy and the Human Sciences* (London, 1985).

connecting personal life to cosmic happenings such as notions of *fate* and *destiny* come under new pressure, and to some extent buckle under it.

The 'Who am I?' question is, of course, connected to the 'How am I to live?' question. Humans are *naturally* moral – not in a biological–genetic sense, but in the sense that the minimal rationality they share leads them to ask: 'How am I to live?'Humans do not simply want to believe that they are good, but want *truly* to be good. Identity is connected not just to meaning, but also to morality; but the two are not completely congruent. Identity is more is-ness, morality is ought-ness. The more complex a society, the more general becomes its moral value system, and the more detachable from any specific identity, such as the religious identity. The average tax-dodging yet devoutly Hindu shopkeeper suffers few qualms of conscience, and the believing Catholic is more inclined now to question Papal infalli-bility. The ability of religious systems to provide a powerful, encompassing and convincing moral canopy weakens decisively in the transition from pre-modernity to modernity, and in the progression of modernity itself.

It is truer today than ever before that humans believe (in religion) not so much because they want to be good, or because they want to search for the truth, but because, above all, they want to locate themselves in society and the world. Both identity and morality move from the realm of the external to the realm of the internal. An external, transcendent system gives way to a more internal, referential system of morality, knowledge and power. In the past, where identity had a more unreflective character, it was more an exter-nal horizon. For the individual today, identity is more an inner horizon; not external authorization, but self-authorship. Personal fulfilment and authen-ticity become more important: one must be 'true to oneself'; one is more concerned about 'feeling good' than striving to 'match a cosmic pattern' or fulfilling one's dharma. Individual failure to live up to the standards, explicit or implicit, embodied in these respective referential systems arouses various kinds of emotions and concerns. In the past, preoccupations and anxieties about such failure led to conjectures about fate, to condemnation, and to feelings of guilt. In the present, the dominant emotion resulting from com-parable failings is not guilt, but shame: 'The more self-identity becomes internally referential, the more shame comes to play a fundamental role in the adult personality.'[92]

While the philosophical and ethical dimensions of different religious systems can in theory find some common ground, and thus claim near-universality, the most important modern function of religious systems – the affirmation and fixation of identity – is inescapably particularist. Is this not fundamentally divisive, and therefore an enduring obstacle to the Enlight-enment aspiration of universalizing the deepest respect for a common humanity? Universalism cannot be counterposed to particularism, but is

---

92 Giddens, *Modernity and Self-Identity*, p. 153.

only achievable through it: 'There is no way of being human which is not *a* way of being human.'[93] Particularism must be the concrete expression of universalism. All identities have boundaries and divide along certain lines, but the relationship between particularism and universalism can differ.

How resistant to entry and exit are the boundaries of different identities? How respectful of equality, despite difference, are they? Progress towards equality across classes and castes requires the progressive disappearance of classes and castes. If aspiring to complete success here is considered utopian, great advances in this direction are not. The white person cannot become black, nor would most men, women or transgender people ever want to change their biology physically; but racial and gender differences can in time cease to matter very much in respect of preference or self-evaluation. The Spanish-speaker can learn Hindi and be equally proud. Particularisms remain, but are conducive to universalist goals through growing acceptance of the principle of equality across differences. But might we ever look to a time when a Muslim can become a Hindu, or a Hindu become a Christian, in relationships of equality, with this fact ceasing to matter very much for the communities in question?[94]

Any hope that this might come about requires that the case for free choice and complete revisability of religious identities be increasingly accepted and respected. And this requires a more modest self-appraisal by religious systems of their place and role in the world. Religious affiliation must increasingly be seen as an option, not as a requirement; one among a range of possible loyalties freely chosen and freely left, without dishonour felt by the community of believers in question. This is not an ecumenism that lays the ground rules for religious coexistence and competition, but one in which competition itself ceases to matter, where conversion between faiths and towards or away from faith is seen neither as collective affront nor as collective vindication.

This goes largely against the grain and tone of religious communities and systems as they currently stand – certainly against that of the world religions

---

93 Cohen, *History, Labour, and Freedom,* p. 146.

94 Religious tolerance in the positive sense is not as evident in the United States as is often made out. When public threat-perception is strong, religious intolerance comes to the fore. So intolerance has been exhibited to Mormons, Jehovah's Witnesses and black Muslims, and has receded when the perception of their threat to 'mainstream values' has receded. The example of the Jehovah's Witnesses is interesting, because a similar controversy was raised in India in the early 1980s.
Just before Pearl Harbor, when Jehovah's Witnesses' children refused to salute the American flag at school (in India they had refused to sing the national anthem), there was a major public outcry. In 1940 the Supreme Court condemned the position of Jehovah's Witnesses. Three years later, when American national confidence was much greater, the Supreme Court reversed its earlier ruling.
Religious tolerance should also mean respect for atheist behaviour. But central to Cold War mythology (for domestic consumption) was the pitting of God-fearing and 'God's-own-country' America against godless and atheistic Communism. Today, religious intolerance is manifested in the demonization of Muslims and Islam – a process not confined to the United States, but growing in Europe and India.

and their communities of believers. It is also incompatible with any notion of the centrality of a particular religious system to a particular culture. It becomes a feasible outcome when the religious function is increasingly privatized, and a desirable one when such privatization is accepted as a positive advance – when religious affiliation becomes, above all, an individual choice. The more secularized and democratic a society, the more chance there is for such a notion of religious modesty, religious equality and religious flexibility to flourish.[95] Insofar as capitalism limits the possibilities of a much more substantive democracy, most contemporary advocates of political secularism who are not Marxists or anti-capitalist socialists, but are concerned to promote what they would call a strong democracy, will not endorse the pursuit of such an ideal, but will content themselves with a minimal though important proceduralism in the relationship between the individual and religion:there should be freedom to convert, without coercion, and freedom of exit.[96]

Identities are psychic filters that shape experiences and emotions. The stronger and more expansive the identities in question, the more they will shape experiences and emotions. Strong experiences frequently help to reshape identities; but not all identities in specific societies are *equally* open to revisability in the light of new experiences. Gandhians can say that the strengthening and expansion of religious identity in civil society through

---

95 Most multiculturalist thinkers, including strong communitarians, would understand 'common culture' as denoting some attribute commonly *shared*, rather than in terms of the more dynamic notion (characteristic of the later Raymond Williams) of something commonly *fashioned*, and will be more inclined to see such a form of religious flexibility – given what they believe is its importance for the culture in question – as undesirable. This may be because they see the religious identity as a 'fundamental attachment' qualitatively different from and more powerful than all other identity attachments. Or it may be because they ascribe a special virtue to belief in the transcendent. Or it may be because to push for the greater individualization and privatization of religious choice is to fall into the trap of endorsing a particular European experience as a universally desirable future goal for non-European societies, whose proper understanding requires an appreciation of the epistemological importance of fundamental cultural difference with a capital D. But what is most common in these stances is the general lack of interest or unwillingness to conceive of a society fundamentally different from a more idealized version of today's liberal-democratic capitalism.

96 However, in the much-praised Indian Constitution, Article 25 clause 4, states the following: 'In this context, the Supreme Court has upheld the validity of the Acts passed by the Madhya Pradesh and Orissa Govts, which prohibited forcible conversion from one religion to another in a manner reprehensible to the conscience of the community and which made conversions by force, fraudulence or allurement an offence.' This endorsement of the Acts by the states of Madhya Pradesh and Orissa, which introduces the 'conscience of the community' as a consideration for sanctioning conversion, is reprehensible, as is the added criterion that conversion by 'allurement' is unacceptable. Hopes for material betterment motivate human behaviour, and there is no reason whatsoever why this should not include religiously related behaviour – for example, the promise of transcending one's lower caste position, or the possibility of greater welfare provision by Christian missionaries. Allurement through advertising, for example, is fundamental to shaping market behaviour in today's drive by the Indian state to promote neoliberal economic development, and in principle calls for no censure by law, let alone constitutionally.

a strengthening and expansion of religion's role will foster a stronger and wider sense of moral decency. Others, who are more critical, say that it is much more likely to shape experiences in ways that divide religious communities and erect barriers between them, leading to a stronger 'Hindu point of view' or 'Muslim point of view', when these should not be the prisms through which many matters need to be viewed.

Gandhians presuppose a strong link between morality and religious identity, which is precisely what has been weakened in modernity. Moreover, since the religious identity is sacralized by reverence, it has a distinctive component of dependency, of near-surrender, sometimes akin to masochism. This makes it somewhat more resistant to rational evaluation and justified criticism of its workings. In a context of religious conflicts and tensions, strengthening and expanding the importance of religious identities in civil society is much more likely to create more, not less, hostility and intolerance.

But what of Weberian despair at the loss of even private meaning in a disenchanted world? Is not the perdurance of religion the result of its faithful provision throughout the ages of meaning to an otherwise meaningless world? And is this not the guarantee of its permanent presence and power, now and in the future? Religion, in fact, is not an indestructibly hardy answer to the dilemmas of meaninglessness, but a non-answer. It has been, throughout pre-modernity, effectively a way of preventing the issue of meaninglessness and meaningfulness being put on life's agenda.

This problem of meaning must be separated from the problem of securing an antidote to the trauma of mortality, of coping with the inescapable transience of a human life. The effectiveness of religion in coping with the fact of mortality did not lie so much in its ability to give meaning, but was more decisively related to the timelessness and repetitiveness of life, its closed and continuous rhythm: '[T]he timeless world did not prompt questions about the meaning of life, since what is obvious (unchallengeable, without alternative) is neither meaningful nor meaningless, but stands outside the realm of meanings'.[97]

Concern with meaning was pointless. Life was not in the hands of the living. It was not 'a task'. 'Life just *was* ...' Religion removed meaning-of-life questions from life's agenda; it did not answer them. Only in modernity does a serious *search* for meaning begin:

Meaning is what is *meant*; there is no meaning unless action is *intentional*, preceded by a move addressed to a purpose. And there is no meaning where there is no freedom of choice between motives nor between purposes, and thus no responsibility for the choice eventually made. Having taken life out of the hands of the living, religions

---

97 Z. Bauman, *Mortality, Immortality and the Other Life Strategies*, pp. 91–2.

endorsed the world which had no room for the vexing questions of meaning.[98]

With the advent of modernity, what stands revealed is not the inadequacy or unsatisfactory character of religion as the answer to the newly perceived problem of meaning, but the revelation that religion has been the *absence* of an answer. What most sociological functionalists and most immortalizers and near-immortalizers of religion seek to do is to *make* religion play a *new* role, even as they insist it is but a continuation of an older role – to push religion forward as the best answer, or at least a good answer, to the 'problem of meaning' in our Age of Doubt.

The quest for meaning is akin to the search for a truth or essence behind appearances. Each of the paradigms – of tradition and religion, of modernity, and of postmodernity – has a distinctive relationship to the notions of progress and meaning, understandings which cannot be combined. One has to choose between these three competing paradigms about the contemporary human condition and their views about the desirable and likely direction of its future.

Pre-modern tradition and religion lack any serious notion of progress. Modernity is seriously committed to progress, even if it must learn not to be too arrogant about its claims and ambitions. Postmodernity consciously rejects the notion and value of progress altogether. The pre-modern way of thinking largely eliminates the problem of meaning from life's agenda. Modernity is the inauguration of a serious search for meaning. Postmodernity is the rejection of such a quest altogether: appearances are all we have. In the first there is the absence of a strong theory of subjectivity based on individuality. In the second there is an affirmation of the self-reflexive subject. In the third there is the denial of subjectivity and the self. Different though they are, the first and the third paradigms can be, and often are, uneasy allies in the common assault on the modernist project, what it stands for, what it aspires to. It is a futile assault. The past cannot be restored, and the postmodernist vision is but a dangerous chimera.

To recapitulate briefly: modernity affects identities in distinctive ways. In modernity we have considerably more and newer identities, not just of language group, kin, religion, caste or even class, but of belonging to the educated, of being consumers, internationalists, nationalists, and so on. Our identities are sharper. The sheer advance in the means of communication and the emergence of census-taking provide a sharper sense of difference

---

98 Ibid., p. 92. Belief in life after death is now an option. The meaning and purpose of death itself changes. Death now has *causes* to be *tackled*. Death is rationalized and segregated. Death is given meaning and made palatable if it comes *after* a 'fulfilling life'. In the West most deaths take place in hospitals. For the urban Indian middle class this is becoming more common, but most deaths still take place at home. Nonetheless, increasingly, death is rationalized as coming after a meaningful and fulfilling life, and not just seen as an unavoidable point of transition in an endless cosmic cycle.

between, say, Muslims and Hindus – a clearer sense of belonging to a religious minority or majority. Our identities are more flexible and revisable. They compete, clash, repel, overlap and combine in new and complex ways.

The religious identity escapes none of these processes. It is relativized by the emergence of more and newer identities. It is sharpened by the collapse of purely localist perceptions, and the recognition of other and different religious identities. Its power is qualified by the new potential for self-revisability of identities. It seeks to coexist or combine with those identities it would not confront, such as nationalism.

The conclusion is inescapable. The decline in the power and importance of religious identity relative to its own past and relative to other identities (whatever the unevenness of this might be within and between societies) is *a fact*. Its continuing relative decline is a *possibility* inherent in the nature of the modern condition. It is also *desirable* that religious systems be more modest, and recognize their reduced role in society. Such modesty is also a precondition for the emergence of a *genuine* religious ecumenism that is compatible with a truly democratic life, and with real religious equality.

On Secularity: A 'Taylored' Vision

Historically, secularization (and the ideology of secularism which intertwines with this process) emerged in Europe in the context of the transition from feudalism to capitalism, the rise of the Enlightenment and of partial de-Christianization. The general understanding of the issue of secularity has ever since been marked by this historical background, with different people assigning different weights to how capitalist modernization, Enlightenment values of humanism, rationalism and materialism, and Christianity relate to the emergence of what can be called the secular age.

In 2007, building on a lifetime of research, Charles Taylor came out with what many would call his *magnum opus*, titled *A Secular Age*.[99] This is a sprawling, untidy work of some 874 pages of remarkable erudition, filled with many a powerful insight. Ever since, it has found both admirers and detractors (much more of the former), and can lay claim to having become an inescapable point of reference for any discussion of secularism and secularization, even as the author was careful to confine the geographical scope of his work to Latin Christendom or the North Atlantic, more commonly referred to as the West.[100] According to Taylor there are three concepts of secularity, two of which – the secularization of many public spaces, and the

---

99 C. Taylor, *A Secular Age* (Cambridge, MA/London, 2007).
100 A major text consisting of commentaries on *A Secular Age* is M. Warner, J. Van Antwerpen and C. Calhoun, *Varieties of Secularism in a Secular Age* (Cambridge, MA/London, 2010). In addition, there has been a veritable torrent of commentaries upon commentaries on Taylor's book.

relative decline in influence of religious beliefs, practices and institutions –
have already been discussed at some length in this chapter.

The third refers to the coming of the secular age in the West, when
there was a fundamental change in the 'conditions of belief, experience and
search' for the spiritual, or what he calls 'fullness'. This no longer has a singular meaning, and its pursuit is no longer restricted to being a reference to
God or to a transcendent beyond. If in a pre-secular era this fullness came
only from outside, in the secular age, for some or many, it could come from
within, that is, immanently. The 'final goal' can now be human flourishing
alone or an 'exclusive humanism'. Taylor's definition of the secular age 'is
one in which the eclipse of all goals beyond human flourishing becomes
conceivable, or better, falls within the range of an imaginable life for masses
of people'.[101]

This is a judgement that can and should be widely accepted. The West
(and not just the West) today is a domain filled with a plurality of ultimate visions, of diverse conceptions of what should constitute the ideal
moral order – an arena in which the religious, the semi-religious, the non-
religious and the anti-religious coexist. There is not just religious decline,
but also the birth of newer forms of religiosity, and even partial reversals
of the trend towards privatization of religion. Taylor's ecumenism with
regard to today's plurality of paths searching for the spiritual or fullness
is in keeping with his distinctive preoccupation with understanding and
respecting multiculturality. It leads him to recognize non-religious forms of
this quest, as well as those embodied in different religions, in ways that are
often highly personalized and even idiosyncratic, and quite apart from the
forms taken by institutionalized religious bodies. These are all indications of
a recomposition of religion and religious behaviour alongside the fact of its
relative decline.[102] The secular age, Taylor says, is here to stay as far as the
West is concerned.

---

101 Taylor, *Secular Age*, pp. 19–20.
102 Taylor imputes to Marx and Marxism what he calls a 'subtraction' argument that
modernity (for Marxists, capitalist modernity) brings about the fading away of older
verities, such as belief in, and service of, God, and as a result a steady progressive clarification of what we and the world are really like. Older goals and allegiances are supposedly
sensibly sloughed off for better, newer ones. This is a mistakenly linear historical account –
empirically invalidated and methodologically unsubtle, to say the least. Taylor fails to
realize that Marx is much more nuanced, indeed dialectical. Insofar as capitalist modernity
does promote greater de-sacralization and secularization of spheres of human existence,
it also introduces a new kind of dehumanizing process with its accompanying illusions,
compulsions and compensations. Marx's writings discuss both processes. In a famous
passage in the *Communist Manifesto*, Marx says: 'All that is solid melts into air, all that
is holy is profaned'. As Wendy Brown points out, he says all that is holy is *profaned* – i.e.
violated and defiled. Capital does violence to human beings and their relations, and this is
not something that Marx approves of or celebrates. This, says Brown, 'is not a subtraction
argument …what capital lays bare is not humanity but itself … what is revealed is not man
or truth but capital's violence toward both man and the sacred'. W. Brown, 'The Sacred,
the Secular and the Profane: Charles Taylor and Karl Marx', in Warner et al., *Varieties of
Secularism*, pp. 92–5.

What has given rise to sharp controversy, however, is his causal narrative of how secularity 3 – the secular age – came about. He largely severs the connection between this and the rise of modernity, certainly as understood by Marx or Weber and their close followers, even as he talks of 'secular modernity'. The source of secularism is said to reside in Christian ethics, or rather, has come from the changes within Christian moral and ethical teachings that have taken place over the last six centuries, and through this process the creation of a newer *secular subjectivity*. Continuity, then, not the ruptures caused by industrialization or Enlightenment rationalism or capitalism, is to be given pride of place in explaining the secularization process, even as this unfolded in an interrupted rather than smooth fashion.[103] Space is given to the impact of the scientific revolution, to urbanization, industrialization and migration (capitalism does not really feature), but as supplementary factors to a causal narrative that is resolutely cultural–ideational, a genealogy of spiritual intentions.

Medieval Christianity, he says, struggled with an inbuilt tension stressing self-transcendence and a degree of human flourishing. What stabilized such an order was the religiously sanctioned acceptance of a 'hierarchical complementarity of functions', albeit of unequal dignity – the clergy prays for all, the lords defend for all, the peasants labour for all.[104] Changing forms of Christianity, the Protestant Reformation above all prepared the way for the emergence of the 'bounded' and 'buffered' self in contrast to the pre-secular 'porous' self, which was intertwined with the enchanted world of spirits and powers, benevolent and malevolent. For the buffered self the mind alone is the source of meaning.[105] This then generated a much stronger momentum to the process of relative disenchantment, whereby a modern individuality of the self emerged – one of 'radical reflexivity' and greater preoccupation with being 'true to oneself'. In short, a religious individualism preceded and promoted a less religious and non-religious secular individualism. Herein lay the story of the spread of an exclusive humanism, with its focus on the human capacity to reorder and make the world progressively better.

Insofar as the individual cannot be separated from the larger community or society, there is a 'social imaginary' at work that operates to stabilize the

---

103 Taylor says this process is discontinuous. In his time frame, changes in Christianity led to a buffered self and some elite disbelief by the eighteenth century. Between the late eighteenth century and World War II, there was a spread of disbelief to masses and the rise of an exclusive humanism, but also of new forms of growing religiosity, such as Methodism, and new spiritual directions within many existing churches including the Catholic Church. Developments after World War II, and especially the cultural revolution of the 1960s, reinforced exclusive humanism, but also saw resurgences of religious faiths.

104 This was the medieval Christian form of cosmization–nomization.

105 Protestantism's rejection of magic, mystery and miracle, its egalitarian idea of the 'priesthood of all believers', and conception of justification by faith alone, made much religious practice irrelevant through the affirmation of ordinary life and the achievement of success in one's everyday vocational activity a possible sign of God's grace. Neither could Catholicism remain immune from this Protestant impact.

existing socio-political order. For Taylor, all social imaginaries require certain conceptions of the unifying moral order.[106] In the seventeenth century, a new vision of the moral order emerged – natural law – and via later thinkers like Grotius and Locke, a new legitimation of political society was provided, one based on equal individuals (rejecting older conceptions of natural hierarchies) having moral obligations to each other, seeking mutual benefit and defending their 'natural rights', even as these were still seen as God-given.[107] What thus began as an elite theory was gradually embedded in a new social imaginary, abetted by the emergence of a 'public sphere' where there is now a more impersonal form of a horizontally mediated citizenry based on the building blocks of discrete individuals, but who also see themselves as belonging to wider, more impersonal entities like the state, the nation, and now to the 'community of human kind'.

What, then, are the most forceful and powerful criticisms of Taylor's project? Three stand out. The first is the peculiarity of his methodology, which is historical and seemingly materialist in seeking to trace over time the changes in the 'background conditions of belief' that give rise to secularism. But modernity, or rather the dominant traditions for understanding the 'conditions for the emergence of modernity' – Weberian and Marxist – are not seriously addressed. If there is at least some reference to industrialization and urbanization as minor causal factors for the coming of the secular age, the importance of the specific forces and compulsions unleashed by the rise of capitalism (print-capitalism gets a brief nod for its help in creating the public sphere) is essentially ignored.

Wendy Brown is not alone in highlighting this lacuna and its negative consequences, but is perhaps the sharpest, in accusing Taylor of an 'odd

---

106 Taylor clearly belongs to the school that places undue weight on value consensus as the main source of order, even as this consensus – for liberal-democratic politics – is not itself religiously founded; and even as its historical and intellectual origins are shaped by the negative fall-out of terrible wars of religion, and by post-Reformation political philosophy from the likes of Grotius, Locke, Kant and others. This approach is not my own, which gives primacy to the combined impact of coercion and the absence of a unifying dissensus. An important criticism of Taylor's understanding of the social imaginary is made in V. Lloyd, 'A Secular Age: What Taylor Misses', at blogs.sscr.org. Lloyd points out that Taylor's notion of the social imaginary binds together 'social practices, norms and supporting ideas' originally created by elites which then spread downwards to become a public common-sense. However, says Lloyd, imagination may bind norms and the ideas that underlie them, but practices 'never exactly follow norms' – i.e. dissensus in the form of all kinds of everyday practices of speech and action diverges from and regularly mocks such norms.

107 Taylor gives due importance to the first articulations of a new moral order in the writings of Grotius and Locke, but does not connect this to the rise of capitalism in the Netherlands and England, and how this influenced the thinking of these two figures on matters of the individual, democracy and rights. For a study of the relationship of Western political thought generally, and of Grotius and Locke in particular, to the nature of Dutch commercial society and England's emerging capitalism, and to their respective social conflicts at the time, see E. M. Wood, *Liberty and Property* (London, 2012), especially Chapters 5 and 7.

representation of historical materialism', one that is a 'markedly thin and mostly unrecognizable version of materialism':

> To begin with, Taylor identifies materialism with a theory of humans driven by economic motivations, an identification that converts materialist analysis from attempting to explain what generates historical conditions to what psychologically animates human action ... One need not subscribe to the idea that human beings are driven by economic or material motives to be a historical materialist; the whole point of a substantive materialism could be said to lie in differentiating human motives or aims from the conditions through which they are shaped, constrained, and enacted. There is, in other words, a crucial difference between reducing humanity to *Homo Economicus* (ironically, it is contemporary neoliberal rationality that performs such a radical reduction) and an account of historical change in which modes of production are a main stage upon which a plethora of human aspirations and capacities are played out. When Marx argues in *The Eighteenth Brumaire* that 'men make their own history but they do not make it just as they please ... under circumstances chosen by themselves', he is plying precisely this distinction, arguing that whatever our motives, our actions and possibilities are conditioned by forces beyond our control, and even our cognition. So a materialist account of historical possibility is interested not in motives for action but in the conditions that produce and contour such motives, the conditions in which our actions are iterated, and the conditions with which our actions interact to produce certain effects.[108]

Capitalism, like nothing else before it, unleashes a dynamic of change that is permanent, rapid and exceptional in its power. This creates new forms of human alienation, so religious reformulations and new fundamentalisms are born. One of Althusser's most interesting contributions was to reject the idea of simple linear historical time, to stress that specific 'levels' have their different and specific historical times within a structure of mutual interaction and influence. Thus there is no simple, unilinear or general pattern of causal relationships which explain how *specific* social formations emerge, secularize or consolidate themselves, even if the capitalist mode of production becomes dominant. This is partly what is meant when talking of the uneven and combined character of capitalist development. Processes of secularization at one level can also help promote de-secularization at another level. In some cases there can be displacement rather than a straightforwardly cumulative process of religious decline.

But capitalist development also raises far more expansive notions of possible human *progress*. Capitalism is also an important secularizing solvent of

---

108 Brown, 'The Sacred, the Secular and the Profane', p. 88.

all religiously based cosmologies, in that it powerfully magnifies the focus on human flourishing as both achievable and cumulative, not to mention its universalizing tendency as its seeks to encroach on ever more domains of human existence and behaviour. Capitalism's dynamic of change a) creates newer possibilities for expanding material prosperity for elites that makes for greater emphasis on secular human flourishing; b) creates much stronger comparative dissatisfactions among the poor with the existing religiously sanctioned order, leading to social upheavals and mass disruptions of a much greater scale than in the past, and which religious practices, beliefs and institutions are less able to deal with; and c) separates the economic from the political in a way that allows more scope and space for democratic mobilizations to emerge, thereby promoting and spreading ideas of egalitarianism and humanism. This separation of the economic from the political is a permissive but not a sufficient condition for such mobilizations to take place, and become effective. But this disjunction also acts to contain the potential thrust of such upheavals as well as to limit the meaning of democracy to a form of political rule by popular representation that should not seriously intrude on to the domain of economic power held by the few. This is not a conception of democracy as a properly institutionalized form of genuine popular rule and empowerment by the citizenry.

Brown makes the point that Taylor fails to come to terms with what she calls 'capital's profanation of the sacred with the extension of market rationality and rationalization to all domains of existence'.[109] Capitalism ignored and underestimated is capitalism accepted. Insofar as Taylor believes that Christians and non-believers in the West share the goal of wanting to deepen human flourishing, he will not take the position that this *necessarily* requires the end of capitalism. Humanizing it in a strongly social-democratic, welfarist direction will do.

The second major line of criticism comes from those, like Saba Mahmoud, who argue that even within Taylor's own terms of reference, wherein Christianity is the source of secularism in the West, no 'self-understanding of Christianity' can hope to be accurate and complete without bringing in its encounters with Eastern Orthodoxy, as well as with the non-Christian and the non-Western world. To ignore this is to parallel the mistake of those who omit the history of slavery and colonialism when talking of post-Enlightenment modernity.[110] Christian missionary work did not only accompany or help the colonial project; it helped to redefine the relationship of Christianity to humanity at large. Greater awareness of the existence of other 'higher' religions relativized the place of Christianity, but also spurred its defenders to emphasize its supposedly distinctive trans-cultural, universalist

109 See W. Brown, 'Idealism, Materialism, Secularism', at blogs.ssrc.org. See also note 103, above.
110 S. Mahmoud, 'Can Secularism be Otherwise?' in Warner et al., *Varieties of Secularism*, p. 286.

calling. Or, as Mahmoud puts it, 'Importantly, the condition of emergence for the 'buffered self' that Taylor tracks was not only an epistemological shift but also civilizational, in that the self-reflection induced by encounters with others was taken as a sign of superiority and uniqueness of West European Christianity.'[111]

The conditions under which the buffered self emerged were also reflective of unequal and oppressively imposed power relations. Contrary to Taylor's own political inclinations, just this sense of 'secular superiority' of the West allows many contemporary liberals and right-wingers to maintain their barely disguised contempt for the more 'primitive' and 'uncivilized' nature of, say, the Islamic world. Claims about secular modernity become ways of disguising, justifying and denying the realities of Western imperialist behaviour.

Finally, Taylor joins those who believe that religious belief in the transcendent provides meaning to an otherwise meaningless world, even as one can strive for 'fullness' in multiple ways, some non-religious. That is to say, he acknowledges that an exclusive humanism is an option in the secular age, and certainly prefers to pitch his tent on a humanist terrain; he believes in the pursuit of human flourishing – but most definitely not in aligning himself with an exclusive humanism. The issue here is not endorsement of a dystopia of obligatory atheism, or of complete exclusion of religious cosmologies, beliefs, practices and institutions, but of priority and primacy. Taylor's position dodges a problem that is determinedly highlighted by Saxton, as pointed out earlier. Today, the combined presence of nuclear and biological weapons (particularly the first) and capitalism (through ecological devastations) constitutes a historically unique threat to the human species, and therefore to the very possibility of future human flourishing. Where belief in the transcendent can provide a degree of comfort and detachment in the face of this reality, it is an exclusive humanism (whether held by believers or non-believers) that provides the strongest nucleus for any wider alliance, that can have the the most single-minded focus on seeking to eliminate these twin dangers to the human species.

One could go further. The more meaningful notion of transcendence, the one that should perhaps preoccupy us much more, is not Taylor's 'going beyond the human', but 'going beyond and transcending capitalism' itself. There is no refuge to be found, at least for this writer, in the chimera of a green capitalism that can somehow ensure permanent ecological sustainability. There are religiously motivated forms of deep ecology, both in certain Western traditions of faith and in certain strands of Hindu philosophical thought. But they are of no consolation, since they rarely if ever distinguish between an unwarranted anthropocentrism and a necessary philosophical anthropology in assessing the relationship between humans and nature. Surprisingly, Taylor has criticized Marxism for being insensitive to the issue

---

111 Ibid., p. 291.

of ecology, for an excessive productivism. If this is a criticism of many in the Marxist tradition, it is acceptable. But he seems unaware of the sensitivity of Marx himself on this score – in his notion of 'metabolic rift' – and of those Marxist currents inspired by these writings that point out that the socialism of Marx has always been far more sensitive to the need for ecological balance than has a capitalism whose fundamental drives are incompatible with maintaining such a balance.[112]

To be an anti-capitalist socialist, or even a Marxist or communist, does not require one to be an atheist or a nonbeliever. Strands of Christian liberation theology are testimony to that. The young Charles Taylor was, in the words of his one-time collaborator, the late Stuart Hall, 'a sort of Catholic Marxist' and an anti-capitalist socialist.[113] The older, and it must be said the publicly and intellectually far more influential Charles Taylor, is more Catholic than Marxist – indeed, more likely to see Marxism (despite some acknowledgement of its virtues) as something of an enemy of his conception of democratic freedom; and he is no longer an anti-capitalist socialist. By 2014, for Taylor, the question of whether a state is capitalist or not is simply of no consequence. What matters is that, for a state to be genuinely secular, it 'can be neither Christian nor Muslim nor Jewish; but by the same token it should also be neither Marxist nor Kantian nor Utilitarian'.[114]

Taylor now categorically insists that religion must not be the prime focus of secularism, but that any genuinely secular regime must aim to 'manage the religious and metaphysical–philosophical diversity of views (including non- and anti-religious views) fairly and democratically', and this is to be done through a reworking of the Rawlsian formula of an 'overlapping consensus' to cover different comprehensive world-views or conceptions of the good life.[115] But unlike Rawls, for whom such a consensus was to be arrived at by a moral reasoning that was secularly founded on the nature of humans as rational beings, Taylor does not see non-religious moral reasoning as in any way superior to religiously founded reasoning for establishing a rights-based society. So, for example, in regard to the 'right to life', he says,'I cannot see how the fact that we are desiring/enjoying/suffering beings or

---

112 See, for example, P. Burkett, *Marxism and Ecological Economics: Toward a Red and Green Political Economy* (Koninklikje, 2006); J. B. Foster, *Marx's Ecology: Materialism and Value* (New York, 2000).

113 S. Hall, 'Life and Times of the First New Left', *New Left Review* II/61 (January–February 2010). Hall's view differs from that of another radical inspired by Catholic teaching, Terry Eagleton, who remains a Marxist and an anti-capitalist socialist. He sees socialism as the political form of the project that the Judeo-Christian tradition at its best also aims at, in its conception of the 'good life' lived according to the virtues of charity and love. Socialism in which the free development of each is necessary for the free development of all is 'politicized love', or the creation of self-realization for all through reciprocity, or 'achieving fulfilment only in terms of each other'. See T. Eagleton, *After Theory* (New York, 2003), p. 222.

114 C. Taylor, 'Defining Secularism', in A. Bilgrami, ed., *Marx, Gandhi and Modernity* (New Delhi, 2014), p. 43.

115 Ibid., p. 31.

the perception that we are rational agents should be any surer basis for this right than the fact that we are made in the image of God'.[116] So, he argues, we should agree on the principles without demanding that 'incompatible but reasonable' world-views should agree on their reasons for arriving at such principles. This is what is required of the overlapping consensus that will guide a modern secular state to pursue and 'maximize the basic goals of liberty and equality between basic beliefs'.[117]

Notice that the call given here is for equality between the different belief systems that are part of the overlapping consensus. The criticisms made by Anderson a decade ago of Rawls's 'overlapping consensus' apply with equal if not more force here as well.[118] Typical of much (but not all) discussion about varieties of secularism, with its preoccupations with cultural differences within liberal democracies, is the insufficient attention it gives to the impact that the uneven and combined character of capitalist development has as it expands globally. Not only is it itself a source of differentiation; it also introduces a very powerful consumerist homogenization across cultural heterogeneities. Besides which, it also universalizes its own ethical principles, such as respect for private property, as the foundation for any democratic society. By ignoring capitalism, Taylor, like many others, never asks how far one should push the pursuit of equality, liberty, fraternity. For him, the strongest candidates for appearing to have 'incompatible but reasonable' comprehensive world-views are religious belief systems.

But while the French Revolution and the Enlightenment talked of the liberty, equality and fraternity of people, Taylor talks of equality between belief systems, clearly believing that universal human rights are embodied in all the world religions despite their textual injunctions to revenge and justified massacres of enemies. Hinduism's connection to caste hierarchy makes its claims to embodying universal principles of equality hard to swallow. As for the possibilities of ethical agreement (though differently propounded) between religions, there is as strong a basis – if not stronger – for claiming that the world religions are in themselves ethically contradictory – not consistent or even striving to be so as belief systems, though some religious experts try to read religious texts against the grain in an attempt to make them so.

---

116 Ibid., p. 46. But modernity's dynamic of change has been such as to demand a regular expansion of rights discourse that has required codification in the language of secular jurisprudence, whose foundational principles are not based on any religion. Taylor does not want a replacement of secular law, but nevertheless does not see any gain to be had by morality being grounded only on the good of humans in this life – what he calls exclusive humanism.

117 Ibid., p. 47. While Taylor believes some measure of institutional separation from religion by the secular state is thereby required, his approach comes close to rejecting that there can be states that are secular but not democratic. In fact, he argues that the Turkey of Atatürk's time is not to be considered a secular state (p. 32).

118 See the chapter on John Rawls in P. Anderson, *Spectrum: From Right to Left in the World of Ideas* (London, 2005).

Secularization Once Again

Of the three notions of secularization originating from the Western experience, the basic dispute concerns the secularization-as-decline thesis. But it also touches on the other two notions of secularization – as relative separation, and as growing rationalization – since the decline thesis incorporates these notions as well.

First, is secularization-as-decline a fact? Much of the argument in the preceding pages has been directed at showing that this is undeniable, at least for the transition from pre-modernity to modernity. In addition, the claim of religion to centrality in modern life is quite implausible. How have opponents reacted? The twin argumentative strategies of the immortalization or near-immortalization of religion, and of insisting on its centrality to culture and society, have already been discussed. Other arguments largely turn on the issues of 'base-line', 'permeation' and 'rationality'.

The idea that modernity brings with it secularization-as-decline, it is said, must assume a base-line whence societies of the past were presumably more religious. This, it is claimed, is the 'myth of the pious primitive'.[119] How do we know this to be so? How can we generalize so extravagantly across the centuries merely from anthropological studies, with all the attendant problems of reading these complex societies as 'primitive' exemplars of *our* past? There is clearly a problem of accumulating proper and decisive historical evidence. But this does not prevent us from intelligently speculating. The base-line argument is something of a formal, technical and abstract objection. Historical evidence (or lack of it) may not convince beyond all doubt about the greater religiosity of past societies, but it certainly does not convince one that the past was more likely to have been less religious. Also, the main critics of the secularization-as-decline thesis try to establish a basic divide between magic and religion along Durkheimian lines, which must be considered unconvincing, to say the least. In the choice between these two assessments of greater or lesser religiosity in the past (allowing for spatial and temporal variations), it is obvious which is the more likely conclusion for students of history.

The base-line criticism thus needs to be bolstered by its upholders with other arguments concerning permeation and rationality. Older, less complex societies do seem to be more permeated by magic–religion than later, more complex societies and civilizations. Modern societies are quite clearly less permeated. There is at least overt shrinkage in the social space occupied by religious influence, whether in institutionalized or non-institutionalized forms. If, in spite of this, it is argued that the secularization-as-decline thesis

---

119 M. Douglas, 'Primitive Thought Worlds', in Robertson, ed., *Sociology of Religion*; M. Douglas, 'The Effects of Modernisation on Religious Change', *Daedalus* III (1982). See also the discussion in Morris, *Anthropological Studies of Religion*, on the structural approach to religious symbolism of Levi-Strauss and Douglas.

is wrong, then this claim can only be validated by redefining secularization to mean something other than decline. This enables one to reject the decline thesis yet accept that secularization (understood only as a form of religious change) has taken place. Declining permeation means growing institution-alization of religion. This, then, is a kind of secularization process that was taking place long before and right up to the advent of modernity. Then a significant development occurs. The very process of institutionalization (reaching its apogee in Christianity, and embodied especially by the Papacy) becomes the precondition for the separation of church and state, and the emergence of the secular state. This, it is usually argued, is probably a posi-tive development.[120] But it does not mean there has been overall decline of religious influence and power in civil society, or in society as a whole (society comprising state, civil society, family, economy, and so on).

There has merely been a reallocation of religious functions, even a secular-ization of religious practices. So Protestantism, and in particular Calvinism, was the generalization of elite asceticism (of monks) to the laity. The Catholic confessional is replaced by the privileged confessional relationship between lawyer and client, doctor and patient. The practice in India of *darshan* (a respectful sighting) of religious leaders can be transferred to political leaders, or leaders in other social fields, such as entertainment and sport. The Guru–*shishya* (disciple) relationship is similarly applicable elsewhere.

Is such reallocation merely a change in the form of religion, which only apparently declines? Or is there an actual reduction of the domain under religious control of any kind, not merely of religion in its institutional form? The answer depends on how one understands this transference of func-tion. Is the fact of such transference enough to confirm the loss of religious power, or are these needs (howsoever institutionally satisfied) derived from within us as religious animals?

Pre-modern relationships and religious systems have always been imbued with principles of strong hierarchy and dependency. Insofar as modernity also brings in a new conception of equality, it clearly has the potential to undermine and destroy older relational patterns – for example, the con-fessional format. The doctor as God is a notion itself under pressure. Even Berger – uneasy, ambiguous and increasingly hostile as he became to the decline thesis – was prepared to concede the fact of *some* secularization of this kind: 'Secularization can be defined as a shrinkage in the role of religion, both in social life and in individual consciousness secularization is a progres-sive loss of plausibility to religious views of reality.'[121]

The attack on presumably modernist concepts of rationality comes, of course, from other quarters (such as postmodernists and anti-modernists) than the one occupied by critics of secularization. But much of the furniture

---

120 Most Western opponents of the decline thesis would accept this. Indian opinion is much more divided, even on this narrow issue of state separation from religious influence.
121 Berger, 'Some Second Thoughts', p. 132.

of argument is the same. How can pre-modern or even 'primitive' thought, or religious thought, be considered irrational compared to modernist thought? And if it is, so what? Is it not the arrogance of the rationalists that leads them to dismiss the importance of the irrational, or of what is beyond rationality, and thus of systems like religion? If we cannot talk of the religiously suffused societies of the past as irrational or less rational, then what is left of the thesis that secularization partly means growing rationality, brought about by more secular systems of knowledge like science? The question of secularization is clearly linked to the debate about rationality and cultural relativism.

Basic to the decline thesis (and not only to this notion of secularization) is the claim that religious systems of thought are less rational than scientific ones, and that modern societies are in some sense more rational because of the impact of the Scientific and Industrial Revolutions. Is this defendable? Obviously it depends on how we understand rationality. But the simple answer is: yes. We have come a long way from the strong foundationalism of the Enlightenment view of reason. We have learned to be more modest. We talk of rationality with a small 'r', and of rationalities in the plural. 'Primitive' thought is not so much irrational as another kind of rationality, comprehensible in its context. But do we simply leave it at that? Are different rationalities and cultures beyond comparison and evaluation?

Rationalities do not simply coexist; they compete and clash. They are what Charles Taylor calls 'incommensurables' which 'somehow occupy the same space'. Insofar as they are incommensurables and obey different rules, they cannot be compared. Insofar as they lay claim to the same space, they can. Magic–religion and science are different kinds of rationalities, and are not comparable. But, insofar as the former makes epistemological claims, which it does – for example, explaining why rain falls – it can be compared with and judged inferior to scientific explanation.

To be rational is to explain. To be more rational is to explain more effectively. To explain is to lay out in best or 'in perspicuous order', the elements that make up the generative or causal mechanism, or the framework of meaning and this is often (though not always) best done through a 'disengaged perspective' – in other words, in a 'theoretical' way. Modern societies are more theoretical than those in the past, and to that extent are more rational.[122] This is not merely an abstract virtue. The proof of the pudding is that superior explanation is inseparable from having a better handle to 'shape' the world.

The contrast is not between irrationality and rationality, but between different and competing rationalities, which forces choice and judgement according to standards. There is the less rational and the more rational, and the possibility of *growing* rationality. Irrationality is generally culture-specific. It is an *inconsistency* that can only be gauged *within* a framework of accepted

---

122 Taylor, *Philosophy and the Human Sciences.*

standards, a contextual irrationality. But there is also *logical inconsistency*, based on universal standards – such as laws of identity, contradiction, negation – just as there are some minimum universal human capacities. Cutting across different rationalities is a common minimum rationality that allows for cultural translation, rational judgement across cultures, change in consensually agreed directions, and 'weak' notions of universal objectivity and progress. Better explanation – progress in rationality – is generally discipline-specific.[123] Knowledge in specific disciplines *does* grow over time and across cultures. Secularization *has* taken place in the transition to modernity.

The real ire of Berger and other sophisticated critics like Taylor is not directed at refuting the *fact* of secularization-as-decline. What they are really against is this idea being seen as a master-trend, a continuing if not irreversible process. This is a well-taken objection, provided not too much is read into it. It certainly does not refute the view that the continuing decline of the importance of religious influence and religious identity is *possible*.

Nor does it mean that substantial secularization has not taken place in non-European societies; or that, even if there is some degree of reversal, it is possible to restore religion to its pre-modern status in culture and society.[124] What it does represent is a salutary caution against (a) assuming that non-European societies will easily or eventually replicate the European secularization experience; and (b) assuming that the existing balance of secular–religious influences is not reversible or that, in the longrun, secularization *must* assert itself.

Within the limits of modernity, the question of further secularization in civil society and the family is more open-ended. It is not clear if the critics of the decline thesis would dispute that, as far as the state is concerned, its secularization might after all be a master-trend. This is connected to another conjecture. Is the democratic state in the long run a master-trend, a process that can claim still more conquests, and whose energies are yet to burn out fully?

Instead of a unidirectional process, more complicated combinations of de-secularization–secularization, of the secular and the religious in society,

---

123 A. Gilbert, *Democratic Individuality* (Cambridge, 1990). Gilbert makes the important point that knowledge is not just culture-specific, but also discipline-specific and open to disciplinary progress and assessment. Aristotle's political and moral philosophies can still speak to us with amazing freshness because of this discipline-specific character. They are not 'imprisoned' in the culture of ancient Greece, and 'untranslatable'.

124 Berger echoed many in feeling that recent religious revivalism was a serious counter to the *general* socio-historical claim of the secularization-as-decline thesis. See Berger, 'Some Second Thoughts'.

However, the *prevalence* of religious beliefs and practices must not be confused with their *importance*. Berger is himself, as in so many areas, more nuanced than others. Since religion is for the individual 'the religious experience', if secularization-as-decline holds, then fewer people are having such experiences. Alternatively, people are having such experiences, but under social pressure are denying it, so that religion is not so much in decline as suffering delegitimation. Berger believed that both were probably happening, but that the second trend might be stronger.

are clearly possible. This could pertain to different spaces, such as state and civil society, where the strength of religious influence in the latter is strong enough to threaten the secularity of the former. As in the early phase of the Kemalist revolution in Turkey, Iran under the Pahlavi Shah's 'White Revolution', or Poland under communist rule, the secularization (of state) – de-secularization (of civil society) could be two moments of the same process. Elsewhere, as in India, the secular and the non-secular simply exist in separate spaces, in a relationship of tension. Indian civil society is much less secular than the civil societies of other democracies. The hitherto diffuse pressure of anti-secular forces in civil society is now being politically organized with such force as to threaten to undo decisively the standard claims to secularity of the Indian state and government.

The secularization–de-secularization combination can also apply to different spaces within civil society (different sectors of social life), or to different groupings. In the UK, for example, there is an uneven spread of religious influence among different ethnic groups. It is growing among British Hindus and British Muslims, but declining among white British Christians, and is perhaps stable among British West Indians.[125]

American civil society is less secular than British civil society. This simple observation tends to be obscured by advocates of secularization as something other than decline. The secularization of consciousness and religious pluralism (as part of a general pluralization of society) is said to represent a unitary process. American religious pluralism emerges out of the privatization of religious affairs. It reflects the individualism of modern life. In fact, the marketization of religion to meet private, therapeutic needs has reached unprecedented levels. According to a number of American Durkheimians the United States is more religiously suffused *and* more secular than Britain, because privatization and pluralization are greater. This apparent paradox, they can claim, is resolvable only if we discard the thesis that secularization represents religious decline. Some have gone on to argue that the United States has a strong Civil Religion decisively influenced by the Big Three faiths: Protestantism, Judaism (in a somewhat Protestantized form) and Catholicism.

Certainly, secularization does mean that religion becomes more private, optional and problematic; and privatization does signify decline relative to the past. But it does not necessarily follow that, the more 'privatized' and marketized religious affairs are, the more secularized a society will be. A public culture dedicated to consumerism means not simply a more privatized society, but also a more consumerized culture, a homogeneity of heterogeneity. This is partly the 'accomplishment' of American religious

125 Turner, *Religion and Social Theory*, argues for just such 'coexistences' and 'combinations' of consolidating and declining religious (and specifically Christian) influences in respect of rich and poor, pagan and Christian 'spaces', atrabilious and attritionist accounts of secularization.

life, of its consumerization of religion. More than elsewhere, the federal-ized democracy of the United States resembles its market model, in which strong consumer lobbies are very active. Religious consumer lobbies in the United States have a social influence foreign to more secularized societies like Britain, regardless of the formally more secular character of the US state and Constitution. The centre of gravity of mainstream American life can swing to religious conservatism more easily and abruptly than in Britain – one of the dangers of having a less secular civil society.

Yet, the religiosity of American public life should not be exaggerated.[126] One says this despite the emergence of the Tea Party, and its impact on the Republican Party. On the one hand, this reflects the growth of certain strands of Christian fundamentalism, partly in reaction to the rise of those Isla-mist currents that act as opponents of US foreign policy, and partly because the trend towards the adoption of greater freedom of individual life-style choices, especially sexual, has actually become stronger. Here the consumer-ized culture of the United States has been a significant spur. The end-result is that the political Right, determined to prioritize the defence of market neoliberalism and all that this brings with it, is pushed, however reluctantly, to accommodate itself to this radicalization of sexual life-style choices. This and other forms of social liberalism can comfortably coexist with neoliberal capitalism and the global hegemonic ambitions of the United States. As for the claims made by the upholders of the Civil Religion thesis, whatever limited credibility this might have had at some point in the past, it can only be further eroded by changing demographic patterns – the United States is becoming less white and less Protestant. Certainly, there are few pertinent lessons for India. The United States as we know it today is almost wholly a modernist construct. Its religious and social life embodies modernist values as few other societies do.

Religious pluralism in India is not in the least connected to the seculariza-tion or rationalization of consciousness, or to the privatization of religious affairs. Both Americans and Indians equate religious pluralism with toler-ance and secularity. But the mediations stressed are fundamentally different. In the United States, secularism is seen as a modernist ideal centred on indi-vidual freedom. In India, secularism is seen as an ancient ideal, and is most assuredly not centred on Westernized notions of individual freedom.

---

126 M. Lienesch, 'Rightwing Religion: Christian Conservatism as a Political Move-ment', *Political Science Quarterly* 31 (1982–83). The late 1970s and early 1980s were supposed to have been the period of rapid right-wing Christian revivalism in the United States. According to Lienesch, claims of such movements were greatly exaggerated. At their peak, listeners to the 'electronic church' numbered 10 million, not the 130 million claimed; Jerry Falwell's Moral Majority had at most half-a-million members, not the 3 million claimed. Nor do right-wing evangelists have as significant an impact on elections as has been suggested.

See also M. E. Marty, 'Religion in America since Mid-Century', *Daedalus* III (1982); R. K Fenn, 'Religion, Identity and Authority', in R. Robertson and B. Holzner, eds, *Identity and Authority* (Oxford, 1980).

The threads of religious pluralism in the US can be woven into the fabric of a Civil Religion that, it is then claimed, covers society. In India, the nature of religious pluralism, the history of religious conflict, the weakness of secularization in civil society, even the weakness of the secular state compared to that in the United States, all make the idea of an Indian equivalent to America's Civil Religion ludicrous. The virtue of the American Civil Religion was that it was more an invocation of God in its common symbols and forms than a sectarian invocation of Christ. In India, the conscious attempt to construct a binding Civil Religion will be another name for, or variant of, an aggressive and intolerant Hindu nationalism.

Secularism as Tolerance

The popular Indian view that secularism means or should mean tolerance is deeply misleading. We know how and why this view emerged.[127] This notion of secularism and secularization rests on three misconceptions: (1) It assumes that serious religious decline has not taken place, and cannot do so. Indian society is said to be permeated by religion. Moreover, the idea of secularization-as-decline is said to be intimately and ineluctably connected to the nature of Christianity, and to its historical trajectory. (2) Its notion of tolerance is utterly inadequate. (3) It involves a sociologically and historically misleading representation of Indian culture, and more specifically of Hinduism.

No society in the developing world, and certainly not India, can escape or retire from the project of modernity. This is most obvious on the economic and political levels, where the market and the apparatuses of the nation-state increasingly sweep aside the pre-modern structures that stand in its way, or push them to mutate or transform themselves in order to survive and flourish. On the cultural level the overall results are more 'mixed', and the range of possibilities greater than in the case of the levels on which the market and the state operate. But here, too, the impact has been profound. What has been said about the relationships between religion, culture, society and identity in the era of modernity applies (in its general thrust and principles) to India as well. There are important specificities – but they *qualify* the fact of secularization and its further possibility; they do not *negate* either. If anything, the desirability of greater secularization in India is stronger than in other countries. No country comes close to having India's scale or depth of religious variation, or stands to suffer more from a serious reversal and failure of secularization. There are no guarantees against this, but the very durability of the Indian democratic and secular state (however weak

---

127 See S. Chandra, 'Secularism and Indian Polity', in B. Chakrabarty, ed., *Secularism and Indian Polity* (New Delhi, 1990); H. Mukhia, 'Communalism: A Study in Its Socio-Historical Perspective', *Social Scientist* 1: 1 (August 1972); H. Mukhia, 'Communalism and the Indian Polity', *South Asia Bulletin* XI (1991).

the democracy and the secularity) is evidence of the strength of modernist efforts and processes. Can Indian civil society be further secularized?

There can be no deterministic answer, but the goal remains something to be fought for. The clear evidence of the growing institutionalization of Hinduism is also in its own way a testimony to the declining permeation of religion in society. Neither Hinduism nor Islam will follow the trajectory of Christianity. But unless one believes that Christianity is both the father of secularization in all its main nuances (decline, disengagement, rationalization) *and* the necessary correlate for its sustenance, there is no logical reason why further secularization must be a failure or an impossibility in India. If that were so, then the best that could be hoped for would be a permanent tension between a somewhat secularized state and a civil society that cannot be further secularized. While the idea of a 'separation of spheres' between the temporal–secular and the spiritual did emerge and develop in premodern Christian discourse, the notion of secularization-as-decline came much later, in the run-up to modernity. This particular seedling is not the unique gift of Christianity, but is much more the result of the emergence of an increasingly autonomous civil society.

If secularization first took place in Christian Europe, can it survive transplantation elsewhere? How strong is the relationship between Christianity and the secularization process? Even in explaining its origin, how much weight should one give to the Christian Reformation, to the developing capitalist mode of production, and to the Renaissance and Enlightenment? In what way were these processes linked? Weber's 'Protestant ethic' thesis assigned decisive impetus to the Christian Reformation – an eminently contestable claim.[128] For all its insights, if Weber's basic claim falls, then Christianity is not quite as strong a source of secularization, modernization and rationalization as he made out. The weight of Perry Anderson's explanation, for example, falls on 'the concatenation of antiquity and feudalism' – on the linkage between the Renaissance revival of the rationalist legacy of Hellenism and the special dynamism of western European feudalism.[129]

Christianity, *pace* Taylor, may only have had seeds of secularization within it; but, even so, what should we make of this? Hellenism, it can be argued, had stronger such seeds, and similar seeds can be found in ancient Indian philosophy and religious discourse. Many religious systems, insofar as their engagement with reality has led to developed doctrine, would almost certainly have such seeds. Peter Berger's claim that the seeds of secularization

128 See, among others, F. Braudel, *Civilization and Capitalism*, 3 vols (London, 1985); S. Amin, *Eurocentrism* (London, 1989); S. Eisenstadt, *European Civilization in a Comparative Perspective* (Oslo, 1987); S. Eisenstadt, 'The Protestant Ethic Thesis', in R. Robertson, ed., *Sociology of Religion*; M. Rodinson, *Islam and Capitalism* (Harmondsworth, 1974); P. Anderson, *Lineages of the Absolutist State* (London, 1979).
129 Anderson, *Lineages of the Absolutist State*.

lay in the Old Testament, to be revived by the Reformation, is extraordinary. According to him, only Christianity had the combination of ethical rational-ism, severe monotheism and an institutionalized church that could lead to secularization. Christianity is the master-key to modern history, the source of secularization, of individualism, of democracy itself.[130]

Since so much hinges on Weber's Protestant ethic in explaining the 'riddle of the origin of capitalism', and thus what many would insist is the primary source of secularization and modernity, one would have thought that most Indian scholars believing in the Christian incubation of secularization (and therefore its alien-ness to India) would rigorously evaluate the adequacy of the Protestant ethic thesis. But there is too much to lose in such further exploration. The idea of secularization as the gift of Christianity is largely taken as given. If it should appear more plausible that capitalist modern-ization (whose original impetus is not derived from Protestantism) is a real force behind secularization, then the intellectual case for the inapplicability of the decline thesis to India is weakened. Indian society will escape substan-tial Christianization; it cannot escape the uneven and combined process of capitalist accumulation. Furthermore, the weaknesses of secular–rationalist modes of thought may owe more to the absence of the equivalent of the European Renaissance than to the absence of Christianity.[131]

Yet, even if one conceded for the sake of argument that the origins of secularization lay in Christianity, and that the Protestant ethic argument is correct, Weber himself would have recognized that, even if it was not the original driver, capitalism had assumed the driving seat. Capitalist mod-ernization, not Christianity, would be the key source of pressure pushing for further secularization and rationalization. Where capitalism goes, some significant measure of secularization will also follow, no matter what our reservations about its durability in, or adaptability to, non-Christian climes.

The second and third misconceptions will be taken together, and the treatment will be brief. A long excursus on the 'nature of Hinduism' will be avoided. It is only after the rise of individualism and individual rights that the terms 'pluralism' and 'tolerance' obtained a strong positive connota-tion. This came about *specifically* in modernity. Yet the two terms have been effectively hijacked to describe a set of pre-modern circumstances in which such positive resonances simply do not fit. Pluralism as a principle of social and political organization emerged in the second and third decades of the twentieth century, as a late Enlightenment reaction to absolutist theories of the state and sovereignty, and in the context of democratic and socialist ideas

130 Berger, *Social Reality of Religion*. There appears to be considerable convergence here between the views of Berger and Charles Taylor.
131 For a corrective to the idea that 'ancient Indian culture', even its 'high culture', lacked a significant secular component, see A. Sen, 'The Threats to Secular India', *New York Review of Books*, 8 April 1993.

about and demands for autonomy. It had nothing to do with the absence or presence of centrally organized religions. Pluralism was related to ideas of 'social intentionality' and 'social design'.[132]

Segmentary, traditional societies are plural, decentralized and static, possessing a certain balance in their structures. Community social life is usually governed by rules of kinship or ritual. There is an ancient pluralism. But modern civil society has a different pluralism, based on an individualist moral culture that is also more secular. The institutional complexes of pre-modern societies are profoundly different from those of modern societies. The new kind of balances required among structures in today's civil societies cannot be achieved without the construction of secular institutions. The alternative in India would be institutions characterized by 'religious patrimonialism'.[133]

To talk of the ancient Indian, or more specifically Hindu, heritage of pluralism is to give a modernist and positive tone to a description that historically cannot bear such weight. Sudipta Kaviraj is perfectly right in saying of this traditional pluralism that it was not much more than the registration of variety.[134] To use his analogy: plant life is plural; it is not thereby tolerant. Tolerance in its positive sense means much more than coexistence.

Also, in ancient or medieval India, the absence of church–state conflict meant that states only had to relate themselves to different religious groupings – hence peaceful coexistence of a passive type, which promoted a certain kind of religious tolerance. The source for this was not just the nature of Indian society, but the character of state behaviour. All states, including the Islamic and the British, followed some version of religious neutrality. Religious segregation in society was the norm, and this was the basis for the tolerance-as-coexistence that prevailed.

Pluralism cannot mean positive tolerance except through conceptual slippages. Religious pluralism of a doctrinal and ritual kind is most strongly characteristic of what has been given the compendium label Hinduism. To imply that Indian tradition and culture always had a heritage of pluralism is really to imply that it is overwhelmingly moulded by Hinduism – a notion of culture that I have already criticized. But even if one were to ignore this near-identification of Indian culture with Hinduism, another series of unwarranted jumps in logic would have to be carried out.

---

132 P. C. Upadhyaya, 'The Politics of Indian Secularism', *Modern Asian Studies* 26 (1992).

133 A. Beteille, 'Secularism and Intellectuals', *Economic and Political Weekly*, 5 March 1994. Beteille mounts a vigorous defence of secular institutions (in both civil society and the state) against critics of modernity and secularism like T. N. Madan. Beteille correctly points out that what is really at issue is not a rejection of secularism or secularization, but the negotiation of the 'terms of coexistence' between the secular and the religious. What he does not add is that, if a secular arrogance of ambition is to be avoided, so too must be a religious arrogance of ambition. Indeed, the new 'terms of coexistence' will have to be weighted in very decisive ways against religious claims.

134 S. Kaviraj, 'Political Culture in Independent India', *Teaching Politics* VII: 1–2 (1989).

The plurality of beliefs, practices and rituals – ritual and *doctrinal* pluralism – is not equivalent to religious–doctrinal tolerance. And religious–doctrinal tolerance is neither equivalent to nor automatically leads to *social* tolerance. The most that can be said about claims for the doctrinal tolerance of Hinduism and the presumed doctrinal intolerance of the Semitic faiths is that both claims, if true, are stimulants (how strong has always to be historically and concretely discerned) to the emergence of different mixes of social tolerance and intolerance. If the monotheism of the Semitic faiths has an exclusionary thrust, it also has a thrust towards egalitarian universalism (the formal equality under God of all believers). If the multiplicity of gods and goddesses, and of forms of worship, in Hinduism encourages a measure of ecumenism, such multiplicity is also a precondition for the existence of the caste system. This is an elaborated system of social hierarchy (intolerance in any modern sense of the term, or tolerance on terms set by superiors) in which moral and religious relativism flourishes.

Of pre-modern India, Kaviraj had this to say: 'Coexistence of numerous local communities which would have liked to impose their ways on others had they the power to do it, is not equal to a situation of pluralism-tolerance. It is a pluralism which represents a powerless intolerance.' For Kaviraj, the internal structure of Hinduism is 'marked more by ineffective intolerance than an ideological tolerance of a positive kind. It led to peevishness and irritation more than mass violence.'[135] The agglomerative, absorptive and glutinous character of what has come to be called Hinduism should not be misconstrued as implying either a natural inclination towards syncretism or a natural propensity to dialogue with other doctrinal or religious systems, or a natural bent towards tolerance. In fact, Romila Thapar has gone further than Kaviraj, stating that ancient India was no haven of tolerance or non-violence when it came to religious conflict. Buddhists were persecuted by Shaiva sects, as were Jains in the south, but these obvious cases of intolerance were masked and 'dismissed as more of a sectarian rivalry rather than religious intolerance. It is argued that the Hindu community as a whole was not responsible for such acts but only one sect among its many.'[136] Moreover, for all Hinduism's claims to ecumenism in respect of beliefs and practices, the persistence of the caste system showed that here the intolerance was directed against the social origin of believers.[137]

---

135 Ibid., pp. 5–7. The late Ashok Rudra, one of India's more eminent Marxist academics, was even sharper. In his 'Myth of Tolerance', in *Seminar* 67 (March 1965), he stated bluntly that Hinduism 'has been tolerant only of such other ways of life and systems of thought and values which consented to let themselves be Hinduised in their fundamentals' (p. 25).

136 See particularly the three chapters in Part II of R. Thapar, *The Past as Present: Forging Contemporary Identities Through History* (New Delhi, 2014). The quote is on p. 121. See also D. N. Jha and M. Dube, 'A Brief History of Religious Intolerance in India', 24 December 2015, posted on the daily Indian news and opinion website, scroll.in.

137 Thapar, *The Past as Present*, p. 122.

The danger of accepting this elision between modern and pre-modern ideas of tolerance is the political disarming of our ability to fight against modern-day religious intolerances. While the myth of Hinduism's intrinsic and unique tolerance sets up an ideal by which one can appeal to 'good Hindus' to reject Hindu nationalism in the name of saving the essence of Hinduism, there is also the danger that Hindu communalism will be explained away as basically a *reaction* to other religious communalisms, since tolerance is supposedly the heart of Hinduism. We can fail to grasp the seriousness of the religious intolerances wracking contemporary India just as we exaggerate the strength of our historical, cultural and religious resources to fight it.

The seriousness of the danger can be exemplified by taking up certain arguments employed by Hindu communal forces. Two apparently winning arguments of Hindu chauvinists have been (a) for the need to rectify the humiliation felt by Hindus about the destruction of temples in the past by Muslim rulers; and (b) that, given the enormous number of such temples that were despoiled, the destruction of the Babri Masjid, and even a few more mosques, hardly balances the historical scales of justice.[138]

What is omitted here is any reference to the decisive changes wrought by modernity. In the past, the despoiling of any temple affronted those loyal to the temple in question. Given the caste-ridden and segmented character of Indian society, most temples so desecrated were places of worship for specific sects, castes and categories of worshippers, though a few had much more open access and wider fame. But the weakness of communication systems alone meant that the scale and depth of the humiliation felt at such acts was controlled and limited. Certainly, it could not compare with what is possible today. Both the scale and depth of anger and humiliation felt by Hindus in India (and even in the Indian diaspora in the West) is incomparably greater than it was at the time when such temple desecrations actually took place. Mass communications, the sharpening of identities and a host of other factors enable the construction of mass anger and emotion on a scale never imaginable before.

The same point applies to the second argument. No matter how many temples Muslim rulers may have destroyed in the past, all of them put together did not weld, and could not have welded, mass emotions among

---

138 While there are certainly numerous examples of Hindu kings destroying Buddhist, Jainist and Vaishnavite temples, Islam's origins as a religion of tribal warriors certainly gave it a 'conquistadorial' edge that distinguished it from the Indic religions, and this affected the behaviour of Muslim marauder-kings and the scale of their depredations in the subcontinent in the period of transition to more settled dynastic rule. Hindu communalists not only ignore shrine destructions by Hindu kings (which were considerable, though not matching the scale of early Islamic marauders); they also ignore the partially 'secular' motives behind such assaults, and usually elide the distinction between kings and ordinary Muslim subjects, implicitly holding the latter, as a community, historically responsible.

Muslims against Hindus in the way that the single campaign for the Ram temple and the destruction of the Babri Masjid has done in respect of Hindu sentiments against Muslims. No past act of temple destruction was ever perceived as, and could have hoped to serve as, a mass rallying cry, a platform for identity-affirmation on such a mass scale for Muslims against the hostile or threatening Other, the 'harbi kafir'.

The reason is simple enough. Modernity is, as never before, the era of mass politics, most certainly since the beginning of the twentieth century. Mass energies, mass collectivities and mass campaigns are forged as never before. Precisely because of the uniquely mass character of identity politics in the present, there is simply no comparison between the politics of symbolic humiliation in the past and that of today; between the politics of shrine-destruction in the past and of today; between the politics of religious identity in the past and today. There is a profound and qualitative difference in the intolerances of the past and those of today. The possibility for mass transformations for human good is also of a qualitatively different order to such possibilities in the past. In this century, both the meridian of mass political good (the institutionalization of political democracy) and the nadir of mass political evil (the horrors of Nazism) have been on display. They are testimony to the uniqueness of modernity and its double-edged potential.

If the intolerances of the present are of such a different order to those of the past, it is elementary wisdom to recognize that the tolerances of the past (negative tolerances at best) cannot seriously be expected to cope with the intolerances of our time. We need to construct new, more robust tolerances. India has its special heritage and its distinctive strengths. It would be foolish indeed not to use those resources. But it will not do to take refuge in extravagant claims about the unique power of the Indian genius, its culture and tradition. The struggle to cope with the problems of modernity will have to be fought on the terrain of modernity itself, and for the most part with the weapons forged in modernity.

We must be clear about our goals and properly assess our means. The notion of secularism or secularization-as-tolerance is neither a proper goal nor an adequate means. The secular state in India must mean a basic separation between state and religion, strengthened by further secularization of state laws, state apparatuses, state personnel and state policies. The effort to secularize civil society in India must mean an effort to reduce religious influence in civil society, reduce the importance of religious identity in much of the pursuits of everyday life, and the increasing optionalization of religious commitment. Overcoming obstacles to these goals is another story altogether. But knowing the direction we must take is some part of the battle won.

3

Communalism, Hindutva, Anti-Secularists: The Conceptual Battleground

Every discourse in India on communalism and fundamentalism, secularism and anti-secularism, Hindutva and its rejection, operates with preconceived notions about culture, civilization, Hinduism, caste, and their inter-relationships. Since these notions are insufficiently probed, they are often implicitly shared. It is not as if political and ideological opponents always or usually have markedly different understandings. Were that the case, Hindu chauvinists and communalists would not so readily attempt to pass themselves off as genuine nationalists or as true secularists, in contrast to Nehruvian 'pseudo-secularists'. Nor could they have succeeded to the extent they have in appropriating for their purposes anti-communal nationalist figures like Mahatma Gandhi. Nor indeed could that other breed hostile to secularism – the anti-secular anti-modernists (or the ambiguous modernists) – have disguised so easily the modernity of their posturings.

Civilization and Culture

Civilization and culture emerge as general social science concepts (independent nouns) in the West in the mid-eighteenth century.[1] Initially, culture was a synonym for civilization, and to this day a strongly culturalist understanding of civilization endures. This is particularly true of India, with distinctive consequences. Civilization contrasts with barbarism. The study of civilizations, then, has been the archaeological–historical study of how the first civilizations emerged and survived. It has also been the study of what sustains many a subsequent non-barbarous or civilized state of affairs. The second type of study has a stronger tendency to use a broader notion of civilization, loosening it from the study of highly specific social formations that characterizes the first approach.

---

1 Williams, *Keywords*, pp. 57–60.

That approach has been strongly historical and well rounded. Civilizations were seen as historical–geographical–economic–political–cultural–social complexes, and not primarily as cultural complexes. Indeed, the unities of such civilizations were seen as dependent on political, social and ecological–economic variables as much as on cultural ones. Such civilizations represent the first great harvest of the leap from ranked to stratified societies. Such social stratification emerged with a new kind of centralizing state in a still admittedly segmentary society, usually with alluvial agriculture helping to generate the necessary economic surpluses.

Colin Renfrew's defining characteristics of a civilization belong very much to this tradition of study. A civilization is an insulation against nature carried out in three ways: (a) insulation against the unknown, meaning a specific religio-ceremonial centre; (b) insulation against time – a writing script; (c) insulation against outsiders – urbanization, a city.[2] A civilization is necessarily characterized by significant asymmetry of power between centre and peripheries. While the cultural dimension of such civilizations can, and usually does, extend itself beyond the spatial and temporal confines of the civilizational cluster itself, it cannot do so ceaselessly. Even its *selective* continuity, or reproduction–transformation, must presuppose a material infrastructure related to its integrating factors of literacy, law and ritual.

Such civilizations emerge, rise, decline and fall. They are eminently historical entities. In such an approach, it would be largely meaningless to talk of any *Indian* civilization, let alone one existing through millenniums. There have only been civilizations *in* India, where India is not any 'natural' territorial entity, but simply an extrapolation backwards in time of the geographical space that came to be defined by British colonial rule.

The second, looser notion of civilization is decisively marked by specific intellectual traditions and discourses in the Europe of the eighteenth, nineteenth and early twentieth centuries, above all by Orientalism, and within it by the German Idealist and Romantic current, with its strong echoes later carried over to post-war American cultural anthropology. The Orientalism that emerged in the period of an ascendant imperialism represented a shift away from the Enlightenment principle of universal equality to the view of the easterner as a separate Other. It was not a complete break. The Other was Europe in infancy. It had a potential for reaching equal adulthood through the grace of colonial paternalism.

But the overwhelming thrust of Orientalist thinking was to endorse the idea of different civilizations with different essences, each evolving in its allotted sphere. The search for such civilizational essences, which were also cultural essences, led to specialized study of the ancient past, when civilizations supposedly existed in pristine form, revealing most clearly their

---

2 C. Renfrew, *The Emergence of Civilization* (London, 1972). See also M. Mann, *The Sources of Social Power*, Vol. I (Cambridge, 1988), p. 74.

essential properties. Two popular disciplines of the nineteenth century, the history of religions (dominated by Idealist philosophy) and comparative linguistics greatly encouraged this approach. It received a further stimulus from two other developing disciplines – biological evolutionism and physical anthropology – taking it in the direction of racial taxonomies.[3] The uniqueness of a civilization was related to the uniqueness of language and to the uniqueness of race, religion being the expressive core of culture–civilization. Language, race, religion became the vital triad. In India it became Sanskrit, Aryan, Hinduism.

Max Weber was to provide new sociological insights into Hinduism. But he was first and foremost a theorist of culture–civilization, and his notions were very much in the eighteenth- and nineteenth-century German tradition of understanding culture as intellectual development, both spiritual and mental. The decisive element in a culture was its world-view, as provided by magic, religion or science. These world-views were the 'switchmen' of civilizations, giving them their respective directional logics. Their dynamics unfolded both through the meanings imparted and in the 'elective affinity' of these world-views with the interests of particular social groups, which then became the main vehicle for the expansion of that world-view. They also influenced the 'practical ethic' of the religion in question, which in turn helped shape the personality of believers.

Many theorists of twentieth-century civilization of a Weberian cast saw civilizations as 'cultural visions' that shaped the activity of particular elites and established the premises of a society, its core values and beliefs. Culture/civilization here is more or less an intangible whole, supposedly built up over centuries around these core ideas and values. It has a soul, spirit, ethos or *mentalité* that remains basically unaltered. In a more materialist rendering that pays more attention to the infrastructure of culture and to the problems of cultural transmission, the virtual isomorphism of culture and civilization is averted. Nonetheless, civilization, above everything else, is said to have a cultural structure, which is the most important aspect of tradition.[4]

---

3 M. Rodinson, 'The Western Image and Western Studies of Islam' (written in 1974), in J. Schacht and C. E. Bosworth, eds, *The Legacy of Islam* (Oxford, 1979).

4 By his own confession, Mann is decisively influenced by Weber's 'general vision of the relationship between society, history and social action'. *Sources of Social Power*, Vol. I, p. 32. So, despite his earlier avowal of Renfrew's understanding of civilization and his repeated assertion of the importance of multi-factor causality, Mann falls prey to a typically Weberian tendency to collapse civilization into culture, even if he pays more attention to the 'organizational power resources' of ideological movements (religion). Mann's understanding of Hinduism is not so much the result of an extensive and impartial study of Hinduism but more a reflection of his desire to 'fit' the study of India and Hinduism into a preconceived structure – his ideological–economic–military–political (IEMP) power model, which is central to his book. So, for Mann, Hinduism is essentially Brahminism, which was the most remarkable 'normative pacifier' in human social history. India, he feels, has long had a cultural unity. However, because of the attention he pays to cultural infrastructure, this unity, he argues, is due more to practical Brahmin power, especially over rituals, than to the distinctiveness of Brahminical ideas and values.

Civilization is a 'structure of tradition' – that is to say, 'a persisting form of arrangements for the handing down of cultural substance (ideas and its products), within a great community'.[5] The transmission of the Great Tradition is carried out by the literati, and its schools and institutional networks; the transmission of the Little Tradition is carried out through local societal structures. Civilization is a relationship between society and culture defined by the latter, but society is where the vehicles of cultural transmission are necessarily located.

At least throughout modern Western intellectual history, there have also been significant contestations of the anthropological, cultural and relativist approach to the study of civilizations, an insistence that change (sometimes dramatic) is as basic as continuity to the cultural dimension of the civilizational entity in question, and that the continuity of political structures may often better explain the continuity of the cultural tradition itself. For example, it is the remarkable continuity of much of China as a political unit, only intermittently broken, that best explains what we call the continuity of Chinese civilization. In the discourse on Western Christian civilization and its 'continuity', many would see Christianity as the enduring essence of Western civilization or society. But there would also be many dissenters from this view. Insofar as the notion of 'Western civilization', across its numerous internal differentiations, is employed by them, it aims to suggest little more than a cultural homogeneity of sorts, indebted undoubtedly to the centuries-long infrastructure of Christianity – a monastic-episcopal economy, dominant educational institutions, an army of missionaries – outlasting its association with the Roman Empire. But this approach refuses to elevate the concept of Western civilization into a primary tool for social understanding and historical investigation for that part of the world.

In modern India's intellectual history, the painting of the notion of civilization has been much more monochrome, for two reasons. First, there was no equivalent of the European experience of Enlightenment humanism

---

But even his emphasis on the infrastructure of culture is lost on most Indian intellectuals who believe in the continuity of Indian civilization. For them, Brahminism has been much more important than Brahmins in explaining India's cultural unity.

One of the most interesting efforts to theorize the notion of a continuous Indian civilization is R. Kumar, *India: A 'Nation State' or A 'Civilization State'?* Occasional Papers, Nehru Memorial Museum and Library, May 1989. Kumar insisted that a civilization be seen as an integrated economic social, political and cultural phenomenon characterized by distinctive traits emerging out of the way its particular mechanisms of wealth-creation, especially its principles of social and political organization and distinctive 'texture of moral values', all knit together. On closer inspection, however, most of the weight for establishing the distinctiveness of Indian civilization comes to rest on expected notions of the longevity and dominance of the caste system, and on the uniqueness of the moral vision associated with Hinduism understood as a 'loosely structured religious system'. These are claims qualified or disputed in my text.

5 M. Singer, *When a Great Tradition Modernizes* (Delhi, 1972). Robert Redfield shares Singer's view of civilization as a 'structure of tradition'. R. Redfield, 'The Social Organization of Tradition', *Far Eastern Quarterly* XV (1955).

and universalism, which promoted more secular and multiform understandings of civilization. Second, the imperatives of colonial resistance decisively marked the terrain and direction of discourse and historical evaluation by Indian intellectuals. In the period before the emergence of a national political movement, cultural self-affirmation required some assertion of Indian 'superiority' in the only sphere where it could be plausibly asserted – that of its cultural–spiritual traditions, which defined its ancient *and* enduring civilization. This was resistance to the West within the discourse of Orientalism, reversed Orientalism becoming an affirmative cultural nationalism.

Later on, for the practical purposes of developing a political (and cultural) nationalism, some discourse of commonness had to be constructed. The concept chosen to bear this burden, so umbrella-like that it could be endorsed by all despite their variant interpretations of its content and foundations, was 'Indian civilization'. The notions of India's civilizational unity and cultural essence were constructions motivated by the political and cultural needs of a developing Indian elite. They did not emerge out of serious empirical historiography. Nor was there ever serious research to objectively corroborate or refute these themes.

Once the idea of the continuity of Indian civilization achieved the force of an axiom, its natural correlate was the idea of India's cultural coherence or unity. How else to explain this continuity in the absence of a coherence itself derived from an essence? The idea of an enduring and cohering essence was vital. Mere uniformities would not be enough to determine a unity. All pre-modern societies are segmentary ones, but these still have their distinctive specificities: the capstone state in China, the more modest state systems in India. The search for essences in India focused on two candidates usually treated as deeply interconnected – the religion of India, and the caste system.

This search for essences was entirely characteristic of Orientalism and of the European Romantics. Societies and cultures had determinate natures, just as Enlightenment science had disclosed a principle of order in the natural world. Human societies were essentialist, objective systems in which the principle of order had to be designed and the designer uncovered. Since culture subsumed society (culture was the more important term), it was cultural essences that had to be discovered. These clearly lay in the pre-colonial past of India. Upon this Indian intellectuals, whether aware or unaware of the influence upon them of Orientalist thinking, were also fully agreed.

But pre-colonial India still accounts for an extraordinarily long stretch of time. Where was its essence to be located? In pre-British India? Pre-Islamic India? Aryan India? Or pre-Aryan India? In short, competing essentialisms have persisted, with no conclusive way of adjudicating between them. However, the major competition has been between those subscribing to Hinduism as the essence of Indian culture–civilization, however the term

'Hinduism' has been conceived, and those claiming that India's essence is represented by a 'composite culture'.[6]

England was the birthplace of Indology, and it was largely empirical. Early admiration for India's intellectual heritage by Orientalists like William Jones, Henry Colebrooke and Charles Wilkins gave way to the more negative appraisals of politicians and administrators like James Mills and Thomas Macaulay, partly to justify the newer phase of post-conquest consolidation. So, after 1850, enthusiasm for Indology shifted to France, and particularly Germany, where it linked with the Romantic reaction against the Enlightenment. It was this Orientalist discourse that most affected subsequent cultural discourse in India. Indology in Germany was closely connected to German Idealism, which focused on philosophy as the heart of culture. The Indian essence was to be found in its ancient philosophical texts, most notably the Upanishads. Or, as in one succinct formulation: 'India is indebted to Schlegel for proclaiming it, with Greece and Germany, the most philosophical of nations.'[7] Unlike post-Enlightenment European philosophy, Indian philosophy had not separated itself from religion or metaphysics. Even its atheistic currents were reactions within this larger framework. European Romanticism prioritized the search for inwardness as the essence of religion. If religion was the natural essence of Indian culture, then a moving spirit, a mystical ethos, was the essence of Indian religion. Such a view not only promoted the belief that Hinduism was the essence of India's civilization–culture, but made Brahminism the defining characteristic of this Hinduism.

At any rate, Indian philosophy had become central to Indian culture. Like nowhere else, it has remained so in the self-perception of most Indian intellectuals, who declaim upon the uniqueness of the Indian experience and legacy. Even those subscribing to the composite-culture view arguing that India reflects fusion of multiple religio-cultural influences have often felt the need to invoke the notion of an enduring ethos expressing itself throughout Indian history, perhaps most clearly articulated and understood in its ancient texts. India was and is the world's most spiritual nation![8]

---

6 R. Khan, ed., *Composite Culture of India and National Integration* (Ahmedabad, 1987); R. Khan, *Indigenous Intellectual Creativity: The Ethos of the Composite Culture of India* (Kyoto, 1978).
The Brahminical view of Hinduism contains two versions of Hinduism's origins. It emerges to prominence in north India with the rise of Aryans (whether or not Aryan presence is explained as indigenous or through migration from the north-west); or in the interaction between Aryans and pre-Aryans.
7 R. Schwab, *The Oriental Renaissance* (New York, 1984), p. 165. For a critical look at Indian Philosophy, see D. P. Chattopadhyay, *What is Living and What is Dead in Indian Philosophy* (Delhi, 1993); D. P. Chattopadhyay, *Indian Philosophy* (Delhi, 1988); D. P. Chattopadhyay, *Indian Atheism* (Delhi, 1991).
8 Even someone as committed to the compositeness of Indian culture as Nehru talked of the 'subconscious mind of India', striving centuries-long for fulfilment–embodiment, and finding it periodically in the reign of 'great rulers' who understood this essentialist spirit–ethos of India. True to Nehru's ecumenism, such rulers were not only Hindu. They included Ashoka (Buddhist), Akbar and Sher Shah (Muslim) and Chandragupta and

The composite-culture argument has never been an adequate counter to the thesis of an essentialist Hinduism. The idea of fusion introduces the Islamic and other experiences, and thus more strongly allows a partly evolutionary understanding of Indian culture. But it still leaves too many unanswered questions. Does the fused substance have more of the properties of one component than the other? What first made this fusion possible, if not the unique and natural syncretic genius of its earliest and original component, Hinduism?[9] Furthermore, as a characterization of what we can call the Indian cultural space, it is no more accurate than its rival, an essentialist Hinduism.

The notion of a cultural space enables us to avoid talking of Indian culture as a unified, singular entity. What we call a cultural space or zone always comprises numerous cultures coming together in complex yet distinctive ways. It is an open, historical, to-be-empirically-determined question as to which sub-space or component is more important and influential than others – for how long, for how far, and in what way? A cultural space in reality is always much more chaotic and messier than are the theories or abstractions about it. The wider the cultural space territorially or in terms of its inhabitants, the more this is so. The idea of a composite culture is simply too neat, too 'composed' a depiction.[10]

Harsha. J. Nehru, *The Discovery of India* (Delhi, London, 1956); J. Nehru, *Glimpses of World History* (Delhi, 1982).

9 Gandhi is quoted (Nehru, *Discovery of India*, p. 136) as saying: 'Indian culture is neither Hindu, Islamic or any other wholly. It is a fusion of all.' This gave Indian culture a broader base, but for him, more than for Nehru, its foundations were unmistakably Hindu.

D. E. Smith, another believer in the compositeness of Indian culture, also says 'Hinduism has indeed provided the essential genius of Indian culture; this cannot be denied.' D. E. Smith, *India as a Secular State* (Princeton, 1963), p. 378.

The debate on composite culture began in earnest in the 1940s, in reaction to the movement for creating Pakistan. It resurfaced in 1959–62, as responses to a series of nationalist studies brought out by the Bharatiya Vidhya Bhavan in India, and to official nationalist studies in Pakistan, notably the four-volume I. H. Qureshi, ed., *A History of the Freedom Movement, Being the Story of Muslim Struggle for the Freedom of Hind-Pakistan,1707–1947*, (Karachi, 1957). The 1962 Indian History Congress devoted its annual session to the question of India's 'composite culture'.

The Constitution, while endorsing the notion of composite culture, also privileges Hinduism, and so-called Hindu culture as its core. Thus, while Article 350A recognizes the necessity for instruction in mother tongues for linguistic minorities, Article 351 stipulates that the Union 'promote the spread of the Hindi language ... as a medium of expression for all the elements of the composite culture ... by drawing wherever necessary or desirable for its vocabulary, primarily on Sanskrit and secondarily on other languages'. A Sanskritized Hindi, not Hindustani (which is shaped by the historic Hindu–Muslim interface), was made a principle medium for promoting a composite culture. See K. M. Chenoy, 'Armed Forces in Northeast India', in R. Samaddar, *Cannons into Ploughshares: Militarization and Prospects of Peace in South Asia* (New Delhi, 1995). See also the two subsections in this chapter on 'National Movement and Constitution' and 'Unprincipled Proximities and Personal Law'.

10 See the subsection in Chapter 2 on 'Culture and Society: The Problem of Order'. It may be noted that those holding to an essentialist Hinduism are cohorts in the 'double fusion' outlined in that subsection.

Even if we were to accept that a religious system was the single most important determining element in a cultural space or sub-space before the advent of modernity in India, this would still not result in the neat synthesis of different religio-cultural uniformities. What is today called Hinduism was itself so diverse that what existed was an enormous multiplicity of cultural spaces and sub-spaces influenced by the principles of behaviour associated with local sects, not by the ordering principles of wider (regional or trans-regional) religious systems. Though Islam possessed a greater degree of uniformity, here also it was the local manifestations of folk or lived Islam that were more important than the ordering principles of an abstract High Islam.

Yet folk Hinduism did not meaningfully synthesize with folk Islam. The artistic embodiments of India's 'cultural synthesis' in art, architecture and music took place at the elite or court level. There was interaction between Hinduism and Islam, between the caste order and the mass of indigenous Muslim converts. The public space of everyday economic and political–administrative transactions was decisively influenced in its norms and values by the social conjunction of high political authority in the hands of Muslim rulers and their allies, and Hindu controllers of craft, production and commerce. The family and domestic space was where religion and the sacred held effective dominance. For pre-modern entities, the norms of the sacred are more important than the norms of the secular and mundane. This more private and meaningful sphere was largely insulated, and remained so despite the efforts and achievements of Bhakti and Sufi saints and mystics. These were at best the exceptions proving the rule. Even their products were for the most part absorbed into a developing Hinduism.

Adjacency and insulation marked the coexistence of Muslims and Hindus, though the caste system always had more influence on Islam (Low and High) than Hindu philosophical doctrine ever did. This did not mean, however, any major merging of ritual patterns within castes. Rather, many Muslim groups (especially artisans) were incorporated as sub-castes, while certain elements of caste-related ritual also entered in a limited way into Muslim households. This was a world neither of sharp polarities and divisions nor of cultural synthesis or social merger.[11]

A cultural zone also has a distinct cultural infrastructure or network of organizational means whose efficacy cannot be separated from its relationship to state power. So a religious system also influences culture *because* it influences the state. Where religious power is concentrated, it is more likely

11 I am in general agreement with Sudipta Kaviraj's characterization of the everyday interface between Hindus and Muslims in pre-modernity. Kaviraj talks of 'fuzzy communities' and 'fuzzy identities', striking metaphorical generalizations, though the actual realities of a given cultural or social space could also reveal instances of less than 'fuzzy', and more than 'fuzzy', communities and identities. S. Kaviraj, 'Religion, Politics and Modernity', in U. Baxi and B. Parekh, eds, *Crisis and Change in Contemporary India* (New Delhi, 1995).

to shape the state and the cultural zone. As it is, Hinduism is such a diffused phenomenon. Separated from the Islamic court, the claim that Hinduism, nonetheless, was a defining influence on Indian culture must imply its integration with caste, the one form of social organization that had a palpably significant effect on Indian life and even on 'outsiders'. The claim must also make of Hinduism's essence an ethos, which, as such, is therefore all-pervading and unstoppable.

Christianity probably had more accumulative influence in pre-modernity over its cultural zone than Hinduism over its 'home terrain', because of its relative doctrinal uniformity, its superior infrastructure and its generally closer connection with state power. It was more able to provide overarching values for Europe's segmentary societies than Hinduism for India's segmentary societies. Contrary to the conventional view, Christianity had more to do with preserving that nebulous entity, Western civilization, than Hinduism did with preserving the even more nebulous entity of Indian civilization.[12]

Caste and Hinduism

Yet the case for the indissoluble connection between Hinduism and Indian civilization was made first by Orientalists, and then by nationalist intellectuals. If the civilization was to be seen as enduring, then the durability of a unified Hinduism had to be unarguably established. One effective way was to convince oneself and others that Hinduism was the 'oldest living faith', and thus India the oldest continuous civilization. What could be powerful and convincing evidence for this claim?

The discovery that the Vedas were the world's oldest texts, transmitted through generations, could certainly be a source of such affirmation, provided the pervasive and formative influence of their philosophical contents on Hinduism through the ages could also be established. Of course, if the Vedas had been read with a more sociological eye, in conjunction with other non-Brahminical or 'second-order' (as they were called) traditional texts, such as Puranas, Buddhist and Jain texts, what emerged would be a more

---

12 Prominent ideologues of Hindutva (but not only them) assign the cause of 'continuity' of India's civilization–culture to the dominance of society over the state (and the dominance of Hinduism in society). This is in contrast to the Chinese situation, where, far more plausibly, it is the greater significance of the state in relation to society that is said to explain cultural (Confucian) civilizational continuity. The states of ancient India are illegitimately reduced to the status of being utterly 'residual', when it is far more sensible to recognize that, within its range, state power is never residual, though its importance vis-à-vis society and its institutions is always variable. In the cruder formulations of Hindutva ideologues, the residuality of the state is said to obey a definite geographical or religious pattern – for example, as between the state systems of East and West, or between Semitic and non-Semitic religious areas. J. Bajaj, 'Introduction'; K. N. Govindacharya, 'Future Vistas'; and S. Gurumurthy, 'The Inclusive and the Exclusive' – all in J. Bajaj, ed., *Ayodhya and the Future India* (Madras, 1993).

accurate and complex picture of major conflict between Brahminism and Shramanism.[13] For the Vedas to play this promotional role for Hinduism, they also had to have an essentialist interpretation. Not surprisingly, within philosophical Hinduism, Vedanta was elevated in importance, and within Vedanta the monism of *advaita* (non-dualist) doctrine was elevated. This was more the preoccupation of nationalist Hindu intellectuals than of earlier Orientalists.

Even if, for the Idealist Orientalist, Hinduism was the mind or ethos of Indian civilization, further confirmatory evidence at the level of social organization was by no means unwelcome. This time, the enduring and 'living' evidence was presumed to be caste. In a move paralleling the construction of the category of Hinduism, caste, too, had to be constructed as a pan-Indian and unified category. Orientalists of the eighteenth and nineteenth centuries, and modern Orientalists like the French structuralists Louis Dumont and Madeleine Biardeau, linked this to the ideology of the Vedas. However, the Vedas talk of varna, but do not mention what is widely understood as, in practice, the caste system – the system of hierarchical jati clusters.[14]

Hinduism, then, was above all the mentality associated with caste. The empiricists among Orientalists focused on jati, the idealists on varna. Both reinforced the idea of an essential, irrational or arational India, even if one perceived this as negative and the other as positive.[15] The essence of India was either external–tangible or internal–intangible. If the latter, then it was no longer subject to the danger of disconfirmation by the requirement of 'adequate' verification. India's essence just is, and always has been.[16] An

---

13 Shramanism is a compendium term for a variety of Buddhist, Jaina and Ajvika sects, all sharing an opposition to Brahminism's beliefs and practices. By 1000 AD, Brahminism had advanced at the expense of Shramanism, but the latter continued in other forms, including Puranic religions, Bhakti, Vaishnavism and Shaivism. R. Thapar, 'Imagined Religious Communities? Ancient History and the Modern Search for a Hindu Identity', *Modern Asian Studies* 23 (1989).

14 L. Dumont, *Homo Hierarchicus* (Delhi, 1988); M. Biardeau, *Hinduism: The Anthropology of a Civilization* (Delhi, 1994). Dumont and Biardeau are modern because they stress the universality of the structure of the mind, and are Orientalists because they see a diversity of cultural essences (themselves rooted in the mind). They see Hinduism's unity, despite its diversity, as resting in core ideas of hierarchy.

The Sanskrit term varna means 'colour', and came with the Aryan migration, where the Aryans were distinguished from the Dasa (meaning those of darker colour). The components of threefold division within the Aryans – priests, warriors/aristocrats and commoners – were all to be separated in status, and not assimilated with Dasas (perhaps for fear of losing Aryan identity), thereby helping to create a fourth category within the varna order of *shudras* distinct from the Brahmins, Kshatriyas and Vaishyas. So, in this sense varna became a legitimizing overlay, and also a novel reinforcement of the jati system, emphasizing at first the Brahmin and non-Brahmin bifurcation, and later probably being crucial in introducing the purity–pollution principle. See R. Thapar, *A History of India*, Vol.1 (Harmondsworth, 1986).

15 Later, Indian scholars promoting a neo-Hinduism, like Sarvepalli Radhakrishnan, former president of India, gave a more rationalist explanation of this essence while retaining its positive value. S. Radhakrishnan, *The Hindu View of Life* (London, 1964).

16 '[C]onstructions of 'Hinduism' are indeed abstract models which never fit all the

internalist essentialism of Hinduism is conjoined to an internalist rendering of the meaning and purpose of caste. Varna is the conceptual purity of
caste, the core of caste being hierarchy. The next step is the idealization of
hierarchy and varna. The tendency towards idealization of hierarchy found
its most famous expression in Dumont's *Homo Hierarchicus.*[17] Caste as the
jati system was the corruption or degeneration or the historically concrete
evolution of varna. Caste, then, was essential to India, and unique. But in its
purest and truest sense it was also strongly positive.

Not all Indian advocates of an essentialist Hinduism accepted the centrality of caste to Hinduism. Some were prepared to accept its separate and prior
genesis to varna, and to see it as an unfortunate accretion that should in fact
be categorically dissociated from Hinduism. Their version of an essentialist
Hinduism would be even more mystical and ethereal, for it could not even
point at this unique social institution as its distorted expression. Caste is here
ignored, rather than rationalized.

The justification of varna has strengthened over the last two centuries,
symptomizing the intellectual popularization of the Brahminical conception
of Hinduism, itself the natural corollary of reform Hinduism. Yet since the
1940s, with the rise of more empirical studies, the idea of caste as a unified
and pan-India category of the country's past has become increasingly unconvincing. The fourfold classification schema of varna seems so obviously the
typical stratification pattern attending the transition from ranked to stratified societies anywhere that it might seem difficult to believe in any specific
connection to the Indian peculiarity of jati. That fourfold classification represents political–military elites; the religious elite; urban low-status groups,
like merchants and artisans; and rural low-status groups, or the peasantry.
A tension often emerges between the first two, expressing itself in variable
institutional and ideological forms. But the Vedic text, the Bhagavad Gita,
does provide the philosophical grounds which not only connected the varna
system to jati but because the former was supposed to be divinely inspired
could provide considerable legitimacy and stability to the hierarchical grada-
tions and internal boundaries of the jati or caste system.[18]

---

actual data of history and frequently appeal to the "Hindu spirit" or some other "reality"
that must be found implied in the data or beneath the surface reality and beneath the
surface meaning attributed to the data by believers, and are therefore also not empirically
verifiable.' R. W. Baird, 'On Defining Hinduism as a Religious and Legal Category', in
A. W. Baird, ed., *Religion and Law in Independent India* (Delhi, 1993), p. 46.

17 See note 14, above. Dumont's notion of the relationship between hierarchical categories (that which encompasses and that which is encompassed, or between larger and
smaller) cannot deal properly with asymmetries of power. His emphasis is on order, not on
oppression. Dumont's study was excessively sympathetic to caste hierarchy. Many Indian
writings, though not as famous or influential, have been more idealizing of caste.

18 Plato's 'noble lie' justified the division between producers, soldiers and guardians
(philosopher kings) as 'natural' since it is based on God-given inborn substances. In the
Gita's version of a noble lie caste hierarchies are supposed to be in accord with divinely
distributed moral qualities so that all must follow their caste determined duties in this life
but there is a future escape route with the processes of karma and rebirth determining

Nevertheless, the view that caste is the precipitate of Hinduism's ideology, an all-encompassing Brahmin-dominated system of hierarchy, has immense problems. Even in our times, M. N. Srinivas reminds us, caste is local in character, and its system of hierarchies is not only qualified by segmentation sideways, but exists as a regional cluster. It is, says Srinivas, only by putting it into the 'Procrustean frame of varna' that one can try to make it national.[19] Caste as ideologically a unified whole based on the principle of hierarchy, whose defining criterion is the purity–pollution relationship is an idealist construct of Dumont and his followers. Those observations of theirs which lend themselves to empirical verification do not receive such validation.[20] Nor does Dumont's claim of Brahmin opposition to and superiority over Kshatriya secular power (the superiority of a purity-defined status to a power-defined status) receive much empirical support. The record on the ground is too varied. Indeed, notions of purity are themselves diverse, and not always expressive of a social hierarchy. They also express a direct relationship between worshipper and deity.[21]

In fact, upward corporate caste mobility at local levels has also been a feature of Indian rural life through the ages, where such possibilities of upward movement were related to factors affecting the local distribution of power, in village and village clusters. In later studies, Srinivas pointed to numbers, property holdings and, in more contemporary times, literacy as factors enabling lower-caste groups – but not untouchables – to move upwards, by adopting 'higher-status' rituals and declaring themselves higher castes. So the locally or regionally 'dominant' caste was often not the Brahmins, or those ritually and religiously defined as such.[22]

The category of the wholly impure – untouchables – is a later accretion to caste, suggesting that the purity–pollution principle is itself a later accretion. Its authoritativeness and spread must have been partly linked to the spread

---

future life possibilities. This comparison between the injunctions of Plato and the Gita appears in M. Nanda, 'Ambedkar's Gita', which was kindly made available to me before its subsequent publication in *Economic and Political Weekly* 3 December 2016.

19 M. N. Srinivas, *Social Change and Modern India* (Delhi, 1966). 'Caste mainly exists and functions as a regional system' (p. 3).

20 Sanskritization means emulation by lower-ranked castes of the behaviour and rituals of upper-ranked castes to secure enhanced status. M. N. Srinivas, who first postulated this with reference to a Brahminical model, has accepted that there are a variety of such models, not only referring to Brahmin but also to Kshatriya castes, at the political apex, that is to say, Kshatriyaization. So Sanskritization does not mean confirmation of a singular Brahmin-dominated caste system, though it does suggest that a more singular Hinduism, strongly influenced by Brahminism, is steadily in the making. The spread of purity–pollution hierarchization is also only partial.

21 C. J. Fuller, 'Gods, Priests and Purity', *Man* 3 (1979). 'Purity and pollution ... define an *idiom* by which respect to Gods is shown' (p. 470). Concepts of purity–pollution are not exhausted by concepts of high and low status, but are 'part of the conceptual apparatus of a highly developed religious tradition' (p. 473).

22 S. S. Jodhka, *Caste* (New Delhi, 2012), pp. 37–42. In parts of north-western India, Brahmins, because poor, were treated as menial castes. See P. Tandon, *Punjabi Century: 1857–1947* (New Delhi, 1961), p. 77.

and consolidation of Brahminical influence within a pre-existing as well as much wider and more variable jati system. Here the line of division is sharp and rigid, and connects to the principle of pollution, even if not only to that. Those in the lower castes, but not untouchables, suffer from impurity in a relative sense. Those who are untouchables are impure in an absolute sense, as well as in a relative sense, with some sub-castes ranked below other sub-castes even though all are in the fold of untouchables. So even those seen as untouchable sub-castes by others higher in caste rankings may not see themselves as defiled, but will see others below them as even more defiled. In the state of Kerala there are those who are not merely untouchable but those whose shadow must not fall on upper castes; and then there are those who are deemed 'unseeable'! Moreover, although there is variation in the proportion of those considered untouchables (from less than 1 percent to close to 30 percent in different states), as well as the intensity of and the forms taken by the defilement that is imposed upon them, untouchability is now a pan-Indian phenomenon, and helps to reinforce the fact of the caste system, understood in all its diversity, as supposedly unique to India.

Diverse patterns of caste hierarchies are accompanied by diverse caste ideologies. There is no overarching Brahminical ideology defining either Hinduism or caste. But the connection between a Hinduism infused (even if in variable doses) by Brahminism and the existence of untouchability is much more difficult to contest or dismiss. Indeed, untouchability has provided an exceptionally strong anchor for the persistence of caste and its finely graded system of inequalities. Psychologically speaking, the category of untouchables, themselves divided into higher and lower sub-castes, both stabilizes and gives emotional compensation to those trapped in the overall system – there is invariably someone even more inferior in status than yourself! This structure of graded impurity is of course sustained by a host of more material factors that put untouchables or Dalits at the bottom of the distribution of wealth and power. The question therefore arises whether the removal of untouchability is compatible with the preservation of the rest of the caste system. B. R. Ambedkar was not the only Indian reformer to believe that one could not be removed without the other. But he was the first Dalit leader to articulate this perspective so strongly, and to insist that Hinduism itself (inescapably Brahminical for him) could not survive without the caste system.[23]

Moreover, that Brahminical ideology has in the last two hundred years spread wider and faster than others, in the process undergoing modification itself. But, leaving that aside, a more materialist interpretation of the caste system in all its diversity, privileging non-ideational factors, is more

---

23 For the best annotated critical version of B. R. Ambedkar's famous text *Annihilation of Caste*, see the text edited and annotated by S. Anand of the Navayana Press (2014), which also carries a powerful introductory essay by Arundhati Roy, 'The Doctor and the Saint', dissecting the relationship between Ambedkar and Gandhi.

appropriate. Romila Thapar has suggested that caste, as the dominant organ-izational structure of Indian society, has changed in relation to changes in environment, access to technology, distribution of economic resources, and kinship patterns. But the ideological rationale for it was relatively constant. Thapar plausibly suggests that the very strength of its ideology of hierarchy (uniquely linking inequality to birth and untouchability) probably reflects the depth of resistance to it.[24] Nicholas Dirks also rejects Louis Dumont's view that a single principle of purity–pollution explains caste hierarchies, whose sources are more diverse.[25]

Where Thapar's argument needs further clarification is in the claim that caste was the dominant organizational structure of ancient India, and there-fore even more so of medieval India. It is only in recent times that forest systems became distorted to incorporate other kinds of socio-economic rela-tions, whether of the market or of caste. But for most of their history, caste relations are to be decisively distinguished from forest–tribal relations. The caste is not a tribe, but emerges because of the transition from nomadic and tribal to settled agrarian systems. Territorially speaking, the 'dominance' of caste is more recent; demographically, it has a longer history.

The tribe is above all a community of ancestry, real or mythical; the com-munity of caste (jati) is not. It is a closed, endogamous status group best understood as a community of function, or more narrowly as a 'marriage circle' – a cluster or network related by lineage or clan, or perhaps in some other way. This remains an area of dispute among even materialist investi-gators of the origins and nature of caste.[26] But the important thing is that caste must be distinguished from tribe (except in more recent times), and that the caste system belongs to settled agriculture and not really to shifting agriculture.

The importance and spread of caste to India is, then, connected to the importance and spread of agrarian systems. This insight provides the possibility of moving towards a more accurate assessment of the histori-cal significance of the caste system. Through the 1950s, 1960s and 1970s, Indian materialist historians were strongly influenced by prevailing currents of Marxism. They were preoccupied with understanding the conditions for the transition to capitalism from pre-industrial agrarian systems. Most histo-ries of ancient India (from the late Vedic age onwards) and of medieval India assumed without much justification the actual and progressive dominance of settled agrarian systems, and therefore the relative ubiquity of the caste system – or, more accurately, of caste systems.

---

24 'A caste society is characterised by hereditary groups ordered hierarchically, asso-ciated with particular marriage and kinship relations and often viewed as performing services for each other.' R. Thapar, 'Which of Us are Aryans?' *Seminar* 364 (December 1989), p. 17.

25 N. Dirks, *Castes of Mind: Colonialism and the Making of Modern India* (Princeton, 2001).

26 M. Klass, *Caste* (Philadelphia, 1980).

A minority current in contemporary Indian historiography has correctly pointed out that the issue is wide open. Indeed, the balance of historical evidence suggests that the agrarian transformation of most of the area we now call India is only a few centuries old.[27] Claims for the widespread dominance of the caste system are greatly exaggerated, at least until more recently. More importantly, it has exhibited fluidity, fuzziness and variety, though efforts at singularizing and unifying its hierarchies have long existed, becoming stronger in more recent times.

What makes caste seem unique to India, whereas the 'bounded' and therefore multiple, and often hierarchical, character of clan and kinship structures is universal, is perhaps the fact that caste is the most *finely graded* form of stratification (both within and between classes) as compared to anywhere else in the world. Insofar as caste at some point in its existence begins to derive sustenance, and thus justification, from Brahminical Hinduism as its particular form of religious sacralization, it appears distinctively and only Indian. But similar forms of clan- and lineage-based stratification within and between classes, receiving other forms of legitimizing anchorage, are widely prevalent. In the Indian case, caste precedes Brahminism and has had a wider geographical spread, indicating that its most powerful roots are materialist rather than ideational and cultural. It is not a singular, all-encompassing system, anymore than is Hinduism. It has been for most of its existence spatially limited, with forest and nomadic India excluded from the jati system. But as caste has spread, developed and changed, so too has Brahminism, the two partially and variably intertwining. Brahminism has provided ideological sustenance for caste formations; and the latter has impacted upon and altered the former, in the direction of greater inclusivity with regard to rituals, beliefs and practices.

The greater adaptability and usefulness of Brahminism to caste in agrarian systems is part of the answer to its overcoming the challenge of Buddhism. It cannot be accidental that Buddhism survived in the northern, eastern and southernmost peripheries of the subcontinent, but not in its more inegalitarian and settled heartlands. Similarly, it has thrived most in the egalitarian village systems of Southeast Asia, but has been only a counter-tradition in the more stratified socio-economic systems of China and Japan. Yet caste, for all its variant forms of imbrication with Brahminical doctrine and values, has always been more important than that doctrine. Islam and Christianity have had to adapt much more to the caste system (s) than to Brahminism.

The history and historiography of Hinduism have long been closely connected. The hows and whys of the construction of the very category of

27 M. Rangarajan, *Environmental Issues in India: A Reader* (New Delhi, 2008), Section I, on pre-colonial India. See also K. K. Trivedi, 'Estimating Forests, Wastes and Fields c. 1600', *Studies in History* 14: 2 (1998). British development of the railway system and canal networks for newly settled areas reduced forest cover at a speed much greater than in the past.

Hinduism have helped to shape the understanding of what it is and was. There have been three basic approaches to characterizing Hinduism.[28] The first was shared by Orientalism and the nationalist Indian response to it. Both talked in terms of differences and essences – of essential differences. Orientalism created a spiritual Hinduism by using prior Brahminical discourse, but in doing so valorized it, along with textual, philosophical Hinduism. Indian intellectuals made worthy the characteristics that Orientalist empiricists saw as unworthy. But they did not dispute the Brahminical

---

28 The sociological approach to the study of Hinduism owes one of its biggest debts to Weber, one of the first major thinkers to attempt a systematic investigation of the 'Hindu social system', and the evolution of Hinduism from ancient through medieval to current times. He looked at the orthodox and heterodox teachings of religious intellectuals, and sought to establish the general characteristics of the Indic religions. Weber spins a sociology out of three concepts: tradition, charisma and rationality. So he talks of three types of religious specialist, three modes of authority, and three kinds of social action. He provided many useful and new sociological insights.

But Weber did not aim to provide a definitive study of the Orient, and its religion and culture. His researches were not free of presupposition, but meant to illuminate and confirm what he already assumed – the uniqueness of Occidental rationalism, for which he had a clear line of explanation. The Orient was characterized, above all, by the absence of the 'spirit of capitalism', and explaining this absence was what Weber was most concerned about.

Like the Romantics, Weber believed in an 'essential India' and in the 'unity of Indian culture–civilization' – a unity provided above all by the Brahminical belief system. But, unlike the Romantics, he was sceptical of this essentialism surviving without grave disruption in the 'disenchanted world' of modernity. Though Weber was aware of popular Hinduism, he saw it as subordinated to overarching Brahminical beliefs in transmigration, karma and the caste system, which for him formed an ubiquitous, coherent whole. He was guilty of too much grand theorizing and too little empirical study. Since for him cultural change preceded and explained social change, the sources of cultural change had to be understood above all else. And this principle of change pivoted on the question of the mentality of believers. Consequently, it was non-verifiable.

Weber's is a study of how salvational strategies emerging from the mentality of believers contributed to the promotion of rationalization processes, where rationalization was understood as disenchantment, specialization and knowledge-accumulation. For Hinduism and the other Asian religions, Weber held that 'the world remained a great enchanted garden ... No path led from the magical religiosity ... to a rational, methodical control of life. Nor did any path lead to that methodical control from the world accommodation of Confucianism, from the world-rejection of Buddhism, from the world conquest of Islam, or from the messianic expectations ... of Judaism.' Thus Indian asceticism, unlike Calvinist Puritanism, was not an asceticism of work. M. Weber, *The Sociology of Religion* (London, p. 270).

Modern-day Weberians, including Mann, have followed Weber in generally seeing religion as a 'belief system', and in assuming that, for the Indian subcontinent: (a) caste was ubiquitous; (b) Hinduism is a singular religious system decisively shaped by a Brahminical contemplative soteriology; (c) this soteriology, anchored by the caste system, has been the great 'normative pacifier' explaining India's continued vulnerability to outside political invasion, and its peculiar imperviousness to external cultural influence.

All these notions are eminently contestable. Mann's chapter on India and Hinduism in the first volume of his otherwise remarkable work, *The Sources of Social Power*, is unsatisfactory.

Göran Therborn points out that Weber's sociology was born of the marriage of German historicism and Austrian marginalist economics, where the former was an idealist tendency promoting a notion of culture as above all a 'value concept'. G. Therborn, *Science, Class and Society* (London, 1980), pp. 279–83.

and singular rendering of Hinduism as such. There was also a difference between the Romantics and many an Indianist. The former saw the essential India (or 'East') as the original depository of what had been lost – not just the Other of Western man, but its other more 'spiritualized' part. The 'recovery' would help constitute a new wholeness of being. The Encounter with Hinduism was also a search by Western man for his other or inner self – not just an intellectual quest, but a therapeutic one.

The initiative for this Encounter and earlier engagements never came from India. It always came from the outside – Greek, Chinese, Arab, and then European. As Wilhelm Halbfass points out, 'There are no Hindu accounts of foreign nations and distant lands. The Indian cultural "colonization" of East and Southeast Asia and the spread of Buddhism are not at all reflected in Sanskrit literature. Even the Muslims ... appear in vague and marginal references.'[29] It was only after the impact of the British, with the Encounter forced upon them, that many Indians began exploring the possibility of some kind of cultural synthesis.

As earlier defensiveness gave way to a more aggressive affirmation against colonialism; the search for a synthesis along the lines followed by European Romanticists gave way to a much stronger assertion of India's intrinsic spiritual–cultural superiority, plain and simple. One current among Indianists – traditional Hinduism, or orthodox Brahminism – had in any case never been that interested either in the Encounter itself or in responding to the West. Reform Hinduism, or neo-Hinduism (which reinforced a Brahminical-leaning understanding of the nature of Hinduism), was much more concerned with so responding, and it did so using a discourse partly shaped by Western precepts. Often, the universalist claims of the West brought forth universalist claims on Hinduism's behalf. There is more Western thought and influence in neo-Hinduism than vice versa.[30]

---

29 W. Halbfass, *India and Europe* (New York, 1988), p. 182. '[W]e find no serious philosophical debate with Islam in traditional Hindu literature' (p. 182). There is only 'silence' and 'evasion'. Outsiders are neither a strong Other nor an inspiration.'The "otherness" is a negative and abstract one; it does not contain any concrete cultural or religious challenges' (p. 187). In the encounter between Islam and Hinduism, the major effort at mediation comes through Sufism, stronger in India than anywhere else that Islam has spread. Islam found it easier to engage in dialogue with non-Brahminic, Shramanic traditions than with Brahminism. The only major (but failed) attempt at a philosophical synthesis of Islam and Brahminism comes from the initiative of the great Mughal ruler Akbar in his Din-e-Ilahi. British rule has far more dialogue with Brahminism, and stresses its importance for 'understanding Hinduism'.

30 Ibid. Halbfass distinguishes between traditional Hinduism and neo-Hinduism: 'What distinguishes Neo-Hinduism and Traditionalism are the different ways they appeal to the tradition, the structures they employ to inter-relate the indigenous and the foreign, and the degrees of receptivity vis-à-vis the West' (p. 220). Neo-Hinduism does much more reinterpretation, guided by Western models and values. It is striking that the major spokespersons on neo-Hinduism, Vivekananda, Aurobindo and Radhakrishnan, wrote primarily in English. Though Gandhi had neither a serious interest nor capability in philosophy, he felt compelled to philosophize, since India's culture and identity were somehow supposed to be linked to its unique philosophy.

Faced with a vast range of rituals, worship and beliefs not readily explainable through Brahminical discourse, there were and remain different views of how best to understand the relationship between Brahminical and lay Hinduism. How inclusive was Brahminism? How did it dominate? Through an ethos discoverable in the ancient and sacred texts and expressed in a true Brahminism, which need not be identical with the current practices and beliefs of existing Brahmins? The origins of popular Hinduism were also in dispute. Was it a degeneration of textual Hinduism, or could it have existed separately from and even prior to Aryan Brahminism, gradually coming into a broadly unified cultural–religious field marked by the 'spirit of Hinduism'?

The lowest common denominator in this understanding of Hinduism was that it was a Brahmin-dominated religious system paternalistically gathering sects to itself so that multiple texts, doctrines, deities and rituals could flourish. But there was nonetheless an overall coherence making of Hinduism, both now and for centuries past, a 'single religious fabric'. Such an understanding promoted a certain kind of history of Hinduism. This was philosophical and art history, or the study of iconography and symbolism. It did not stimulate a sociological study of Hinduism, and only later anthropological research somewhat qualifies this established research perspective by bringing popular Hinduism closer to the centre-stage.[31]

A second approach concedes more ground to folk or popular Hinduism. In most versions there is talk of a Great Tradition, which is more doctrinal and uniform, and pertains to the upper social strata; and of a Little Tradition, encompassing the diversity of folk or lived Hinduism. But the Great and Little Traditions interact, the former influencing the latter more than vice versa, fostering the emergence, ideologically speaking, of a graduated hierarchy of religious values, practices, beliefs – even of deities. Here the metaphor of the 'jungle of Hinduism' is more widely used, and Brahmins are seen as the forest's guardians (equipped with the more powerful tools of Brahminism) rather than as the gardeners of this jungle. While a more singularized Hinduism is emerging, this process is not best understood through categories like the Great and Little Traditions when applied to the past. Even today, the degree of internal uniformity or coherence implied within the Great and Little Traditions, respectively, is much less than the usages imply.

Attempts at empirical validation in fact reveal variant and competing Great Traditions. Moreover, the so-called Little Tradition is so diverse that to categorize such diversity under a single label, 'Little Tradition' or 'Popular Hinduism', misleadingly implies that it nonetheless 'belongs' to one religious field, itself broadly partitioned into two interlinked categories of the Great and the Little. A more radical and sceptical approach expresses

---

31 Thapar, 'Imagined Religious Communities?'

its unhappiness with these analytical terms, and is even more emphatic in its stress on the importance of popular Hinduism.[32]

This second way of understanding Hinduism differs from the first in rejecting the idea of a Brahminical–philosophical–mystical essence. It pays far more attention to the anthropology of 'Hindus', and thus to popular, lived Hinduism. In its most radical variant, the heart of this popular Hinduism is considered to be the worship of deities who can exercise power over humans in desired ways for the worshipper. Worship is a 'contract of power', with obligations on both sides. Here, Hinduism is an extremely worldly religion, though like all developed religious systems it has its philosophies and its more ethereal speculations. But, for all its differences with the first approach, here also there remains the rock-bottom insistence that Hinduism is a *comprehensible whole*. It does possess at the most fundamental level a necessarily abstract but real unity, which expresses itself in shared organizing principles and structures.[33]

Only a third approach categorically rejects the idea that Hinduism, even today, can be understood as a comprehensible whole. It is simply too diverse, not only in terms of its range of beliefs and practices, but also with respect to variations in its understandings of supposedly shared concepts, such as the existence of differing notions of karma and transmigration–reincarnation. The term 'Hinduism' is best seen by social scientists with no strong political or cultural axes to grind as a compendium category, or as a plurality of 'intersecting clusters' with no central or essential belief or practice that is commonly shared.[34] As Thapar says, 'The position I would take is that there were Hindu religions (in the plural) using Hindu simply as a term that defines an area; and possibly up to a point defines the culture

---

32 C. J. Fuller, *The Camphor Flame* (Delhi, 1992).

33 Ibid. Fuller's is a contemporary anthropological, not historical, study. He readily subscribes to the view that, caste is pan-Indian, and he assumes that this has long been so. Caste, after all, is the expression of the deepest unifying principle of Indian society, namely hierarchy. Fuller believes in a 'mainstream Hinduism' in which Brahminism is the single most important 'evaluative norm'. Bhakti is not an egalitarian deviation from it. It embodies the same quest for individual release – salvation, but makes it more democratically available. It does not socially confront caste. It maintains the unequal guru–disciple relationship so common to mainstream Hinduism. Most of the founders of Bhakti sects and movements were ascetic renouncers, indicating its concurrence with traditional status values, where the renouncer is evaluated as higher than the Brahmin.
This is an interesting and provocative thesis. Certainly, Bhakti has been incorporated over time into a more Brahminized Hinduism, itself undergoing a loosening and modification of its Brahminism. Whether Bhakti has always been like this is best left for historians to decide. The historian Romila Thapar has a much broader view of Bhakti, stressing its diversity of beliefs and practices (Thapar, 'Imagined Religion Communities'). Political scientist Sudipra Kaviraj sees Bhakti as the exception to mainstream forms of the Hindu–Muslim interface (Kaviraj, 'Religion, Politics and Modernity').

34 The compendium view is that of Romila Thapar ('Imagined Religious Communities'), while the second is advanced in W. Doniger, *The Hindus: An Alternative History* (Noida, 2009).

but not completely.'[35] Wendy Doniger rejects the Hindu nationalist claim that Hinduism was unique to or dominant in India (as a geographical unit) at *any* time in history, whether before the Indus Valley civilization, in the time of the Vedas, before the rise of Buddhism, or after its decline in the fifth century CE. Her clusters approach 'does not endorse any single authoritative or essentialist view of what Hinduism is; it allows them all. Any version of this polythetic polytheism (which is also a monotheism, a monism and a pantheism) including this one' is not to be taken as authoritative.[36] The very notion of Hinduism was quasi-political in origin, and this has directed research into it, and made the compendium understanding of Hinduism the least popular (among Indianists) of contending interpretations.

But it would be mistaken to leave it at that. The most important *process* that has been taking place over the last few centuries, greatly accelerated since the twentieth century, has been the construction of a more singular Hinduism, or what Thapar has called a 'syndicated Hinduism'. This syndication process is not the monopoly of any single cultural or political 'syndicate'. It has had a number of sources, and those participating in its construction have had different understandings of how it had to be done, and why. But the most chauvinistic construction of monolithic Hinduism existing today can trace an important part of its lineage to earlier currents of reform Hinduism and neo-Hinduism. For Thapar, this syndicated Hinduism is a garbled form of Brahminism, with a 'motley of values' from other sources, like the Bhakti movements and Puranic rituals.[37]

No assessment of contemporary Hinduism should ignore its intrinsic diversity, and hence the resources it possesses to counter this ongoing singularization. Nor should it fail to see that this process is already taking place and has gathered pace. Indeed, on balance the centripetal efforts unleashed by those constructing a more essentialist and uniform Hinduism have made significant headway. Those content to emphasize the natural diversity of Hinduism – the insuperable obstacles to the construction of a Hindu community and therefore to the consolidation and growth of Hindu communalism – need to think again. What has already been achieved in this

---

35 R. Thapar, 'Interpretations of Indian History', in G. Sen, ed., *Perceiving India*, Delhi, 1993.

36 Doniger, *Hindus*, p. 29. In the end Doniger contents herself with analysing and portraying certain selected themes and practices contained within, or dispersed among, some of these clusters. Despite Doniger's obvious admiration for the diversity of beliefs and practices of Hindus, and for their 'worldly wisdom and sensuality', unsurprisingly, her book was banned by the Modi government not long after it came to power in 2015, as a distorted and offensive portrayal of Hinduism.

37 R. Thapar, 'Syndicated Moksha', *Seminar* 313 (September 1985). According to Thapar, syndicated Hinduism draws largely on Gita, Vedantic thought and some aspects of the Dharmashastras, as well on other sources. For a more recent and powerful restatement and elaboration of her arguments on syndicated Hinduism, see Chapter 9, 'Syndicated Hinduism', in Thapar, *The Past as Present*.

respect is dangerous enough. Whether or not things can get worse is an eminently political question.

Modernity provides multiple possibilities. The forces of secularization and democratization lead to a more relativized Hindu identity, to an acceptance of a more modest social role for Hinduism, and to greater plurality and choice even in religious behaviour, in keeping with Hinduism's naturally large range of variations in this respect. A variety of other forces, both communal and non-communal, push for a more singular religious system. Ultimately, this process is of less significance than the issue of secularization of civil society and the secularity of the Indian state. Even a singular Hinduism need not present a serious danger if it is accompanied by a reduction in the importance afforded to religious identity in social life – in other words, by greater secularization. The long-term evolution of what we call Hinduism is not, in itself, the most important political issue. What is are the ways in which distorted interpretations of Hinduism, and of India's past and present, are used to construct false and dangerous political, social and cultural ideals, and programmes for their achievement.

Hinduism's Mystique of Tolerance

Hinduism's mystique of tolerance rests on two central pillars, which on closer inspection disclose extremely shaky foundations.[38] It is based on the plural coexistence of multiple faiths, religious practices and beliefs both within 'Hinduism' and between it and the 'non-Hindu' religious systems; and it is based on philosophical doctrine. In neither case do 'facts' speak for themselves. Tolerance is neither axiomatic nor self-evident. 'Facts' were interpreted to mean incontestably self-evident truths, and both the interpreters and the interpretations belong to the period of the Encounter between East and West, and to its aftermath of reform Hinduism and neo-Hinduism. The mystique of tolerance is a modern construction to serve modern purposes.

The 'constructors' did recognize that, if their judgement of overall tolerance was to stand, then it had to represent a balance between that religious system's ideology (here taken to mean simply beliefs, doctrines) and its social structure. What was remarkable, however, was the way in which obvious intolerances in both domains was ignored or rationalized away. If caste was the social structure associated with Hinduism, how could its obviously intolerant character be wished away? Yet it was, usually through its rationalization as a degeneration of a pristine system of order: varna. Take this remarkable disclaimer by Sarvepalli Radhakrishnan: 'The institutions of caste illustrate the spirit of comprehensive synthesis characteristic of the Hindu mind with its faith in the collaboration of races and the cooperation of cultures. Paradoxical as it may seem, the system of caste is the outcome of

---

38 See also the subsection 'Secularism as Tolerance' in Chapter 2.

tolerance and trust.'[39] Swami Vivekananda, Gandhi and Sarvepalli Radhakrishnan all justified the historical references to caste and varna, claiming that caste later degenerated. They rejected caste in this form, insisting that only in its pure form (varna) was it central to Hinduism. But they remained silent about how varna, though a historical phenomenon, could nonetheless be conceptually pure. However necessary a system of order might be, and however useful and positive it might be deemed, all historical systems of order have their defects and their patterns of oppression, subordination and exploitation. Moreover, as historical systems they are necessarily subject to change, and always encounter some degree of resistance from those subordinated. They can be stable but not harmonious. All ideological attempts to paint them as harmonious result in a social bias towards notions of tolerance defined on elite terms.

Even when the claim refers only to religious tolerance, not to a wider social tolerance, it is still not sustainable. Strong rivalries between Brahminism, Buddhism and Jainism have been characterized wrongly as minor sectarian rivalries within a common fold. As Thapar reminds us,

> The insistence on the tradition of religious tolerance and nonviolence as characteristic of Hinduism, which is built on a selection of normative values emphasising Ahimsa, is not borne out by historical evidence. The theory is so deeply ingrained among most Indians that there is the failure to see the reverse of it when it stares them in the face. The extremity of intolerance implicit in the notion of untouchability was glossed over by regarding it as a function of caste and society.[40]

What most distinguished pre-modern India from other parts of the world was not tolerance, but the scale of its religious pluralism – a pluralism that has never meant much more than religious coexistence. Such coexistence was found elsewhere and in other histories, but nowhere else embodied by a comparable range and intricate variety of beliefs and practices. However, everywhere the general terms of religious coexistence are substantially a function of the relationship between political and religious elites, for both strive to secure popular loyalties, and are thus competitors for power, however much the arrangements for organizing that competition may vary. Those terms change when the relationship changes. This has been the history of religious pluralism in India, as much before as after the advent of Islam. Religious coexistence in India has been a sociological phenomenon, not primarily a religious one. Ignoring this leads to improper conclusions. And even here one must not elide the history of religious intolerance in the past. There were religious and sectarian antagonisms in ancient times between

---

39 Radhakrishnan, *Hindu View of Life*, p. 93.
40 R. Thapar, *Cultural Transaction and Early India* (Delhi, 1987), p. 15.

Brahmins and Buddhists, Shaivites and Vaishnavites, Shavism and Jainism. The notion of Hinduism's 'innate' tolerance was a construct initially of Westerners like Francois Bernier, Johann Gottfried von Herder, and even Immanuel Kant, as well as of Orientalists like William Jones, influenced as they were to some degree by the Romantic glorification of ancient India. Coming later were the nineteenth- and twentieth-century Indian champions of Hinduism's 'unique' tolerance – Dayanand Saraswati, Ramakrishna Paramahamsa, Swami Vivekananda and others.[41]

Insofar as religious conversion is seen as some kind of obstacle to religious harmony, and therefore to coexistence, much has been made of Hinduism's refusal to convert, said to derive from its doctrinally plural nature.[42] Yet Brahminism and many a 'Hindu sect' have engaged in conversion. This is so obviously the case that the widespread insistence that classical Hinduism (pre-modern Hinduism) abstained from conversion is another example of that wilful blindness that elsewhere leads many to proclaim the natural tolerance of Hinduism despite the existence of the caste system and of untouchability. There is no way, for example, that Hinduism could have spread to Southeast Asia, to become as influential as it did for centuries, without such conversion practices. The ludicrous alternative is to believe that the overwhelming bulk of Southeast Asian followers of Hinduism were the descendants of an original Hindu migration.

The point is not that Hinduism does not convert, but that its conversion process is very different from that of the Prophetic religions. There is rarely a fixed point of conversion, or a formal mechanism.[43] The will to convert existed, but Hindu social arrangements – the absence of church and caliph – did not provide much of a basis for coercive mechanisms to emerge capable of carrying out such an ambition. Too much should not be made of this

---

41 See D. N. Jha and M. Dube, 'A Brief History of Religious Intolerance in India', 24 December 2015, posted on the daily Indian news and opinion website, scroll.in

42 Ambedkar has argued in *Annihilation of Caste* that Hinduism did transform itself to become pan-Indian, especially after the decline of Buddhism began. If it later moved away from being a 'missionary religion', this was primarily because the caste system itself presented the biggest obstacle. Inculcating beliefs and practices in new converts is not as important as their social emplacement in the new religious community. Here the difficulty was in what caste or sub-caste one should place the new recruit. Ibid., p. 254.

43 Currents in neo-Hinduism such as the Arya Samaj, being a more Semitized form of Hinduism, have introduced a formalized system of conversion – the Shuddi, or purification ceremony. Today, explicitly Hindutva currents carry out what they call *ghar wapsi* or 'returning home'. This is conversion presented as a re-conversion to an original Hinduism, but takes the form of a purification ritual. That is to say, the conversion represents a shift from being of impure faith to the purity of Hinduism. The contempt displayed for other faiths does not sit well with claims about the remarkable tolerance of Hinduism so strongly espoused by the acolytes of Hindutva.

Proselytization is more a function of social factors than of doctrinal impulses. This is why Indic religions have proselytized in their own fashion, while Zoroastrianism turned sharply inwards because of its distinctive history. The strictures against conversion are so severe that the very survival of the Parsi Zoroastrian community is at stake. There are fewer than 90,000 Parsis in the world today.

absence. Even in the Semitic religions, conversion was primarily through processes not involving coercion. But that Hinduism lacked such coercive arrangements, and that conversion was more exemplary than emissary in character, did make it different in important ways from Christianity and Islam. Hinduism did not require one to 'invade' another space or to 'reject' it. It has had no equivalent, after all, to the jihads and the Crusades.

Nonetheless, the connection of Hindu religious elites to secular political elites – in other words, the question of power – was certainly important in explaining the spread of Hinduism in Southeast Asia and elsewhere. The adoption of forms of Hinduism by local rulers would undoubtedly have hastened even the exemplary process of conversion among a king's subjects. And the elite adoption of such Hinduism was often connected to calculations of how it might enhance their social, political and cultural authority.

Other factors no doubt help to explain conversion at the popular level. These are all matters for historical-sociological investigation. But there is little room for the view that Hinduism lacked an impulse to spread and convert. Even within South Asia, Brahminism expanded through distinctive processes of accommodation and inclusion. Here again, provided the picture is not overdrawn (lived Christianity and Islam have also involved major accommodation to pagan and non-Islamic practices, beliefs and rituals), there is an important difference between Brahminism and the Semitic faiths, the former having had a much greater flexibility in its processes of incorporation.

But tolerance is not an alternative name for this flexibility, or internal coexistence of variant practices and beliefs, any more than it is the name for an external coexistence between sects and religions. The issue of coexistence of different religious communities is simply too complex to be grasped adequately by a notion of tolerance. Moreover, neither pluralism nor tolerance can have the same meaning in pre-modernity as they have when they are connected to modern notions of equality and democratic rights.[44] In pre-modern India, states may have been 'tolerant' of religions, but justice was based on a principle of inequality. Religious and other minorities might have enjoyed protection and special rights, but were not on a par with majorities. Under Islamic rule, it would not be correct to see Hindus as a collectively oppressed 'majority' since Hinduism itself is comprised of many minorities.

Brahminical Hinduism's claim to doctrinal tolerance is based on its distinctive approach to the question of truth. Unlike the revelatory religions, it advances no propositional truth claims. It does not do without a notion of

---

44 How can a traditional pluralism 'which does not involve any theory of consent or responsibility ... be called even remotely democratic?' is the apt poser in S. Kaviraj, *Political Culture in Independent India*, seminar paper for the Indian Political Science Conference, Patiala, December 1978. 'Traditional Hinduism presupposes an irreducible cosmologically established inequality of human beings and a fundamentally hierarchical structure of society which leaves little room for the mutual recognition of free persons and their individual rights and choices.' Halbfass, *India and Europe*, pp. 410–11.

truth altogether, but operates with a much more flexible one than the revelatory religions. Correspondingly, it can avoid the sharp polarity of notions
of good and evil more typical of the soteriologies of Christianity and Islam.
Good and evil are seen as different facets of a common entity, and ultimate
quests are seen in terms not of the final triumph of good over evil, but of the
transcendence of both. This is a soteriology conducive to contemplation,
not activism.[45]

Doxa is not as important here. Hinduism is marked much more by a
process of dialogue with itself, a kind of internal philosophical ecumenism.[46] But if this is a form of philosophical tolerance, it also expresses a
form of philosophical intolerance: internal dialogue is important, but not
dialogue with others, or with other 'truths'. What, then, is the notion of
truth in Brahminical Hinduism? Are there elements or degrees of truth in
other religions? Or are there equal, multiple truths? Though Vedantism can
be interpreted as subscribing to the latter, it most certainly plays around
with the former notion. Indeed, there is a strongly held notion of truth
being one, yet having many levels, so that not all people can have the same
perception of truth or of reality. An egalitarian relativism is here partnered,
even subsumed, by an overriding arrogance.

This describes both Hinduism's understanding of society and its relationship to other religious doctrines. Thus, different individuals (and groups)
occupy different 'levels' in relation to the ultimate truth, which is in principle an attainable object. Different people are at different stages of spiritual
growth in the quest for perfection, and these differences are somehow
connected to, and reflective of, the individual's actual condition of life.

This philosophical Hinduism is not syncretic in terms of religious doctrine, but essentialist. It does not enter into dialogue with other truths, but
avoids such dialogue, or even the preparatory manoeuvres for a philosophical
synthesis.[47] You have your truths and I have mine – and mine is the deepest

---

45 If the frame of mind this inspires among believers has its merits, it also has its
problems. Liberation theologies or their indigenous equivalents remain alien to Brahminism, with its authorization of varna and caste. But it is not alien to India. Ambedkar's
Buddhism can be understood as an indigenous form of such liberation theology. See
G. Omvedt, 'Hinduism, Social Inequality and the State', in D. Allen, ed., *Religion
and Political Conflict in South Asia* (Delhi, 1993). Omvedt also points out that 'anti-
Hinduization' movements, though widespread, tend to be invisible because they neces-
sarily lack a single focus. They take a variety of forms – Dalit struggles, Veerashaivism,
Sikhism, tribal movements, etc.

46 While Vivekananda, Aurobindo and Savarkar seek to effect a philosophical closure
of sorts, Gandhi and Tagore are truer to this internal ecumenical philosophical tradition.

47 By the nineteenth century, European philosophy had been substantially secularized.
'True' philosophy was separate from religion and metaphysics. It was also open-ended.
Not so Indian philosophy. In the Hindu renaissance of the eighteenth and nineteenth centuries, even the earlier traditions of critical argumentation against religion and metaphysics
were largely bypassed. Indian philosophy, with exceptions like Lokayata, contains finished
doctrinal structures not open-endedly 'asking questions and pursuing knowledge'.
Of the ancient, enduring philosophies, Greek philosophy continues to be of far more
contemporary relevance than Indian, undoubtedly because it is more secularly grounded.

truth! That is its credo. The essence of this Hinduism is also the essence of all religions. This 'doctrinal tolerance' does not seriously reflect on other 'truths', but merely includes them hierarchically or perspectivally. Halbfass, in describing the interface between traditional Hinduism and other religious doctrines, had it right.

This process illustrates the potential and the limits of the traditional Hindu way of dealing with 'heterodox' teachings. It leaves room for many different views and standpoints, but always tends to include them in hierarchic or perspectivist schemes, and to subordinate them to one ultimate truth – frequently that of Advaita Vedanta. The 'other' teaching is usually not recognized in its otherness, but claimed as an aspect of, approach to, or aberration from the truth contained in its own doctrine.[48]

Such a claim of doctrinal tolerance not only disguises its distinctive intolerance, but justifies a belief in its own superiority. The claim that both Hinduism and Indian culture are uniquely characterized by a 'unity in diversity' is but another form of this same mask.[49] Even the composite patriotism of Indian nationalists fed into this distorted catholicity of a Brahminical Hinduism.[50] The great redeeming grace of Hinduism lies not so much in

---

Ancient Greek religion had no notion of transcendence comparable to that in the Indic religions. See Chattopadhyay, *What is Living and What is Dead in Indian Philosophy*.

48 Halbfass, *India and Europe*, p. 191. Hinduism is 'all religions in one', not 'one religion among many'. Other religions accepting inter-religious differences of a fundamental kind may each claim to be the best. Philosophical Hinduism, especially in the hands of practitioners of neo-Hinduism, will simply not accept such fundamental differences. It therefore pushes not for any modern form of secular coexistence, nor for confrontation, but for an 'inter-religious understanding' on its own terms.

49 The unity-in-diversity argument often endorses a hierarchical and ultimately Brahminized conception of unity. Bengali incorporates the notion of *adhikari-bheda* – of each caste, sect, religious community having its distinct norms (dharma) and niche in a hierarchical structure. Many religious intellectuals have played around with this perception, such as Ramakrishna and Rabrindranath Tagore, in his Swadeshi phase. It was given a more philosophical cast by some writings of Vivekananda and Radhakrishnan. The notion of 'composite culture' tends towards this hierarchized conception of 'unity-in-diversity'.

50 There were also differences among proponents of neo-Hinduism. For Vivekananda, the philosophical monism of Vedanta was decisive, and the 'true' Brahmin remained his human ideal. For Radhakrishnan, Hinduism in its deepest sense was a 'feeling' beyond morality and metaphysics. For Gandhi, the essence of religion was morality and truth, though his understanding of the latter would undergo evolution. From an initial commitment to 'God is truth', he later committed himself to 'Truth is God'. He moved from a more personal notion of the ultimate to a more impersonal one, closer to the Brahminical philosophical tradition of belief in a Formless Essence or Cosmic Spirit – a non-embodied, all-pervasive consciousness beyond morality. This was Hinduism as the eternal, all-encompassing religion.

All three subscribed implicitly to notions of Hinduism's intrinsic, if unstated, religious superiority. All opposed conversion (though for different reasons), indicating their deep unease with modern notions of individual rights. Only Gandhi, the most self-questioning of the three, would seriously try to move away from his earlier position, when he had believed that 'Hinduism was the most tolerant of all religions' and that 'what of substance is contained in any other religion is to be found in Hinduism', to a more tortured realization that such claims were incompatible with any genuine notion of the equality of all religions. Looking for a common essence to all religions, Gandhi would find it in

its philosophy or in its Brahminism as in the simple ecumenism of its largely non-Brahminical and popular forms of existence.

Hindutva

The closest English translation of the term 'Hindutva' would be 'Hindu-ness'. But it is a broader term than Hinduism, and connects to the kind of answers given to the questions: Who is a Hindu? What are the properties that are constitutive of Hinduness? It was in the period of colonialism that religious communities began to be sharply defined. Who did the defining and how they did it became major political issues serving definite political interests. If British colonialism had an interest in defining an India of different religious communities that shared few cultural characteristics, and were often at loggerheads with each other, anti-colonial nationalists had their reasons for defining and understanding matters differently.

This issue was obviously connected to matters of nation and nationalism. Nationalists had many more reasons to claim that India had been a nation, culturally if not politically, submerged if not actually realized, long before British rule. To have accepted that it was British rule that constituted an Indian nation in any meaningful, unified sense of the term would have been politically and emotionally disarming. Emerging nationalisms invariably invent a past for themselves. The first phase is the stipulation of a strong and enduring cultural nationalism. The questions 'Who is a Hindu?' and the 'Who is an Indian?' were inescapable ones that required answers, in this process of constructing competing versions of cultural nationalism.

---

his constructions of truth and non-violence. But his understanding of these terms would remain imprisoned within the idiom of Hinduism. Nonetheless, with genuine sensitivity, Gandhi would say, 'Tolerance may imply a gratuitous assumption of the inferiority of other faiths to one's own and respect suggest a sense of patronizing whereas ahimsa teaches us to entertain the same respect for the religious faith of others as we accord to our own.' M. Gandhi, *Collected Works XLIV* (Ahmedabad, 1964), p. 166.

According to one biographer, after 1930 Gandhi forswore any statement that might suggest the superiority of Hinduism. J. F. Jordens, 'Gandhi and Religious Pluralism', in H. G. Coward, ed., *Modern Indian Responses to Religious Pluralism* (New York, 1987). At the same time, Gandhi's self-questioning was also reflective of a profound self-obsessive streak, wherein he basically argued with himself rather than carrying out serious intellectual and rational engagement with others. The truth was what he perceived it to be at any particular moment, and it was this that guided him. A landmark study of Gandhi's political and spiritual thought, with the latter guiding the former, is K. Tidrick, *Gandhi: A Political and Spiritual Life* (London/New York, 2008). This iconoclastic study has never received the attention it deserves from Gandhi's scholarly admirers, whether at home or abroad – no doubt because it constitutes a major and more negative re-evaluation of Gandhi's life and practice. It is no accident that one exception in this regard is Arundhati Roy, in her introduction to the Navayana annotated edition of Ambedkar's *Annihilation of Caste*, which constitutes a much more critical evaluation of Gandhi vis-à-vis Ambedkar. See the exchange between the Mahatma's grandson, Rajmohan Gandhi, and Arundhati Roy in the pages of the *Economic and Political Weekly*: R. Gandhi, 'Independence and Social Justice' (11 April 2015); A. Roy, 'All the World's a Half-Built Dam' (20 June 2015); R. Gandhi, 'Response to Arundhati Roy' (25 July 2015).

Answers to the question 'Who is a Hindu?' had to be sought precisely because there was no self-evident and universally acceptable answer, but instead multiple and overlapping ones.[51] But the question most preoccupied the Hindu cultural Right. This was a radical, modernist current to be distinguished from Hindu traditionalists and conservatives. They were out to remould the 'Hindu community' and 'Hindu society', not to conserve it. The operative term for them was not 'Indianness' but 'Hinduness', or 'Hindutva'. The 'foreigner' was not the non-Indian, or simply the outsider beneficiary of colonial rule, but all those not fully assimilated into Hinduness.

Many Indian nationalists, to a greater or lesser degree, saw Hinduism as a vital, indeed decisive, part of Indian culture, and therefore of an Indian cultural nationalism. Like the Hindutva Right, they also sought to remould Indian society, and even the 'Hindu community'. But their respective versions of cultural and political nationalism were significantly different, and so also were their programmes and visions for India as an independent state.

The differences did not centre on the issue of Hinduism and how best to understand it. The first important synthesizer and proponent of Hindutva, Veer Savarkar, saw this as a racial, cultural, religious–spiritual unity – a unity of culture and territory.[52] Hinduism was a part of Hindutva, but Savarkar would not give it as prominent a role as did M. S. Golwalkar, the second head of the Rashtriya Swayamsevak Sangh (National Volunteer Corps).[53] What united the proponents of Hindutva before independence, and unites them now, is not agreement on specific definitions, but common assent to a certain *chain of reasoning*.

Figures like Vivekananda and Gandhi, whose views, lives and teachings are in so many ways markedly different from – indeed opposed to – political Hindutva, can nonetheless be appropriated, with a degree of plausibility, to serve Hindutva interests. While such figures never subscribed to Hindutva's full chain of reasoning, they did implicitly or explicitly endorse some links in that longer chain.[54] There lies a major dilemma for all those who would

---

51 G. Pandey, 'Who of us are Hindus?', in G. Pandey, ed., *Hindus and Others: The Question of Identity in India Today* (Delhi, 1993).

52 V. D. Savarkar, *Hindutva: Who is a Hindu?* (Bombay, 1969). For Savarkar, Hinduism is the -ism of Hindus, and applies to all the religions of the land of Hindus (including Sikhism, Jainism, Buddhism), where a Hindu is defined as one whose holy land and motherland (*Bharat Mata*) is the same – Hindustan or Bharat.

53 M. S. Golwalkar, *We or Our Nationhood Defined* (Nagpur, 1966).

54 Gandhi and Vivekananda both believed that a distinctive ethos constituted the essence of Hinduism.

Whereas the Hindu cultural right – the RSS, for example – says it 'respects' Muslims because they were originally Hindus, i.e. *in spite* of their adherence to Islam, Gandhi respected Muslims *because* he respected Islam. At the same time, the source of Gandhi's respect was more his *abstract* commitment to, and respect for, all religions. When he retreated from the abstract to the concrete, Gandhi's observations about Muslims tended to fall into stereotypes. One extreme example of this tendency was his reference to the Muslim as a bully, at the time of the Moplah rebellion in Malabar in the 1920s.

promote an opposition to Hindutva from within the discourse of Hinduism and neo-Hinduism.

This basic chain of reasoning goes as follows: ethos/spirit is the heart of Hinduism, which is at the heart of, or coterminous with, Hindu culture (which defines Indian culture), which is at the heart of the Hindu nation (which defines the Indian nation). Four concepts – ethos, religion, culture, nation – are the key elements in this discourse. Not only is Hindutva's understanding of each extremely unsophisticated, but its understanding of the connections between them is absurdly determinist. Enough has surely been said so far about why this is so.

Cultural nationalism is always constructed, and constructed with purposes in view. It is the judgement of these purposes – of their value and the possibility of their attainment – that provides us with a basis for assessing competing cultural nationalisms and making alignments. Since there is no fixed entity called the *true* cultural nationalism, it cannot be 'uncovered' by historical study. But this is not to say there are not better, more accurate ways of understanding Indian culture and history. There clearly are, and these can provide no solace to the claims of Hindutva. But it *is* to say that an Indian cultural nationalism is neither 'naturally' a Hindu nationalism nor 'naturally' a secular nationalism, or a composite nationalism. What it is and will be is what we fight to make it become.

Hindutva operates with another tight reductionism. If India is to become strong, then it must acquire cultural confidence. This confidence comes from the people recognizing the country's true cultural roots. For all the crudity of these formulations, they contain a hint of one noteworthy understanding. Cultural confidence may not be the key determinant, but it is certainly conducive to the construction of a generally strong and healthy India. What we mean by 'strong and healthy' and what we mean by 'culture and cultural confidence' are precisely at issue. The best conception hinges on an understanding of culture (certainly culture in modernity) that lies beyond the ken of Hindutva.

The priority of strengthening the cultural resources of a country or society always preoccupied the late Raymond Williams. Throughout his life, he subjected the notion of culture to constant interrogation. In this process he began to draw a distinction between what he had once treated as synonymous – 'culture in common' and 'common culture'. He came to endorse the latter, and to argue that strengthening cultural resources meant moving closer to the deepening and institutionalization of a 'common culture'.[55] Where 'culture in common' could be read as a form of cultural essentialism, 'common culture' could be understood as its opposite – always open, plural, ordinary, changing, expanding.

---

55 R. Williams, *Resources of Hope* (London,1989). See 'The Idea of a Common Culture' pp. 32–38. See also Williams, *Culture*.

Hindutva is distinctively Indian, but in insisting that we possess a culture in common (a cultural essence), and that what prevents us becoming culturally stronger as a nation is our refusal (more accurately, the refusal of some – Muslims and secularists) to recognize this essence and build upon it, Hindutva is no different from the cultural chauvinisms of other countries, East or West. The political ideologies presenting implied threats to 'uncomprehending' minorities – of Thatcherite racism ('we are being swamped'), neo-Nazi anti-Semitism in Western Europe, Islamic fundamentalism, and Hindutva forces – are structurally isomorphic: 'If you do not recognize, understand or appreciate that this is our culture in common, then you are guilty of weakening, damaging, even betraying our nation/culture, and we don't like it, and will not let you get away with it.'

The construction of a genuine common culture characterized by ever greater openness, plurality and ordinariness has a global dimension, as well.

If Hindutva is anti-secular, there is also an anti-secularism that claims to be anti-Hindutva. But before taking up this form of anti-secularism, I will examine the discourse on the nature of Indian secularism.

Indian Secularism

Amid the various forms taken globally by the secular state (and the conceptions of secularism underlying them), where does Indian secularism and its conception of the state stand? Secularism, in its original and broadest meaning, refers to a change in the foundations of moral behaviour, and its implications for the general organization of human society, going beyond the specific issue of the state's secularity. Here is where the issue of secularization is identified as also that of secular humanism, as an ideal to be pursued for the purposes of promoting human flourishing in this world and no other. The narrower meaning is a reference to the state and its independence of, and separation from, religious power, institutions, personnel and influence.

But how far is this separation and state autonomy to go, given the historically concrete circumstances in which so many secular states emerged? This is where the encounter with and debate over 'varieties of secularism' has taken place, strongly reinforced by the post-colonial emergence of secular states outside the West. Given the country's unmatched religious diversity, it is not at all surprising that Indian scholars have made important contributions to a globally expanding discourse on secularism despite, as well as because of, the disagreements between them. One of the more systematic Indian attempts at theorizing 'political secularism' generally, and Indian secularism in particular, has come from the pen of Rajeev Bhargava, through a series of essays spanning over two decades, from the beginning of the 1990s to the present.[56] While he expresses personal sympathy for ethical

---

56 He is currently senior professorial fellow at the Centre for the Study of Developing

or normative secularism, and therefore for a universal secular humanism founded on the rational autonomy of humans, his attention has always been more strongly focused on political secularism and state secularity. Indeed, its value and necessity is to be separately justified from the pursuit of an ethical secularism.

If the valorization of this disjunction is a gain – enabling Bhargava to provide an impressively elaborated taxonomy of different secular states, and therefore an appreciation of the 'distinctive' character of Indian secularism – it also represents a loss, in that the state–religion interface tends to become the self-contained domain of enquiry, and the one in which one must most strongly work to maintain the stability or improve the secular quality of the state. There is less focus on, and therefore a more blurred vision of, the relationship between secularization in society, or of the necessity to develop a more secular public culture, in order to sustain the secular state. The more positively one evaluates the actual and potential contribution that religious world-views and practices can make to the goals of human emancipation, the less interest there will be in (even reluctance or opposition to) the project of promoting the further secularization of society, even of societies that are more suffused by a popular religiosity.

Political secularism is value-based, and most existing secular states are based on principles of religious liberty and religious non-discrimination; the latter through exclusion of religion or through the state's exercise of neutrality, however this might be understood.[57] Religious liberty does not mean people are free to do whatever they religiously believe, for this will clash with the secular state, which must intervene to separate the acceptable from the unacceptable. Final powers of legal arbitration must rest with the state, which thereby draws the boundary lines. The secular state must, implicitly or otherwise, evaluate religion, and the way in which it draws such boundary lines (given specific histories) can reflect anti-religious hostility, indifference, or a range of more positive assessments of religion – and, it must be said, of religious diversity, given possible changes in the religious composition of populations.

Bhargava has perceptively identified three levels of this state-religion interface: (i) at the level of ultimate ends; (ii) between institutions and personnel; (iii) in law and public policy. At the first level, the separation must

---

Societies in New Delhi, of which he was formerly director. He has also been faculty professor and head of the Centre for Political Studies, JNU, and of the Department of Political Science, University of Delhi.

57 Bhargava talks of 'amoral states' or 'self-aggrandizing states' whose rulers seek to maximize power and wealth and are not value-based in the right way – for example, colonial Britain with its 'civilizing mission'. See R. Bhargava, *The Promise of India's Secular Democracy* (New Delhi, 2010), p. 76. Clearly, his focus is on the inward-turned side of the Janus-faced state – on whether its citizenship rights are defined irrespective of religious affiliation and loyalties. According to longstanding traditions in international relations, the external (mis)behavior of advanced capitalist democracies like the United States is justified as unavoidable in an anarchic and amoral world order.

be complete. The aim of the secular state cannot be to pursue salvation for its citizens. If the core principles of state secularity are to ensure religious liberty and equal citizenship regardless of religious affiliation, then there must be a basic separation, at the second level, between organized religious power and influence and organized political power. It is at the third level that the variations will arise, but all variants must respect the stipulated core principles – absence of religious hegemony over the state, religious liberty, and civic equality in relation to religious affiliation. A secular state need not be democratic, but a democratic state must be secular. It is true that the degree of secularity, in terms of separateness, is not an indicator of the degree of democracy. But, despite the fuzziness of the relationship between state secularity and democracy, it is important that neither term is so defined as to erode the claim of the former being necessary but not sufficient to achieve the latter.[58]

From these minimal but crucial criteria, Bhargava constructs three models of actual secular states, before turning to India. The first is the French, in which there is 'one-sided exclusion', whereby the state can intervene to help or hinder religion (witness its restrictions on the dress codes of Muslim women and Sikh men) but not vice versa, even for Catholicism. The second model is that of the United States, in which there is 'mutual exclusion'

---

58 Taylor's unease with what he calls the 'independent ethic' of secularism – one that is grounded in common human attributes independent of religion or culture, such as autonomy and rationality, leads him to propose a 'hybrid' approach that would ground a 'universal political ethic' on values of freedom, equality and popular sovereignty that he believes are part of various religious traditions with which one can form an overlapping consensus. But this common political ethic or 'mode of secularism' demands that there be 'political freedom'. So, for Taylor, Atatürk's Turkey was not secular. See the arguments presented in C. Taylor, 'Modes of Secularism', in R. Bhargava, ed., *Secularism and its Critics* (Delhi, 1998); and C. Taylor, 'Defining Secularism', in A. Bilgrami, ed., *Marx, Gandhi and Modernity* (New Delhi, 2014), p. 31.
    On the other side, there are the four preconditions for democracy spelled out in A. Stepan and G. B. Robertson, 'An Arab More than Muslim Electoral Gap', *Journal of Democracy* 1:413 (2003), pp. 30–44: 1) Useable state; 2) free and fair elections with freedom of speech and to organize; 3) elected governments free from any 'reserve domain' to appoint powerful political officers and to make public policies; 4) must not *systematically* [my emphasis] erode the democratic constitution, rule of law and citizen's human rights. Stepan, furthermore, endorses the view held by R. Dahl, A. Lijphardt and J. L. Linz that secularism is not a necessary condition for a democracy. See, in particular, A. Stepan,'The Multiple Secularisms of Modern Democratic and Non-Democratic Regimes', in C. Calhoun, M. Juergensmeyer and J. Van Antwerpen, eds, *Rethinking Secularism* (New York, 2011). Such a view allows Israel to be designated a democracy. For a powerful rebuttal of such a view, see the public speech by the late Ronald Dworkin, titled 'E. H. Thompson Forum on World Issues (2009)' at youtube.com. Dworkin distinguishes between a 'religious tolerant state', one that has an established religion but is tolerant of dissenting religions and no religion, and a 'secular tolerant state', which has no religion but tolerates religion (s). Israel is of the first kind, its Basic Law (which stands as its constitution) defining it as Jewish. It cannot show equal concern and respect for all citizens in law regardless of religious affiliation. Indeed, a democratic nation-state must be viewed by all as a state that in principle respects them equally. Instead, Israel embodies a merger of religion and nationalism that constitutes a profound intolerance of its non-Jewish citizens.

at the third level. The third model characterizes many European states, which have a formal religious establishment whose power over the state – barring certain left-over policy and legal biases from the past – nonetheless respects the core principles of political secularism. These are 'moderate secularisms' that are flexible in matters of policy and law, as is Indian secularism; but these European states, like France and the United States, can and should learn from how India has dealt with religiously diverse pressures and claims.

So the defining characteristic of the Indian state is a 'principled distance' that is non-sectarian but not indifferent, let alone hostile, to religion, and is therefore more open to accommodation in the state–religion interface in *both* directions. On the one hand, it is willing to intervene in the name of securing or promoting decent values of peace, harmony, freedom and equality based on respect for all religions. On the other hand, the Indian state is sensitive to the need for differentiated citizenship and group rights, both cultural and religious, since religious liberty, for Bhargava, applies not just to the individual but to a community's right to their own religious practices, albeit that these practices are made subject to respect for certain 'basic individual rights', among which is the right to individual exit; and that these rights – for example, gender equality – should not be overridden in the name of group values, identity or security. 'Should', however, is an appeal, and is preferred here to the sharper injunction of 'must'. Unsurprisingly, the whole area of religious community rights and practices as they exist in India today – the issue of religious personal laws – has raised disputes about how justified it is to take a strongly positive view of Indian secularism as a supposedly principled doctrine.

It is true that Indian secularism is distinctive. Principled distance, says Bhargava, exists informally in the practices of the United States and France, but, by not being explicitly endorsed or embodied in their constitutions and laws, does not alter existing doctrinal beliefs and formulations. It is in this respect that the Indian Constitution and law is said to be superior, and provides a vital platform for better practice.[59] Clearly, the existing con-

---

59 S. Kaviraj, who is highly appreciative of Bhargava's understanding of Indian secularism, rightly points out that, unlike in the case of Europe, where the emergence of the secular state preceded by more than a century the establishment of full-suffrage democracies, independent India had self-consciously and simultaneously to design, justify and ensconce secular and democratic principles in its Constitution, which would then serve as the foundation stone of its newly freed polity. It is this that makes its secularist doctrine a more sophisticated one. At the same time, the Constitution, following as it did the trauma of Partition, had to prioritize the securing of interreligious harmony. India's was, in the words of Bhargava, a 'contextual secularism'. In Europe and India severe interreligious strife was a powerful stimulus to the formation of a secular state. New rulers could then be more confident of voiding such future interreligious violence. S. Kaviraj, 'Languages of Secularity', *Economic and Political Weekly*, 14 December 2013. But India's secularity, more strongly influenced by democratic values, paid attention to 'intra-religious domination' as well; hence, according to Bhargava, there is a conscious articulation of the need for intervention according to positive values.

ceptualizations in European and American secularisms are not adequate to dealing with growing religious diversity in anything but an ad hoc, often uncharitable and biased manner. Islamophobia is growing in the North Atlantic and Europe, as elsewhere, and a litany of biases can be recited. In the UK, numerous Christian schools are state-funded, while Muslim applications for similar support are turned down. Permissions to build mosques are often refused in Germany, Italy and elsewhere. Muslim burial grounds have been denied in Denmark. In certain countries in Europe, it is difficult to establish *halal* butcheries. Swiss cantons have ruled out minarets. French restrictions on dress codes have already been mentioned. A deeper problem underlying all this is that the Western image of itself as embodying superior values of liberal democracy, because of its particular secular traditions, acts as a major barrier to the moral and intellectual introspection necessary for making its societies more tolerant and humane. To his great credit, Bhargava, perhaps more than anyone else, has highlighted this lacuna through his work, which is all the more persuasive because of its theoretical and analytical acumen.[60]

The deficiencies of Western secularism should be clear. But what about the possible problems with Indian secularism as doctrine and principle, going beyond the issue of the obvious gap between theory and practice, which Bhargava himself would be among the first to highlight? Certainly, given the reality of the rise of Hindu communalism to the point where the BJP has secured an absolute majority to rule at the centre, Indian secularism is currently in crisis. Many other Indian secularists would agree with Bhargava that this is no reason to abandon the principle of secularism in India, nor simply to denigrate it in the manner of Hindutva ideologues proclaiming the supposedly unique tolerances of Hinduism, and therefore the virtues of 'Hindu rule'. But this does not mean that the value and potential of Indian secularism, as embodied for example in the publicly much venerated Constitution, cannot undergo a sharper and more critical scrutiny than its admirers are generally wont to countenance.

The National Movement and the Constitution

Outside the ranks of the Sangh and its ardent followers and acolytes, it is difficult to deny that anti-Muslim communalism (like casteism and sexism) is to a considerable degree institutionalized in, both the apparatuses of the state and the structures of society. Admittedly, having a Constitution and therefore an official doctrine that declares the state to be secular provides a benchmark that at least de-legitimizes religious discrimination, making it easier to publicly condemn, expose and fight. Few would argue, given

---

60 See also R. Bhargava, 'How Secular is European Secularism?', in Bilgrami, *Marx, Gandhi and Modernity*; and R. Bhargava, 'Reimagining Secularism: Respect, Domination and Principled Distance', *Economic and Political Weekly*, 14 December 2013.

institutionalized forms of racism in the United States and those that prevailed in former apartheid South Africa, that abandoning apartheid as an official state ideology made no difference, or that the racist realities of the United States and apartheid South Africa may simply be equated. But how helpful – that is, how progressive – is the Indian Constitution, even as it declares itself secular?

As a general rule, strongly positive assessments of the secular thrust of the Constitution are allied to more sympathetic assessments of the functioning and dominant ethos of the Constituent Assembly, which in turn would flow from a more appreciative judgement (whatever one's criticisms or reservations) of the Congress-led National Movement that eventually set it up. Contestation over the meanings and values to ascribe to Indian secularism start here. Within the Congress, one can discern three currents. There were those, like Nehru, who expressed a rationalist secular humanism largely divorced from religion. Ambedkar, outside the Congress, shared this perspective. Others, like Madan Mohan Malaviya, were Hindu nationalists (Sardar Patel and Lala Lajpat Rai were not much better), who agreed substantially, though not completely, with the beliefs, values and aims of the even more aggressive and uncompromising currents of Hindu nationalism outside the Congress. Meanwhile, Gandhi (often the key arbiter amid the internal tensions and rivalries) expressed a 'multi-religious nationalism' as the key to securing harmony and respect amid religious diversity. Nevertheless, for him too, the ultimate source for creating this supposedly remarkable 'blend' lay in the uniquely accommodative character of Hinduism. For Gandhi, this was best understood as a long-enduring culture (rather than a religion), which made Muslims, despite their allegiance to a more closed religious framework, every bit as Indian as were Hindus, whose numerical majority nevertheless established the crucial socio-cultural ballast for Indian unity.

The internal relationship of forces within the Congress would of course be affected by developments in the wider political arena. In fact, the term secularism really entered Indian political discourse only in the 1940s – a testimony to its meaning being shaped by prior discourses on 'national unity', majority–minority relations, and concerns about communalism.[61] If British rule helped to define religious groups – in a way quite different from the

---

61 This late entry of the term secularism is pointed out in S. Tejani, *Indian Secularism: A Social and Intellectual History* (New Delhi, 2007). It also says that the term 'communal' originally carried no negative connotation, referring only to various 'communities of interest' beyond religious groups. It is was with the Morley-Minto reforms of 1909, which proposed separate political representation for distinct groups, that the term came to be identified with Muslims as a minority religious group mobilizing for its specific interests. From being an umbrella term for various groups, it came to denote an 'unfortunate particularity' counterposed to developing conceptions of nationalism itself, according to Tejani, being inordinately shaped by Hindu popular movements in western India (but spreading elsewhere) for cow protection, Ganpati festivals, and celebratory freedoms for processional activities when passing nearby mosques.

past – as *political* categories, this trend was carried forward and deepened by both the early stirrings of a proto-nationalist movement that adopted these categories, and by British constitutional reforms that extended local and provincial representation and powers to Indians, but sought to establish the greater stability of central colonial rule by sustaining these demarcations as befitting divide-and-rule tactics, and favouring conservative elites as more loyal satraps.

There is no doubt that the Congress-led National Movement was a Hindu-inflected one, and therefore having biases towards upper castes as well. Gandhi's willingness to abide by the Lucknow Pact of 1916, which promised separate electorates for Muslims and Sikhs, contrasted sharply with his rejection of the same for untouchables (the Poona Pact of 1932). Clearly, the cross-caste 'organic unity' of Hinduism was far more important to him than the stipulated organic unity of a multi-religious India. Hindus had to remain, politically speaking, a numerical majority, and so untouchables had to be denied the status of a political minority.[62] Muslims could be accepted by the Congress as a political minority as long as they remained so. The Congress leaders were predominantly upper-caste Hindus, most comfortable with the ideas, idioms and values of a Brahminical Hinduism (whose intellectual forbearers were Vivekananda and Aurobindo Ghosh), hence the strong thrust to make Hindu identifications nationalist ones.[63] At the same time, Congress claimed to be a kind of all-India secular expression of the Indian people, irrespective of religion, which ruled out association with the Muslim League on any terms not strongly tilted towards the Congress. Partition, of course, put paid to an earlier willingness to allow Muslims separate representation as a political minority.

Could the Congress be held largely or primarily responsible for causing Partition, the blame for which was otherwise pinned wholly on the Muslim League – and by association, on anti-national communal tendencies within the Muslim community? Certainly, the fact of Partition would crucially shape the understanding of how a secular Indian Constitution should be drawn up. It is true that the Constituent Assembly, to which fell the responsibility to draw up the Constitution, and which met from 1946 to 1949, mainly comprised upper-caste Hindu men, and was politically dominated by the Congress. But to what extent did this create a Hindu and upper-caste

62 On 21 August 1932, in the context of the controversy that led to the Poona Pact, Gandhi wrote the following to Sardar Patel: 'The possible consequences of separate electorates for harijans fill me with horror ... [They] will create division among Hindus so much so that it will lead to bloodshed. Untouchable hooligans will make common cause with Muslim hooligans and kill caste Hindus.' R. K. Prabhu and U. R. Rao, eds., *Collected Works of Mahatma Gandhi*, Vol. 1, p. 469 (Ahmedabad, 1967).

63 G. Balachandran, 'Religion and Nationalism in Modern India' in K. Basu and S. Subrahmanyam, eds, *Unravelling the Nation: Sectarian Conflict in India's Secular Identity* (New Delhi, 1996). Balachandran points to 'the confident assumption held by the majority of the Congress leadership that national solidarity was inherently a quality of India's (Hindu) cultural heritage' (p. 100).

bias in the Constitution, given that liberal and democratic principles and values played a significant part in shaping the final outcome?

For some, the eventual compromise was an honourable, even admirable one: 'Indian secularism is an ethically sensitive negotiated settlement between diverse groups and divergent values.'[64] Again, the wisdom of Gandhi and Nehru enabled them to join forces powerfully to ensure that the principle of political secularism be enshrined in the Constitution, even as the latter believed in ethical secularism while the former did not.[65] For other upholders of secularism, the 'Nehruvian secularism' of the Constitution has proved in hindsight to be a failure, at most a 'holding operation' against the tides of communalism. What was not delivered was any acknowledgement of the reality (without commending it) of religious communitarian voices in politics, which should have been properly organized on a 'statist site' in a creative dialogue. This would have allowed moderate voices to come to the surface, to forge an 'alternate substantive secularism emergent rather than assumed'.[66] Instead, with Gandhi no longer in the forefront, Nehru's modernizing Congress adopted an 'Archimedean' stance, because the Congress believed itself to be representative of all communities.

The problem with pinning hopes for the emergence of a superior secular consensus from inter-community dialogue is that a number of difficulties stand in the way. Even if the state is to take responsibility for filtering final community representatives, power inequalities would remain between participants. Can the state also be assumed to be socially so neutral that it would push strongly for the triumph of fair and honest adjudication? What if the basic assumption of an overlapping consensus – that there can be a consensual arrival at provisions incorporating fundamental values, even if the reasoning behind them differs – is mistaken, and there are stubborn incommensurable factors deriving from the different religious world-views of the participants – or, at least, they understand this to be the case?[67]

There are, then, voices that are significantly more critical of the compromises that took place during the drafting of the Indian Constitution, and therefore over the final outcome achieved. One of the more interesting of

---

64 R. Bhargava, 'Rehabilitating Secularism', in Calhoun et al., *Rethinking Secularism*, p. 109 – repeated in his 'Reimagining Secularism' (p. 87). For his elucidation of the multi-value virtues of the Constitution, see in particular his 'Rehabilitating Secularism' and his 'India's Secular Constitution', in A. Vanaik and R. Bhargava, eds, *Understanding Contemporary India: Critical Perspectives* (New Delhi, 2010).

65 Kaviraj, 'Languages of Secularity'.

66 A. Bilgrami, 'Secularism, Nationalism and Modernity', in Bhargava, *Secularism and Its Critics*, p. 400.

67 Pandey perceptively identifies these problems, but nevertheless places his hopes in the state and public eventually recognizing that India is a land of 'multiple minorities'; thus the language of majority and minority is to be abandoned, but not, it seems, replaced by Enlightenment values stressing the primacy of the individual. See G. Pandey, 'The Secular State and the Limits of Dialogue', in A. D. Needham and R. Sundarajan, eds, *The Crisis of Secularism in India* (Durham, NC/London, 2007).

these voices is that of Meera Nanda. She has compared the US Constitution
and its 'wall of separation' with the secular character of the Indian state
and Constitution. In the case of the United States, she points out that the
insertion of a wall of separation was the result of an alliance between radical
Protestant sects like the Baptists and Methodists, concerned to protect
themselves from interference by the state, but also from the use of state
power by the dominant Protestant churches lined up against them on doctrinal and other grounds, and by those like Jefferson, Paine and Madison,
who were more inclined towards a secular humanism and wanted to prevent
faith from encroaching on the state. Where others might see an overlapping
consensus working positively in the Indian context, Nanda sees a compromise between more secular humanists, like Nehru, and neo-Hindu advocates
(among whom she includes Gandhi), whose intellectual inspiration came
from the neo-Vedantism of Vivekananda and Aurobindo. Along with others
inside and outside the National Movement, the shared 'common sense' of
this group was that *sarva dharm sambhavam* (equal respect to all religions)
constituted the foundation of Indian secularism.

To the extent that it took nearly two centuries for a full-suffrage, democratic US state to emerge after the Constitutional declaration of American
secularity, there was time for a significant absorption by the main Protestant
churches of Enlightenment values, and of the validity of scientific enquiry
into nature. This allowed for a certain privatization of religion, for a disenchantment from nature, and for a more secular public culture of modern
pluralism and tolerance to emerge. This is far from complete among the
US population, and is now under threat. But this relative secularization of
American society is a fact, and has taken place to a much greater extent than
in India, where popular religiosity is far less leavened by the ingredients of
secular humanism; in short, ethical humanism has made greater ground in
the United States than in India. Whatever one may think of Nanda's comparative perspective on how the US and Indian constitutions have emerged,
and of their impact on state secularity, she is, along with this writer, one
of the very few contributors to the Indian debate on secularism who has
focused more on the process of secularization, and stressed this dimension
as having a more determining effect on the overall nature of the polity. That
the Indian secular state and Constitution also reflect a compromise is seen by
some in highly positive terms, because they are less concerned than Nanda
with the negative implications of the gap between ethical secularism and
political secularism, or between the secularization of society and the secularity of the state. So, while Nanda is appreciative of the strengths of the state
and the Indian Constitution, she is also more critical of the deficiencies in its
making and of its content.

The Constitution is seen as having a 'mixed' character, with serious deficiencies that would not be adequately captured, but were instead glossed
over by the notion of 'principled distance'. One of the consequences of this

mixed nature is that the Indian courts would have to be repeatedly called upon to pass judgements on the legitimate boundaries and content of such state behaviour, whether by intervening or by refraining from doing so. It is probably accurate to say that these judgements over a range of issues during the history of independent India have been positive – upholding values of egalitarianism and non-discrimination – but also negative. On balance, the courts have, in my view, legitimized rather than de-legitimized Hindu beliefs and practices, thereby playing into the hands of Hindutva forces. One of the most shocking and disturbing examples of this was the Supreme Court ruling on Hindutva in December 1995. The issue concerned Hindu nationalist appeals to voters to support the party and candidates of Hindutva that were committed to making India a Hindu *rashtra* (nation), and not to give their votes to others not sharing this view. Formerly, such appeals had always been disallowed as violating the legal prohibition on soliciting votes on the grounds of religion. The three-judge bench, headed by Justice J. S. Verma, ruled that this did not violate the law or Constitution, because of the distinctiveness of Hindutva and Hinduism, which was not a religion but the way of life of all Indians! This enabled the BJP election manifesto of 1996 to declare that the true meaning of Hindutva as the essence of Indian secularism had now been made clear.[68] A political ideology had thus been equated with a faith.

That, for him, this ruling was inspired by the Constitution was made clear in a subsequent interview given by Justice Verma, in which he declared that 'secularism in the Constitution is merely a reaffirmation and continuation of the Indian (i.e. Hindu) way of life'.[69] He is not alone in this kind of thinking. A former president of India, S. Radhakrishnan, when vice president, in 1956, had this to say: 'the religious impartiality of the Indian state is not to be confused with secularism or atheism. Secularism as here defined is in accordance with the ancient religious tradition of India. It tries to build up a fellowship of believers...based on the principle of unity in diversity'.[70] Neither Verma nor Radhakrishnan are, or were, admirers of the Sangh; far from it. But this overlap in thinking about secularism exists. The actual 'mixed' character of the Indian Constitution has meant that, up to the 1980s, the forces of Hindutva – namely, the Sangh – would criticize the

---

68 For the judgement itself, see judis.nic.in. In April 1996 another three-judge bench said that this ruling was not final, and that the matter should be cleared up by a future, larger judicial bench headed by the chief justice. Despite another such declaration of intent by the Supreme Court in February 2014 – that is to say, some nineteen years after the judgement – to this day this has not taken place. The delay is inexplicable and very damaging, since understanding secularism in the Constitution as fundamentally distinct from and indeed opposed to Hindutva should be a political, moral and legal imperative. The Sangh has of course greatly benefitted from this failure.

69 See M. Nanda, *The Wrongs of the Religious Right* (New Delhi, 2005), p. 45, where the quote is from an interview appearing in G. J. Jacobsohn, *The Wheel of Law: India's Secularism in Comparative Constitutional Context* (Princeton, 2003), pp. 206–9.

70 P. C. Chatterjee, *Secular Values for Secular India* (New Delhi, 1995), p. 103.

secular thrust of the Constitution as being anti-Hindu. Subsequently, they have found that it is more politically profitable to reinterpret the Constitution's secular thrust as confirmation that they represent the true secularists, as opposed to the 'pseudo-secularism' of leftists or others opposed to them. The Sangh now declares that it wants to further secularize the Constitution, which recognizes that Hinduism is the essence of Indian secularism, and to present themselves as the true correctors of the weaknesses of the Constitution in, for example, not having a uniform civil code. Secularism is now being counterposed to minority rights.

Yet another area – apart from the contentious issue of a Personal Law (which will be taken up later) – in which the ambiguities of the Constitution have been interpreted by the courts to help strengthen Hindutva is in the matter of conversions. During the drafting of the Constitution, Ambedkar wanted to restrict the meaning of 'freedom of religion' to freedom to worship, unhappy as he was about the sanction that could otherwise could be applied to Hindu 'practices' such as *sati* and child marriage. Hindu conservatives were opposed to Ambedkar for the same reason. Hindu nationalists in the Constituent Assembly, with Gandhi's agreement, opposed proselytization, implicitly affirming a Hindu past and also showing a dominant concern with preserving Hindu unity. Others more attuned to liberal and modern values, as well as Christian and Muslim members, were of course supportive of the right to convert. The final compromise formula allowed freedom to 'profess, practice and propagate', where 'propagate' was clearly understood to mean freedom to convert, though it was made subject to 'public order, morality and health'.

But, from the 1960s onwards, a number of states, beginning with Madhya Pradesh and Orissa, passed anti-conversion laws that banned conversions by 'force, fraud and allurement'. This conditional clause is itself controversial, to say the least. In 1977, however, a Supreme Court ruling endorsed these state laws, declaring that the freedom to propagate does not necessarily allow for conversion, as a matter of right. More states legislated their own Freedom of Religion Acts to restrict, control and scrutinize conversion efforts.[71] While 'allurement', or inducement, is a fundamental feature of existence of citizens in a market economy, and is seen as compatible with the freedom of choice of individuals as consumers or job-seekers, the desire to enhance one's social status, overcoming the stigmas of caste or the desire to make one's life better through access to education, health care, employment, and so on, are thereby stigmatized as motivating factors behind conversion – although the turn to religion has for most people always been inseparable from the need to cope with the secular needs of everyday life. There is in fact no rational justification for proscribing 'allurement'. Fraud is

---

71 G. Vishwanathan, 'Literacy and Conversion in the Discourse of Hindu Nationalism', in Needham and Sundarajan, *Crisis of Secularism in India*.

also a difficult concept. Some states, through their particular religious bills, have interpreted this to define fraud as including both promises of heaven and warnings of hell.[72] But does it apply to the behaviour of the plethora of Hindu 'godmen' and 'devis' who carry out 'miracles' and promise various spectacular benefits, material and spiritual, to attract a large following for themselves or for their particular sects? Hardly! If force refers only to the exercise or threat of physical violence in some form, then its proscription would be justified. But force can take various forms short of the exercise of physical force, with conversion then being seen as a beneficial trade-off for the disadvantaged.

What seems quite evident is that these legal restrictions on conversion are primarily – indeed overwhelmingly – meant to deter conversions away from Hinduism, to either Islam or Christianity. Hindu missionary work is widely seen as pursuing 're-conversion' to an 'original' faith or religious–social status, and has never invited, in doctrine or practice, similar restraints or indictments by Indian state authorities, at either the central or provincial levels.[73] It is difficult to avoid the conclusion that the Constitution itself contains far too many implicit or explicit Hindu biases.

---

72 U. Baxi, 'Siting Secularism in the Uniform Civil Code', in Needham and Sundarajan, *Crisis of Secularism in India*.

73 The record of the authorities in dealing with communal violence in India where the overwhelming majority of victims have been primarily minorities – occasionally Christians, but mainly Muslims (and also Sikhs in the 1984 riots that followed the assassination of Indira Gandhi by her Sikh bodyguards) – is an abysmal one. This applies both to the courts and to the police and paramilitary apparatuses. For the pusillanimous behaviour of the first, witness the failure, since 1949 to the present, to deal with the whole Babri Masjid–Ram Janmabhoomi issue; a good survey is given in S. Gopal, ed., *Anatomy of a Confrontation* (New Delhi, 1992), especially the chapter on 'Legal Aspects of the Issue', by A. G. Noorani. Note also the way in which state-level courts have failed to mete out punishment to wrongdoers in riots and pogroms affecting minorities, despite the reports of independent commissions of inquiry. The 2010 Allahabad High Court judgement partitioned the land on which the former Babri Majid stood, onto which, in 1949, Hindu idol figurines were originally illegally smuggled, and where a makeshift Hindu temple was constructed in 1992, after the illegal demolition of the mosque. This partitioning was done in such a manner as to effectively legitimize these illegal actions. See 'The Ayodhya Judgement Verdict/orders-ramjanmabhoomi', at indialawywers.wordpress.com. In March 2015 this issue was taken to the Supreme Court, so a final decision has yet to be made. Justice so delayed is justice denied, and it is highly doubtful whether, given the general political climate, any Supreme Court will have the courage to demand the removal of the makeshift temple.

At the same time, there is a vast literature available about the role of various actors in communal riots and pogroms in India. Among the most faithful chroniclers and analysts of these events was the late Asghar Ali Engineer. See his *Communal Riots in Post-Independence India* (Hyderabad, 1984); *Communalism and Communal Violence in India* (Delhi, 1989). See also O. Khalidi, *Khaki and Ethnic Violence in India* (New Delhi, 2003); K. S Subramanian, *Political Violence and Police in India* (New Delhi, 2007), especially Chapter 7, 'State-Sponsored Violence Against Muslims in Gujarat 2002: A Case Study of Police Partisanship' (Subramanian is a former senior police officer).

Unprincipled Proximities and Personal Laws

'Hindu-tainted' is the term used by a scholar, Pritam Singh, to describe the Constitution, in an article where he detailed the various elements of such bias.[74] It is not the case that these elements have not been separately pointed out by others, but Singh's article has the important merit of bringing these criticisms together, and thus providing a comprehensive and coherent focus on the issue of what, it can then be argued, is a more systematized Hindu bias in the Constitution, thus raising stronger doubts about the secular nature of the National Movement that preceded it. Singh says that he is not arguing for a 'rigidly fixed template of secularism' for assessing the Indian Constitution, but that he wishes 'to question the complacency of Indian secular opinion about the secular foundations of the Indian republic'. More controversially, he does not believe that the Constitution has ideological or political utility for fighting the forces of Hindutva, despite its 'admirable and historically progressive features'.[75]

There are criticisms of the Indian Constitution that do not come from its Hindu biases, such as the fact that it has a strongly centralized character prioritizing territorial unity by denying the right to self-determination for the north-east, and even formally allowing for the acquisition of further territory beyond its 1947 boundaries to become part of India. But this does not mark it out from other bourgeois democratic constitutions, and this issue will not be taken up here.

The very first Article of the Constitution refers to 'India, that is Bharat'. The insertion of the latter term was an explicit demand of Hindu nationalist members of the Constituent Assembly, reflecting as it did a pre-Muslim past of presumed Hindu glory, when the whole peninsula was 'Bharat-Varsha', or the land of the legendary King Bharata. Indicative of a Hindu assimilationist

---

74 P. Singh, 'Hindu Bias in India's "Secular" Constitution: Probing Flaws in the Instruments of Governance', *Third World Quarterly* 26: 6 (2005), pp. 909–26. See also T. Mahmood, 'Appeasing the Majority', *Times of India*, 18 July 2013. Giving added weight to Mahmood's criticisms of the 'non-secular character' of many Constitutional provisions is the fact that he was a former chairman of the National Minorities Commission and an ex-member of the Law Commission of India. He warned that longstanding Muslim educational institutions enjoying 'minority status', and therefore by law able to enrol a much higher proportion of Muslim students, would be attacked for this. Promoting secularity would be the excuse for trying to deny 'protective discrimination' to Muslims and Christians. The Modi regime, in seeking to take away the minority status of two such major central universities catering to both Muslims and non-Muslims, namely Aligarh Muslim University and Jamia Millia Islamia, has shown him to be quite prescient in this regard.

75 If Bhargava would certainly demur from such a conclusion, the legal expert Upendra Baxi commends the 'vibrancy of vision' of a Constitution which, like no other before it, sought an 'explicit and comprehensive transformation of a traditional society', but adds a warning that there is 'sufficient ground for anxiety concerning the potential for justice in Indian constitutionalism'. U. Baxi, 'The (Im)Possibility of Constitutional Justice: Seismographic Notes on Indian Constitutionalism', in Z. Hasan, E. Sridharan and R. Sudarshan, eds., *India's Living Constitution: Ideas, Practices, Controversies* (New Delhi, 2002), p. 55.

drive, the Hindu Code Bill of 1955 included in its definition of – Hindus – Sikhs, Jains and Buddhists. This has given rise at times to protests by all three communities. Under the guise of concern for animal husbandry, the Directive Principles called for 'prohibiting the slaughter of cows and calves and other milch and draught cattle'. This was a clear concession to upper-caste Hindu members of the Assembly; directed against Muslims and Dalits, it is a form of spiritual imposition.[76] Many states of the Union banned cow slaughter, and the latest Modi government has extended the ban on slaughter of both cows and bulls to Maharashtra, which was not subject to it.

While India has a large number of official languages, only Hindi has been given the status of National Official Language, specifically in the Devanagari script, a Brahmin-dominated script that was not as widely used at the moment of independence as the Kaithi script, which was perceived by upper castes as closer to Hindustani than to Sanskrit. Sanskrit, in turn, was also given a special status in the Constitution, as the principal source for the development of the vocabulary, grammar and phonetics of Hindi, whose spread was deemed a duty of the Union of India to promote greater national unity. Sanskrit is the mother tongue of a few hundred people, but is emphasized in the Constitution, while a number of tribal languages, such as Santhali, Bhilli and Lammi, each spoken by well over a million people, are completely ignored. Other widely spoken languages of north India, including Braj, Avadhi and Maithili, have been relegated to the status of 'dialects' of a Sanskritized Hindi.[77]

Before turning to the contentious issue of personal laws and how compatible their preservation is with Constitutional commitment to secularism, I should address the fundamental issue of caste itself. Many have highlighted the fact that untouchability is banned by the Constitution, and this is said to be a hallmark of its commitment to social justice. *But caste itself has not been Constitutionally banned; nor has there been, nor will there be, any amendment accepted that calls for this.* Yet this is something of a crucial litmus test regarding the extent to which the Constitution is 'Hindu-tainted'.[78] Caste discrimination was outlawed, but there is no constitutional call for abolishing caste itself – implying that the *existence* of caste, as distinct from practices of discrimination, is acceptable. Affirmative action for lower-caste Hindus was sanctioned, and then under pressure extended to Dalits among Jains and Sikhs. But Dalit Christians and Muslims remain excluded to this day.

No doubt there will be those who say that no purpose would be served by an Indian Constitution banning something that is so deep-seated, and

---

76 K. Ilaiah, 'Cow and Culture', *The Hindu*, 25 October 2002. See also K. Ilaiah, *Buffalo Nationalism: A Critique of Spiritual Fascism* (Kolkata, 2004).

77 A. Rai, *Hindi Nationalism* (Delhi, 2002); P. Brass, *Language, Religion and Politics in North India* (London, 1974).

78 For all his criticisms, Pritam Singh is not alone among analysts of the Constitution in failing to call attention to this lacuna.

will persist no matter what the Constitution declares. Again, many would claim that making such a declaration would detract from the sobriety of the Constitution's provisions, which must relate to the reality of Indian society if they are to furnish a tool for the further improvement of that society. This will not do, and in my view constitutes a form of special pleading to cover up a serious and unwarranted deficiency.

Article 15 of the Constitution's Fundamental Rights prohibits discrimination on the grounds of 'religion, race, caste, sex and place of birth', but this is far from adequate even as a statement of principle. Elimination of discrimination based on sex and race obviously does not entail the elimination of differences of sex and race as biological facts. But caste is not a biological fact, and to call for the end of caste discrimination without demanding the elimination of the caste system itself makes no sense, since it is by its very nature a hierarchical system of graded inequality of dignity and status, related to accidents of birth. Any Constitution that is committed in principle to equal respect of its citizens and to equal dignity cannot remain silent on this issue. But to have outlawed the caste system itself would have meant confronting a Brahminical understanding of Hinduism, if not Hinduism in its entirety. It would have meant attacking a religiously sanctioned belief system of birth-based inequality and discrimination. To avoid enacting such a ban is not just to pretend, but to formally promote the illusion, that caste discrimination can somehow be overcome while the caste–varna system remains intact. Here, 'respect for religion' could be interpreted to justify non-interference. But the failure to interfere reveals not just a weakness of democratic values, but a special bias towards the dominant religious system of the country in its beliefs and practices – in other words, a secular failure as well. Even with regard to the specific issue of untouchability, can this evil be eradicated short of eliminating the caste system itself? Apparently the Indian Constitution thinks so.

All debate about the secularity or otherwise of the Constitution has had to address its preservation of personal laws for Christians, Parsis and Muslims, as well as the only partial reforms undertaken of Hindu family laws – the question of the absent Uniform Civil Code (UCC). This absence had much more to do with concerns about how best to deal with the religious–cultural sensitivities especially of Muslims, by far the largest religious minority. It also reflected the fact that there was a relative lack of concern with issues of gender justice, which really only come to the forefront much later, after the emergence of an autonomous women's movement in the late 1970s. Matters were subsequently made more complicated for both the advocates of greater secularism and for those supporting the struggle against gender oppression by the Sangh's adoption in the 1980s of the call for a UCC. In making this call the Sangh is claiming first, that this absence of a UCC reflects the state's anti-secular bias and that the bodies affiliated to Sangh are the true secularists in contrast to 'pseudo-secularists' who by not pushing wholeheartedly for a UCC are appeasing (partly for vote bank purposes) a socially backward Muslim minority. Second, that this state failure shows a lack of equal treatment between Muslims and Hindus, and therefore constitutes a 'discrimination' against the latter, who did undergo some reform of family laws under the Hindu Code bill of 1955. Third, that it shows up the contrast between Muslims and the more humane, tolerant, modern and non-communal character of Hindus, who had accepted the need for reform. In fact, the purpose of the 1955 Bill was more to homogenize culturally diverse Hindu practices in keeping with a desire to project a more uniform Hindu community than answering concerns about gender equality.[79]

Given this rise of Hindu communal forces and the threats it posed, one consequence was a heightening of identity politics among Muslims more generally, and across the gender divide. It became more difficult to view a UCC as only or primarily an issue of gender justice (after all, much remained to be done for Hindu women as well), and not interfering from the 'outside' to change or replace Personal Law has come to be seen as respecting in principle the rights of a minority to maintain its own cultural resources. Moreover, the Indian women's movement, recognizing that gender-just laws have the best chance of being accepted by men, and therefore women, in religious communities when they are not seen as an imposition from outside, has also moved towards stressing the necessity of 'reforms from within' for all religious communities. In this way, it has sought to make the issue one of pursuing gender justice among all religious communities, and separating themselves from the Sangh, whose call for a UCC is primarily a stick with which to beat Muslims and Islam. Unsurprisingly, the women's wings of the forces of Hindutva, with its overall commitment to preserving patriarchal and martial values, have remained aloof from the intense debates and struggles waged historically by the progressive women's movement for changes in specific laws, relating, for example, to dowry, rape and domestic violence.

But what has been achieved by such piecemeal reforms is limited and very far from sufficient. There is no incompatibility or strategic contradiction in pursuing step-by-step reforms while also postulating a more comprehensive programme, such as a model UCC, as a way of placing stronger pressure on concerned authorities and winning more supporters to the cause. However, earlier efforts by the women's movement to adopt this side-by-side strategy, which included the formulation of just such an overall model UCC, have been reduced to the more limited aim of a purely step-by-step approach pressing for reforms from within the religious community. But what of the possible support to be derived in this struggle for greater gender justice from the provisions of the Constitution? Given that all constitutions are

---

79 F. Agnes, 'The Supreme Court, the Media and the Uniform Civil Code Debate in India', in Needham and Sundarajan, *Crisis of Secularism in India*.

products of their times and circumstances, the failure of the Indian Constitution to contain a UCC has come to be seen by many secular progressives and social activists as unavoidable, and not in itself an indictment of the document. After all, in the section on Directive Principles, Article 44 specifies that the state 'shall endeavour to secure for the citizens a uniform civil code throughout the territory of India'.

And there is the rub. First, what was historically unavoidable should not be presented as a virtue of Indian secularism. The absence of a UCC in the Constitution was over-determined by both the relationship of Congress leaders to the Muslim Ulama and by the 'soft' Hindu nationalism that shaped the thinking of so many of its members in the Constituent Assembly.[80] Second, the real question is why the state founded by this Constitution has never seriously moved in the direction which Article 44 says it should have done. According to the legal scholar, Upendra Baxi, 'endeavour' here should mean something like 'initiating a process with a view to concluding' a UCC. Six-and-a-half decades later, there has been no such serious process initiated. This could take the form of a regularized and systematized conversation between leaders of religious communities, which the state would play a major role in organizing and sustaining. It could involve financial, economic and other forms of support to those seeking to opt out of community, personal and customary laws but fearful of the adverse consequences of doing so. What forward movement has there been that can enthuse those who believe reform from within is the only way to proceed? Why have the Constitution and the state founded upon it proved unable to generate a serious forward momentum in this regard?[81]

To raise these questions is not to dismiss as inconsequential or as a charade such secular characteristics as are possessed by both the Constitution and the state, but simply to call for a better assessment of the strengths and weaknesses of Indian secularism, and for a more balanced comparison of it with the secularisms of Western states in liberal democracies. The centuries-long reality of great religious diversity has shaped the nature of Indian secularism, and does provide important lessons for the secularisms of Europe. But the tendency to make more of this diversity than it deserves is best avoided. The eminent historian of ancient India, Romila Thapar, provides salutary advice in this regard:

---

80 N. Rajan, *Secularism, Democracy, Justice: Implications of Rawlsian Principles in India* (New Delhi, 1998), Chapter 4. See also M. Nussbaum, 'On Equal Conditions', in M. Hasan, ed., *Will Secular India Survive?* (New Delhi, 2004), pp. 45–6: '[I]t was a mistake all along to exempt personal laws from the scrutiny of fundamental rights … To allow compromise here is to allow compromises with the very foundations of citizenship and the equal dignity of citizens.'

81 Baxi, 'Siting Secularism in the Uniform Civil Code'. The Supreme Court is the guardian empowered to defend through its interpretations the 'basic structure' of the Constitution. Here Baxi raises an important point: does this 'basic structure' need to be changed in the light of the feminist critique, since the Constitution is in his words 'logically self-contradictory', forbidding gender discrimination and yet preserving personal laws?

The Indian view of secularism generally speaks only of the coexistence of religions. That I find inadequate. What are often quoted are the Asokan edicts where Asoka speaks about the need for all sects to honour each other and, specifically, to honour the other person's sect. And in recent times, therefore, it is often said that Indian civilization is a civilization where all religions were and are honoured. However, it is not enough to say that the coexistence of all religions means a secular society unless there is also an insistence on the religions having equal status. If we associate religions with a majority community and minority communities, as we invariably do, then these distinctions assume a lack of equal status.[82]

Yes, inter-religious tolerance at the level of many culturally related practices of everyday life is greater in India than in Europe. But even here there should be no exaggeration, since there are aspects of everyday life in which it is today's India that can learn from Europe. For example, there has never been any justification for the legal ban on cow slaughter that is upheld by a large majority of Indian states, especially given the diverse eating habits of various religious groups and citizens. During the term of the latest Modi government at the centre, the Maharashtra government (also ruled by the BJP) has for the first time extended this ban to include bulls and bullocks, while a rising crescendo of voices organized by the forces of the Sangh in civil society everywhere call for making even the possession and eating of beef (including buffalo meat), if not illegal, then certainly a sign of anti-Hindu degeneracy that must be publicly opposed and condemned. In late September 2015, a Muslim family in western Uttar Pradesh, very close to the national capital, was attacked by a mob merely on the basis of rumours that they had kept and eaten beef in their home. The father was beaten to death, and one son in critical condition after this assault had to be hospitalized. This event came in the context of a dramatic spike in small-scale communalist attacks throughout Uttar Pradesh, overwhelmingly by Hindu groups against Muslims, in the months preceding and following the 2014 general election.[83]

European notions of secularism do need to change, to abandon their fixed templates and assumptions of superiority, developing a more expansive sense of what it means to respect religious freedoms and their expressions in public and even political life. This must also go along with a greater awareness of what should not be accepted in the name of a liberal conception of freedom of expression. The cartoon controversy and much of the reaction to the tragedy surrounding the killing of the journalists of *Charlie Hebdo*, the

---

82 See R. Chakravarti, interview with R. Thapar, *Frontline*, 18 September 2015, pp. 12–13.

83 See 'Dadri: Outrage after Mob Lynches Man for Allegedly Consuming Beef', *Indian Express*, 30 September 2015.

French satirical magazine, highlighted this problem. Satire must avoid forms of hate speech and portrayal. Here context always matters, and what may be permissible for one community is not necessarily so for another. Satire should be about 'afflicting the comfortable and comforting the afflicted'. Islamophobia is the new form of racism in Europe, and Muslims there suffer from various forms of discrimination and injustice. Satirical portrayals that are offensive to many or most Catholics in France cannot justify the same towards Muslims there, because Catholics do not constitute a community that suffers anything close to the kind of hostility, discrimination and public prejudice that is currently directed at Muslims.

But then there is the other side of the picture. Everyday inter-religious cultural acts of tolerance are essentially of a passive nature. When it comes to active forms of dangerous physical intolerance between religious sects and groups, whether individually or collectively orchestrated, the record in India is far, far worse than in Europe or in the democracies of North and South America. Indian secularism is part of a political set-up that is domestically far more anti-democratic and violent, in that it involves the repeated large-scale killing of minority religious groups, especially Muslims, by perpetrators who invariably escape punishment. Nor can the apparatuses of the Indian state be absolved from culpability.[84] Indeed, in no other liberal democracy has a far-right political entity come to power at the national level four times – in chronological order, first for a few days as a minority regime, then twice in coalition, and finally with a majority of its own. If nothing else, this is testimony to the fact that the Sangh Parivar's vicious communalist ethos has come to represent an established 'common sense' in India's polity and society.

A key lesson that can be drawn from this comparative reality is that, in the longer run and in a deeper sense, it is the quality of secularity in society rather than that of the state that is most important. Nanda has repeatedly stressed the point that popular religiosity of a certain kind in the wider society (when it is not associated with a liberation theology or a millenarianism that prioritizes resolution of the secular plight of the poor and downtrodden) does constitute a potential danger. The iconography, beliefs and rituals of Hindutva as a religio-political movement are not different from those of popular religiosity, and do attract followers in their own right. The bases of support for the BJP will vary, and does not necessarily express hostility to the Muslim as religious other. But this appeal is present at various levels, and the Sangh Parivar can be widely seen as a 'faith protector', and as a supporter and 'dignifier' of the Hindu believer.[85]

Besides, where the breadth and intensity of popular religiosity is high, this reality is a significant factor contributing to the emergence of religio-political

---

84 See note 74, above.
85 Nanda, *Wrongs of the Religious Right*.

movements. Countries at roughly similar socio-economic levels but with much lower levels of intense popular religiosity will not have a similar scale or depth of religio-political movements. Their emergence is thus not to be seen simply as a reaction to, or displacement of, socio-economic frustrations. Religiosity is, or at least can be, an independent causal factor. Theological conservatism tends to promote political conservatism. Ultimate beliefs can count for more than socio-economic concerns.[86] Evangelical Hinduism on Indian television and elsewhere does not automatically translate into support for Hindutva politics, or for the Sangh. But it certainly creates a stronger ground for such support to emerge, and the Hindutva movement knows this – which is why it endorses and promotes deeper and wider public religiosity.

There is a 'quiet faith' that is more privatized, individualized and mellow, as distinct from a 'loud', publicly asserted faith. Nanda is correct to suggest that subdued religiosity is more characteristic of the West (despite variations between different countries) than of India, and that this is reflective of the greater influence and popular diffusion of Enlightenment values, which has helped to promote a more secular public culture. One must respect belief in the sacred and transcendent for its capacity to enable believers to cope with life and improve it, individually and collectively. But its claims of positive intervention by supernatural forces in shaping reality must, like other empirical claims, be put to evidentiary tests. On this terrain of belief, one should accept that 'there are no divine commandments in nature, morality and politics', and concede the importance of scientific reason, which entails a willingness to subject the content of religious metaphysics to investigation, allowing for the possibility of falsification, while rejecting the non-falsifiable.[87] Nanda believes that rationalist and popular science movements have been important tools in the effort to secularize Indian society, but the discourse on Indian secularism has not sufficiently respected this need to develop scientific reason or promote a popular 'scientific temper'. This is one Constitutional injunction, she believes, that has been casually dismissed or ignored by far too many secularists, who have otherwise bent over backwards to try to find all kinds of virtues in religious discourses, even where these do not exist.

One does not have to afford the same degree of importance that Nanda does to rationalist confrontation with religious beliefs as part of the wider process of generating a cultural transformation in order to applaud both her determination to highlight the central importance of the further secularization of Indian society and her emphasis on scientific reasoning, as well as other Enlightenment-inspired values, that are capable of being universalized to create a better world order.

---

86 See N. Keddie, 'The New Religious Politics: Where, When, and Why do "Fundamentalisms" Appear?', *Comparative Study of Society and History* 40: 4, pp. 696–723.
87 Nanda, *Wrongs of the Religious Right*, p. 59.

Anti-Secularism

The term 'anti-secularism' here refers not to all anti-secular forces, but to a much narrower grouping taking its distance from both communal-fundamentalist Hindutva forces and from the secularists opposed to them. As such, it is not a serious political force guiding any identifiable party or organization of any major consequence. However, it does describe an intellectual current that has gained ground in Indian academia and among NGO activists, and has influenced the general public discourse on matters pertaining to communalism and secularism. It claims to represent a third position opposing communalism and its various manifestations, but not in the name of a supposedly Westernized concept of secularism and the secular state. Instead it proposes a more useful and 'authentic' indigenism, which seeks to oppose communalism and the various forms of perversion of religion through endorsement and utilization of the resources within India's religious traditions.

In the eyes of many a secularist, however, this approach is seen as having a damaging political effect – as legitimizing, implicitly when not explicitly, the assault by communal forces (above all political Hindutva) against the current level of secularity of the state. It is seen as reinforcing a false solution already pervading the public discourse – the idea that a secular state should be one that enjoins and prescribes the showing of 'equal respect to all religions' (*sarva dharm sambhavam*) rather than maintaining a basic separation of state apparatuses from religious influence and religious institutions; and that a state which maintains this kind of distance is necessarily anti-religion, or very likely to be so, and is therefore repressive, totalitarian, and so on.

L. K. Advani, a former head of the BJP who is said to have coined or at least first publicized the term 'pseudo-secularism', often publicly stated that a true as opposed to pseudo-secular state would be a state practising *sarva dharm sambhavam*, with the added rider that a Hindu *rashtra* would be truly secular because of the unique tolerance of Hinduism. Not all anti-secularists share this vision of Hinduism's unique tolerance. But they do endorse the view that, if the notion of a secular state in India is to be meaningful, then it must adopt a more authentically indigenous notion of active organization of religious toleration.

The three most important spokespersons for this anti-secularism are Bhiku T. Parekh, T. N. Madan and Ashis Nandy.[88] If there are certain similarities in their thinking and writing, they also have their important differences and distinctive ambiguities. Anti-secularism is not a strongly consistent and

---

88 Bhiku T. Parekh is emeritus professor of political philosophy at the University of Westminster and a life peer. T. N. Madan is honorary professor of sociology at the Indian Institute of Economic Growth, New Delhi. Ashis Nandy is senior honorary fellow at the Centre for the Study of Developing Societies, New Delhi. 'Anti-secularist' and 'anti-secularism' are not terms that Parekh or Madan would necessarily use to describe themselves or their views.

coherent discourse. It is still united more by what it is against than what it is for. But in this discourse, ranging over six general themes, there are common points of reference. These six general themes are: the issue of modernity; understandings of culture, civilization, religion and Hinduism in regard to Indian society past and present; secularism and secularization; particularism and universalism; individualism and communitarianism; and neo-Gandhianism.

All three share similar basic understandings of culture and civilization, and of religion's relationship to Indian culture, though they differ in their assessments of Hinduism (and Islam). They express varying levels of unease with modern concepts of democratic individualism, and place different amounts of stress on the importance of religiously rooted communitarian values as a preferred counterpoint. All three express sympathy for Gandhi's vision and thought. They are neo-Gandhians, but differ over what Gandhi-ism is, and over the precise value of that legacy. Parekh and Madan hold to what can be called an essentially culturalist theory of modernity, which is the main source-bed of the 'multiple modernities' school. Madan clearly says that modernity has many beginnings, while Nandy relies more on an anti-modernist 'competing universalism'.[89]

The most intransigent of these anti-secularists – the one who would not hesitate to describe himself as such, is Ashis Nandy. He is also the most uncompromising in his hostility to history, to the project of modernity, and the one most determined to read Gandhi as an anti-modernist. Neither Parekh nor Madan would go so far as to write off the project of modernity altogether, and both seem more concerned to conjoin religion and moder-nity. In contrast to Nandy's unremitting hostility to secularism, Madan is noticeably more ambiguous about it. Parekh is more sober and judicious in assessing Gandhi and Gandhiism, and his own preferences are more often to be read off from the sympathies and reservations expressed in his explicatory narratives about political leaders like Gandhi and Nehru. If many of Nandy's observations are infuriating, extreme and unbalanced, many are also provoc-ative, stimulating and insightful. Of the three, Nandy's views have been the most influential, and in some ways politically the most dangerous.

Madan, Parekh and Nandy are cultural essentialists, and that essence is religion. All the problems of double fusion (the cultural programming of society, with religion the cultural programmer) or analytical conflation of culture and society are faithfully replicated in their writings.[90] In Parekh they can be gleaned from his treatment of Gandhi's thought. All three immor-talize and glorify religion. There is the standard bifurcation of religion into good and bad – religion-as-faith and religion-as-ideology, true religion and mere religiosity – enabling them to deflect all criticism of religious failings

---

89 See T. N. Madan, *Images of the World: Essays on Religion, Secularism and Culture* (New Delhi, 2006), Chapter 1.
90 See subsection 'Culture and Society' in the preceding Chapter 2.

as largely irrelevant because inapplicable to what is the true subject matter. Culture is understood as a 'whole way of life', but is also importantly connected to issues of cognition and indigenous forms of knowledge. Each thinker varies in how he understands culture's 'structure of coherence'.

For Madan, culture has key themes or 'dynamic affirmations', which are the principal source of the 'character, structure and direction' of a cultural complex. They give it a 'civilizational distinctiveness'.[91] For all three, civilization is understood only as a long, enduring cultural complex. Parekh sees civilization as 'a shared body of values, attitudes, ways of looking at the world and forms of social relationship'. According to him, 'A common civilizational basis was ... not only available in India but formed the ineliminable substance of its collective life.'[92] For Nandy, Indian civilization is so inclusive of all other faiths that he avoids claiming special centrality for Hinduism; it is a 'confederation of cultures'. For Madan there is no disputing Hinduism's pivotal role in Indian civilization. Parekh's Gandhi also wishes to broaden the notion to include other religious–cultural contributions, but Hinduism clearly has a pre-eminent role.

Religion is either inescapably central to or even constitutive of Indian society, past and present. Both Madan and Nandy frequently endorse the second, more extreme formulation. But where Parekh is sceptical about Hinduism having an essence of its own, and sees popular Hinduism as 'institutionalized bargains', as a power contract, Madan has a more forthrightly Brahminical understanding. Beneath diversity, he sees a unity based on a common code of ethics, and on certain axial beliefs like dharma, karma, artha and kama.[93] There is also a unifying syncretism at the level of action. But since 'civilizational distinctiveness' for Madan necessarily requires a worldview that certain favoured social strata are more likely to possess, there is no embarrassment in acknowledging Brahminic pre-eminence or the centrality of Brahminism and Vedic philosophy to Hindu thought. Like Dumont, Madan sees the 'secret of Hinduism' in the dialogue between renouncer and man-in-the-world.[94]

---

91 T. N. Madan, *Non-Renunciation: Themes and Interpretations of Hindu Culture* (Delhi, 1987).

In this cultural and civilizational continuity, the principle of tradition is the principle of continuity; so, for Madan, 'modernity must be defined in relation to, and not in denial of tradition'. T. N. Madan, *Tradition and Modernity in the Sociology of D. P. Mukherjhee* (Lucknow, 1977), p. 23.

As for upholders of secularism in India, 'in traditional or tradition-haunted societies they can only mean conversion and the loss of one's culture, and if you like, loss of one's soul'. T. N. Madan, 'Secularism in Its Place', *Journal of Asian Studies* 46: 4 (November 1987), p. 754.

92 B. T. Parekh, 'Nehru and the National Philosophy of India', *Economic and Political Weekly*, 5 January 1991, p. 39.

93 Dharma – has multiple meanings relating to behavior in accord with duties, law, virtues, proper conduct. Artha- meaning, goal, purpose. Karma – past deeds determining successive existences. Kama – desire.

94 Madan, *Non-Renunciation*.The absence of this Brahminical slant in Nandy must

Madan's own studies on Muslims and Hindu Pandits in Kashmir have clearly shaped his understanding of Hinduism and Islam.[95] It is the former that possesses most resources for promoting the kind of secularism he most admires, namely inter-faith understanding and religious tolerance. The usual stereotypes regarding Hinduism's tolerance are echoed in his writings. Thus Madan did not much talk of Hindu communalism in his earlier writings, since there is for him no such thing as a Hindu community. He rarely mentioned Hindu nationalism, but was candid about his view that the Indian state 'panders' to the minorities: 'The notion of minority status as privilege is not slander in today's India but a social and political fact. And it is one of the very major reasons why Indian secularism has run into difficulties.'[96] But the anti-Muslim carnage of 2002 in Gujarat did lead Madan to more forcefully distance himself from the forces of Hindutva, and more clearly acknowledge the dangers it presented.[97]

Nandy would never have made that kind of a statement about minority pandering. For him religious faith is the operative notion. Religious systems may differ in the degree of syncretism they encourage, but Nandy largely abstracts from the specificities of any particular religious system when seeking to explain the essentialism of Indian culture and civilization. He is content to understand Hinduism as a combination of classical and folk Hinduisms, where the interrelationship is open to shifting balances. Similar strains are to be found between the classical and folk forms of other religions. Madan's attitudes to secularism and secularization are marked by significant ambiguities, even confusions, which in his later responses to critics are not fully addressed.[98] He knows the kind of secularism he favours – *sarva dharm*

---

partly explain the contrast in his and Madan's positions regarding the issue of caste quotas in the Mandal Report. Madan opposed Mandal; Nandy rightly and courageously supported it.

95 T. N. Madan, 'Religious Ideology in a Plural Society: The Muslims and Hindus of Kashmir', in T. N. Madan, ed., *Muslim Communities of South Asia* (Delhi, 1989); Madan, *Non-Renunciation*; T. N. Madan, *Family and Kingship* (Delhi, 1989). See also 'Introduction' in T. N. Madan, ed., *Religion in India* (Delhi, 1991). From these studies, Madan is convinced that the peaceful coexistence of Hindus and Muslims, at least in Kashmir, can only be based on mutual economic interdependence, political pragmatism and ideological compromise and cannot go any deeper than this.

96 From the mimeograph of T. N. Madan's inaugural public lecture, 'There's Tricks i' th' World: Whither Indian Secularism?', at the International Conference on Religion, Identity and Politics: India in a Comparative Perspective, held at the University of Hull, 24–26 October, 1991. Also published as 'Whither Indian Secularism?', *Modern Asian Studies* 27 (1993), p. 667.

97 As should be clear, Madan pins considerable hopes on the potential of inter-religious compromises to secure greater harmony. So it is perhaps not surprising, though certainly disturbing to this writer, that he seems to approve the advice given by the eminent Parsi jurist and lawyer, Fali Nariman, in regard to resolving the Babri Masjid–Ram Janmabhoomi issue. Nariman said that Muslims should let a Ram temple be built in Ayodhya, as 'this would not be an act of surrender but an act of statesmanship – for the greater good of the greater number' of Muslims. F. Nariman, 'Giving Isn't Giving In', *Hindustan Times*, 14 August 2003. The quote appears in Madan, *Images of the World*, p. 51–52.

98 These responses, as well as further ruminations on themes broached earlier, appear

sambhavam. But since he (like Parekh) seeks to assert religion's centrality to modernity (at least in India), and he does not reject modernity (as Nandy does), Madan is conspicuously unsure what to make of secular humanism as an ideology, or secularization as a process. Madan does not successfully negotiate between the various meanings of secularization. Thus he can see it as having only a peripheral relation to religion. It is a process of 'empowering human agency', as contrasted to supra-human agency, and as such something that has been going on everywhere and throughout the ages. It would appear, then, to bear no special relationship either to modernity, or to any particular religious system. Yet Madan also insists that secularization is the distinctive gift of Christianity.[99] What are we to make of this?

In one attempt of his at giving a clearer definition of secularization it is said to be a term ; 'useful in describing certain processes that are as old as human culture: the processes by which, step by step, human beings have reduced their dependence upon supra-human agency and narrowed down the areas of life in which religious ideas, symbols and institutions hold sway'.[100] However, the process of relative decline of religious influence is not as old as human culture, but receives a qualitative acceleration with the emergence of modernity. Furthermore, in this definition there is, if not a stipulated connection, certainly a clearly implied conjunction between the enhancement of human agency and the reduction of religious influence.

Elsewhere, however, Madan insists that religions enhance human agency by being the source of humanity's deepest values, and therefore are themselves an important expression of the secularization-empowering process. Perhaps Madan means that secularization is a capacious term describing a number of processes, some as old as human culture and to be judged positively (enhancing of human agency), and others not so old, and not to be necessarily judged as positive (the relative decline of religious influence). But what happens, then, to his implied connection between the two? Madan seems unaware of such ambiguities. Certainly the definition does not square with his claim that secularization is a gift of Christianity.

In making this claim, Madan has in mind the tendencies towards the greater privatization of religious concerns. Christian (Protestant) discourse legitimizes and endorses this privatization, and thus promotes it. This is unlike the Indic religious discourses. But even if this is so, it does not warrant the strong claim that secularization is the gift of Christianity.[101] It has multiple sources of birth and sustenance. Capitalist modernization and

---

in Part I of Madan, *Images of the World*, especially in Chapter 5, 'Secularism Revisited: Doctrine of Destiny or Political Ideology'.

99 Madan endorses the views of Peter Berger and David Martin. P. Berger, *The Social Reality of Religion* (London, 1973); D. Martin, *A General Theory of Secularization* (Oxford, 1978). See Madan, 'Whither Indian Secularism?'

100 Madan, 'Whither Indian Secularism?', p. 669.

101 Madan is too influenced by Berger's understanding of Protestantism, individualism and secularization.

democratic discourses originating in the Enlightenment also come into the reckoning. Just how Enlightenment values, capitalist modernization and reform Christianity come together helps explain the emergence of processes of secularization. Given these multiple sources of birth and continuity, it cannot be complacently argued that the absence of a dominant Christian discourse means secularization is very weakly implanted in India, for both capitalism and democratic discourse have developed real roots in the country.

Madan can hardly deny that secularization has taken place in India and is continuing. This, he would say, is a value-neutral fact.[102] Insofar as it means more empowerment of human agency, he can hardly be against it. Insofar as it also means a relative religious decline, he cannot make it fully clear to his readers what he makes of this. This will remain so until he deals with the unresolved tension between the two themes within his own understanding of secularization of 'enhanced empowerment' and 'religious decline'. There are times when he expresses open hostility to secularization. Secularization as a process of privatizing religion acts to undermine the good society that must have religion and religious-based morality at its centre. Secularization creates, by way of a reaction, fundamentalism and religious fanaticism, in that the 'excesses of the one feed the other'.[103]

Logically, then, his position should be a clear opposition not just to the 'secularization thesis', or to what some secularists or forms of secularism say, but to the very process of secularization. Some way should be found either to halt and reverse it, or to separate its positive, empowering aspect from its negative aspect of religious decline, presuming this is possible. This would require from Madan a much clearer, more coherent and consistent *attack* on secularization.

At other points, Madan does suggest that promoting secularization or 'expanding human control over human lives' (which, he says, is proceeding weakly in India) does require a narrowing down of religious influence.[104] He further suggests that the Indic religions, not being revealed truths, are open to self-questioning and thus to such secularization. To promote it, then, requires not Christian-inspired secularism, distinguishing between the secular and the sacred spheres of existence. Secularization in India, he says, needs to be promoted not by an anti-religious interpretation of secularism, but by a secularism meaning 'inter-religious understanding'.

But all this leaves unanswered questions. The Western notion of secu-larism is not, as Madan accepts, necessarily anti-religious. But by clearly delineating the secular from the sacred, it insists that 'religion must be put in its place', which is narrower and more modest than in the past. If this interpretation of secularism is transported to India as part of democratic dis-course, how does it thereby become anti-religious, even if (like democratic

---

102 Madan, 'Whither Indian Secularism?'
103 Madan, *Images of the World*, p. 2.
104 Madan, 'Whither Indian Secularism?'

discourse itself) it is alien to indigenous traditions? Or is it that what is not an anti-religious ideology in Christian societies is automatically so in India, where religious systems are more holistic?

Moreover, how does an ideology of interreligious understanding *reinforce* a secularization process that demands that *all* religions in India adjust to a more modest role and space? Promoting interreligious understanding may help organize the terms of coexistence between religious systems. But secularization, insofar as it requires a reinforcing ideology, wants one to legitimize and justify its *gaining* of more 'secular' space at the expense of *all* forms of religious influence. This is about organizing the terms of coexistence between the secular and the religious, and not about organizing the terms of coexistence between religious systems. There is no obvious passage from the latter to the former. These are *contending* interpretations of what secularism should mean, pertaining either to contending interpretations of secularization or to contending stands (for or against) on an agreed interpretation of secularization. None of these ambiguities is resolved by the simple differentiation that what Madan is attacking and rejecting is not secularization as empirical fact (which is indisputable) but that formulation of the secularization thesis which is so narrow and extreme as to claim that there cannot but be everywhere, as modernity progresses, a continuous and inevitable decline of religious influence in social and public significance.[105] The discourse on secularization is wider and more complex than Madan allows for, even among Marxists.[106]

Thus similar ambiguities pervade his treatment of secularism. With more accuracy, the ideology of secularism is said to have its roots in Christianity. But it is also, he says, the gift of the Enlightenment, which is not quite the same thing. How important the distinction is depends on how Madan understands the connection between Christianity and Enlightenment, itself a contentious historical issue. Since, as Madan notes correctly, in its origins and in most of its dominant versions the ideology of secularism was not, and is not, anti-religious, he has no reason to be against 'secular humanism'. He says he is more concerned to point out its limitations. When secularism is made out to be more important than it can or should be, it creates problems. Moreover, 'extreme' secularists who are against faith, or are obsessed about the importance of a scientific temper, are the real danger. Whatever one thinks of this caution, the ambiguities remain. Now it seems the problem is the immodesty of secularism and secularists: 'It is important to recognize that one of the major reasons for the rise of religious fundamentalism all over the world is the excesses of secularism, its emergence as a dogma, even as a religion.'[107] Presumably a more modest, undogmatic secularism would be fine.

---

105 Madan, *Images of the World*, Chapter 1.

106 Madan seems to think that there is a particular 'Marxist' view on secularism and secularization, which there is not.

107 Madan, 'Whither Indian Secularism?', p. 695.

The problem in India, says Madan, is that the Western-inspired notion is an alien, un-rooted ideology which has, furthermore, not received real backing from the state. A secularization process not receiving strong support from a popular ideology of secularism will be weakly institutionalized.

Here the villain of the piece would appear to be the inadequacy, not the iniquity of secularism. It has been the naive imposition of a minority, according to Madan. Is secularism a failure because it has been imposed and found wanting, indeed detrimental? Or because it has never been seriously pushed or institutionalized?[108]

In other formulations, Madan is far more hostile to secularism. In India, secularism is impossible as a credo because of mass adherence to religion; it is impractical because the neutrality of a secular state is not feasible; it is impotent because it cannot counteract fanaticism and fundamentalism. Secularism is also bereft of true morality, promoting only instrumental values. It is 'moral arrogance and political folly'. Like many others seeking to conjoin religion and modernity for the good of the latter, Madan sees religion as providing meaning in an otherwise meaningless world. He admires Weber for highlighting that science and rationality cannot give answers to the key questions concerning the purpose of life and how it should be lived. Kudos to Durkheim, as well, for his great insight that has, according to Madan, stood the test of time, namely: 'the idea of society is the soul of religion', even as 'art, law, science move out of the ambit of religion'.[109]

There is secularism as 'political ideology', which is related to Enlightenment ideology, which he sees as homogenizing and committed to the dystopian search for human perfectibility, where others might see it more modestly as providing a powerful and necessary impulse and drive for cumulative social improvement. There is secularism as 'world-view' and as 'societal blueprint'. He has reservations about all three, but also says he is not for the abandonment of the secular state; nor does he totally reject ideologies and

---

108 In a specific response to my criticism here, Madan has said that, yes, the ideology of secularism has not made progress and has met with indifference and opposition and, yes, the state has not done enough – by which he means that it has 'relied excessively on the Constitutional (legislative and judicial) route' and not paid enough attention to using the educational process to create an ethos of secularism, which cannot be 'enacted' by legislative fiat. (Madan, *Images of the World*). In my critique of Nandy, written at the same time as that of Madan, I had already stressed this point, and cited in it support of the foremost critic of this failure, namely the educationalist and secularist Professor Krishna Kumar, who has since retired as head of the Department of Education, University of Delhi. One of his key arguments for promoting a more secular education was that Indian education was too much characterized by the guru–shisya (devotee) relationship drawn from religious practices, which should be student- and not teacher-centred. This secular emphasis has more to do with altering the process of teaching than with pushing the content of secularism as an ideology, and is fundamentally at odds with the way Hindu religious texts – much admired by many, including Madan – have been transmitted across the generations. See *Furies*, p. 170 and endnote 81,

109 Madan, *Images of the World*, p. 6. Madan does not mention, as also moving out of the ambit of religion, the capitalist economy as perhaps the most powerful single ingredient in the secularizing solvent of modernity.

institutions embodying secular values. He also likes the distinction made by Bhargava between political secularism and ethical secularism, endorsing the first conception. What he meant by his 1987 article on 'Secularism in Its Place' is that a modern secularism must find its appropriate means of expression in the specifically Indian setting. Not only does this mean it must appreciate and use the great resources of religious toleration that have been such an important part of India's long history, but that the defence of such an Indian secularity must not be advanced on the grounds of secularism, but based on the virtues of religious tolerance. At the same time Madan is also somewhat sceptical about how much can be achieved by interreligious dialogue in India. The three-language formula put forward for education in all states has failed because most have not been interested in learning another Indian language besides their own. Similarly, most religiously minded people in India take little interest in the other's religion. The careful reader of Madan is left confused as to whether he believes the secular state has done too much or too little.[110]

And what of secularization? Has this, too, been a failure? Understood conventionally, it has clearly proceeded apace, and Madan suggests as much. But he also misreads growing religiosity as indicating the failure of secularization, citing the upsurges of politico-religious movements, starting from the late 1970s, as in Iran, Poland, Nicaragua, and so on. No doubt the rise of Islamist currents would also be cited in support of his argument, although the political dimension in 'political Islam' is more important than the religious one. This is itself reflective of the pressures imposed by a secularizing modernity that leads to new complexities in the religion–modernity relationship. Here Nandy is closer to the mark, recognizing that modernist processes (including secularization), by 'de-permeating' religion and permitting its 'narrowing' institutionalization, can create the basis for more extravagant yet sharpened expressions of religiosity, which serve to mark a religious identity and assert it against the 'Other'. Nandy goes further, insisting that this is what modernity and secularization will (not merely can) do. But the point is that, contrary to Madan, growing religiosity of this kind is compatible with (but not a logical outcome of) growing secularization. It is not a refutation of it. Perhaps Madan means that the 'failure' lies not in secularization failing to take place, but that, having taken place, it has failed to do good.

Also, the heavy propagation of any ideology or philosophy of secularism is not vital for extending the secularization–modernization process. The US has maintained a secular state for well-nigh two centuries without such ideological–philosophical affirmation. There is no paradox here. Secular-humanist values are a subset of a wider democratic–individualist framework of values. They institutionalize themselves as the latter do. But

---

110 Madan, 'Secularism Revisited'.

institutionalizing a strong secular state is much easier than institutionalizing a strong, secular civil society. Western social scientists advocating a stronger connection between religion and modern life are rarely, if ever, opponents of the secular state, which is correctly seen as a bulwark against religious fanaticism and fundamentalism. But they are also deeply sympathetic to the view that religion can provide a highly positive social and public input into coping with the 'plight of modernity'.

This is where the principal source of Madan's own uncertainties lies. He is justifiably deeply dissatisfied with the condition of modernity. He believes the discourse of rights is inadequate, indeed 'hedonist', because it does not speak of duties and obligations. It cannot give what religions provide – a collectively shared vision of the good and meaningful life based on commonly held ultimate values. This is a constant refrain to be found in Nandy as well, but one which leads him towards an intransigent anti-modernism. Madan, by contrast, is not willing to adopt a strident anti-modernism.

Nevertheless, his intellectual and political posture is still one-sided. Madan focuses on the presumed inadequacies of secularism and secularization, on the limitations of modern notions of liberalism and democracy. He does not focus on the profound inadequacies of religion and religious systems in coping with the problems of modern life. He attacks secularism for refusing to recognize that religion cannot be 'put in its place', or substantially privatized. It is by its very nature totalizing. But, ironically enough, secularism is attacked for its own totalizations, for being both alien (Western in origin) and culturally arrogant – seeking to become part of the common sense of a culture in which it has no roots. Other modernist notions, like democracy and economic development, have taken root for better or worse in India. But the speed and depth at which this has come about are issues he bypasses.

While Madan raises the problem of cultural untranslatability as a criticism of secular pretensions in Indian society, he does not seriously explore it. How does he justify his own essentialist understanding of culture and Hinduism, given contending traditions within a culture or religious system? What about untranslatability between religious–cultural systems themselves? How does this square with assumptions of meaningful tolerance between such systems?

No religious system has a natural claim to the values of gender equality or citizenship democracy. The point is not to deny or decry this, but to see religious systems, and more importantly cultures, as capable of evolving and changing. Such values, though originally external to religious discourse, can be 'translated' into and internalized within that discourse and into the larger culture. In much the same way, it is not enough merely to note the absence of values of secularism (once judged positive) in Indic religious discourses or cultures. Nor is it adequate to dismiss the struggle to internalize or 'indigenize' these values as something impossible or not worth the effort. This is not just to denigrate secularism; it is also to denigrate the open-ended possibilities in cultures and in a cultural space. Such determinism is always much more likely to arise from a perspective of cultural essentialism, with its usual corollary – the implicit or explicit, the more or less exuberant, defence of a cultural relativism.

Modern pluralism requires both secularism and religion 'knowing their places'. The issue is not an outright rejection of one or the other, but how best to negotiate their terms of coexistence. The totalizing claims of religious systems make it difficult, though not impossible, for it to move in this direction. This impulse to coexist is not internal to Indic religious systems; it comes primarily from the secular transformations that have been part of capitalist modernization in India.

Previous coexistence between religions in India is not a result of, but in spite of, each religion's totalizing claims. This coexistence represents 'lived tolerances', in which there is neither mass understanding or mass curiosity *across* faiths. One cannot simultaneously demonize the supposed totalizations of secular discourse and sanctify the totalizing claims of religion, all in the name of constructing a desirable pluralism.[111] Madan's desire, in some ways laudable, to resurrect a 'moral community' of the old Durkheimian kind (via the resources of religion) is reflective of the Nostalgia Paradigm shared in some significant degree by all anti-secularists. It is an unsophisticated replay of the present-day debate in political philosophy between liberalism and communitarianism, in which the best liberalism and the best communitarianism find considerable common ground.

It is more unsophisticated because it fails to grapple adequately with modernist possibilities and transformations. The construction of a 'moral community' in a more secularized modern world is far more problematic because of the sharpening of social conflict, the emergence of competing ideologies, the range and depth of individual freedom, and the great variety in conceptions of the good life. A moral consensus is more easily attainable with respect to means (fair and impartial procedures, the values of

---

111 In a fine critique of Madan, André Beteille stresses the importance of negotiating the 'terms of coexistence' between the secular and the religious. He is not for dispensing with either. Does Madan really oppose the secularization of social institutions such as universities, firms and administrative bodies? Does he really endorse the totalization of religion? Is not this totalization more the ideal of the religious intellectual than a fact on the ground? Do not 'the totalizing aims to which Madan has referred vary greatly from one religion to another; and within the same religious tradition, from one historical phase to the other'? A. Beteille, 'Secularism and Intellectuals', *Economic and Political Weekly*, 5 March 1994, p. 565. Beteille also points out that secular institutions cannot show 'equal respect to all religions' by accommodating them equally or on an unlimited basis. This is simply unworkable.

In his reply, Madan clearly gives ground. He clarifies that he is attacking those secularists who believe religion is fake and evil. He also admits to overstating 'the holistic character of traditional religions'. But it was in the name of this holism that he attacked secularists and the standard notion of secularism, and not just the minuscule group who feel religion is fake or evil. T. N. Madan, 'Secularism and the Intellectuals', *Economic and Political Weekly*, 30 April 1994.

compromise) than to goals. Madan (like Nandy) fails to accept that religions are never unproblematically the source of the deepest or ultimate values. Religious systems have acted to stabilize and hierarchically organize by selecting from the *existing range* of values available. The deepest values are not self-evidently the same within a cultural space, or across its various social strata. Nor do different religious systems have the *same* ultimate values. These are never a fixed set discovered or grounded once and for all by the world religions. There is a historicity of the value systems associated with the respective world religions.

The search today for a commonly shared conception of the good is entirely legitimate. But it is a far more onerous task than the anti-secularist immortalizers of religion assume. And it is inconceivable without the healthy institutionalization of the much frowned upon (by them) modern discourse of rights. Madan, however, would prefer to place his hopes on what he calls a 'participatory pluralism'.[112] On the one hand, this would be a *modus vivendi* involving dialogue and compromise through respect for the fundamentals of all faiths. The ideology of secularism should be reworked 'as an ideology of participatory pluralism based on values of dignity (equality of rights) and freedom of conscience'.[113] His secular Indian state would be Gandhi's uniform treatment of all religions – *sarva dharm sambhavam*, whereby the Constitution should deny financial assistance to all religions even where their existence would require state support. As Gandhi said, a religion that cannot exist without state support does not deserve to exist. That a religious minority might be oppressed and that it might require special rights not given to others is here implicitly frowned upon.

Moreover, 'freedom of conscience' is not to be taken as endorsing a licence for conversion. Madan is no advocate of conversion. Here, he is on the same side as many a Hindu nationalist, and critical of 'unfair' conversions, where the meaning ascribed to 'unfair' goes well beyond simply physical coercion to include other nonviolent means. In this respect, he is not unhappy with the state laws that have laid down restrictions on conversions by proselytizing religions. Madan considers Hinduism to be a non-proselytising religion. It is not a surprise, then, that he harbours great admiration for Gandhi, whom he sees as an exemplar of participatory pluralism. Madan is not a cultural relativist; indeed, he goes to considerable lengths to explain lucidly and sensibly why such a position is mistaken.[114] He does believe in transcultural absolutes where values are concerned, and therefore in the communicability of such absolute or fundamental values and principles across faiths as the

---

112 First given detailed treatment in T. N. Madan, 'Perspectives on Pluralism' *Seminar* 484 (1999), pp. 18–23.

113 Madan, 'Secularism Revisited', p. 140.

114 Madan, 'Perspectives on Pluralism'. Most of this text is taken up with explaining why his participatory pluralism is not a form of cultural relativism, and in criticizing those who would see the relationship of Hinduism to other faiths in terms of the former's intrinsic superiority, i.e. its hierarchical inclusion of the virtues and truths of other religions.

bases on which socio-political agreements can be forged. This then is his stated lodestar – 'a universal, spiritual (non-secular) humanism'.[115] Insofar as Gandhi is the figure who has exemplified this, it was he who most sought to establish the material grounds for this participatory pluralism through shared labour (the spinning wheel) and trusteeship.

Leaving aside the ugly class paternalism of the latter notion, this is really all we get by way of elaboration of how Gandhian wisdom might help to create a meaningful modern, Indian secularism. Madan admits that his notion of participatory pluralism needs further clarification and development. In the end, he refers to Isaiah Berlin's value pluralism, in which different ends are sought but rationality and communication can allow shared understandings, sympathy and cross-cultural learning to emerge. One might be forgiven for thinking that all this amounts to very thin gruel indeed when it comes to coping with today's reality in India and elsewhere.

Anti-Modernist Stridencies

Those who are not interested in conjoining religion to modernity but are stridently anti-modernist are not concerned about establishing the importance of tradition within, and for, modernity. They want to establish the incompatibility of modernity with tradition and culture. To accept modernity, however critically, is somehow to be anti-culture. Conversely, to be an anti-modernist is to be profoundly concerned with culture. And this stance of anti-modernism is a meaningful political choice today because, even in the face of the undoubted power of modernists and of modernizing processes, it speaks for a still enormously powerful constituency, the authentic Indian masses for whom culture and therefore tradition remain paramount.[116] This is the brief that Ashis Nandy has chosen to argue.

Nandy's understandings of religion, culture, society and civilization are not markedly different from those of many a culturalist or immortalizer of religion. But his distinctive twist lies in how he uses these notions to indict modernity as irredeemably tainted: 'Culture ... is a way of life and it covers, apart from "high culture", indigenous knowledge, including indigenous theories of science, education and social change.' Or, elsewhere: 'a culture, in the sense of traditions, represents the accumulated wisdom of the people – empirical and rational in its architectonics, though not in every detail'.[117]

---

115 Madan, 'Perspectives on Pluralism', p. 21.

116 Meera Nanda has called this posture of Nandy's a neo-populism that is as old as modernity itself. Indeed, it is *only* as old as modernity. See her fine critique, M. Nanda, 'Is Modern Science a Western, Patriarchal Myth? A Critique of Populist Orthodoxy', *South Asia Bulletin* XI: 1–2, 1991.

117 A. Nandy, 'Culture, State and the Rediscovery of Indian Politics', *Economic and Political Weekly*, 8 December 1984. For a confused attempt to deal with the various meanings of culture, see A. Nandy, 'Culture as Resistance', *Times of India*, 10 December 1994. It highlights once again Nandy's determination to promote a notion of culture that is

Here culture, not society, is the important term. Society is conceptualized in terms of culture. Culture may mean 'way of life', but what is most important about this 'way of life' are the various forms of 'indigenous knowledge' or 'traditions', meaning 'accumulated wisdom'. Tradition, if you like, is a 'matter of the mind'. Religion's strength is that it is a 'total theory of life' which has to invade public spaces, and must have a theory of transcendence. What is civilization, or, more particularly, Indian civilization? For Nandy, it means 'a culture dominated by religious consciousness that has not competed for the minds of men but offered itself as a lifestyle within which other lifestyles can be accommodated'.[118]

Civilization is above all a culture.[119] Culture is above all a distinctive sensibility, a mentality, a special sense of self (Nandy claims the pre-modern self is 'fluid'). It is accumulated wisdoms, including accumulated theories of all kinds – of indigenous science, culture, oppression, and so on. It is a traditional world-view in which metaphysics is vital because it is perennial philosophy answering perennial problems in a way that situates individual and society as microcosmic expressions of the cosmic–universal order.[120]

And religion has been the source of this distinctive sensibility. Most of the time, Nandy sees religion as virtually isomorphic with culture. Occasionally he sees it as merely central to culture. But religion, too, is above all a matter of the mind and self, of experience and feeling or thought.[121] Thus, to under-

---

definitionally anti-modern – conceiving it, for example, as itself a resistance escaping the discourse of resistance allowed by modernity.

See also two solid critiques of the culturological approaches of anti-modernists: S. Joseph, 'Indigenous Social Science Project', *Economic and Political Weekly*, 13 April 1991; S. Joseph, 'Culture and Political Analysis in India', *Social Scientist*, October–November 1991.

118 A. Nandy, *At the Edge of Psychology* (Delhi, 1980) p. 113.

119 There are universal core values, and they are found in those special, large accommodative traditional cultures we can call civilizations. What is distinctive about civilizations is how they synthesize the package containing these universal core values. See A. Nandy, *Traditions, Tyranny and Utopias* (Delhi, 1987): 'All civilizations share some basic values and such cultural traditions as derive from man's biological self and social experience. The distinctiveness of a complex civilization lies not in the uniqueness of its values but in the gestalt which it imposes on these values and in the weights it assigns to its different values and sub-traditions' (p. 22). A culture also has a definite patterning; so cultural change operates within certain essentialist constraints. 'A culture is not a grocery store ... A culture is an interconnected whole with some strong interconnections and some weak ... Within it you have some options only if yet others are not exercised' (p. 120). Given this patterned and essentialist notion of culture, Nandy handles issues of cultural contestation *within* a tradition in expected ways, abstracting from issues of power and ideology. Such tensions simply represent 'a dialectic between the classical and the folk, the past and the present, the dead and living'. Nandy, 'Culture, State and the Rediscovery of Indian Politics'. Both cultural conflicts and social tensions are underplayed in the interests of presenting a more or less harmonious picture of traditional societies.

120 A. Nandy, 'Cultural Frames for Transformative Politics: A Credo', in B. T. Parekh and T. Pantham, eds, *Political Discourse* (Delhi, 1987), p. 243.

121 For the immortalizer of religion, the religious consciousness is not so much a historical form of consciousness as an ineradicable element in the structure of consciousness.

stand a civilization is to understand a culture, or cultures, which is also to understand a religious system, or systems, and thus to understand the mind of an authentic inmate of that culture. Nandy's own discipline of psychology is thus privileged above all other disciplinary vantage points for developing a general understanding of culture, civilization and society, provided one follows him in recognizing that true psychology is not an engineering but a philosophical enterprise. It is the study of the art of self-realization. This is the psychologist as social thinker, not social engineer.[122] But could it be that becoming a serious social thinker might require strenuous efforts to develop other disciplinary, skills including those of history?

Not for the aggressively anti-historical Nandy. What holds for the study of traditional societies holds for the study of modern ones. Modernity is also, above all, a 'state of mind'. Indeed, it is a diseased state of mind, a 'pathology' that has become particularly acute since the 1950s and 1960s. Colonialism, too, was above all a state of mind, which is why it has not ended. Modernizers represent the continuity of the colonized mind. Since modernity is a pathology, all of its forms are diseased beyond hope. Critical modernists are therefore feeble counter-players or 'ornamental dissenters', who should never be mistaken for serious critics.[123]

It is ineffable not because of the inescapable limitations in our cognitive powers concerning the workings of the mind, but because of its 'core' location in the psyche.

122 A. Nandy, 'The Politics of Application and Social Relevance in Contemporary Psychology', in Baxi and Parekh, *Crisis and Change in Contemporary India*.

Personality encompasses identity, but is not equivalent to it. Efforts to understand personality owe much to the insights of both the psychoanalytical and cognitive approaches to identity and personality formation. The psychoanalytical approach stresses 'objects of authority', the 'arational' roots of identity-fixation, and the 'fixity' of identities. It is more determinist than the cognitive approach, emphasizing the key role of typical authority figures in a typical family set-up, which in turn may be taken to express the typicality of the cultures in which such families are embedded. The psychoanalytical tradition has significant differences concerning how much importance it affords to cognitive understandings of personality and identity-formation, and how much flexibility there is in personality-construction. In the cognitive approach, the family will not be so central a mediating link between culture/society and the personality; nor will the 'typicality' of a family set-up be so readily assumed.

The more determinist currents within psychoanalytically influenced psychology gravitate towards more essentialist and reductionist views about the relationship between culture/society and personality. For Nandy, there are distinctive personality configurations for distinctive cultures, and an Indian self that reveals its distinctiveness – for example, in favouring non-violent ways of resisting in crisis situations. For the distinctive Indian self to exist, there has to be a distinctive Indian family cutting across such social categories as caste or class. So the gender division becomes all-important in personality-formation, and there will be a distinctive Indian way in which the Indian individual objectifies his or her relation, especially, to the mother.

123 A. Nandy, *The Intimate Enemy* (Delhi, 1983). His characterization of critical modernism borders on caricature. He sees the range of such criticality as extremely limited. He claims it does not challenge the epistemology of science, when in fact there is an extremely lively dispute about what science is and how special and useful it is. Critical modernists are supposed to take the nation-state system for granted. What does this mean? Are modernists united in lauding it or believing it to be irreplaceable? Critical modernists are not supposed to have any serious problems with the urban–industrial vision, and argue

Since entities like culture or modernity possess 'typical' mentalities, they can be analysed and understood through the study of 'typical' representatives of that culture or mentality. The culture of 'critical traditionality' (Nandy's ideal) is thus *represented* by the thought and personality of Gandhi. Time and again, Nandy uses this technique of making an individual personality or a personality-type *stand in* as an expression of larger social processes. These are his favoured taxonomies of culture and society. Such an approach has a long pedigree in post-Weberian Western social science. But this has not fazed Nandy, whose project is avowedly to 'recover' an indigenous social science.

Nandy is concerned most of all with the 'cultural psychology of Indian politics'.[124] Were this endeavour perceived only as a modest peep providing partial and limited insights into such complex matters as modernity, then one could even be highly grateful for some of the insights received. But instead it leads in his hands to the construction of a grandiose paradigm of anti-modernism, forging an Alternative Science – another theory of universalism that will compete with and oppose Enlightenment universalism itself.

Nobody can accuse Nandy of not thinking big. No doubt this 'large vision' has been one of his main attractions. But it is a form of big thinking that abjures the scholarly prerequisites of developing substantial expertise across disciplines. It is not the psychological or philosophical, but the sociological approach to studying religion, culture and modernity that has the strongest natural affinity with developing such interdisciplinary skills. However, Nandy considers the sociology of religion to be like a theology of science, which suggests that, though he may have thought about theology and science, he has not thought much about sociology, let alone the sociology of religion.

It is not just that what Nandy does not know, or want to know, adversely affects his vision. There are problems enough in what he claims to know. Take his conception of religion and its relationship to culture. Our understanding of culture must recognize the distinction between religion-as-faith and religion-as-ideology. He says that this distinction may be inappropriate, indicating that he is aware that faith and ideology are not, in real life, separate water-tight compartments. But this has never been more than a mere doffing of the cap in the direction of a complex reality, because Nandy constructs a comprehensive intellectual edifice on the flimsy foundations of its being a real, living distinction.

This point needs to be clarified. It is not illegitimate to make a conceptual distinction between religion-as-faith and religion-as-ideology. But because, in reality, the two are not separable (any more than are culture and society), the purpose and justification for making such conceptual abstractions or

---

primarily about who would be the most desirable elites! See Nandy, 'Cultural Frames for Transformative Politics'.

124 Nandy, *At the Edge of Psychology*.

simplifications is that they can enable us to understand the complexities of real life more accurately. If one takes recourse to abstractions like religion-as-faith and religion-as-ideology, it is only justified intellectually if one does so not merely to show how the two aspects of religion are different, *but also to show how they are connected.*[125]

This Nandy has never seriously attempted to do. He cannot. It would wreck his intellectual project, devastating the foundations on which he has constructed his understandings of religion, culture and secularism. The *analytical* separation of faith from ideology must never be misrepresented as an *actual* dichotomy. But, precisely because he does this, Nandy comfortably articulates a series of sharp dichotomies: religion-as-faith versus religion-as-ideology – the former is good, unblemished religion; the latter is bad, blemished, indeed not even genuine religion; there are the traditional masses, with one kind of mind-set, versus the modernizing–secularizing elites, with another. Whatever its partial insights, this method is the enemy of sobriety and balance when it comes to assessing issues concerning religion, culture, society, secularism, secularization and modernity.

The way in which Nandy defines his two concepts of religion is very revealing:

> By faith I mean religion as a way of life, a tradition which is definitionally non-monolithic and operationally plural. I say 'definitionally' because unless a religion is geographically confined to a small area, religion as a way of life has to in effect turn into a confederation of a number of ways of life, linked by a common faith having some theological space for the heterogeneity which everyday life introduces.[126]

A number of things strike the reader. To be 'non-monolithic' and 'operationally plural', to have 'space for heterogeneity', are all positive attributes. To possess these *by definition* is to render religion-as-faith impervious to negative criticism. There are no negative references or clauses serving as any kind of counterweight to the wholly positive evaluation of faith. This is not a neutral definition, but a positively loaded one, ruling out *judgement* of faith. Since religion is a 'way of life' – indeed, the larger religions are a 'confederation of a number of ways of life' – religion is present where ways of life exist. This is, once again, to immortalize or near-immortalize religion. There is no entertaining the possibility even that religion might be a historically contingent phenomenon in certain times and places. If it is bad and unrewarding to assassinate religion by definition, is it justified to glorify and immortalize religion by definition?

125 For a more thoughtful conceptual use of the distinction between religion-as-ideology and religion-as-faith, see R. Bharucha, *The Question of Faith* (Delhi, 1993).

126 A. Nandy, 'The Politics of Secularism and the Recovery of Religious Tolerance', in V. Das, ed., *Mirrors of Violence* (Delhi, 1990), p. 70.

Let us go further. Since culture, too, is a 'way of life', and a 'large' or 'world' culture is also a 'confederation of cultures', we have an understanding of religion that is virtually isomorphic with the understanding of culture. Is this a sensible way to go about grasping the relationship between religion and culture? In the case of religion, Nandy takes the analytically reasonable (though unnecessary) step of distinguishing between religion-as-faith and religion-as-ideology, but fumbles his attempt to explain or understand reality by refusing to investigate the ways in which faith and ideology are connected or inseparable, as they undoubtedly also are.

But in the way he handles the relationship between religion and culture, he makes the opposite error. Here, he analytically conflates two concepts, which it is not just reasonable but necessary to separate in order to understand how, in reality, religion and culture are and are not fused. This is because the fusion is never total. The geographical zones of religion and culture do not coincide; nor does the former fully permeate the latter. The relationship between the two is more flexible and retractable. Analytical separation of the two is here a necessary but not sufficient condition for more clearly understanding their relationship.

Since Nandy recognizes that world religions span world cultures, he also operates with a notion of world culture that does not occupy the same space as a world religion, though both are understood as 'confederations of ways of life'. Thus, he is fully prepared to speak of cultures divided by the same faith – for example, Iranian Islam and Indonesian Islam. Nandy says these two Islams are not isomorphic but interlocking – a sensible enough formulation. But this does not follow with any logical clarity from his own theoretical precepts. On the one hand, there is the isomorphism or near-isomorphism of his definitions of religion and culture. On the other, there is a recognition that culture is broader than religion, so that, though the latter may be central to the former, culture shapes religion in their fusion as well. Thus, different cultures can be divided by the same faith.

In short, Nandy can certainly say some sensible things about cultural change, but this is despite, not because of, his theoretical constructions. So, in his handling of the relationship between religion and culture, he veers between seeing them as isomorphic, and thus seeing religion as merely central to and inseparable from culture. This is still a cultural essentialism (hence incapable of dealing adequately with issues of cultural change) in which the religious essence is itself the cultural essence, or an indispensable part of it.

However, Nandy also wants to allow for what was once peripheral in a culture to have the capacity to become, in changed circumstances, newly central. So traditional cultures should also be seen as having such dynamic resources. And if traditional cultures have such a capacity, then, given his determinism about the link between religion and culture, traditional religious systems must also have this internalized capacity. This particular track of Nandy's thinking runs somewhat counter to the others.[127]

These confusions and inconsistencies are never faced squarely; nor are the difficulties and complexities in the handling of entities like religion and culture seriously negotiated. At most, they are rationalized away by means of conceptions of the essential flexibility of faith systems, or the unique fluidity of the traditional self, and so on. The reason is simple. Nandy's definitions and arguments about religion and culture do not aim to explore, in as open-ended and balanced a way as possible, this immensely difficult terrain. They are basically conceptual sticks with which to beat the 'anti-culture' and 'anti-tradition' elements of modernity, which he identifies above all with politics (the state) and science (rationality).

As for his definition of religion-as-ideology: 'By ideology I mean religion as a sub-nation, national or cross-national identifier of populations contesting for, or protecting non-religious, usually political or socio-economic interests. Such religion-as-ideologies are usually identified with one or more texts which, rather than ways of life of the believers, then become the final identifiers of the "pure" forms of the religion.'[128] This definitional reliance on texts provides 'a set of manageable operational definitions'.[129] Here, Nandy's definition is neutral. But religion-as-ideology is made, by definition, *non-religious*. It is a 'secular identifier' connected to the pursuit of secular interests. Such identifiers do their job of demarcating populations by linking themselves to the 'purity' or dogmatism of texts, rather than to the openness of lived religion – religion-as-faith, as a way of life. Since the latter is definitionally good, religion-as-ideology, which contrasts so strongly with it, can be considered for most purposes as bad – though, strictly speaking, it is not defined as such. But of course, time and again, Nandy expresses his hostility to, and criticisms of, religion-as-ideology. At the same time, this really has nothing to do with 'true' religion or faith. It is, moreover, a secular identifier.

---

127 While Nandy does not budge from a determinist notion of the religion–culture link, he does occasionally adopt an approach to cultural change that does not square with the essentialism of most of his formulations concerning culture. Interestingly, this surfaces most clearly when he deals with Gandhi's intervention into Hinduism and Indian cultural anti-colonialism. Nandy wants to appropriate Gandhi as a 'critical traditionalist' or 'critical insider'. Gandhi, says Nandy, tries to make central to Hinduism what was earlier peripheral. If this claim is true (which is disputable), then it represents an attempt at phenomenal religious or cultural upheaval. Hence a certain unease on Nandy's part with the adequacy of labelling Gandhi a 'critical traditionalist'. Since Gandhi's dramatic intervention is to be seen as expressive of the internal resources for change possessed by Indian culture, this culture has to be redefined in the direction of greater flexibility. A cultural situation is now described as much more of a process: 'The two processes of inflow and outflow determine at a given point of time Indian culture, rather than a rigidly defined set of practices or products surviving from the society's past.' Nandy, *Traditions, Tyranny and Utopias*, p. 153.
128 Nandy, 'Politics of Secularism', p. 70.
129 Ibid.

Nandy uses the word 'usually' in two places in this definition, each time to cover his back, as it were, because he has avoided introducing one very important word into this definition: culture. Nandy talks of how these identifications and demarcations are made for the purposes of contesting or protecting 'usually, political or socio-economic interests'. What about cultural interests? Can religion-as-ideology provide identifiers for contesting or pursuing non-religious cultural interests?

Since Nandy uses the word 'usually', it would seem that he has to concede that, at least occasionally, religion-as-ideology serves the purposes of relating to non-religious cultural interests. But is the absence of any specific reference to cultural interests accidental? Given Nandy's strong culturalism, his insistence on the umbilical cord between religion-as-faith and culture, his stance on the natural anti-culturalness of modernity, and his view that it is in modernity, especially late modernity, that religion-as-ideology becomes more widespread, he wants to concede as little ground as possible to such notions as the existence of significant non-religious or secular cultural interests.

When 'usually' appears on the second occasion, referring to texts rather than ways of life, Nandy again exhibits an uncertainty. Could religion-as-ideology be at least occasionally identified not with one or more texts, but with the 'ways of life of the believers'? But if this were so, religion-as-ideology could be connected to aspects of faith and 'true' culture. Then this connection would have to be evaluated. If it is judged good, then he weakens the argumentative force of his asserted dualism of religion-as-ideology, bad; religion-as-faith, good. If it is judged bad, then he can be read as allowing for the possibility that faith itself (and culture) can be deeply tainted with ideology.

In his defence of popular faith, Nandy also takes up the cause of myth. When believers (or non-believers) give increasing importance to the claims of science over myth, they reinforce the ideologization of religion. They refuse to understand the power and value of myth, its role in the structure or system of faith. Nandy has a real point here, but the deeper problem is his own. When objects become sacred and mythical, their secular meanings recede greatly. They never completely disappear, and can resurface or affect manifest or latent meanings in peculiar ways. But when something becomes a mythical entity its significance is *overwhelmingly* derived from some transcendental presence.

This process of constructing sacredness is always a process of investing properties that can *only* belong to humans in something beyond humans, and this is always a 'false' construct, though it can have real and positive value. But this 'falseness', central to myth and faith, is supported by a network of institutions and practices which itself is always characterized by asymmetrical relations of power between real people. The construction of a structure or system of faith and its forms of expression cannot be separated from the construction of a system of ideological power, though it cannot be reduced to that either.[130]

Nandy might be able to 'resolve' these ambiguities and justify his symptomatic silences. But it is doubtful that he is even interested in trying, since the logic of such a venture, once embarked upon, would put at risk the integrity of his anti-modernist project itself.

For someone as hostile to secularism and secularization as Nandy, his use of these terms is remarkably casual. He generally assumes that secularization and secularism have an invariant relationship. When secularization advances, so does the ideology of secularism.[131] So a criticism of the latter can stand in as criticism of the former. In reality, it cannot. The secularization process and specific histories of modernization and nationalism have generally been more important for explaining the emergence of secular states than the ideology of secularism. This is why so many essentially secular states have religious–monarchial trappings, and why sentiments or traditions of anti-clericalism vary so much.

In India also, there has been a real disjunction between the two. It is one of the myths of many an anti-secularist that the Westernized concept of secularism has been too dominant in public and political discourse. This, they claim, has been the source of communal and other evils. But since India is populated by more than Westernized elites, and its 'public space' is wider than that defined by these elites, there is the 'revenge' of the masses against the elites, and of their culture against elite organized politics. Elite hegemony is being contested. Nandy's own endeavour is to recover the still-living traditions of religious and ethnic tolerance 'from the hegemonic language of secularism popularised by westernised intellectuals'.[132]

In fact, most Westernized intellectuals in India have been quite confused

---

130 R. Bhargava, 'Objective Significance in Critical Theory', in Parekh and Pantham, *Political Discourse*.

Myth transforms a world of facts into pure signs. It invests nature with properties belonging only to humanity. So the confrontation of science with nature was necessarily 'intercepted' by the confrontation of science with myth. Any attempt at an unbalanced (exaggerated) defence of the value of myth, such as Nandy's, has to launch an unbalanced attack on science.

Nandy would heartily endorse Clifford Geertz's mistaken claim that 'the ideologization of religion begins when the certainty of faith totters'. The ideology of religion was always there in pre-modernity when faith was not tottering. In the absence of competing ideologies and of serious doubt about religion's totalizing claims, the ideological dimension of religion was rarely seen as such. But it is also true that, in modernity, the ideological dimension of religion can become more important. There is a 'thinning' of the religious consciousness that enables mass mobilization through sharing of a few 'thinned' beliefs. This is not the replacement of faith by ideology, but a transformation of the nature of faith (and ideology), and of the religious consciousness itself.

131 The advance of secularism here means some people or institutions (the state) push it more strongly, not that the ideology becomes more successful in securing adherents. For Nandy, as secularization advances in late modernity, the ideology of secularism becomes less successful, with people turning to religious faith to find meaning.

132 Nandy, 'Politics of Secularism', p. 69.

about what is or should be meant by the 'language of secularism', rarely negotiating clearly between the Indian and Western notions, nor possessing much clarity about the Western notion, seeing it more as some vague principle of statehood than as an ideology of morality centred on a humanist individualism. As for its popularization or its construction as a hegemonic political or public discourse, this is way off the mark. Neither the state nor the 'secular elite' has even seriously tried to make it popular, to vernacularize it, or to attempt to give it wider and deeper roots.[133]

Even in its Indian version, calling for *sarva dharm sambhavam,* or equal respect to all religions, it has never been popularized. Those hostile to the Enlightenment-inspired notion of secularism and partial to the Indian version have simply assumed that the Indian masses (or at least Hindus) *naturally* believe and endorse such a meaning of secularism. This is not true, and 'lived tolerances' should not be construed as meaning that the ordinary Hindu or Muslim has *equal* respect for all religions, or believes that this should be an important principle of statehood, or that the Indian state can or does behave accordingly. This debate on what is the most appropriate notion of secularism is itself essentially an elite affair.

One of the areas in which the ideology of secularism (stressing the values of secular, humanist individualism) could have but has not been systematically promoted is in education. Even after 1947, Indian education, public or private, has never seriously promoted the attitude that religious authority could be questioned, even though religious authority (Hindu or Islamic) has no specific hierarchy or clergy. Secular education tries to put the learner, not the teacher, at the centre of the learning process. In India the teacher–pupil relationship reproduces the hierarchical 'learning' relationship sanctified by existing religious traditions. So when 'secular' values or principles are presented (primarily in textbooks), they serve only as a mark of distinction, a way of saying that secular India is different from non-secular Pakistan – or that the properly educated Indian, by being secular, is different from the ignorant and superstitious masses. The term 'secular' here serves as a political or social marker, little else.[134]

The failure of secularism is hardly the failure of an ideology. It is essentially the failure of a ruling class that used secular ideals as means of seeking legitimacy, but which largely ignored the social tasks associated with the development of a secular society.[135] Had India's elites really tried to make secularism a *hegemonic* discourse, they would have behaved very differently. Post-independence education did not even promote 'Indianness' except as 'canned patriotism'.

---

133 S. Kaviraj, 'On the Discourse of Secularism', in B. Chakrabarty, ed., *Secularism and Indian Polity* (New Delhi, 1990).

134 K. Kumar, 'Secularism: Its Politics and Pedagogy', *Economic and Political Weekly,* 4 November 1989.

135 Ibid., p. 2,476.

How, then, can something so weakly implanted as secularism in India do so much damage? Does a suspicion on Nandy's part that this might be the case explain his failure to define secularism as precisely as he does his two concepts of religion? Nandy attacks secularism and secularization in two steps. First, he treats secularism as a synecdoche, seeing it not as a narrow ideology of morals but as a wider ideology of statehood, thus making the secular state complicit with the arrogances of the nation-state system. Second, he believes that 'to accept the ideology of secularism is to accept the ideologies of progress and modernity as the new justifications of domination'.[136] Secularism is an ideology that legitimizes both those who exercise state power and the structures of the state itself, because it promotes the view that the irrational, religious masses lack the rationality of modernizers, and because the state is crucial for modernization. It is the modern ideology of statehood – nothing less.[137]

This is not correct. There are a number of modern ideologies of statehood, perhaps the most important being nationalism. Most of them are secular, but not all. A religious nationalism or a religious pan-nationalism is also a modern ideology, and can be an ideology of statehood. But secularism itself is not an ideology of statehood. It is an ideology that endorses a particular *principle* of modern statehood, a principle that emerges historically as part of the *modern democratic revolution*. That is why, even etymologically, the word secularism appears long after the words 'secular' or 'state'. This is a new principle of democratic individualism, and any consistent assault on secularism – for example, by Nandy – will also to some extent assault modern notions of democracy and individualism.

Secularism is an ideology not of statehood, but of ethics.[138] It separates ethics and religion by grounding morality in the human individual, and not in some transcendent sphere. It thus allows for a relationship between politics (state) and ethics separated from religion. This creates room for

---

136 Nandy, 'Politics of Secularism', p. 90. Apparently, secularism and reasonable notions of progress and modernity cannot go hand-in-hand with rejection of justifications for domination!

137 Since specific states have been ethnophobic and ethnocidal, Nandy does not hesitate to claim that secularism is definitionally 'ethnophobic' and 'frequently ethnocidal'. Ibid.
The secular state ignores the difference between good and bad religion. Secularism limits the democratic process because it separates culture from politics, thereby 'truncating the political personality of the citizen'. Secularists are a sad lot who can be classified as follows: (a) secularists as elite modernisers; (b) innocent secularists who are what they are on ideological and moral grounds; (c) secularists as social climbers wanting to be *au fait* with the modern world; (d) the *genuine* secularists, who cynically manipulate religion for expedient secular purposes. Ibid.
Once again, the classification scheme simply comes out of Nandy's head, and corresponds to a typology of character traits organized by him as a psychologist and social critic.

138 R. Bhargava's distinction between political and ethical secularism was already implicit in Holyoake's original coinage of the term 'secularism'.

introducing new norms into state constitutions. A secular state is one that avoids legitimizing any particular set of ethics or moral codes associated with any particular religious system or world-view. Such a secular morality is possible because of common and universal features of humanity, and is codified in the form of modern secular, not customary, law.

A secular state, then, would have three necessary and sufficient attributes. In the relationship between religion and the individual, it enshrines the right to freedom of worship. In the relationship of the state to the individual, the notion of citizenship is primary, and cannot be conceived of as linked to any fixed property or attribute of any particular individual or group. Regarding the relationship between religion and the state, the latter should be religiously non-affiliated and impartial. Formal non-affiliation is not as important as practical impartiality through the basic separation of religious and state power. These principles are so obviously conducive to democratic governance – a secular state being its necessary but not sufficient condition – that it is difficult to see any basis for the objections to it.

The importance of such norms for good governance was clear to Gandhi, and in this sense he was all for the secular Indian state. But what Gandhi – and indeed Nandy – could not accept is the *ethical premise* of the secular state. Thus Nandy attacks this premise, claiming that a secular public morality is greatly inferior to a religion-based public morality. He does not directly contest the validity of the three specific attributes that define the secular state. Gandhi was more explicitly in favour of such a secular state, and Madan, for one, pays more attention to this attitude of Gandhi's than does Nandy.

Nandy focuses instead on the call for public space to be devoted to the dialogue between the religious and the secular. And he tries to make out that secularism, as an ideology of statehood, sees the state as 'the ultimate reservoir of sanity', and therefore as the 'ultimate arbiter among different religions and communities'.[139] This is an unsubtle caricature. The modern secular state claims ultimate arbitration powers only in matters of conflict between religious claims and secular constitutional law, on the assumption that such law (on which the state is constituted) is humane and just. Such secular–democratic law does not make the state the 'ultimate arbiter', but establishes a new equilibrium between state and civil society.

This represents a *redistribution* of powers of arbitration, where *finality of authority* is no longer absolute (because sacred), or singularly or oligarchically located. The secular–democratic state is part of a new political arrangement of checks and balances fundamentally different from the balancing principles and institutions of pre-modern, segmentary societies dominated by customary law. Both the state and the institutions of an emerging civil society thereby become more important. Much of political life is represented by the shifting balance of forces between the two. Furthermore, mass forms

---

139 Nandy, 'Politics of Secularism'.

of cultural politics become more powerful and more possible in modernity, especially in 'late modernity'.[140]

How does Nandy argue against the ethics of secularism and the ethical premise of the secular state? How does he defend the claim that a religion-based public morality is superior to modern secular notions of public and political morality? He does this by rejecting the idea of any moral progress, and the claim that the modern notion of equality is a new moral value of the utmost importance. It is the 'ultimate' moral values that are crucial, and these are to be found in all the major religious systems. They therefore pre-date modernity. The practical human and social expression of such ultimate value systems would be the principle of *tolerance*, and not some recent acquisition, such as the principle of equality.[141]

Religious systems are peculiarly gifted with the ability to promote and institutionalize tolerance because all such religious systems share a belief in the importance of *transcendence*. Belief in transcendence expresses a distinctive psychology of the believer. In vibrant religious–cultural systems, the believer has a 'fluid self', a 'configuration of selves'. This construct is fluid because it incorporates the self, the non-self and the anti-self. There is an empirical, perishable self as well as an imperishable, transcendent self – and thus a distinctive 'wholeness of the self', which the more well-bounded self of modernity undermines.[142]

All that is valuable in modernity may be incorporated as a 'subset' in a reinvigorated and critical traditionality.[143] This is possible because India remains a traditional society, and a traditional civilization and culture, or cultures, with a modern, secular state whose further encroachment must be halted and reversed. We must invest our hopes in inter- and intra-religious dialogue, to lead us to a more worthwhile existence. So the religious community must be seen as a, if not the, principal political and social unit in the construction of the desired anti-modernist project.

After allowing for all qualifications and nuances, these last four paragraphs represent Nandy's basic credo. It is a credo which, in virtually every major respect, rests on mistaken assumptions and understandings. While the principle of transcendence is central to all major religious systems, it is not confined to them. It is a part of all human cultures, including cultures not recognizably religious, as well as cultures in modernity.[144]

---

140 One could reasonably ask: Late for what? But this characterization is certainly preferable to the claim that we are in a 'postmodern' era.

141 Final authority in matters of inter- and intra-religious conflict should rest with the appropriate religious authorities, and not with the secular state.

142 Hans Mol and Georg Simmel would both meet with Nandy's approval, since they hold that modern individualist rationalism makes the self 'brittle', weakening its sense of 'wholeness'. See subsection on 'Religion in Modernity' in the preceding Chapter 2.

143 Nandy, 'Culture, State and the Rediscovery of Indian Politics'; A. Nandy, 'Counter-Statement on Humanistic Temper', *Mainstream*, 10 October 1981.

144 Life is about connectedness, since death is the end of connectedness. The search for connectedness is what the principle of transcendence is about. It is thus innate to

Furthermore, what religious systems mean by transcendence *differs*. Religious systems, contrary to the view of anti-secularists, do not have the same ultimate goals, values and visions, but have different and often competing ultimaticities. This issue is repeatedly dodged by those who would invest so much in inter-faith dialogue and accommodation.[145] Religious systems have different metaphysics, even different understandings of what constitute the 'perennial' questions. In modernity, the notion of transcendence does not and cannot disappear. There are simply many more ways than ever before of thinking about and coping with it.

The psychology of the self does bear a determinate relationship with the society in which it is embedded. But the most important divide is not between the Eastern and Western self, or between the Hindu and the Islamic self, but between the pre-modern and modern self. All talk by Nandy of the special fluidity of the pre-modern self is utterly mistaken.[146] The pre-modern self is not a more fluid but a more *diffuse* self, because of the lack of sharp boundaries. But the range over which the self is diffuse is limited by the much more *static* character of the world the pre-modern self inhabits.

The more static pre-modern world gives rise not to a more fluid or revisable self, but to a more static and diffuse self, which, precisely because it is diffuse, allows the religious dimension and the religious idiom to dominate in ways that they no longer can, or should, in modernity. It is the more dynamized world of modernity that gives rise to the more dynamized self, which is more self-reflexive, more well bounded in its various selves, but also more fluid and revisable. The static self is not a more autonomous or flexible one. Its moral horizon is a more externally determined one, and is

---

humanness, but its forms are variable. Religion is but one form – and modern, more secularized culture also copes, albeit in different ways, with the issue of transcendence. What the best ways of dealing with it are is a question that is answered historically, not eternally – thus, not always through religion. See Z. Bauman, *Mortality, Immortality and Other Life Strategies* (Oxford, 1992).

145. Inter-faith dialogue is usually something undertaken by the most liberal elements among religious elites or intellectuals. The dialogue rarely goes beyond the level of platitudes – 'different paths to a common goal', and so on. For the sake of harmony and ecumenism, the issue of conversion is usually skirted, for any aggressive defence of the importance and the right to convert would raise matters threatening such artificially constructed ecumenism-as-tolerance. The advocates of neo-Hinduism, like Gandhi, who had high hopes for what inter-faith dialogue might achieve, cannot accept a strong defence of the right or necessity to religiously convert. Nor can Madan. To convert is to convince, which demands shared agreement on norms of right and wrong, truth and falsehood. The impossibility of inter-faith dialogue ever arriving at such shared norms means the dialogue is confined to courtesies, to the search for similarities in doctrinal meaning, listening to and respecting differences, rarely involving vigorous argument, contestation, discussion or strong judgements. There is no democratic way of reaching a higher synthesis, for *democratic* dialogue means reasoned argument based on shared norms of judgement. The end-result of such inter-faith dialogue may be a better understanding by participants of other faiths, and proclamations of overall harmony, but it invariably leaves the bulk of believers of any particular religion comfortably untouched.

146 Nandy, 'Politics of Secularism'; Nandy, 'Cultural Frames for Transformative Politics'.

constituted not by the abstract ultimate values of a large religious system but by the detailed and specific injunctions of local culture and sect affiliation.

The modern self is more morally sceptical, flexible and questing. The complexity of self-perception and self-definition is necessarily linked to the complexity of social life itself. The moral horizon in modernity is more internally constituted than externally given. Even the faithful believer has to move in this direction.

Nandy is free to interpret the pre-modern self as a more wholesome self, conducive to the development of social tolerances.[147] But when he claims that the way forward in India is to try to recover those sources of tolerance in 'traditional ways of life', all he offers by way of a programmatic perspective is that we look seriously at the philosophies, theologies and symbolisms of such tolerances. What Nandy does not ask us to do is historically investigate the *contexts* in which those symbolisms and philosophies operated, so as to get a better idea of their functions and purposes.

Nandy, for all his admiration of India's past, will not undertake a subaltern history to arrive at, for example, a Dalit's-eye-view of India's so-called tolerant past, or a gendered view of patriarchal societies and patriarchal religions.[148] If he has to concede the fact of such traditional forms of oppression, he will in more conservative moments echo Ananda Coomaraswamy's claim that pre-modern caste oppression was never as bad as modern class oppression; or, in his more radical moments, endorse Gandhi's inversion of the traditional values associated with caste hierarchy as the furthest one can go in fighting it.[149]

---

147 All that is required to sustain the 'authentic innocence' of a critical traditionality, Nandy feels, is to update the theories of evil and oppression that all major religions and cultures have. Such cultures have a language of continuity in which change is incorporated within a larger framework of continuity, which Nandy, for one, feels is desirable. There is a language of spiritualism containing idioms concerning oppression and its analysis. The language of self is concerned with matters of self-control, self-realization, power over the self. Nandy believes these languages provide enough resources to cope with life today and to create an adequate and meaningful existence.

148 Individualism erodes patriarchy. Nandy, who opposes modern individualism, has always sought to make light of patriarchy. One of the most important gains of modernity is how gender discourse, especially in recent times, has transformed notions of the good and desirable, and of acceptable social roles, beyond the ken of traditional societies. See Nandy's convoluted attempt to condemn sati, yet attack modern feminism by defending the subtlety of the philosophy of sati, in A. Nandy, 'The Human Factor', *Illustrated Weekly*, 13 March 1988.

149 Nandy, 'Cultural Frames for Transformative Politics'. For black anti-racists, as for anti-caste Dalits, the inversion of traditional values associated with racism and casteism has never been the ultimate goal, for the battle is not in the mind alone, and such inversion is itself a defensive posture. This inversion is but a means of affirmation and mobilization to eradicate racism and casteism as objective structures of oppression. Eventually there should no longer be the necessity for such an inversion. Eradicating racism and casteism are modern goals related to modern notions of equality. No wonder Nandy is uneasy about this and supports the approach of Gandhi to caste, rather than that of the fully modernist Ambedkar, who sought to abolish caste, not reform it. That Ambedkar, rather than Gandhi, is the more important figure for Indian Dalits does constitute a minor

Among the weakest points in the anti-modernist and anti-secularist case is the programmatic alternative they offer. How is *sarva dharm sambhavam* to be institutionalized, or to embody such multi-religiosity? Or can it practise 'equal respect to all religions' without embodying such multi-religiosity?[150] References to Gandhi's vision and injunctions to learn from him cannot compensate for this lack of a programmatic perspective. Nor will it do to cite the possibilities inherent in inter-faith or inter-community dialogue conducted by its 'best' representative figures or institutions.[151] At most, they are sometimes a valuable source for interreligious crisis-management.

If there is no common notion of transcendence, but only competing visions of it, and of 'true morality', and of the 'genuinely good life', then what reason is there to presume that inter-faith dialogue is more capable than the procedural principles of liberal-democratic individualism of providing commonly accepted standards for how to organize and participate in a public and political moral life? Even those modern-day communitarians wishing to accommodate different styles of religious reasoning through an 'overlapping consensus' insist that the state, to be humane and democratic, must have a *moral core* that is non-negotiable.[152]

The most fundamental mistake of anti-modernists like Nandy, or ambiguous modernists like Madan and Parekh, is their refusal to recognize that India was long ago 'condemned' to modernity. India is neither a traditional society nor one in transition from tradition to modernity. It has long been pursuing its own form of modernity, shaped by its distinctive institutional and other legacies. But these 'traditional' legacies of caste and religion do not operate in traditional ways, nor mean what they once did.

In a typical conceptual dualism, Nandy talks of the distinctive mind-sets of the ordinary village Indian and of the Westernized, urbanized Indian. This is the obvious corollary of his claim that the typical inhabitant of traditional India has a distinctive psychology ('configuration of selves') separate from that of the no-longer-traditional Indian. That traditional Indian who thinks in fundamentally different, arationalist or non-rationalist ways from the secularized, rationalist Indian is 'authentic' and in tune with the enduring ethos and culture of India. This, again, is quite mistaken.

There is merit in the argument that the mind-sets of urban elites and rural masses are not quite the same in the weights they attach to different ways

---

source of embarrassment for Nandy's self-positioning as an articulator of authentic Indian aspirations.

Nor is Nandy much interested in looking at the sources of tolerance in modernity itself, to see if they can better deal with modern-day intolerances.

150 Bhiku T. Parekh has some sense of the difficulties, but does not delve seriously into the issue. Parekh, 'Nehru and the National Philosophy of India'.

151 See note 93, above.

152 C. Taylor, oral seminar presentation at Jawaharlal Nehru University, Delhi, Autumn 1993, on how a multicultural overlapping consensus could help strengthen a democratic polity.

of thinking and articulating. But there is no sharp dichotomy, only a weakly sloping trend-line linking the two social poles of elites and masses. Thought or argument by analogy, axiom, assertion and logical procedures coexist in the same person, but they combine in different ways. Of these, only reasoned argument can operate according to commonly accepted standards of judgement, and thus provide the basis for genuine and uncoercive intellectual conversion. The elite mind-set is not distinguished from the popular mind-set by being 'rational' as opposed to 'arational'. Indeed, the middle-class professional can be equally 'arational' and dependent on axiom, assertion or analogical forms of thinking in certain spheres of life. Similarly, the popular mind-set can and does exhibit similar variations in ways of thinking in different spheres of existence and responsibility in everyday life.

The ordinary villager is, in fact, closer to the urban professional in her mind-set than she is to the mind-set of her ancestors. The mass awareness, unleashed by modernity, of the depth and range of possibilities for change in one's life makes certain of that. The ordinary Indian has internalized an awareness of the possibility of material progress (be it the value of literacy, or the desire for electricity connections at home) that makes the values and goals, the very psychology and personality, of the ordinary Indian fundamentally different from that of her predecessors.

The resulting fact that there can be *levels of mass discontent* that have no equivalent in the past, and that shape and influence Indian political and cultural life in ways bearing little comparison to what was conceivable in that past, already testifies to the uniquely *modern* character of Indian society today, and to the expectations it releases.[153] Gandhi could not be what he was, and could not have the effect he had, except in the context of a modernity that decisively shaped his own mind-set and that of the mass constituency he sought to influence. Gandhi introduced *completely new themes* into Indian cultural, and Hindu religious, discourse. He did this in a *very short span of time*. And he had *mass effect*. All the three aspects emphasized here are conceivable only within the framework of modernity.

Anti-modernism is *not* non-modern, and Critical Traditionality is an oxymoron. The resources for criticism within traditional societies are inherently limited. The unique character of tradition was its givenness and 'overwhelming' character; the impossibility of recognizing itself as just a tradition. Modernity de-traditionalizes tradition, leading defenders like Nandy to do what was never required even of traditional society's elites – to rationalize, justify and defend tradition. The absence of any radical notion of change

---

153 It is only in modernity that education, leisure and health become 'basic needs'. It is only in our times that poverty becomes eliminable, that crime, sickness and madness become 'correctable', and, for better and worse, there emerge 'sequestrating' institutions for them. A. Giddens, *Modernity and Self-Identity* (Oxford, 1991). The authentic Indian masses seem to have no problems in welcoming and visiting good hospitals which do not practise only indigenous medicine.

or progress meant a corresponding absence of a referential horizon (even imagined – even the utopias of tradition could not be so radical) by which to carry out serious criticism of traditionality.[154]

Nandy, of course, denies this. His is not just a lost cause, but a non-existent one. The only feasible choices available are either an arrogant, overbearing modernity, or a critical and modest one. Those rejecting both and insisting on the necessity of a mythology of Critical Traditionality, or anti-modernity, should at least acknowledge that this is (and can only be) a modern myth. They should not pretend that it represents some kind of continuity with the pre-modern past, and that there are therefore long-enduring resources on which to build.[155] If Gandhi is the great exemplar of anti-modernity or Critical Traditionality, then search anywhere in India's pre-modernity – there will not, and cannot, be a comparable figure.[156]

---

154 Nandy has a baseless fear. If modernity is the only fate for India, then the modernizer–Westerner becomes the privileged one who best knows India's future, as well as its past, since the West has been through that past (of tradition). This justifies an 'imperialism of categories' whereby the modern Westerner or their Indian clone seeks to understand India's past, present and future. A. Nandy, 'Self as a Political Concept', in P. C. Chatterjee, ed., *Self-Images, Identity and Nationality* (Shimla, 1989). India is pursuing its *own* form of modernity. The West holds no mirror to its past or future. Indeed, the best Indian political science has always been preoccupied with the distinctiveness and peculiarities of the Indian political system, despite the Western origin of its democracy. Moreover, good conceptual tools, regardless of their origins, can survive intelligent transfer and use elsewhere. The problematicity of applying 'Western' analytical categories is paralleled by the problematicity of applying 'Indian' analytical categories to India. The Nandy type of indigenist anti-modernism enjoys popularity in Western academic circles partly because it constitutes an inverted form of privileging the West. By rejecting the idea that India has left traditional society behind and is pursuing its own kind of modernity, it reinforces the standard Western prejudices about India today as indeed a pre-modern society that can only either go its pre-modern way or ape the West. A *critical Indian* modernity is ruled out, to the comfort of old-fashioned Western conservatism.

155 In a pre-modern, timeless and repetitive world, ahistorical remedies can apply; the reinterpretation of myth to serve purposes of careful, slow and limited reform may work. It cannot be anywhere near adequate to cope with contemporary India's problems. Nandy's refusal to see this means he has immunized himself in his own mind against reasoned refutation. Either his myths are more plausible for the reconstruction of a more humane Indian society, or someone else's are. But since his audience both at home and in the West is influenced by reasoned argument, Nandy will, perforce, resort to such forms of logical discourse, even if he will not be bound by their conventions of propriety and judgement. Nandy, *Intimate Enemy*.

156 Parekh's understanding of Gandhi is superior to that of Nandy. Where Nandy sees him as a critical traditionalist, Parekh, more cautiously if still mistakenly, sees him straddling critical traditionality and critical modernity, but closer to the first. He sees Gandhi's thrust as, in many ways, a 'secularized, activist Brahminism', whereas Nandy strongly underplays the influence of Brahminism on Gandhi. What for Parekh is a weakness is for Nandy (given his methodology) a strength. Gandhi sees groups as only a collection of individuals, and therefore understands the dynamics of individual change as unproblematically applicable to the dynamics of group change. Self-improvement is the route to group improvement. Parekh is more sensitive to the failure, not of Gandhi, but of Gandhiism. Finally, Parekh is not so sanguine about the ahistorical Gandhi, especially in his perception of the Hindu–Muslim problem: 'A view of history that left out history itself could hardly be expected to unite those haunted by it.' B. T. Parekh, *Gandhi's Political Philosophy* (London, 1989), p. 190. *Hind Swaraj*, which Gandhi wrote in 1909 expressing his

Nandy is so determined to preserve this illusion of a viable Critical Traditionality that he makes such brazen claims as that certain values, like human dignity, freedom, non-violence and equality are beyond history and culture. Are modern notions of freedom and equality even the same as pre-modern notions, let alone inferior? Or can what is good in modernity, such as civil liberties, survive as a subset within a more authentically Indian traditionalist setting? How is the modern principle of equality to survive as a 'respected' subset within a pre-modern shell whose defining substance combines the principle of hierarchy with an anti-liberal communitarianism?

The great irony in this defence is that Nandy displays a weaker understanding of traditionality and the past than he does of modernity and the present, even though his understanding of modernity is also deeply flawed. This is because the *critical edge* of his thinking applies overwhelmingly to modernity. At least he tells us what is bad about it. By contrast, despite all talk of a critical traditionalism, his weighing and assessment of the past is overwhelmingly positive. In justifiably attacking the arrogances of modernity – of science, for example – he ignores the arrogances of religion. Worse, he often pretends there are no such arrogances.

Modernity is not the enemy but the *accelerator* of cultural pluralism, of all kinds of pluralism. Where, as in pre-modernity, there are few claimants to authority, and the religious system often enjoys near-omnipotent status, pluralism simply cannot mean what it means when there are multiple authority systems and none can claim the near-omnipotent status of a religious system.

Science with a capital S does represent a potential danger here. But opposing this danger does not mean swinging to the other extreme. Nandy's critique of Big Science is more useful than his criticisms of secularism. But when he denies that science has a special epistemological status, he is wrong. Science has rational and unique methods of reasoning, but these operate more as values than as rules. They are also uniquely powerful in regard to the natural world. The material products of science are themselves one of the most powerful forms of evidence we have of a cross-cultural, anti-relativist and universalist system of knowledge. Yet the self-reflexive awareness of the best science that knowledge is value-laden can also attenuate the claims of science itself. This self-reflexiveness comes from its strongly *theoretical* character. And theoretical forms of rationality, though certainly not the only or always best forms of rationality, *are* a special form of it.

Compare this to the non-self-reflexiveness of non-science. One of Nandy's more delightful aphorisms points out that if astrology is the myth of the weak, science is the myth of the strong. More soberly reflected upon, the rejoinder would be 'Well, not quite', and the 'not quite' is very important. Nandy says that science must be put in its place and regarded as one

---

vision for India and which he never repudiated, is the most systematized expression of his anti-modernism. That Gandhi had an explicitly anti-modern project does not make him a non-modern.

among many imperfect traditions of humanity. One can only applaud in agreement (provided its epistemological uniqueness is not denied). But such modest pluralism is capable of becoming the dominant common-sense only in modernity. There is a special pluralism inherent in the discourse of reason, and any paradigm as hostile to rationality as Nandy's, and yet insisting that it will be democratic, is dangerously contradictory.

Without reason, analogy, axiom and assertion can pass for argument. And assertions can be refuted only with other assertions. Thus, such theories risk devolving into authoritarian non-theories akin to religions. Far from being impenetrable, it is reason that has the potential to have an open texture, and to be accessible to all who will participate in the discourse. It is faith and intuition that cannot be challenged.[157]

When Nandy insists he is immunized from professional criticism, that his own myths can be challenged only by more plausible myths, he is simply expressing his commitment to an authoritarian and deeply anti-democratic form of discourse.

Anti-secularists are religious communitarians who (like communalists and fundamentalists) see the relationship between individual and society as primarily based not on rights, but on 'moral responsibility' and 'consensus'. Though they are generally less hostile than religious fundamentalists to the idea of individual rights, both are programmatically unspecific about how personal freedom will be organized in their respective social utopias.

One major difference, however, is that the anti-secularists are much more adamantly opposed to centralized state power, believing that a decentralized polity is vital. To check and unburden the encroaching state, there should be a looser federation of associations based on 'natural communities'. Among communitarians, religious or otherwise, there are significant variations on how anti-state or anti-modern such arrangements should be. But, in the Indian context, they generally agree on what these 'natural communities' are, though they may differ on which are more important.

These are jati, caste, religion, tribe and village – each treated as largely undifferentiated and subjected internally only to 'traditional' critique. These are key communities apparently, because each and every self is an embedded self, and these are the most widespread and 'natural' forms of embeddedness. It is this embeddedness that furnishes purpose and meaning. The individualism (often caricatured as atomism) of modern life and political discourse would seek to destroy something profound and precious – this embeddedness. The religious community is one such natural community of embeddedness. Only by giving more responsibility to this community, already one of the organizing principles of social life in India, can we move towards a more tolerant, democratic and humane order.[158]

---

157 J. Grant, 'I Feel Therefore I Am: A Critique of Female Experience as the Basis for a Feminist Epistemology', *Women and Politics* 7: 3 (1987), p. 113.

158 Nandy's neo-Gandhianism means he shares his mentor's view of what constitutes

While every self is always an embedded self, modern life demands the ability to negotiate between different selves, to revise and change embedded selves, and the respect for the right to do so. The communities we are born into represent our first contexts of choice, our original cultural set. It is important to have this, but not vital that it remain unchanged for any given individual. Individual rights have ontological and ethical priority over collective rights and powers, because collective rights to self-determination, or collectively binding consensus, must first presuppose individual freedom to decide whether and in what way to belong to a particular community.

That is the message of the modern discourse of freedom, which proclaims its superiority over other (pre-modern) discourses of freedom and autonomy. This does not deny the inescapability of being an embedded self, but expresses that here, too, a new freedom, a new pluralism, a new openness can operate. It is a message that will remain powerful and appealing. Endorsing the value and importance of having a particular cultural community does not automatically entail endorsing the characteristics of any particular cultural community. Nor does it mean endorsing confinement within it.[159] Those who would struggle for a humane future must reject the siren song of anti-modernism. It leads to a dangerous and disastrous seduction.

A Subalternist's View on Secularism

The title of this subsection, insofar as it is a reference to the one major reflection by Partha Chatterjee on the specific issue of secularism, could be criticized as inaccurate. Yes, Chatterjee was – and continues to be seen as – a major figure and theorist of what has come to be called the Subaltern Studies school. But he also wrote something of an epitaph for Subaltern Studies in 2012, where he said it was time to move on to new projects for newer times, which should nevertheless make use of the insights that Subaltern Studies had provided, and to address some of the questions it had thrown up but could not adequately answer.[160] Chatterjee was right. Subaltern Studies had moved on. Many of its leading lights, including Chatterjee himself, had made, from their point of view, a natural progression into locating their work in the broader field of postcolonial studies, whose signature themes included rejection of Eurocentric universalism and its 'colonizations'

---

proper justice. Customary law is said to be superior to modern law because the litigant is treated not as a 'passive object' but as an individual in a given community. Judgement of the litigant's behaviour should aim, above all, at promoting introspection and, therefore, self-correction. This is a conception of justice not as fairness but, above all, as a contributor to self-mastery.

159 W. Kymlicka, *Liberalism, Community and Culture* (Oxford, 1989); C. Gould, *Rethinking Democracy* (Cambridge, 1988); G. Mahajan, 'Cultural Embodiment and Histories', in Baxi and Parekh, *Crisis and Change in Contemporary India*.

160 P. Chatterjee, 'After Subaltern Studies', *Economic and Political Weekly*, 1 September 2012.

of the conceptual categories required to think and write the histories of non-European 'alternative modernities'. The postulation of cultural Difference (with a capital D) has now become the guiding beacon for engaging in this important task.

This is precisely why Chatterjee's views on secularism are taken up here, along with those of Madan and Nandy. While Chatterjee shares their valorization of the religious community as a key political actor in Indian democracy, unlike them he positions himself on the political Left. He is neither as dismissive of Marxism as Madan nor, like Nandy, an anti-modernist; he has, if anything, a more postmodernist sensibility. Yet, in the broad convergence between their views on secularism, they have helped to channel their separate allegiances into a broader intellectual–political current that declares itself to be anti-communal but sees a Western-tainted conception of secularism, insofar as it impinges on Indian reality, as very much part of the problem. This is enough reason, then, for including a critique of Chatterjee's most direct attack on secularism in his article 'Secularism and Tolerance'.[161]

This article developed the trajectory that had been well established in his book, *The Nation and Its Fragments*.[162] There, Chatterjee completed his slide into culturalism, and through it towards ever greater sympathy for indigenism. To the binary contrast between colonialism and indigenous community were added other polar contrasts, such as material/spiritual, outer/inner and world/home. In each of these binaries, the second term had become the more important – the realm of true autonomous thought and struggle, itself cultural as opposed to political or economic. Struggle on the terrain of the 'material' or 'outer' or 'world' had become a form of surrender to the defining principles of colonial discourse itself.[163] His last chapter, on 'Communities and the Nation', was a sustained effort to theorize community and to counterpose the 'narrative of community' (not of class) to the 'narrative of capital', itself identified with and standing in for the narratives of universal history.

This effectively paved the way for him to accept the 'religious community' as a primary political unit for the purposes of contesting the purportedly unjustified hegemony of the secular state. At the heart of Chatterjee's article on 'Secularism and Tolerance' is the attempt to expose and then resolve a

---

161 P. Chatterjee, 'Secularism and Tolerance', *Economic and Political Weekly*, 9 July 1994.

162 P. Chatterjee, *The Nation and Its Fragments: Colonial and Postcolonial Histories* (Delhi, 1994).

163 S. Sarkar, 'The Decline of the Subaltern in *Subaltern Studies*', in his *Writing Social History*, (New Delhi, 1997). Sarkar points out that, even while elevating struggle by protagonists within the 'inner domain', Chatterjee does not take up the struggle against indigenous patriarchy, or say anything about the rich history of the anti-caste movements of Periyar, Phule and Ambedkar in his long chapter, 'The Nation and its Out-castes'. Similarly, neither workers nor capitalists constitute 'fragments' of the 'Indian nation' worthy enough to be given the independent attention he otherwise gives to women, peasants and outcastes.

fundamental 'impasse' well expressed by the current dilemma of what to do about the issue of a Uniform Civil Code (UCC), given the communalist Hindu Right's assault on the anomalous existence of Muslim Personal Law in a supposedly secular Indian state. This, says the Hindu Right, is evidence of the secular state's 'minorityist' bias towards Muslims.

Chatterjee's stance, like that of Nandy, is a third position, against both the Hindu Right and Indian secularists. But he looks not to pre-modern indigenist arrangements for a solution, but to as-yet-untried ones. Before explaining and justifying his proposed resolution of the problem, Chatterjee attacks Indian secularism, seeking to show that there is no incompatibility between the political agenda of the Hindu communalist right and the preservation of a secular Indian state. The Hindu Right, after all, does not attack secularism as such, but 'pseudo-secularists' and the 'pseudo-secular' state, showing that it is quite happy to live with a secular state.[164] Is it not plausible that political Hindutva's talk of 'pseudo-secularism' is the tribute vice pays to virtue? That for all its flaws, Indian democracy has a real authority and prestige not easily challenged? That, for all the lack of clarity about what Indian secularism does or should mean, it is generally realized that the preservation of the democratic state is in some crucial sense linked to its secular character? And that to respect Indian democracy is in some way to respect secularism? With respect to the issues of both secularism and democracy, the Hindu Right prefers not a frontal attack, but to *redefine* democracy as majoritarianism, and secularism as tolerance, in order to present itself as more truly secular and democratic.

As for the issue of Indian secularism, the Hindu Right can much more profitably seek to co-opt for itself an existing notion of secularism that is already widespread within the public discourse, and use it to justify its political project. The notion of secularism as tolerance is thus appropriated by the Hindu Right, and then used to justify the construction of a Hindu *rashtra*, since Hinduism is widely considered (not only by the Right) as the most tolerant of religions.

Chatterjee ignores such lines of explanation and the adoption of such strategies on the part of the Hindu Right. Had he taken them more seriously, he might also have been more inclined to question Hinduism's claim to a special tolerance. Insofar as he talks of defending 'the duty of the democratic state to ensure policies of religious tolerance', he plays into the hands of political Hindutva, even if his own elaboration of what such tolerance should mean might not be acceptable on various counts to the Hindu Right. So the real problem is not the Hindu state, or Hindu *rashtra*, but the secular state itself! But to make the secular state a problem and assign blanket

---

164 '[The] Hindu Right is directed not against the principle of the secular state, but rather towards mobilising the legal powers of the state', Chatterjee, 'Secularism and Tolerance', p. 1,768. Or: 'The majoritananism of the Hindu Right, it seems to me, is perfectly at peace with the institutions and procedures of the "western" or "modern" state' (ibid.).

responsibility for this to India's modernists and secularists, Chatterjee has to argue that this category of modernists and secularists possesses a consistent understanding of secularism, when patently it does not.[165]

Different contexts did give rise to different meanings of secularism in India, as distinct from the West, as Chatterjee also recognizes. These contentions, moreover, created confusion and affected the secular character and behaviour of the Indian state. It is not, as Chatterjee contends, that differences centred only on how applicable an agreed notion was. These confusions had pertinent effects. India's state laws were based on Western liberal-democratic and secular principles, but qualifications to it (the absence of a UCC) and the actual *behaviour* of the Indian state towards its religious communities have had not a little to do with conflicts about the most appropriate notion of secularism.

The Western notion was a guideline, but there was little understanding of its core characteristics or of its incompatibility with National Movement–derived notions of secularism as a principle of tolerance uniting religious communities. Precisely because of such confusions, the word 'secular' was not included in the Constitution when it was first drawn up, but only introduced by Indira Gandhi in 1976, during the Emergency, to legitimize her rule. In reality the secular state's behaviour has represented an admixture of Western and Indian notions.

Having correctly enunciated the basic principles of a secular state in terms of the founding values of liberty, equality and neutrality, Chatterjee sees the Hindu Right's pressure for a UCC as expressive of a dilemma the secular state cannot resolve. For is not the Hindu Right's demand for a UCC in the name of equality an encroachment on the principle of liberty in whose name the cultural rights and identity of Muslims should be respected? The secular pressure for a UCC thus plays into the hands of the Hindu Right: secularism is compatible with authoritarianism. Chatterjee never suggests that the establishment, piecemeal and cumulative, of the most gender-just laws, whether or not they are finally and formally embodied in a UCC, would itself represent the deepest threat to Hindu communalism's basic perspectives regarding the family – that such 'best' secular laws would in fact be incompatible with political Hindutva.

This dismissal of secular possibilities allows him to attack with a clearer conscience the very paradigm of Enlightenment democracy as incapable of handling cultural diversity and freedom because it is steeped in rights discourse. Chatterjee is fully cognizant of the individual–communitarian debate in modern political theory. But he rules out the search for multiculturalism on the basis of a fundamentally agreed set of universal values, and the idea

---

165 '[T]he the proponents of the secular state in India never had any doubts at all about the meaning of the concept of secularism; all the doubts were about whether that concept would find a congenial field of application in the Indian social and political context'. Ibid., p. 1,769.

that a collective's right to its culture must also presume that the collective in question recognizes that it, too, must operate in a culture of rights. All such efforts at reconciling the best liberalism with the best communitarianism are, for Chatterjee, unconvincing and unacceptable. 'None of these liberal arguments seems to have enough strength to come to grips with the problems posed by the Indian situation.'[166]

Chatterjee endorses the claim that, since the very notion of the self or individual is to be questioned or rejected (the 'decentred self'), the individual cannot be the locus for anchoring a discourse of rights.[167] Since Chatterjee does not reject a rights discourse altogether, not only can a cultural community have its own distinct rights to do what it wants, it need not give reasons for this:

> Thus, when a minority group demands a cultural right, it in fact says, 'We have our reasons for doing things the way we do, but since you don't share the fundamentals of our world-view, you will never come to understand or appreciate those reasons. Therefore, leave us alone and let us mind our own business'.[168]

This brazen defence of extreme group relativism is actually undertaken in the name of wanting to secure a truer democracy. To provide a theoretical gloss on what would otherwise be seen as an incoherent relativist free-for-all inimical to any notion of democratic political governance across communities and individuals, Chatterjee takes up a Foucauldian notion of 'governmentality', but frankly admits to using it in his own way. For Foucault, governmentality was a specific form of disciplinary power cutting across the state–civil society divide, in which a 'modern regime no longer retains a distinct aspect of sovereignty'.[169]

But Chatterjee's purpose in reorganizing this concept is to argue something else: where governmental technologies do not hold sway, there you will not find applicable its 'juridicial sovereignty'. The 'inner' domain of the cultural community (or religious community, where the identification of religion and culture is no longer considered problematic) can and should remain aloof from the tyranny of state-imposed laws. When a community refuses to give reasons to the state for 'not being like you', it is actually democratically resisting the incursion of the 'technologies of governmentality'.

The community, here the religious community, has become the desired locus for advancing the democratic process. Legislating independently on

---

166 Ibid., p. 1,774.
167 '[A]rguments about the need to hold on to a universalist frameworks of reason ... tend to sound like pious homilies because they ignore the strategic context of power in which identity or difference is often asserted'. Ibid., p. 1,774.
168 Ibid.
169 Ibid., p. 1,775.

family and other matters, the community need not give reasons to 'outsiders'. But to be tolerant it must give reasons to itself through some public and representative process – in other words, it must be accountable to its own constituency. However, the mechanisms of accountability here would seem to be no different from those operative elsewhere. Presumably some notion of a universal, adult franchise would exist even if the 'universe' is the cultural community. Presumably each person's vote would count as much as another's – a smuggling in of the individual as the key political unit, at least for some public regulative purposes. Antipathy to the overbearingness of state forms has only resulted in the endorsement here of the overbearingness of a community form itself perceived in much the same way as a state-in-itself.[170]

The crucial issue in regard to such proposed 'legislative autonomy' for the religious community is the matter of the individual's right of exit. Does a Muslim woman, for example, have the right to reject the application of even an agreed internal consensus on Sharia, and opt instead for some other framework of non-community-based secular law? At this point of dispute, what laws apply? This is the crux of the matter. And even many who would not wish for a UCC, and who insist that reforms to Personal Law within a religious community should be the strategic 'line of march', would nonetheless agree that, at a point of dispute with an uncoerced disputant, secular laws should prevail, where these should be made as gender-just as possible.

Chatterjee does not directly address this issue, but the thrust of his argument opposes this as well as the (temporary, qualified or otherwise) right of exit. The religious community must be left to reform itself. To fears that this would mean endorsing existing relations of unequal and exploitative power, Chatterjee says that history confirms the strong possibility of such reforms, and that such aloofness and non-interference is preferable to the unacceptable arrogances of state imposition.[171] Where once Chatterjee would emphasize, in opposition to all essentialisms, the constructed character of communities, he has now come close to politically essentializing and reifying the religious community.

The individual belongs to multiple communities, and communities and their values, norms and commitments often clash and compete. This forces into the open issues of choice and judgement, and therefore raises questions about identifying the unit that has the right of choice, and arriving at a criterion (which be suitable across all communities) for judging such conflicts. In the name of an anti-individualist, anti-humanist, supposedly truer

---

170 Sarkar, 'Decline of the Subaltern'.
171 Chatterjee cites in his own support the history of the Shiromani Gurdwara Parbandhak Committee (SGPC), an elected lay body that has emerged as a major public regulatory force for Sikhs. The growing power of the SGPC among Sikhs has been part of a process in which the very definition of a Sikh and of a Sikh community has become more exclusive and undemocratic. The growing importance of the SGPC has reflected and promoted the process whereby the values and beliefs of one section – the Khalsa (unshorn) Sikhs – have become more dominant.

democracy, Chatterjee would have us, in effect, endorse the traditional networks of pre-Enlightenment collective oppressions, albeit with a modernist twist. He has joined forces with religious communitarians for whom the relationship between the individual and the community is to be based not primarily on rights, but on consensus.

In the specific area of Muslim Personal Law and the issue of a UCC, Chatterjee's strategic line is simply reactionary, contrary to the effort to widen the scope of application of gender-just laws, and represents a step backwards from what even many progressives working for internal reforms among Muslims would want. This is not the way to fight Muslim or Hindu communalism. It is, of course, a way to fight further promotion of secularism and secularization in India.

Communalism, Religious Fundamentalism and Religious Nationalism

The anti-secularist, anti-modern, postmodern or postcolonial thinker puts most blame for communalism or religious fundamentalism on secularism and modernity. These evils, it is claimed, are the reactions to the secularizing and modernizing processes that have been mistakenly seen as solutions, rather than for what they actually are: the causes. For the psychologically minded anti-modernist, these evils of communalism or fundamentalism (like so much else) is a particular state of mind or expression of a distinctive personality type. Fundamentalism is the response of self-hating believers to a secular, desacralized world. And this self-hatred or 'inner threat' is projected as an 'outer oppression' by some identified group, the despised Other.

But whether it is the anti-secularist, the secularist or the communalist religious activist, their respective understandings of communalism represent different ways of navigating over a large terrain that has common references or indicators. Some of them are like double-headed arrows, each pointing in opposite directions. The result is a wide variety of ways of defining or charting the phenomenon of communalism.

Choosing the best chart is a matter of where one is trying to get to. How best to understand communalism is related to one's wider intellectual and political projects. This does not mean a complete relativism; there are better and worse charts. But no single chart will provide all the best possible angles for surveying how the land lies. This may become clearer when we look at the references – the dyads and binary contrasts – that have shaped the various constructions of the concept of communalism.

Certainly, a greater awareness of the complexities and difficulties involved in any such attempt at concept-construction has made me more reluctant to advance even a provisional or working definition of communalism in just a few sentences.[172] I would now prefer to point out these dyads, look at some

---

172 This is something I was more prepared to do earlier. A. Vanaik, *The Painful*

of the choices of direction taken in each case, and simply explain my own preferences.

There are at least eight such dyads:

- *Modern–non-modern*: Is communalism a modern or non-modern phenomenon?
- *Singular–plural*: Is it a term applicable to a society with a single dominant religion, or only to those with significant religious pluralities?
- *Political–non-political*: Is it a political phenomenon or non-political – or both, but operating at different levels?
- *Individual–collective*: Is it operative at the collective level only, or at the individual level as well?
- *Religious–non-religious/secular*: Is it a secular phenomenon, or is it significantly related to religion? And if so, what does this mean?
- *Religious–ethnic*: Is it specifically religious, or more generally ethnic?
- *Essentialist–non-essentialist*: Is it an essentialist characteristic of India or the East, or non-essentialist?
- *Negative–neutral*: Is it to be understood as negatively charged, or should it be evaluatively neutral?

Choices in respect of a particular dyad cannot be easily separated from biases and choices in respect of others, and are part of the overall framework of values and perceptions that define one's own intellectual and political alignments.

Take the question of communalism's modern or non-modern character. Anti-secularists would without hesitation insist on the modernity of communalism. Others would say it depends on what you mean by communalism, and suggest that certain dimensions of it have a significant pre-modern history. Still others would associate the rise of communalism not with modernity per se, but with changes in the pattern of modernity. Communalism, then, is a modern phenomenon; but if modernity is its necessary condition, it is not a sufficient one.

As an adjective, the word 'communal' is mostly used with reference to consciousness and conflict: communal consciousness and communal conflict. For those who see modernity as constituting a profound and decisive rupture with the past, neither the forms of consciousness nor of the conflict within it can be seen in quite the same way as in pre-modernity. The use of communalism as a 'bridging' term, applicable with equal felicity to phenomena in the past as to our present, would not help us to grasp the distinctiveness of the problems of the present.

With some justification it could be argued that, while communal conflict was a significant feature of the past, communal consciousness was not. This

---

Transition (London, 1990), p. 157.

might seem comparable to saying that class conflict has been a feature of all stratified societies even if a strong class consciousness was infrequently associated with such struggle before the advent of industrialization. But the comparison is not tenable, unless one reduces 'communal' to a synonym for the term 'religious', so that communal conflict and communal conscious- ness mean nothing other than religious conflict and religious consciousness. This would empty the concept of any distinctive value. Moreover, the actual emergence of the term and the development of a discourse of communalism are roughly concurrent with the constructions of the discourse of coloni- alism, and then of nationalism. It is a modern construction meant to serve modern purposes, though different architects have had different projects in mind.

The communal riot as an archetypal form of communal conflict precedes colonial rule, but not by centuries.[173] It was also comparatively rare. Though references to the Muslim community and the defence of its interests are to be found under Mughal rule, the consciousness of belonging to a pan- Indian entity – the Muslim community – was for most Muslims extremely vague and weak, and subordinated to other, more local loyalties and forms of community consciousness. As communal consciousness sharpened during and after colonialism, the character of communal conflict also changed significantly.[174]

Situating communalism as a modern phenomenon also raises a series of other issues, and creates its own theoretical biases. It cannot, then, be an Indian essentialism. It was not a basic feature of India's past, and is not equivalent to other kinds of supposedly essentialist factionalism, such as trib- alism or casteism. British colonialists who saw it as such were making it part of an Orientalist discourse that justified their own civilizing mission. Not being an essentialism, communalism is a concept that in principle is gen- eralizable to other shores and climes. There is no reason why it cannot be used to analyse the travails in the Balkans and elsewhere in Europe, except that the international relationship of political and intellectual forces that helps determine what discursive terms are used, and where, can hardly be expected to allow this.

An existing Western usage of the term 'communalism' is strongly positive and expressive of communitarian as opposed to individualist (self-centred) longings, because the history of Western modernity has been different.

---

173 C. A. Bayly, 'The Pre-History of Communalism? Religious Conflict in India, 1700–1860', *Modern Asian Studies* 19 (1985); H. Mukhia, 'Communalism and the Indian Polity', *South Asia Bulletin* XI: 1–2 (1991).

174 Mukhia, 'Communalism and the Indian Polity'. Mukhia points out that com- munal consciousness is not simply the creation of colonialism, and that its first stirrings emerged earlier, under medieval Mughal rule. This is to equate communal consciousness with community consciousness, and to allow for a neutral evaluation of the terms 'com- munal' and 'communalism'. His article can also be read as affirming that such communal consciousness cannot have the sharpened and mass character that it has in modernity.

Nationalism there was much more a secular phenomenon, because it had already been preceded by the institutionalization of a democratic, secular discourse questioning the claims of Christianity and the Church.

Even where a strong connection between religion and nationalism existed, the ideal of a secular state was not questioned.[175] Except for the former Yugoslavia and Albania, Europe was uniformly Christian. Religious nationalism, not communalism, was the issue. The key contrast was between Europe's centre and peripheries, between the zone where national identity was less aggressive because more secure, and where it was not. Religious identity as collective public consciousness was much less important in the centre.[176] Insofar as today's religious map of Europe has changed since 1648, it is because of mass migration from former colonial possessions and intra-EU movements, not because of any dynamic arising from within Christianity to change this as it once did through generating mass enthusiasms and conversions of the formerly uninitiated or uninterested. This lost appeal is itself indicative of Christianity's relative decline, and the emergence of a secular state and a more secularized society. For these rather than for any essentialist reasons, communalism has become a term confined primarily to South Asia.

Should it apply only to where two or more major religious systems exist, or even where there is no such plurality? If the latter, then there are two likely corollaries: (1) communalism is more likely to be a substitutable expression for religious fundamentalism or religious nationalism; (2) it need not even refer specifically to a religious grouping, but can be used to refer to some other ethnic grouping, or even to an altogether neutral concept of 'community', ethnic or otherwise.

In both cases, the special value of such a concept becomes submerged. The moment communalism is seen as a term that applies when there is a plurality of religious (or other ethnic) groups, then it is likely to express some kind of tension *between* groups, to be a negative conception of communalism. It is

---

175 In India, 'We are secular not because we had begun to question the rule of religious injunctions but because we saw in secularism a way of holding our many religious identities together.' M. S. Gore, 'Secularism and Equal Regard for All Religions', in Chakrabarty, *Secularism and Indian Polity*, p. 158. In India it was the presumed commonality of religions, not the frank recognition of differences between religious sects, that justified the secular state.

176 Religion connects with nationalism through origin myths of the nation, in a process that was strong in Scotland, Poland, Belgium, Ireland, Iberia, Serbia, Bulgaria, Romania and Greece. In France, Italy and Czechoslovakia it had to contend with liberal secular nationalism. Where the origin myth is old and there has been little external threat, as in England and Holland, religious consciousness is more dormant. The relaxed unions between nation and religion are where this is based on glory: Holland, Spain, Sweden, Austria, England. It is not so when the union is based on threat and suffering: Greece, Cyprus, Poland, Belgium, Ireland, Croatia. There is more ambiguity where there are plural religions (much of the former Yugoslavia, Albania) and where ecclesiastical authority was opposed to national unification (Germany, Italy). Martin, *General Theory of Secularization*, Chapter 3.

something unpleasant, unwanted, even condemnable. This is the way Orientalists used it, and the way most Indian nationalists perceived it. It is the
direction taken even by the Indian anti-essentialist and modernist construction of it (mainly in the 1920s and 1930s). There is no good reason why we
should not continue to so use it, though there have been attempts to give it
a more neutral imputation.[177]

A more debated theoretical or definitional issue, however, is whether
communalism should be understood in ways that make it structurally
modular. Can it not describe a range of group tensions? Here it becomes a
term of ethnicity rather than of religion alone.[178] While there is no a priori
reason for saying that this use is illegitimate, problems do arise. If we make
communalism the equivalent for any kind of negative 'communitarianism',
then certain theoretical tendencies surface. We are deprived of any specific
term with which to analyse interreligious tensions and conflicts in modernity. It becomes more difficult to think about how interreligious tensions
differ from other kinds of inter-ethnic tensions: the specificities of religious
power and influence are obscured. The tendency, already strong, to believe
that communalism really has very little to do with religion is reinforced.
At most, religious identity becomes a boundary marker for the politics of
communal mobilization. This is far and away the dominant tendency in the
definitions and understandings of communalism held even by those committed to Enlightenment notions of secularism and the secular state.

---

177 Communalism is 'that phenomenon we might define as a politicized community
identity'. S. Freitag, *Collective Action and Community* (Delhi, 1990), p. 6.
178 The late Khushwant Singh and Bipan Chandra saw communalism on the individual level as a 'state of mind', which, for the latter, is also a false consciousness. It is 'a
feeling of belonging to a particular community which has a sense of exclusion towards
all others and an unfair preference for your own community'. K. Singh, 'Dangers of
Communalism in Contemporary India', in K. Singh and B. Chandra, *Many Faces of Communalism* (Chandigarh, 1985), p. 35. Singh also felt such a definition was adequate at the
collective level, expressing a collective state of mind. Chandra saw communalism at the
collective level as an ideology or a specific doctrine whose communal character depended
on the degree of separateness and hostility it postulates towards the 'Other'. So there
are the beginnings of a communal ideology when there is a consciousness only of collective secular interests; a liberal communalism when these are seen as separate and distinct
from other communities; and a full-blown communalism when such interests are seen as
opposed to, and threatened by, other communities. B. Chandra, 'Communalism – The
Way Out', in ibid., pp. 45–6. By making communalism an ideology, Chandra depersonal-
ized it. It can now become the property of a more impersonal entity like a party, and thus
become institutionalized. This is an advance on the 'state of mind' notion of communalism. Also, 'Communalism in the contemporary Indian context is a deep, almost visceral
form of antagonism and antipathy between communities of differing cultural, ethnic,
linguistic and/or religious identities.' R. E. Frykenberg, 'Hindu Fundamentalism and the
Structural Stability of India', in M. E. Marty and R. S. Appleby, eds, *Fundamentalism and
the State* (Chicago, 1993), p. 236.
    For Dipankar Gupta, communalism is not a religio-political phenomenon but an
ethnic-separatist one. This is why he believes Hindutva as the form of Hindu communalism is actually 'Hindustanitva', or Hindustan-ness, i.e. primarily about keeping India
united. D. Gupta, 'Communalism and Fundamentalism', *Economic and Political Weekly*
XXVI (1991).

Take the following definitions of communalism, which, unlike the broad ethnic notion, do stipulate a connection to religion. It is 'the functioning of religious communities or organizations detrimental to the interests of other groups or the nation as a whole. The term usually invokes some kind of political involvement.'[179] Or, 'Communalism is taken here as a political doctrine which makes use of religio-cultural differences to achieve political ends.'[180] There is Jawaharlal Nehru's definition of communalism as 'a narrow group mentality basing itself on a religious community but in reality concerned with political power and patronage for the interested group'.[181] In this approach, the conceptual slide into notions like good and bad religion, true religion and false religiosity, religion-as-faith and religion-as-ideology, is greatly strengthened.

Communalism can, on this understanding, only be perceived as an overwhelmingly *secular* problem, having fundamentally secular sources, though opinion can be divided on whether there should be secular or anti-secular solutions. The central location for investigating the problems of communalism becomes simply the non-religious or contra-religious processes of modernity. This should not be the conclusion in an argument that rightly stresses the modernity of communalism. The true terrain is the changing relationship of religion and religious systems to other processes in modernity.

Both sides of the equation linking the religious and the non-religious have to be seriously investigated. It is not modernity per se, but changing scenarios in modernity and the changing responses of religious systems, that are the problems. The worldwide resurgence of religious fundamentalism, religious nationalism and communalism is a feature arising from the fourth, not the third, quarter of the twentieth century. Temporally and spatially specific critiques of the forces operating within modernity, religious and non-religious, are called for, not general or ahistorical critiques of either religious systems or modernity.

Like other negative phenomena, such as racism, sexism and casteism, communalism operates at both the individual and collective levels. At the individual level, it is an attitudinal problem that is socially derived. There are racial, sexist and casteist prejudices and communal consciousness or biases. But where caste identity presupposes the existence of a strongly institutionalized system of caste oppression, the existence of racial, sexual and religious identities and self-awarenesses does not axiomatically presuppose the existence of strongly institutionalized racism, sexism or communalism – though, concretely speaking, the institutionalization of patriarchy has been universal. In the case of racism and communalism, different societies can and do have different degrees of institutionalization of such evils, and the differences are often qualitatively significant.

---

179 Smith, *India as a Secular State*, p. 454.
180 P. Dixit, *Communalism: A Struggle for Power* (Delhi, 1974), p. 1.
181 Nehru, *Discovery of India*, p. 387.

It is at the collective or institutionalized level that the problem is most seriously posed, and must be primarily confronted. Moreover, a collective resolution of the collective problem of communalism is not the sum of the individual resolutions of individual problems. An understanding or definition of communalism that sees it in more or less this fashion, which does not sufficiently distinguish between the individual and collective aspects as two different types of problem (with the line of causation running from the social to the individual), will not be very helpful in providing a programme for combating it.

This is a major problem with all 'state of mind' definitions of communalism. Since the problem has to be tackled at this wider, more public level, the Indian academic discourse has also, for the most part, seen communalism as a political phenomenon. This is eminently sensible because its political thrust makes it particularly dangerous. But it is also a social and cultural phenomenon, which is what gives it the political force it has. It operates not just in and around the state, but in civil society as well. It has to do not only with the constructions of politics, but also with the constructions and affirmations of religious identity. It is not only political systems, structures, institutions, elites and personnel that are to blame, but also religious systems, structures, institutions, elites and personnel. It is not just secularization in modernity that is the problem, but also competitive de-secularization in late modernity, or the striving to extend the reach, power and importance of religious institutions, ideologies and identities at the expense of secular equivalents.[182]

Modernity makes communalism possible, yet also carries the antidote for it. This is never a permanent cure, but it can be a stable and increasingly effective one. Communalism is the sharpest expression in a religiously plural society of the failure to establish a proper balance between the secular and the religious – in other words, the terms of coexistence. The initiative in this ongoing effort has always rested with secular forces.

The religious map of Europe remained unchanged for centuries, until the mass migrations into Europe after the process of de-colonization began. The religious map of the world will also no longer change, except of course through mass migration, which brings its own multiculturalist problems and newer dilemmas for secularism and the secular state. But the era when any world religion could be said to possess the internal dynamism enabling it to greatly expand its sphere of influence is gone for good. The Christian,

---

182 Religious discourse is not communalist discourse. It only provides the alphabet, or perhaps some words, from which the ugly sentences of communalist discourse are constructed. But religious discourse must also be seen as only one kind of discourse, language or alphabet system among others in a modern, secular society. It is a discourse that must recognize its limited applicability. When it intrudes into other domains where other languages (and alphabets) are more fitted – i.e. when it becomes legitimized as an acceptable discourse on the terrain of modern politics – then it widens the field over which communal discourse operates. This is true even when, in that domain, it can be used to fight communal constructions of its 'alphabet'.

Islamic, Hindu and Buddhist worlds will no longer grow at the expense of each other, though within each of these spaces there certainly can be changes in the internal relationship of forces between churches, sects and branches.[183]

In short, no world religion can any longer be said to possess a distinctive dynamism of its own. The exceptional power of the West and of Westernization does not give Christianity any reason to believe it can ride piggy-back to make newer conquests. It is not the distinctive gifts of religious systems that explain the recent (and fluctuating) resurgence of religio-political movements and ideologies, but the specific weaknesses of secular processes in various parts of the world. Once, a world religion expanded because for both secular and religious reasons it was better able to address the needs of potential believers. Today, there is only the turning away from secular failures to whatever is at hand within an existing religious system. This indicates not the enduring dynamism of religion, but more its value as a compensatory mechanism in modernity.

This resurgence is, above all, a reaction to a failed modernization. Religion-related movements are usually most aggressively political, widespread and dangerous where the failure is most acute. That is why, though Christian fundamentalist movements are on the rise in the advanced Western world, they do not represent as serious a threat for these societies as Islamic fundamentalist or Hindu communal or Buddhist revanchist movements do in theirs. This failure is a many-sided one, expressed in inadequacies of socio-economic development, weaknesses of political democratization, and ideological disarray. These religion-related movements take different forms, varying in their explicitly political character and their obsession with state power. Not all are religio-political movements, and among the latter political ambitions vary. Some others are religious revivalisms, and some have more to do with social reform. Yet others combine elements of some or all of the above.

Religious fundamentalism has become an inaccurate term of convenience to describe all such religion-related movements. Not all religious fundamentalisms are religio-political movements. A host of Christian fundamentalist currents are largely unconcerned about the public domain of politics. While all communalisms and religious nationalist movements are religio-political movements, they are not always religious fundamentalisms. And not all communalisms are religious nationalisms, as is demonstrated by Muslim communalism in India. Where religious fundamentalisms and nationalisms need not posit hostility to a 'religious other', communalism does. So even when a communalism, such as Hindu communalism, is also a religious nationalism, it is not only that.

---

183 While Protestantism has made considerable gains in Latin America over recent decades because of conversion (mainly to right-wing, US-based evangelical sects), the United States as the world's largest immigrant society is becoming less Protestant.

To handle these differences effectively, religious fundamentalism must not be characterized too sweepingly. It need not be defined pejoratively. One person's fundamentalism is another's normality. Nor should it be perceived in an overly political fashion.[184] Where the secular state is secure, religious fundamentalism does not make state power its focus, or, even if it does, it has little scope for serious headway.[185]

Religious fundamentalism is best understood as a label for those movements stressing either a return to or reinterpretation of foundational sacred texts, in order to resolve contemporary political, social or personal problems. Fundamentalism can be reactionary – but it is not conservative: it does not seek to conserve what already exists. Hinduism and Buddhism, not being scriptural religions, could not give rise to religious fundamentalisms, therefore. But the kind of religio-political movements that do arise – Hindu communalism, Buddhist communalism or nationalism – nonetheless share many aspects of fundamentalist movements.

They both fight on the terrain of modernity itself, and not on the ground between tradition and modernity. They are most certainly not atavisms. They both employ the mass politics of religious appeal. Their means of mobilization are invariably modern. They pursue goals that are modernist and anti-modernist, but never non-modernist or pre-modernist. Their thrust is, on balance, directed against secularism and the secularizing process, and against political democracy. They share common attitudes to science, using science's own disclaimers about its provisionality, contingency and falsifiability to claim that it cannot be true knowledge, which only religion can provide.[186] Much of what has been said here would apply to most religious nationalist movements and ideologies.

What is common to all these religio-political movements is that they are each greatly inspired in their reform agendas by religious faith (they are not just political manipulators of religious identity markers), and not only by secular ambitions. They are, therefore, invariably far more precise in their programmatic injunctions concerning education and family life (which usually carry negative implications for gender justice) than they are in regard

---

184 Mark Juergensmeyer feels the political dimension must be brought into the centre of any conception of religious fundamentalism. But this seems largely because of his preoccupation with religious nationalism and his unconcern with less political forms of religious fundamentalism. M. Juergensmeyer, 'Why Religious Nationalists are not Fundamentalists', *Religion* 23 (1993).

185 '[T]he success[es] of fundamentalisms in reimagining the nation and remaking the state have occurred primarily if not exclusively in states in which the public–private distinction ... has not been written into the Constitution and protected by laws and judicial rulings ...[I]n polities in which some form of church–state separation has been adopted, fundamentalism seems less likely to dictate the course of national self-definition – unless and until the fundamentalists undergo a process of moderation. This is most apparent in the case of Christian fundamentalists in the USA.' Marty and Appleby, *Fundamentalism and the State*, p. 640.

186 The more extreme elements would advocate at least supplementing secular science with Islamic or Vedic science.

to reforming the macro-structures or systems of political and economic life. Even in modernity, the family is where religious influence remains greatest.

Religious nationalism contrasts with secular nationalism. It need not but can be a fundamentalism. It is more benign than communalism. The 'Other' it opposes are secularists or secular nationalists, not necessarily a 'religious other', hostility to the last named being the basic characteristic of communalism. But most religious nationalisms today are strongly negative. They have a definite authoritarian thrust, though it is flexible and variable. There are shifting combinations of the religious and the secular, the democratic and the authoritarian.[187]

Religious nationalism is a distinctive hybrid in which the more important defining element is the noun. Religious and secular nationalisms are two different forms of cultural nationalism, incompatible because of their irreconcilable differences on the issue of individual rights. But religious nationalisms cannot be a *complete* replacement for a secular nationalism, because of the nature of nationalism itself. The latter has not just a cultural dimension, which can be answered by either a religious or a secular candidate, but also a political dimension, which is secular in character. This usually, but not always, acts to temper the fervour and thrust of religious nationalisms, which is why the small minority of religious nationalist states that exist do not altogether outlaw secular values, institutions or laws, but incorporate them in variable ways.

Secular nationalism, especially if it is also a democratic nationalism, has resources of strength which are often underestimated. While the number of religious nationalist movements is growing, the number of religious nationalist states is not growing anywhere near as fast. Such movements do not have things all their own way. Religious loyalties are not equivalent to national loyalties, though religion and nationalism have in so many ways quite a similar structure.[188] Religious loyalty operates with a notion of believership. Nationalism does not just represent a community of believers, in which the principle of believership can be religiously or secularly based; it is also a community of citizens operating with a uniquely powerful political (and secular) principle of legitimacy and empowerment: citizenship. It is the unique power of nationalism that explains why, in modernity, religious

---

187 'Political Islam' is the term used by Mahmood Mamdani, because it is the politics more than the Islam that is the dominant characteristic, with its appeal to Islamic-inspired injunctions for organizing modern life being highly variable between different groups, sects and movements. See his excellent study, M. Mamdani, *Good Muslim, Bad Muslim: America, the Cold War and the Roots of Terror* (New York, 2004).

188 Such a 'structure' comprises doctrines, myths, ethics, ritual, experience, and social organization. Both religion and nationalism have the power to invoke martyrdom and sacrifice on a large scale. M. Juergensmeyer, *Religious Nationalism Confronts the Secular State* (Delhi, 1994). Juergensmeyer mistakenly sees 'secular' nationalism as having the same structure as a religious system, when it is actually nationalism itself that has this. Similarly, in the term 'religious nationalism', he sees the adjective as the defining element. The result is a failure to address adequately the unique power of nationalism.

systems seek to co-opt rather than confront nationalism in the name of some 'higher' transnational religious loyalty. Despite religion's claims to transcendence, should it seek through confrontation to 'transcend' nationalism, it will lose out.

Of course, a fuller explanation of the unique power of nationalism would have to probe more deeply than I have done here. It would not be enough simply to point out the similar structures in nationalist and religious systems. To what extent is nationalism a replacement for religious affiliation made powerfully appealing precisely because the structures and symbols of this affiliation are akin to religion or kinship? On the other hand, if nationalism has been *more* powerful than a religious system in our times, the weight of explanation is more likely to fall on the fact that it is a *political* community as well as a culturally imagined one.[189] I suggested above that the empowering principle of citizenship has been one such crucial factor. But this hardly exhausts the exploration of the political sources of nationalism's unique strength.

Indeed, the intensity of belief and commitment that the nation can evoke, to the point of demanding and securing the sacrifice of one's life, may itself have as much to do with the fact of its being a *nation-state*, a 'community of political destiny', a 'community of life and death', because of the possibilities of wars between nation-states. Where membership is a matter of fate (belonging to a nation is not usually chosen, and is thereby similar to religious and family membership), and where it also carries risk because such affiliation can demand the ultimate sacrifice, then such a community also possesses for its believers a distinctive purity. Here, the possibility of war gives the nation a special grandeur, and the fact of war gives it 'a precise, univocal and resolutely imagined identity'.[190]

Behind religion's inability to match the appeal of nationalism, then, are political weaknesses that go beyond merely the issue of citizenship. But this, nonetheless, remains a serious lacuna that needs to be registered.

Religious systems cannot override a political arrangement in which the modern, empowering principle of citizenship operates. The nation-state is not the only form such a political arrangement can take. Nor should we assume that the nation-state system will endure long into the future. But the search for alternatives is still in its infancy. Meanwhile, there are still progressive forms of nationalism that can be counterposed to religious nationalism. To reject religious nationalism, even in this era of globalization, does not require us, automatically or always, to reject nationalism itself.

---

189 B. Anderson, *Imagined Communities* (London, 1991). In Anderson's phrase, the nation was an 'imagined political community'. But most of his own efforts went into the exploration of the nation as an imagined cultural artefact.

190 For a thoughtful discussion on the strengths and weaknesses of Anderson's justly famous work, see G. Balakrishnan, 'The National Imagination', *New Left Review* I/211 (May–June 1995), p. 68.

But if nationalism provides resources to check the absolutist tendencies of religious systems, nationalism, because it usually legitimizes the authority of the state, can also promote the tendential absolutism of the state itself. Thus, religious nationalism can also mean the dangerous marriage of two such absolutist-prone systems. It is not just any kind of secular nationalism that can effectively confront religious nationalism, but *democratic* nationalisms that can do so. The struggle for democracy – the deepening institutionalization of human rights and the expansion of popular empowerment – is among the most powerful counter not only to religious nationalisms, but also to religious fundamentalisms and communalisms.

All these religio-political movements have arisen in response to the many-sided failure of capitalist modernization. It is the resurrection of a more effective and sensitive modernization project that will most weaken the evils of such religio-political movements and ideologies. If the construction of such an alternative modernization project is considered inseparable from the task of deepening democracy and pursuing socialism, then the anti-communal struggle in India becomes an integral part of this wider anti-authoritarian and anti-capitalist project.

The most effective way to promote the various themes of secularism is not always to do it directly. The secular discourse is a subset of the wider discourse of democracy and equality. It is this discourse (with strong socialist references) that is most important, and should be ideologically promoted. How the major principles of a secular outlook should be promoted is related to how best to organize propagation of a general democratic discourse. One major aspect of the discourse of secularism has to do with emphasizing and justifying the necessity of a secular state. This theme should be directly propagated in myriad ways. The message here is that the existence and strengthening of a secular state is the necessary but not sufficient condition for the existence and strengthening of a democratic system.

Another aspect of this discourse has to do with the secularization of civil society – namely, the ways in which religious loyalties must accept a more modest role, and come to terms with secular institutions, affiliations and norms of functioning. Here, the motifs of privatizing and optionalizing religion mean more than merely a basic separation of religion from the state. These are not themes that fruitfully lend themselves to any direct agitprop approach. Indeed, this would be counterproductive. Here, it is the institutionalization of greater democracy, social and gender equality, and economic progress in civil society that is most important. The ideological complement to this is the propagation of a general discourse of democracy, welfare and equality in which the specifically secular aspects are incorporated. Even if such a general discourse were to avoid explicit references to being anti-capitalist or pro-socialist and confine itself to social-democratic and 'green development' perspectives, measures and demands, it would be profoundly subversive, since, in this writer's view, this is not compatible with the preservation and continuation of capitalism, whose future ravages would be much sharper in the countries of the developing world, like India. But space in this ideological struggle must also be made for rationalist movements that try to promote a scientific outlook towards nature, and therefore cannot but mount an explicit critique of certain forms, norms and beliefs of popular Hindu religiosity, in particular.

Progressives can have differences about how much weight should be given to such exercises and efforts in the overall secularizing strategy of confronting the forces of political Hindutva in civil society, since this will lead to false accusations that secularists are anti-religious when the effort to promote the ideology of secularism is really part of the larger project aimed at promoting democratization of thought, behaviour and institutions. But it is not an arena that should be ignored. Certainly the forces of political Hindutva, by their very hostility, do not ignore this terrain of discourse.[191] Nanda, more than anyone else, has emphasized this in her various writings: 'All components of popular religiosity – the view of the world, rituals, and ethics – serve as rules of grammar that Hindutva parties share with the everyday Hindu believers of all castes ... Hindutva may not be a distortion of "real" religion designed to dupe and manipulate the "innocent" masses ... that Hindutva may actually have a significant amount of popular consent'.[192]

Her argument is that far too many believe that Indian nationalism will be all the stronger if its citizens are educated to understand its distinctiveness, in that it rests on a 'civilizational idiom' that is ultimately rooted in Hindu

---

191 In August 2013, N. Dabholkar, founder of the Committee for Eradication of Superstition in Maharashtra, and a former vice-president of the Federation of Indian Rationalist Associations, was gunned down in daylight. In February 2015 the same fate was meted out to G. Pansare, also of Maharashtra, who died of his injuries, and who was a close friend of Dabholkar. Pansare was a member of the Communist Party of India, and a respected writer critical of superstitions and historical myth-making. Again, in August 2015, M. Kalburgi, a Kannada writer and scholar also critical of superstitions and idol-worshipping, was shot dead. All three aroused the ire of upper-caste Hindu far-right groups, and all three had received a number of death threats prior to their deaths. At the time of writing, the culprits in all three cases have yet to be punished.

192 M. Nanda, *Prophets Facing Backward: Postmodernism, Science and Hindu Nationalism* (Delhi, 2004), p. 48. See also M. Nanda, *The God Market: How Globalization is making India more Hindu* (Noida, 2009), where she highlights the developing 'state–temple–corporate complex'. By this she means the deepening partnership between the neoliberal Indian state, the corporate sector (predominantly Hindu) and the religious Hindu establishment to nurture the popular religiosity of the majority. This, she avers, is particularly so in the areas of education where the official commitment to secularism does not prevent state support to three types of Hindu traditionalist institutions. In the first kind, Vedic science courses are taught and there is training of priests. In the second case, land grants are given to tax-exempt ashrams and temples for setting up deemed universities offering courses in various secular subjects like conventional science and engineering. Financial support is also given for the setting up of dispensaries, hospitals, public reading rooms, and so on, for the lay public. In the third category, apart from giving financial support, public sector infrastructure projects are diverted to meet the needs of religious festivals, pilgrimages, and even forms of religious tourism. All this is aimed at benefiting the majority religion disproportionately.

metaphysics. This Hindu metaphysics does not allow for a separation of the sacred from the profane, even the extent this has happened in Christianity. Allegiance to this 'holist metaphysics' means reinterpreting secularism and democracy in ways that make it compatible with this idiom that, in turn, legitimizes Hindu nationalism: 'A scientific critique of metaphysics is uniquely important in the case of Hinduism because the dominant Vedic and Vedantic traditions treat God as immanent in nature and therefore allow no demarcation between the supernatural and nature, the super-empirical and the scientific.'[193] Nanda is certainly on the mark in pointing out how, unlike other forms of revivalism in the other world religions, it is in Hindu nationalist revivalism that we find an obsession with wanting to make modern science verify the metaphysical assumptions of Vedic Hinduism. Prime Minister Modi, no less, in a reference to Ganesh – the deity with a human body and an elephant head – made a point of publicly stating his belief that plastic surgery (he meant transplantation) was known to Indian ancients, as well as stem cell research and space travel.[194]

Where the Sangh Parivar aims to reinterpret the values of secularism and democracy to conform more closely to the social values and beliefs of popular Hindu religiosity, should not secularists seek to change social values and beliefs to conform more closely to the modern norms, values and beliefs of secularism and democracy? If so, this means the secularization and democratization of society is the key task – one demanding that religious systems learn their place in this new dispensation. They have no inherent dynamic leading them to endorse or practically reinforce modern principles of pluralism and democracy. The world religions are historically shaped entities bearing the marks of that shaping. But this does not mean they are incompatible with such modern principles.

It does mean, however, that religions have to *learn* how to become compatible, and to accept the costs and consequences of what this entails. That is what the ideology of secularism (insofar as it would deal with the issue of secularization of civil society) would demand, and it is easy to see how religious activists, from communalists to anti-secularists, can distort this message into a purportedly anti-religious one. This distortion is most effective when religions are directly exhorted to learn their place. They are least effective when religious systems are indirectly pushed to adopt more accommodating and modest postures because of the practical virtues and benefits that attend the progressive institutionalization of democracy and justice (in the widest sense) on the ground.

---

193 Nanda, *Prophets Facing Backward*, p. 50.
194 Maseeh Rahman, 'Indian Prime Minister Claims Genetic Science Existed in Ancient Past', *Guardian*, 28 October 2014. See also M. Nanda, *Science in Saffron: Skeptical Essays on History of Science* (New Delhi, 2016), where she both acknowledges ancient India's genuine contribution to science and subjects to critique misrepresentations by the likes of Vivekananda, a much-revered philosopher of Vedantic Hinduism.

This is the best approach for India's secular activists to take in their confrontation with the various communalisms existing, at least in regard to their operations in civil society. Of these, Hindu communalism is far and away the most dangerous. Muslim communalism in India is more socially and spatially restricted, and not linked to any pan-Indian Islamic movement. Muslim communalism in a particular locale promotes the organizational growth of Hindu communalism in the same place, while the reverse does not necessarily apply.[195] But this should not justify a perspective of first tackling Hindu communalism and then worrying about the others. All communalisms have to be tackled together, because they all feed on each other, even as we are aware of the special power of Hindu communalism to change the fabric of Indian society. It alone can bring about a highly authoritarian and centralized form of rule: the Hindu state. Moreover, the attempt to impose its specific view of pan-Hindu unity will greatly weaken the social fabric of India by reinforcing not just communal but also caste oppression, as well as weakening territorial unity.

This Hindu communalism, organizationally represented by the forces of the Sangh combine, is not to be equated with Hindu nationalism. Nor is its ideology purely one of Hindu nationalism. Hindu communalism, in its systematized hostility to the Muslim 'Other', and in its larger project for social and political change, is much more. It is a deeply reactionary and strongly authoritarian far right movement, having a corresponding ideological thrust, whereas Hindu nationalism comes in many kinds. It is entirely legitimate to talk of Gandhi's Hindu nationalism and that of other nationalist leaders and currents. But it would be utterly mistaken to brand Gandhi's perspectives as communal, to doubt his anti-communal credentials, or to deny his remarkable capacity to mobilize anti-communal campaigns.

Many of Gandhi's perspectives were in conflict with modern conceptions of secularism, and to that extent weakened the struggle for it. But being anti-secular, or behaving in ways that weaken secularism, is not the same as being communal or behaving communally. Though, in a general and long-term sense, failing to strengthen the secular state or promote secularization strengthens the communalist dynamic, there is still space for non-secular means of discourse and behaviour (with their limitations and dangers) to contribute to the struggle against communalism. They cannot constitute the *strategic* perspective in the struggle against communalism, but can provide a partial and important tactical resource.

Hindu communalism gives rise not to just any kind of Hindu nationalism, but to the most vicious form of it available in India. By using this term as a self-description, the forces of the Sangh combine give themselves a more benign image than they could ever deserve, as well as implying continuities

---

195 J. Alam, 'Muslim Communalism', *Economic and Political Weekly*, 2 June 1984. See also his *Who Wants Democracy?* (New Delhi, 2006), especially Chapter 4, 'Muslims: The "Joker" in the Democratic Pack'.

with other, less pernicious forms of Hindu nationalism. As for Hindutva, it is an important part of the wider ideology of Hindu communalism – perhaps its most coherently organized part. But it is not the whole of that ideology.

Hindutva is the intellectual anchor of the ideology pursued by the most vicious form of Hindu nationalism, which is itself a major part of the overall project of Hindu communalism.[196]

---

196 The Sangh combine is also pragmatic. The sentiments cultivated among Hindus against the Muslim 'Other' range from righteousness to deprivation to fear. When the first is cultivated, the open text of the message is religious solidarity, and the submerged text is antagonism. K. N. Pannikar, 'Conceptualising Communalism', *Seminar* 394 (June 1992). Given the different though related conceptions of Hindutva, I have preferred not to align myself with Savarkar's particular definition but to see Hindutva (as laid out in the earlier subsection in this chapter) as a wider, more abstract intellectual construct having political resonances. Political Hindutva is a term I have used to describe the forces of the Sangh combine, whose ideology, being more politically driven, is guided by but different from Hindutva. (See Chapter 5, below, subsection on 'Deconstructing Sangh Ideology'.) I make no claim that this is the only useful way to deal with the notion of Hindutva, or to draw out appropriate relationships between it and the forces of the Sangh combine. For convenience's sake, I have sometimes simply used the term Hindutva when I mean political Hindutva and not the more abstract intellectual construct. But the context makes it clear when I am resorting to this equivalence, and should prevent confusion.

PART III

4

The Threat of Hindu Communalism: Problems with the Fascist Paradigm

Contending Paradigms

Any attempt to render the historical phenomenon of fascism conceptually serviceable for contemporary purposes – for example, analysing Hindu communalism – must cope with the necessity and difficulty of establishing a 'fascist minimum' embodying its main dynamics. A set of defining characteristics – properties, preconditions – and methodological injunctions has to be articulated. This must, in part or whole, constitute a core and heuristic recognized as such by social scientists and general analysts. Along with supplementary theories, it should be accepted as a dominant model amid competing theories and paradigms, vindicating itself as a fascist paradigm. If total consensus is not demanded for the heuristic or 'fascist minimum' (because we are dealing with a research programme in the *social* sciences), too little agreement will not do either – framing just one among numerous angles of vision of fascism.

Stanley Payne has listed eleven different ways of attempting to theorize the phenomenon of fascism. The list is reflexive and open enough to include the approach of those scholars sceptical about even seeing fascism as a generic phenomenon, who would abjure the theorization of it altogether.[1] One can impose taxonomic discipline on this methodological largesse. Broadly speaking, there are Marxist and non-Marxist approaches, each with their intra-paradigm divergences. This is especially so for the latter, which lack any positive theoretical principle of unification. Yet there is some large and important ground of agreement in both research programmes:

1. Fascism in power, the fascist state, is a distinctive form of the modern state.[2] Its distinctiveness lies in its extreme centralization of political power

---

1 S. G. Payne, *Fascism* (London, 1980).
2 H. A. Turner, Jr, 'Fascism and Modernization' *World Politics* 24 (1971–72). Turner

and, as a logical corollary, its exceptional degree of autonomy from other major power actors and forces.[3]

2. The two undisputed examples of fascism in power were Italy and Germany, though the latter had a unique Nazi twist.[4] These two regimes

---

insists on taking German fascism's pastoralist themes at face value. The Nazi regime, had it lasted, would have revealed its anti-modern thrust more clearly. Nazism wanted the products of industry, but without becoming an industrial society; its policy of *Lebensraum* was aimed at achieving just such an 'authentic' folk-German anti-industrial society, serviced by non-Germanic industrialized regions. Turner also sides with those who argue that fascism in Italy was not an agent of modernization. (See A. Hughes and M. Kolinsky, 'Paradigmatic Fascism and Modernization', *Political Studies* 24: 4 [1976]). As late as 1938, only 33 per cent of the national income came from industry, while between 1921 and 1936 industrial employment rose from 24 per cent to only 28 per cent, and agricultural employment fell only from 56 per cent to 48 per cent. However, Payne (*Fascism*) and A. J. Gregor in his rejoinder to Turner are much more persuasive. (See A. J. Gregor, 'Fascism and Modernization', *World Politics* 26 [1973–74]). Even before Mussolini, Italy was sixth in the world economic ranking. Comparisons with pre-1913 and post-1949 growth rates do not take into consideration the enormous dislocation of World War I; nor do they adequately credit Mussolini's significant performance in the context of the Great Depression. For Gregor, without Mussolini's modernization of agriculture and prior industrialization, the post-1945 Italian economic miracle would not have been possible.

Barrington Moore insists that fascism protected the interests of big agriculture in Italy at the expense of agricultural labourers and small peasants. The number of owner-operators dropped by 500,000 between 1921 and 1931, while that of 'cash-and-share' tenants rose by 400,000. In power, German Nazism junked its pseudo-radical agrarian populism, since a strong war economy could only be built on the basis of industry. B. Moore, *Social Origins of Dictatorship and Democracy* (Harmondsworth, 1966), pp. 450–52. This dispute over the modern or anti-modern character of fascism is confined to bourgeois analysts. Marxists all agree on the modernizing thrust of fascism, even if as a movement it feeds on the anti-modern sentiments of deeply dislocated social layers. At bottom, the existence of this dispute reflects a key problem area in bourgeois thinking on fascism: What weight to give to economic structures and goals in any assessment of fascist movements and regimes? This problem is exacerbated by the methodological presumption in favour of ideology and organizational style as the defining elements of fascism.

3 Most Marxists, perceiving fascism as a 'solution' to an extreme form of capitalist crisis, accept that the price capitalist ruling classes have to pay is their substantial 'political expropriation'. Certainly, the Nazi state's determination to carry the war beyond 1944, when it was clearly lost and Germany could have sued for reasonable peace terms (the motivation of the Officer's Plot against Hitler in that year), and the economic 'irrationality and costliness' of Hitler's unflinching pursuit of the 'Final Solution', strongly confirm this fact of the Nazi state's exceptional autonomy from the class interests it was ultimately supposed to serve. Differences between Nazism and Italian fascism – the greater importance of Hitler's party in the party-state of German fascism added to the autonomy of the German state – expressed themselves in the particularly aggressive expansionism of Nazi foreign policy.

Nicos Poulantzas is one Marxist not prepared to concede that much (relative) autonomy to the fascist state. N. Poulantzas, *Fascism and Dictatorship* (London, 1974). This derives from his understanding the state not in 'organizational-realist' terms as a distinctive set of apparatuses but as a 'social relation' – i.e. as the condensation of the balance of various class forces. Accordingly, the fascist state expresses a realignment in the 'power bloc' whereby big monopoly capital achieves hegemony. Such a 'condensation' of class forces would not be possible if the state as a 'social relation' were not relatively autonomous from specific classes and class fractions. For all its theoretical fruitfulness, the alternative approach – which, unlike Poulantzas, refuses to dissolve state power into class power – has proved more insightful in understanding state relationship to class power.

4 E. Weber, *Varieties of Fascism* (New York, 1964). Weber insists on drawing a

and states with their antecedent movements, plus the plethora of National Socialist and fascist movements, parties and groups in Europe during the inter-war period, constitute the primary empirical data for all attempts at theorizing fascism.

3. Fascism is a strong form of authoritarian nationalism. Fascism is always an authoritarian nationalism, but the reverse does not hold.

There are fascist movements and fascist states, fascism in opposition and fascism in power. The first major difference between non-Marxist and most Marxist approaches has been that the former, in seeking to draw up a 'fascist minimum' or 'essence', has focused much more sharply on movements, while the latter has focused on the characteristics of the fascist state: fascism in its presumably mature and certainly most dangerous and powerful form. Since ideology and ideological appeal are much more central to the existence and growth of fascism as a movement, it is hardly surprising that non-Marxist approaches are much more strongly pivoted on the elucidation of fascism's distinctive ideological themes and organizational principles. Ideology, organization, even philosophy become the principal criteria and obsession of such theorizations.[5]

The 'true' nature of a movement lies in its aspirations, not in its practices, which necessarily involve compromises. To be fascist is, above all, to have an ideology that, in its pristine form, qualifies as fascist. This still does not fully resolve the problem of establishing a 'fascist minimum' capable of achieving a strong consensus. What ideological elements or themes should be included and excluded? Fortunately, the problem has been made more manageable.

Payne has outlined a viable method for establishing a 'fascist minimum' in such a framework – the right way to go about things. His three-part model comprises (a) fascist negations, (b) generic ideological motifs and goals, (c) special and common features of style and organization. With regard to the first, all fascisms would have to incorporate explicitly in their ideologies anti-liberalism, anti-democracy and anti-communism, or anti-Marxism. The shorter the list of negations, the more extended the list of qualifying candidates for the status of fascism is likely to be. However, some theorists have insisted on including other negations, such as anti-conservatism and anti-pacifism.

What would be the indispensable ideological motifs and goals? These might be (a) treating the state as an 'absolute' or near-absolute; (b) the goal

---

qualitative distinction between Italian fascism and National Socialism, especially in its German form. But even for him there are enough common reference points to incorporate both under the rubric of 'varieties of fascism'. Where Mussolini's fascism is supremely pragmatic, Nazism is more theoretical and doctrinaire: 'Fascism is pragmatically activist. National Socialism theoretically motivated or, at least, expressed. Both aim to conquer power and that center of power which is the modern state' (p. 143).

5 See, for example, the metaphysical meanderings of E. Nolte, *Three Faces of Fascism* (London, 1963).

of empire, or an aggressively expansionist foreign policy; (c) the primacy of some collective principle or unit of belonging subsuming individual autonomy and universalist values, and generally requiring construction of some collective 'Other' as the enemy;[6] (d) extreme authoritarian nationalism; (e) an apocalyptic perception of deep 'civilizational crisis' requiring construction of the 'new man', which is more important than any new programme. It is the *mystique* of a fascist movement rather than its programme that makes it a radical inspirational project.

These are the following common features of style and organization:

1. Charismatic leadership would seem to be central to all fascisms. The leader embodies the inspirational ideal. Indeed, it is precisely the relationship of the leader to the masses that embodies the superior, because more 'direct' and plebiscitary, democracy of fascism.[7]
2. There is the exaltation of youth and the youthfulness (relative to leaders of the traditional right-wing parties) of fascist leaders. A real generational gap prevails.[8]
3. Violence is glorified, and political behaviour and relationships are militarized.
4. Political meetings are carefully choreographed to arouse mass emotions through evocative symbols.
5. Masculinity is stressed.

As this example of an elaborated 'fascist minimum' might suggest, such a non-Marxist approach has attractions for many a Marxist who has also made similar ideological–organizational comparisons to justify the designation of fascism in a given case. But even such a worked-out fascist minimum leaves enough scope for never-ending disagreements over how best to characterize a specific movement, party or group. The content of the postulated

---

6 This is too loose a formulation for those analysts (Marxists and non-Marxists) who insist on some race theory, such as anti-Semitism as indispensable to fascist ideology – i.e. a race–culture–nation symbiosis. However, the 'original' fascism of Italy did not really fall into this category. Mussolini's Blackshirts prided themselves on not having an anti-Semitic strain in their fascism. Only in 1938 did Italy, under German pressure, introduce a formal anti-Semitism into the fascist programme. Jews were proportionally over-represented in Italian fascism.

If there was an element of 'Catholic fascism' in Italy, there was no equivalent of 'Christian fascism' in Nazism. Indeed, many European fascisms were explicitly secular in their thrust, just as others (the Iron Guard Movement of Romania) had a semi-religious mystical aspect. The Falangists of Spain produced no race ideology, instead taking their ideology from the church. The attempt to form a Fascist International in 1934 foundered on disagreement over racism, and anti-Semitism in particular. (Payne, *Fascism*.)

7 For Weber, the unifying element is the leader. He 'is not so much the representative of his people as its medium' (*Varieties of Fascism*, p. 81).

8 In 1933 Hitler and Mussolini were forty-four, Oswald Mosley (Britain); thirty-seven; Jacques Doriot (France), thirty-five; Roman Corneliu Zelea Codreanu (Romania), thirty-one; José Antonio Primo de Rivera (Spain), thirty; and Léon Degrelle (Belgium), twenty-four.

minimum will be continuously disputed, with demands for revision, amendment and deletion, stipulating that the minimum be filled out differently.

Fascist movements have more in common with each other than fascist – or semi-fascist, neo-fascist or proto-fascist – regimes. There have also been many more fascist movements than regimes. This fact, it is widely believed, provides a more confident basis for generic speculation or theory-building. But if non-Marxists in one sense find it easier to make generic claims, they are also in another sense less pressured to do so. No indissociable link is postulated between the capitalist accumulation process and the fascist phenomenon. As it is, the bourgeois state as an autonomous entity 'above' classes (whatever its possible class biases) renders nugatory the search for some distinctive relationship between class power and fascist state power. Non-Marxists readily concede the importance of recognizing the class or social base of the fascist movement or state – the refracted influence on the fascist entity of the petty bourgeoisie or middle classes; but that is a different matter.[9]

Some will readily recognize the importance of incorporating a significant 'socio-economic dimension' into the study of fascism, but it is overwhelmingly Marxists who subscribe to an agency theory of fascism, insisting that it serves the interests, especially and decisively when in power, of dominant classes other than the petty bourgeoisie. In the best Marxist expositions, it is recognized that fascist agents are *self-appointed* and far from being the pliable servitors of the big bourgeoisie.

Non-Marxist approaches to the study of fascism, then, are highly flexible, and employ a variety of modes. They can perceive it as a generic phenomenon, or refuse altogether to see it as such. If the latter, they can insist that fascism is the result of unique national histories, of Italy and Germany for example, where contingency and the unforeseeable accidents of history play a decisive role. So Nazism peaked by 1932, and was then declining but for the rise of Hitler to chancellorship, which is explained contingently; hence the reversal of fortunes for Nazism and its accession to power. But even if fascism is accepted as something generic, expressing itself in 'varieties of fascism', there can still be a whole range of answers to the question: How generic? It has been seen as an inter-war European phenomenon, and only that.[10] It has been seen as a political phenomenon linked decisively either

---

9 There is even a theory held by Talcott Parsons of fascism as an autonomous middle-class movement, and this in its most developed form is Seymour Lipset's theory of the 'radicalism of the centre'. S. M. Lipset, *Political Man* (New York, 1960), Chapter 5. For the view that fascism is not a petty bourgeois movement, see M. Mann, 'Class Politics in the Twentieth Century', *New Left Review* I/212 (July–August 1995). This claim was subsequently further developed and justified in his later book-length study of fascism, M. Mann, *Fascists* (Cambridge, 2004).

10 This is the view articulated in Nolte, *Three Faces of Fascism*; Payne, *Fascism*; and R. de Felice, *Interpretations of Fascism* (Cambridge, MA, 1977). Strong dissenter from the view that fascism is an intra-European phenomenon only can be found in B. Zachariah, 'A Voluntary Gleichschaltung? Perspectives from India towards a non-Eurocentric

to political ideology or to problems of development and modernisation. If the former, then it is easy to conclude that fascism is itself a subset of a larger political phenomenon of totalitarianism. This is a widely held view among non-Marxist analysts of fascism.[11] If the second, then in principle fascism is of more general world significance, and could well surface in other times and places than inter-war Europe.

The non-Marxist attempt to construct a paradigm of fascism therefore offers a series of differently positioned windows from which to view the

---

Understanding of Fascism', *Transcultural Studies* 2014: 2. Zachariah prefers the term 'fascist repertoire' to 'fascist minimum', to which he argues 'India[ns] contributed independently rather than imitatively' (p. 67). When it comes to identifying the key elements of this 'generalizable' repertoire, what is offered is well-trodden ground: 'The repertoire tends to include an organic and primordial nationalism involving a controlling statism that disciplines the members of the organic nation to act as, for, and in the organic (or *völkisch*) nation that must be purified and preserved. It is in the service of preserving this organic nation that a paramilitarist tendency towards national discipline is invoked. The coherence of the repertoire is maintained by inciting a sense of continuous crisis and alarm about the potential decay of the organic nation if discipline and purity is not preserved' (ibid.).

11 The concept of totalitarianism had a decisive impact on historical and political research. It uncoupled fascism from the nature of capitalism and bracketed the study of fascism with the study of Stalinism. Bourgeois theories now searched for *fundamental* similarities between the fascist and Soviet states (Stalinist and post-Stalinist), abstracting from their different socio-economic structures. Since Mussolini was the first political leader to self-consciously describe the Italian fascist state as 'totalitarian', this subsumption by the concept of totalitarianism could claim a certain historical legitimacy.

The other decisive step in identifying the Stalinist political system as totalitarian was more dubious. Trotsky first pointed to totalitarian similarities, but only in a restricted sense. 'A totalitarian regime, whether of the Stalinist or fascist type, by its very essence, can only be a temporary transitional regime. Naked dictatorship in history has generally been the product and the symptom of an especially severe social crisis, and not at all of a stable regime. Severe crisis cannot be a permanent condition of society. A totalitarian state is capable of suppressing social contradictions during a certain period, but it is incapable of perpetuating itself.' L. Trotsky, *In Defence of Marxism* (New York, 1940), p. 13. For Trotsky, the totalitarian dictatorship had to give way rapidly to the Bonapartist dictatorship.

Hannah Arendt took over Trotsky's use of the concept and allied it with the psychological insights of the Frankfurt School to make it a characterization of a prolonged and stable dictatorship. To protect post-1945 Third World dictatorships befriended by the advanced democracies from a similar charge, other theoretical steps were taken by analysts from Carl Friedlich and Zbigniew Brzezinski to Karl Popper. First, the totalitarian state's existence was linked to the existence of an official totalitarian ideology like fascism/Nazism or Marxism, unlike that of merely 'authoritarian' states. Second, the totalitarian state was invested with the property of extreme political immobilism. Unlike authoritarianisms, there could be no transformation from within or above, while the potential for such endogenously inspired transformation did exist in authoritarian regimes.

The bankruptcy of the totalitarian paradigm was never more obvious than after 1989. But Western victory in the Cold War has led to rapid internalization of the concept of totalitarianism within the ranks of its former opponents in the former Soviet bloc. Only those who believe that the authority or longevity of concepts is primarily a function of intrinsic merits or the protocols of intellectual and logical consistency need be surprised by this. For a good critique of theories of totalitarianism, see M. Kitchen, *Fascism* (London, 1976).

phenomenon. This, it could be claimed, is one of the strengths of this kind of intellectual tradition, respecting the multiplicities of causations and correlations in history. But many of the best non-Marxist studies do consider it a generic phenomenon, certainly for inter-war Europe, even as they are more sceptical of the likelihood of its re-emergence in contemporary times and places. Two texts, namely Michael Mann's *Fascists* and Robert Paxton's *The Anatomy of Fascism*, both published after the turn of the new millennium in 2004, stand out as widely accepted, seminal works themselves based on an extraordinarily comprehensive survey of the previous literature on fascism.[12] One is by a renowned sociologist, the other by an eminent historian. Neither sees himself as a Marxist, and both accept the 'imperative of definition', though Mann does this explicitly at the beginning of his text and Paxton only at the end of his. Nevertheless, the methods they adopt to study the phenomenon of fascism, and therefore their respective encapsulations of the fascist phenomenon, are fundamentally different.

Mann and Paxton

Mann focuses on fascist movements, not on regimes. He finds himself in close agreement with those other thinkers and writers for whom ideology is central in defining fascism.[13] He also goes some way with those who emphasize the values held by fascists, such as the idea of 'palingenesis' or of the re-birth or regeneration of a nation, race or people by populist ultra-nationalism.[14] But since Mann sees this as characteristic of even milder nationalisms, for him values *plus* organizational forms are the key to understanding fascism: 'Fascism is the pursuit of transcendent and cleansing nation-statism through paramilitarism.'[15] So there must be an 'organic nationalism' postulating an internal or external enemy to be cleansed culturally and/or politically. There will be a 'radical statism' manned by a party elite loyal to a supreme leader expressing the popular will. This state is necessarily corporatist, absorbing classes and interest groups into state institutions. After all, was not the slogan of Mussolini 'Everything in the State, nothing against the

---

12 Mann, *Fascists*. R. O. Paxton, *The Anatomy of Fascism* (London, 2005). The first has a twenty-one-page bibliography, the second a twenty-nine-page bibliographical essay

13 R. Eatwell, *Fascism: A History* (London, 1995); R. Eatwell, 'On Defining the Fascist Minimum: The Centrality of Ideology', *Journal of Political Ideologies* 1: 3 (1996), pp. 303–19; R. Eatwell, 'Universal Fascism? Approaches and Definitions', in S. U. Larsen, ed., *Fascism outside Europe* (New York, 2001).

14 R. Griffin, *The Nature of Fascism* (London, 1991); R. Griffin, *Fascism* (Oxford, 1995); R. Griffin, '"The Primacy of Culture": The Current Growth (or Manufacture) of Consensus within Fascist Studies', *Journal of Contemporary History* 37 (2002). See also G. L. Mosse, *The Crisis of German Ideology: Intellectual Origins of the Third Reich* (New York, 1964); G. L. Mosse, 'The Genesis of Fascism', *Journal of Contemporary History* 1 (1966); G. L. Mosse, *The Fascist Revolution* (New York, 1999).

15 Mann, *Fascists*, p. 13.

State, nothing outside the State'?[16] A fascist movement necessarily provides a transcendent vision of a new world or society – this is its utopian dimension, its revolutionary call. Finally, there must be paramilitarist violence outside the state – which does little to stop it – that thereby builds a 'battle-hardened comradeship'.

True to Mann's classic IEMP (ideological/economic/military/political) neo-Weberian model, he says that fascism arose in Europe because of crises at all of these four levels, and promised solutions in each case. Clearly, a crisis condition of great severity is central to Mann's preconditions for the rise of fascism. Here he joins most Marxist scholars and thinkers, but he differs from them in not seeing fear of working-class power and the need to destroy it as central to the fascist project. The fact that the working class was strongly attacked in Italy and Germany was an 'over-reaction' by panicky old regimes and sections of the dominant elites, which explains their support to the fascists. Mann's definition of fascism as a movement, then, is part of the broader liberal tradition, though he provides his own content to the 'fascist minimum'. His distinctive and most important contribution, however, lies in his showing that the social base of fascist movements went well beyond the petty bourgeoisie and was much wider, including students, ex-soldiers, jobless intellectuals, lumpen proletarians, small shopkeepers, white-collar workers, public-sector and state employees, higher and lower level school teachers. True, the industrial labour force for the most part were largely though not completely immune to fascist appeal.[17]

Paxton is one of the few non-Marxist scholars who methodologically insists that fascism can only be grasped as a *process* – that to properly grasp it as a unified entity requires examining it in *all* its stages. He enumerates five such stages: (a) the creation of movements, (b) its rooting within the political system, (c) the seizure of power, (d) its exercise of power, (e) its longer-term fate. This approach is very close to that of the best of the classical Marxist approaches – that of Trotsky and his post-war intellectual–political inheritors, which are taken up below. The crucial point is that Paxton insists, contra Mann and many others, that the characteristics of fascism in power must be taken into consideration precisely because fascist-like movements may or may not debouch into a fascist dictatorship whose form and content is quite distinctive, historically appearing only in Italy and Germany, and

---

16 Ibid., p.7.
17 As will be seen later, there is a marked similarity in the key properties traced by Mann and by the German Marxist Arthur Rosenberg, who went into exile in 1933 and wrote his study, titled 'Fascism as a Mass Movement'. Certainly, several decades later Mann has provided strong confirmation of Rosenberg's insight that the social base of fascism, contra many a Marxist of the time, went well beyond the petty bourgeoisie and was more multi-class. Rosenberg's essay was first published in German (Karlsbad, 1934) and translates as 'Democracy and Socialism: Fascism as a Mass Movement'. Subsequently an abbreviated edition appeared in Wolfgang Abendroth, ed., *Faschismus und Kapitalismus: Theoren uber die sozialen Ursprunge und die Funktion des Faschismus*, (Frankfurt, 1967).

must not be confused with other far-right forms of authoritarian rule, or with military dictatorships.[18]

That is to say, fascist forces dramatically change their characteristics in the very process through which they become major players able to challenge for and achieve state power, then to fulfil and complete an evolving fascist project that is not written into their 'genes'. Paxton explicitly warns against any biological analogy: key characteristics are not located once and for all in the early movement phase, which then reveal themselves in their full splendour as the movement grows. This would be to assume that there is an 'original' blueprint at the time of 'birth plus early nurture' – that the hallmark of fascism resides in its ideology and in the way it mobilizes. There is here a clear recognition of how the very interaction between an evolving context and the putative fascist entity alters both context and entity: that it is the fascist situation that matures. For Paxton, 'A definition that does full justice to the phenomenon of fascism must apply to the later stages as effectively as it does to the earlier ones.'[19]

Precisely because he pays attention to fascism in power, Paxton talks of the 'dual state' – a 'normative' one bound by bureaucratic rules, procedures and promotion, versus a 'prerogative' state in which the executive is less bound by the compulsion of existing administrative routine. There were variations, therefore, in how the tensions between party and state, between party and bureaucracy, between older elites and the fascist elite, played themselves out in Italy and Germany – more state than party in Italy; in Germany more the party-state, with Hitler more unbound and dominant in relation to the older elites and inside the party itself. But unlike authoritarian military regimes, which want a passive, demobilized public, the fascist dictatorship wants active and enthusiastic consent from its citizenry, albeit 'controlled'. Fascism thus had to be not just imperialist, but a 'war-making imperialism' to deepen its internal strength and roots, as well as to make its geopolitical mark by gaining territory and resources. This drive to war was not just functional, but expressive of the superiority of a race or people. Mann, too, emphasizes the symbolic aspect of violence as a basic value of fascism, but much less its instrumental purpose.

Dylan Riley, in an excellent review of both Mann and Paxton, highlights their key differences.[20] Mann, like many others (including some Indian

---

18 Even Mann accepts that there is a certain spectrum of far-right forms of the capitalist state, from conservative authoritarianisms like Portugal and Spain, where smaller fascist groups and elements were subordinated, to one-party modernizing authoritarianisms of all kinds, such as in a Japan absent any serious mass movement from below that is in anyway similar to those in inter-war Europe, to military dictatorships of various kinds.

19 Paxton, *Anatomy of Fascism*, p. 206.

20 D. Riley, 'Enigmas of Fascism', *New Left Review* II/30 (November–December 2004). Riley's own distinctive and original contribution to fascism studies came with his *The Civic Foundations of Fascism in Europe: Italy, Spain and Romania* (Baltimore, MD, 2010), where he highlighted how the existence of civic associational life enabled fascist mass mobilizations, and therefore no straight line could be drawn from the existence

Marxists), believes that the very fact that historical fascism saw many more movements than regimes means a generic theory must emerge out of the study of what is common to the movements. This actually leads to a much more static notion of the 'fascist minimum'. On the other hand, Paxton's comparative approach leads him to insist (to Riley's approval) that the very fact that only two fascist regimes emerged means that any dynamic, rounded, balanced and appropriate understanding of fascism cannot be derived from a study of the wider range of movements only. Moreover, where Mann believes fascism is revolutionary in its transcendent appeal and strong utopian thrust, Paxton, with Marxists, believes fascism is counter-revolutionary. Where Mann believes fascism has a coherent ideology, Paxton sees it as an eclectic mishmash, though ultra-nationalism and 'rebirth', but not racialization of an enemy, are fundamental themes. Where Mann dismisses the idea that fascism is a key response to the power of the Left, Paxton makes the threat of left power basic to fascism's appeal to elites and much of the public, as well as stipulating that it shapes its behaviour both as a movement and when in power. Interestingly, both Mann and Paxton, while not completely ruling out a contemporary resurgence of fascism, believe it is highly unlikely (beyond parties and movements that are pale imitations) because of the solidity of liberal democracy in Western Europe, North America and Japan, consigning 'fascist-like' but not necessarily 'fascist' developments to the developing world.[21]

Is There a Meeting Ground?

Is there any meeting ground between Marxists and non-Marxists on this issue of defining fascism? Given that there are fierce intra-Marxist disputes on this score, there are occasional crossovers, as we will see in the left debate on Indian fascism. But, with rare exceptions, non-Marxists do not assign quite the same weight to socio-economic factors in their overall explanatory framework.

The fulcrum of classical Marxist approaches has rested on the economic function of fascism, on the fragile nature of the relationship of class forces that make the 'fascist option' available, and its success possible or probable. Common ideological referents gleaned from the movement phase of fascism before it emerges as a new form of the bourgeois state can certainly feature in the delineation of a Marxist fascist minimum. But they are not clinching arguments for characterizing the 'fascist danger'. Analysis of the economic preconditions for fascism has to be given greater importance. In

---

of a rich and varied life of civic association to the assurance and stabilization of liberal democracy.

21 'Hindu nationalism does spawn off some fascist tendencies but is not really fascism' (Mann, *Fascists*, p. 373); 'But neither Islamism nor Hindu Nationalism is really fascist. This is for a simple reason. They really *are* political religions' (ibid., p. 374).

addition, and just as important, is the precise evaluation of the social balance – the relationship of class forces, in a context of prolonged economic crisis of extraordinary depth, between capital and labour, and the relationship of forces between class fractions and constituents of the ruling class bloc, coalition or alliance.

That this should be the central focus in investigating the possibilities of fascist victory when potential candidates for such status are in opposition – i.e. in the movement phase – must seem at first glance a major aberration. Surely it is ideological appeal that most explains the continuing growth of a mass movement and of a fascist political formation? Surely it is this growth that then alters and destabilizes the relationship of class forces, and not an existing instability or crisis in class relations that explains the rise of a fascist movement? Is that not putting the cart before the horse? Certainly, the growing power of a fascist movement is itself a powerful input into the forcible and sometimes drastic rearrangement in the distribution of class power, even at the apex. But it is the existence of a prior crisis in class relationships, both within capital and between capital and labour (which must necessarily play itself out on the social and political terrain), that gives a decisive fillip to fascism. Whatever the mediations, refractions and lags, the crisis must reveal itself in class tensions and antagonisms and in the turmoils of political parties, both internally and in their relationships with each other.

It is this prior crisis that creates the 'space' for the rapid growth of fascist formations, even though their origins and initial growth can be, and usually are, independent of these developments. The latter operate backstage, as it were, of the more visible terrain of political contestation. The rapid acceleration and growth of fascist political formations is never a straightforward function of fascism's ideological message, but feeds powerfully on pre-existing social dislocations of an abnormally serious kind.

Fascism is so extreme a form of the bourgeois state – one where its 'freedom of action' in relation to the dominant classes is so great – that only the most extreme crisis conditions drive the dominant class, or sections of it, to endorse this 'solution'. To put matters as clearly as possible, to understand the fascist phenomenon requires us to grasp it in motion, to see it as a *unity of three moments*. This unity must encompass the study of fascism 'out of power' – ascertaining the key characteristics of party and movement; of fascism 'in power' – ascertaining the characteristics of form and behavior of the fascist state; and of the transition from 'out' to 'in', of the key contextual factors that made the transition possible.[22]

A longstanding criticism by non-Marxists (and sometimes by 'unorthodox

---

22 Though Paxton shows no interest in the writings on fascism of Trotsky, Bauer or Thalheimer, or in those of the post–World War II generation of anti-Stalinist Marxists, his method of analysis of the fascist phenomenon remains closest to theirs, and does receive deserved appreciation from left quarters. See, for example, J. Wolfreys, 'What Is Fascism?' *International Socialism*, Autumn 2006; Riley, 'Enigmas of Fascism'.

Marxists') is that such a perspective can never give adequate weight to ideology or politics, or to the principal fascist actor itself. No doubt the linguistic turn in the social sciences, with its emphasis on the 'autonomy of political discourse', has shaped more recent studies of fascism that focus on ideas and ideology. Considering that much of the best post-war work by Marxists has been in the area of ideology and politics, this charge is not strong. But there is a point beyond which fewer Marxists than non-Marxists will go in elevating the importance of the ideological–political. Most charitably, one can simply acknowledge that both Marxist and non-Marxist approaches have their distinct virtues and shortcomings. A non-Marxist can argue that political movements, especially those like fascism, are no doubt influenced by but autonomous of class forces. It may be difficult, but is nonetheless possible, for them to arrive at power regardless of what ruling classes decide. In a democratic order, this is even easier than otherwise, given the mass character and thus the legitimacy of such a movement.

The weakness of this proposition is that if a fascist movement can arrive at government power 'against the wishes' of dominant classes or class fractions, it can hardly rule except within constraints set by the necessity of reproducing capitalist social relations on an expanded scale. There is a point beyond which it cannot go 'against the wishes' of the dominant classes and expect to stabilize the fascist state – in other words, its own existence. Fascist movement aspirations do not automatically become fascist regime policies, or even options. Fascism is as fascism does, and for the fascist party in power this is not endogenously or unilaterally determined.

In the end, choice of paradigm is determined by one's balance-sheet judgement regarding the comparative merits of the two basic approaches.

Marxist theorizations of fascism have a definite cast. They are 'agency' theories (however sophisticated) with a functionalist bent. Class conflict and balances must remain crucial points of reference. Fascist formations are perceived as conscious or inadvertent agents for some section of ruling capitalists – more inadvertently in the movement phase, more consciously when in power. In striving for, achieving and retaining power, fascist formations carry out a crucial economic (and social–political–ideological) function for the favoured classes or class fractions, and for the capitalist system as a whole. The problem with functionalist arguments is well known. They are rarely decisive except where the mechanism that bears the burden of 'functional explanation' is specified. They usually, at best, count as persuasive secondary evidence for the validity of a stipulated proposition.

It is hardly surprising, then, that non- and anti-Marxists remain sceptical of the Marxist approach. These sentiments are reciprocated by their Marxist counterparts, and with good reason. Bourgeois theories have never provided so compelling a picture of the socio-economic dynamics of fascism. The dialogue between Marxists and non-Marxists over fascism, more than half a century after its appearance, remains a dialogue of the deaf, whatever the limited exchange of insights. The roots of this deadlock are clear enough. Marxists are inescapably committed to the idea of social existence as a 'complexly structured totality' that includes the notion of intention and directionality, in the weak sense. The economy influences other 'levels' in ways not equivalently reciprocated, at least in capitalism, even though the 'level of the economic' can never be purely economic. It 'determines', where determination is akin to the conception of Raymond Williams as 'exerting pressures and setting limits'. No more, perhaps, but certainly not less. This does not necessarily lead to an economic reductionism, but it does mean a special weight, however qualified or mediated, is placed on economic and class factors.

This is alien to the methodological habits and traditions of non-Marxists. Moreover, for Marxists, states in capitalist societies, at least, are axiomatically class states; so, too, is the fascist state. If non-Marxists disagree with the Marxist theorization of the fascist state, it is because they disagree fundamentally with the Marxist theorization of any bourgeois state or state in capitalist society. Unless Marxists develop the conceptual tools that establish the capitalist and class character of the state independently of functionalist argument, and are able to validate this analysis empirically in concrete cases, they cannot decisively win the argumentative battle with unbelieving liberal or conservative theorists of the modern state – though neither will they lose it.

Marxists may believe that the balance of plausibility rests strongly with them. But the grey area of theoretical and empirical uncertainty that exists provides a not dishonourable escape route for those who are against the caricature of Marxism but genuinely unconvinced of the legitimacy and efficacy of the Marxist approach. Marxists may be justified in believing their approach to be superior; but they do have an enduring difficulty sustaining this claim to superiority beyond all reasonable doubt in the court of intellectual appeal. It is likely, given the nature of the social sciences (the impossibility of controlled experimentation), that conclusive 'proof' of the validity of the notion of the class state may not be possible. But better Marxist theory should be able to persuade non-Marxists not because it will offer conclusive proof, but because it offers qualitatively better explanation and the possibility of better prediction. To opt for the Marxist paradigm in the analysis of fascism is already to have opted intellectually for a Marxist approach in the social sciences. It is within the Marxist paradigm – or, more correctly, the historical attempts to construct such a paradigm – that the rest of the discussion will be situated.

The Marxist Paradigm: The Tensions Within

Their insistence on the indissoluble link between capitalism and fascism means Marxists are naturally predisposed to discover a theory of fascism, to be inveterate genericists, to treat it as a phenomenon fully capable of occurring and recurring beyond the temporal and spatial confines of inter-war Europe. It may not actually so recur, but it is capable of doing so. But the global historical record since 1945 has created a certain inadequately explored tension.

The first fascisms appeared, assumed power, or achieved threatening proportions in inter-war Europe. For Marxists, there was a clear association between advanced capitalisms and imperialisms and the danger of fascism. It was not a coincidence that such movements were strongest in the countries ruled by the defeated empires of World War I. But after 1945, despite the occasional emergence of 'fascistic' or 'fascist-like' organizations in the OECD countries, it is precisely this zone that has seemed most inoculated against anti-democratic authoritarianisms, let alone fascism. This is especially so after the transition to bourgeois democracy of Portugal and Spain in the late 1970s. Fascist-like formations have been pressure groups helping to shift the political centre of gravity rightwards (especially in regard to certain policies, such as race and immigration) in certain advanced democracies during certain periods, but little else.

The zone in which capitalist authoritarian nationalisms have flourished has been the Third World or (as it is now more frequently referred to) the 'developing world' or the 'global South'. Hence the question: Can there be fascisms in this part of the world? If so, what are their preconditions and principal characteristics? In the light of such experiences, what modifications are required when elaborating a fascist minimum (otherwise based heavily on the properties of classical fascism) to make the notion of fascism more relevant to the second half of the twentieth century? Is such a step legitimate? Are we dealing with 'functional substitutes for fascism', rather than fascism proper? How significant, anyway, is the difference between the two?

An important Marxist tradition remains hostile to such spatial extension. Fascism is a feature not just of capitalism in crisis, but of capitalism in crisis in its imperialist stage, and prevails among imperialist countries only. Brutal authoritarianism in an advanced, imperialist country has a global and historical significance of a *qualitatively* different order than in a non-imperialist, dependent capitalist country. Fascism is a form of 'international reaction' in a context of close correspondence of interests between national capitals (led by their bigger battalions) and the nation-state. Fascist rivalry flows from and exacerbates inter-imperialist rivalry. Trotsky, Mandel, Gramsci, Togliatti and Poulantzas all saw militarism and an expansionist foreign policy as intrinsic to fascism.[23] The fascist temptation was strongest where the link in the imperialist chain was weakest: among the weaker, latecomer imperialisms.[24]

---

23 L. Trotsky, *The Struggle Against Fascism in Germany* (London, 1975), introduced by E. Mandel; P. Togliatti, *Lessons of Fascism* (Rome, 1970); N. Poulantzas, *Fascism and Dictatorship*. See also D. Beetham, *Marxists in the Face of Fascism* (Manchester, 1983).

24 The weakness is the result of the overall effect of accumulating economic, political

Such expansionist politico-military behaviour was promoted not just by economic imperatives, but also by ideology.

There is an enormous difficulty in establishing a fascist minimum that encompasses the central dynamics of classical inter-war European fascism and also those of post-1945 global South candidates for fascist status. This partly explains why, within the Marxist tradition, theories of a 'universalist' fascist threat or possibility are undeveloped and scarce. The continent where authoritarian nationalist capitalist regimes have emerged time and again, enjoying a fairly long run, has been Latin America. Yet the generic concept that seems most appropriate to explaining the Latin American experience, whether authoritarian or quasi-democratic, has been 'populism' not 'fascism'. The term 'populism' has no single accepted meaning, and is the site of much dispute. But in all versions its differences with classical fascism are marked.[25]

---

and ideological contradictions, and not just of relative economic backwardness in relation to other imperialist powers.

25 Populism has been understood as political movement, as ideology, or both. G. Germani, *Authoritarianism, Fascism and National Populism* (New Jersey, 1976), says the Latin American middle class supported various populisms because there was no threatening working class beneath it. Latin American authoritarianisms were quite different: 'The main difference between the Latin American variety and the classic type of fascism consists in the fact that the active role in promoting and eventually establishing an authoritarian regime was usually assumed by the military not by the middle classes, which, however, under certain conditions gave their support to it' (p. 73).

A. Hennessy, 'Fascism and Populism in Latin America', in W. Lacquer, ed., *Fascism: A Reader's Guide* (London, 1976) says that six distinctive features of European fascism are absent in Latin America: (1) There has been no total war in twentieth-century Latin America as a pre-fascist 'dislocator' of society. The absence of war means that soldiers lack a military function, are more involved in civilian affairs, and are less tolerant of armed rivals. Populism links up through patronage with the 'marginal men', hence fascism holds less appeal for the latter. (2) Catholic culture is ubiquitous, and the church happy with its links to 'traditional' conservatives. (3) There is a weak Left in Latin America. Moreover, there is urbanization without much industrialization. Clientelism controls the urban discontented. (4) Reactions to cultural crisis after World War I (anti-liberal, anti-Europe, anti-US) moved to nativism (Indianismo) and Hispanismo. (5) The preconditions for fascist economic autarky were not there. Latin American countries were primarily exporters, having a limited domestic market. (6) Only in the seventies was there student and youth support for the Right.

M. Löwy, ed., *Populism in Latin America*, Notebooks for Study and Research, No. 6 (Amsterdam, 1987) also gives a useful typology of theories of populism in Latin America. According to him, Gino Germani conceives of populism as the 'political manifestation of traditional and authoritarian masses out of step with modernisation' (p. 3). Torcuato di Tella, says Löwy, sees it as the product of a 'revolution of expectations'. A whole *dependencia* school (Francisco Weffort, Octavio Ianni, F. H. Cardoso, R. M. Marini) sees populism as the expression of a distinct economic cycle – the period of import-substituting industrialization.

E. Laclau, *On Populist Reason* (London, 2005) says: 'Populism is, quite simply, a way of constructing the political' (p. xi). It is a 'mode of articulation' of varying ideological, social and political content. So fascism is one variant of right-wing populism using certain 'populist interpellations' to challenge the existing power bloc. For Löwy, a provisional Marxist definition would be populism as a multi-class 'political movement expressed in diverse organisational forms (party, trade unions, various associations, etc.) – under

The crucial point of contrast, however, is that the middle class of post-1945 global South countries is located in a qualitatively different class matrix than that of inter-war Europe, and has a different character. The Latin American experience has given rise to a different kind of political movement and regime. Hence the generic label 'populism'.

For a Marxist wishing to justify the possibility of Third World fascisms, one possible theoretical route to take would be to see it as a political outcome that emerges in certain cases and for certain reasons, but is a potential embedded in the general dynamics of the capitalist modernization process. Fascism is not, then, the 'specific conjuncture of the class struggle' (Poulantzas). It need not share most of the characteristics of classical European fascism that went into the making of the classical Marxist theories, of which the most outstanding were those of Trotsky, Gramsci, Thalheimer and Bauer. The fascist phenomenon becomes not so much a *recurring temptation* of a capitalist system in periodic crisis as a *point of transition* in the historical development of capitalism. Such an approach rescues and enhances the possibility of developing world fascisms in our times, but greatly minimizes (if not negating) the possibility of fascism's recurrence in the advanced metropolitan countries.

Such an approach sacrifices the complexities of a multi-causal explanation of fascism for a more single-minded focus on the socio-economic necessities of capitalist industrialization and the imperatives imposed on the modernizing state. But in the hands of its most skilled practitioner to date, Barrington Moore, it has been fruitful. Moore replaced the wide fish-eye lens of analysis with a deep-focus lens, greatly extending the time-span for studying the possible emergence of fascism in a particular case. His study of its preconditions stretches backwards well beyond the vision of even the most reputed Marxist students of classical fascism. Moore might not qualify as a 'Marxist' historian–sociologist. But he is taken as the most eminent representative of a left approach with very strong affinities to Marxism, because he shared a similar commitment to rooting the story of political evolution and state transformations in class struggles and imbalances.

For Moore, fascism was a latent possibility in almost all the major societies (except the United States), and also in societies undergoing modernization

---

a bourgeois/petty bourgeois leadership and the charismatic leadership of a caudillo' (*Populism in Latin America*, p. 3). Its ideology is anti-imperialist and anti-communist. Such movements are ideologically heterogeneous, with right-wing nationalists, sometimes crypto-fascist wings, a hegemonic nationalist reformist centre, and a crypto-socialist leftwing. Populist regimes are Bonapartist (posing as above classes), resting sometimes on employers and army, sometimes on trade unions and popular mobilization. They pursue nationalist industrial development (ibid.).

Whether understood as a movement or an ideology, populism remains an imprecise concept. Löwy's definition makes Latin American (and Third World) populism very different from the original turn-of-the-century rural populism of Russian Narodnism and North America, and also rules out the possibility of First World populism, with its clearly defined relationships between capital and labour.

today.[26] Though he employed the comparative method, he still generalized on the basis of too few case studies (England, France, the United States, China, Japan and India), even if these are major ones. Moore excused himself from providing similar case studies for Germany and Russia (as well as for Italy), citing the excellent material already available, and stressed that he did refer to them to illustrate his comparative case studies. Latin America and Africa are completely excluded, which certainly damages any effort to theorize the broad principles, landmarks and contours of the development process and its associated political and state forms. Even so, he provides rich and thought-provoking fare.

Moore designates pre-war Japan an Asian fascism, instituted between 1938 and 1940. What were the distinguishing points of fascism – the points in common between Germany and Japan? National mobilization was decreed, radicals were arrested, political parties were dissolved and replaced by the Imperial Rule Assistance Association – a rather unsuccessful copy of a Western totalitarian party. Shortly thereafter, Japan joined the anti-Comintern Triple Alliance and dissolved all trade unions, replacing them with an association for the 'service to the nation through industry'. Thus, by the end of 1940, Japan displayed the principal external traits of European fascism.[27] Fundamental anatomical commonalities are also elucidated.

Both Germany and Japan entered the industrial world at a late stage. In both countries, regimes emerged whose main policies were repression at home and expansion abroad. In both cases, the main social basis for this programme was a coalition between the commercial and industrial elites (who started from a weak position) and the traditional ruling classes in the countryside, directed against the peasants and the industrial workers. Finally, in both cases, a form of rightist radicalism emerged out of the plight of the petty bourgeoisie and peasants under advancing capitalism. This right-wing radicalism provided some of the slogans for repressive regimes in both countries, but was sacrificed in practice to the requirements of profit and 'efficiency'.[28]

---

26 Moore, *Social Origins of Dictatorship and Democracy*, Chapter 8, 'Revolution from Above and Fascism', pp. 433–52.

27 Ibid., p. 301.

28 Ibid., p. 305. Moore also cites differences between Japanese and European fascism. In Germany the army housed the traditional elite, who were unsympathetic to Nazism but did Hitler's bidding. In backward Japan, the agrarian sector was more important and the army was more sensitive to pressures from the countryside and from urban small business. There was no 'sudden seizure of power', no rupture with constitutional democracy, because Japan had no democratic phase comparable to the Weimar Republic or pre-Mussolini Italy. Japanese fascism found existing political institutions more congenial, and evolved more naturally within them. Japan had no plebeian supremo, though the Emperor served as an abstract national rallying point. Nor did it have a mass party. Japanese fascism was not the culmination of the growth of a mass fascist movement, but a 'respectable fascism' from above – respectable because, in the takeover by high government officials, popular elements, namely the anti-capitalist popular Right, were excluded. Finally, there was no policy of mass terror and extermination against any specific segment

For Moore, the key to understanding all twentieth-century fascisms is the scope provided for 'plebeian anti-capitalism'. The three routes of successful modernization have been: (a) capitalist development via a bourgeois revolution 'from below', which is most conducive to establishing strong democracies; (b) peasant revolutions (Russia and China) leading to communist modernization; and (c) reactionary capitalism leading to authoritarian states, culminating in certain cases in fascism (Italy, Germany, Japan) and carrying out a revolution 'from above'. India is a fourth route, fitting into neither of these courses, and negatively confirms Moore's thesis. It has a weak bourgeois democracy with a weak economy, representing stagnant modernization.[29]

The solution to the riddle of development and modernization (with its associated political forms, from democracy to the spectrum of authoritarianisms ending in fascism) is found in the countryside. Lord and peasant, not bourgeois and worker, are the key actors in the story. Always and everywhere, the peasant and the countryside pay the highest price (dislocation, transformation and contribution) for industrialization and the rise of the modernizing state.

The economic compulsions behind the rise of fascism lie not in the imperatives of surplus-extraction from the worker in the city, but elsewhere. There must exist a labour-repressive agrarian system, and the crucial preconditions for democracy (spelled out elsewhere by Moore) must be absent.[30] These are the necessary though not sufficient conditions for the emergence of fascism. Such labour-repressive systems can be of two types: either capitalist extraction of necessary surplus from the countryside keeps traditional peasant society intact but squeezes more out by using servile or semi-servile labour in larger units of cultivation, or there is plantation slavery or its functional equivalent. In Eastern Europe the reintroduction of serfdom was a 'halfway form'. Where there are American-style family farms or a mobile agricultural labour force, or where a pre-industrial or pre-commercial agrarian system exists but there is a 'rough balance between the overlord's contribution to justice and security and the cultivator's

---

of the indigenous population. Loyalty and obedience were secured by deploying a combination of coercion and traditional symbols of authority.

29 Moore's book takes us up only to the mid 1960s. It is debatable whether the subsequent durability of Indian democracy and its steady if unspectacular growth up to and beyond the turn of the new millennium would have led him to a serious revision of his assessments.

30 Moore's famous five conditions for stable democratic development are as follows: (1) There should be a balance between crown and landed nobility: neither too strong a crown nor too independent a nobility. (2) There is a turn towards an appropriate form of commercial agriculture by the peasantry or landed aristocracy. (3) The landed aristocracy is weakened – its political hegemony must be broken or transformed, so that the peasant becomes the commercial-minded farmer, and the landed upper classes part of the rising capitalist class, or be swept aside. (4) There is no aristocratic-bourgeois coalition against peasants and workers. (5) There is a revolutionary break with the past. India has some of these features, notably (3) and (4), and hence only a weak and conflict-ridden democracy.

contribution in the form of crops', there is no labour-repressive system. India does not fit into the category of any of Moore's labour-repressive agrarian systems. Moore's chapter on India is particularly weak on its post-independence agrarian structure and evolution.[31] The rural petty bourgeoisie (rich farmers and aspiring capitalist family farmers) may be susceptible to Hindu communalist demagogy, but they can hardly constitute the base for 'plebeian anti-capitalism' or be strongly responsive to pseudo-radical pre-capitalist appeals glorifying the idealized peasant of the past.

The most remarkable thing about India is the persistence of the peasantry, the huge prevalence relative to other rural classes of family farmers, and the limited and slow polarization of classes in the countryside. There is no Indian equivalent of the small German peasant in hock to city-based middle-men and brokers. The only serious candidate for fascist status in India – the Sangh combine – has felt no need to orient its ideology specifically to the small peasantry. The peasant is not a key motif in that ideology.

Moore's second necessary condition for the emergence of fascism is a reactionary coalition between an industrial and commercial class (too weak to take power itself) with a landed aristocracy and the bureaucracy of an authoritarian – for example, monarchical – state. Competition from more technically advanced capitalist rivals throws the landed upper class into crisis, and pushes it to use 'political levers' to preserve its rule. This leads to an authoritarianism (with some democratic features), but not yet to fascism. It is the *failure* of these authoritarian regimes to solve the burning problems of the day – specifically, rapid capital accumulation – that is decisive. They are unable or unwilling to carry out fundamental structural changes, most importantly the dramatic overhaul and modernization of agriculture in ways ultimately incompatible with the preservation in the old form of the 'reactionary' coalition or the earlier 'labour-repressive agrarian system'. Where a regime seeks to modernize but is not able to transform the social structure, then, provided the other preconditions for fascism exist, the fascist state is the 'solution' to this problem. It is the developmentalist 'revolution from above'.

While his book remains an outstanding work of comparative historical sociology, time has not been kind to Moore's overall perspective. The sources of capitalist development, of political democratization and of a variety of forms of authoritarianism have been too various and too complexly interrelated to be covered by Moore's broad yet patchy brush-strokes. The uneven spread of democracies, the numerically limited but nonetheless dramatic successes of capitalism in the Third World, and the collapse of communism in the Second World all suggest that many more 'basic' forces are at work than are allowed for by Moore's framework of analysis.

---

31 Daniel Thorner's works were among the earliest accurate characterizations of India's agrarian structure. For a collection of his writings at various moments, see D. Thorner, *The Shaping of Modern India* (Bombay, 1980).

Not only is the specificity of the phenomenon of fascism lost in his model; it also represents a step backwards from those Marxist analyses of fascism which, although also pivoted on class power and extraction of economic surplus, were urban-oriented as well as insistent that other non-economic factors and social relationships had to be part of any derived fascist minimum. For Moore, fascism is a 'revolution from above' rather than a 'counter-revolution from below'. Thus he can see it as a reactionary but forward movement in resolving the historical problems of modernization. Not surprisingly, Moore, unlike Marxists, is unconcerned with the programmatic perspectives (strengths and weaknesses) of forces opposing fascism, or whether they could have triumphed and fascism been avoided. In that sense, his is an academic rather than political engagement with fascism. Had he included case studies of Italy and Germany, this omission would have been near-impossible. Choosing not to include these two paradigmatic cases of fascism says much about the teleological and objectivist bias in his methodology.

Given that he understands fascism as a revolution from above, there is little reason for him to consider its 'movement' or popular character as crucial to its emergence. The 'revolution from above' may be facilitated and significantly marked by a 'fascism from below', but this is not crucial to it. In his scheme of things, there can be 'fascisms from above', as in Japan.

For all his sensitivity to socio-economic factors, Moore's approach has a serious problem which tends to align him with non-Marxists like Nolte, whose method otherwise could not be more distant from his own. Moore rejects the idea of fascism as a counter-revolution, which Marxists aver. They may not all agree on distinctions between conservatives, reactionaries, the radical Right and fascists. But to call fascism a counter-revolution is, above all, to insist that it is a rescue operation. It is the most radical form of social and political surgery, whose primary goal is to protect the most crucial existing ligaments of class power. That which is already the most powerful segment of the capitalist class (or alliance) must remain so at all costs. It might be legitimate to stretch the classical notion of fascism (always a fascism from below) to incorporate the possibility of a 'fascism from above'. Chile after the coup against Allende could be a candidate. But this would still have to be a 'counter-revolution from above', and not a 'revolution from above'.

The notion of Third World or global South fascisms may be valid, but it still awaits theorization that is a qualitative step forward from Moore's model. Moreover, the latter is at a tangent to the existing tradition of serious Marxist analysis of fascism, from where it indubitably emerged. Moore does not build on these perceptions, but bypasses them. It is doubtful whether that is the most promising way forward for those insisting on the contemporary validity of the concept of fascism in both the developing and developed world.

The Classical Marxist Views

In historical retrospect, the analyses of Trotsky, Gramsci, Thalheimer and Bauer stand up best. They grasped more accurately than others the properties of the phenomenon they were dealing with, gauged the threat more seriously, and put forward the best programmatic perspectives of their times. It is hardly surprising that what is common to their respective analyses is more important than their differences. One of the most serious efforts at theorizing fascism in the post-war period was undertaken by Nicos Poulantzas. Perhaps his unusual sensitivity to the problem of authoritarianism and the fragility of the democratic state in Western Europe, while others were much more preoccupied with the question of the durability of bourgeois democracy and its dampening effects on working-class revolutionary fervour, had much to do with his Greek origins.

Trotsky's approach to fascism was the single most impressive effort by any major Marxist thinker. The late Ernest Mandel, the most important systematizer of Trotsky's thought after Isaac Deutscher, has presented Trotsky's 'theory of fascism' as a unity of six elements, each having a certain autonomy, but together forming a 'closed and dynamic totality':[32]

1. The rise of fascism expresses a severe social crisis of capitalism not necessarily coinciding with a conjunctural crisis. This is capitalism's inability to accumulate in the 'old' way at a given level of real wages, productivity, access to raw materials, markets, and so on. The economic function of a fascist seizure of power is to dramatically raise the production and realization of surplus value for decisive sectors of monopoly capital.
2. Bourgeois democracy is a highly unstable form of rule resting on a 'highly unstable equilibrium of economic and social forces'. When this is disturbed, as it must eventually be, then there has to be greater centralization of executive power. Fascism entails an extreme degree of centralization wherein the bourgeoisie is 'politically expropriated' to serve the economic interests of the big bourgeoisie.
3. However, neither a standard form of centralization of power, such as a military dictatorship, nor a 'pure police state' or absolute monarchy, has the capacity to atomize or demoralize for long a conscious, numerically strong working class, and thus prevent elementary class struggles. Only a fascist movement can do this by mass terror and systematized physical assaults on the working class *before* the seizure of power. The fascist dictatorship only *completes* the job of atomization, demoralization, control and surveillance of the working class in civil society.
4. Such a mass movement only arises on the basis of a petty bourgeoisie large sections of which are falling into despair.[33] The ideology of such a

---

32 See E. Mandel, 'Introduction', in Trotsky, *Struggle Against Fascism in Germany*.
33 A corrective to this typical view of the social base of fascism held by the majority

movement must (a) be extremely nationalistic, (b) be vocally anti-capitalist, and (c) have an intense hatred for the organized working class. Such a movement grows by cutting its teeth on (physically attacking) working-class organizations.

5. The fight to shift the relationship of forces decisively between the fascist and workers' movements must take place *before* the fascist seizure of power. In this civil war, the working class, fighting for its life, also has chances of victory. It is this 'openness' of the civil war situation and its 'risks' – the 'all-or-nothing' character of the situation – that makes the big bourgeoisie accept 'political expropriation'. Civil war is a real possibility because the acuteness of the socio-economic crisis affords the working-class movement real opportunities for victory as well.

6. The fascist seizure of power both *completes* the fascist project and *initiates* a transmutation of the state into a Bonapartist dictatorship requiring an abandonment of the demagoguery of the 'movement' phase, and the assimilation of its cadres into a bureaucratized state apparatus. The petty bourgeois base systematically shrinks as the 'monopoly class character' of the fascist party becomes more evident. The all-or-nothing character of the fascist dictatorship leads it to seek to do on the world market what it has done domestically: revise the conditions for surplus production, extraction and realization by the monopoly bourgeoisie. This necessarily leads to foreign military adventure.

Trotsky's theory of fascism applies only to considerably industrialized countries in late capitalism. It assumes the country in question is not a semi-colonial, backward or semi-capitalist country. The decisive class actor behind fascism is not foreign capital or its representative or subordinate fractions, but the domestic 'big bourgeoisie', or sections thereof.

Social democracy saw aggressive counter-mobilization against fascism as 'too provocative' and counterproductive. It also gave too much explanatory weight to the conjunctural economic crisis, and too little to the structural crisis of capitalism. 'Third-period' Stalinism did not recognize the independent character of the fascist mass movement, and was too inclined towards a conspiratorial view of fascism as the result of the machinations of the most aggressive sections of the big bourgeoisie. Its false theory of 'gradual fascisization' of the state under Weimar rule, or 'creeping fascism', disregarded the ruptural character of the fascist victory, and was first cousin to the now discredited 'social fascist' view of social democracy.

The post-1935 Comintern perspective underlying the Popular Front strategy saw fascism as the 'open dictatorship of monopoly capital'. Fascism was viewed as a new stage in the process of the expansion of executive

---

of Marxists at the time, including by Trotsky, is given in Mann's work. The middle class, more broadly conceived, is the key base, even as support for the mass movement extends somewhat both upwards and downwards from it. See Mann, *Fascists*.

power, when in fact it was a *special form* of the strong executive or 'open dictatorship', characterized not just by 'traditional' repression but by the destruction of all workers' organizations. The Dimitrov thesis still saw fascism as a 'defensive' measure, a 'counter-offensive', thus underestimating its staying power and failing to realize that its victory presumes the decisive defeat of the working class. Fascism was not a 'counter-offensive' but an 'offensive' of the big bourgeoisie. The Seventh Congress Communist International thesis viewed the relationship between big capital and the fascist party deterministically, and so was ill-prepared for the flexibility and freedom of the latter, particularly in foreign policy.

Antonio Gramsci shared most of Trotsky's propositions and conclusions. Gramsci (and PalmiroTogliatti) saw fascism as a mass movement of the petty bourgeoisie violently attacking working-class organizations. Its strength was the consequence, not the cause, of working-class and Left defeats. Big property used but did not control the fascist movement. Once in power, fascism attacks its own petty bourgeois base. But, unlike Trotsky, Gramsci, like August Thalheimer, sought the explanation for military expansionism abroad less in economic compulsions than in the need for a diversionary and unifying policy to cope with the internal contradictions of the fascist state, partly arising out of the tension between the aspirations of the petty bourgeois base and the interests of the big bourgeoisie.

While Gramsci never had as 'rounded' a theory of fascism as Trotsky's, he offered a more developed understanding of the ideological dimension of fascism via his notion of hegemony. Both Gramsci and the Frankfurt School-inspired studies on the mass psychology or social pathology of fascism help fill a lacuna in Trotsky's analysis, which underestimated the strength of fascism's nationalist appeal.[34]

Otto Bauer, and especially Thalheimer, were close to Trotsky's theory. Like Trotsky, both saw the victory of fascism as coming *after* the ebbing of the revolutionary flood.[35] Their major difference with Trotsky and with each

---

34 For a helpful analysis of the strengths and weaknesses of bourgeois psychological theories of fascism and those of the Frankfurt School, see Kitchen, *Fascism*. The latter had the merit of pursuing explanations of mass and not individual psychology. They also sought to uncover the socio-economic dynamics of mass psychology and the external roots of the 'authoritarian personality'. Those inclined to individual psychology (the 'fascism within us' school) were more preoccupied with the psychological make-up of fascist leaders.

For the sophisticated way in which Gramsci tries to grapple with Italian fascism's ideological–cultural specificity, and to understand its mobilizational capacities in relation to the distinctive socio-cultural history and character of Italy, see A. Ahmad, 'Fascism and National Culture: Reading Gramsci in the Days of Hindutva', *Social Scientist* 21: 3–4 (March–April 1993). In a parallel move to Gramsci's, Ahmad examines elements of Indian culture, past and present, that help account for the 'nostalgias' and 'cravings' that can be manipulated to build what he considers an Indian fascism.

35 'But in reality fascism did not triumph at the moment when the bourgeoisie was threatened by the proletarian revolution: it triumphed when the proletariat had long been weakened and forced onto the defensive, when the revolutionary flood had abated. The

other was over Bonapartism. Thalheimer had a view of Bonapartism closer to Marx's own, seeing it as the extreme power of the executive in special circumstances. Fascism and Bonapartism were different, but had many similarities. So Bonapartism should be the starting point for developing a theory of fascism. He was also less certain about rejecting the 'creeping fascism' thesis, and thus more prone to devaluing the capacity of the working class to resist it.[36]

Trotsky refined the notion of Bonapartism, arguing that there were two types – a highly unstable and a more stable one. The unstable, preventive Bonapartisms were the Brüning and Papen governments preceding Hitler, which held the balance between Left and Right, trying to contain fascism's threat to the bourgeoisie (its political expropriation) while seeking to utilize it against the working class. The more stable Bonapartism was the Hitler regime. But this, too, was relatively unstable in the longer run, because it had to turn against its petty bourgeois base. Gramsci and Togliatti agreed, though they did not see it as a Bonapartism but as the unavoidable transformation of a *fascist* state in power.

These classical Marxist theories also have their enduring weaknesses. The social base of fascism went beyond the narrowly defined petty bourgeoisie. Another weakness was one they could not be blamed for, being denied the luxury of historical retrospect which alone could have enabled important refinements to their theories. Nazism was a distinctive form of fascism in which the importance of the 'Führer principle' was exceptional. Mussolini

---

capitalists and large landowners did not entrust the fascist hordes with the power of the state so as to protect themselves against a threatening proletarian revolution, but so as to depress wages, to destroy the social gains of the working class, to eradicate the trade unions and positions of power gained by the working class.' O. Bauer, 'Der Faschismus' in W. Abendroth, ed., *Faschismus und Kapitalismus*, pp. 153–4.

Poulantzas makes the same point. The decisive defeats of the working class must come before the seizure of power. The bourgeoisie first attacks the 'real relationship of forces' on which working-class gains rest, and only after this (via fascism) does it attack the gains themselves. Where Poulantzas can be faulted is in insisting that even the beginning of the rise of the fascist movement must presume a series of working-class defeats. Initially, a fascist phenomenon (in Italy, for example) can grow and bring in a stratum of working-class unemployed, uprooted, and so on, not because the organized working class is attacked or 'defeated' in certain confrontations, but because it is too fragmented, demoralized or misled to realize the necessity of challenging it. See C. Sparks, 'Fascism and the Working Class', *International Socialism*, Autumn 1978.

36 Kitchen (*Fascism*) has criticized Trotsky on Bonapartism, preferring Thaiheimer. The key difference is that Trotsky, in the course of theorizing fascism, also began to develop the idea of Bonapartism in an independent direction. The value of this initiative is demonstrated by the subsequent frequent use of Bonapartism by Marxists in the developing world to examine a series of state forms that combine extreme executive power with the state having considerable autonomy from dominant classes, yet, unlike Marx's version, not resting unproblematically on an internally incoherent petty bourgeoisie and peasantry. Marx's belief that such a peasantry would have to plump for bourgeois or working-class political leadership or else seek Bonapartist identification is belied by the numerous examples of it finding its own forms of political expression, and often following its own distinct course, regardless of the pressures of the bourgeoisie and working class.

came to power within three years of the formation of the Italian Fascios. Hitler came to power after a much longer period of incubation, growth and consolidation of German fascism as a mass movement. Marxists like Trotsky underestimated the importance of 'charismatic' authority and of the 'Führer principle' that was carried over from the Nazi party to the Nazi state. The stronger the fascist party – the stronger the movement it led – the easier it was for its 'personal authority' to make this transition. Gramsci's brief comments on 'Caesarism' offered more hints about the possibility of such an outcome in Germany. But these were hardly more than hints – a variation on the theme of Bonapartism that was the common currency of these classical Marxist theorists of fascism.[37]

These Marxist theories of classical European fascism operated within certain distinctive parameters, which either no longer operate or can only do so in critically amended ways. These parameters have rarely been spelled out. But a general sense of unease with the validity of the classical theories of fascism certainly marked the work of Nicos Poulantzas. He preserved the idea of fascism as a recurring tendency in advanced capitalist societies (and only there), but at the price of a 'dilution' of its force and threat. His key formulations are that fascism emerges from a 'specific conjuncture of the class struggle' and is a specific form of the regime in an 'exceptional state'. Exceptional here means not 'rare in occurrence' but 'emphatic in degree'. The exceptional capitalist state is exceptionally bureaucratized. It is that state in which physical repression and its apparatuses become more important than legitimizing apparatuses. Repressive apparatuses also have their own legitimacy. Fascism differs from other forms of the exceptional state, such as

---

37 See I. Kershaw, 'The Nazi State: An Exceptional State?' *New Left Review* I/176 (July–August 1989). According to Kershaw, the traditional elites continue to be outflanked by the fascist party after it comes to power not only because of the mass popularity of the fascist party, but because of their own relative weakness. Their power, expressed through their support for fascism in crushing the working class, is a destructive one. They have little capacity to construct a stable new state, hence their need for the fascist party in power if other right-wing parties are much weaker. Kershaw's argument does help to answer something that is otherwise a puzzle: the peculiar stability–instability as well as continuing and remarkable autonomy of the fascist executive, years after the fascist seizure of power.

Both Trotsky and Gramsci stressed that fascism in power attacks its own petty bourgeois mass base and merges itself into the state apparatuses, hence its growing instability as it prepares for its own transcendence. This is what underlay Trotsky's view of fascism transmuting into another kind of Bonapartism of a more stable kind than the pre-fascist 'preventive' Bonapartisms (a view criticized in, for example, Kitchen, *Fascism*). Trotsky's clumsy formula of a stable or relatively more stable Bonapartism reflected a remarkable intuition. The fascist state might undermine its own base, the fascist party might merge into the state apparatus, and the traditional elites and the fascist party evolve a new partnership reflecting a stronger convergence of interests. Nevertheless, the state under fascist leadership would still be a Bonapartism (more autonomous, and with a much stronger, centralized executive power than the normal bourgeois state), and yet more 'stable' in its authority than Marx's use of the term 'Bonapartism' would convey. Kitchen (*Fascism*) fails to recognize the superiority of Trotsky's intuition compared to the more conventional usage of Bonapartism by Thalheimer and Bauer.

Bonapartism or military dictatorship, not by its relative autonomy (which, believed Poulantzas, is less than in Bonapartism) or by the urgency of its economic function, 'but by the forms it used, the radical changes in the ideological state apparatuses, and their relationship to the repressive apparatuses of the state'.[38]

Poulantzas gives valuable emphasis to the idea of fascism as a response to an ideological crisis of legitimacy, but at the price of devaluing its economic function. His notion of fascism emerging as a serious option because of the crisis of the conjuncture without requiring a more prolonged structural crisis (the Great Depression, for example) means it can emerge after 1945 and in the post-boom West. His concept of the exceptional state, spanning the range from milder to harsher varieties of authoritarianism, makes it a more feasible possibility than otherwise in the advanced countries.

However, says Poulantzas, the kind of 'pure' political crisis of the conjuncture that is required for fascism to come to power is so rare that fascism proper is highly unlikely in the contemporary capitalisms of the advanced countries. Fascism is a 'live' tendency and a recurring factor. But, realistically, what emerges are different kinds of exceptional state having different combinations of the characteristics of fascism and non-fascist authoritarianisms.

The Basic Parameters

What were the basic parameters of classical fascism that, in part or whole, may no longer obtain? Eight such parameters can be listed.

1. The enormous dislocation of a continental-scale modern war whose physical, ecological, social, economic and political devastation had until then no close historical approximation. The core cadres of all the most active European fascist movements and parties included the declassed, war veterans, lumpens and unemployed. World War I and the inter-war interregnum were widely perceived as the epitome of a deep 'civilizational crisis'.

The cultural nationalisms that emerged in inter-war Europe, and the loss of self-confidence among large sections of the petty bourgeoisie and of the intelligentsia, were rooted in this palpable sense of civilizational decline – the end of the *belle époque*, the run-up to World War I, its frenzied aftermath (the decade of the twenties) and the onset of the Great Depression. In contrast, the cultural nationalisms of the colonized world were the reactions of indigenous elite and middle-class intellectuals to the colonial experience itself. Though the cultural nationalisms of inter-war Europe manipulated themes that had emerged decades earlier, even before the turn of the century, the cultural nationalisms of the colonized countries (because of their link to

---

38 Poulantzas, *Fascism and Dictatorship*, p. 52.

a progressive project – the stirrings of anti-colonialism) were to have an organic growth, a wider spread and a more lasting appeal.

2. The sense of 'civilizational decline' expressed itself in popular and elite disillusionment with liberalism and the liberal order. It was only through and after World War II that liberalism was to stage a remarkable and unexpected comeback.[39] Inter-war Europe was *uniquely* fertile ground for the message of anti-liberalism and anti-democracy so central to fascist ideology.

3. This receptivity to anti-liberalism and anti-democracy was connected to a disbelief in the durability of bourgeois democratic structures. The stated or unstated assumption of all classical Marxist theories of fascism was that bourgeois democracy might be the most desirable and effective of all forms of bourgeois rule, but it was an exceptional state of affairs, inherently unstable. Nothing left Marxists as unprepared for the course of the post-war era in the metropolitan heartlands as this facile and utterly mistaken assumption.[40] While there is a relationship between economy and polity – the stronger the economy, the more feasible a bourgeois democratic form of the state – this is not axiomatic. In the weak, dependent economies of the developing world, the overall historical trend so far has been opposite to what Marxists should have anticipated if they believed in the instability and exceptionalism of bourgeois democratic rule, all the more so for backward economies. Authoritarian rule in the developing countries has been increasingly punctuated by quasi- or controlled- or guided-democratic experiments. Inconceivable to pre–World War II Marxists, even military dictatorships have held largely unrigged elections and stepped down when their legitimacy or that of their political puppets has been repudiated.

In the last two decades, over 800 million people in the former Second and Third Worlds have moved towards quasi- or near-democracy.[41] Political liberalism has never enjoyed greater or more universal appeal, and the democratic idea (albeit in bourgeois form) has become a material force of such strength that *explicit* anti-liberalism and anti-democracy have less chance than ever of popular, or even middle-class endorsement.

In functioning democracies, right-wing movements seeking popular support more often than not cloak their anti-democratic character, apologize for or disavow occasional 'excesses', and rationalize their demands and behaviour as expressions not just of the popular will but of the *democratic* majority. Only to the detriment of their populist ambitions would such movements campaign on an openly anti-democratic platform. Where fascism promised to usher in authoritarianism in full sight through the

---

39 See P. Anderson, *A Zone of Engagement* (London, 1992).

40 Pre-war Bernsteinian social democracy did articulate a more optimistic assessment of the durability of bourgeois democracy. But this anti-capitalist social democracy rapidly debouched into the anti-Marxist, pro-capitalist social democracy of the post-war period, its legacy briefly revived only with the emergence of Eurocommunism.

41 Anderson, *Zone of Engagement*, p. 350. But as this democracy has spread, it has also 'thinned'.

front door, today's radical or 'fascistic' Right will bring it in surreptitiously, through the back door.

This is an important point. The character and mood of a right-wing movement's social base (even among the petty bourgeoisie or middle classes) is very different when its leading party campaigns openly on a comprehensively anti-liberal and anti-democratic programme and when it does not. This is so even if the party trains its cadres in a spirit explicitly hostile to the ideology of liberalism and bourgeois democracy. The potential for mischief and evil of such right-wing formations is qualitatively greater when it wins popular support for what it actually is, and not for what it pretends to be. It is not an adequate counter-argument to point to the experiences of participation and involvement in democratic processes by fascist parties in the fascist era, or to the examples of their dissimulation of an anti-democratic thrust and message. Propaganda about the essential bankruptcy of the liberal-democratic model, the believers in this notion and the *believability* of this notion were all of a qualitatively different order in the 'fascist era' than in the post-1945 era. Mussolini openly espoused totalitarianism, giving it a positive content. Hitler and others presented fascist *dictatorship* as a superior, transcending form of 'truer', more meaningful mass democracy and mass self-expression.

Insofar as a fascism in power would insist upon a 'monopoly of political representation', ruling out any multi-party democratic system of operation no matter how 'guided' or 'controlled', this does raise the question of how to assess far-right parties in Europe and elsewhere which today swear by the preservation of a democratic set-up. Kevin Passmore, in a lively little book, like the overwhelming majority of non-Marxists, also defines fascism in terms of its ideology, organization and programme, and expresses his scepticism in this regard about contemporary forces of the far right in Europe, for example in Italy and France.[42] Contemporary far-right groups accept electoral democracy and globalization through the expansion of free markets – the antithesis of corporatism. He goes further: 'Where fascism sees the destruction of democracy as a precondition for the triumph of ultra-nationalism, the contemporary extreme right attempts to ethnically homogenize democracy and reserve its advantages for the dominant nationality.'[43] Passmore calls this a 'racist national-populism' more akin to South African apartheid, whose aim was the permanent inferiorization of an ethnic minority.

So much water has now flown under the bridge, so strong remain the negative historical memories of fascisms and 'totalitarianisms' in power, and so strong are the myriad contemporary re-creations of such memories

---

42 K. Passmore, *Fascism: A Very Short Introduction* (Oxford, 2002). For Passmore, fascism means primary loyalty to the nation; that all policies, including economic policies, are suffused with an ultra-nationalism; implacable hostility to socialism and feminism; and the presence of a charismatic leader and a mass militarized party.

43 Ibid., p. 90. One might consider whether this is a not inapt depiction of the Hindutva project.

that no putative fascist force in our times can pursue the ideological course adopted by the fascisms of the past. They cannot, to their mass base, openly proclaim their allegiance to an anti-democratic *fascism* or an anti-democratic *totalitarianism* – in other words, to a fundamentally anti-liberal, anti-democratic project. Nor can they pursue a second course, legitimizing use of such labels in public discourse by redefining them to convey a 'softer', 'more positive' or 'more *truly* democratic' content. Such is the historical discredit attached to them.

This differs sharply with the fate of such terms as socialism and Marxism. Here the historical record has pushed many subscribing to the transformative project labelled socialism to redefine the notion to make it 'softer' and 'more democratic', even to reduce it to a subset of democracy. But the label itself has not been abandoned. Indeed, can any kind of meaningful socialism ever be brought about without clinging to the term itself? Those influenced by discourse theory and the presumed importance of 'interpellation' should ask themselves what kind of fascism or totalitarianism can be brought about when the very use of such 'names' or terms has become impermissible. Why this impermissibility? What are its consequences for the construction of the transformative project that fascism promises?

The usual way out of this 'difficulty' for 'unorthodox Marxists' or 'post-Marxists' committed to the notion of Third World and Indian fascisms but influenced by discourse theory and the presumed 'irreducibility of the ideological–cultural' is simply to ignore its existence, although it emerges from the very terms of their own theoretical framework. For all the emphasis of this school on the 'collective construction of identities' by culturally authoritarian mass movements and cultural discourse, the development of what is to all intents and purposes postulated to be a *fascist* mass movement owes nothing at all to the construction of a self-consciously *fascist* mass identity, which is clearly absent. Such movements are *objectively* fascist and totalitarian. This might be acceptable to Marxists, or to others who take seriously the notion of objectivity, but is certainly at odds with the biases and analytical practices of this school itself.

In left circles in India less influenced by discourse theory, preserving the validity of the fascist paradigm can involve a shift towards acceptance of the 'fascism from above' perspective. Such fascisms may be facilitated in certain cases by a mass movement from below, which need not be openly anti-working class in its behaviour or self-perception, but is *objectively* so.

4. The underestimation of the strength and durability of bourgeois democracy after 1945 by Marxists was, of course, the natural correlate of an obverse error – the overestimation of the 'structural crisis' of capitalism. The remarkable productivity of late capitalism and its ability to learn from its mistakes (preventing a repeat of anything approximating the Great Depression) has thrown all earlier anticipations out the window. Whatever its contradictions and problems, 'actually existing capitalism' has proved itself more

capable of coping with them than 'actually existing socialism' (its principal systemic rival) showed itself to be in coping with its own.

The kind of socio-economic dislocations that were the preconditions for the growth of fascism in inter-war Europe have not been approximated any-where in the heartlands of advanced capitalism. Marxists of the inter-war period believed not just that there would be relative poverty and inequalities in the advanced countries, but that there would be absolute impoverishment on a mass scale. Though cyclical upswings were likely, and severe defeats for the working class via fascism could usher in a more sustained upturn, the longer-term prospects for the global capitalist system were bleak, even though there would not be any inevitable breakdown.

Decades after the end of the 'long boom' (itself never anticipated), the prospects of fascisms coming to power remain dim. Though new and stronger authoritarian pressures are visible in certain countries of Europe, the overall climate is still nowhere near as disturbing as in the 'fascist era'. It is more to the former Second and Third Worlds that fascism-watchers have shifted their gaze. Despite the incomparable strengths of the Marxist critique of capitalism as an economic system, it has still to properly grasp existing capitalism's sources of productivity and dynamism.

5. It was this acuteness of the capitalist structural crisis between the wars that explained the attractions of the fascist option for sections of domestic big capital, particularly its finance wing. What is more, this crisis operated in a global framework in which imperialist competition for expanded eco-nomic control over raw materials and markets was rife. Success in expanding economic control was crucial for coping effectively with the structural crisis in its national manifestations. And this effort by competing national capitals was inseparable from expanding political (and therefore, in the final analysis, military) control by competing national states

For the Marxist theorists of classical fascism, the typical form of inter-im-perialist competition and conflict was territorial expansion through wars, particularly by imperialist latecomers. Fascism or military dictatorship, with its much greater centralization of political and military power, was one of the more effective ways of preparing and conducting this inter-imperialist rivalry. The economic stake of World War II was global pre-eminence, and it was the United States which, coming out of that war, achieved and retained that status for several decades.

The usefulness of this vision of global economic imperatives did not outlive the inter-war period. Such have been the changes in global capital-ism that territorial expansion through wars is not only atypical of modern inter-imperialist rivalry, but almost inconceivable. The presence of a power-ful Soviet-bloc rival which contained such inter-imperialist tensions was not the key factor. Even after the collapse of communism, full-scale wars between imperialist powers and conquest of territory are processes clearly belonging to a bygone era.

Even Marxists sense as much, but have yet to properly theorize why, as part of the larger task of adequately theorizing imperialism in its new phase. For Marxist theorists of fascism in this new phase of imperialism, what are the strong compulsions, if any, for the fascist option to emerge and triumph in the metropolitan countries?

6. The classical theory of fascism was linked to the classical theory of imperialism (Hobson, Hilferding, Lenin). The core principle of imperialism remains unchanged: the expansionist compulsions of capital. But the forms, mechanisms and correlates of this expansionism have varied. It is here that the assumptions of the classical theory of imperialism have proved inadequate. For Lenin, 'It is beyond doubt …that capitalism's transition to the stage of monopoly capitalism, to finance capitalism, is connected with the intensification of the struggle for the partition of the world.'[44]

What is this connection? Economic partition, in particular of the supply and demand of raw materials, would require political partition.[45] The classical theory's over-emphasis on the importance of territorial expansion flowed from its under-emphasis and lack of recognition of finance capital's dynamism, In the classical theory, technical innovation as a source of profit was downgraded and subordinated to cartel agreements and manipulation of financial markets as far more important sources of profit.

The most important feature of an expanding capitalism after World War II, however, has been the growing, indeed primary, importance of technical innovation. Control of knowhow, not so much of raw materials or markets, has become central to the capitalist accumulation process on a global scale. Political stability and the preservation of capitalist social relations have become far more important for imperialism outside its territorial heartlands than direct political or military control. Control over technology and knowhow has superseded in importance the expansion of control through direct ownership, thus allowing more complex forms of cooperation and competition between monopoly capitals, transnational corporations and smaller capitals, domestic and foreign. The attitudes of imperialist capital and states towards authoritarianism in the former Soviet bloc and the global South are diverse. When rolling back revolutions and the influence of the USSR was the primary obsession, imperialist support for Third World authoritarianisms was often very strong. The key purpose was not specific economic compulsions of making profits in these countries, but the more general purpose of preserving capitalist social relations and preventing political challenges to this order – in other words, making the world safe from communism.

---

44 V.I. Lenin, *Imperialism: The Highest Form of Capitalism* (Moscow, 1916 [n.d.]), p. 131.

45 Lenin stated this connection between economic and political partition, but never actually *proved* its necessity. It assumed strong congruence of interests between finance capital and the state, and the existence of finance capital in national blocs.

But political stability was often better served through the institutional-ization of quasi-democratic or near-democratic regimes, especially when it became clearer that the threat of steady communist expansion was greatly exaggerated. The natural preference of imperialism in the developing world is neither authoritarianism nor democracy, but political stability, where this is a function not simply of strong rule by preferred dynastic leaders but also of the strength of popular democratic aspirations among the ruled.

Since Marxists hold that, in most of the global South, domestic capi-tals are dependent capitals, the interests of the entities they are dependent upon, namely foreign capitals (more precisely segments of foreign ruling classes), become crucially important. Any Marxist attempt to theorize fas-cisms among the countries of the global South has to factor in this external dimension. Why should foreign capitals having controlling positions in the dominant-class coalitions or ruling-class alliances of specific developing world countries want to encourage, not just the authoritarian option, but the specifically fascist one? If fascism is the 'resolution' of the acute eco-nomic–political–ideological dilemmas of the hegemonic component of the biggest and most powerful segment of capital in the ruling-class bloc, coa-lition or alliance, then it must be the resolution of the dilemmas of foreign capital or its representatives that plays this crucial hegemonizing role. In a *dependent* capitalist country, foreign capital plays the crucial hegemonizing role in the ruling power bloc or class alliance.[46]

Fascisms in the developing world, it would appear, are ultimately rooted not in the needs of indigenous bourgeoisies, but in those of the advanced capitalist world. But most of the developing world (barring certain 'emerg-ing economies' to be counted on the fingers of two hands) – while remaining an important source of profits for metropolitan-based capitals – has become secondary. It is the 'intensive' processes of accumulation within the OECD countries, plus the emerging economies (of which China is the most import-ant, though India, Brazil, Turkey, Indonesia, Russia and a few others also figure), that has become central to the accumulation processes of global capitalism.

---

46 If India is not perceived as a dependent capitalist country, then the economic impetus to fascism, it could be argued, is derived solely internally. But where, then, is the *severity* of the economic crisis driving the Indian bourgeoisie or key sections of it towards fascism? Most left-wing critics of the New Economic Policy correctly point out that there was no deep structural crisis necessitating this turn. It was an attempted 'long-term solution' to a short-term crisis, and an effort of substantial sections of the Indian big bourgeoisie to broker more favourable terms of economic collaboration with trans-national corporations. Will political Hindutva be the attempt to resolve in a 'fascist' way a coming economic crisis of great magnitude and reject strongly such collaboration as weakening Indian big capital? Considering that the forces of the Hindu Right are increas-ingly supportive of such collaboration and of the greater entry of foreign capital, as per the dictates of neoliberal globalization, this is not a serious viewpoint. However one looks at India – as a dependent capitalist country or as a rare, independent capitalist country in the developing world – there is no convincing economic rationale for emerging fascism, though there may be for emerging or deepening authoritarianism.

7. All mass communist parties of the non-Maoist and non-Castroist type had their origins before World War I, or between the two world wars. Not a single new mass communist party of the orthodox type emerged after World War II. Only two such parties – the South African Communist Party (SACP) and the Communist Party of India (Marxist) or CPI (M) – remained stable or continued to grow. But even that momentum has been lost in recent years, with the CPI (M) finally voted out of power after a thirty-four-year period of rule in the province of West Bengal. This decline is true of the Maoist or Castroist currents wherever they emerged as mass parties. Nepal may be the only Maoist exception, but the fortunes of its Maoists have also taken a serious downturn in recent times. It is a dismal picture contrasting sharply with the first half of the twentieth century, when, whatever their temporary vicissitudes, socialist-, communist- and Marxist-inspired working-class movements were a powerful and growing force, and communism an ideology with a vibrant and strong appeal. The 'actuality of the revolution', to use Lukács's phrase, by which was certainly also meant its imminence, was no mere rhetorical slogan. There was justification for an equable revolutionary optimism. The fascist option made sense in the context of this powerful systemic threat to the rule of capital, especially where the working-class threat and the possibility of its rapid mass radicalization were so real and strong.

In the post-war era, the overall historical trajectory has been towards the domestication and de-radicalization of the working-class movement worldwide, with but few exceptions. Even in Brazil, the Workers' Party, having ascended to government and ruled for a prolonged period, is no longer the force it used to be when in opposition. Social democracy and orthodox communism are both in historic decline, with their political centre of gravity more to the right than at any time in their respective histories. The loss of élan in socialist ideology and the loss of self-confidence in all the organized currents of socialism and communism are unmistakable, especially after the collapse of communism in 1989 and China's subsequent economic trajectory. The revival of the socialist agenda and restoration of the 'actuality of the revolution' are clearly matters of the 'long haul'.

In what used to be called the First World, the working-class movement is nowhere a systemic threat, and has yet to replicate its earlier, more radical credentials of the inter-war or immediate post-war period. This may not be a permanent situation, but the prolonged absence of such a radical pressure on the system must affect one's evaluation of the prospects and possibilities of fascism, now and in the foreseeable future. In the former Second World, the general direction of a 'transition to capitalism' is unwavering, only its pace and manner perhaps being in dispute. A stabilization of the 'transition to democracy' is much more problematic, and many parts of it continue to show unacceptable authoritarian features. A further authoritarian involution of the state in some cases can hardly be ruled out, nor barbaric forms of state behaviour that might warrant the label fascism (as a term of abuse). The re-formation of nation-states and the redrawing of territorial boundaries may be on the agenda – witness Georgia and Ukraine. But it is the similarities with the pre–World War I, pre-fascist period, rather than with the inter-war 'fascist era', that are more striking. There are no signs anywhere of the kind of working-class threat that might evoke an extreme fascist response. In no eastern European country is there a working class that looks likely to be radicalized quickly. It is reformist parties that may even eschew the label of socialist or communist that hegemonize the working class. These parties express whatever level of class unity and independence has been forged in the post-communist phase. Even such minimal class-political independence of a reformist type may not emerge in certain countries, where the US model of two main bourgeois parties, liberal and conservative, rather than conservative and social democratic, might be institutionalized.

In the developing world, with few exceptions, the working class is divided in its political loyalties between an array of forces. Explicitly working-class or Left parties have to contend with populist parties that often have as strong a working-class base, if not stronger. In few developing countries is there an independent and fairly united working-class movement that represents a major political threat to bourgeois rule. In some of the more industrialized of these countries, including India and South Korea, they are little more than a significant pressure group. Only in Latin America in the 1970s did working-class power pose a grave threat to bourgeois domination. Chile under Allende was the foremost example. Pinochet's counter-revolutionary coup and subsequent dictatorship did not have many of the properties of a 'fascist option' or seizure of power. There was no mass fascist movement resting primarily on the middle classes defeating the working class decisively before ascending to power. There was no fascist party with a distinctly fascist ideology, which grew rapidly before making its bid for power. But one crucial function of fascism was certainly displayed. The working class was brutally crushed with all its organs smashed because the hegemony of the ruling classes was gravely threatened by the logic of Allende's reforms and the rapidly mobilizing social base of his government. This crushing took place not via a movement, but by the military, not before but after a coup. The precise designation of this experience and of the Pinochet dictatorship – whether it exemplified semi-fascism or fascism, or simply brutal military authoritarianism – clearly takes second place to the function carried out by the new post-Allende regime.

But the 'fascistic' traits in the political process culminating in Pinochet's coup were in direct proportion to the strength of the revolutionary threat posed by the Chilean working class. If the Chilean counter-revolution carries one lesson, it is that the character and behaviour of authoritarian states not provoked by the rising power of a unified and independent working class will be different in very significant respects from those that are so provoked. Repressing and subordinating the working class within a one-party state may be one property of fascism. A number of Third World regimes, including Iraq under Saddam Hussein, might therefore have been said to have fulfilled this condition, but these are not fascist dictatorships. Many developmentalist dictatorships have had much the same relationship with the working class. Here, it has usually been the *prior* weakness of the working-class movement, its relative isolation and limited spread in a largely backward economy, that has facilitated the institutionalization of such a relationship when the party-state dictatorship or military dictatorship was formed. This is clearly quite different from the counter-revolutionary character, the 'last-ditch rescue operation', of fascism. Nor does it approximate to fascism's 'unity of three moments.

8. The eighth feature of fascism in inter-war Europe was the 'squeezing of the middle classes' of town and countryside. Two pressures kept the vice in place. First was the class-polarizing effect of capitalist industrialization. In the towns this would mean the steady proletarianization of the lower rungs of this middle class as the relative size and objective strength of the working class grew. In the countryside, the small peasant would lose out, and the peasantry would not persist. The other factor behind the squeezing process was the growing conflict between capital and labour, pushing the vacillating petty bourgeoisie to choose sides. Nonetheless, this shrinking middle class was the only mass base for the bourgeoisie. One of Trotsky's key insights was that the self-consciousness and self-confidence of this stratum would determine the particular *form* of bourgeois rule. There is thus a crucial relationship between the insecurities of this layer and the brutal nature and policy direction of dictatorial rule.

The second half of the twentieth century has shown that here, too, the assumptions of the classical Marxist theories of fascism have been shaken. In much of the global South, the most striking feature has been not the more or less rapid disappearance of the small-landholding farmer but the remarkable 'persistence of the peasantry'. In the towns the middle classes have usually had little pressure from below from a working class that has been undeveloped and fragmented. This middle class has been a major base for populist movements, and important layers have often been the driving force behind progressive reform movements. Far from being squeezed, this middle class has been more easily incorporated into ruling oligarchies via the state bureaucracy. As late industrializers, most developing countries had a higher proportion of the middle class within their overall class matrix than was the case for the early industrializers of the West at a comparable point in their modernizing process.

Insofar as populism is a more useful generic label to attach to a variety of political movements and regimes in the developing world, it is surely because of the greater role played by these middle classes in the political evolution of their societies. The natural pattern of political development in the advanced societies has been the emergence and consolidation of sharply etched class parties, obviously so in programme and composition, because the working class and the peasantry largely achieved class independence. Multi-class nationalist political formations have been the norm in much of the developing world precisely because workers and peasants have not achieved the same degree of class-political independence.

In the advanced countries, the post-war developments have created an intellectual controversy about what has been called the 'embarrassment of the middle classes'. Is the sociological record such as to refute classical Marxism's polarization thesis – the dominant two-class model? There is no clear answer. According to one Marxist definition of class as necessarily structured by a relationship of exploitation, it is still possible to argue that the polarization thesis holds.[47] But no Marxist will dispute that, if the working class has grown absolutely and proportionately, it is also more segmented internally than ever before by criteria of skill, education, gender, race, wages, conditions, and so on. If indeed the middle class has objectively been squeezed by the processes of late capitalist accumulation in the advanced capitalist world, this also seems to mean much less than it did earlier. The growing segmentation of the working class beneath it, whose upper layers overlap with the lower reaches of the middle class, has immensely complicated the question of sustaining, let alone deepening, the unity and class independence of that proletariat. The subjective pressure of the working class on the middle class has been significantly defused, no matter what its 'objective' constriction.

The social, economic and political evolution of capitalism has made the usefulness of the fascist paradigm more, not less problematic. In the post-war era, only the most blatantly 'neo-Nazi' and 'neo-fascist' groups have been referred to as fascist by a wide consensus within Marxist circles. These formations self-consciously trace their lineage to the inter-war fascisms. But the thrust of their public propaganda and campaigning is not the 'fascist solution' to the 'civilizational crisis' of their times, or the construction of the 'new man', but a super-patriotism focused on racist and anti-immigrant xenophobia. Since their fascist potential is not to be gauged solely or even primarily by their internal ideology and organization, and since much of their base is working-class youth, they have also been characterized more cautiously and sensibly as pre-fascist or potentially fascist formations whose ideology contains dangerous fascist themes.

The memory and awareness of what the historic experience of fascism has meant and the practical experience of prolonged bourgeois democracy are powerful vaccines within the working class (and even the petty bourgeoisie) against the fascist temptation. Neo-fascist groups have secured mass support

---

47 For detailed arguments in support of the 'polarization thesis', for the 'new class' theories, and for Wright's 'contradictory class locations', see E. O. Wright, ed., *The Debate on Classes* (London, 1989).

for their racist and xenophobic programmes and activities, but there is no easy transition from this to widespread support for fascism proper.[48]

If there is widespread but not total consensus on the characterization of some groups and parties in Europe as fascist, there is no consensus on the characterization of movements or regimes as fascist. No single movement and no single authoritarian nationalist regime anywhere has secured such a consensually agreed label in the post-war period. The fascist era was, above all, an era of fascist movements, not regimes. If, in its heyday, it is the rarity of fascist victories that was so striking, what reason is there to believe that fascist movements or fascist regimes are likely to be less rare and more frequent in an era when the preconditions for their emergence, growth and victory are weaker or absent? Is not the absence of consensus over the validity of the fascist label for any single post-war movement or regime reflective of the absence of the fascist phenomenon itself?

The frequent resort by Marxists (and some non-Marxists) to adjectival qualifiers of fascism – semi-fascism, neo-fascism, quasi-fascism, proto-fascism or fascist-like – is revealing. They suggest both unease and pugnacious insistence. Fascism, Marxists are adamant, is a recurring phenomenon. But it has recurred in forms which leave one uncertain just how fascist they are, or even whether they belong to the genus. Such hyphenated fascisms are sometimes used simply to suggest that *some* characteristics of *some* fascist entities of the past exist in its contemporary lookalikes. This usage has descriptive value, but hardly offers much in the search for a contemporaneously relevant theory of fascism.

There is a stronger interpretation of the meaning of such hyphenated fascisms. The political entities so described – parties, groups, movements, regimes – are seen as possessing the 'fascist essence', the 'inner logic' of fascism. It is another thing that this logic may be prevented from 'maturing' into the more recognizably fascist entities that are historically familiar. To talk of the 'inner logic' of a fascist entity or of its degree of maturity is to perceive it as equivalent to a 'fascist organism'. This presumed homology of political or social entities with biological ones has often caused havoc in Marxist thought. It is misleading here as well. This 'inner logic' is not equivalent to the fascist minimum. The 'logic' or 'principal dynamics' of fascism subsumed by the notion of the fascist minimum are never the result of the

---

48 In Italy during the 1990s, the Italian Socialist Movement, with allegiance to a fascist past, transformed itself into a self-consciously right-wing Catholic conservative party, changing its name to Alleanza Nazionale. It calls itself post-fascist and declares commitment to electoral democracy, talks of racial equality (while attacking immigration), and has a leader, Giancarlo Fini, who many would say is not more rightist than the former premier, Silvio Berlusconi. In France the National Front does not have a mass paramilitary wing, presses for more use of referendums and more powers for parliament over the executive, and supports free-market liberalism, while railing against immigration and cultivating Islamophobia. It has a woman, Marine Le Pen, as leader, which is unthinkable for any fascist force, which is necessarily anti-feminist and ineradicably masculinist. See, among others, Passmore, *Fascism*.

evolution (unblocked or otherwise) of some 'organism' marked by its infant or adolescent or even adult characteristics. *The fascist minimum is always the complex structuration of characteristics both internal and external to the 'fascist protagonist' in a given context.* The contextual or 'shaping' factors are more important than any 'inner logic' or 'essence' of the 'fascist organism'. It is the fascist *situation* that 'matures'. The putative fascist entity does not have an all-powerful self-propelling dynamic of its own. To insist that fascism must be seen as a 'unity of three moments', that it is a phenomenon in motion, means it must be perceived in its process of full development, and therefore in its totality – which is the opposite of a static and acontextual approach.

Parties and movements may be pre-fascist or potentially fascist. It is difficult to see how they, or regimes, can be proto- or semi- or quasi-fascist, except in a superficial descriptive sense. Perhaps they could be called 'functional substitutes for fascism'?[49] But which functions are fulfilled and which left out? And how effective is the 'substitution' when these functions are left out? What are the forms of substitution, and why? Is this not an attempt to salvage a thesis that is increasingly less defensible, where the refutation is re-described as confirmation? For example, in order to explain the economic successes of far-east Asia, their Confucianist cultural 'ethos' has been labelled a 'functional substitute' for the Protestant ethic. Most of the movements and regimes likely to be so labelled are in the developing world. Are we not in danger of getting lost in our own theoretical maze because we are determined to see things through some kind of fascist prism, or its optical substitute? There is no developed theory of Third World fascism except Moore's. And the classical theories cannot be transposed to the developing world without distorting their essential character.

Fascism as a descriptive term of abuse will no doubt live on, and have a certain rhetorical–political value. Fascism as a label for contemporary political phenomena claiming only that the phenomena so described share some (possibly important) properties with the fascist phenomena of the past can also be an acceptable usage. But Marxists might also ponder whether the time might not have arrived to abandon fascism as a conceptual tool of contemporary relevance. From a different starting point, then, and following a very different route of historical self-evaluation, a 'Marxist theory of fascism'

---

49 See D. Pizzo, 'The Museumization of Fascism', *Comparative Studies of South Asia, Africa and the Middle East* XVIII: 2 (1998). Pizzo was one of the few to engage directly, seriously and fairly with my arguments when it was first presented. Pizzo, while recognizing the difficulties of developing a general theory that could incorporate the notion of Third World or developing country fascism, tries to do just that. He holds that 'fascism is a radical form of "emergency surgery" to save the most fundamental structures of global capitalist accumulation during periods of acute crisis.' Such a counter-revolution, he argues, can happen in a developing country: 'The latter would constitute a form of Third World fascism – one could call it "neo-fascism" or label it a "functional substitute for fascism" to emphasize the very real differences from the classical fascist states, but it can and should be situated inside a larger, universal fascist paradigm' (p. 96).

might reach the same conclusion as some of the non-Marxist theories of fascism. Fascism was a generic phenomenon, but one that was ultimately confined spatially and temporally to inter-war Europe. Do not geographically universalize its presence. What we need is not a new, more developed or refined theory of fascism, but newer and better ways of understanding newer, even generic, phenomena thrown up by the capitalism of our times. Knowing what to select and discard from the historic repertoire of Marxist concepts to interrogate the present is always a tricky affair. Discarding the concept of fascism might risk serious error for one must not rule out the possibility of a fascist turn should a genuine threat posed by working class power emerge somewhere. Yet there are those on the Marxist left who believe this might be a liberating decision.[50]

The Left Debate on Indian Fascism

The debate on fascism in India has been active for close to twenty-five years. If one were to venture a tentative chronological starting point for this, it would likely be the Sangh Parivar's Babri Masjid demolition campaign, which reached its culmination on 6 December 1992 with the destruction of the sixteenth-century mosque. That this has been an overwhelmingly Left debate whose major contributors have been those who consider themselves Marxists of one stripe or the other, or at least have been decisively influenced by Marxism, is not surprising. For the one thing, common to this Left, whether or not they agree that fascism exists in India, is their recognition that the forces of the Sangh do not simply constitute a right-wing force but belong to the far right, and thereby distinguish themselves from all other bourgeois political formations in the country, barring the Shiv Sena.[51] Liberal commentators, for example, would generally consider the Sangh to be currently a right-wing force which, despite the protestations of its leadership, has a somewhat communalist anti-Muslim, and therefore anti-secular, thrust, which it should definitely shed. The BJP is generally seen as more

50 V. Kaiwar, 'Comments on Fascism and Functional Substitutes for Fascism', *Comparative Studies of South Asia, Africa and the Middle East* XX: 1–2 (2000), pp. 125–7. Kaiwar is one Marxist who argues that the time of fascism may well be over. We live in a period when modernization has 'overtaken all survivals of pre-modernity of the inter-war variety', and when the conflicts of our time, and their resolutions, will be of a very different order than those of even the fairly recent past. Today's 'Jamesonian post-modern era', in which there is no alternative horizon remotely visible or imaginable in the way it once was to an ever-globalizing capitalism, means its failings and contradictions will have to be addressed in a conceptual vocabulary that may require us to jettison any notion comparable to fascism.

51 The Shiv Sena emerged in the 1960s as a chauvinist body pursuing a 'sons of the soil' programme in the state of Maharashtra against all non-Maharashtrians, particularly South Indians, who it claimed were taking away jobs and diluting Marathi culture. It is a purely regional, far-right force and, despite subsequently adopting a Hindu nationalist agenda to expand its geographical and social base, remains a small regional force with pockets of influence, but otherwise tailing the BJP at best.

moderate than the RSS, over which it should be prepared to exercise a stronger moderating influence. Were the BJP and the Sangh as a whole to move in this direction, then this body could emerge as an Indian–Hindu equivalent of European Christian Democracy – a socially conservative but basically modernizing force that is sufficiently committed to the preservation of the basic elements of a liberal democratic polity – and, given this tilt towards the bourgeois centre, might better deserve the appellation 'centre-right'.

One will only deal here with those writers who have explicitly declared that the Sangh is a fascist entity, and that therefore an Indian variant of fascism exists.[52] Excluded from this survey, then, are those who are more cautious and uncertain, and thus prone to use terms like neo-fascism, semi-fascism or even 'semi-fascism in-the-making'. This greater hesitancy springs from a) their sense that the preconditions for the rise of inter-war fascisms in Europe – a severe social and economic crisis related in large part to World War I and later to the Great Depression – are not present here; b) the fact that there has not for a long time been any serious working-class, peasant or left-organized pressure from below in India; and c) the fact that the BJP in power did not establish anything like a dictatorship, let alone of the fascist type.[53]

What is common to the criers of 'fascism in India' is much more a set of absences than anything positively embraced, which is the following: that there exist ultra-nationalist forces of Hindu communalism that 'racialize' the 'enemy' (Muslims) and mobilize violence against it, and therefore constitute the Indian variant of fascism. The common set of absences however, is the result above all of a method of analysis that rejects the view that fascism must be understood as a complex unity of three moments, or that (as Paxton would say) one can only define or call a phenomenon fascist after evaluation of it as a process encompassing all its phases, and the circumstances shaping it, from movement to dictatorship and its rule thereafter. Among those surveyed here, either the relationship between movement and accession to state

---

52 There are those who distinguish between the fascist RSS and the BJP, which they say is not a classically fascist party. But this means little, since the RSS is seen as the parent body exercising sway over all the main organizations within the Sangh, which as a whole can then be justifiably characterized as fascist. Given that it would not be possible to deal with all such writers and analysts, I cannot avoid the charge of being selective and biased in choosing those I believe have been the more systematic in their arguments and claims.

53 In my view this sobriety is only to be commended. See D. Pizzo, 'Museumization of Fascism'; D. Pizzo, 'A Continuing Discussion on Fascism, Globalization, and the "Third World"', *Comparative Studies of South Asia, Africa and the Middle East* XX: 1–2 (2000), pp. 119–25. See also my reply to his initial response, 'Reply to Pizzo', in the same issue. See also Bernard D'Mello, 'Where is the Magazine? Indian Semi-Fascism and the Left', *Economic and Political Weekly* XLIX: 41 (11 October 2014). Here semi-fascism is itself seen as a process, not yet characterizing the Indian state under BJP rule but a future possibility, depending upon what policy directions this government takes and how successfully or otherwise it is resisted at this level, as well as in civil society where the cultural–ideological battle remains crucial. Organizationally, what is required, D'Mello says, is a United Front of left parties, including all those non-party-affiliated bodies opposed to neoliberalism, Indian imperial ambitions, US imperialism and Hindutva. Matters thus remain open.

power and subsequent rule is completely severed, or the link is uneasily or half-heartedly postulated. But in neither case is the fascist label abandoned or qualified.

Nor has the fact that no pattern of central rule even roughly equivalent to the authoritarianism of the 1975–77 Emergency period emerged between 1998 and 2004 been allowed to promote serious rethinking, let alone abandonment, of the fascist label. In the early 1990s when, during the Babri Masjid campaign, cries of the fascist danger surfaced most strongly from the ranks of the Left, those who warned of a BJP-led government emerging in the future pulled no punches in claiming this to be a mortal threat to Indian democracy. Insofar as such an outcome would be coalition rule, albeit led by the BJP/Sangh, direct analogies were drawn with the electoral rise of fascist-led coalitions under Mussolini and Hitler, in which the other parties of governance were soon discarded. No consolations, it was warned, should thus be sought for in the assumption that coalitional compromises would provide decisive protection. There were also no predictions then of the survival of the existing state, albeit with its peculiar mix of authoritarianism and democracy, let alone that the fascist Sangh would quietly accept electoral defeat and resign itself to remaining out of central power for a period of quite uncertain length.[54]

Notwithstanding this outcome, all that seems to have occurred subsequent to the BJP's first stint in power at the centre is a form of theoretical self-inoculation. Some minor adjustments or refinements by this group to their earlier analyses may at most be required to better fit the facts. In fact, the first period of BJP-led NDA rule can even be said to have provided confirmation, not refutation or embarrassment, of their pre-existing theoretical predispositions. They can now more strongly than ever assert that fascism is essentially a 'step-by-step' process, a 'creeping' or 'slow-motion' phenomenon. Moreover, this period did provide, it is claimed, strong evidence of the veracity of their characterization of fascism – namely, the 2002 Gujarat pogrom. Just as, between then and 2015, the rise of a personality cult around Narendra Modi could be said to further confirm the appropriateness of labelling the Sangh fascist, even as the earlier absence of a Führer-like leader did not in any way diminish the earlier accuracy of that characterization. The fascist organism, it seems, is clearly maturing!

Other abandonments include the following. The context of inter-

---

54 Since I had consistently dissented from the view that a fascist danger was imminent, I argued that, even with the BJP coming into power, they were capable of launching anti-Muslim pogroms and generally raising communal strife to hitherto unprecedented levels, but that, nevertheless, there would be serious constraints, both domestic and international, allowing for considerable democratic space to persist. As far as I am aware, there were no similar anticipations emerging from those who then stressed the reality of the fascist presence, fearing what the Sangh's accession to power might bring. All rationalizations about the persistence of a democratic space seem to have been made post facto, and not preceding the 1998 election results.

imperialist rivalries that marked classical fascism – indeed, the fact that imperialist behaviour and war-making is basic to fascism – is no longer deemed relevant. That fascism was an extreme form of international reaction resulting from the aspirations of a late-industrializing imperial power, is ignored.[55] Unlike the views of classical Marxists like Trotsky, a universal theory of fascism must mean its geographical universality and possible emergence anywhere. It is further noticeable that the central point of Marxist reference for those participating in the Indian debate and adamant about the presence of fascism is never Trotsky. This is both remarkable and understandable. Thinkers like Italy's Antonio Gramsci and Germany's Arthur Rosenberg made their theoretical interventions after the accession to power of fascists in their two countries. Not only did Trotsky analyse as no one else had the danger of fascism in Germany well before its accession to power; he also provided the key political perspective – the United Front of Left parties – for preventing its rise to power. I fully concur with Perry Anderson's perspicacious judgement: 'Trotsky's writings on fascism represent the only direct and developed analysis of a modern capitalist state in the whole of classical Marxism.'[56] For those close to or inside the Stalinized mainstream left parties in India, silence on, or at most grudging acknowledgement of, Trotsky's merits as a writer or leader is *derigueur*. For these parties, it is the reference to the Dimitroff thesis at the Seventh Congress of the Comintern in 1935 that is important. But, for others outside this mainstream, this absence of reference is related precisely to their preoccupation with the movement phase and refusal to factor the key characteristics of fascist dictatorship into their definitions. Their reference points from the past are Gramsci, Reich and Rosenberg, and Sartre and Poulantzas in the post-war era.

What about fascist corporatism? Fascist corporatism meant significant state control over both economy and society. Economic and other social departments organized to incorporate employers and workers with these 'corporations', not so much competing with each other as, with state mediation, negotiating with each other. Private property remains, as do disparities of income and wealth between classes. But such state corporatism would repress the working class and better direct the economy and society in the direction (including war) that the state and its project of 'national harmony and loyalty above all else' would want. The association between top state managers and business would be close, but one where the relationship of forces would favour the former. The relationship of forces among state

---

55 That the 'ultra-nationalism' of the RSS and Hindu Mahasabha never led it to participate in the National Movement for independence from British colonial rule, or even openly to espouse anti-imperialism, has always been an embarrassment of sorts for those labelling them as fascists. Indeed, they were in many ways supportive of the colonial power. No matter; the magic wand of re-description can come into play. They were perhaps a form of 'subordinate fascism', or better still 'subaltern fascism'. See K. Srinivasan, 'A Subaltern Fascism?' in J. Banaji, ed., *Fascism: Essays on Europe and India* (New Delhi, 2013).

56 P. Anderson, *Considerations on Western Marxism* (London, 1984), p. 119.

managers, between the top party echelons and the administrative bureaucrats outside or nominally in the party, would vary. In Italy, statism rather
than the party was relatively more important than in Germany, where it
resembled more of a 'party-state'. Among the Indian Left, either the issue
of fascist corporatism is ignored, since it could not be squared with the neoliberal reality of today, which is also very much the project of the far right in
India and elsewhere, or there is the claim that the state is being corporatized
àla fascism – but here the meaning is the very different one of corporations
wanting the state to promote neoliberal, market-based policies, and being
increasingly able to get their way.

The focus here will be on the writings of four major participants in the
debate on fascism in India, namely Dilip Simeon, Jairus Banaji, Aijaz Ahmad
and Radhika Desai.[57] As has already been made clear, I believe all four, in
talking of an Indian fascism, are making a category mistake. Nevertheless,
there remains the responsibility at least briefly to summarise their arguments,
so that the reader is better placed to make up her own mind, or if so inclined
to follow up on the references provided. But there is an additional reason
for wanting to do this. Each of the four have also displayed some distinctive
merit that has helped to enrich the debate overall and, requires in its own
right a measure of recognition. Simeon and Banaji share much common
ground. There is some overlap between Simeon's two key articles of 1986
and 2013. In the first, he states: 'Communalism is the Indian version of
fascist populism and racist nationalism.'[58] The features that make it a fascism
are (a) its postulation of a glorious past which can serve to create an aspi-
rational ideal in the near future; (b) its postulation of an internal 'enemy'
– Muslims on one side, Hindus on the other; (c) murder squads; (d) the
use of democratic space and institutions to destroy democracy; and (e) the
creation of a 'symbiosis between the state and the bestial personality that is
the hallmark of fascism'.[59]

Simeon, in insisting that communalism and racist nationalism represent

---

57 The texts relied upon are D. Simeon, 'Communalism in Modern India: A Theo-
retical Examination', *Mainstream*, 13 December 1986; D. Simeon, 'The Law of Killing:
A Brief History of Indian Fascism', in Banaji *Fascism*; J. Banaji, 'The Political Culture of
Fascism', paper presented in Mumbai in September 2002, available at sacw.net; J. Banaji,
'Preface', 'Fascism as Mass Movement: Translator's Introduction', and 'Trajectories of
Fascism: Extreme-Right Movements in India and Elsewhere', in J. Banaji, ed., *Fascism:
Essays on Europe and India*; J. Banaji, 'Interview', *Hard News*, April 2013; A. Ahmad,
'Fascism and National Culture: Reading Gramsci in the Days of Hindutva', *Social Scien-
tist* 21: 3–4 (March-April 1993); A. Ahmad, 'Colonialism, Fascism and Uncle Shylock',
Frontline (17 June 2000); A. Ahmad, *On Communalism and Globalization: Offensives of
the Far Right*, 2nd edn (New Delhi, 2004); A. Ahmad, 'India: Liberal Democracy and the
Extreme Right', in L. Panitch and G. Albo, eds, *Socialist Register 2016* (London, 2015);
R. Desai, 'A Latter-Day Fascism?', *Economic and Political Weekly* XLIX: 35 (30 August
2014) and 'The Question of Fascism', in the Harper Collins compilation, *Making Sense
of Modi's India*, (New Delhi, 2016).
58 Simeon, 'Communalism in Modern India', p. 10.
59 Ibid., p. 11.

fascism, is not referring to that of the Hindus alone, but also to the communalisms of Muslims and Sikhs, since Partition was related to the rise of the ideas of both Hindus and Muslims as separate nations, while in the 1980s the Sikh nationalism of the Khalistan movement emerged. In both articles, but especially in the later one, he provides a very serious and perceptive account of communalism in both its Hindu and Muslim variants, describing and analysing its emergence in the colonial era, its social roots, and the selective appropriation of certain values and beliefs from the broader spectrum of Hindu and Islamic traditions of practice and belief, which are then manipulated and homogenized to construct the discourses of communalism and reactionary nationalism that climaxed in Partition. Unsurprisingly, the later article, which was able to digest the rise and fall of the BJP-led NDA government of 1998–99 and 1999–2004, adds a discursive element absent in the earlier text. To understand fascism, he says, do not bring in the features of it as a regime, but recognize it by its ideas and its features as a mass movement. To bring in regime features when the movement or entity seizes 'absolute power' or 'total power' (both terms are used) would be mistaken. How much truer, then, would be this definitional injunction when the Sangh at the centre was unable to replicate the absolute character of fascist rule in Hitler's Germany or Mussolini's Italy. Fascism proper exists in India even as there are more complex combinations of, and coexistences between, constitutionality, certain democratic practices and structures, a growing authoritarianism, and instances of institutional decay. Indian fascism also continues on its way, but how prolonged a period of continuity it will enjoy one cannot really say.

Wherein lay the distinctive merits of Simeon's contribution? He was among the very first on the Indian left at a time, in the mid 1980s, when the Sangh was seemingly floundering politically – the BJP had secured only two Lok Sabha seats in the 1984 general elections – to warn of the grave and growing danger presented by Hindutva precisely, because the sourcebed of its ideas and values was centuries old and deeply rooted. He was thus among the first to investigate and uncover its many intellectual and cultural roots, attacking along the way various justifications given even by the likes of Ambedkar and G. Adhikari of the Communist Party of India for the acceptance of Partition. Inspiring others to focus more effectively on the dangers of Hindutva and to grasp the roots of Indian communalism (majority and minority) has been his important contribution – not his ruminations on Indian fascism.[60]

---

60 Simeon is not alone in having recourse to the study by Marzia Casolari, 'Hindutva's Foreign Tie-up in the 1930s: Archival Evidence', *Economic and Political Weekly* 35: 4 (22–28 January 2000), to show that there were connections between both the RSS and Hindu Mahasabha with Italian fascism. But it is important to understand that, insofar as various groups outside Europe were influenced by early-twentieth-century fascism, their imitation was by their own lights – borrowing some features, modifying some, ignoring others. The RSS, for example, for decades before and after 1947, abjured struggles for

Banaji, more than anyone else, has been responsible for introducing into the Indian debate the insights of Arthur Rosenberg, as well as providing perspectives drawn from William Reich and Jean-Paul Sartre. All-important, for him, is the necessity of grasping 'the political culture of fascism', to seeing the sources of its presence in India today. The real strength of Rosenberg's argument was his insistence that historical fascism as a mass movement was not a movement of the petty bourgeoisie or lower middle classes, but a wider multi-class movement incorporating wage employees, white-collar workers and sections of the intelligentsia. The weight of the middle classes compared to workers was greater overall, but this did not suffice to make it a petty-bourgeois movement, even if these layers were more susceptible to its appeal. Decades later, a number of academic studies have largely confirmed this insight of Rosenberg's, made at a time when he had no benefit of either historical hindsight or the study of accumulated empirical data. For Rosenberg, the basic ideas of fascism pre-date it, and are found in conservative and radical-right groups of all kinds, such as the belief in an 'organic nationalism' of a particular 'people', 'race' or 'ethnicity' whose nationalist 'rebirth' or 're-generation' (it was glorious once) requires ethnic cleansing. Fascism as a mass movement allied to the existence of stormtroopers carries out this violence against an internal enemy. Deep-seated racism was not a feature of Italian fascism, but Banaji is no exception among a wider tendency among the Indian Left that has made a racialized enemy central to its understanding of fascism.

Nevertheless, Banaji's appropriation of Rosenberg is partial and selective. For Rosenberg, the existence of crisis conditions for the rise of fascism was central. Fascism, he believed, was a movement in the interests of big capital in an era of inter-imperialist rivalry, and in power would pursue economic protectionism – in other words, it had a crucial economic functionality and purpose. World War I and the Great Depression caused deep social turmoil in Germany, enabling 'anti-liberal nationalist tendencies' to gain the 'upper hand' and create the space for 'storm trooper terrorism'. Banaji pays hardly any attention to these parts of the scaffolding of Rosenberg's thought and analysis that pushed the German to identify fascism as a mass movement practising violence. If Banaji might welcome as a truism across space and time the statement by Rosenberg that 'Fascism is the most recent example of ... anti-liberal bourgeois mass movements',[61] he would also be more inclined to dismiss as a specific observation about Germany with no durable definitional value another: 'Fascism is nothing but a modern form of

state power, seeing civil society as the main terrain (aloof from the corrupting influence of state control) for carrying out the Hindutva transformation of India. This has not prevented many on the Indian left from nevertheless insisting that the RSS was from its inception a fascist force.

61 Banaji, *Fascism*, p. 26.

the bourgeois-capitalist counter-revolution wearing a popular mask.'[62] Also ignored are Rosenberg's curious, vague and obfuscating claims about 'legal fascism', and his belief that there co-existed no less than *three* different forms of fascism in Germany.

Banaji is adamant that any assumption that there has to be a grave capitalist crisis, with its attendant class-related tensions, as a precondition for the rise of fascism as a serious force, is to be discarded. Nor does fascism have to have serious economic functionality for big capital. Fascism, he avers, must not be seen as a 'cataclysm' or even as an 'abnormality'.[63] Rather, it is a brooding possibility that can surface anywhere, precisely because authoritarian structures, old and new, exist everywhere as a normal feature of societies and, through processes of socialization and physic formation of human beings, create the conditions for fascism to obtain mass appeal. For Banaji, the key to understanding fascism lies in understanding its political culture. He draws inspiration from three sources – Rosenberg, Reich, Sartre – and identifies three levels of this political culture.

From Rosenberg comes the recognition of fascism as a mass movement appealing across classes through a body of ideas picked from a pre-existing mélange of illiberalism, conservatism, nationalism and racism. From Reich one gets an understanding of why there is this susceptibility to the fascist message. This is because of the social bases for the construction of the authoritarian personality. In different societies, different structures of social repression promote subservience to hierarchical authority – for example, caste in India. But the sexual repression and oppression of women (though patriarchal forms and practices may vary) is a constant across societies. From Sartre comes an understanding of why large masses engage in pogroms and violence against the defamed, racially defined target groups.[64]

It therefore follows that this political culture must be countered at three levels. First, there should be resistance to nationalism and nationalist

---

62 Ibid., p. 23.

63 Pothik Ghosh, while appreciative of Banaji's emphasis on political culture and mass psychology, does express a certain unease about his 'ascetic culturalism', which neglects 'historical materialist criteria'. Ghosh warns against counterposing fascism to liberalism when underlying the rise of both is capitalism. See *Correspondence (Journal of the Indian Institute of Marxist Studies)* 1 (March 2003). Similar unease with the distancing of fascism from capitalism is found in an article in the same issue by R. Kumar, 'Counter-hegemonic Discourse Against Fascism – Issues and Debates'. Kumar reasserts the strong connection between fascism and the capitalist system. He is unhappy about compartmentalizing fascism as a political and cultural phenomenon 'divorced from economic or social aspects'. One does not have to accept Comintern instrumentalism to insist upon fascism's connection to capitalism as an 'emergency form', and also to analyse how it comes to state power via popular mobilization. Kumar, who accepts that the Sangh is fascist, nevertheless asks whether the Indian state is fascist. Does it have fascist tendencies? What can be the forms of fascism – i.e. is communalism its only form here? Does servility towards the whole social set-up necessarily require one Führer-like figure?

64 Banaji is not alone in ignoring the Italian situation, nor that in both Italy and Germany fascists attacked the independent organizations of the working class, which has not occurred in India.

temptations. In the era of globalization, Banaji has strong things to say about the economic nationalism of the Indian Left, but claims: 'The nationalism of the fascist right is also deeply isolationist and its rhetoric against international capital even more xenophobic.'[65] One wonders what he would make of the Sangh now. While sections of the Left continue to push for a form of economic nationalism, albeit leavened with greater receptivity to foreign capital, the 'fascist' Sangh is greatly enthusiastic about foreign investment and neoliberalism, and even Modi's 'Make in India' slogan is one that seeks to invite the entry of foreign capital. The occasional Swadeshi rhetoric is all but passé, and not taken seriously even within the Sangh. If Banaji rejects the idea of counterposing a secular and democratic nationalist project against Hindutva, it is because he sees nationalism per se as the problem.

At the second level, one must pursue the democratization of everyday authority structures from school to family to workplace, but especially struggle against sexual repression and women's oppression. Insofar as this suggests that the permanent defeat of far-right forces requires a much wider and deeper struggle to overcome capitalism, patriarchy and a host of other oppressive social structures, it will receive assent from many progressives as a long-term goal. But shorter-term strategic perspectives are also required. Here, the question of possible alliances comes up (see below).

At the third level, storm trooper violence must be countered by one's own organized forces outside the state, which is usually passively complicit. This is easier said than done, but the sentiment is admirable.

Finally, as would be expected, Banaji distinguishes between fascism and fascist dictatorship, allowing for the fact that, even if the former comes to power, the latter might not happen. The emergence of a fascist state, with its extremely centralized character is, he says, made extraordinarily difficult (but not impossible) by the reality of an India that is so 'fragmented on geographic, cultural, political and economic lines'.[66] Enough has already been said about such conceptual bifurcations between movement and state, and the inflationary spiral they create for the use of the label of fascism.

What, then, of the virtues of Banaji's approach? He certainly stimulated, in independent left circles, further study into Hindutva and the political culture it helps to create.[67] His rejection of the Comintern's instrumentalist

---

65 Banaji, *Fascism*, p. 6.
66 Interview with J. Banaji by S. Naqvi, *Hard News*, April 2013, p. 36.
67 See M. Jal, 'Fetishism of Hinduism and Its Secret Thereof: A Retort to the Indian Fascists', *Economic and Political Weekly* 1: 15 (11 April 2015). Clearly influenced by Banaji's work, Jal argues that one cannot effectively alter the mass psychology so conducive to the rise of Indian fascism, particularly in the era of neoliberal capitalism, without confronting head-on Hinduism and the social foundation of caste hierarchy. To fight Indian fascism effectively, we have to annihilate the caste system i.e., Marx and Ambedkar to be co-joined along with Fanon and Freud – an 'Indian Fanonism'. Jal believes that Marx's notion of the Asiatic Mode of Production provides a fruitful approach because it recognized that India could not be understood through the lens of feudalism or in the same way as European societies and thus could allow caste (which was central to Ambedkar's

understanding of fascism as expressing above all the power of finance capital has also been salutary. But there are strong grounds for seeing his introduction of Sartre's insights as being his most important contribution. Why do large numbers of people not confined to the middle classes engage in such mass violence – as in Gujarat in 2002, where Dalits and Adivasis participated in the anti-Muslim pogrom? Or, even if they do not participate, why do they nevertheless approve of such violence? Banaji uses Sartre's work on seriality and fused groups to explain how masses are manipulated by 'command groups', but using a 'manipulation' that is successful precisely because conceptions and values concerning 'national regeneration' *through* violence against the 'enemy' have been deeply internalized by the practitioners of that violence, even as the mob remains a serialized one, an 'inert instrument' of a 'directing group': 'Thus for Sartre, the passive complicity that sustains the mass base of fascism is a serial complicity.'[68] This emphasis on a mass 'passive complicity' that accepts and justifies the violence carried out by organized groups has proved a welcome counterpoint to those approaches that have been more strongly based on the material–instrumentalist gains that are supposedly anticipated by participants in mob violence – as well as to the presumed centrality of the networks that are said to constitute 'institutionalised riot systems'.[69]

Unlike Banaji and others who focus only on fascism as a mass movement, Ahmad does see it as connected to economic structure and class relations, and believes that the status of, not Germany, but Italy as an early-twentieth-century 'semi-industrialized' society offers more by way of 'analogue and resonances' for understanding Indian fascism. Gramsci's importance, according to Ahmad, lies in the fact that his prison writings were focused not so much on the dilemmas and difficulties in bringing about a socialist revolution in the West, where parliamentary democratic structures were more entrenched in society – which is how Western Marxists and scholars have mostly read him – as on how and why fascism could triumph and establish its ideological hegemony.

Italy had both an imperial and a classical ancient past, and religion, more than language, provided its social cement. Hindutva also claims an ancient unity and imperial past, in which the Rajput and Maratha empires are cited, along with mythic histories such as those in the *Ramayana* epic. In both cases, Ahmad argues, themes supposedly residing in the popular culture of

---

thinking) to be given much more importance. Moreover, caste is also a mental illness, a psychosis and the Indian worker is a 'divided' and schizophrenic self. This is where the insights of Fanon and Freud come in and it becomes vital to think of ways to carry out a psychic cleansing against the cultural-political efforts of the fascism of the Sangh Parivar. Jal further argues that we will also need to reject Gandhi and Gandhiism, even if the Gandhian vision of the Indian nation is not the same as the fascist vision of the nation.

68 Banaji, *Fascism*, p. 223.

69 See the P. Brass, *Forms of Collective Violence* (New Delhi, 2006); P. Brass, *The Production of Hindu–Muslim Violence in Contemporary India* (New Delhi, 2003).

past centuries are used for the purposes of fascist mobilization. Cognizant of the usefulness of the 'base–superstructure' metaphor, where the former is seen as establishing the 'conditions of possibility and setting the limits' of the latter, ideas and values of the past that had a certain 'rationality' because they were once more strongly connected to the economic division of labour – such as patriarchy, and for India caste as well – will continue to persist despite their much lesser contemporary 'rationality' as long as the necessary structural transformation of the economy has not been made. They will remain as components for the construction of a newer 'common sense'.

Gramsci, says Ahmad, realized that the popular upheavals from below that followed 1789 in France, and then elsewhere, created a new elite awareness that the rising bourgeoisie must compromise with the landed aristocracy (Germany and Italy) to nullify the potential of workers and peasants struggling strongly against them. The task then was one of carrying out certain reforms and concessions over a prolonged period of time – the 'passive revolution'. Insofar as this required national consolidation, a more pathological nationalism of a 'supra-historical nation' would arise unless challenged by subaltern resistance. In India, as Ahmad perceptively points out, this took the form of a 'spiritual national unity', pushed in milder or stronger versions by a host of figures from Nehru to Gandhi to Vivekananda, and others who gave it a more explicit and aggressive 'Hindu nationalist' content.

The idea of fascism occurring where a bourgeois revolutionary process is blocked or incomplete enables its use in the Third World. So 'Hindutva-type fascisms' are movements or regimes of 'backward' bourgeoisies that have become 'prematurely senile'. In Third World countries – which would include India – fascism comes after the nationalist bourgeois project has collapsed, when the indigenous bourgeoisie can no longer be independent (as it perhaps tried to be under the Nehruvian model of development) but becomes subordinated to the more powerful imperialisms, such as the United States, as the pre-eminent financial, technological and military force. So fascism for Ahmad does have an economic function – a restructuring which the liberal state may not be able to carry out. But this is not the corporate restructuring, as of classical fascism, but a neoliberalism that reinforces the dependency of the Indian bourgeoisie on imperialism – reflecting the failure of the bourgeois revolution in India.[70]

In his text of 2004, when it became possible to assess the record of the Sangh in government, Ahmad drew further conclusions. Indian fascism comes to power, he says, only because the Left is isolated and the liberal centre has collapsed. Certainly, in the 2014, elections both the Left and the Congress were marginalized as never before. But it is not clear whether, in

---

70 Indian big capital, or the big bourgeoisie, for a long time now can hardly be adequately characterized as dependent. More complex relations are at play between the Indian corporate sector and foreign transnationals. Indeed, sections of Indian big capital are themselves significant and growing players on the world market.

explaining the formation of the 1998–2004 governments or that inaugurated in 2014, Ahmad believes the Congress represents that 'liberal centre'.
He also claims that saffronization and neoliberalism amount to a 'full-scale
counter-revolution of sorts'.[71] If calling this a 'counter-revolution' helps
strengthen his Marxist credentials when declaring the Sangh to be fascist,
the 'of sorts' suggests a hesitant unease with calling it 'full-scale' in the first
place. This ambivalence arises again when Ahmad rightly insists that German
and Italian fascism should not be treated as 'models' (read: static Weberian ideal-types), but that fascism should be seen as a 'general tendency'
anywhere, thereby reflecting national specificities. Hence, he defends and
reaffirms a claim made much earlier, that 'every country gets the fascism
it deserves'. This is, in my view, a misleading claim, for reasons that have
already been explored at some length. But what is surprising is that Ahmad
could have said, following his own argumentative logic, that 'every country
gets the fascist tendency (or far right) it deserves'! This much more modest
and qualified claim would have obtained much wider consensual agreement
from Marxists of all stripes. And, of course, Ahmad too has to acknowledge
that Indian fascism, though certainly a fascism, has not broken with democracy even when in power.

Finally, what are the distinctive merits of Ahmad's contributions? They
are considerable. First, there is a lot to be said for his claim that Gramsci's
writings were focused as much on fascism as on the problems facing socialist
revolution in the West, if not more. Second, his reading of Gramsci successfully highlights the similarities in the cultural construction of Italian fascism
and Hindutva. This is particularly valuable because, where others were preoccupied with emphasizing the centrality of a *racialized* internal enemy
to be ethnically cleansed, and therefore with analogies with the German
case, Ahmad refuses to ignore or downplay the relevance of the political
culture of the original fascism of Italy. Third, Ahmad insists on there being
an economic function that does bring in the issue of the 'class relationship of
forces', and at least implies that fascism has to try and alter this by physically
assaulting the organizations of the working class and the Left – though the
absence of this behaviour in the Indian context is not remarked upon. This
may be because it is more of a latent threat, given the willingness and ability
of the BJP also to work with the institutional framework of liberal democracy, even as it seeks to erode it from within as it carries out its 'long march
through the institutions'. Fourth, Hindutva has to be fought on the terrain
of the 'national-popular' – through the construction of a positive nationalist
agenda. Nationalism per se is not to be abandoned or castigated. Fifth, he
insists that many of today's fascisms are of a fundamentally new type compared to the classical fascism of the inter-war years – and now operate in
a context where the dominant reality in far too many places is the relative

---

71 Ahmad, *On Communalism and Globalization*, p. xiv.

feebleness of the Left and the supineness of the working class 'beaten back by neoliberal successes in the reorganization of capital'. This insistence has been the spur to his providing, more than anyone else on the Left, a series of acute insights into the subtle and (most importantly) *original* workings of the organizations of the Sangh in the 'low-intensity' liberal-democratic set-up of India today.[72]

Radhika Desai does call the Sangh fascist, on the basis of its having storm troopers and because of its movement characteristics – the more so since the Sangh, in Modi, now has a more Führer-like figure. But the question-mark placed at the end of the title given to her paper suggests she is uncertain of there being now or in the future a fascist state, which she, following Poulantzas, considers the strongest form of the 'exceptional state'. As things stand, Desai recognizes that the Indian state is not that, and she further acknowledges that the classic Marxist parameters for the growth of fascism and the instalment of a fascist state – namely a deep crisis of capitalist accumulation, and a serious threat from a strong Left and working class – are absent. At the same time, Desai believes that, though the neoliberal state is not equivalent to the fascist corporatist state, its continuation will ensure massive problems of capital accumulation. Neoliberalism is stuck in its 'austerity phase', and has to try 'legitimizing a capitalism it can no longer revive'.[73]

Unlike Banaji, Desai does see fascism as an abnormal state of affairs. A fascist, or even an exceptional, state has to be more autonomous of the control of the big bourgeoisie – which, however, in India today is supporting the BJP in power precisely because it expects and hopes thereby to increase its control and influence. So how might matters move in a progressively more fascist direction, culminating in a fascist or fascist-like state? Even in the absence of a strong working class or Left resistance, the social turmoil caused by the Sangh pushing ahead with its destabilizing agenda – abrogating Article 370, imposing a Uniform Civil Code, building the Ram Temple at Ayodhya – would gain the necessary assent from the ruling classes to become that kind of a state. While recognizing that the Congress may be in terminal decline, she does not see the BJP becoming the 'normal' party of bourgeois rule in the way that the Congress was.

Desai's most distinctive contribution is her account of the decline of the Congress, which clearly paved the way for the electoral rise of the BJP and

---

72 Ahmad, 'India: Liberal Democracy and the Extreme Right', pp. 190–1. For Ahmad, the *'general question'* – his emphasis – is 'what would fascism look like if it came to a democratic industrial country that had no powerful working-class movement to oppose it?' While I strongly demur from his extension in this way of the fascist label and paradigm, his concrete analyses of the nature of the far-right beast in India is to be both appreciated and admired. *Socialist Register 2016*, for all the different understandings presented about how and whether the far-right forces of today are to be seen as forms of fascism, remains a valuable survey of the current context that has seen the rise of such forces worldwide.

73 Desai, 'A Latter-Day Fascism?', p. 49.

Sangh. Here she emphasizes the crucial role played in class terms by what is called the 'provincial propertied classes' (PPCs), which emerged from the middle castes to become capitalist farmers and local industrialists, and whose representative parties emerged in various regions – hence the somewhat misleading label 'regional parties'. These classes and castes first abandoned the Congress and set up their own alternative political formations, which were then prepared to ally with the BJP, and on several occasions did so. Now, in many cases, large parts of this social base are gravitating towards the BJP. Thus, Desai – not content merely to identify the character of the social base that has rallied behind the BJP's communal campaigns – has been among the first to provide a picture of the changing class configuration behind its rise.

Yet, contrary to her view, this very change in class support for it only reinforces the view that the BJP and Sangh are being normalized, and therefore may well remain the central point of political reference of the Indian polity for some time to come. This new normality is of course disturbing, considering its far-right character; but preserving this status also acts somewhat to contain its anti-democratic thrust. This is not any source of consolation. The authoritarian drift already prevalent, and contributed to for so long by the rule of the Congress, is further strengthened by the rise of the Sangh. This is bad enough, and deeply worrying, but it is not a fascism, nor a fascism-in-the-making.

The trajectory of the far right in Europe offers lessons that carry some relevance for India and elsewhere in the developing world, since these formations can trace their lineage much more directly to the classical fascisms whose properties – by analogy and selection – have formed the basis of similar claims about the far right in the developing world. Here Enzo Traverso has been one of the more perceptive writers on the European history of fascism.[74] In an excellent overview of the changing character of the far right and racism in Europe, he argues that contemporary racist discourse is no longer 'hierarchical' and 'racialist', but 'differentialist and culturalist'. Today's inheritor parties of inter-war European fascist forces have changed in western Europe, certainly, into a new 'de-fascistized' far right. In Italy, Gianfranco Fini, of the Future and Freedom Party, presents his organization as being positioned on a liberal and reformist right, critical of the excessive conservatism of Berlusconi and the cultural obscurantism of the Northern League. The National Front in France is headed by a woman, Marine Le Pen –

---

74 E. Traverso, 'The Hate Factory: Xenophobia and Racism in Europe', *International Viewpoint* 438 (July 2011), at internationalviewpoint.org. Banaji commends Traverso's 'brilliant little book' *Understanding the Nazi Genocide: Marxism After Auschwitz*, (London, 1999) as one of those that 'forced the more thinking elements of the left to reconsider classic Marxist accounts of classical fascism' (*Fascism: Essays on Europe and India*, p. 217). It is doubtful, however, whether he would share, even with specific reference to Europe, the trajectory of thought taken by Traverso.

inconceivable for the inherent macho-ness of fascist forces.[75] In Holland, the late Pim Fortuyn, who publicly declared himself to be gay and was one of the key figures of the far right, combined xenophobia with individualism and the defence of women's rights.

This western European far right has favoured the global expansion of the neoliberal order, criticized the welfare state, supported the tax revolt of the well-off, endorsed economic deregulation, and, most interesting of all, valorized individual freedoms, abandoning the cult of the state. Islamophobia is the new cement of western Europe, the new racism making Muslims the entity that is not capable of being assimilated within the so-called national community. As Traverso says, this 'de-fascistized' far right is a form of radical populism, and in being so crosses the border between the right and the far right. It can be inferred from Traverso's analysis, then, that this far right is not about *destroying* representative democracy, but about seriously *restricting* its distribution of rights – stigmatizing, inferiorizing and discriminating against the 'enemy' ethnic minority. Even allowing for the potential of further and stronger excesses by the Indian far right, in a democratic context that is considerably weaker than those of western Europe, might this description not capture much of the essence of the Sangh Parivar as a radical right-wing authoritarian populism? The Sangh could then be seen as a 'de-fascistized' far right in Indian conditions? There are those who would see fascist dangers in many forms of radical right-wing populism, and there are those who would insist – as this writer does – that the distinctively fascist danger lies at the *extreme* end of the spectrum of radical populisms of the right: the furthest right of the far right.

Hindu Communalism and the Question of Fascism

It might appear strange that a text whose ostensible purpose is to 'situate' Hindu communalism has so far paid little attention to its concrete manifestation: the forces of the Sangh combine and their collective ideology. But, if the fascist paradigm itself is inappropriate or of very limited value for situating not just Hindu communalism but a whole host of political phenomena, particularly in the developing world, then it hardly helps to delineate the 'essential' features of the Hindu communalist Right to see how they 'fit' the fascist design or label. Investigating the validity of the fascist paradigm is the primary level of exploration.

At the secondary level – investigating the 'fascistic' features of the organizational structure, style, behaviour and ideology of the Sangh combine – the disputations are endless, and assessment inconclusive. There are important

---

75 Though the Sangh remains a patriarchal organization, the intense macho-ism of fascism is of another order altogether, and this does not square easily with the fact that there are a significant number of women who are public spokespersons of the BJP, and that some are present in the higher echelons of the BJP leadership.

dissimilarities as well as similarities: the absence in the Sangh Combine of any truly charismatic leader until the rise of someone like Modi, who might more plausibly fit the bill but is certainly no youthful contemporary of the fascist leaders of the past; the absence of *explicitly* anti-liberal, anti-democratic and anti–working-class themes in its campaigning; the absence of any verbal anti-capitalist demagogy (*swadeshi*, or emphasis on indigenous production, is not its equivalent); the absence of any orientation to the theme of a 'generational revolt' – and so on. No doubt a list of similarities can also be generated. When there is no accepted theory of fascism, no accepted set of objective criteria, the assignment of 'fascist' emphasis and weight must remain arbitrary – the method a solipsism.

Though all fascist formations and movements must compromise in pro-paganda and tactics, their pragmatism has definite limits. They draw support from all classes, but are not *simply* a form of authoritarian populism. They do not 'loosely unify', but polarize society and politics. They have a mass but minority support. It is not an accident that, where fascist parties did come to power – Italy, Germany and Spain – they did so in right-wing coalitions that they either subsequently dominated and destroyed (Germany, Italy) or were subordinated to and absorbed into (the Falangists of Spain).

Fascist formations win ideological and political hegemony because their decisive victories are achieved on the non-ideological terrain. The tempo of their forward movement is convulsive and mercurial. They grow rapidly, but also fade out quickly if they do not achieve power, for the extreme crisis situation on which fascism feeds is by its very nature an unstable one crying out for a 'solution', and getting it in one form or another – socialist, democratic, authoritarian or fascist. Extreme crisis can never be a durable or normal condition of any society. Once in power, however, the tenure of the fascist state can be much prolonged, even as the character lines dividing a fascist state from less extreme forms of authoritarianism become blurred.

In post-colonial societies, the political vehicles of religious fundamentalism or religious nationalism are not fascist formations but, at most, potential fascist formations. I have argued that the conditions for the realization of that potential do not exist, and are not likely to surface. While the fascist state in India would necessarily be Hindu nationalist, the Hindu communal and nationalist state would not necessarily be fascist. It is noteworthy that, of the range of Islamic states that do exist, from the 'harder' varieties in West Asia to the 'softer' ones in the Malay–Indonesian zone, it is very difficult to get away with classifying even one as properly fascist. This is not a clinching argument, but it illustrates the variant possibilities regarding theocratic, confessional or denominationalist states, and the range of combinations of the secular, the democratic and the authoritarian in structures, policies, laws and practices in states that are otherwise all religiously affiliated, and therefore in some key respect institutionally discriminatory and undemocratic with respect to their non-Muslim citizens. Israel manages to combine functioning bourgeois democracy for Jews with institutionalized discrimination against, and often brutal repression of, Palestinians. But it is not a fascist state.

There are those who have succumbed to the temptation to call Iran a clerico-fascist regime. Gilbert Achcar, the Marxist scholar, in an outstanding article, rejected this characterization, explaining the difference between Islamic fundamentalism and fascism by specific reference to the Iranian Revolution of 1979, and to other such movements.[76] Where fascism is linked to big capital, Khomeinism in Iran was linked to the traditional commercial bourgeoisie and *bazaari*. The Iranian revolution was against big private capital that was linked to imperialism. The mass movement was anti-imperialist, meaning that revolutionaries and fundamentalists had a 'common enemy', which is inconceivable when one assesses the relationship between leftist revolutionaries and fascist forces. Where fascist ideology is based on ultra-nationalism – and, for many analysts, on racist exclusion – Khomeinism, and Islamic fundamentalism more generally, is indigenous to Muslim societies and inspired by a centuries-old set of beliefs. Nor is it ultra-nationalist in the way fascism is, but is instead committed to a trans-nationalism of Muslims everywhere, or of the world as a whole. Foreign rule is opposed in the name of Islam, not in the name of the nation. The United States, therefore, was the 'Great Satan' more than the 'Great Imperialist'.

Islam, says Achcar, is at heart a political religion, and in the eyes of Islamists must remain so. So the secular demand for separation of religion from politics at the level of the state is deemed anti-religious and anti-Islam.[77] Turkey is the one country that was not directly dominated by foreign rule. Kemal Atatürk alone attacked, not colonialism or imperialism, but the Sultanate, and therefore pushed for a 'hard secularism'. Other radical nationalist and basically secular movements, such as Nasserism, never explicitly criticized Islam or the religious order, preferring to give formal allegiance to Islam in a common struggle against foreign rule and influence. Finally, Islamic movements suffer in their ideology from an inescapable anti-modernism, reflected in their Sharia injunctions and inspirations relating to the family, education and gender. Fascism is a much more modernist creed, concerned with creating a 'new man' and a 'new society' rather than seeking to revive older 'social virtues'.

Following from Achcar's perceptive description of 'political Islam', one notes the similarity with Hindutva, in that both have difficulty with the aspirations today concerning popular demands, even within their own social

---

76 See S. Jaber (the pseudonym then used by G. Achcar),'The Resurgence of Islamic Fundamentalism', *International Marxist Review* 2: 3 (Summer 1987).

77 Many would say that, similarly, Hindutva is the politicization of Brahminical Hinduism. Votaries of Hindutva would likewise say that their opponents are anti-Hindu and anti-Hinduism, except that Hindutva co-opts the notion of secularity itself, but a secularity understood above all as tolerance not as separation.

bases, for greater personal autonomy in life-style and behaviour – especially, but not only, in the field of sexual relations.

If the weakness of the fascist paradigm calls for abjuring its use, this renunciation is made easier if one can see a plausible alternative paradigm. One can also understand the rise of the Hindu communal Right as a specific Indian manifestation of a generic phenomenon, but not one that belongs to the genus of fascism.

An Alternative Paradigm

Only the most rudimentary outlines of an alternative paradigm will be attempted here. From the end of the third quarter of the twentieth century, in all major zones – formerly the First, Second and Third Worlds – there has been a dramatic rise in the politics of cultural exclusivism and xenophobia. Ethnic separatism or hatred have been sentiments on the increase.

Across the globe, the politics of cultural exclusivity have taken four major forms. First, there has been the rise of religious fundamentalisms – not just Islamic, but also, though less powerfully, Jewish and Christian. Second, there has been the growth of Hindu nationalism and communalism, and what with some caution might be called Buddhist nationalism and revanchism. Third, there has been the rise, especially in the former Second World, of irredentist nationalisms – the unfinished business, it might seem, of the death throes of the Habsburg, Tsarist and Ottoman multinational empires put into deep freeze by communist victories in the USSR, Yugoslavia, Eastern Europe and the post-Yalta Cold War glacis in Europe. Fourth, the spreading and swelling carbuncles of racist and anti-immigrant xenophobia have been clearly evident in the First World.

In all these forms, the nation is either the focus or arena of contestation, the dominant point of reference. It is in the name of fulfilling the nation's destiny that the most barbarous political acts (those that most easily evoke the accusation of fascism) are justified. Why this centrality of the national unit? So international a phenomenon must have, to begin with, generic and global causes. Moreover, the temporal bunching of its irruption in these varied forms is too close for it to be dismissed as a temporal coincidence. Its primary roots are surely the crisis of late-twentieth and early-twenty-first-century modernity, albeit differentially mediated by the dilemmas of capitalism in its liberal-democratic guise in the First World, in the collapse of communism in the Second, or in the relative failure of developmentalism in the Third.

Though an all-round crisis, it has a distinctive cultural dimension. From the midtwentieth century onwards, there has been an unprecedented rise of cultural politics involving contestation over norms, values and meanings. This in turn produces conflicts over questions of identity, since norms, values and meanings have to be felt and lived. Of course, both the content and frequency distributions of cultural politics have been uneven. So, too, the lessons imbibed from a global historical experience – of world wars, fascism, the decline and rise of liberal democracy, anti-colonial movements, the rise and decline of communism, the spread of consumer capitalism, the growth of mass communications networks, and so on. But what, then, is the universal experience of modernity?

It is a recognition of the unavoidability of constant flux, the permanence of change. Modernity institutionalizes the principle of radical doubt. It weakens, where it does not destroy, the absolute authority of tradition, including religion. It provides a plurality of claimants to authority. Modernity creates the self-reflexive personality, for whom existential dilemmas can be more intense because there are no longer any easy answers. The certainties of custom and tradition are replaced by the uncertainties of reason and knowledge, the ambiguities of progress, and of development and fulfilment – whether of the society one lives in or of the self. Even as religion and religious identity are relativized and compartmentalized, the preconditions for their resurgence are also created.

The devastation of older values, ways of life, forms of belonging, and even of recently acquired values, ways of life and communities is traumatic enough. It is made bearable if what replaces what has been destroyed is 'better' – if the promise of greater fulfilment, empowerment and emancipation is believable. It is the fading of this Enlightenment promise of interrupted, uneven but nonetheless continuous progress that has provoked a new kind of social disorientation and cultural despair, whose forms vary geographically, and are preceded by different histories, rooted in different combinations of the old and the new. The dangers and threats they pose differ in intensity. But everywhere the fall-back positions are the same.

When the future appears bleak, when neither steady generational progress nor the possibility of successful social transformation is believable, the incorrigible past is the only source of guaranteed security. The imagined communities of ethnicity, nation and religion (of which the most important is the nation) provide the most sought-for continuities with that past. Of these, it is the community of the nation that can subsume other identities, because in its modern form, the nation-state, it is the prime locus of power. These three are the communities one is born into, that one can escape from only with the greatest difficulty, that one can belong to with the greatest ease, without *doing* anything in order to belong.

Eric Hobsbawm had this to say about this kind of imagined belonging:

After all, nobody can change the past from which one descends, and nobody can undo who one is. And how do men and women know that they belong to this community? Because they can define the others who do not belong. In other words by xenophobia. And because we live in an era when all other human relations and values are in crisis, or at least somewhere on a journey towards unknown and uncertain destinations, xenophobia looks like becoming the mass ideology of the 20th-century *fin de siècle*. What holds humanity together today is the denial of what the human race has in common.[78]

Like much else, the politics of cultural exclusivism are qualitatively less destabilizing in the advanced world than elsewhere. These negative cultural movements, primarily racism and anti-immigrant xenophobia, have come into the foreground recently. They were preceded (from the 1960s to the mid 1980s) by an extraordinary and unparalleled flowering of progressive movements and struggles over ecological and peace issues, against race and gender discrimination, and for freedom of sexual orientation and life-style. As Gramsci had suggested in his writings on Fordism, ideology and culture became more than ever the arenas of struggle in modern capitalism.

Unanticipated by him or by other Marxists, these struggles were accompanied by a relative quiescence of the traditional working-class movement. The politics of identity have overshadowed the politics of class. Culture had become a dominant, if not pre-eminent, terrain of social struggle, the pre-occupation of the 'new social movements'. The end of the 'long boom', the transition from what some have called Fordism to post-Fordism, marked a new phase – the rise of conservatism and neoliberalism, the partial containment and domestication of the new social movements, the growth of nationalist xenophobia.

Part of the reason is socio-economic decline. When the national cake no longer grows as fast, or it stagnates (the collapse of the cake is no longer feared), then whether you 'belong' or not determines your entitlement to a share. Capitalism in its best liberal-democratic garb still delivers the goods, but not enough of them and to not enough people. In the increasingly multi-ethnic societies of the West, it is inter-ethnic competitions that have grown fiercer. But the failure is not simply economic. Social disorientation also means a loss of sense of community. When the old links have been disrupted, what are the values that can bind people together?

In the more secularized West, with its more settled nationalisms, the preferred options have been the ethnic communities of race and language. In the former socialist world, what else is there for the ordinary citizen to fall back on except ethnicity and religion, separately or together? Here, cultural chauvinism is not just nationally xenophobic, but often separatist. Serbian and Croatian nationalisms are not proto-fascisms, however barbaric their activities have been in Bosnia. They are brutal attempts to forge new collectivities of meaning and political coherence along the lines of administrative convenience left by the collapsed socialist order. As such, they are not the

---

78 E. Hobsbawm, 'Whose Fault-Line Is It Anyway?' *New Statesman & Society*, 24 April 1992, p. 26.

simple revival of the old, pre–World War I nationalisms. That socialist order ultimately failed to provide a stable new principle of collective belonging – loyalty to the socialist nation-state or to the socialist multinational state. It could not even provide the 'Fordist' prosperity of advanced capitalism, or transit to a technologically more advanced 'post-Fordist' era.

The former Second World saw no equivalent to the cultural politics of the period from the 1960s to the 1980s in the West. The politics of life choices could have no secure foothold when the agenda of the politics of life chances was so under-fulfilled, and independent political life was not allowed to exist.[79] When it was finally allowed to surface, cultural politics moved along the tracks already laid out – the formally legitimized, ostensibly self-determining 'nationalities' of what had formerly been Yugoslavia, USSR, Czechoslovakia, and so on.

In the Third World, the failure is the faded promise of the post-colonial project. The basic content of these anti-colonial nationalisms was negative, defined primarily by what they stood against rather than by what they stood for. Since the colonized entities were rarely culturally homogeneous, neither for the most part were the emerging 'new' nations of this developing world. The cultural content of these nationalisms was not a settled question. It would remain a part of the post-colonial agenda, and its composition, organization and trajectory would be marked by the relative successes or failures of that project.

In India, Hindu nationalism was already an important stream in the wider flow of anti-colonial cultural nationalism. But it is the decay of the post-colonial project as originally defined that best explains the subsequent rise of reactionary authoritarian populism embodied in the Sangh combine. It is not the newness of its ideological themes or messages, but the new receptivity to older, quite familiar messages that most explains its rise. It is not the slow 'Long March' of Hindu communal ideology and its disseminating organizations that best explains its rising popularity, but factors outside the purview and control of the Sangh combine. This new receptivity is grounded not in pre-fascist preparations or seedings of the economy and polity (the New Economic Policy, whatever else it means, does not mean that), but in the collapse of the Nehruvian Consensus – the name that best defined the post-colonial project in India. The institutional embodiment of that project was the Congress, whose historic decline forms the crucial backdrop to the story of how and why Hindu communalism has grown.[80]

The guiding principles of the Nehruvian project included socialism, secularism and democracy. As the consensus collapsed, the guiding principles

---

79 See A. Giddens, *Modernity and Self-Identity* (Cambridge, 1991).

80 See S. Kaviraj, 'On State, Society and Discourse in India', in J. Manor, ed., *Rethinking Third World Politics* (London, 1991), for a perceptive critique of the Nehruvian Congress failure in the realm of the 'cultural reproduction' of its guiding principles, i.e. its failure to establish it as the Gramscian 'common sense' at the base of Indian society.

themselves were called into question – the first and second openly, by the Congress itself and by the Sangh, respectively; the third surreptitiously. The first meant a vague but important commitment to social justice. The second meant a commitment to the preservation of a non-denominationalist and religiously unaffiliated state.

The danger, then, is the discarding not of the Nehruvian project, which was clearly flawed, but of the principles that underlay it. Yet the appeal of Hindutva and its reactionary political encasement is precisely that it promises to provide a new project altogether, based on very different guiding principles. It offers no *overall* socio-economic, political and cultural–ideological programme. On the economy and foreign policy (the discarding of nonalignment and the pursuit of a strategic relationship with the United States), the Sangh has followed more aggressively in the footsteps of the Congress. Its distinctive focus is overwhelmingly on the cultural-political front, its promise deceptively simple. If the nation is to be strong, it must be culturally united through a clarification, acceptance and consolidation of its nationalist 'essence'. It is a new understanding of the past that provides the best means for handling the future. Knowing who we are, individually and collectively, somehow suffices in establishing, and guiding us towards, our destination.

This is a perspective that seeks not to 'solve' the crisis of modernity as it applies to India, but only to cope. It offers neither revolution nor counter-revolution, but a programme of neoliberal consolidation and cultural retrenchment. Cultural exclusivism and xenophobia are not means to the creation of a new, more powerful and transformative project, but the end-goal, the project itself – which will, of course, result in an even more 'degraded democracy'.

Does It Make a Difference?

How significant a difference does accurate theoretical characterization of a phenomenon make? Given a bottom-line agreement that politically institutionalized Hindutva is a dangerous and pernicious phenomenon, that it is responsible for barbarous actions akin to those perpetrated by fascists of the past, and that its coming to power would further reinforce the authoritarian drift of the Indian state, does it really matter if it is explicitly defined as fully or partially fascist, even if there is no strict theoretical warrant for either label?

This cannot be answered in any straightforward fashion. The significance of the difference between a truer and more false characterization, between political rhetoric and theoretical accuracy, varies according to the purposes of analysis. There are three aims that analysts separately can emphasize – explanation–understanding, prediction and practice – though all explanatory–interpretive frameworks have their own predictive and practical policy biases, if only implicit.

The first is in some ways the most important. The best test of a theory in the social sciences is its explanatory and interpretive power. Failure in prediction of an outcome or the inability to formulate or effectively apply practical solutions to a problem does not suffice to disqualify or discredit a theory or paradigm, as long as its explanatory and interpretive power is greater than that of rivals. The very nature of the social sciences makes the link between the range and plausibility of explanation and efficacious application of its directives or orientations a much more tenuous affair than the equivalent linkage between pure and applied fields in the natural sciences.[81] Whatever the failures of Marxism in prediction, or as a guide for social transformation, its explanatory–interpretive power relative to other paradigms guarantees it a major presence in the social sciences.

To know or understand phenomena more accurately is of great epistemological value its own right, whatever the practical or other consequences might be. But when it comes to political phenomena, and especially if these are of a contemporary kind, then the extra-explanatory consequences of different types of explanation are usually real enough, even if of uncertain and varying significance. A good social science theory or paradigm must above all furnish a superior explanation and understanding of the matter in hand. The arguments laid out in this chapter have sought to show why the paradigm of fascism fails to perform well in this task. But better theories or paradigms should also have a reasonably strong tendency to make better predictions in comparison to worse theories or paradigms. And better predictions or assessments about the future behaviour of the political phenomena in question should make it easier to find better means of coping with them. Whether or not we consider Hindu communalism and the forces that embody it to be fascist certainly makes some difference to political anticipations and practical perspectives.

Again, the differences in regard to anticipations are likely to be less significant, less diverse, and less detailed than those on the level of explanatory–interpretive rivalry. The further one moves from 'pure' explanation to 'practice' (via predictions and anticipations), the *less* likely are paradigm differences to matter significantly. This does not mean such differences cannot be significant, but only highlights a general tendency inherent in the nature of the differences between more theoretical and more practical endeavours.

The fascist and non-fascist views of self-described Hindu nationalism do have different analytical logics, giving rise to different conjectures and practical injunctions. Some of these differences will be addressed later, after

---

81 None of this should be taken as endorsing the view that it is possible or even desirable to separate theory from practice. A theoretical orientation is invariably based on a prior practical orientation, even if this is unarticulated. But, as in the natural sciences, there is a difference between the 'context of discovery' or the more value-laden fixing of an agenda of theoretical–historical inquiry, and the 'context of justification', the existence of 'objective' protocols for evaluating better or worse theories and histories.

discussing the third aim: the practice that is derived from one's theory. A political practice aimed at combating a threatening phenomenon must have a shorter-term as well as a longer-term perspective. Sometimes this can be seen as the division between tactics and strategy. On other occasions, the short-term goal is of such paramount importance – for example, preventing the Sangh combine from achieving state power – that it, too, is seen as requiring a distinctive strategy.

The 'art' of political practice is different from the 'science' of theoretical analysis. The best theorists are rarely the best political strategists, and there is no straightforward relationship between best or good theory and best or good strategy or practice. Theoretical differences are in an important sense less significant than programmatic differences, and are usually secondary to the latter.[82] Programmatic agreement is more valuable than theoretical agreement. Precisely because there often is such agreement despite theoretical–analytical differences, practical alliances between, and collective action by, disparate political forces is possible.

Programmatic perspective and practical strategy are directed *distillations* of theoretical wisdoms. They involve a drastic reduction in the number of variables that have to be accounted for in order to make theoretical insight *operational*. They also call for intellectual gifts of evaluation, other than theoretical–analytical expertise of the usual kind. The operational significance of the theoretical differences may sometimes be small, or even negligible.

Any political *strategy* must do certain things. It must first determine the principal aim – for example, defeating the forces of political Hindutva. It must then break down this principal aim into a series of more specific objectives that are in some sense more strictly time-bound – for example, preventing the reactionary Hindu Right from gaining state power, or expanding further from its existing strongholds, or advancing on the ideological front. Corresponding to these objectives, priorities have to be established. Actual and potential resources that can be deployed to achieve these priorities and objectives have to be assessed, and rational courses or plans of action charted and adopted to connect potential means and desired objectives. And all this must be done within an overall understanding of the constraints of the system, of what is feasible at a given moment as well as over a longer timespan.

Over a longer period, differences in theory become more important, since they are the *primary* and *general* way in which operational strategies –

---

82 It is only sectarianism that prevents political forces that have programmatic agree-ment, but theoretical differences, from working together in practice. Thus, within Left circles, theoretical differences over the nature of the USSR and its ruling stratum should have been subordinated to the common programmatic agreement on opposing the Soviet system, and believing that only a radical overthrow of its ruling stratum could release a sufficiently powerful forward momentum towards a socialist alternative. Instead, the implosion of the USSR saw a transition, by and large, in which the old elite became the new one.

political programmes and practices – are affected. In attempting to prevent the Sangh combine from coming to power, theoretical rivalries may well translate into significant differences of political practice, even in the short run. But perspectives for defeating the forces of political Hindutva for good – for destroying its social roots in the longer run – will likely be much more significantly affected by theoretical differences over the phenomenon's very *character*.

Some Political Conjectures

For a Marxist to believe that the forces of Hindu communalism embody the threat of an Indian fascism is to give the struggle to prevent it from coming to central state power an exceptional gravitas. It is to give it an apocalyptic charge, to believe that the working-class movement will be crushed before the accession of fascism to power; or, *à la* Pinochet's Chile, that it will be so crushed immediately upon or soon after fascism's seizure of state power. Fascist dominance in power may, however, be preceded by a coalitionist interregnum in which fascism briefly 'marks time'. In all Marxist notions of fascism, its accession to more or less full state power represents the *culmination* of the logic of fascism, not just an early transit point on a political trajectory that *ultimately may* lead to fascism. That is too open-ended a formulation, and is alien to any Marxist notion of fascism that bases itself on the lessons of the fascist era. Such an open-ended formulation may be in consonance with an understanding of the forces of Hindu communalism as authoritarian, reactionary and anti-secular, and even as potentially fascist – but not as fascist already.

Clearly, a major difference of political perspective emerges from the two contesting (fascist and non-fascist) paradigms. One will more greatly emphasize the drastic curtailment or elimination of any democratic space for opposition once 'fascism' comes to power. It follows that the opposition must resort to primarily clandestine forms of struggle, and that mass and legal forms of resistance are near-impossible in the short and probably medium term. Only slow, molecular, underground forms of resistance can create the conditions for the subsequent and painful emergence of more collective and large-scale forms of resistance. In a very basic sense, the 'political game is lost' if political Hindutva comes to state power. Its anti-Muslim character (even including state-endorsed anti-Muslim pogroms) is secondary to a more fundamental logic: the destruction of even the possibility of *any* organized resistance on any significant scale.

The logic of such a perspective should be to align the widest possible spectrum of 'anti-fascist' forces. In propaganda, it would be a dereliction of political responsibility not repeatedly to highlight the 'fascist' threat *behind* the outward garb of political Hindutva, of selling this 'truth' about its real character, however reluctant its potential consumers (and fascism's prime victims, the working class) might be to see things this way. One of the most striking aspects of the fascist era was the lag in consciousness of the leadership behind the rank-and-file of the organized working-class movement, which had an intuitive hostility to the fascist threat and was more aware of its danger. (Even in Allende's Chile, the working class was much more sensitive than the political leadership to the imminent possibility of a military coup, and clamoured for armed self-defence, which Allende and his fellow leaders opposed.) However, the organized working class in India does not see the forces of Hindu communalism in this way, though much of the leadership of the various left-wing political formations does. This does not lead these leaders to reject the notion of fascism, but apparently makes the task of convincing the working-class movement and other oppressed sectors of the specifically fascist danger all the more urgent, though extraordinarily difficult.

An alternative view might see the forces of Hindu communalism as viciously authoritarian and capable of launching anti-Muslim pogroms, fomenting civil strife at a hitherto unknown level, and so on – though as non-fascist, or at best pre- or potentially fascist. Such a view would be more inclined to predict that the scenario, even after the formation of a Bharatiya Janata Party government, would be very different. It would be more inclined to emphasize the significant domestic and international constraints preventing any rapid elimination of all democratic space for open and mass forms of resistance. Precisely because the decisive battles to crush all democratic and working-class opposition have not been waged, there would continue to be significant prospects for delaying, halting and even reversing the extent of authoritarian degeneration. The securing of government power by political Hindutva would be a qualitative defeat for democratic, secular and anti-communal forces. But the political game would not have been lost, and there would still be much to play for.

Such a perspective would have a more open-ended and flexible view of the range of outcomes and degrees of authoritarianism possible. The state's authoritarian evolution would continue to depend on the unforeseeable outcome of continuing political struggles and pressures. At the same time, those holding such a perspective would, as much as the anti-fascists, seek to build the widest possible secular and democratic front to prevent this reactionary right-wing populism from coming to power in the first place.

Apart from its rhetorical value, the use (certainly the excessive use) of the label 'fascist' would be seen as misleading, and possibly counterproductive. It would imply 'extreme' outcomes if political Hindutva were to continue rising, rather than suggesting the longer menu of options that would presumably be the truer and more open-ended reflection of the reality on the ground. This could disorientate the organization of opposition to the Hindu communal Right.

Over a longer time-span, the differing paradigms would also tend to suggest something else. The focus of the fascist paradigm is the question of state power – its loss to fascism (with all its baleful consequences) or other-wise. An alternative approach which refuses to situate these proponents of Hindu nationalism within the fascist paradigm is much more likely to see the principal danger as residing not in something that lies *behind* Hindu communalism, or in some fascist core *contained within* or *hidden in* Hindu communalism, but as Hindu communalism *itself*, as the specific manifesta-tion of the politics of cultural exclusivity and radical right-wing reaction.

The long-term, and in a sense more basic focus would be not on the potential or likelihood of a 'fascist' suborning of the state, but on politicized Hindutva's deep roots and growth in civil society, well beyond the ques-tion of its capacity to appropriate the state. In a sense, the phenomenon is *more deep-rooted* than fascism, *more enduring* and *more difficult* completely or comprehensively to destroy. The ultimate decay or defeat of the Hindu state would not have the same decisively damaging effect on Hindu com-munalism as the ultimate decay or defeat of the fascist state has on the forces of fascism. The effect of the demise of a Hindu nationalist and communal state on this Hindu communalism would almost certainly be less complete than that of the demise of the fascist state on fascism. Its 'traces' would be stronger and longer-lasting; indeed, they would be more than just 'traces'.

Whereas fascism in civil society is the prelude and the *preparation* for fascism coming into power, this relationship does not hold so tightly between Hindu communalism in civil society and the Hindu state. The task of secularizing Indian society is a much more arduous one than that of simply preserving or deepening the secular and democratic character of the Indian state.

The analysis presented in the above paragraphs, which was initially out-lined before the BJP came to power in 1998, has not only stood the test of time, but constitutes a powerful refutation of the views of those who have resorted to the term 'fascist'. In order to retain credibility, the latter them-selves now have to argue a) that Sangh fascism is a longer-term danger, and is of a 'creeping' or 'slow-motion' or 'accumulating' or 'gradualist' kind; b) that the crucial terrain of struggle if one wants the permanent defeat of the Sangh is civil society; c) that, even if the Sangh ascends to power, the degree to which democratic institutions, rights, norms, laws, practices, and so on, will be dismantled is uncertain.

As far as I am aware, before 1998 and the formation of the first NDA government at the centre, none of the four whose work I have focused on here (nor many others who have described the Sangh as fascist, or believed that fascism had arrived in India) have provided anything explicit, in writing, resembling the kinds of anticipations presented here, or argued why the overall scenario outlined above would be the most likely.

At the same time, whatever the label one uses to describe the Sangh, the way it has behaved while in power at the centre means there is now, in 2016, much greater agreement about the nature of the danger the Sangh represents to the Indian polity. Thus, despite continuing theoretical disagreements, when it comes to programmatic and practical issues concerning how to fight the Sangh – what the spaces are that would remain available; the possibilities for the use of existing institutions of the state and civil society; the resort to popular mobilization – the differences have substantially narrowed. The main area of practical and programmatic dispute on the Indian Left now has to do with the question of identifying which are the available forces with which one should forge principled alliances to confront the Sangh. Chief among these questions is that of how, and whether, to relate to the Congress on this matter.

The Problem of Alliances

The two kinds of strategic alliance for opposing the Hindu communalist Right – corresponding to the fascist and non-fascist paradigms, respectively – are the 'anti-fascist' front and the 'secular and democratic' front. But each can have different meanings for different people, including Marxists. Within the Marxist tradition, there have been two distinct and competing candidates for the best means of fighting 'fascism'. There is the United Front, formulated in the course of the first four Congresses of the Third International, and developed further by Trotsky; and the Popular Front, developed in 1935, at the Seventh Congress of the Comintern.

The United Front concept envisioned a *unity in action* of the main working-class parties, in a context in which (unlike in the Third World with its populist parties) the characterization of working-class parties (communist or social-democratic) was unproblematic. This unity, with the assent of the respective party leaderships, could not be based on any 'common long-term programme' between revolutionary and reformist forces, but was focused on common *specific* goals to defend common interests. Since 'unity in action' and 'common experiences in action' were crucial for developing greater self-awareness and self-confidence within the working class in relation to class opponents – including fascists – the United Front should extend to all forms of working-class organization – unions, for example, as well as parties.

Structures to facilitate such 'unity in action' should not be artificially imposed, but instead based on the forms of class unity that already exist or are periodically thrown up in struggle in specific contexts. Moreover, the United Front must under no circumstances entail an 'ideological non-aggression pact'. Revolutionary organizations must remain free to carry out ideological warfare against reformist ideas. Such a proviso clearly creates practical difficulties, and is more likely to be acceptable where the revolutionary wing of the labour movement is of significant weight.

In two countries of the developing world, China and Nicaragua, where strategic fronts were instrumental in ensuring victorious revolutions through nationalist and democratic struggles, these fronts, while true to one fundamental principle of the classical United Front, nevertheless violated another. The revolutionary party or force in the strategic front retained its organizational and military independence, but at the same time the Front incorporated a major bourgeois political formation. They were, in effect, Popular Fronts, but the significant weight and organizational independence of the revolutionary component was the guarantee against successful betrayal by the 'bourgeois partner'.

The Popular Front perspective was different from that of the United Front. It, too, sought at its core to unite the working-class movement, with its divided political loyalties; but this was to be integrated with the effort to create the widest possible unity of all forces, including bourgeois political parties and other formations opposed to fascism. Thus, three concentric circles were envisioned, each with a different level of unity: first, the front of working-class parties, with strong unity; then a broader and looser anti-fascist front of parties; and then an even looser national front including all anti-fascist elements. A possible fourth circle was an even looser international front against fascism.[83]

The problem with the Popular Front approach is its political under-determination, and therefore its capacity to incubate a variety of approaches to how such alliances were perceived and organized. When used by Stalin as a subordinate instrument of his foreign-policy goal of protecting 'socialism in one country', or in Spain, Popular Frontism justified disastrous opportunist alliances – especially when the working class could strike for victory. And yet, as in China and Nicaragua, when interpreted and carried out differently (keeping in mind some of the key principles of the United Front policy), it proved remarkably fruitful.

One of the central problems of the United Front perspective is its limited usefulness in countries where the working class is not hegemonized in its large majority by working-class parties. In situations of political urgency or crisis, where working-class parties are clearly not strong enough, even in combination, to triumph on their own, it is not a serious strategy for meeting the *imminent* threat or changing the overall relationship of forces decisively in its favour – though it can be useful in the narrower task of revolutionary party-building.

---

83 See E. Hobsbawm, 'Fifty Years of Peoples' Fronts', in his *Politics for a Rational Left* (London, 1989). See also P. Rousset, *The Chinese Revolution, Pt. II*, Notebooks for Study and Research (Amsterdam, 1986). Rousset uses the same metaphor of concentric circles to describe Mao's successful 'united front' strategy for defeating the Japanese and rapidly expanding the Chinese Communist Party's mass base. He perceptively points out that, contrary to traditional Trotskyist criticism of anything that smacks of Popular Frontism, the danger inherent in Mao's strategy was not opportunism or conceding too much to bourgeois cohorts. It was sectarianism, since the Chinese Communist Party was the nucleus of the whole concentric arrangement, and would brook no fundamental challenge to its authority in the name of socialist or democratic principles of pluralism, whatever its tactical 'concessions'.

Since, in most Third World countries, such hegemonization of the proletariat (urban and rural) by specifically working-class parties is a rarity, and
the proletariat itself (understood even in the broadest sense as all wage
earners) may not be a significant majority of the general population, the
strategy is something of a non-starter. In the Indian context, to believe that
the working-class parties of the Left (the CPI, the CPM – far-left Maoist
groups), even if they could get together in a United Front, could *on their
own* alter the relationship of forces *decisively* against the reactionary Hindu
Right's current political onslaught, is frankly absurd

The Popular Front represents a far more realistic project. But it embodies
a strategy fraught with dangers, some of which are so grave as to render the
whole strategy, in certain circumstances, counterproductive. It is a double-
edged strategy, but in most developing countries – certainly in India – one
cannot simply counterpose the United Front to the Popular Front. The
latter, understood as operating at different levels or 'circles', leaves room for
many on the Left or far Left to pursue a classical United Front strategy as
part of a wider Popular Front strategy. But the bigger and more influential
the Left party or organization, the more it has seriously to reckon with the
question of alliances with which bourgeois parties and organizations and
with what reservations?.

The Popular Front must be pursued by the big actors on the Left, but
with their eyes open, in full recognition of the risks involved. First, a Popular
Front must never be based on some 'common longer-term programme'
shared with bourgeois parties. It is a unity only against a common enemy.
Second, since such fronts are neither socially nor politically homogeneous,
they are always fractious. Even the common goals specified will, for some,
be an initial step in the quest for a deeper unity, while for others they will
represent the furthest they are prepared to go.

Popular Fronts, then, are likely to be brief political interludes. Furthermore, the internal relationship of forces between Left and bourgeois parties
affects the Front's trajectory. The weaker the Left is politically and organizationally, the greater are the chances of its being used and discarded by
its temporary allies, and thus also the prospect of the experience proving
counterproductive for the Left and its social base. These are real dangers and
real problems. The Popular Front is guaranteed neither to succeed nor to
fail. But where working-class parties *on their own* are not strong enough to
succeed solely through a United Front policy, properly articulated Popular
Fronts cannot be ruled out purely on the basis of an abstract theoretical
principle treated as a historical Holy Writ. Too much has happened in the
last fifty years and more. Such Fronts are most likely to succeed where the
goal is short-term and limited, and where the Left goes into them in some
strength, with its organization independent, its critical faculties alive, and its
eyes open.

In India, some concretized expression of the Popular Front strategy is unavoidable at both the extra-electoral and electoral levels in order to contain and push back the forces of the Hindu Right. Such a general strategic perspective could be endorsed both by some who insist that the Sangh combine embodies fascism and by those who believe it does not. Whether one subscribes to the fascist paradigm or not, this apparently does not have to make a significant difference to choice of strategy. In practical terms, the 'anti-fascist Popular Front' and the 'secular and democratic front' can converge on the same arrangement, even as their different nomenclatures indicate different evaluations of the nature of the main threat.

The stumbling block here is the question of the bourgeois centrist parties – the old Janata Parivar which has spawned a number of parties, bigger and smaller in Bihar, and parties such as the Dalit-based Bahujan Samaj Party (BSP) and the Samajwadi Party (SP) in Uttar Pradesh, as well as various other regional parties that are not part of today's National Democratic Alliance (NDA). Although it enjoys a parliamentary majority on its own, the BJP still welds together the NDA by giving its members minor positions in government. Are those outside the NDA to be part of the 'anti-fascist front' or 'secular front', or not? Regional bourgeois parties in the post-bifurcated Andhra Pradesh from which the new state of Telengana has emerged while Tamil Nadu, West Bengal, Orissa and Karnataka, also have to be taken into account. But some of them, even if not part of the NDA, prefer to keep their options open with respect to Modi's currently incumbent BJP. So the establishment of an *effective* all-India anti-communalist or 'anti-fascist' pole of political reference is by no means easy or certain.

The question of the Congress is pre-eminent. Marxists upholding the fascist paradigm are torn between those who see the Congress as a flabby, authoritarian-inclined but nonetheless anti-fascist force, and those who see it as so much responsible for the rise of Indian fascism, and insufficiently distant from the Sangh combine in its nature, as to disqualify it from any involvement in a strategy to combat fascism.

Those (Marxists and non-Marxists) who reject the fascist paradigm as applicable to today's India have the task of assessing the 'secular' character of the Congress, or at least of judging its commitment to the preservation of India's as-yet-religiously-unaffiliated, non-denominationalist state. I believe that the rise of Hindu communalism is best seen not as the rise of an Indian fascism, but as the consequence of the collapse of the post-colonial project institutionalized in 1947. The decline of the Congress has been the condition for the rise of the Sangh combine, as also for the rise of all other parties. But its political and moral degeneration on all fronts has benefited and legitimized the BJP and Sangh the most. Unlike the programmatic communalism of the cohorts of the Sangh, that of the Congress has been pragmatic and opportunistic. Though this means its secularism has also been opportunistic, rather than completely absent, the Congress has repeatedly failed the most important test of its 'secular integrity'. Various communal riots have taken place under its watch at the centre, and at the level of the states; in almost all cases the perpetrators have gone unpunished.[84] Despite the destruction of the Babri Masjid in 1992, Congress governments at the centre, fearful of losing the 'Hindu vote', have never taken serious steps against the growth of Hindutva.

Though the Congress was the political force primarily responsible for the institutionalization of the Indian state in 1947, and for its continued existence as a weakly secular and weakly democratic state (despite its super-vision of the authoritarian interlude of 1975–77), it is most responsible for the turn towards economic neoliberalism. This economic right-turn is of course not possible without a corresponding turn to the right at the political and ideological levels, thereby further nourishing the political field for the rise of other right-wing tendencies and forces. In fact, though the Congress was for so much of its post-independence life a bourgeois-centrist force – a classic populist-type party containing left and right factions; – over time, and well before the 2014 general elections, it has transmogrified into a much smaller, clearly right-wing party, while retaining a measure of social-democratic rhetoric.

A successful struggle to defeat Hindutva decisively cannot be waged without repudiating neoliberalism and all that comes with it, including the foreign policy turn towards a strategic alliance with the United States. What this means is that the Congress cannot be a strategic partner against the Sangh, even though very specific issue-based fronts can of course be entered into with it. Furthermore, its decline is now so dramatic and its weakness so profound that, in the near future, it might easily sink into irrelevance. Concomitant with the dramatic decay of the Congress is the crisis of the mainstream Left, which still constitutes the main battalions in opposition to the forces of Hindutva. Yes, this mainstream Left is today better seen more as social democratic (being pressed by internal and external forces to move further rightwards) than as communist, which it is only in name. Even so, it is actually the principal legatee of the older principles of the Nehruvian con-sensus, and as such more strongly and consistently opposed to Hindutva than the other bourgeois parties. Parties and groups further to the left (leaving aside the underground and politically extremely insular Maoist groups) are much smaller in membership and possess far fewer resources; but, given their political commitments, are indispensable allies in the common strug-gle against Hindutva. Since the Left as a whole will have to constitute the solid core of any broader secular and democratic front, there is every reason

---

84 I am not referring here to the Congress-led pogrom of 1984 against Sikhs in Delhi, and elsewhere in the north, following the assassination of Indira Gandhi by her Sikh bodyguards; nor to the greatest ever massacre of Muslims in independent India, when in 1948 Nehru sent the army to overthrow the Nizam ruler of Hyderabad. The reference is rather to the dismal record from the early 1960s onwards, when there have been com-munal riots all over the country in which Muslims have been by far the most numerous victims.

for the coming together in action of this wider spectrum of the left, along with the other progressive groups in civil society and social movements that realize defeating the Hindu Right is both a precondition for achieving their own demands and a fundamental necessity of our times. This is the principal short-term, and perhaps medium-term challenge that the Indian left must address.

5

The New Modi Regime

The 2014 Elections

There are numerous reasons why the 2014 general elections to India's lower house of parliament, the Lok Sabha, constituted a post-independence landmark event. But the most important is that they signified for the first time ever the replacement of the Indian National Congress by the Hindutva-motivated Bharatiya Janata Party (BJP) as the *central point of reference* of the Indian polity. The BJP has replaced the Congress as the preferred vehicle for carrying on the right-wing agenda of domestic and foreign capital. Moreover, the new prime minister, Narendra Modi, had, as chief minister of Gujarat state in February–March 2002, overseen (and for many was directly implicated in) the eruption and prolongation of one of the worst anti-Muslim pogroms since independence. If India is as secular and democratic as so many liberals make it out to be, then that alone should have permanently disqualified him from reaching his current position.[1] This denouement carries profound implications for the foreseeable future. But first, what do the voting patterns that produced this result tell us?

Of the 543 elected seats, the BJP achieved (to its own surprise) a majority of 282, its highest-ever tally, while the Congress (never before getting less than a 100) was reduced to 44. The regional allies of the Congress gave the pre-poll coalition of the United Progressive Alliance (UPA) 15 more seats; while the pre-poll regional allies of the BJP – the Shiromani Akali Dal of Punjab (4), the Telegu Desam in the south (17) and the Shiv Sena in Maharastra (18) – helped raise the National Democratic Alliance (NDA) total to 336. The BJP can rule on its own terms, and has handed over only minor ministerial berths to its allies. Its previous high-water mark was in 1998, with 182 seats and a 26 per cent vote share. This time it secured 31 per cent

---

1 Precisely this assumption led many after the BJP's election failure in 2009 to under-estimate the depth and spread of communal sentiment in its milder and more virulent forms, and therefore to dismiss the future prospects of the BJP, and particularly of Modi as a potential prime minister. Since I did not share this underestimation, I feared a BJP comeback, with Modi as its possible prime ministerial candidate though not as a single majority party. See my 'India's Paradigmatic Communal Violence', *Socialist Register 2009* (Pontypool, 2008), p. 150.

overall, but obtained a simple seat majority – although previously, whenever a party has secured a ruling majority, the vote share has varied between a low of around 41 per cent and a high of around 49 per cent. What does this signify about the BJP victory?

Even allowing for the disproportion between seats and votes inherent in a first-past-the-post electoral system, this was an exceptionally large imbalance, reflecting the fragmentation of the non-BJP vote. With the Congress getting around 19 per cent, regional parties still garnered half the votes polled. It could therefore be argued that the regionalization of the Indian polity inaugurated in the 1991 elections still holds. This view gains credibility from the fact that the key to the BJP's success came from its unexpectedly good performance in two key north Indian states (neither ruled by it): Uttar Pradesh, where it won an extraordinary 71 out of 80 seats on a 42 per cent vote share; and Bihar, where it won 22 out of 40 seats with a vote share of 29 per cent. Without these two states, the BJP would not have crossed the 200-seat mark. In Uttar Pradesh, though the Samajwadi Party (SP) was only 1 per cent short of its score in the 2009 elections (23 per cent), its seat tally fell from 23 to 5, while the party of Dalits, the Bahujan Samaj Party (BSP), lost all of its 20, seats despite carrying 20 per cent of the vote. In Bihar, regional forces again got reasonable vote shares but lost out seat-wise.

It is true that the BJP benefited from a fragmented opposition vote, but one should not underestimate the extent of its breakthrough, magnified as it is by the precipitous decline of the Congress. The latter has no representation from fourteen out of the twenty-nine states of the Union. The BJP is now the only national party making inroads into newer states, and even into the former left bastions of West Bengal and Kerala. In West Bengal, where the Left Front ruled for thirty-four continuous years (1977–2011) under the leadership of the Communist Party of India-Marxist (CPM), the BJP received 17 per cent of the vote, compared to the CPM's 22.5 per cent, and each picked up two seats, while the regional Trinamul Congress Party (a former breakaway from the parent Congress) swept thirty-four out of the forty-two seats available. In Kerala, the BJP almost did the unthinkable when it came close to winning one seat, and for the first time crossed the 10 per cent vote-share mark.

If geographical extension was one big gain, another has been its social advance across castes, classes and tribes (Adivasis). In Jharkhand state, where the tribal population, at 27 per cent, is more than triple the national average, the BJP won twelve out of fourteen seats. In Uttar Pradesh, the country's most populous state, the BJP won around three-quarters of all upper-caste votes and over half of those of the intermediate castes (whose upper layers are largely landed upper and middle peasantry) or 'Other Backward Classes' (OBCs), other than in the Yadav community, which remained loyal to the SP; and 40 per cent of the Dalit vote, barring the Jatavs, who remained loyal to the BSP. In Bihar, a similar story prevailed among upper castes, with the

BJP also securing over half of the lower OBC vote and one-third among Dalits. Lower castes and lower classes broadly overlap. The one social group that remained relatively immune to the Modi appeal were, of course, the Muslims (overwhelmingly poor and educationally backward, they form approximately 14 per cent of the country's population). In fact, for the first time ever, a majority ruling party will not have a single Muslim MP. Apart from this group, much of what should be the natural class constituency of the Left voted for the Right.

Any attempt to rectify this drift must understand why this happened. In the absence of class-mobilizing politics by the Left, Modi's promise of better development and governance proved highly attractive. Over the last two decades there has been some 'transformation' of class politics, but it has been by and for the Right. Of the various processes whose complex interweaving has most shaped the Indian polity over the last three decades – the forward march of Hindutva and of the intermediate castes, Dalit affirmation, Muslim ferment, regional assertiveness – the one with the most explicit class referent is the emergence of the misnamed but growing 'middle class'. Currently comprising the top 15 to 20 per cent of the 1.2 billion population, it has provided the most important base for the rise of reactionary right-wing politics, whether practised by the Congress or by the BJP.

Is the geographical and social expansion of the BJP vote an exceptional, one-time affair due primarily to proximate factors like the remarkable nature of the election campaign waged by the Modi-led Sangh Parivar? Certainly, the communal riots in Uttar Pradesh of Autumn 2013, in which the hand of the Sangh is widely suspected, helped polarize the elections that followed in that state and elsewhere. Moreover, even apart from Modi's own indefatigable efforts – between September 2013 and midMay 2014 he traversed some 300,000 kilometres, and in the last two months held a daily average of four or five rallies or meetings – this campaign set new standards in the deployment of money-power, technological gadgetry and cadre mobilization on the ground. The total expenditure by government, parties and candidates, projected at Rs. 30,000 crore (probably less than the reality), compares with the $7 billion, or Rs. 42,000 crore, spent during the US presidential election of 2012. The BJP easily took the lion's share of monies given by the corporate sector (big and medium) strongly biased towards the candidature of Modi, as the authority figure who could fast-track policy clearances in its favour, as he had done during his long reign in Gujarat as chief minister.

To this money power was added the massive use of social media messaging, of hologram technology to project 3D images of Modi to some 1,350 locations, as well as the manpower of the RSS for face-to-face mobilization on the ground. The Congress's campaigning, led by an uninspiring Rahul Gandhi as heir-apparent, was but a pale shadow of this. The BJP high command divided 428 contested constituencies into 'favourable', 'battleground' and 'difficult', assigning more cadres to the latter two for patrolling several hundred thousand polling stations. Voter addresses and telephone numbers were centralized and distributed accordingly with the aim of ensuring a very high turnout, especially of the young.[2] This calculated strategy paid off. Since 1991, whenever the turnout has been over 60 per cent, the BJP has done better. This time the turnout, at 66 per cent, was the highest ever. Among the close to 100 million first-time (18 to 22 year-old) voters, there was a 68 per cent turnout – of which the BJP received the biggest single share.

One could argue that India is following in the steps of advanced industrialized democracies, where even in parliamentary systems the mediatization of electoral politicking has meant greater personalization as well as presidentialization. Discussion of programmes and the choices to be made between them – what elections are classically supposed to be about – takes a back seat to public relations skills in messaging. This is not to say that differences between what contending parties claim to stand for are unimportant. But in a media-soaked context without class mobilization and the political confrontations flowing from this, the way in which these specificities are articulated or obscured can become decisive. In contrast to past elections, this time the central appeal was not even a policy promise, but a highly personalized one of giving power to a 'strongman saviour' who would then resolve all basic ills.

The Longer View

However, there are more fundamental reasons for the BJP's and Modi's ascent. It is the culmination of a process that had been going on since at least the late 1980s, with a neoliberal turn in the economy being accompanied by the rise of a Hindutva-influenced consolidation of 'common sense' socially and a stronger authoritarian inflection politically. These developments have all been normalized, and now define the limits of the 'acceptable' range of mainstream discourse on what policies and practices should be followed at the central and provincial levels. The prime culprit is of course the Congress Party, whose long-term historical and historic decline through its acts of omission and commission set the stage for the emergence of these developments. In a comparative sense, the Congress's decline broadly mirrors the trajectory taken by its 'nationalist populist' equivalents in Latin America, where, after prolonged periods of rule – for example, Peronism in Argentina, Vargism in Brazil, the PRI in Mexico, APRA in Peru, MNR in Bolivia, and Acción Democrática in Venezuela – such formations either went into oblivion or transmogrified into smaller, explicitly right-wing parties. But in a few of these countries this created the space where, unlike in India so far, left-wing

---

2 News report, 'RSS cadre return to camps after poll battle', *Times of India*, 22 May 2014.

formations grew much stronger, and successfully contested state power precisely because they struggled to transform oppressive class relations.

In the developing world, national-populist bourgeois parties with both left and right factions, mediated by a stabilizing centre, were a characteristic of the phase of import-substitution industrialization within the space created globally by systemic Cold War hostility. Once the former gave way to free-market fundamentalism and the Soviet bloc was no more, the new consensus, in India certainly, was that neoliberal globalization was not just the only but the best direction to take, with mainstream debate confined to how 'welfarist' a face it should have. On the economic front, it was the Congress that, even in the 1980s, embarked on the neoliberal journey (legitimized after 1991), and then also initiated the search for a closer strategic relationship with the United States and Israel. The fact is that, by the 1970s, the Congress had lost the organizational structure that had emerged out of its role in the struggle for independence, through which intermediary bodies headed by powerful local and regional leaders kept it connected to the grassroots. The degeneration continued thereafter, with its elite leadership moving steadily away from even the old Nehruvian rhetoric claiming to promote state-led development.[3]

Given the social character of the Indian state as it has developed over time – where now Indian and foreign big capital together outweigh the landed elite – this turn further to the right was not at all surprising. It could only have been countered effectively if there was organized class resistance from below, which of course the Congress would not pursue. The non-Congress regional parties were aligned to their own local rural and urban elites, while the BSP found itself mired in an identity politics – abjuring, cross-caste, lower-class mobilization. The Congress had become a vast electoral machine whose activists, lacking any ideological commitment or inspiration, were effectively silent except at various election times – local, regional and national. The glue that held the Congress together was its ability to come to power at various levels, and thereby sustain the clientelist links that substituted for its not having any internally democratic structure or vibrant culture of political discussion and debate. The 'family dynasty' was crucial because only it could serve as final arbiter in the factional conflicts within. Unlike the ideologically driven, cadre-based Sangh and left parties, electoral fortune or misfortune plays a decisive role in its very survival and well-being.

Ruling classes in capitalist democracies ideally want two 'safe' contending parties, so that one or the other can act as the alternative when public discontent with the politics of class war from above becomes too destabilizing.

---

3 Unlike East Asia, India never established a 'developmentalist state'. See V. Chibber, 'Reviving the Developmental State?', *Socialist Register 2005* (Pontypool, 2004); V. Chibber, *Locked in Place: State-Building and Late Industrialization in India* (Princeton, 2003).

So there can still be corporate and media support for the Congress. But this alone cannot resurrect a decaying entity that has to find its own political resources to generate stronger public support, and of this there are as yet no signs. The BJP and the Sangh are in a better position. Neoliberal globalization does not diminish the importance of states, but actually requires states to play the crucial role of stabilizers and legitimizers of its expansion. There is thus a dialectic between the international and the national. Growing trans-nationalization of market relations can happily go hand-in-hand with the assertion of nationally particularist right-wing politics and ideologies. This is where the Indian specificity of Hindutva comes in, and has disproportionately influenced the dominant form of Indian nationalism. This would not have been possible if the Sangh had not been capable of mass mobilizations and of steady, long-term work in the pores of civil society to win adherents and activists to its cultural and political messages of Hindu unity as the way to 'making India strong'.

The Congress not only did not resist the Sangh's activities in this regard, but abetted this process through its own pragmatism, periodically assuaging communal elements among Hindus, Muslims and Sikhs. In retrospect, a crucial turning point was when the Congress failed to confront the Sangh's mass campaign to demolish the Babri Masjid in Ayodhya, Uttar Pradesh – a campaign that openly defied the Constitutional commitments to secularism, leaving a trail of riots and communal violence against Muslims. After it was destroyed in 1992, amid a political rally that developed into a riot involving 150,000 people, there were further riots, leading to deaths in Uttar Pradesh and elsewhere. The Congress could have forcefully prevented this demolition, but did not; nor were top Sangh leaders ever punished. Indeed, in 1991, the Congress government had enacted a 'Place of Worship (Special Provisions) Act' to protect the shrines of all communities from communal vandalism, but kept the Ayodhya Babri Mosque out of its purview. The official Liberhan Commission, set up shortly after to investigate the demolition, was supposed to submit its report in three months; it actually submitted its final Report seventeen years later, in 2009. The Report indicted all the top Sangh leaders, including the 'pseudo-moderate' former prime minister, Atal Behari Vajpayee, as privy to this criminal conspiracy. Not only did these leaders go unpunished; Vajpayee is now widely portrayed even by 'secular liberals' as something of a 'statesman'.

The underlying reality is that, even allowing for Congress's ineptitude and culpability, the Sangh's Hindutva project could never have advanced as it has if the social and political soil had not long been fertile for its flourishing. Those liberals who have repeatedly waxed eloquent on the virtues of the National Movement, the secularity of the state, and its 'remarkable' Constitution have never been prepared to admit this reality.[4] For millennia,

---

4 See the two subsections concerning the biased character of the Indian Constitution in Chapter 3, above.

'Hinduism' was little more than a compendium label for multiple sects with various beliefs and rituals possessing no unifying thematic. The Gandhi-led National Movement introduced the poison of religiously inspired appeals that were necessarily oriented towards mobilizing the majority Hindus. Both before and after Gandhi, there has been a steady process of what the eminent historian Romila Thapar has called 'syndicated Hinduism'. This has entailed the more or less systematic consolidation of an ever-widening Hindu self-consciousness across castes.[5]

Yet, despite the growing popularity of some Hindutva themes and the Modi victory, the Indian polity remains in deep flux. The incredible social, cultural, religious and geographical diversity of the country, and therefore the creation of a remarkable range of sectional loyalties and identities, have not prevented the cross-caste and cross-region 'Hindu' mobilization from achieving such remarkable success. Not only the Babri Masjid–Ram Janmabhoomi movement (the greatest mass mobilization since the days of the independence struggle) but the dramatic escalation in the frequency and scale of communal rioting and other incidents, has had a powerful religiously polarizing effect across other social divisions. If this extreme sectionalism has proved a problem for an explicitly class politics, this has had more to do with the failure of the Left to mobilize on all the lines of non-class oppressions within the broader working class, as precisely the way to generate the widest possible class unity. The lesson that the success of Hindutva holds is that the decisive factor is not the objective reality of immense social diversity, but the subjective question of how one tackles it through the politics of mass mobilizations.

Six Processes

The persistence of this flux means that, though the Right has gained so much traction over the last decades, it remains the case that the ruling classes and their acolytes have not found the political recipe that can enduringly stabilize their rule. There continues to be too much turmoil from all sorts of tensions, including intra- and inter-class tensions, even as the wider matrix of social instability and political uncertainty has been shaped for a long time now by six other intersecting processes:

1. The continuing forward march of the intermediate castes (or 'Other Backward Classes' in official jargon, to which category over 50 per cent of Hindus belong). What has been called the 'provincial propertied classes' (PPCs), mostly belong here, and provide leadership and direction for this broader social layer of OBCs.[6] The concerns of the PPCs are not those of the

---

5 R. Thapar, *The Past as Present* (New Delhi, 2014), Chapter 9.
6 The term 'Provincial Propertied Classes' comes from the work of Radhika Desai. See R. Desai, 'Hindutva's Ebbing Tide?' in S. Ruparelia, S. Reddy, J. Harriss and S.

Most Backward Castes (MBCs) within the category of OBCs, whose conditions are quite terrible. PPC dominance has blocked alignment of MBCs with the poor Dalits and Muslims with whom they share so many forms of deprivation. Even before Modi, the BJP gained electoral ground among OBCs, though this varied from state to state. Though there are BJP chief ministers of states drawn from OBC ranks, Modi himself is the first BJP leader who is also an OBC. He represents a certain pole of attraction, but this is still no guarantee of stable loyalty to the BJP from the various caste groups, higher and lower, that make up the OBC community. Regional political parties and their influences come into play here.

2. Unprecedented Dalit assertiveness. Quota policies in central and state government jobs and educational institutions, and the fact that no party would dare seriously to challenge this policy (also extended to OBCs) is proof of how effective Dalit mobilization has been. But what this quota policy has done is to create a significant middle and even a small upper class among Dalits who provide the leadership, whose orientation is different from that of the lower and lowest Dalit sub-caste ranks. These upper Dalit layers and their progeny benefit most from the quota policies. Even as it is a good thing that the Indian middle and upper classes have become socially more diverse, this very diversity also acts to promote and consolidate policies that favour these very classes. Thus many of these Dalit beneficiaries can see value in aligning themselves with their class brethren and their political vehicles, to the point where many laud the virtues of neoliberal capitalist development as a liberating force for the Dalits generally. That a near-majority of Dalits are agricultural proletarians, while the majority of agricultural proletarians are not Dalits, has not led to efforts by the parties of Dalits – the most important being the BSP – to build a cross-caste class alliance of landless labourers, which is the best way to promote the interests of the most oppressed Dalits.

Rather, there is a merry-go-round of shifting electoral alliances between the BSP and others, which has included the BJP, and the pursuit of symbolic politics through the invocation of Ambedkar. There is a double irony here. Ambedkar turned to Buddhism as the way out of the caste system. But Dalit assertiveness is taking the form of asserting its own caste power and status, rather than showing any determination to finish off the caste system. Nor, so far, is there any mass conversion to Buddhism of Dalits, the majority continuing to remain within the Hindu fold. The Sangh under Modi, meanwhile, is systematically seeking to appropriate Ambedkar himself as a great leader and visionary who poses no problems for making a great Hindu India that encompasses Buddhists, Jains and Sikhs, as against 'external' potential traitors like Muslims, Christians and communists. The BSP, playing similar

Corbridge, *Understanding India's New Political Economy* (New York, 2011); R. Desai, 'A Latter-Day Fascism?' *Economic and Political Weekly*, 30 August 2014.

symbolic political games regarding Ambedkar, finds itself on the back foot in the face of this Hindutva appropriation and glorification of the Dalit leader, although Ambedkar himself excoriated Brahminical Hinduism in no uncertain terms.

3. Unprecedented Muslim ferment. Not so long ago, it made great sense to argue that local Muslims had more in common culturally with local Hindus than either with more geographically distant Muslims or Hindus in India, to the point where many would deny the existence of any serious trans-regional Hindu or Muslim 'community consciousness'. This is no longer the case. The syndicalization of Hinduism, abetted by the revolution in mass communications, has deepened and widened the sense of belonging to a particular religious community. That a plethora of Hindu religious and 'spiritual' leaders with their respective mass followings have overwhelmingly endorsed the Sangh as protector of the Hindu community and its collective interests has reinforced this trend. The fact that Muslims have been the principal victims of numerous and continuing communal riots and incidents, small and large, in which the culprits are hardly ever punished, has created an ever wider consciousness of Muslims in India being a besieged community.

Of all religious groups, Muslims are the most urbanized, and of the urban population the poorest in per capita terms.[7] Economic decline of the old Muslim elite and one-time aristocracy in the north, the replacement of Urdu by Hindi as the official language, and the fears generated by communal riots in which they have overwhelmingly been the main victims, have considerably accelerated their ghettoization and segregation. In the past, urban India always operated a form of segregation by religion and caste, but there was still a reasonable interface created by significant functional, and to some degree cultural exchanges, leading to a resilient and relatively peaceful sharing of urban space – more certainly in the cities of the south and east than in the north and west. But after repeated riots, a much greater influx of richer Muslims into poorer Muslim areas has taken place juxtaposing enclaves and slums for example, in Ahmedabad, Gujarat after the 2002 pogrom, but also in other states. This has meant (a) greater collective security, with increased capacities for resistance against communal assaults; (b) some advances in commonly shared health and education facilities for poorer Muslims; (c) a more united form of 'strategic voting' at election times for non-BJP parties. But the downside is (a) higher land prices, which help to push out poorer Muslims; (b) stronger economic and cultural–religious connections with the Gulf states and Saudi Arabia; (c) the reinforcement of a much stronger sense of separation among Muslim youth from 'Hindu'

---

7 The last report of the National Council for Applied Economic Research to focus on the plight of Muslims, which came out in 2009–10, revealed that 31 per cent of urban Muslims lived below the poverty line, as did 20 per cent of rural Muslims, while their rate of poverty decline is lower than for Hindus, let alone Sikhs and Christians. The average annual income of a Muslim family was Rs. 28,500, which is close to that for Adivasis and Dalits.

India.[8] The rise of Islamophobia worldwide, combined with the entry on a much greater scale of externally funded preaching of more radical Islamist currents, has also made the situation worse. So much so that it is only in the last five years or so that there have emerged home-grown Muslim terrorist groups and individuals. The closed circle of Hindu–Muslim antagonistic behaviour that feeds on itself has thus strengthened.

4. The forward march – albeit interrupted from time to time in its tempo and geographically uneven in its impact – of Hindutva. This trajectory is not determined by the electoral ups and downs of the BJP. There is no other force remotely comparable in scale or depth to the multiple organizations of the Sangh doing its ideological groundwork within India society. The Congress, through its pragmatic communalism, unlike the programmatic communalism of the BJP, nonetheless paved the way for the rise of Hindutva. This raises the question of how far back one must go in order to understand the roots and catalysts of Hindu nationalism. It should be understood that Hindu nationalism has existed in various forms, many different from Hindutva and even critical of many of its ingredients, though not in wholesale opposition to all its themes and arguments. Widespread throughout the intelligentsia, the media, and most political parties, including parts of the Left, are beliefs in Hinduism's uniquely tolerant character; in its being the essential core of the 'national culture'; in the unmatched philosophical wisdoms of its ancient texts; in the virtuousness of the varna system, as distinct from the caste system; and in how it contrasts with the more aggressive character of Islam – combined with a tacit agreement to ignore the Hindu biases in the much-celebrated Indian Constitution. What is downplayed, if not ignored, is that Indian society is not secular, and that the Indian state is only weakly secular in principle, but communal in so much of its practice, regardless of which party holds power at the centre.

Most Hindus today are not hostile to Muslims, but they are largely indifferent to their difficulties. Their socioeconomic plight was highlighted by the Sachar Committee Report of 2011; but its recommendations for affirmative action through quotas for Muslims, as are given to Dalits, tribals and OBCs, was ignored by the Congress government. Where the Sangh has succeeded is in creating a situation in which, if secularism is emphasized in public discourse by politicians and other prominent figure, this is now seen as a tiresome trope reflective of a desire to 'appease' or reassure Muslims that they are on their side. The invocation of secularism shows unconcern, and is therefore 'unfair' to other religious communities, and indeed is something of a diversion from recognizing the everyday problems and difficulties they face. The Aam Aadmi Party (AAP), which wanted to appeal to the widest cross-section of the public, predominantly Hindus of all castes, including

---

8 C. Jaffrelot, 'In, and Out, of the Ghetto', *Indian Express*, 15 January 2015. See also L. Gayer and C. Jaffrelot, *Muslims in Indian Cities: Trajectories of Marginalisation* (London, 2012).

those who might otherwise support the BJP, deliberately avoided this discourse in its public pitch to the citizens of Delhi, and thereby reaped strong electoral dividends. This diminishment and cheapening of the discourse of secularism is itself a significant indicator of the ideological advances made by Hindutva.

5. The regionalization of the Indian polity. For most of the history of independent India, there has been a single party that could claim to be the only national force. It was first the Congress, followed for a short period by there being two contending forces, and now it is the BJP alone. It was at the provincial level that opposition forces reflecting the complexity and diversity of Indian society emerged and flourished. The first-past-the-post electoral system, contra Duverger's law, did not stabilize two- or three-party competition at the centre, while coalition governments involving regional parties did not always collapse, but often lasted out their full terms. There have been two types of regional parties – those that, by their very nature have no trans-regional ambitions, and those that do, but because of their geographically, linguistically or socially sectoral characters have not yet succeeded in becoming a significant force at the national level. With the exception of the Left, itself a regional force, none of these other parties has seriously worked out national-level or international-level programmatic perspectives. Their need for good relations with either the Congress or the BJP means they have been willing to let those parties make the running on such extra-provincial issues. This has been the case even when they have been coalition partners at the centre, where they have traded in their support for specific provincial rewards.

This regionalization will persist as long as a macro-level liberal-democratic framework is in place. The BJP has made regional advances, but two- or three-party competitive systems at the provincial level will endure. One major reason why smaller regional parties do not oppose the first-past-the-post system in favour of some form of proportional representation at the centre is that this reform would also necessarily take place at the provincial level, undermining their own chances of securing single-party rule, or at least dominance, in a state coalition government. What is now likely is that the strongest challenger to the BJP at the centre in future elections may well be a stitched-up coalition of regional parties. It remains to be seen whether any one of these regional forces, which now include the Congress, could become a significant force nationally. After the Bihar election results of November 2015, there is much talk of Nitish Kumar, the chief minister of that state, becoming a potential prime ministerial candidate at the head of some stitched-up coalition to fight the next general elections. While there is now considerable mediatization and personalization of elections even in parliamentary democracies, having a popular leader at the head of such a coalition would not, on its own, be enough to nullify the advantage the BJP has in being the only national party.

For survival purposes, in the face of BJP advances regional parties now have to consider coming together more seriously. But this does not mean that they can avoid the even sharper divisions or difficulties that would emerge, given the narrow and sectoral interests and visions that have historically shaped them as political formations. On the much wider terrain of the national and international arenas, their distinctive contributions have been more limited.[9] Whether this can change programmatically and ideologically, or whether one or more parties can grow nationally and yet maintain their existing social loyalties, remains to be seen. Hitherto, what has made coalition governments at the centre viable has been the existence of one party, either the BJP or the Congress, that has acted as the national-level hub for the arrangement. Neither the Janata government of 1977–80, the V. P Singh and Chandrasekhar governments of the 1989–91 period, nor the Deve Gowda Gujral governments of 1996–98 were able to survive a full term.

6. Finally, the rise of the 'Indian Middle Class' (IMC), which in fact is an elite category of mass proportions. Its character and importance in shaping elite nationalism have already been discussed (see Chapter 1). This layer, as we have seen, is the social base for the continuation and deepening of the neoliberal economic agenda – which, however, is the very agenda thats pursuit will create the biggest problems for the Sangh effort to establish strong, expanding and enduring popularity, and the most likely source for growing public dissatisfaction. This is precisely why a closer look at what the Modi government has been doing in this regard is necessary.

The Unfolding Agenda

More than two-and-a-half years have now passed since Modi's national victory in May 2014 – enough time to have provided concrete evidence about where his government is heading on domestic and external fronts. Make no mistake: in power is not a mere religiously conservative right-wing (or right-of-centre) government that is insufficiently committed to secularism, as many a liberal commentator would have it. The BJP is a far-right party, and is the electoral-political wing of the Sangh Parivar, whose parent organization is the RSS – easily the largest, most strongly motivated, and geographically most widespread cadre-based organization in the country. The Sangh has multiple front organizations which, along with the RSS, have been operating for decades in the pores of civil society, and this collective body is now stronger than ever before. What makes the Sangh distinctive from all other political forces is its ideology of Hindutva – that is, its commitment to a very exclusivist form of Hindu nationalism, holding that India

---

9 Sanjay Ruparelia, in his study of the three non-Congress, non-BJP governments of 1977–80, 1989–91 and 1996–98 has suggested that all three pursued distinctive policies, promoting a more 'cooperative federalism' and better relations with neighbouring countries of South Asia. S. Ruparelia, *Divided We Govern: Coalition Politics in Modern India* (New Delhi, 2015).

must recognize itself as above all a Hindu nation for which a Hindu state, in all but name, is required if it is to secure its historic mission of achieving national and global strength and prestige.

The BJP's communal character does mean that, though it is basically following the same foreign policy direction as the previous UPA governments – namely, deepening ties with the United States to contain China; coming closer to Israel; expanding its nuclear arsenal and seeking entry into the Nuclear Suppliers Group – it has added its own imprint. Modi has been determined to promote himself as an international statesman and made official visits to more than 60 countries so far. No other Indian prime minister has been so peripatetic in so short a period of rule. These travels have had much more to do with Modi wanting to overcome his international 'pariah' status after the Gujarat pogrom (where despite his command responsibility he has gone unpunished) and to pose as a global statesman, than with having to make diplomatic deals at the very highest levels with all the countries visited.

In June 2016, Modi visited the United States for the third time since becoming prime minister, and signed 'foundation agreements' that included the commitment to finalize in the near future the Logistics Exchange Memorandum of Agreement (LEMOA), which will give the United States, for the first time, free access to several bases on Indian soil. Worse, according to one media report there is a secret accord 'outlining a joint strategy to deal with "specific situations" in the Asia-Pacific region in the future.' This, says the report, is tantamount to an undeclared strategic alliance – undeclared since Indian claims to pursuing an independent policy towards China, in particular, would not then be that credible.[10] As for Israel, the Sangh's abiding hostility to Muslims and Islam gives an ideological as well as strategic dimension to New Delhi's tie-up with Tel Aviv. Modi will almost certainly be the first Indian prime minister to visit Israel officially. Disappointment with Nepal's turn towards secular republicanism will be greater, and general annoyance more strongly expressed in various ways.

A dose of muscularity has also been added to Modi's foreign policy vis-a-vis Pakistan. There is a domestic dividend here in that those sections not enamoured of his party's anti-Muslim orientation can nonetheless come around to approving his kind of more aggressive nationalism when it comes to dealing with Pakistan. On September 18 there was a cross-border attack (presumably carried out by the militant group, the Jaish-e-Mohammed) on an Indian army cantonment that killed 19 Indian soldiers. Modi who had not spoken out even once on what had been happening in Kashmir where the Indian armed forces had been brutally assaulting civilians since July, immediately declared this a terrorist act.[11] Unlike previous administrations

---

10 A. G. Noorani, 'The Secret Accord', *Frontline*, 22 July 2016.

11 In early July a young militant, Burhan Wani, described by the Indian authorities as a wanted terrorist, was killed in a joint operation by the army and Jammu and Kashmir

who for the most part did not publicise such attacks nor their own cross-border retaliations, Modi sought to make as much political capital at home as he could. Eleven days later the Indian army carried out its own cross-border night attack on armed Pakistani personnel. While the Pakistan government denied that any such attack had taken place, perhaps to tone down military tensions, New Delhi released some pictures of the said raid and deliberately publicised it as a 'surgical strike' by a government which unlike its predecessors would more aggressively defend Indian nationalism.[12] The periodic playing of the 'Pakistan card' and the cultivation of Islamophobia by reference to the 'terrorism threat' here and abroad carries a great risk. Cross-border raids from the other side against Indian army camps are very unlikely to stop. Responding militarily whenever such raids happen or even doing so when there are no such raids but simply to teach the 'Pakistan enemy' a lesson for its 'persistent terrorism' can certainly promote the domestic popularity of Modi at times when he feels he most needs this; for example, whenever the forthcoming state elections in 2017 and 2018 are imminent. But since the marginal benefit of raising such calls to rally around the Indian flag progressively diminishes, there is always the danger that the military responses ordered by Modi become progressively stronger and riskier creating precisely an escalatory dynamic of military tit for tat that becomes ever more difficult to control on both sides.

However, if the effort to eventually establish a Hindu Rashtra is to have real chances of succeeding, then it is above all what the Sangh and the BJP government do domestically that counts most. It is this terrain that therefore needs to be examined most seriously.

Basic Strategies

Various steps need to be taken if the desired Hindu Rashtra in substance is to come much closer to being realized. In his first speech after victory, Modi declared his intentions by calling on the public to give him two full five-year

---

police. Immediately after, not only did several thousand people attend his funeral, but protests and demonstrations flared up in Kashmir Valley and were repeatedly fired upon by official forces. What is noteworthy is that the northern army commander, Lt. Gen. D. S. Hooda, made light of the current level of insurgency, saying that, while there were 7,000-odd militants in the 1990s, the figure now for the number of such militants was only around 200. It did not occur to him that this constituted an extraordinarily powerful and standing indictment of the Indian government that today retains well over half-a-million armed personnel of all kinds in Jammu and Kashmir, making it the part of the world that had the worst ratio of civilians to armed personnel. See the interview report by R. Singh, 'This Phase Will Soon Pass, Things Are Calming Down, Says Top Army Commander', *Hindustan Times*, 12 July 2016. Fatal firing on protestors continued for some time, even after this assurance that matters had 'calmed down'. Over the next few months, the civilian death toll rose to over 80, and those injured by army and police firing was well over a thousand.

12 For the escalatory dangers posed by such publicized 'macho-ness', see my '5 Points as to Why the "Surgical Strike" Might Not be the Best Move', September 30, 2016, at catchnews.com.

terms, so that he could carry out a glorious transformation of India. That at the very beginning of his first term he should be asking for a ten-year mandate was indicative of his determination to fulfil a long-term agenda, which is to normalize BJP rule, just as Congress rule at the centre was taken as natural for almost two decades after independence. The transformation he seeks is not so much on the economic front. Here the BJP and Sangh (with some minor internal dissent) will basically follow in the footsteps of their Congress/UPA predecessor governments – namely, the continuing pursuit and consolidation of neoliberalism. It is on the political, socio-cultural and educational fronts that the most serious institutional changes are required if the dream of establishing a Hindu Rashtra (to which Modi is and always has been deeply committed) is to be realized.

First, politically, the state-based (and national) strategy is to try to finish off the Congress and expand BJP influence – hence its call for a 'Congress-Mukt Bharat', or Congress-free India. Nationally this would, if accomplished, further reinforce the view that there is no alternative to the BJP for ensuring stable central rule, no matter what one's reservations about it might be. At the provincial level, this means adopting great flexibility in the forging of temporary alliances for specific purposes, while all the time building from below through the activities of the various Sangh fronts and the RSS *shakas*, or local branches. What may give the BJP hope that the Congress will continue to go downhill is that, in whatever states the Congress was formerly one of the top two parties but then lost this status, subsequently it has never been able to retrieve it. The BJP, on the other hand, despite ups and downs, has made an entry into states where it previously never had a significant presence, even to the point in some cases of now being a major contender for provincial rule. This has been the case in Jammu and Kashmir (where for the first time ever it is part of the ruling coalition), Karnataka, Haryana, West Bengal and Kerala. The assembly elections in 2015 – first in Delhi, which saw the victory of a newcomer, the Aam Aadmi Party or AAP (Party of the Common Man), and then, later in the same year, the victory in Bihar of the regional party Janata Dal United or JD (U), led by Nitish Kumar, the reigning chief minister – were clear setbacks. Subsequent state elections in 2016 in Assam, West Bengal, Kerala and Tamil Nadu saw the BJP come to power for the first time ever in Assam (inaugurating its entry as a major political player into the north-eastern region), and obtain also, for the first time ever, one seat in the Kerala assembly. This geographical extension more than compensated for its failures in Tamil Nadu and West Bengal, where the Left Front's electoral performance was disastrous – worse than that of the Congress, with which it had forged a seat-sharing arrangement in advance of the polls.

Both the BJP electorally and the Sangh politically and ideologically have gained ground upwards and downwards. Shedding its past economic nationalism to become a fervent advocate of economic neoliberalism, the BJP has gained considerably greater support from the corporate world, from social elites and from the top 15 to 20 per cent of the population – the so-called Indian Middle Class (IMC), whose upper sections enjoy, in terms of purchasing power, rough equivalence with the middle classes of the advanced West, and whose lower sections aspire to reach that level, and live in fear of slipping downwards. Support from lower social ranks has also grown. Part of the reason for this is simply the failure of other political forces. But the positioning of the Sangh as a 'protector of Hindus', as a 'guardian of the faith', and the promise of cultural mobility upwards that Hindutva holds out to 'middle castes' (but also for sections of the Dalits and Adivasis) through its invocation of Hindu unity, cannot at all be discounted in a context where daily sufferings, and the alienation they cause, provide fertile grounds for the turn to greater religiosity on the part of a wider public. Many of the elements that make up the discourse of Hindutva have become something of a new 'common sense', widely tolerated and even accepted by a much larger and broader constituency.

The BJP/RSS already has its sights firmly on trying to win the next general election, scheduled for 2019 but which can be called earlier. Success would give the Sangh the space, time and the confident ruthlessness to ram through much more on its larger Hindutva agenda, whatever the opposition, which it could then expect to be even more demoralized. This is where the results of state assembly elections to be held in 2017 in Punjab, Uttar Pradesh, Uttrakhand, Goa and BJP-ruled Gujarat, and in 2018 in Madhya Pradesh, Chattisgarh, Rajasthan (all currently BJP-ruled), will serve as a crucial indicator of its prospects. The BJP must hold fast in the above four states where it is already ensconced, which is quite likely given that its main opposition there is the enfeebled and directionless Congress. But this is not enough. It must make a breakthrough in Uttar Pradesh, whose population would qualify it as the fifth-largest country in the world.

The main players besides the BJP for the February–March 2017 elections in Uttar Pradesh are the SP and the BSP, with the Congress a distant fourth. The BJP will bank on solid votes from the upper castes and substantial sections of the OBCs (since Modi himself is an OBC), and on the non-Jatav sections of the Dalits. The Jatavs are the single biggest subcaste among Dalits in UP accounting for fourteen per cent out of the total twenty per cent Dalit population in the state and constitute, unlike the remaining six per cent of Dalit subcastes, a solid base for the BSP. Moreover, Sangh cohorts can be fully expected to ratchet up communal tensions nearer the polls by various means. These efforts might certainly include the instigation of riots involving injuries and killings, from whose polarizing effects it can realistically expect to derive some benefit. The anti-incumbency factor may work against the ruling SP, which over the last several elections has garnered the bulk of Muslim support and at this time of writing is on the verge of splitting into two parts; one headed by the personally popular Chief

Minister, Akhilesh Yadav, and the other by his father who built up the original SP, Mulayam Singh Yadav. Since Muslims and Dalits together make up almost 40 per cent of voters in the state, the obvious strategy for the BSP's Mayawati is to forge just such a support base, which would make her the front-runner in the electoral sweepstakes. This is, no doubt, why she has decided to field Muslim candidates for the 404 assembly seats.[13] But this means serious rivalry between the SP and BSP, with no guarantee that she can wrest sufficient Muslim support from the former 97 even if it splits Akhilesh Yadav and the Congress are forging an electoral alliance which may well prove enough to win over most Muslims in the state.

But even if the BJP were to lose in Uttar Pradesh, there is still the problem of how to confront it electorally at the national level. It is as yet not clear whether some kind of 'third' or 'federal' front of regional and smaller parties, including those of the mainstream Left, can be formed to challenge the BJP later. The Congress is now much weaker in its ability to act as a hub around which others might coalesce, and the latter may not now even want to elevate Congress importance in this way. Then there is the fact that, in the absence of programmatic cohesion, it is fear of the BJP eventually making inroads into their own regional bases that constitutes the principal glue for bringing these parties together. But who would be the accepted leader and prime ministerial candidate, given that a number of regional leaders in the bigger states consider themselves to have roughly equal if not higher status? Nitish Kumar is not a 'natural' choice. Besides, the BJP will also make efforts to woo some of the regional forces to its own NDA coalition with promises of benefits, should it achieve central rule once again. In such a scenario, defeat for the BJP in Uttar Pradesh would be the most important factor in helping to create the momentum towards stitching together some kind of collective front that could challenge the BJP in the next general election with any reasonable prospect of succeeding.

Second, if the BJP can on its own become electorally more popular than it currently is, then it can expect to attract other regional allies who would also be more compliant. Here the aim would be to obtain enough support to ensure a two-thirds majority in both houses of parliament. This can then allow it via proposed amendments to carry out a substantial reworking of the Constitution, if the better route of calling for a Second Constituent Assembly is not possible. That the the latter idea is being seriously considered in the RSS is a fact. During the Ram Janmabhoomi campaign, one of the key strategists in the BJP was K. N. Govindacharya, a long-time RSS *pracharak*. He dropped out of favour in the BJP because, as a staunch ideologue, he has been a strong critic of the BJP's 'moderation'. Once a bitter critic of Modi, Govindacharya now talks of just such a constitutional re-write, because he

---

13 Ramendra Singh, 'UP assembly polls: BSP nominates 97 Muslim candidates, its highest ever', Indian Express, 4 January 2017.

sees Modi's majority BJP rule as behaving much more in line with RSS aims and ideology.[14] As it is, on July 19, 2016 the Citizenship Amendment Bill was introduced into the Lok Sabha to change the impartiality of the Citizenship Act of 1955 by allowing illegal migrants from certain minority religious communities – namely, Hindus, Jains, Sikhs, Budhists, Parsis and Christians – from Afghanistan, Pakistan and Bangladesh to stay on in India and after a waiting period of six years (reduced from eleven years in the 1955 Act) become eligible to apply for Indian citizenship. Excluded of course are illegal Muslim migrants who can be imprisoned or deported. The Bill is currently sitting with a Joint Parliamentary Committee so final outcomes are yet to be decided. But the intention of the BJP-Sangh is clear – to move towards establishing an automatic 'right of return' for Hindus in south Asia and perhaps later elsewhere. Like Israel's Law of Return for the world's Jews, it is the symbolic aspect that is all important. Most of the Hindu diaspora will, of course, not return for good but the idea that India is essentially a Hindu nation will have been indirectly legitimized.[15]

Third, economically, the aim is to consolidate business confidence and strengthen the support base of the IMC by pursuing further reforms to loosen the play of market forces, while reserving key controversial Hindutva demands – building the Ram Janmabhoomi temple at Ayodhya, repealing Article 370 (not possible without a two-thirds majority in both Houses), pushing a Uniform Civil Code (where the uniformity is much more important than enhancing gender justice for all religious communities) – for later on in this term, or for the second successive five-year term of rule.

Fourth, for a range of issues, predominantly but not solely cultural-ideological, the BJP-Sangh is determined to try and alter *the general terms of public discourse* by use of government-controlled media, through social media activism by Sangh supporters, by the deliberate floating of provocative statements and the carrying out of acts to *test the waters*, as it were, to see how far one can go. There is also a plan to use the states (especially where the BJP is in power) as laboratories for policies that might become national. These are the three legs of its domestic strategic tripod. In regard to the testing of waters and the effort to alter the public discourse, there is a division of labour between the government and the Sangh organizations, whose foot-soldiers, anyway emboldened by the Modi triumph, are to be given substantial leeway in this respect. This leeway includes the use of physical violence and coercion, which except in very rare cases will not invite punishment by law enforcement agencies, subordinated as they largely are to their bureaucratic and political masters. Central to this effort at altering

---

14 V. Gopinath, 'RSS Ideologue Govindacharya: We Will Rewrite the Constitution to Reflect Bharatiyata', 20 June 2016, at thewire.in.

15 See S. Baruah, 'Who Can Become An Indian Citizen?', *Indian Express*, 28 November 2016; and L. Garg, 'If India Wants to Remain Secular, the New Citizenship Bill isn't the Way to Go', 21 September 2016 at thewire.in.

public discourse is the systematic dissemination of propaganda and agitation not only to conflate Hindu nationalism with Indian nationalism, but also to project the BJP and the Sangh as the 'true' upholders of the 'unity and integrity' of the country, and therefore of a distinctively Indian nationalism that can attract those not otherwise sympathetic to Hindutva politics.

Here, the Sangh has made a very conscious assault on the principle of freedom of speech, finding it most easy to get away with this when it is done in the name of curbing 'anti-national sentiments'. Here is where the issues of Kashmir, Pakistan and terrorism come in. Central universities like Jawaharlal Nehru University (JNU) and Hyderabad Central University (HCU) are among the very best in India. Not surprisingly, therefore, they also house substantial numbers of radical students. Many of those in JNU and HCU, in the first half of 2016, held campus meetings protesting the army's behaviour in Kashmir and elsewhere; or called for self-determination in Kashmir; or protested the hanging of one Afzal Guru, who was accused of being a collaborator (on highly contestable evidence) in the 2001 armed assault on the Indian parliament. They have attracted legal charges ranging from unlawful disruption all the way up to sedition; the latter charge being made on the basis of archaic colonial laws that have been retained in independent India. Nor have some of these students been spared from physical assault by Sangh goons, as well. In HCU, the mistreatment of Dalit students by top administrators brought in by the new government led to the tragic suicide of a bright young Dalit scholar, Rohith Vemula, whose extremely moving letter outlining why he was taking this drastic step made national headlines, causing some embarrassment to even the central government. But there was no *mea culpa*, no rectification of the circumstances that had led to Vemula's death, and no concession to student demands to remove permanently the obdurate vice-chancellor of HCU, under whose aegis all of this had happened.[16] In the case of JNU, the anti-national tag against radical left stu-

16 Rather than take serious steps to rectify the conditions in HCU that led to the suicide, BJP officials have claimed that Vemula was not actually a Dalit despite legal evidence to the contrary; as if his not being a Dalit would somehow justify their inaction. In early July 2016, four Dalits were publicly flogged in Una, Gujarat by a squad of some 40 'gau Rakshaks' or 'cow protectors' because they were doing their duty of skinning dead carcasses. In the BJP ruled states like Gujarat and especially after Modi came to power at the centre, the number of such vigilante squads has risen greatly as also their public confrontations with those – mainly Dalits and Muslims – involved in such disposal and other activities related to the leather trade. This attack at Una was videoed and went viral leading to a massive social boycott by Dalits in Gujarat who refused to carry out this necessary function while nationally there was a huge media uproar and widespread condemnation of the flogging by the opposition parties. Though Gujarat has a Dalit population of less than 3 percent, it is in the top half of all states when it comes to the record of atrocities against them. The Gujarat administration under the chief ministership of Modi did nothing to improve matters. Modi made no comment on the incident for nearly a month but when he finally decided to break his silence in a televised address on August 6, he, as is his wont, sought to rhetorically dramatize and exaggerate his 'personal concern', publicly declaring 'shoot me, not my Dalit brothers'. See A. Barman, 'For a Nervous and Angry Modi, the Cow is Now a Political Animal', 9 August 2016, at thequint.com. On the dismal record

dents, rather than arousing mass anger against the injustices done to them, probably enjoyed widespread resonance and acceptance among the general public in Delhi and beyond, since it too had become a 'national' issue. Again, all this took place under the aegis of a newly appointed vice-chancellor close to the Sangh.

The fallout from these and earlier government and Sangh efforts at proscribing free speech (whether in the form of public meetings, film documentaries, newly published books, or otherwise) in the name of preventing or opposing 'insults' to the 'Hindu-Indian' nation has been twofold. First, it has created an atmosphere in which there will be much greater self-censorship on the part of those who would otherwise intervene in the public discourse in support of liberal values. Among the NGOs which have been legally entitled to receive foreign funds there are a few that intervene to highlight human rights abuses or otherwise support progressive struggles in civil society. Some of these have seen their legal sanction to receive foreign funds arbitrarily withdrawn. In general, independent human rights activism is discouraged while the autonomy of the National Human Rights Commission was also sought to be undermined.[17] This is a statutory body comprising a Chair and seven other members which hitherto has always excluded any politician from membership. But for the first time ever this government pushed for a BJP vice-president, Avinash R. Khanna, to be appointed to the NHRC. Fortunately, public pressure led to him withdrawing his candidature and it remains to be seen what the BJP will do next.

There will also be more kowtowing in the media to this government – already noticeable among TV news channels. All this can only help the ongoing effort at 'Hinduizing' the public sphere. Second, the BJP/RSS has decided that presenting itself as the most ardent defender and builder of nationalism against others, less fervent or even disruptive, may be a winning pitch that it should take up in both the forthcoming state assembly and general elections.

Fifth, the government plans to accelerate the assault on Naxalites by

---

of Gujarat, see M. Macwan, 'Atrocities, Discrimination Led to Wave of Anger in Gujarat' in *The Hindu*, July 22, 2016.

17 In early November 2016, the police in BJP ruled Chhattisgarh booked Professor Nandini Sundar of Delhi University and 10 other eminent public intellectuals and civil society activists for the murder of a tribal in the area of Bastar where there has long been a substantial presence of Naxalites. The absurdity of the charge is revealed by the fact that not only was it made several months after the death but that none of the accused were in the Bastar region when the death took place. Though the charge is being contested in the courts and unlikely to get any purchase, not only is there undue legal and financial harassment of the accused but a message of strong discouragement is being sent to other social activists not to carry out investigation of police behavior in Naxal areas. Sundar has worked extensively on Maoism and her petition to the Supreme Court in 2011 succeeded in getting the police-backed vigilante force – the Salwa Judum comprising tribal youth – disbanded as an illegal and unconstitutional body. See R. Mishra, 'DU Professor Nandini Sundar Booked for Murder of Chhattisgarh Tribal', *Hindustan Times*, 8 November 2016; also available at m.hindustantimes.com.

bringing in more para-miltary forces into the picture as well as stationing army training camps in Maoist areas and creating officially sanctioned armed groups, actually thinly disguised vigilante groups from among disaffected tribals. The army is not supposed to involve itself in fighting the Maoists but can justify going after them on grounds that their training activities have been disrupted in one way or the other. In short, this government aims to be even more ruthlessly repressive than the previous UPA governments vis-a-vis the Maoists no matter that this will lead to greater suffering among the Adivasis who constitute the sea in which the Maoists swim

Sixth, there is the effort to suborn the judiciary to the new government. Initially the attempt was to establish a new National Judicial Appointments Commission (NJAC) which failed because of the Supreme Court ruling against the proposed format, which would have given the executive veto powers over appointments at the top courts. While the existing collegium system, whereby Supreme Court judges make appointments at the Supreme Court and High Court levels, is seriously flawed and needs to be changed, the proposed NJAC would have been disastrous. But the central government has not given up, and there is an ongoing tussle over the specific terms of the 'memorandum of procedures' regarding appointments to High Courts up and down the country, whereby the government can try through the back door to block undesired appointees by the Supreme Court collegium.[18] The end result is that necessary judicial appointments have been held up creating an ever worsening backlog of untried cases and with no signs yet of the stand-off between the Supreme Court and the executive ending.

Seventh, is the policy of silent approval and public reprieve. While on some occasions ordinary Sangh activists have been hauled up after public protests against their hate speech, senior BJP members, including MPs and even a union minister, have got away with delivering hate-speeches against Muslims.[19] So it should come as no surprise that BJP governments both at the centre and in the states have gone beyond ignoring and excusing such acts to give reprieves of some sort to senior officials in the party, bureaucracy and police who have proved their loyalty to the Sangh, or to Modi personally, even if they have been legally indicted for their involvement in communal riots, terror bomb blasts, or what are called fake encounters, where extrajudicial murders of unarmed 'suspects' have taken place.[20] A

18 Press Trust of India, 'Executive–Judiciary Relationship in Tatters: Cong', 11 July 2016, at ptinews.com.

19 U. Majumdar, 'Hate Speech Divides BJP in Agra', 4 March 2016, at outlookindia.com.

20 In May 2016, the National Investigation Agency (NIA) dropped all terror-related charges against Sadhvi Pragya Thakur in the Malegaon bomb blast of 2008, in Maharashtra. The then NIA public prosecutor, Rohini Sailan, had earlier in the year withdrawn from this case, stating that she had been pressured to 'go soft on the accused'. On 28 June the Special Mumbai Court nevertheless denied her bail, effectively rejecting the NIA's 'clean chit'. Press Trust of India 'NIA Acted Like "Shield" to Accused in Malegaon Case: Ex Prosecutor', 30 June 2016, at ndtv.com. The NIA also diluted charges against other

former Deputy Inspector General of police in Gujarat, D. G. Vanzara, jailed in 2007 on charges of conducting fake encounters, was released on bail in February 2015. Earlier, when in jail, in his resignation letter from the services, he said of Modi, then the Gujarat chief minister: 'My God has betrayed me.' Implicated as being complicit with Vanzara was Amit Shah then the home minister in Gujarat, and the person closest to Modi from their years together in that state, who is now party chief of the BJP. He was discharged in December 2014 (after Modi became prime minister) by the Central Bureau of Investigation (CBI).[21] The messages being sent by such behaviour are obvious: those pushing the Hindutva agenda by hook or by crook, by aggressive and even violent means, would be protected.

Eighth, is Modi's deliberate adoption of a style of public communication that is declamatory and bombastic but most importantly a one-way mono-logue pitched directly to the public through radio, the print, electronic and social media. On one hand this reflects the fact that Modi is a deeply inse-cure, vindictive and extremely authoritarian personality, who seeks to rule at the centre in broadly the same personalized way that he ruled in Gujarat – by centralizing as much power with himself and a small, trusted coterie that is beholden to him. He consciously sidelines those who might present a political challenge to him. So the Prime Minister's Office (PMO) has now become a major decision-taker for matters that would otherwise lie outside its purview. For all his oratorical skills in Hindi, his mind-set is that of a rigid ideologue steeped in the verities of Hindutva. His general understanding of a range of state policy matters is limited; and he does not possess the sup-pleness of mind or argument that would enable him to respond effectively and immediately in face-to-face encounters with interlocutors determined to carry out serious scrutiny or criticism of his government's views and deci-sions.[22] It is noticeable that he does not bother to attend parliament on a regular basis to open himself up to questioning by opposition MPs, and it is highly revealing that, in more than two years of rule so far, he has not held a single public press conference, as distinct from giving the odd interview to a

---

high-profile figures close to the Sangh, like the RSS member Swami Aseemanand, accused of a bombing in 2007 on the Samjautha Express train, in which sixty-eight people were killed – mostly Pakistani Muslims returning home via the Indian land border destination. In a taped interview with *Caravan* magazine (later denied), Swami Aseemanand had stated that a series of deadly blasts between 2006 and 2008 were sanctioned by the RSS. See A. Swain, 'Why Saffron Terror is Not a Myth', 26 June 2016, at scroll.in.

21 Sabrangindia, 'Controversial Cop Vanzara Asks Sons of Mughals to Quit India', 6 March 2016, at sabrangindian.in.

22 For a recent sober biography, in which the author also carried out a series of personal interviews with Modi but avoided hagiography, and maintained a critical perspective, see N. Mukhopadhyay, *Narendra Modi: The Man, The Times* (New Delhi, 2013). Modi was appointed (not elected) chief minister of Gujarat in 2001 by the Sangh hierarchy without ever having contested any election to public office before that. He had always been the organization man par excellence for the RSS, and then for the BJP. He joined the former in the early 1970s, was deputed to the BJP in 1987, and became general secretary of the party in 1998.

selected journalist. In fact, when he has given a one-to-one TV interview to a critical interlocutor, he has invariably made gaffes of one kind or the other.

On the other hand, this pattern of communication is also a deliberate and calculated one. Modi seeks to present himself to the Indian public as one, who in contrast to his predecessors, is both a man of more humble origins therefore at one with the masses, and also a leader that is more courageously determined to protect and promote the Indian nation. He therefore stands above the government and even his own party as the protector of the people and the very medium through which its collective will is expressed. If this is one personality trait that reminds one of fascist leaders of old, there is another.[23] No other Indian prime minister has sought (in an almost Goebbelsian manner) to inundate the print media and billboards throughout the country with his picture. These reproductions do not simply appear in government advertisements of the schemes he has announced after May 2014, but also for a host of other government schemes no matter how minor. The government-owned All-India Radio national broadcaster carries a monthly political sermon by Modi which community radio set-ups also are encouraged to carry. The PMO monitors the social media on a daily basis and puts out messages on the Twitter accounts of Modi personally and that of the PMO. During the 1975–77 Emergency Rule, an acolyte of Mrs. Gandhi put forward the slogan – 'India is Indira and Indira is India'. Without explicitly saying as much, this is precisely the subliminal message of himself that Modi wishes the Indian public to accept.

The economy

The Modi regime, far from seeking to alter the basic neoliberal trajectory, has sought to reinforce it. The government's budget for 2016–17, released in March 2016, made this amply clear. The fiscal deficit must be reduced while 'incentives' – i.e. tax deductions – must be given to capitalists and the wealthy. So the priorities are to lower corporate taxes; restrain government borrowings; let public expenditure be based on residual tax initiatives, namely more indirect taxes; sell off public assets in part or in whole; reduce public investment; and ease entry for foreign investors.[24] By reclassifying

---

23 The well known political psychologist and social theorist, Ashis Nandy shortly after the Gujarat pogrom of 2002 recalled how, more than a decade ago, he and another social scientist Achyut Yagnik had carried out an interview with Modi, then a small-time RSS and BJP functionary and how disturbed he had been. 'It was a long rambling interview but left me in no doubt that here was a classic, clinical case of a fascist ... I still remember the cool, measured tone in which he elaborated a cosmic conspiracy against India that painted every Muslim as a suspected traitor and a potential terrorist. I came out of the interview shaken and told Yagnik that, for the first time I had met a textbook case of a fascist and prospective killer, perhaps a future mass murderer.' A. Nandy, 'Obituary of a Culture', *Seminar* 513, May 2002.

24 As it is, only around 3 per cent of the population pay personal income tax, and 50 per cent of large companies pay little or no tax. Corporate tax, on paper, is 30 per cent, but is actually 23 per cent or less when not altogether avoided. See V.K. Marla, 'Shhh ...!

budget headings, the Modi government tried to pretend it was enhancing allocations for agriculture, when this was not the case at all.[25] India's agrarian crisis is wide and deep. With banks prioritizing credit for big capital and retail loans for upper- and middle-class households, small and medium farmers have had to turn to moneylenders. As a result, outstanding debt of cultivators to private moneylenders rose as a proportion of total agricultural debt from 17.5 per cent in 1992 to 29.6 per cent in 2013. This government shows little interest in implementing the National Food Security Act, which subsidizes basic food items in the public distribution system, preferring to move towards direct cash transfers for purchases in open rural markets. Agricultural R&D as a proportion of the total agricultural GDP is 31 per cent in India, as compared to 65 per cent in China, 49 per cent in Thailand, 38 per cent in Bangladesh, and 37 per cent in Indonesia. The allocation for the world's largest employment scheme, which comes under the Mahatma Gandhi National Rural Employment Guarantee Act (MGNREGA), is, even in nominal terms less than what was provided previously. This is the case even though, instead of the promise of assured employment for one hundred days each year for all jobseekers being carried through, for a number of states the average is barely forty days – to say nothing of how often there are unwarranted delays in making wage payments.[26]

It is certainly true that it is the Congress that has had the single biggest share of rule at the centre during the last two-and-a-half decades, and must therefore shoulder the bulk of the blame for the highly lopsided character of the Indian economy. Just how bad things are in rural India became clearer after the preliminary results of the first Socio-Economic Caste Census (SECC) were made public in mid 2015. In three out of four rural households, no one earns more than Rs. 5,000 a month, while 56 per cent of rural households own no land. Only 3 per cent of rural households have at least a single member with a graduate degree. Half of rural India is illiterate, and more than half have minimal or no skills in reading and writing. Though the SECC is mandated to visit every rural household, many forest-dwellers, nomadic communities, distress migrants, bonded workers, and so on, escape visitation, making SECC data something of an underestimate of the actual levels of poverty and deprivation.[27] Given all this, where has the Modi government sought to put its particular stamp on Indian economic development? There are three areas: 1) the land question; 2) the opening up to foreign investment, hence Modi's call to 'make in India'; 3) promoting

---

Don't Talk about the Economy!' 8 May 2016, at countercurrents.org. The tax-to-GDP ratio is among the world's lowest – 13.2 per cent in 2015–16, and projected at 13.1 per cent for 2016–17.

25 See the issue of *Frontline* magazine of 1 April 2016, the whole of which is devoted to examining the budget.

26 Ibid.

27 H. Mander, 'Many Degrees of Hopelessness in India's Villages', *Hindustan Times*, 30 July 2015.

labour-market flexibility as the way to generate more jobs, especially in manufacturing and the industrial sector.

The land question

Shortly after coming to power, the Modi government sought to change the Land Acquisition Rehabilitation and Resettlement (LARR) Act of 2013 to make matters much easier for all kinds of private appropriators, investors and 'entities', and not just for private 'companies'. Consent clauses requiring a large majority of the affected population to agree to land acquisition for both private and public–private projects to be set up were to be removed. The range of activities that the private sector could pursue on land acquired were extended, as also was what the government could do under the principle of 'eminent domain'. There were to be no public hearings or social-impact assessments. A number of distinguished economists, including those who are critical of neoliberalism, have supported the need for such government acquisition to help private investment, even if they have disagreed with specific provisions of the 2013 Act, or the proposed Modi ordinance and then Bill. Their central argument is that you cannot avoid 'development displacement', so proper compensation should instead be ensured, with prior social impact assessment to target those affected, while the range of purposes for which acquisition is required for the benefit of private investors should be filtered, avoiding the disruption to productive agriculture caused on land producing multiple crops.

A powerful, but very much a minority perspective is that a pro-market neoliberal government has deliberately decided to become a 'land broker' that is heavily biased towards the private sector, and uses its power to get land for that sector, instead of leaving matters purely to market negotiation between potential buyers and sellers.[28] This is because, in that case, buyer competition would raise prices much higher than government-assessed rates of compensation, and contiguous land acquisition would be jeopardized by a few holdouts, or even one. Finally, farmers and rural groups might simply not be willing to sell their land, either out of opposition to the particular project in question, because of the lack of other earning options, or because possessing land provides rock-bottom security.

The argument of the government's opponents is that a) the government is not being a fair arbitrator, but exercising a not-so-disguised and biased form of extra-economic coercion; and b) this is not a way of promoting an 'agrarian transition' – a process of creating the initial conditions for capitalism – but simply profit-seeking within capitalism, where the land itself is far more important than the labour released for supposedly industrial employment

---

28 See the powerful riposte of M. Levien, 'From Primitive Accumulation to Regimes of Dispossession: Six Theses on India's Land Question', *Economic and Political Weekly*, May 30, 2015.

and development. The experience of what has so far been achieved over the decades by government allocation of land for Special Economic Zones, along with large tax breaks for developers, is quite revealing. Up to December 2014, 491 SEZs were approved. Despite land acquisition having been completed, only 40 per cent are now operational.[29] What is more, there has in the last two decades been a major increase in the levels of exploitation of the country's mineral, forestry and marine wealth for domestic and export purposes. There is the push for industrial farming and the land consolidation that this would require, as also for corporate-controlled farm-to-shop linkages. Similarly, large-scale mechanized trawling is being promoted in coastal waters, as is larger-scale fish and shrimp farming. These efforts to link government to big corporate interests that Modi is keen to strengthen (given his style of governance in Gujarat) have caused immense suffering to the rural poor – particularly to the landless, to Adivasis and fishing communities. Not surprisingly, there has been a rise in struggles among precisely these sections against corporate interests, particularly in mining, and this is a major reason why the Modi government has gone after those progressive NGOs (Greenpeace India, among others) that provide support and a voice to these struggles. If these support structures of popular movements are weakened or destroyed, and their advocates muzzled, then it becomes possible later to pursue the activists directly on the ground.

If the Modi government has had to backtrack on its attempt to amend the LARR Act, that is because of the lack of a sufficient majority in both houses of parliament. However, in keeping with the government's strategy of trying to do at the level of states what it cannot for the moment do nationally, a Joint Parliamentary Committee has been set up and states urged to pass their own laws by making use of loopholes in the central law, which formally cannot be violated by state laws.

Foreign investment

In 2014–15, agriculture accounted for around 17 per cent of GDP; industry for around 30 per cent, of which the contribution of the manufacturing sector was around 17 per cent (a jump from the previous financial year, but no better than what had been achieved in the mid 1970s); while the rest, around 53 per cent, was accounted for by the services sector. For all the Modi hype about 'make in India', the share of manufacturing is not only lower than in China, but also in Malaysia, Thailand and Indonesia. Overall investment has remained stagnant, at around 30 per cent, compared to the peak year of 2007–08, when it stood at 38 per cent. What about FDI inflows and outflows? The inflow was better than the previous year, totalling US $45

29 U. Chatterjee, R. Murgai and M. Rama, 'Employment Outcomes Along the Rural–Urban Gradation', *Economic and Political Weekly*, 27 June 2015.

billion, but outflow was US $30.9 billion. So 26 per cent of the outflow went to the Netherlands, 14 per cent to Singapore, 12 per cent to Mauritius, 11 per cent to the Virgin Islands, and 2 per cent to the Cayman Islands. These are all tax havens of one kind or the other. As for the remainder, Mozambique accounted for 7 per cent, the United States for 6 per cent, the UAE for 5 per cent, and the UK for 4 per cent. As for the inflows, 27 per cent came from Mauritius, 21 per cent from Singapore, 11 per cent from the UK (which has jurisdiction over the British Virgin Islands and the Cayman Islands), 5 per cent from the Netherlands, and 4 per cent from the United States.[30]

It does not take a genius to recognize that these tax havens are serving as conduits for a great deal of round-tripping by Indians making illicit transfers abroad, in order to avoid taxes and capital controls. This includes monies made from bribes and kickbacks, and from human and antiquities trafficking. The government loses a great deal by way of revenue, but pats itself on the back for encouraging foreign investment, a great deal of which is volatile portfolio investment. What is rarely emphasized in the public media is that, between 2004 and 2013, around US $510 billion went out as black money, while between 2000 and 2015, according to the Finance Ministry, India received US $392.2 billion. Multinational enterprises including big Indian corporates were the key culprits in this illicit outflow, using transfer pricing to hide profits and submitting false invoices for goods (misinvoicing for services and illegal private-exchange racketeering has not been taken into account in arriving at the outflow figures), depriving the Indian government of *direct* tax revenues. This is one major reason why the earlier UPA government and Modi's have both pushed for an *indirect* Goods and Services Tax (GST).This proposal has now been passed and becomes official policy but severe problems of fine tuning and implementation remain given that states will lose much of their autonomy to tax and spend in response to changing local needs.[31]

This FDI inflow goes largely to skill- and capital-intensive sectors, so that its employment impact is limited. In descending order of importance, the sectors are services, telecoms, trading, automobiles, software and hardware,

---

30 See Eximbank,'Presentation on India's International Trade and Investment', eximbankinda.in, last accessed 5 December 2016. Owing to the Double Tax Avoidance Agreement between India and Mauritius, incoming flows to India from this 1.2 million–population tax haven island are not taxed; hence the lure of round-tripping for the Indian wealthy. Of all FDI between 2000 and 2015, 34 per cent came from Mauritius – easily the single biggest source of FDI. See G. Sampath, 'The Hidden Wealth of Nations', *The Hindu*, 21 January 2016. See also Y. Aggarwal, 'FDI Reforms: A Lot of Concerns Remain', *Asian Age*, 24 June 2016. Aggarwal points out that, in 2015, China's total stock of FDI was around US $2.7 trillion, or ten times greater than India's. Up to February 2016, FDI inflows into India were mainly in services (US $5.95 billion), followed by software and hardware (US $5.83 billion), trading (US $3.67 billion) and automobiles (US $2.44 billion).

31 G. Sampath, 'Playing Games with the Taxman', *The Hindu*, 11 January 2016; and A. Ranade, 'The Age of GST Dawns', *The Hindu*, 4 August 2016.

pharmaceuticals, and finally miscellaneous mechanical and engineering goods. What has happened is that the Indian pattern of neoliberal development has increased all kinds of inequalities – regional inequality between poorer and richer states, between social classes, and between cities and the countryside.[32] Where FDI goes to reflects and reinforces these inequalities. Maximum FDI goes to Maharashtra, Gujarat, Tamil Nadu, Andhra Pradesh and Karnataka, while select higher-income cities are specifically targeted, such as Ahmedabad, Bangalore, Chennai, Hyderabad, Delhi, Mumbai and Pune. Modi may wish to claim credit for the fact that India, with ninety-seven dollar billionaires, has now replaced Russia as the country with the third-highest number – though it still trails China (430) and the United States (537).[33]

The job deficit and labour market flexibility

The Achilles heel of the Indian economy throughout the period of liberalization has been the enduring job deficit, in terms of both quantity and quality, especially but not only for women. Between 1983/84 and 1992/93, employment increased by an annual average of a little over 2 per cent. Between 1993/94 and 2004/05 this fell to 1.85 per cent, while between 2004/05 to 2011/12 it fell to 0.5 per cent. The latest available data (up to 2011/12) shows a total labour force of 483.75 million, of which 48.9 per cent were employed in the farm sector and 24.3 per cent in industry, with services absorbing 26.9 per cent. The share of females in the labour force was 33 per cent in 2004/05 but had fallen to 27 per cent by 2011/12. This may be partly explained by higher enrolment of females in secondary education, but is still far below the share of female jobs in China and Brazil.[34]

---

32 Taking into account the 12 largest states having eighty five per cent of the population, the gap between the richest and poorest states (measured in terms of per capita net domestic product) has dramatically increased since 1990 when neoliberal policies really took root. In 1960 the top three states were 1.7 times better off than the bottom three but in 2014 this becomes three times greater. Kerala with the highest per capita is now four times richer than Bihar with the lowest. This gap between richest and poorest province within a country is among the highest in the world. Moreover, the overall trend shows a widening and not a narrowing. See P. Chakravarty and V. Dehejia, 'The Gap Between Rich and Poor States', *The Hindu*, 5 September 2016. As for wealth differences, the share of wealth held by the richest one per cent of Indians has gone up from 49 per cent in 2014 to 53 per cent in 2015 to 58.4 per cent in 2016. In 2000 this one per cent held 36.8 per cent of the country's wealth. Their share has risen in just 16 years from a third to three-fifths today. The richest ten per cent of Indians increased their share of the wealth pie from 68.8 per cent in 2010 to 80.7 per cent in 2016. See M. Chakravarty, 'Richest 1% of Indians Now Own 58.4% of Wealth', *Hindustan Times*, 24 November 2016.

33 According to the Human Global Rich List of 2016, twenty-seven more were added in India, out of ninety-nine to the global total. See P. Pandey, 'India Adds 27 New Billionaires', *The Hindu*, 25 February 2016.

34 A. Maira, 'Jobs Growth and Industrial Policy', *Economic and Political Weekly*, 23 August 2014. See also C. Rangarajan, Seema and Vibeesh E.M., 'Developments in the Workforce Between 2009–10 and 2011–12', *Economic and Political Weekly*, 7 June 2014. What the National Sample Survey data show is that 60 million jobs were created between 1999 and 2004 but only 27 million between 2004 and 2010, even though average growth

Uniquely in India, however, unemployment rates rise with levels of formal education. This testifies not so much to deprivation for the educated, but to the lack of marketable skills created by the educational system that, on the whole, is poor in quality as well as failing to serve enough people. In India, among 15 to 29 year-olds in 2011/12, the unemployment rate stood at 19 per cent; for those with secondary level education the unemployment rate was 4.6 per cent; for non-literates it was 2.3 per cent. Moreover, the proportion of those of a working age having secondary education was 19 per cent, as compared to 61 per cent in China, 48 per cent in Brazil, and 46 per cent in Indonesia. But when it came to the proportion of graduates, India, with 8 per cent, had the same rate as China, Brazil and Indonesia.[35]

Modi's stated goal is to raise the share of the manufacturing sector to 25 per cent by 2022, and create 100 million new jobs. He believes he can do this by changing labour laws as they are currently framed at both central and state levels. The aim of these changes is to make it easier for employers to hire and fire, and more difficult for workers to unionise, register, and gain recognition, while easing off on government monitoring of whether firms are observing existing rules and norms in their workplaces. As it is, in 1983 the state of Uttar Pradesh made it easier for firms to retrench workers without having to secure government permission. Where once this freedom applied to firms with less than 100 workers, this was scaled up to include all firms with less than 300. In 2006, Andhra Pradesh removed application of this rule in SEZs, as did Gujarat, where Modi had previously held power. Since 2014 Rajasthan, which is ruled by the BJP, has amended three major laws – the Industrial Disputes Act, the Contract Labour (Regulation and Abolition) Act, and the Factories Act – all in favour of capital.[36]

This is the supply-side formula of neoliberal economic thinking, which has not yet worked throughout the post-1991 'reform period'. What it has done is to increase the proportion of those on contract and of casual workers, even in the manufacturing and organized sector of the workforce. Between 1992 and 2001, the share of contract and temporary workers in Indian manufacturing doubled, with considerable substitution of those directly employed.

---

rates were higher in the latter period and even higher after 2010, but employment absorption even weaker. The latest 2016 quarterly survey by the Labour Department analysing trends in the employment-intensive sectors of textiles, leather, metals, automobiles, gems and jewellery, transport, IT/BPOs, and handlooms and powerlooms (where there is a preponderance of less government-favoured small and medium enterprises) lends further credence to the idea that this is the overall pattern. Its data for the sectors surveyed shows average rates of employment absorption declining even when compared to the low levels of the past. So rates in 2013–15 were worse than those in 2011–13, which in turn were lower than those in 2009–11. R. Jaganathan, 'Growth No Longer Means Jobs', *Times of India*, 11 July 2016.

35 Maira, 'Jobs Growth and Industrial Policy'.

36 See A. Sood, P. Nath and S. Ghosh, 'Deregulating Capital, Regulating Labour: The Dynamics in the Manufacturing Sector in India', *Economic and Political Weekly*, 28 June 2014; K. Chandra, 'Ad-Hocism in the Decisions to Modify Labour Laws', *Economic and Political Weekly*, 26 July 2014.

Between 2003/04 and 2009/10, the number of contract workers among those employed in the organized sector rose by 12.3 per cent, compared to a rise of 5.1 per cent among those directly employed.[37] Real, as distinct from nominal, wages hardly rose between 1990 and 2011, because of inflation, especially in food prices. But higher-ranking staff and managers did very well. According to a study by the Annual Survey of Industries, the share of wages to net value in enterprises was 25.8 per cent in 1990/91, but down to 11.9 per cent in 2011/12. In 1990/91 wages were 64 per cent of total emoluments (which figure includes the additional 36 per cent of salaries, commissions and bonus payments to managers and whose share of total emoluments have been rising over time.); in 2011/12, 46 per cent.[38]

The neoliberal argument for increasing labour-market flexibility is of course that labour itself will benefit through more and better jobs, because 'excessive' protection reduces economic efficiency, raising the cost-burden on firms because of their having to follow cumbersome, outdated and detailed rules. But when one considers that only 3 per cent of the Indian workforce is unionized, while most trade unions are under respective party control, and that 7 per cent are in the organized sector, where most labour laws apply, the idea that eliminating labour-market 'rigidities' in an economy where 93 per cent are in the unorganized or informal sector will generate mass prosperity is the most extraordinary of claims. There are five big union federations: the Congress-affiliated Indian Trade Union Congress, or INTUC (33.3 million members); the BJP-RSS affiliated Bharatiya Mazdoor Sangh, or BMS (17.1 million); the CPM-affiliated Centre of Indian Trade Unions, or CITU (5.7 million); the CPI-affiliated All India Trade Union Congress, or AITUC (14.2 million); and the Hind Mazdoor Sabha, or HMS (9.1 million), formerly affiliated to the socialist parties but now claiming to be independent. Their membership is largely passive, and figures not easily verifiable. But the biggest problem is that these federations are rivals in securing workers' loyalty, making united actions much more difficult, infrequent and short. Meanwhile, their leaders' obedience to party imperatives often trumps collective labour interests. During the Congress-led UPA governments, INTUC did not seriously oppose, let alone stop, the government's neoliberal onslaught. In September 2015 one of the largest ever one-day strikes took place, called by four federations against the Modi government's labour plans. The BMS stayed out of this nationwide stoppage.[39]

It is also true that Indian labour laws have for a long time been observed more in their breach than in their practice by both Indian firms and foreign

---

37 Contractualization in government jobs is growing rapidly. As much as 44 per cent of all government jobs are now temporary, and the ratio is rising, with their wage levels almost the same as those for contractual labour in the private sector. See C. Jaffrelot, 'Solution Is the Problem', *Indian Express*, 24 June 2016.

38 Sood et al.,'Deregulating Capital'; Maira, 'Jobs Growth and Industrial Policy'.

39 G. Sampath, 'Labour in the Twenty-First Century', *The Hindu*, 20 February 2016.

TNCs. Firms get around these 'rigidities' in various ways – through hiring contract labour; shifting state location; leasing in small firms, since, even in the organized sector, most laws do not apply to units having less than ten workers (which, incidentally, account for 97 per cent of all units); sub-contracting former in-house activities; and developing capital-intensive technologies. Contract workers are forbidden in 'core' and 'perennial' activities, but this prohibition is routinely flouted without much fear of ret-ribution.[40] This dismal situation has not stopped the Federation of Indian Chambers of Commerce and Industry (FICCI) and the All India Organi-zation of Employers (AIOE) from circulating a paper, 'Suggested Labour Policy Reforms', that demands further dilution and negation of the existing structure of labour protection – miserably weak both in law and, worse, in enforcement. What employers want – although informal workers enjoy no formal legal protection from the country's 144 labour laws, which are applicable to even non-unionized workers in the organized sector – is the ability to employ ever more informal workers, but without affording them any protection, thus entrenching and legitimizing their status as informal.

The organized workforce within manufacturing is only 10 per cent of those employed, and it is estimated that four-fifths of new jobs created in manufacturing will be in the unorganized sector. The central issue is not what to do about labour market rigidities, but what to do about its huge informal sector of 93 per cent unorganized labour, where 71 per cent of informal workers are given no written contract, 71 per cent get no paid leave, 72 per cent no social security benefits, and 42 per cent are temporary.[41] Neither the Modi regime nor its predecessors have any considered perspective to offer on this front. Rather, the focus is on containing, weakening, and where pos-sible crushing worker resistance from both the organized and unorganized workforce. Contract workers have fought for wage revision, the regulariza-tion of their employment – even while remaining within the unorganized sector – and equal pay for equal work. In modern industry in the organized sector, worker violence has risen as a counter to the increasing violence of employers relying on hired muscle and a police force almost always biased in favour of capital owners and their political and other supporters. The balance of class forces has long favoured capital. In the post-1991 period, the frequency of strikes has fallen, while the average duration of work stoppages has increased. Between 2000/01 and 2009/10, man-days lost to lockouts, at 170 million, far outweighed those lost to strikes, at 84.05 million. For all the talk of an 'inspection Raj' shackling the entrepreneurial

---

40 R. Kapoor, 'Creating Good Jobs: Assessing the Labour Market Regulation Debate', *Economic and Political Weekly*, 15 November 2014.

41 P. Rustagi, 'Informal Employment Statistics', *Economic and Political Weekly*, 7 February 2015. The details come from data compiled by the National Sample Survey Office in their report, *Informal Sector and Conditions of Employment in India*, (New Delhi, 2012).

spirit, the inspection rate in factories fell from 63 per cent in 1986 to 17.8 per cent in 2008. Meanwhile the courts have shifted against labour, giving rulings to curb agitations, demonstrations, bandhs or shut-downs (not officially termed as strikes), strikes, work-to-rules, go-slows, and so on – usually in the name of protecting the rights of citizen-consumers and denying the rights of citizen-producers.

The Modi government is in the process of redrafting various major pieces of labour legislation. But no trade union federations (not even the BJP-controlled BMS) or any other labour organization has been invited to be part of this drafting process. There is a case for rationalization and simplification of what is perhaps the world's lengthiest list of labour laws – not for the promotion of neoliberalism, but for the better protection of workers. Here the National Labour Commission has put forward some sensible ideas about the pruning of these laws, and their reorganization into five clear categories – namely those dealing with a) industrial relations, b) wages, c) social security, d) safety, and e) welfare and working conditions. Of course, there is a vital need to bring vast sections of unorganized, especially casual, workers under the ambit of protective laws.[42] But for this to happen there will have to be struggles from below, as it certainly will not be provided as largesse from above.

Demonetization

The fourth area where Modi has carried out a dramatic change in economic policy, but unlike the three discussed above, this has much more to do with his political ambitions than with anything else. On November 8, 2016, Modi announced that 500 rupee and 1,000 rupee notes would, starting immediately, no longer be legal tender. The declared justification for such a move was that this was the single greatest step ever taken (naturally only by the 'great helmsman' of this administration) to combat corruption and the black or shadow economy caused by bribery and the ill-gotten gains of the crooked, and by the non-payment of taxes on hidden incomes of the wealthy, who by no means are a completely separate category from the former. Considering that by value, this amounts to nullifying 86 per cent of all cash in circulation in the Indian economy, its devastating impact can well be imagined. A grace period of 50 days up to December 31, 2016 was given for the general public to deposit such notes in their accounts in banks and post offices up to a certain total limit not exceeding Rupees 250,000 (anything more would arouse suspicion of being black money holders who would then be investigated). Such notes it was said could also be directly exchanged for existing 100 rupee notes, again up to strict daily and weekly limits per person. Since bank penetration is overall only around 53 per cent

---

42 Chandra, 'Ad-Hocism'.

of the adult population and therefore a huge chunk of the working population do not have bank accounts, the result has been a significant slowing down where there is not altogether a halt to the daily and weekly earnings and activities of many of the poorest sections of society especially in the informal sector.[43] Huge queues appeared at banks and ATMs throughout the country further disrupting work patterns and reducing production. All this suffering was greatly exacerbated by the fact that not enough new notes of 500 and 2,000 (there are to be no new 1,000 rupee notes) had been printed in preparation for this move. Indeed, it became clear soon enough that several more months running well into 2017 would be needed to print out enough notes as banks regularly ran out of enough cash to meet daily and weekly demands and had to shut down repeatedly. Despite Modi's public promise on Nov. 8 that the limit for direct exchanges of 500 and 1,000 rupee old notes after November 24, 2016 would be raised, all direct exchanges (though not deposits) of these old notes were in fact abruptly ended after that date – evidence of how badly prepared his administration and the Reserve Bank of India (RBI) had been. Clearly, there was far from enough printed supply from government mints to meet immediate, let alone short and medium term needs in the future. Certain payments for government utilities like water and electricity, for college and school fees for hospital treatment were still allowed in old notes but even here refusal by receiving bodies was common while limits were also imposed on how much of one's *own money* one could withdraw from banks – an extraordinary violation of a citizen's financial freedom and right. No other country has ever demonetized so suddenly and on such a scale. The full scale and depth of the negative economic consequences caused by this demonetization will only become clearer well into 2017.

The early responses of most of the media and of the general public was to applaud the move even as it would cause some hardship. However, as the ill-prepared character of the move became clearer and the general suffering more extended in time, there was a growing sense even among the media that its implementation left much to be desired, and that it might turn out to be a gamble that could cost Modi politically while the economy, despite government assurances to the contrary, would go into some kind of a downspin of as yet uncertain duration or degree. But if there is to be a greater public awareness of what the really important purposes behind the move are then the official reasons given for demonetization – fighting corruption and attacking the black economy – have to be shown as quite misleading.

For a start, is Modi, the anti-corruption crusader, himself untainted? In an explosive article, Paranjoy Guha Thakurta, the editor of the prestigious *Economy and Political Weekly* said 'Documents seized by the Income Tax

---

43 See A. Pathak, '10 Reasons Why BJP's Demonetization Is An Unmitigated – And Politically Motivated – Disaster', 14 November 2016 at huffingtonpost.in.

Department in private corporations imply pay-offs were made to the PM and leading politicians' when Modi was chief minister of Gujarat.[44] According to these official documents individuals associated with the founder chairman Subrata Roy of the Sahara Group of companies distributed some Rs. 115 crore between May 2013 and March 2014 – the months leading up to the 2014 general elections – to Modi, Shivraj Singh Chouhan, the chief minister of Madhya Pradesh, Raman Singh, the chief minister of Chattisgarh (both were then and currently are BJP-ruled states), Shaina NC, the treasurer of the BJP in Maharashtra, and Sheila Dikshit, the former Congress chief minister of Delhi. However, the income tax department and the Central Bureau of Investigation are not carrying out any investigations while there were rumours that the government had a 'cover up' plan ready claiming that an angry employee of the Sahara Group made up these documents to blackmail the boss, Subrata Roy. The NGO, Common Cause took the matter up with the Supreme Court requesting that it order an investigation. Given the immensely high stakes involved and perhaps mindful of the message that would be sent even if it ordered an initial probe, the SC ruled that the documents provided could not be authenticated beyond all doubt and refused the request.[45]

All major political parties get unaccounted funds from the private corporate sector with the exception so far of the AAP party. During Modi's campaign for the 2014 general elections he made anti-corruption a major plank feeding on the national furore created by the Anna Hazare and Kejriwal led campaign of 2011. On his first day in office on 28 May 2014 Modi set up a special investigation team (SIT) under a retired SC judge to look into black money. The most important discovery by this SIT was malfeasance of the Adani Group of companies based in Ahmedabad, Gujarat whose chair Gautam Adani, is known to be very close to Modi. It was Adani's chartered plane that Modi used in his campaigning around India. This Group, allegedly through over-invoicing of imports, is said to have stashed away over Rs. 5,000 crore in tax havens abroad. The Enforcement Directorate (ED) of the government was pursuing the case but after Modi's ascension at the centre the officer heading the Ahmedabad branch of the ED was removed while two senior officers in Mumbai overseeing the investigations were forced out of the agency.[46]

As for dealing a major blow to the black or shadow economy, it is nothing of the sort. Estimates of the black economy in India vary from a low of

---

44 Paranjoy G. Thakurta, 'Did Modi Receive Over Rs. 55 Crore From the Sahara Group as the Chief Minister of Gujarat?', *Economic and Political Weekly*, 19 November 2016

45 K. Rajagopal, 'SC Refuses to Order Probe into "Sahara-Birla Papers"', *The Hindu*, 26 November 2016.

46 See J. Joseph, 'Modi, Adani and Black Money. Where's the Investigation Going?' excerpted from his book *A Feast of Vultures: The Hidden Business of Democracy in India*, (Noida, 2016) and also available at thewire.in.

around 22 per cent (still much higher than most other economies) to a high of over 70 per cent of GDP.[47] There is black wealth and black cash that is circulating in and outside the white or legitimate economy. Black wealth is held as gold and jewellery, real estate, or sent abroad with some resting in foreign accounts and some of it round-tripping back in laundered form for making investments in the legitimate economy. This black wealth, which is the biggest component, is unaffected by demonetization. The cash component – black money – is only between five to six per cent of total black assets and even a large part of this cash will get laundered.[48] To seriously weaken the hold of the black economy several other measures would need to be taken such as arresting and indicting the really big guns who illegally transfer funds out, tackling real estate speculation, gold hoarding and trading, the financial nexus between politicians and corporates regarding election funding, policy-related bribery, the kickbacks in major arms deals, the mass scale of tax avoidance (only 3 per cent of Indian pay personal income tax and the tax to GDP ratio is a low 16 per cent), and so on. In fact, what Modi has done is to divert attention away from the real sources that generate black money and assets.[49] Why then has he taken such a step?

Modi was the principal organiser in Gujarat for the Ram Janmabhoomi campaign and the skills he showed then were to propel him soon enough to a national-level status as organiser and secretary within the BJP. In that campaign various means were adopted to somehow give ordinary households and individuals a sense of belonging and participation, and therefore a stronger emotional investment in the great political cause of erecting a Ram Mandir at Ayodhya, even as they were not going to be activists involved in campaigning or in the processions and street mobilisations around the

47 The low estimate is by a World Bank Study by F. Schneider, A. Buehn and C. E. Montenegro, *Shadow Economies all Over the World* (Washington, 2010) also available at documents.worldbank.org This study is up to 2006/07. Another study carried out by the Indian government's National Institute for Public Finance and Policy commissioned in 2014 estimated the size of the black economy as 70 per cent of GDP. Despite being a confidential report it was accessed by sections of the media and thereafter widely cited. See the interview of Arun Kumar by M. Roshan, 'This is Tough, But Done For The Wrong Reasons' 16 November 2016 at caravanmagazine.in.

48 Interview by P. Ball with former chief statistician of India, P. Sen, 'Demonetisation is Not Going to Curb Black money ... It's Like an Income', *The Asian Age*, 20 November 2016. According to one report, Indians living in India in 2015–16 illicitly exported US $83 billion, second only to the Chinese. M.Guruswamy, 'How Modi Played his Trump Card', *The Asian Age*, 10 November 2016.

49 The criticisms of why demonetization will not succeed in seriously curbing the black economy are growing. A good starting point for understanding the nature of the black economy and why this is the case, see A. Kumar, *The Black Economy in India* (New Delhi, 2014). Also P. Patnaik, 'Demonetisation: The Lies The Government Weaves As It Abandons Reason', 23 November 2016 at thecitizen.in. For a summary of outside responses by the likes of Larry Summers, the *New York Times,* the *Economist* and others see, Gayeti Singh, '"Worst Mistake of PM Modi's Career": World Media and Economist Decry Demonetization Havoc in India', 23 November 2016 at thecitizen.in. The *Frontline* issue of 9 December 2016 titled "Monumental Blunder' on its cover, carries a range of articles criticizing the manifold implications and consequences of demonetization.

issue. Collecting small (even very small) amounts of money from households visited by Sangh cadres, calling for a brick or material to be gifted for eventual building of the temple, or requesting a couple of chapattis to be cooked and given to feed marchers in a procession due to come around nearby – these were all ways of making this emotional connection wider and stronger. This demonetization, precisely because it affects almost everyone, has allowed Modi to appeal to, and nourish, the class resentment that the vast majority of the public naturally feels towards the wealthy few who flourish the most in the black economy. It is not that this rich segment will suffer greatly or that their future involvement in such activities will end once matters settle down with the new notes in place; or that the black economy will collapse. What is important is the short-term perception that just as Modi has declared war on Pakistan sponsored terrorism on the foreign policy front, he has now on the economic front declared another kind of war on a widely accepted evil and is calling for mass support for a nationalist cause. Even though the traditional base of the BJP and Sangh – the small and medium entrepreneurs and traders who are outside the tax net will be hit with different degrees of severity – this political loss is more than made up if Modi can succeed in swinging the vast majority of poorer Indians into supporting and admiring him. In the last twenty years the social base of the BJP and Sangh has extended upwards from its traditional base. If he can now substantially extend this support downwards he will have done what no other leader of the Sangh Parivar has succeeded in doing. Corollary short term benefits are certainly not to be sniffed at – can the Modi persona, amplified by the media in its various forms, be enough to give the BJP electoral victory in UP? Even if demonetization creates widespread disillusionment with the BJP *after* the UP elections, this will be more than bearable providing the BJP either wins or becomes the single largest party in UP. Of all the main contending parties there, only the BJP has not projected any single local leader as its candidate for chief minister-ship of the state should it win. The BJP is banking on Modi who has already started doing what he likes most – going on the campaign trail in UP.

However, insofar as this politically motivated step of demonetization has created and is creating economic turmoil and widespread hardship of a kind that was never anticipated by Modi or by his small coterie of key advisers, this is one gamble that could rebound against him even before the forthcoming elections of Spring 2017. Modi may well wish to make another populist gesture like announcing that to alleviate public hardship a certain sum, say Rs. 10,000, will be deposited from the exchequer in all Jan Dhan accounts but it is doubtful if this can be carried out before the Spring elections or even whether the government will do so afterwards. This is because it would mean raising the fiscal deficit which will warn outside investors not to come in and would also go against the grain of current neoliberal economic policies. But for short term politically expedient reasons it remains a possibility. In August 2015, Modi announced his Jan Dhan Yojana (Peoples Money Scheme) for financial inclusion of the poor, namely the members of 75 million households hitherto without bank accounts. The scheme was to open up zero-balance accounts in mainly the nationalized banks that could then be accessed for savings deposits, insurance, pensions and limited overdraft facilities. By June 2016 some 200 million such accounts were said to have opened up but about one-third were duplicate accounts of those already having other accounts. There are also a very large number of inoperative and dormant accounts continuing to have zero-balance or just one rupee as a face saving addition by the banks themselves. The total cost to the government of such a move would be inconsequential given its overall budget but it will certainly not compensate in any way for the damage done by demonetization to the economy.[50] But perception is all, and it here that Modi wants to win the battle. Whether or not his political gamble of demonetization succeeds remains to be seen.

Communal efforts

It is in the domain of public culture and education that the forces of Hindutva have always marked themselves out from all other parties and political currents. The previous NDA governments, in which the BJP did not have a decisive majority, had to move more cautiously. The Modi regime has been much more determinedly aggressive. And it is in this domain that the three-pronged strategy – testing the waters, altering the terms of discourse, using the states as laboratories – has been most actively deployed. At times, when the public reaction, domestic and/or international, has been strong enough to make Sangh initiatives politically counterproductive, some measure of damage control has been attempted – through carefully moderated criticism of a kind that will not put off the Sangh's core constituency of hard-line Hindutva-ites.

In regard to educational and cultural institutions of all kinds, the plan is simple: to put Sangh loyalists into positions of control and authority in each case. This is done wherever such appointments are to be made by the central or state governments (where the BJP is in power); or, where this cannot be done directly, to use government pressure. Coming under the scope of the Sangh, then, are heads and senior personnel of central and state universities and research institutions; bodies empowered to determine the content of textbooks for government schools at central and state levels; cultural academies of various kinds; archival centres; training institutes, from the select and prestigious Indian Institutes of Technology to those institutes producing film and television graduates; censorship boards, and so on. Besides this,

---

50 See A. Srivas, 'Twenty Crore Bank Accounts Opened', 3 May 2016 at thewire.in After demonetization was announced many of these accounts received a sudden influx of deposits indicating that in large part through middlemen and for a small commission these accounts were being used by black money holders to launder their hoards.

the Sangh has its own network of schools (the biggest such private network in the country), whose curriculum it can substantially determine and then have approved by its own state governments. In July 2016, the central government announced that it would institute a cultural mapping of artistes of various kinds into three categories – 'Outstanding', 'Promising', and 'Waiting' – for the purposes of sanctioning official funds and trips abroad. This, of course, is a way of introducing its own system of patronage to win over loyalty from within the cultural sector.[51]

Since the Sangh does not have a penumbra of intellectual heavyweights around it, too many of its appointments lack essential credentials, or even credibility as serious scholars or administrators, thus arousing public criticism and sometimes strong opposition within the institutions, as for example in the case of the Film and Television Institute of India, JNU and HCU. More specific protests by university students against interventions by either BJP governments or the RSS student wing, the ABVP, which seeks to suppress their freedoms of association and speech, have taken place in Allahabad, Benares and Chennai. Such public criticism is usually dismissed as coming from politically motivated figures comfortable with earlier dispensations, which were highly biased and routinely appointed leftist intellectuals. In short, what the government is now doing is rectifying an earlier bias. On the whole, this counterargument is not very persuasive, because too often the mediocrity and unsuitability of various appointments is so blatant. But that is not stopping the Modi government from going ahead with what has rightly been called its 'long march through educational and cultural institutions'.

It is of course easier for the Sangh to carry out this strategy at the level of BJP-ruled states. So the Haryana government has made readings from the Bhagavad Gita compulsory in schools. In Gujarat, in the autumn of 2014, nine new books were introduced into 42,000 elementary schools, free of charge, as supplementary readings (for the grades from one to twelve, that is, up to the completion of high school). They are the work of Hindu right-wing ideologues. Dina Nath Batra, an RSS *pracharak* and head of the 'Shiksha Bachao Andolan Samiti' (a Hindutva body, whose name when translated reads as the 'Committee and Movement to Save Teaching') wrote eight of them. Batra has been instrumental in pushing the Bhagavad Gita

---

51 Planned for September–December 2017 is a jamboree organized by the RSS's cultural wing, the Sanskar Bharti, that will be the Sangh's version of a Nobel Prize ceremony. If each Nobel Prize is worth 8 million kronors or Rs. 6.24 crore, the total worth of all the Indian prizes to be given away will exceed that, amounting to Rs. 68.7 crore. These eleven prizes will be named after eminent Indian personalities – Mahatma Gandhi for the category of Human Rights, Buddha for Peace, Sardar Patel for International Unity, Kalidas for Literature, Aryabhatta for Science, Adi Shankaracharya for Social and Spiritual Unity, Bhimrao Ambedkar for Social Upliftment and Harmony, and so on. This event, to be repeated every three years, will be held on the campus of Benares Hindu University. The purpose is to woo intellectuals of high calibre, and to present the Sangh as the dedicated and true admirer and guardian of national pride and stature.

into the curriculum in Haryana, and was responsible, through pressing lawsuits against their publishers, for the ban on Wendy Doniger's *The Hindus: An Alternative History*, in February 2015, and for forcing Orient Blackswan to withdraw Megha Kumar's book on the Ahmedabad riots, *Communalism and Sexual Violence: Ahmedabad since 1969*. His own books carry a foreword by Modi, which states that his 'inspirational literature will inspire students and teachers'.[52] Modi himself has publicly declared that ancient India had mastered the transplantation of body parts (though he referred to it as 'plastic surgery'), and wrote the preface for another book of Batra's which declared that stem-cell research and travel by aeroplane were a reality in ancient India, as revealed in Hindu epics.[53] In Madhya Pradesh, the *surya namaskar* – morning invocation to the sun – has been introduced into the curriculum of government schools, and was made compulsory. This was also the case in Rajasthan, which sought to extend it to private schools, though court rulings have since clarified that this can only be optional.

On 31 October 2015, a five-member committee comprising four bureaucrats and one favoured academic was set up to bring out what is now called the T. S. R. Subramanian Committee Report, to serve as the basis for a new education policy. It was submitted on 27 May 2016 to the government, which has not so far made it public, arousing suspicions that, before widespread public scrutiny and discussion is possible, but after consultations with some state governments, it might be quietly finalized and pronounced as policy. The drafts were to be sent to state governments, but the education minister Ashok Chowdhary, of the non-BJP government of Bihar, pointed out that no draft had been sent to his office, even as the former central human resources and development minister, Smriti Irani (now replaced in a recent cabinet reshuffle), castigated Bihar for not sending in its suggestions. However, the report was procured by *Frontline* magazine, and two of its recommendations are particularly disturbing. It talks of the necessity of 'value education' being integral to teaching. This is a long-standing obsession of the Sangh, and is shorthand for inculcating and indoctrinating Hindutva values and beliefs in school children from early on. At the

52 Gaurang Jani, professor of sociology at Gujarat University, has said: 'The move to infuse right-wing ideology in mainstream curriculum has been started by printing books with a religious bias using taxpayers' money. If the books are received without major opposition in Gujarat, they will introduce such books at the national level as well.' See R. Kumar, 'Hindu Right Rewriting Indian Textbooks', Aljazeera, 4 November 2014, at aljazeera.com.

53 On 25 October 2014, at a gathering of medics, while inaugurating the H.N. Reliance Foundation Hospital in Mumbai, Prime Minister Modi said: 'Mahabharata says Karna was not born out of his mother's womb. This means people then were aware of genetic science. There must have been a plastic surgeon who fixed an elephant's head on Ganesha.' See 'Modi @Reliance Hospital Opening: 'Plastic Surgeon May Have Fixed Elephant's Head on Ganesha', 25 October 2014 at rediff.com>news. See also A. Mukul, 'Ancient Gyan Is New Edu Policy?' *Times of India*, 22 December 2015; also available at timesofindia.indiatimes.com.

university and tertiary level, the report calls for curbing student involvement in politics, meaning that educational institutions should effectively ban or otherwise prevent such activities. This can clear the way for the ABVP, which is affiliated not to the BJP but to the RSS which claims to be a cultural, not a political organization.[54]

Outside of education, there is the sphere of public argument and moral norms. What do we find here? There is an attempt to push a Hindu agenda of some kind on various fronts. The ground is being prepared for a national ban on cow-slaughter. Many states already have this ban, but some have gone further, extending it to bulls and bullocks. After the Modi accession, Maharashtra has just carried out this extension. There is no ban on having beef in the home, but Mohammed Akhlaq was assaulted and killed by a mob of Hindus in his home in Dadri village, not far from the capital region, based on the mere suspicion of his possessing beef. While this incident made international headlines and provoked widespread condemnation of the barbarity, it also had a religiously polarizing effect locally. Rationalizations of and excuses for this heinous act were offered by senior BJP leaders, and calls made for a wider discussion about the need to respect Hindu sentiments; as if such an injunction could justify condoning this cold-blooded murder or the soft-pedalling of criticism of it. Once again, the aim is, to make respectable in public discourse the kind of rationalisations that would once have been thought outrageous.[55] Meanwhile, eggs, an important source of protein, were removed from midday school meals in Madhya Pradesh – yet another example of the Sangh's 'food fundamentalism'.

The 'Ghar Wapsi' or 'homecoming' programme has gained momentum, and is much more openly espoused by the organizations and footsoldiers of the Sangh since Modi's victory. Despite the constitutional provision for freedom to practice religion, which includes the right to propagate, it is subject to restrictions concerning not just forcible conversion, which is justifiable, but also for conversion by 'fraud' and 'allurement' – terms that are

---

54 Between 2003 and 2013, the ABVP grew in membership from 1.1 million to 2.2 million, and after the 2014 election victory jumped to around 3.2 million, making it the largest student body in the country. It has 9,800 units in universities and colleges throughout the country. It is stronger in the northern Hindi belt, but also in the non-Hindi speaking states of Karnataka, Telengana, Andhra Pradesh, Maharashtra and Gujarat. It is weakest in Punjab, Haryana, Tamil Nadu, Kerala, West Bengal and the north-eastern states. At the national and apex levels, the top posts are held by RSS members or *pracharaks*. The ABVP's main messages to students are preserving the unity and integrity of the country, opposing Naxalism and 'anti-national' intellectuals, the indigenizing of syllabuses to reflect traditional values, i.e. those of a Brahminically influenced Hinduism. See D. Tewari, 'Behind ABVP's Confidence, Govt. and Growth', *Indian Express*, 24 February 2016.

55 'Controversial Statements by BJP Leaders on Dadri Lynching Incident', *New Indian Express* (online), 4 October 2015, at newindianexpress.com. Among the leaders cited were Mahesh Sharma, the union cabinet minister for culture, Sanjeev Balyan, the union minister of state for agriculture, Sakshi Maharaj, a Hindu religious leader and BJP MP from UP, and Sangeet Som, a BJP member of the UP state assembly.

ill-defined, and therefore a proscription much more difficult to justify. In fact, this vagueness allows for arguments and rulings that charitable and educational institutions, particularly of Christians operating in Dalit or tribal areas, constitute a form of fraud and/or allurement, and are therefore illegal. Although Christians, according to the last Census, in 2011, comprise only 2.3 per cent of the population, Christian-run networks covering the areas of education, recreation, and social and health services, account for more than 20 per cent of all such autonomous structures in civil society – many being among the best in their respective fields, and therefore a challenge to various Sangh institutions and their efforts to expand their influence by addressing the secular needs of the public. Moreover, though these institutions at the apex remain under Christian or church control, the large majority of them offer widespread employment to members of all communities, while their services are available to all. Their presence in fact constitutes a powerful secularizing force, and presents an obstacle to communal forces. For this reason, as well as the concern over possible conversions in tribal and poor rural areas, Christians, even though they are such a small minority, are an anathema to the Sangh.[56]

Seven Indian states have anti-conversion laws on their books, which are clearly aimed at preventing conversion of Hindus by imposing various restrictions, such as having to seek prior permission from designated authorities. There is also a certain correlation between states having anti-conversion laws and those having a higher frequency of attacks on Christians.[57] 'Reconversion' to Hinduism is not considered a problem in the same way; indeed, the anti-conversion law of Chattisgarh is explicitly amended to allow for this. The 2006 bill passed by the state assembly and as yet neither affirmed nor rejected by the central government says that the return of a person to his ancestor's religion or own original religion is not a conversion. This 'reconversion' to Hinduism is accompanied by a purification procedure – clearly implying that the prior, non-Hindu religion is a form of impurity! A senior minister has called for a debate on whether there should be a national anti-conversion law. Another way of testing the waters was the claim made in February 2015 by RSS chief, Mohan Bhagwat, that Mother Teresa's charity work was primarily motivated by the desire to convert. Here, given the furore that then emerged, damage control was exercised, and there was no further stoking of these particular embers.

There have been a number of other areas in which communalist provocations have been carried out by the Sangh. Christmas Day has been renamed 'Good Governance Day'. Rakhi, a Hindu–Sikh custom with a somewhat patriarchal flavour, celebrating the protection of sisters by their brothers, was declared a national holiday in August 2015. There has been a deliberate

---

56 See A. Vanaik, 'Step Back, Christian Soldiers', *Telegraph*, 8 November 1999.
57 See CSW briefing, 'India: Anti-Conversion Legislation: Summary of Concerns', *Christian Solidarity Worldwide*, November 2006, at cswusa.org.

attempt to appropriate certain Congress leaders, such as Madan Mohan Malaviya and Sardar Patel, and even Gandhi, all of whom who did subscribe to some Hindu nationalist ideas. The more explicit secular nationalism of Nehru makes his appropriation in the same way untenable. The purpose of these selective appropriations of Congress leaders is obviously to refurbish the image of the Sangh as the country's historically most staunch nationalists, although the RSS consciously chose to remain outside the greatest expression of Indian nationalist commitment – the struggle for independence from British rule. The attempt to appropriate Ambedkar as someone who shared certain Hindutva views flies in the face of all that he wrote and believed in. But this is considered politically necessary to win over Dalits to the Sangh fold – a tactic that has not been without some success.

On Republic Day 2015 there appeared in the media government advertisements of the preamble of the Indian Constitution, which referred to the pre-amendment version where the words 'secular' and 'socialist' were absent. Uproar led to this being declared an 'accident', but then the union minister of telecommunications, Ravi Shankar Prasad, called for a public debate on the issue of secularism in the Constitution, indicating that, once again, this had been a deliberate testing of the waters. The new government appointed P.B. Acharya, a former RSS *pracharak*, as governor of Assam. Though occupying a seat that is officially supposed to be non-partisan, he has lost no time in declaring that 'Hindustan is for Hindus', and that, while Hindus leaving Bangladesh are welcome as 'refugees', poor Muslim migrants are not; the usual term to describe the latter – a term that now has widespread and unthinking currency in mainstream Indian media – is 'infiltrators'.[58]

One area where the Sangh, like most conservative right-wing currents worldwide, finds it less easy to win over adherents is with regard to its moral policing. In the Indian context, this leads to public intimidation of even Hindu women adopting what is considered 'Westernized' behaviour and dress. More open and relaxed interaction between the sexes (celebrating Valentine's Day, for example) and greater freedom in the matter of sexual orientation is also opposed. But here the Sangh is more on the defensive. While the media generally approves of the right-wing turn economically and politically, including in foreign policy, this approval is also generally accompanied everywhere by a greater endorsement of 'social liberalism'. That is to say, together with neoliberalism comes a market-based notion of 'freedom as choice' – in other words, the pursuit of a more personalized, consumerist lifestyle. But in India there is one area of moral policing that is less frowned upon, precisely because of the ideological inroads made by Hindutva – the contrived and artificial anger against 'love jihad', or the claim that Muslim

---

58 See Times News Network, 'Hindustan is for Hindus: Assam Guv', *Times of India*, 22 November 2015.

men are luring Hindu women into love marriages, thereby endangering, among other things, the Hindu population, since the Muslim rate of reproduction is deemed greater than that of Hindus. This is an absurd argument, but it nevertheless has wide appeal.[59]

Businesses, which often include crony capitalists favoured by the government, have an aversion to large scale-riots or pogroms, which are disruptive and negatively impact investor confidence home and abroad. The strategy has therefore been to shift towards the promotion of smaller-scale communal incidents of various kinds, where the injury and death count is low, and more likely to escape the radar of the national media, but still has a strong if localized polarizing effect. Nevertheless, there has been a higher frequency of attention-grabbing incidents of communal violence since Modi came to power. Apart from the killing of Akhlaq in Dadri, of a Muslim youth and software engineer, Mohsin Sheikh in Pune on June 2, 2014, are the killings of the two rationalists (who had reported earlier threats from right-wing extremists to the police, but to no avail) G. Pansare in Maharashtra, in February 2015, and M. Kalburgi, in nearby Karnataka in August 2015. At the time of writing, none of the culprits have been brought to book. Churches have been attacked in the capital region, while, according to an *Indian Express*, report there were 600 communal incidents in Uttar Pradesh in the ten weeks following the May 2014 general elections.[60]

Shortly after his victory, Modi ordered the Information and Broadcasting Ministry to start carefully monitoring issues trending in the social media. In particular, there was to be a close vigil on people tagging Modi by name in blogs, tweets and Facebook posts. This obviously creates the possibility of data being passed on to intelligence agencies like the Intelligence Bureau, whose former head, A. Doval, is now the National Security Advisor at the PMO; to the Research and Analysis Wing; and to the Central Monitoring System, which is a clandestine electronic mass-surveillance data-mining programme. Modi has not proposed privacy legislation that would protect personal data from abusive use by government authorities.[61] In fact, a stronger surveillance state is being constructed. An earlier measure instituted by the previous UPA government is important here. This was the effort to give each citizen a unique identification number and card, courtesy of

---

59 According to the 2011 Census, since the last census, in 2001, the Hindu population had declined by 0.7 per cent, to 79.8 per cent of the total, while that of Muslims had risen by 0.8 per cent to 14.2 per cent, the percentage of Christians remaining the same. The fall in the fertility rate of Muslims is greater than that for Hindus. The anti-conversion programme of Hindutva is not just dangerous and dishonest on its own terms, it is also hype. See Firstpost, 'India Has 79.8% Hindus, 14.2% Muslims, Says 2011 Census on Religion', 26 August 2015, at firstpost.com.

60 A. E. Suresh, 'Express Investigation Part-I: Over 600 "Communal Incidents" in UP Since LS Results, 60% Near Bypoll Seats', 9 August 2014 at indianexpress.com.

61 For a sample of the most viciously communalist public statements made by Modi before his premiership – and never retracted – see the carefully documented essay by legal expert A.G. Noorani, 'India's Sawdust Caesar', *Frontline*, 25 December 2015.

the Unique Identification Authority of India, on the basis of quite detailed personal information on each person's mobile nos., occupation, residence, family details, and so on. This is also called the 'Aadhar' card. In one respect, this is part of the neoliberal project of facilitating the targeting of welfare schemes, to avoid universalizing such benefits. The effort to make it *compulsory* to have such a card in order to receive certain benefits has not been stymied by the Supreme Court. But the process of expanding the net of Aadhar card–holders is going on, as is its linkage to certain consumption rights, even though these cannot technically be denied to non-card-holders. The real danger is the database that will result. Despite official assurances that this huge reservoir of personal information will not be misused, in the Aadhar legislation as it stands there are no guarantees of recompense against possible misuse, while crucial exceptions are laid down that can allow secret surveillance and the elimination of the assumed privacy of those investigated. District judges (who, unlike judges at higher levels, can be much more easily pressured by the government) can sanction access to this database for the government without disclosure to or discussion with the person or persons affected. Furthermore, a joint secretary authorized by the government can do the same 'in the interests of national security'. There is also no public or independent oversight committee to monitor the operation of Aadhar. All this is a clear violation of the UN Report of 2014 on 'The Right to Privacy in the Digital Age'–but so what![62]

The long-standing 'Trishul' (Trident)

What about the three major demands that the BJP and the Sangh have long made? These are calls for the abrogation of Article 370, for the implementation of the Uniform Civil Code (UCC), and for the construction of a huge Ram Temple at the very site in Ayodhya where the Babri Masjid was destroyed in defiance of the Supreme Court and the Constitution. These demands have not been abandoned, but placed on the backburner. In one sense, they have served their main purpose. These demands generated a huge swell of support, and fed into a process of mass mobilization that succeeded in propelling the Sangh into the power it now holds. But until the Sangh and BJP become so dominant that they can change the Constitution (for which they will need two-thirds support in both houses of parliament), they cannot abrogate Article 370. This Article formally provides for very considerable autonomy for Jammu and Kashmir. In any case, in practice that autonomy has been greatly eroded. But since, for Hindutva, Muslims (who are in a majority in that state) must prove their loyalty to India by giving up claims to special treatment, abrogation will remain a longer-term goal. Meanwhile the permanent state of emergency and armed repression of Muslims in Kashmir Valley continues.

---

62 See C. Arun, 'Privacy Is a Fundamental Right', *The Hindu*, 18 March 2016.

As for pursuing a UCC, the reason for raising this demand has never had anything to do with concern for Muslim women and children, but was a way of highlighting the differential treatment of Muslims, which was therefore 'unfair' to Hindus. Uniformity for the purposes of 'national integration' was the theme being played upon, the implication being that Muslims, by not 'integrating', were weakening the country. Moreover, by constantly evoking the issue of a UCC in judgements concerning disputes over Muslim personal law, but rarely in disputes over Hindu personal law, the judiciary has reinforced the communal view that Hindus have reformed their laws, setting a standard for others, while minority communities not carrying out such reform are somehow anti-national.

Political Hindutva has no commitment to a genuinely gender-just UCC. In fact, a UCC would necessitate the abandonment of many current Hindu laws and practices regarding marriage and divorce, succession, matrimonial property and adoption rights. For all its talk of a UCC, the women's wing of the RSS has never involved itself in the generation of more gender-just laws, as the broader women's movement has sought to do. The kind of common civil code acceptable to it would be based on Hindu codes interpreted in a loosely Brahminical fashion. In such a situation, not surprisingly, the very idea of a common civil code is seen by large sections of the Muslim population as motivated by anti-Muslim sentiment.

Today the issue has become so deeply communalized that secular progressives have become divided and ambivalent about this vexed issue. Among progressives, there are currently factions favouring four different approaches:

1. Introducing a compulsory common code, irrespective of what it is called – a UCC, a common civil code, a gender-justice code, or whatever. The anti-women aspects of all personal laws should be done away with, while certain inoffensive customary and cultural practices can be retained. All persons would be governed by such a code.
2. Providing a UCC that would be optional, not compulsory. In a first variation, the civil code exists alongside personal laws, and it can be accessed at any time in one's adult life. A second variation assumes everyone is born under a common civil code, but can at any time opt to be governed by a particular personal law – what has been called 'reverse optionality'. This would actually legitimize a reactionary choice, weakening efforts to move society in a more progressive direction.
3. Amending existing personal laws in line with gender equality. Formulating a common civil code should be avoided. And these amendments should emerge from within the community in question when they are able to command widespread support.
4. Retaining personal laws and operating a common civil code, but passing a number of laws cutting across personal laws in specific areas – for example,

a common matrimonial property act applicable to everyone. A start in this direction could be made by taking up those areas where personal laws have nothing to offer, such as in access to matrimonial property, matters of domestic violence, the compulsory registration of marriages, and so on.

Not all of these positions are mutually exclusive. One might ultimately want a compulsory UCC but prefer an optional UCC for the time being. Or one might prefer a phased, piecemeal legislative approach, rather than a package legislation. The common ground is that all progressives agree on changes in gender-unequal provisions, whether in personal or existing secular laws. This emphasis on having the 'best' secular and personal laws also undermines the perspectives of political Hindutva, which cannot tolerate such a dramatic transformation of Hindu codes – although these have been reformed to a greater extent than has Muslim Personal Law.

There is little disagreement about how such laws and provisions can be formulated – through the active involvement of feminists and progressive women's groups, female disputants with respect to personal laws, and legally skilled personnel. There is more disagreement about how such laws will be brought into force – which agencies will be responsible, whether their intro-duction will be phased, and so on.

While all movements of social reform within a religious commu-nity should be encouraged, can they alone determine the availability and scope of the best secular laws? The answer seems obvious: they cannot. If current circumstances render a compulsory common civil code communally counterproductive, as a transitional measure there could certainly be the institutionalization of a 'best' optional civil code, whether legislated piece-meal or in a single package. Anyone can opt for it at any time, its provisions being superior to personal law or tribal custom in any matter of dispute. Such an approach is politically practical in the short term, and would rep-resent a significant advance for secularism over what exists today. It is a perspective that the Left and progressive parties, for example, could collec-tively mobilize around.

But the ultimate goal of a common civil code applicable to all must be maintained. Religious and customary laws (which are community-based) cannot be reformed to be compatible with modern notions of equality and liberty without losing their character as recognizably religious–traditional laws. Nor should the diversity and plurality of Indian society be made an excuse for justifying the existence of a permanent plurality of personal laws.

Once a universally applicable body of democratic law governing family life, gender and interpersonal relationships within a country has *replaced* the bulk of religious and customary laws, it can through a process of constant reform be progressively made more open, tolerant and accommodating of changing social mores. It is an illusion to imagine that one can achieve such a 'body of law', cultivating an open-ended, tolerant and plural legal structure, through some process of stitching together various personal laws, which can somehow each be reformed so as to be compatible with modern democratic principles of jurisprudence. Undertaken in the name of preserving plurality and diversity, it will rationalize and disguise the existence of the principles of hierarchy and patriarchy that are to be found in all pre-modern systems of community laws and codes. An important recent article points out that the state of Goa has a common civil code that is secular. It was imposed by the former colonial administration of Portugal in 1910, but has been accepted by all religious communities in that state, and could serve as a template for the country as a whole. It would need to be updated and significantly amended to take into consideration more modern forms of property and the more egalitarian principles that are now supposed to guide conjugal relations and their possible break-ups. Its key features (which would be unacceptable to the Hindutva brigade) include the compulsory registration of marriages to *precede* any religious ceremonial sanction; communion of assets, legally giving women an equal share in their husbands' assets; equal treatment of sons and daughters; 50 per cent of assets going to children ; deed of succession; registration of wills – and so on.[63] The Goan example highlights the fact that anti-patriarchal breakthroughs can *follow the prior imposition* of secular laws. It has not eliminated patriarchal behaviour in Goa and it denies freedom of personal judgement regarding disposal of one's assets after death, but there is far more protection for women and children there in law and practice.[64]

Finally, it has proved more difficult, certainly at an all-India level to mobilize people to help build a Ram Temple, beyond the make-shift one that currently exists and which, although illegally constructed, no government at the Centre has had the courage to remove. It was easier to mobilize negative emotions of hatred and anger at an all-India level against a symbol of presumed injustice. Of course, the temple's eventual construction would make it the most powerful symbol of the pre-eminence of Hindutva in India, and it will therefore remain a cause to be pursued. As might have been expected, after the electoral defeat in Bihar but before the state assembly elections of 2016 in Assam (which the BJP won), West Bengal, Tamil Nadu and Kerala (all four went to separate regional parties) the VHP in particular has sought to raise the communalist temperature by bringing building material

---

63 The Goa code applies only to marriages registered in Goa. Regarding inheritance by children, in the absence of a will, 50 per cent of assets of the deceased will go to the spouse and the remaining to other legal heirs, presumably children. In case there is a parental will, 50 per cent goes to the surviving spouse, 25 per cent to children and the remaining 25 per cent as per the will. This does mean that the freedom to dispose of one's estate through a will is restricted which can also be considered undemocratic. A deed of succession is a formal decree by a civil court that those so identified are the legal successors entitled to the estate of the deceased. This is required whether or not a will exists.

64 See P. R. deSouza, 'Politics of the Uniform Civil Code in India', *Economic and Political Weekly*, 28 November 2015.

to Ayodhya for the construction of the temple, while the RSS and BJP – in the typical Sangh style of giving different messages to different audiences – have stated that they are going to wait for the long-pending Supreme Court ruling.[65]

Though this *trishul* has been deployed to arouse mass grievances and anger against India's Muslims, the longer-term aim of the Sangh is not to create a civil war situation in which there might be mass genocide on a scale to match what Hitler did, or what the colonial powers carried out against the inhabitants of Africa or the New World. At any rate, that is not the intention of Hindutva, which is instead a) the establishment of a Hindu state in all but name – one that reinterprets democracy to mean a majoritarianism in which 'Hindu interests' are to be prioritized; and b) the permanent inferiorization of Muslims and Christians in India. The latter should understand that they live in a 'Hindu India', all the stronger culturally and politically for being so. If they can accept this quietly – or, better still, collaborate in the construction of the project – then they can get on with their lives as second-class citizens. Otherwise they will have to face the consequences!

Confronting Modi and the Hindutva Project

There are points that must be borne in mind in the effort to confront and defeat Modi specifically, and the Hindutva project generally. First, this is a long-term struggle. Second, it is a struggle that has to be fought primarily at the level of civil society. Yes, government authority in the hands of Hindutva forces at the central and state levels is a serious danger in its own right, as well as a powerful contributor to communalist expansion and consolidation beyond it, in society at large. But merely replacing the Modi government at the centre, or the BJP provincial governments, welcome though all this would be, is not enough. Hindu communal prejudices and practices are too deep and widespread, and have themselves reinforced Muslim communal behaviour and mobilization, creating a certain action–reaction cycle.

There are thus two strategies – one for the short to medium term, the other for the longer term. The more immediate one is to erode the credibility of the Modi regime and that of the BJP state governments, and help replace their rule. The longer-term one is to bring about the steady secularization of Indian civil society, and the institutions and practices it comprises. However, one must not separate either the shorter-term or longer-term struggle from the wider struggle against neoliberalism, and for greater democracy and social justice in all forms – in other words, from the pursuit (incremental or otherwise) of measures to bring about a more foundational transformation of Indian society and polity.

---

65 PTI News Service, 'Ayodhya: VHP's First Lot of Stones for Ram Temple Arrives, Police on Alert', *Indian Express*, 21 December 2015.

The great weak spot of the Modi regime was pointed out earlier. His inability to provide enough decent jobs to meet the basic livelihood requirements of the large majority of the population may be his undoing. Modi has cleverly sought, both during his election campaign and after, to place periodic references to the goals and values of the Hindutva agenda within a broader, repetitive discourse of development for all – hence his slogan: 'Good days are coming!' He knows that he is more likely to make significant advances in carrying out that communalist agenda if he can also succeed in providing greater mass prosperity. It is therefore here, in the gap between the promise and the performance, that mass discontent will grow over time. But if this is the necessary condition, it is not a sufficient one for translating discontent into strong opposition to his regime. Here, living politics will come into play. In times of turmoil – and there will be very considerable turmoil – the danger always arises of the Sangh being able to find a way of diverting mass anger at governmental failures. A constructed 'nationalist anger' against domestic and/or external scapegoats can be a powerful force – a possible prelude to the imposition of greater authoritarian rule from above.

What are the ways of combating it? One is for progressive forces to try and usurp the developmental and nationalist discourse. The emphasis cannot just be on opposing Hindu nationalism or condemning neoliberal globalization, but must also spell out the features of an alternative 'democratic nationalism'. At the first level, it means politically ensuring freedom from fear of physical assault on grounds of caste, class, gender, religion, race, and so on. At a second level, it means promoting the personal dignity that comes from respecting, and therefore institutionalizing different cultural rights and freedoms in the name of cultural empowerment and equality, so that the message driven home is one of cultural and national inclusiveness, as against the promotion of a cultural essentialism. The late Benedict Anderson used to say that either one treats nationalism as an inheritance – as something belonging to the past – in which case there will always be disputes about what is the 'proper inheritance' and who are the 'proper inheritors' (which can easily escalate to produce bitterness, hatred and violence); or one sees nationalism as an ongoing political project belonging to the present and future, in which case nationalism is what we will make of it. This is all the more necessary now that the Hindutva brigade is very consciously and systematically trying to usurp the banner of nationalism per se. In confronting this manoeuvre, the key is the creation of a far more secular and democratic, and therefore inclusive, nationalism than exists today – so that more and more citizens recognize, contra Hindutva, that there are and must always be different ways of being Indian.

At a third level, it means calling for the highest priority to be given to establishing a minimally decent life for all. This means going beyond the 'poverty discourse' to demand the provision of decent jobs that can provide basic sufficiencies of food, shelter, clothing, education, healthcare and leisure. The purpose of putting forward what is currently a wish-list is basically to up the ante – to seize the discourse of development and redefine what development means, and thereby also to highlight unjustified inequalities of income, wealth and therefore of power. This is necessary because it is not so much absolute levels of misery, but comparative dissatisfactions (much more easily generated, given the mass-communication tools of our time) that provide the stronger impulse to popular action.

This does not mean that the specifically communal dimension must not be addressed. To secularize civil society in India does require a diminution of public religiosity.[66] Rationalist and popular science movements have been an important tool in the effort to secularize Indian society, but the discourse on Indian secularism has not sufficiently respected this need to develop scientific reason or promote a popular 'scientific temper'. Certainly, the Hindutva brigade understands this better than many secularists, bending over backwards to try to find all kinds of virtues in religious discourses, even where these do not exist – hence the Sangh's calculated assaults on rationalists.

The most effective way to promote the various themes of secularism is not always to do it directly. The secular discourse is a subset of the wider discourse of democracy and equality. It is this discourse that is most important, and should be ideologically promoted. How the major principles of a secular outlook should be promoted is related to how best to organize the propagation of a general democratic discourse. One major aspect of the discourse of secularism has to do with emphasizing and justifying the necessity of a secular state. This theme should be directly propagated in myriad ways. The message here is that the existence and strengthening of a secular state is a necessary but not sufficient condition for the existence and strengthening of a democratic system.

The other, even more important aspect of this discourse has to do with the secularization of civil society – the ways in which religious loyalties must accept a more modest role, and come to terms with secular institutions, affiliations and norms of functioning. Here, the motifs of privatizing and optionalizing religion mean more than merely a basic separation of religion from the state. These are not themes that lend themselves to any direct agitprop approach. Indeed, this would be counterproductive. It is the actual institutionalization of greater democracy, social and gender equality and economic progress in civil society that is most important. This is why I have argued above that progressives must redefine development to show even more starkly the limitations of the Modi regime. Progressives can have differences about how much weight should be given to such exercises and efforts in the overall secularizing strategy of confronting the forces

---

66 See the section on 'Unprincipled Proximities and Personal Laws', in Chapter 3.

of political Hindutva in civil society, since this enterprise will lead to false accusations that secularists are anti-religious when the effort to promote the ideology of secularism is really part of the larger project aimed at promoting democratization of thought, behaviour and institutions. But it is not an arena that should be ignored.

In the forging of progressive forces – parties, movements and groups – is there a place for Congress and non-BJP parties? In regard to the Congress, it is important to recognize that it has itself paved the way for the rise of Hindutva, and has not hesitated to play a 'soft Hindutva' card from time to time. It must therefore not be seen as a *strategic* ally against Hindutva. If the Congress cannot ever align with the BJP, this is simply because to do would be its death knell. A fundamental distinction must be made between seeing it as the BJP's competitor for power and as a serious opponent of Hindutva politics, which it is not. And it is the latter that counts most. Much the same can be said for the other regional parties. Unlike the Congress, which historically has been the central point of national reference, regional parties have at various times accommodated to and made alliances with the BJP. This has been for pragmatic reasons, but again reflects the weakness of their supposedly secularist commitments. No tears should be shed, then, for the decline of the 'secular' Congress. This decline has created the space not just for the right but for centrist forces and for a rejuvenated Left to grow. But what about the newcomer – the Common Man Party, or AAP?

The newcomer

A centrist push has come from the newly formed Aam Aadmi Party (AAP), or Common Man Party. The AAP was basically thrown up by the largely urban-based, middle-class anti-corruption movement that erupted in April 2011 and lasted for more than a year, with especially large mobilizations in Delhi. The symbolic leader of the anti-corruption movement was a culturally conservative Gandhian, Anna Hazare, who runs a 'model village community' in Maharashtra. But the real organizers were the group around Arvind Kejriwal, a former civil servant turned social activist. The campaign ended with a Congress promise to pass an Act setting up a powerful and independent monitoring body and Ombudsman to check corruption. Unlike Hazare, who places himself above party affiliations, Kejriwal and his cohorts felt that a new party had to be created to cleanse the body politic, and that the time was now opportune. In late 2013, the AAP was formed (after much grassroots activity) precisely to fight state assembly elections in Delhi at the end of December 2013, very much with an eye to the forthcoming general elections.

Eschewing the presentation of a full-fledged programme, the AAP concentrated on opposing corruption, including the illegal corporate funding of parties, or bribes for personal or policy favours.[67] It cleverly produced seventy local manifestos for each of the seventy assembly seats in Delhi, focusing on concerns such as protection against crime and harassment, and the cheap and adequate provision of water and electricity. It used the internet and social media innovatively to make transparent its own funding through high-volume small donations directly from the public, as well as for getting across its party messages and recruiting members for a nominal fee. Large numbers of middle-class youth and professionals of all ages joined it in Delhi, while it also had a national impact. To the surprise of all, it won twenty-eight seats to the BJP's thirty-two and the Congress's eight in the Delhi assembly.

Initially insisting it would never take support from either the Congress or the BJP, it took the reins of the Delhi government with the Congress's agreement, only to resign after a stint of forty-nine days on flimsy grounds, essentially because it wanted to concentrate on mass campaigning in the general elections. President's rule on Delhi was then imposed, with the Congress and BJP both wanting to wait till after the general elections before calling for the capital's next assembly elections. The AAP's basic strategy, even before it fought the Delhi elections, was that its breakthrough there (it was hoping to get a majority on its own) would give it the credentials to fight the general elections, where it could then hope to make a dramatic showing by garnering between twenty and forty Lok Sabha seats through simultaneous recruitment and campaigning on a mass scale. With such a performance, the AAP could expect to become a major contender for government by the 2019 elections. The assumption was that a political breakthrough would not have to come through the slow accumulation of members and credibility through years of activity, or through proof of performance at the provincial level. Rather, sheer mass disillusionment with both the BJP and the Congress would immediately produce a wave in favour of the new anti-corruption party.

This particular gamble failed. The electronic and mass media that first strongly welcomed it turned against it, citing its flip-flop in Delhi, which had also dismayed many of its own supporters as well as other onlookers. Even as it declared itself in support of the market system and capitalism generally, the AAP's decision to attack crony capitalism – and therefore some of the biggest business houses in the country – alienated the corporatized media. The fact that the AAP also saw itself as a movement-cum-party that would regularly resort to protest actions like mass sit-ins to press its demands made it suspect

---

67 Only the vaguest idea of what AAP stands for can be gathered from the main political document, a pocket-sized book of 145 pages, authored by its principal leader, Arvind Kejriwal, called *Swaraj* (Noida, 2012). This is a somewhat rambling text whose principal thrust is that decentralization of power to the municipal and *panchayat* levels is the key to solving all major problems of the people – a modernized version of Gandhian perspectives.

according to elite standards of 'sobriety'. Moreover, standing candidates in over 400 constituencies meant there was little check on their quality, with only Kejriwal having national brand recognition. Its comparatively minimal resources were also stretched to the limit. It obtained a nationwide vote share of 2.3 per cent, and only 4 seats (all from the state of Punjab); not bad, perhaps, for a first-time entrant, but way below its expectations.

Nevertheless, being a fresh, seemingly honest and untainted force that had yet to be tested, it continued to enjoy credibility in the capital region, and swept the February 2015 Delhi elections (obtaining sixty-five out of seventy seats), to the considerable shock of the BJP and of Modi himself, who put his personal reputation as vote-catcher on the line by personally campaigning strongly in these local elections in a way that no previous prime minister had ever done. Despite starting off so brightly and now having a full five-year term of incumbency, the AAP was soon faced with external and internal problems. Internally, the lack of democratic transparency in functioning (Kejriwal is accused, with some justice, of often being author-itarian) led to a split, inconsequential in numbers, but made more publicly significant and damaging by the departure, amid mutual criticisms, of some of its high-profile figures, including the progressive Supreme Court lawyer, Prashant Bhushan, and the internationally known academic and former public spokesperson for the party, Yogendra Yadav. Both were also part of the original 'brains trust' that had set up the party in the first place.

Externally, given the peculiar arrangement for Delhi, whereby there is a division of power between the lieutenant governor of Delhi and the Delhi assembly and executive, the cooperation of both is required if successful policy formulation and application over a whole range of areas is to take place. The lieutenant governor, Naseeb Jung, (replaced in January following his resignation for personal reasons) was seen by AAP as largely following the dictates of the central government, thereby acting as a powerful and deliberate constraint on the party's capacities to fulfil its policy promises to Delhi residents. There is much merit in this argument, but AAP is also seen as guilty of making unwarranted excuses and seeking to shift the blame for its own failures and difficulties. So BJP hostility is a large part of the story, but not the only factor. On the whole, the AAP is still being tested in the public eye, and no definite verdict as to its future prospects can yet be pronounced. But its performance in Delhi has generally been better than that of its predecessors. Through subsidies, electricity bills have come down, as promised. There is easier access by the public to government officials, including to the top party echelons. An important start has been made in delivering on the promise of establishing 1,000 Mohalla or neighbourhood health clinics, with doctors regularly tending to the local communities and providing free or cheap supplies of medicine.

Having learned from its 2014 fiasco of standing candidates everywhere, the AAP has now developed a more promising strategy. It will proceed more slowly, focusing on the two states of Punjab and Goa – particularly the former. Punjab suffers from multiple crises – agrarian problems, including soil erosion, a rapidly declining water table, huge and rising debt burdens on small and middle peasants; mass drug consumption among the youth; utterly inadequate health and higher-education facilities; and social exclusion and oppression of Dalits, who constitute 30 per cent of the population, which is the highest in any state. Disillusionment with the ruling SAD-BJP coalition, and memories of Congress failures in the past, mean the Aam Aadmi Party, which has campaigned actively in the state, is poised to become the biggest electoral force. Success for the AAP would give it the springboard to become the most likely centrist replacement at the national level for the Congress, and the Congress and the BJP understand this. What favours the AAP now and in the future is that it remains as yet untainted by its past performances.

How will it evolve programmatically? What seems clear from its efforts so far is that it aims to present itself as a 'non-ideological', pragmatic, problem-solving entity. It deliberately retains an ideological fuzziness ('neither left nor right', say its leaders) and aims to challenge both the Congress and the BJP, but particularly the latter. If it can only do so by outflanking both not from the right but from the left, it still remains unclear how far to the left it will tack. After the departure of Yadav and Bhushan, both more social-democratically inclined, it is more likely that AAP will remain within the confines of a neoliberalism with a human face.

There is a lesson here to be learned from the experience of Latin America, where, in Brazil, Bolivia and Ecuador, new parties have developed out of social movements based on the factory working class and/or the poor peas-antry and/or the indigenous population. This gave those parties a solid core base whose concerns were reflected in their programmes and social character of their activists. Operating from this position of relative strength, they then sought to attract sections of the middle class. The AAP trajectory has been the reverse. First attracting middle-class activism, it has sought to extend its appeal downwards. It wants to grow as a movement-cum-party, but also wants to avoid sharp class and caste conflicts – in short, to be a something-for-everybody, centrist force. Whether it will survive and grow as such, whether it can be pulled significantly leftwards, or whether there will be a substantial left-directed breakaway grouping that wants to engage in more transformative class actions from below, are still imponderables. As for secularism, this is a language the AAP generally avoids, though it will make references to abiding by the Constitution. Some of its earlier leaders have left to join the BJP, while the party has no compunctions about welcoming into its ranks former BJP members. It is certainly opposed to communal violence, and has not so far played the religious card in the way that the Congress has often done.

The only political force then that has been consistently and ideologically committed to opposing Hindutva, despite its pragmatism and sometimes unprincipled behaviour, is constituted by the parties of the Left. This much is clearly understood by the Sangh, which is why it cannot appropriate figures of the Left as it can those of the Congress or other parties; why it identifies communists along with Christians and Muslims as the 'external' enemies of Bharat; and why there can never be formal alliances with it, such as the BJP has had with other regional parties like the Janata Dal and BSP – or even quiet offers of support, such as the BJP has extended to the Telegu Desam or AIDMK, and would be willing to extend to the DMK if the merry-go-round of shifting alliances permits it. What is possible are alliances on *specific* issues between the Left and the Congress and other regional parties against the BJP and Sangh. There is even room for various trade union federations to join with the BMS on specific issues concerning the labour movement. Just as for elections, tactical agreements of various kinds can be forged. Weakening and reversing the electoral trajectory of the BJP/ Sangh is obviously a short- and medium-term necessity. But this is very different from believing that there can be a long-term strategic alliance between all or most current anti-BJP forces to defeat the Hindutva project.

Indeed, what has been argued here is that the struggle to decisively de-communalize Indian society cannot be separated from the struggle to transform the whole of India in a far more egalitarian and democratic direction. To the long-term transformative project of Hindutva, nothing less than a long-term project of counter-transformation, and not just resistance, is required. This raises the question that even secular progressives in India hardly ever pose: Can this 'decisive de-communalization' and 'sufficient secularization' of Indian society, and therefore the establishment of a 'strongly secular state', be achieved within the framework of Indian capitalism, or is this effort tied to the pursuit of an anti-capitalist and socialist alternative? Here the issue of regenerating the Indian Left necessarily comes in not as a precondition, but as itself a process of possible development emerging out of this very pursuit.

What this implies is that the longer-term struggle to defeat Hindutva and the broader neoliberal project requires the emergence of a much stronger Left that can act as the principal hub of a wider network of forces to carry out this task successfully. Once the issue becomes not just one of anti-communalism but one of anti-capitalism, or more precisely the need to pursue an alternative to it even if the shape of the end-state or goal is far from clear, then opposing Hindutva becomes connected to making the case for that socialist alternative, and to the building of an anti-neoliberal front as the transitional programme. Some tentative thoughts in this regard will now be presented, in the hope of generating a wider and deeper discussion.

Secularism, Socialism, and the Building of an Anti-Neoliberal Platform

Although civil society in India is weak, its institutions are developing. It is an area of contestation in which consciously secular forces are weak and lack backing from a state that has not sought to mount any serious challenge to the expansion of religious influence outside its domain. The struggle lies between, on the one hand, an expanding, self-confident political Hinduism and an orthodox Islam engaged in a powerful operation of retrenchment within a psychologically besieged Muslim community, and, on the other hand, the secular mechanisms of expanding market relations, modern technology and science, corporate and non-corporate bureaucratization, urbanization, and class divisions and struggles in industry and agriculture. In crucial areas of civil society, such as education, health, recreation, welfare services, the private media, and even trade unions and political parties, secularization has been extremely slow and uneven. In the face of all this, it is disturbing that Indian secularists are mostly prepared to ignore civil society in favour of a one-sided stress on strengthening the secular nature of the state, hardly supplemented even by ideological campaigns in support of a secular interpretation of Indian nationalism.

What was possible in the West is not possible in India. The struggle to defeat communalism decisively, to eliminate it as a danger, is inseparable from the struggle to dismantle capitalism and replace bourgeois democracy with a deeper socialist democracy. Why should this be so? Is this claim not a retreat to a Marxist dogmatism that has been clearly refuted by reality – a return to a utopian millenarianism that has been in practice the source of a tragic ideological and political totalitarianism? These are large issues, and to make a case for a Marxist vision of socialism in the new millennium – after 1989 and all that – would take us far from our immediate area of investigation. Suffice it to say that the most powerful assault on the idea that liberal-democratic capitalism is the 'end of history' cannot but make recourse to the wellsprings of classical Marxism, to its analytical resources and its alternative vision of the future. Far from being outdated, the quest for a global alternative to capitalism is made more urgent than ever by the three evils of mass immiseration and horrendous inequalities when there is no longer a global scarcity of resources to address them; the possibility of nuclear or biological warfare; and the ecological crisis which, like the prospect of nuclear/biological war, for the first time ever threatens the very existence of part or all of the human species.

In India, the connections between its specific forms of capitalism, liberal democracy and communalism are so strong that progressive secularization can no longer be confidently visualized as the more or less inevitable outcome of an Indian 'long march' of capitalist modernization and liberal-democratic consolidation. Under capitalism, a necessary but by no means sufficient condition for secular advances in civil society – especially in the fields of health, education, child care and recreation – is the creation of a strong welfare state on the model of the best of the western European countries, although these welfare states have now themselves run into deep trouble. Strong welfare states were never a gift from above, from a prospering capitalist or ruling class, but everywhere represented the fruits of the pressure that a well-organized and united labour movement could bring to bear on a given state or ruling-class order. In the countries of advanced capitalism, where the relationship of forces between capital and labour has been historically inclined in favour of the former, as in the United States, welfarism has been the weakest.[68]

In India, which has a claim to having one of the most fragmented labour movements anywhere, state welfarism, to the degree that it was encouraged, was the result of the Nehruvian social-democratic vision. That era is now gone for good, and in the new climate of market-friendly economic development even a prolonged Indian economic miracle will not lead to a substantial welfarism from above. In fact, the established trend is towards the further privatization of healthcare, education, social security insurance, and so on. In such a situation, the existing division of responsibilities between the capitalist state and religious institutions in civil society is likely to be strengthened. Religion as a social power has always derived much of its strength from its ability partially to redress material and secular needs. Such an order reinforces particularist religious (and caste) loyalties. Hindu communalism has the material infrastructure of the RSS and its offshoots; orthodox Islam, too, has its own infrastructure of religiously controlled schools, sports clubs, cultural organizations, presses, credit agencies, work cooperatives, and so on, while more financial resources are coming in from the reactionary Islamic states of the Gulf region.

If capitalism knows how to utilize existing divisions to ensure its reproduction and stabilization, bourgeois democracy reinforces communal divides, since effective political competition means subordinating normative ideals to the practical task of the successful organization of pressure. It means moving along the path of least resistance, mobilizing on the basis of existing identities and given levels of consciousness. If caste and religious community feelings and structures are already strong and socially effective, then these are likely to be reinforced by the way in which electoral competition operates. This has been the Indian experience, where even centrist, 'secular' parties have sought to work with, rather than against, more overtly communalist bodies.

---

68 B. S. Turner is among the few writers to have stressed the structural differentiation in respect of 'existential dilemmas' of how religious responses to 'meaning of life' questions tend to be more intellectualized for dominant classes and more mundane – related to questions of health, terrestrial power, security and wealth – for socially more insecure and oppressed classes. His 'corporeal sociology of religion', influenced by Foucault, insists on linking existential questions to the biographical history of our bodies. The theory and practice of health is thus linked to the theory and practice of religion. B. S. Turner, *Religion and Social Theory* (New Delhi, 1991).

A long-term programme for de-communalizing India must give the highest priority to the building of secular counter-institutions in civil society, and to promoting a more secular popular culture. To erode in this way the social importance of religious identity is to seek democratization in its classical rather than 'liberal' sense. It implies the progressive erosion of power differentials between individuals and between groups, whether that power is social, economic or political in form, and whether the groups are classes, castes or other communities.

If the limited form of empowerment provided by national citizenship can be so corrosive of religious loyalty, or so effective in pushing religious and religio-political structures into a more wary and respectful appreciation of it, then it is not unrealistic to believe that qualitatively higher levels of such empowerment can further narrow the space of religious loyalty – or else push it in a direction where the value of religious loyalty, fervour and belief becomes increasingly based on its commitment to an egalitarian universalism that is not essentially ideological or transcendental in character. This would be nothing short of a profound secularization of the religious mission itself – as is the case with liberation theology.[69]

How a socialist transformation might be brought about in a liberal-democratic capitalist order is still the most important unresolved strategic problem. But an indispensable part of such an overall strategy is the building of democratic *and secular* counter-institutions in civil society through a multiplicity of localized struggles and single- and multiple-issue movements coordinating and uniting such struggles through appropriate structures, programmes and action networks. Since no realistic assessment of these times can ignore the fact that the mass appeal of socialism is weaker than at any time since 1917, is it the case that anti-communalists in India are doomed at best to carrying out a long-term holding operation for secularism? To argue that capitalism and bourgeois democracy in India cannot be the preconditions for the eradication of communalism is not the same to argue that there is no other scenario for the future than communalism's progressive escalation, or India's inexorable descent into a communalist, authoritarian nightmare.

It is conceivable that weakened but enduring bourgeois-democratic structures will coexist with communal tensions and more institutionalized patterns of discrimination against non-Hindu minorities, in much the same

---

69 The Indian anti-secularist has not hesitated to cite Christian liberation theology in her support. But a chasm separates the two. For the anti-secularist, the principal lines of demarcation are between believers and non-believers, the secularist and the non-secularist, the indigenous and the alien. At no point is she prepared to appropriate as her fundamental line of demarcation the operative principle of liberation theology at its best: the *social* divide between rich and poor, oppressor and oppressed. Characteristically, liberation theology sees Marxism as a valuable resource and Marxists as actual or potential allies, while the anti-secularist sees Marxism and Marxists as prisoners of a Western episteme, and therefore dangerously misled and misleading, or at best irrelevant.

way as racism and bourgeois democracy in the West have coexisted – though this analogy should not be stretched too far. (Politically thinned as Western democracies have become by the neoliberal turn, they are more securely anchored and far less violent domestically than the political structures of the 'world's largest democracy'.) Moreover, such a perspective presumes that the challenge posed by the forces of Hindu communalism will at least be contained. The short-term task of de-communalizing the purely political terrain and preserving the secular state has become all-important. The BJP and the organizations behind it must not stabilize themselves in power at the centre. Unless secular political forces prevent such a denouement, the longer-term and more fundamental task of successfully secularizing civil society is hardly conceivable.

Here, the issue of caste becomes vital. Caste is an identity more deeply felt than class, and has an emotional resonance stronger still than that of religion, because the social roots of caste oppression are deep and its social consequences all too real. But it matters a great deal how caste struggle is conducted, who leads, and in what directions. In one case we have the politics of the current Dalit leadership and of the lower rungs of the OBCs, which is about creating bigger and stronger lower-caste upper and middle classes that can then wield greater leverage on middle- and upper-caste elites in the joint project of rule. In the other case we have an attempt at cultural and psychological upliftment through the construction of a broader Hindu identity, which will also seek to stabilize class rule through assurances of greater social diversity among elite layers. In no case do we have as yet a lower-caste upsurge that seeks to transform capitalism, or even institutionalize a system of universal and quality provision of basic welfare needs. For in that case a cross-caste class alliance among the poor and oppressed of all kinds would be required. Among his own constituency, Ambedkar as an iconic Dalit leader to be admired has been separated from Ambedkar as a Fabian socialist and political liberal to be followed.

The first and undoubtedly most prolonged phase in pursuing an anticapitalist alternative would be the construction of an anti-neoliberal platform, not just because of what it would achieve if successful, but also because of its mass radicalizing impact – emerging from what demands it would not be able to achieve, despite their obvious reasonableness and desirability.

In Modi's first victory speech he called for a public mandate of ten years to complete his promised 'transformation'. The challenge, then, is to build a broad anti-neoliberal platform to prevent and reverse this Hindutva-ized far right class project. Where does the Left figure in this effort?[70] The parliamentary left of the CPM and the CPI – separated by bureaucratic rivalries, not irresolvable programmatic differences – suffered their worst ever defeat,

---

70 For a more comprehensive treatment of the Indian left, see my 'Subcontinental Strategies', *New Left Review* II/70 (July–August 2011).

securing nine and one seats, respectively, in the 2014 elections. Long-term co-optation into the system reduced this left to trying, when in provincial power (in West Bengal and Kerala), to become 'better' managers of cap-italist development, even after its neoliberal turn, and otherwise to being a 'responsible' opposition nationally. The collapse of Stalinist communism put an end to an already ongoing process of ideological demoralization of its cadres, rendering this Left for the most part not capable (as it once was) of leading large-scale and sustained mass mobilizations (although it remains involved in a few progressive grassroots struggles here and there). This loss of interest in and capacity to pursue such politics of mass protest is its real dilemma. In programmatic and policy terms, the Left has become, in all but name, a social-democratic force drifting rightwards domestically, but is still more staunchly secular than any other parliamentary rival. It does not, however, oppose the state crackdown on 'Naxalites', or defend the right to full self-determination in Kashmir or the north-east. But it maintains a stance against Western imperialism (its criticisms of Russia and China remain muted) that keeps it to the left of European social democrats.

Indian Maoism for the most part rejects electoral involvement. The CPI-ML (Maoist) is rooted among the poorest and most deprived Dalits and especially Adivasis of central India. It has waged armed struggle against the state for decades and survived, even grown, with a membership estimated in a few tens of thousands. But it fails to recognize the basic strategic dilemma facing Marxist revolutionaries everywhere: how to bring about a fundamental transformation in class power in liberal-democratic capitalist societies, even if the strength of their 'best political shell' (as Lenin called it) of liberal democ-racy varies. To be sure, in India liberal democracy is weak and brutalized. But even so, it is still meaningful and real. Moreover, even in backward cap-italisms, armed apparatuses of the state are strong and can look for outside support whenever seriously threatened. Ruling classes have learned that, if quick victory is not possible, prolonging the war plays into their hands. Internal divisions arise among the insurgents, and their mass base becomes war-weary. As it is, there is a disjunction between the Maoist base, which looks primarily for concrete, near-term improvements in livelihood, and the more uncertain, remote and ideologically driven aim of the leadership to capture state power. Over the last few years, there have been many more defections and captures from the middle and higher levels of leadership. It is quite possible that the party has passed its peak of strength and influence, and is in decline. Certainly, the Modi government promises to crush it ruthlessly.

How, then, is an anti-neoliberal platform to be generated? Neoliberalism emerged through a transformation of class relations in favour of capital and against labour so great that derailing it would itself require so great a count-er-shift in the class relationship of forces as to almost certainly put the issue of moving towards a 'twenty-first-century socialism' on the agenda. Striving for a reversion to the post-war social-democratic heyday would clearly now be chasing chimera.[71] Raising standard social-democratic demands, such as universalizing free quality healthcare and education, and the provision of social security, cheap and adequate public transport and housing, and so on – precisely because they are not fully achievable – then become crucial spurs for generating an anti-capitalist momentum. This would be reinforced by the call for the spread of more direct forms of public participation and democratic decision-making, along with existing representative institutions themselves needing change, as for example in moving towards some kind of proportional electoral system in India.

Indian economic development, even under the new government, will guarantee rising discontent, not least because the Modi promise of jobs for all jobseekers will fail. Two statistics say it all: 93 per cent of India's work-force is in the informal sector (compared to Brazil's 55 per cent); and the number of jobs generated by each percentage-point increase in economic growth in India actually fell radically between 2000 and 2010.[72] Capital intensity is rising in all sectors. This means that Modi's goal to raise consid-erably the proportion of industry's contribution to output (from around a quarter of GDP now) will not produce enough jobs, and even those created will be mostly informal and casualized. Accelerating the large-scale industri-alization of agriculture, forced land acquisitions for industry and real estate, and more ruthless exploitation of marine, forest and mineral wealth will worsen the plight of the landless, of small and marginal farmers, and of Adivasis and fishing communities, as well as causing greater ecological dev-astation. Although over time the rural population will become a minority, it will remain substantial.

Moreover, there will be no 'disappearance of the peasantry' even as class divisions become sharper. The migration of more family members to expanding urban slums in search of livelihoods in the informal sector creates stronger living links between town and country. Many of those who would contest urban class disparities and participate in struggles for the 'right to the city' are connected to their family members in rural households who do farm and off-farm work outside towns and cities. Thus, there is a living link that can connect urban demands and more traditional demands for land redistribution, and secure rural off-farm jobs and decent wages.[73] Fleshing

---

71 For all the justified criticisms from the Left of his dismissal of Marxist economic thinking, Thomas Piketty does have the inestimable merit of recognizing (from within the mainstream of neoclassical economics itself) that the 'golden age' of social democ-racy is an unrepeatable exception. See T. Piketty, *Capital in the Twenty-First Century* (Cambridge, MA, 2014).

72 The employment elasticity of output between 2000 and 2010, when India had high average growth rates, actually fell from 0.44 to 0.01. See S. Mehrotra, A. Gandhi, P. Saha and B. K. Sahoo, *Joblessness and Informalization: Challenges to Inclusive Growth in India*, Institute of Applied Manpower Research, Planning Commission, Government of India, December 2012, p. 10.

73 D. Harvey, *Rebel Cities: From the Right to the City to the Urban Revolution* (London, 2012).

out such a broad programme for generating a mass-struggle momentum from all oppressed sections is vital. But the main issue is how to generate the forces that can wage a prolonged and collective fight for it.

In India, the transformation of class relations of power must necessarily also be refracted through struggles around other identities of gender, caste, and ethnic demarcations of various kinds. Though the majority or near majority of Dalits are agricultural proletarians, the majority of the latter are not Dalits. This means cross-caste class solidarities must be built. But this is not what the BSP, the main party of Dalits being led by middle-class aspirations, has so far sought to do. But progressives must nevertheless try to engage with that base through and besides its leadership. One great nightmare for the forces of Hindutva and the dominant classes they chiefly cater to is the coming together of Muslims, Dalits, Adivasis and the most oppressed lower rungs of the OBCs or backward castes who, in class terms, have more in common with each other than with others, and easily constitute a numerical majority in the country. The point is not to create a mere electoral bloc through promises of sectoral favours. This has been done in the past by both regional parties and the Congress, but does not endure because, even as special group needs are to a limited extent addressed, common class needs are not.

Localized agitations in some socially mixed areas against some common oppression, like unwanted mining operations or large-scale land displacements and takeovers, have led to collective organization and struggle. There are many such important struggles going on, but it has not been possible to bring them enduringly together, even as this is increasingly seen as necessary by many of the leaders of such struggles and by the radical Left. A mere stitching-together of an artificial coalition – united only by the periodic meetings of representatives passing public resolutions or solidarity messages, or even agreeing to put forward an agreed list of electoral candidates – will not do. Real solidarity has to come through collective struggles, not just around the problems of one's own group but through involvement in the struggles of others. The first kind of struggle raises sectoral consciousness; the second, a wider consciousness of the need for deeper change, a better appreciation of who one's allies are, and a greater sense of self-confidence.

This problem of bringing together the politics of the singular and the universal has always required an organizational framework which, like a spider's web, has activists who are fanned out in different areas of struggle, and yet are integrated enough to be able to share experiences and understandings. This requires developing the capacity to shift personnel and resources in accordance with the differing tempos of struggles and the opportunities for rapid advance that arise on one or another front. There is no single party that can play this role today in India. But there are a whole host of groups and social movements that can help form the components of an anti-neoliberal platform. Nor should the existing Left be immediately written off. The very shock administered by the scale of the right-wing Hindutva advance may spark a process of more fundamental rethinking and reorganization. In the best-case scenario, the parliamentary Left would recognize that it must completely jettison its Stalinist legacy organizationally and programmatically; forsake its governing ambitions and the compromises they necessitated; concentrate on re-energizing its existing cadres by making extra-parliamentary activity its primary preoccupation; and play a non-manipulative and dedicated supporting role in progressive struggles that are already taking place. Internally, there should be a complete revamping to promote freedom of discussion with the party constitution changed so as to guarantee tendency and faction rights; and there should be proportional representation at all levels of the leadership pyramid for such groupings (if they exist), as well as for women, Adivasis and lower castes, in proportion to their membership.

The Maoists would need to realize that their current armed struggle strategy is a dead end, learn from the wider non-Maoist, anti-Stalinist Marxist traditions, and come above ground to struggle, even as they may wish to retain the defensive capacity to protect their social bases effectively against the eventuality of oppressor violence. The Indian state has on occasion called for a dialogue with Maoists, raising the possibility of mutual agreement on roughly these terms. This may well be a deception, and certainly the current government seems more determined to eliminate the Maoists physically. How long the Maoists can survive under this onslaught, and how frustrated the government might become at its relative lack of success, is dependent on the strength of the loyalties of the mass base towards the Maoists. There are limits to how far the state can drain the 'sea' in which the Maoists thrive, unless that sea on its own becomes progressively smaller. This means there may well emerge opportunities for the state to prefer dialogue and agreement. If so, these opportunities should be explored. Should New Delhi come to feel in due course that the military balance is so strongly tilted in its favour as to assure early victory, it will no longer be interested in such an accommodation.

A more realistic scenario perhaps is that the CPI, CPM and CPI-ML (Maoist) will not carry out such self-transformation. In this case, a new Left will emerge through a process of splits (this has already happened to the student wing of the CPM), re-compositions, realignments and fusions through extended dialogue and collaboration between small far-left groupings (of which India has quite a few) that are outside the shadow of, and critical of, the big three. This will involve seriously exploring the possibility of engaging with the Bahujan Samaj Party (given its Dalit base), with other more independent minded Dalit groups outside of the BSP and with any left breakaway from the AAP.[74] There is the obvious need to work with the range

---

74 Jignesh Mevani is a young lawyer and a highly articulate Dalit activist who has emerged as the principal leader of Dalits in Gujarat after the Una incident by organizing various mass rallies and processions. Unlike any other Dalit leader in the country, he has

of progressive social movements, peace groups, progressive medics, lawyers, teachers, the more radical NGOs, and so on, up and down the country. These cover the whole range of concerns, from civil liberties to the rights of Adivasis, Muslims, sexual minorities, oppressed ethno-national communities in Kashmir and the north-east, the political under-representation of women, domestic violence, public harassment and workplace discrimination of all kinds. Struggles continue against the progressive degradation of nature that is negatively affecting livelihoods and posing potential dangers caused by 'big development', from big dams and nuclear power stations to the proposed scheme to interlink major rivers.

Let us also not forget that the information and communications revolution has meant that the visibility and awareness of inequalities of income, wealth and power are greater than ever, arousing much stronger comparative dissatisfactions and anger. Mass struggles in other parts of the world now have rapid knock-on effects – witness the flurry of protests involving occupation of public spaces in country after country not so long ago, even if the specific demands raised were different. Many of these struggles appear not to belong to the arena of class conflict, yet they do. Indeed, they must be taken up. Capitalist ruling classes nationally (as in India) and internationally are far more homogeneous, despite all of the cultural, social and regional differences that exist between and among them. Their lines of coordination are smoother and shorter, their capacities for uniting when required quicker. In contrast, those they oppress are far more heterogeneous in their concerns, their lines of communication dispersed and weaker, their broad unification much more difficult to achieve. But it is because there is ultimately a class homogeneity underlying this great heterogeneity that it is possible for them to coalesce. When this happens on a sufficient scale, a revolutionary transformation of class and social relations can take place. Indian progressives know that times of great adversity are also times of real opportunities and possibilities. The future of India remains open and the nemesis of Hindutva is by no means assured of long-term ascendancy or final victory.

spoken about the need to go beyond 'anti-caste sloganeering', to not get 'bogged down in identity politics' and to fight for economic justice as well as social justice; and that Dalits should see the left as their ally which in turn must work to win the trust of Dalits. He has declared the need for poor OBCs, Muslims, Adivasis, Dalits and trade unionists to form a coalition against the Sangh Parivar. Land reform for the landless is at the top of his reform agenda. See G. Sampath, 'Material Issues are at the Heart of Dalit Politics, says Jignesh Mevani', *The Hindu*, 23 September 2016; also available at thehindu.com.

Index

339–40, 348, 385; and Congress-led pogrom against Sikhs, 340n84; and cow protection, 361n16, 382; against Dalits, 361n16; and destruction of Babri Masjid, 78, 163, 205n73; domestic violence, 209, 387, 406; and ethnic cleansing, 89, 315; and ethno-national oppressions, 83, 315; and genocide, 390; and glorification of in fascism, 274; and Gujarat Pogrom, 78, 82, 84n56, 87–8, 89, 91, 217, 311, 318, 343, 351, 355, 365n23; and Hindu-Muslim riots, 84, 85; and Japanese fascism, 287–288n28; and mass violence, 89, 162, 212, 318; against Muslims, 46, 48, 59, 60n43, 68, 70, 72, 74–5, 78, 84–91, 205n73, 211, 212, 217, 310, 311n54, 333, 334, 340n84, 343, 348, 351, 385; and Partition, 32, 83–4, 87; and physical violence and coercion, 360, 361; political violence, 83, 87–90, 363; and rath yatra (chariot tour), 70; and riots, 41, 48, 57, 60, 72, 74–5, 79, 84–6, 88–90, 205n73, 254, 318, 339–40, 345, 348, 349, 351, 363, 385; and Sangh Parivar, 84, 88, 89, 90, 348; secessionist violence, 83; by the state, 64, 74–5, 83–90, 212, 303–4, 317, 363–4; and terrorism, 4–5, 51, 90n65, 315, 352, 355–6, 361, 363, 378; and Uttar Pradesh, 89, 345, 348; against women, 83, 87; worker violence, 373; against working-class, 292, 320, 373

Weber, Max: and capitalism, 130, 160, 180n28; and meaning of life, 106, 137, 141, 221; and modernity, 145, 146; 'Protestant ethic' thesis of, 159, 160; and religion, 101–2, 108, 110, 141, 159, 160, 167; and society, 129, 167
Western world: and Christian Democratic party, 66, 310; and Christian Europe, 159, 173, 255; and Christianity, 131, 148–9, 159–60, 168, 258–9; and civilization, 165, 173; and communalism, 254–5; and democracy in Western Europe, 280, 291; and Encounter with Hinduism, 181, 185; and ethnic communities, 328; and far right in Europe, 322–3; and fascism, 18, 21, 296; and France, 196, 197;

and imperialism, 149, 402; and Indian diaspora, 163; and inter-war Europe, 296–7; and Islam, 4, 149, 212; and Islamophobia, 198, 212, 307n48, 323; and migrations into Europe, 255, 258; and modernity, 96, 149, 254, 305; and nationalism, 40n14, 254; and the Other, 166, 181; and racism, 307n48, 400; and Renaissance, 159, 160; and Romantics, 166, 169, 170, 180n28, 181, 187; and secularism, 12, 14–15, 37, 101, 148–9, 210, 219–21, 247, 249; and secularization, 36, 96, 97, 143, 144, 152, 155, 159–60; and the secular state, 98, 194, 197n59; and socialist revolution, 318, 320; and struggles from 1960-80, 328, 329; and the welfare state, 398; and western and eastern Europe, 30, 97n5; and Western democracies, 82, 97, 243n154, 400; and Western Europe, 107–8, 146n107, 194; and Western political thought, 146n107, 198
Williams, Raymond: and cultural power, 123; and culture, 7–8, 101, 120, 122–3, 131, 140n95, 193; and economy, 283
women: and domestic violence, 209; and feminism, 298n42, 307n48, 388; and France's Marine le Pen, 307n48, 322; and Hindutva, 83, 209; Hindu women, 43, 209, 384; and indigenous patriarchy, 247n163; and lack of a Uniform Civil Code, 208, 209; Muslim women, 196, 251, 386; and oppressive social structures, 68, 316, 317; and political representation, 405, 406; and Rashtriya Sevika Sangh (national women's wing), 41, 387; and Uniform Civil Code, 387, 388; violence against, 83, 87; and women's movements, 84, 209
World Hindu Council, 41, 44–5, 67; coalition of, 69; and mass mobilizing pilgrimages, 68; and Ram Janamabhoomi campaign, 69–72; and Sangh Parivar, 70
World War I, 272n2, 284, 285n25, 296, 303, 310, 315
World War II, 20, 145, 272n3, 297, 300, 301